Library of
Davidson College

PHILOSOPHIA

PHILOSOPHICAL TEXTS AND STUDIES
WIJSGERIGE TEKSTEN EN STUDIES

edited by / onder redactie van

PROF. DR. C. J. DE VOGEL EN PROF. DR. K. KUYPERS

Uitgaven van het Filosofisch Instituut der Rijksuniversiteit te Utrecht

1. L. M. de Rijk, Ph. D., *Petrus Abaelardus, Dialectica*. First complete edition of the Parisian manuscript.
2. B. L. Hijmans Jr., Ph. D., 'ΑΣΚΗΣΙΣ. Notes on Epictetus' educational system.
3. L. M. de Rijk, Ph. D., *Garlandus Compotista, Dialectica*. First edition of the manuscripts.
4. Prof. R. H. Popkin, *The History of Scepticism from Erasmus to Descartes*. Part I.
5. Leo Elders S. V. D., Ph. D., *Aristotle's Theory of the One*. A commentary on book X of the Metaphysics.
6. L. M. de Rijk, Ph. D., *Logica Modernorum, vol. I*. A contribution to the history of early terminist logic.
7. W. N. A. Klever, Ph. D., ΑΝΑΜΝΗΣΙΣ *en* ΑΝΑΓΩΓΗ. Gesprek met Plato en Aristoteles over het menselijk kennen.
8. A. C. van Geytenbeek, Ph. D., *Musonius Rufus and Greek Diatribe*.
9. J. Mansfeld, Ph. D., *Die Offenbarung des Parmenides und die menschliche Welt*.
10. W. van Dooren, Ph. D., *Het totaliteitsbegrip bij Hegel en zijn voorgangers*.
11. Dr. J. Louet-Feisser, *De wijsbegeerte en het wetenschappelijk beroep op de feiten*.
12. C. J. de Vogel, Ph. D., *Pythagoras and early Pythagoreanism*. An interpretation of neglected evidence on the philosopher Pythagoras.
13. Leo Elders S.V.D., Ph.D., *Aristotle's Cosmology*. A commentary on the De caelo.
14. Dr. Th. de Boer, *De ontwikkelingsgang in het denken van Husserl*.
15. C. de Deugd M. A., Ph. D., D. Litt., *The significance of Spinoza's first kind of knowledge*.
16. L. M. de Rijk, Ph. D., *Logica modernorum, vol. II*.
    Part I. The origin and early development of the theory of supposition.
    Part II. The origin and early development of the theory of supposition. Texts and indices.
17. Theo Gerard Sinnige, Ph. D., *Matter and Infinity in the Presocratic Schools and Plato*.
18. K. Kuypers, Ph.D., *Verspreide geschriften*. Deel I. Mens en geschiedenis; Deel II. Wetenschap en kunde.
19. C. J. de Vogel, *Philosophia*, Part I, *Studies in Greek Philosophy*.

PHILOSOPHIA

PART I

Studies in Greek Philosophy

by

C. J. DE VOGEL

professor of Ancient and early Christian
philosophy in the University of Utrecht

ASSEN, MCMLXX

VAN GORCUM & COMP. N.V. - DR. H. J. PRAKKE & H. M. G. PRAKKE

© *1969 by Koninklijke Van Gorcum & Comp. N.V., Assen, The Netherlands.*

No parts of this book may be reproduced in any form, by print, photoprint, microfilm or any other means, without written permission from the publisher.

ISBN 90 232 0733 5

Printed in The Netherlands by Royal VanGorcum Ltd.

TO HAROLD CHERNISS
in token of
a long and solid friendship

PRÉFACE / PREFACE
VORWORT

Ce volume n'est pas un simple recueil d'articles déjà publiés. Il y en a de tout nouveaux – tels les trois chapitres de la section des *Pythagorica* et le chapitre IX sur les points controversiaux chez Platon –, et d'autres qui n'ont paru dans aucune langue européenne plus accessible que le néerlandais – tels le chapitre VI (paru uniquement en japonnais à Tokio), et les chapitres XVII (uniquement en néerlandais) et X (en japonnais et en néerlandais). Tous ceux qui restent ont été plus ou moins remaniés, quelques uns légèrement, d'autres d'une telle façon que des passages plus ou moins importants en ont été récrits entièrement.

Quant aux chapitres XI et XII qui datent tous les deux de 1948-49, bien que d'abord je n'aie pas eu l'intention de les faire reproduire dans ce volume, autant plus qu'ils ont été traduits en allemand pour paraître dans un volume sur les ἄγραφα de Platon qui sera publié par la *Wissenschaftliche Buchgesellschaft* à Darmstadt, le fait que j'ai dû m'y référer plus d'une fois dans quelques autres chapitres du présent volume, tandis que l'éditeur allemand m'a fait savoir que son volume projeté ne paraîtra que vers la fin de 1970, m'a fait décider de faire réimprimer ces articles dans leurs formes française et anglaise et de les insérer dans les *Platonica* de ce livre.

Si la plupart des chapitres de ce volume ont été écrits soit en français soit en anglais, on en trouvera l'explication en partie dans les liens culturels qui m'attachent à la France depuis mon séjour à l'École Française d'Athènes de 1932-34, en partie aux circonstances politiques qui, dans les années immédiatement après 1945, m'ont orientée vers l'emploi du français ou de l'anglais plutôt que vers l'allemand, bien que ce fût là la langue qui depuis de longues années m'était la plus familière.

Actuellement, puisque les liens culturels entre la Hollande et l'Allemagne sont entièrement rétablis, il n'y a plus aucune raison d'éviter la langue allemande. La raison pourquoi j'ai traité ici du livre important de M. Burkert en anglais est d'une tout autre nature: c'est que j'ai écrit en allemand un compte rendu de ce livre pour la revue allemande *Gymnasium*, article non encore paru au moment où je prépare ce volume pour la presse. Certainement j'avais plus de choses à dire à propos du livre de Burkert que je n'ai pu faire entrer dans un petit compte rendu. D'autre part, j'ai voulu éviter la doublure. Voilà les raisons pourquoi j'ai écrit mon chapitre sur Burkert en anglais, – et celui sur Philip, dont j'ai fait un compte rendu en anglais (non encore paru) pour le *Journal of Hellenic Studies*, en allemand. Ce chapitre allemand est là pour deux raisons: non seulement pour éviter la doublure, mais aussi, et même en premier lieu, comme symbole.

Das einzige deutsch geschriebene Kapitel dieses Buches ist von der Verf. mehr oder weniger wie ein Symbol gemeint: sie war der Meinung, dass in diesem mehrsprachigen Band die deutsche Sprache nicht fehlen sollte.

For the reader's convenience I shall mention in a note to the title of each chapter, the year it was first written and, if it was previously published, where and when.

To this volume which is entirely concerned with Greek philosophy, I gave the title of

ΦΙΛΟΣΟΦΙΑ

Part 1, *Studies in Greek Philosophy*

I intend to follow it up later by a second Part, which will deal with subjects concerning Greek and Christian thought, Patristic and Medieval philosophy. I hope to achieve this within the next three years.

Utrecht, July 1969
C. J. d. V.

CONTENTS

INTRODUCTORY CHAPTER

Chapter I	*Some reflections on the term* φιλοσοφία	3

PYTHAGORICA

Chapter II	*Les fragments dits de Philolaus*	27
Chapter III	*An important German work on Pythagoras and the Pythagorean tradition: Walter Burkert, Weisheit und Wissenschaft* (Nürnberg 1962)	78
Chapter IV	*Nochmals die Pythagorasfrage: J. A. Philip, Pythagoras and early Pythagoreanism*, Toronto 1966	92

SOCRATICA

Chapter V	*Who was Socrates?*	109
Chapter VI	*Was Socrates a rationalist?*	131

PLATONICA

Chapter VII	*Examen critique de l'interprétation traditionnelle de la philosophie de Platon*	155
Chapter VIII	*Platon a-t-il ou n'a-t-il pas introduit le principe de mouvement dans son monde intelligible?*	176
Chapter IX	*Some controversial points of Plato interpretation reconsidered*	183
Chapter X	*What was God for Plato?*	
	(1) The problem, in the judgment of Ancients and Moderns	210
	(2) The Demiurge and the good World-Soul	225
Chapter XI	*La dernière phase de la philosophie de Platon et l'interprétation de Léon Robin*	243
Chapter XII	*Problems concerning Plato's later doctrine*, (1)	256
	(2)	274

ARISTOTELICA

Chapter XIII	*Did Aristotle ever accept Plato's theory of transcendent Ideas?*	295

Chapter XIV	*A propos des premiers chapitres de la Métaphysique d'Aristote*	331

PRAENEOPLATONICA

Chapter XV	*On the Neoplatonic character of Platonism and the Platonic character of Neoplatonism*	355
Chapter XVI	*La théorie de l'ἄπειρον chez Platon et dans la tradition platonicienne*	378

NEOPLATONICA

Chapter XVII	*The monism of Plotinus*	399

EAST AND WEST

Chapter XVIII	*The motive of eternal change in Greek and later Western philosophy compared with Indian thought*	419

INDICES

	Index of names	434
	Index of subjects	437
	Index of Greek words	445

INTRODUCTORY CHAPTER

CHAPTER I

SOME REFLECTIONS ON THE TERM ΦΙΛΟΣΟΦΙΑ [1]

Since both the concept of philosophy and the term itself are of Greek origin, it is reasonable to begin by raising the question of what the Greeks meant by it. It is still too frequently done that some modern school concept of philosophy is used as a standard and applied to the Ancients. Then it is said, for instance, that the early Greek "philosopher" Pythagoras, who according to the tradition was the first to use that term, should not be considered as a philosopher at all, since his kind of wisdom does not come up to the modern standard. Socrates, Plato and Aristotle, no doubt, will satisfy certain essential requirements; but I am afraid they will be found to have regarded and practised philosophy on at least as many points in a way that is entirely strange to the modern view of what it should be. Aristotle may turn out to be the most satisfactory representative of "philosophy" among the Ancients. But Socrates and Plato will definitely be found not to fit into the preconceived framework at all. And as far as Hellenistic philosophy is concerned, and still more the "philosophers" of the later centuries of Antiquity, those of the Roman Empire, no doubt they will be said not to have been philosophers at all, the former because they may appear to have been more concerned with ethical-practical questions than with pure theory, the latter because to them religious experience might seem to have been more important than theoretical thinking. To the modern philosopher who comes to the Ancients with his standard of what philosophy should be, that might seem to be the end of all.

[1] These "Reflections" were first written in Dutch, Febr.-March 1959, and spoken before the audience of the Dominican Fathers at Nijmegen on March 7 (St. Thomas) of that year. They were published in Dutch not before 1967 in the author's volume *Theoria* (v. Gorcum, Assen). They appeared in English in a revised form in the first number of the *International Philosophical Quarterly*, N.Y. 1961. The present chapter varies from both previous editions.

INTRODUCTORY CHAPTER

In view of all this, then, I wish to begin at the beginning and raise the question of what the Greeks themselves meant by that newly invented and somewhat technically applied term, and what they expected from the implied kind of mental training.

THALES

It is generally accepted that Greek philosophy begins with Thales of Miletus; but placing the starting point here is not a matter of modern interpretation; it is an ancient tradition.

Aristotle, who was the first to give a fairly elaborate survey of the history of Greek philosophy up to his own day, begins his exposition by stating that the older philosophers sought for a material principle, an archetypal stuff, from which everything comes and into which it returns, so that, while things arise and perish, the original stuff remains.

He calls Thales "the founder of this kind of philosophy"[1], since he taught that water is the principle from which everything arises.

Looking back over the intervening twenty-five hundred years, we may well wonder why the Greeks called Thales the first philosopher. Why not Homer or Hesiod in whom we already find certain elements of an explanation of the universe? The answer to this question is not too difficult. For the Greeks "philosophy" was an attempt at a *rational* explanation. Granted that it did not realize the complete elimination of mythology all at once, yet it certainly did strive after such an elimination, and it did so consciously.

Yet this characteristic by itself is not sufficient to throw full light on the ancient Greek view of philosophy. There are other aspects that must be taken into account, among them the note of *universality*. "Philosophy" also meant to them an explanation of the whole of things. While the note of rationality distinguished it from poetic imagination, universality set it apart from the special disciplines, such as engineering, historiography, or geography. But it is by no means correct to say – although one hears it often enough – that philosophy simply meant "science" in the widest sense, the different disciplines having been detached and separated from it only gradually, and this hardly before the time of Aristotle. No doubt, there is a certain amount of truth in this almost traditional statement; for both mathematics and astronomy were practised in the Pre-Socratic schools, and had their place also in Plato's Academy; moreover, Aristotle was

[1] Aristotle, *Metaph.* A 3, 983 b 20.

a great biologist. Yet it should be realized that already in Plato's day mathematics was practised as an independent science, along with musicology, and that Plato situated the mathematical sciences, including astronomy, in his system of higher education as *preparatory* studies, preceding philosophy properly so-called, whose technical name was "dialectic".

Again, neither medicine nor historiography nor geography, all originating in the sixth and fifth centuries before Christ, were ever considered to belong to philosophy. Thus Thales, who, according to Herodotus, served ably in the army of Croesus as an hydraulics engineer, was not on this account called a "wise man" by his contemporaries.

But even rationality and universality do not sufficiently characterize the ancient Greek view of philosophy. Both Plato and Aristotle (our oldest sources) recount stories about Thales – legends, we might call them – which provide interesting sidelights on his personality that are too easily discarded by modern criticism. But the Greeks felt that such stories revealed something essential about Thales as a philosopher. One of these is the famous anecdote recounting how the learned man, absorbed in the consideration of some astronomical problem, fell into a pit and was laughed at by a pretty Thracian servant-girl[1]. The incident is supposed to illustrate the mentality of the philosopher who "does not know the way to the market-place".

Still another story is found in Aristotle's *Politics*[2]. Thales used to be reproached for his poverty, since it provided evidence that philosophy was of no use. But on one occasion when the philosopher had foreseen through his knowledge of the stars that there was going to be a great harvest of olives, he hired all the olive presses in Miletus and Chios for a small price, since no one bid against him, and held them until the time of the harvest when the sudden demand for many presses enabled him to let them out at a large profit. In this way he demonstrated that it is easy for philosophers to be rich – if they like... But this is not the thing that interests them.

The same story is told in a shorter form by Diogenes Laertius, who gives as his source Hieronymus of Rhodes, a third-century Peripatetic (later a dissident and opponent of the School). This gives us no right, however, to regard the story as of Hellenistic invention, made up to illustrate a view originating in those days. Nor are there any grounds

---
[1] Plato, *Theaet.* 174a.
[2] Aristotle, *Polit.* I 11, 1259a9ff.

for holding that Aristotle invented it. It is much more probable that both stories, that of the pit and that of the olive presses, come from an older tradition, though it is not possible for us to trace it back further. This much is certain: for the Greeks it was an essential feature of the philosopher not to be interested in the things of ordinary life. The fact that they attributed this attitude of mind to philosophers even as early as Thales reveals their own conception of philosophy and of those who practised it. It involved an intense concern for the things of the spirit, which, in turn, implied a certain detachment from outward things, including money and honour.

XENOPHANES, PYTHAGORAS

Thus, the aged Xenophanes despised the glory of the champions of the Olympic games, holding his own wisdom to be of higher value than the physical strength of men and horses[1]. Pythagoras lived with his disciples in a kind of monastery where property was put in a common stock. No doubt the descriptions of the Pythagorean community at Croton, given by Iamblichus many years later, should be read with certain reservations[2]. What is certain is that the "Pythagorean life" (for which Plato says[3] Pythagoras was especially loved, adding that "to this day it distinguishes Pythagoreans from the rest of the world") was a form of ethico-religious education. By reflecting on number – not only as a principle of order in the cosmos but as a principle of human knowledge – by the practice of music and musical theory, and by ritual purification and abstinence from certain foods, the Pythagoreans sought to attain a purification of the soul and an inner harmony.

It appears from this that philosophy was considered by the ancient Pythagoreans not at all as mere intellectual activity. Certainly intellectual activity played an important part in it, but this does not seem to have been the real purpose of the Pythagorean community life. Rather, what was cultivated by means of the intellect was a spiritual and moral elevation of the human personality. It was believed that such elevation could be reached by abstract thinking, aided by certain psychological effects ascribed to music. The real purpose, then, was to bring the immortal soul to the highest possible perfection.

---

[1] Xenophanes, fr. 2.
[2] Iambl. *V.P.* c. 17 ff.
[3] *Rep.* X 600 b.

ON THE TERM ΦΙΛΟΣΟΦΙΑ

It is apparent that for Pythagoras and his followers the philosophical life implied detachment from material goods exactly as we shall find it later in Socrates and Plato, and even, to a certain extent, in Aristotle.

In Cicero's *Tuscalanae*[1] we find the well-known story recounting how Leon, the sovereign of Phlious, asked Pythagoras what his trade or discipline was. Pythagoras replied that he had neither trade nor discipline but that he was a philosopher. When the ruler asked him what this term meant, Pythagoras replied by offering the analogy of the Olympic games. Three kinds of people are found there: 1. those who take part in the games – and these strive after honour; 2. a large number of people who come for trading – and these are concerned with gain; finally, 3. a group which comes only to look on. These last are the purely disinterested observers. Analogously, three kinds of people may be distinguished in ordinary life: the great mass of men interested in material gain, a special group concerned with high posts and honour, and finally, a small group striving neither for honour nor for gain, but in an attitude of utter disinterestedness seeking only after truth and knowledge. Such is the philosophos.

Modern philosophers sometimes seem to think this answer rather odd or, in any case, hardly satisfactory to one of our contemporaries who might chance to ask what philosophy means[2]. But do they not underrate the value of this truly Greek expression of what the philosophical attitude towards life is and should be? Of course, *we* may decree that philosophy is not an "attitude towards life" at all and that it has nothing to do with it; but this should not blind us to the fact that for the Greeks that is precisely and emphatically what it was. Nor should it be said, as it has been, that the story of Pythagoras' reply to Leon apparently sprang from the generation after Aristotle when the "three lives theory", created by Aristotle, became a hotly debated question. Since Cicero found the story in Heraclides Ponticus, it is certainly not of post-Aristotelian origin; neither was it simply invented by Aristotle. On the contrary, it represents a view that was current with Socrates and the Socratic circle, with Plato and the Academy. But we have good reasons to assume that Pythagoras actually called himself a "philosophos"[3], and that he did conceive

[1] V 3, 8-9.
[2] As an example of this attitude the reader may find a comment on the above cited passage of the *Tusculanae* in the inaugural address of the late professor W. Wiersma, held September 1958 to the University of Amsterdam.
[3] The reader can find my arguments on this point in my book *Pythagoras and*

philosophy in the sense indicated in the above story: to him and to his disciples philosophy was *theoria*, but this implied a certain personal attitude towards life, an attitude of inner freedom, of distance from the things coveted by the majority of men: money and material goods, comfort and pleasure of the senses, even honour and high regard in the eyes of men.

SOCRATES

When confronted with a figure like Socrates, the professional philosopher of today will often say that he admires his behaviour and attitude towards life "even though such an attitude has nothing to do with philosophy". The fact is, however, that for Socrates himself it not only had something to do with philosophy but it was the most essential part of philosophy. Let us listen to Socrates speaking to his judges:

> If you now released me, Sirs, and said, "Socrates, now we shall not listen to Anytus but let you go – on this condition, however, that you will not be concerned any more with this kind of investigation; and if you should be taken in the very act of doing so again, you will die" – supposing you let me off on these terms, I should say to you: "Men of Athens, I honour and I love you, but I shall obey God rather than you, and as long as I have breath and shall be able, I shall never cease to philosophize and to exhort you and make clear to everyone of you I ever meet, saying, according to my habit: "Dear friend, you who are an Athenian, an inhabitant of a city great and glorious in wisdom and in strength, do you not feel ashamed of heaping up the greatest amount of money and caring for glory and honour, but not for insight or truth or how your soul may reach the greatest possible perfection?"[1]

This was what a philosopher should care for in Socrates' opinion. Thus, Socrates, and Plato after him, found here the criterion for distinguishing true and false philosophy: the former leads men to

Early Pythagoreanism, van Gorcum, Assen 1966, p. 96-102. Important is Heraclitus fr. 35, which cannot be explained in a satisfactory way unless it refers to a contemporary or somewhat older philosopher, who was known to have called himself by that name, and was referred to by Heraclitus ironically.
[1] Plato, *Apol.* 29 c-e.

moral improvement, the latter (called 'sophistry') never succeeds in making men better than they were[1].

When Socrates was in prison awaiting execution, his friend Crito came to offer him an easy escape and a safe refuge in Thessaly. To this suggestion Socrates replied: Of what have I always been speaking throughout my life? What principles did I lay down, founded on rational reflection? Were they not that we should not care for the opinion of the crowd but only for that of the experts; that the soul is of higher value than the body; that what matters is not merely to live but to live well; that goodness, beauty, and justice are the same; that we should never and in no respect do wrong, and, lastly, never return wrong if anyone has wronged us? This is what I used to say, and are these principles not still valid?[2] Crito answered that they were. Well, then, said Socrates, if this is so, I cannot run away, for then I would wrong my greatest benefactors: the laws of the city under whose protection I have been born and lived my life.

It would be very strange indeed to hold that this behaviour had nothing to do with Socrates' philosophy. Rather, it must be said that for Socrates, and doubtless for Plato, "philosophy" meant not only rational reflection, but an utter obedience to the principles thus laid down. To these thinkers philosophy may have been pure theory, but it was pure theory *ruling practical life.*

PARMENIDES, HERACLITUS, DEMOCRITUS

But let us return to the Pre-Socratics. After Pythagoras we come to the great Parmenides, "venerable and awful", as Plato calls him[3], borrowing a phrase from Homer. In the *Theaetetus* Socrates is represented as according to Parmenides a place apart; he is willing to criticize others, including Eleatics, but he wishes to make an exception for Parmenides. In his youth Socrates had met Parmenides who was then an old man, and he appeared to him "to have an absolutely noble depth". We do not know anything of Parmenides' life. What Plato relates in the *Theaetetus* may be a fiction. But this much we can say for sure: The author of Parmenides' poem must have been an introverted type, withdrawn from external things and directed toward that eternal, unchanging, transcendent world which can be reached

---

[1] Plato, *Gorgias* 502e2-503d3; 515b6-517a6.
[2] Plato, *Crito* 46b-49e.
[3] *Theaetetus* 183e.

only by abstract thought. To him the reality of the spiritual world was so overpowering that *our* world, the world of motion and change, sank for him to the level of appearance. It is inconceivable that such a philosopher should not have had that detachment from temporal things which for the Greeks was the very essence of philosophy.

In the case of Heraclitus we know something more. We know, for example, that he went his own way, solitary and proud. To the extent that his semi-materialistic mode of thought allowed, he was, in his worldview, a cosmic spiritualist, even as Pythagoras had been. Like all the ancients, Heraclitus regarded thought not as a mere abstraction but as a power governing personal life. He himself was dominated by the idea that man in his spiritual being is rooted in divine Reason to which he must conform both his thoughts and actions[1]. It may safely be said that, as with so many other Greek philosophers, his attitude toward life reflected a certain egocentric, more or less ascetic spiritualism. When we come to those thinkers for whom we have more ample sources, I hope to show that this is, in fact, the characteristic attitude of all those whom the Greeks called "lovers of wisdom" and honoured as such.

Such a demonstration might seem to offer the least hope of success in the case of an indubitable materialist like Democritus, who not only explained the physical world as a mere mechanical process but also declared in his ethical aphorisms that the most important thing in life is to keep one's *euthymia*, i.e. a pleasant frame of mind[2]. Yet here, too, appearances are deceptive. The moral teaching of Democritus, which might seem at first glance to be a kind of hedonism – and in a sense, no doubt, it is – turns out to be an exhortation to soberness and moderation of desire[3], to keeping within bounds[4] and detaching oneself from external things, such as money, goods and the pleasures of the senses. Happiness, says our philosopher, lies not in these things, but in the inner man[5]. To these assertions Democritus even adjoined the principles of an ethics of a purely interior life, such as was developed in the Stoa at a later date: morality is not in the deeds we do, but depends entirely on the inner disposition of the subject[6].

---

[1] *Heracl.*, fr. 1, 2, 112, 114.
[2] Democr., fr. 3; fr. 191.
[3] Id., fr. 283, 284, 286, 210, 211.
[4] Id., fr. 191, 286.
[5] Id., fr. 170, 171, 146, 40, 77; cf. 189.
[6] Id., fr. 62, 96, 244, 264.

ON THE TERM ΦΙΛΟΣΟΦΙΑ

SOCRATES AGAIN

When we come again to Socrates, we find that Aristotle represents him as the founder of a philosophy of the concept and of a certain method of logic. But, as Gaston Bastide has observed, if Socrates was aiming at satisfactory definitions, his life as a philosopher was a complete failure, since he did not succeed in forming any[1].

Bastide was by no means the first to attack Aristotle's view of Socrates. Some twenty-five years before, Heinrich Maier had published an important work at Tübingen in which he tried to show that Socrates was on no account to be regarded primarily as the founder of a philosophy of the concept; what really interested him was not universal definitions but the individual soul of the concrete man. Socrates' calling was far higher than the one Aristotle ascribed to him, and he might well be called a missionary and pastor, practising the cure of souls[2]. The true purpose of his life was an ethico-religious one, which was to make his fellow-citizens morally better than they were; and this work he regarded as his service to God.

The few passages I have cited above may suffice to prove that Maier's thesis was not entirely unfounded. Yet essentially he was wrong, as wrong as Aristotle had been. For if the latter made Socrates a one-sided rationalist, omitting his moral preoccupations and his religious attitude towards life, Maier denied him the very intellectual core of his whole work and method. The fact is that for Socrates philosophy was a rational and methodical reflection, aiming at a clear view of the concepts which we continually use in the field of morals. But the method meant to him a "rendering an account of oneself", leading people to a true grasp of moral principles. And for him these principles appear to have been rooted in a transcendent order[3]. Therefore, since for him the vision of transcendent truth, which was the goal of intellectual investigation, was of an absolutely overpowering force, he was convinced that the reflection on oneself and moral principles cannot fail to lead one to a better, i.e., a more religious life. It would be more religious because "good" and "right" are rooted in a suprahuman, let us say, a divine order. That is why Socrates conceived

---

[1] G. Bastide, *Le moment historique de Socrate*, Paris 1939.
[2] H. Maier, *Sokrates*, Tübingen 1913.
[3] See Plato, *Apol.* 41 a-d; *Crito* 54 bc. Cp. Xenophon, *Memorab.* IV 4, 12-25. For further explanation, see the section of *Socratica* in the present volume, ch. 5 and 6.

his task as a kind of mission, fulfilled in the service of "the God"[1].

It might be concluded then that Socrates intended to attain moral improvement *by means of rational reflection*. But I would be unwilling to argue that – since "the end is superior to the means" – "apparently" for Socrates moral improvement was the really important matter, while the intellectual process was "just the means". By such an interpretation one would surely misunderstand Socrates. He never regarded the rational method, which *was* philosophy, properly speaking, as subordinate. Intellectual clearness was to him an ideal, a matter of supreme value. But this clarity, i.e., knowledge, was never exclusively a matter of the intellect. He considered it essential to knowledge, that it be the *ruling force in man*[2].

This basic conviction was the foundation for the famous principle that "no one sins willingly". Socrates could never have held such a principle – and it is certain that he did hold it – unless he had been profoundly convinced of the active and transforming power of a perfectly clear insight into the nature of our moral principles. Thus, had anyone contradicted him by maintaining that, if intellectual clearness is of supreme value in itself, it would follow that moral improvement neither belongs to nor adds anything essential to this value, Socrates would, no doubt, have answered that intellectual clearness is not intellectual clearness and that knowledge is not knowledge unless it functions as the ruling force in man. Therefore, true insight into moral principles leads necessarily to moral improvement; not – he might have added – that intellectual clearness as "the means" would be subordinate to moral improvement as the real aim, but that it is *a power governing the individual man, a sovereign power which, as such, implies moral improvement*. Thus, for Socrates, moral improvement could not be detached from intellectual clearness, nor could the latter exist without the former. The two are correlative.

PLATO

Much the same can be said of Plato. He follows his master in holding that a philosophical view of moral principles, i.e., a strictly noetic grasp of a transcendent Reality, is a powerful force, capable of transforming human personality and of elevating it to a superior state. On this level "social virtue" is evidently implied, but is also surpassed by

---

[1] Plato, *Apol.* 28b-31c.
[2] See, e.g., Plato, *Protag.* 352b-d.

the burning intensity of the spiritual life, i.e., by gazing on, or even "touching", the eternal Truth¹.

> "In that state of life, dear Socrates", said Diotima, "if anywhere, life is worth living for a man, when he contemplates Beauty-itself. If you ever see that, it will appear to you to be not of the level of gold and garments and beautiful young people, at the sight of whom you are now quite upset and willing – you and many others with you – always to see and be together with the object of your love, if possible without eating and drinking – just contemplating and being together with him. What do you think would happen if it were given to anyone to see the Beautiful-itself, pure and unmixed, not spoiled by human flesh and colours and a lot of other mortal nonsense, but if he were able to see divine Beauty in its perfect unity of form? Do you think that life would become vile when a man looked in that direction and contemplated That by the faculty proper to It, and lived with It? Or do you not think, she said, that only there will he be able, seeing Beauty with that eye by which It can be seen, to produce true fruits of virtue, not phantoms of it, since he is in contact with Truth itself, not with a phantom? And would it not be given to him, on having produced true virtue and having fostered it, to become beloved of God and, if ever any man may, immortal?"²

Again, in the *Phaedrus* myth, only purified souls are able to follow the gods in their flight onwards, and in their company to glimpse the supercelestial place in which dwell absolute Justice, Temperance, and Knowledge³. Once more, this is the spiritual vision of transcendent Truth towards which the training of well-endowed young people is directed in the *Republic*. Nothing less depends on this training than the well-being of the commonwealth, that is, of the whole population of the city; for only those who live in contact with eternal Truth and

---

¹ In *Phaedo* 82 a-b "social virtue" (δημοτικὴ καὶ πολιτικὴ ἀρετή), such as temperance and justice, which come to man by custom and by training, without presupposing philosophy and higher spiritual insight, is opposed to higher virtue which is founded on philosophy and implies a purification of the soul that must be as complete as possible. This is exactly what we read in Plotinus, *Enn.* I 2, 4-6.
² *Symposium* 211 d - 212 a.
³ *Phaedr.* 247 a-c.

finally attain to the vision of the supreme Good will be able to realize something of the Good in human life and lead others in its service.

This leading principle of Plato's *Republic* is founded on the firm belief in a perfect and transcendent Reality. This belief was a *rational* one, for the existence of such a Reality must necessarily be assumed to explain the existence of the sensible world and the fact of human knowledge, including the knowledge of moral principles.

What then was Plato's "concept" of philosophy? It is clear that for him philosophy consisted in seeking eternal truth and in living as much as possible in its presence. Such a definition implies many things: first, a superior physical, intellectual, and moral endowment; secondly, a strict and elaborate training in developing these talents; and, finally, a way of living in accord with that lofty Reality, the contemplation of which constitutes the very purpose and achievement of the philosopher's discipline. Further arguments are hardly needed to show that for Plato philosophy was pure theory; but pure theory always implied a certain style of life which included detachment from external things, freedom from desires, and a life conducted according to the promptings of the spirit.

STOICS AND EPICUREANS

Is it an innovation, then, when, within the Stoa, philosophy is compared to a fertile field whose encircling fence is logic, whose soil is physics (including metaphysics), and whose harvest is ethics? Or is it so new when we find that, among the Stoics, ethics comprises not only theoretical reflection but also an implied style of life? The only question that might be raised is this: Did pure theory retain the place of primary interest among the Hellenistic philosophers which it occupied in Plato and Aristotle, or was not theory cultivated in this period for the sake of practice, and physico-metaphysical insight sought in behalf of a certain attitude towards practical life? Thus we are told by Seneca that the true aim of philosophy is to form a man's character and to enable him to stand firm against all the blows of fortune[1].

If the question be put in this form, I should reply that in the post-Aristotelian Schools and even for Plotinus at a later date, philosophy is still that *essential unity of theoretical research and its fruits in personal life* which we found it to have been, in our earlier investigation, for

---

[1] Seneca, *Epist.* 104, 21-24; cf., e.g., *Nat. Quaest.* III, Praef. 10-14.

Socrates and Plato and shall find it to have been, in a measure at least, for Aristotle. A man like Epicurus was surely very far from considering philosophy as an exclusively theoretical discipline, without any consequences for practical life. But in this case two observations must be made. The first is that in Antiquity Epicurus was generally regarded as quite the opposite of a scholarly person. And though Cyril Bailey has amply shown that this verdict does scant justice to the highly ingenious views reflected in Epicurus' elaboration of the atomic theory, while recently Mr. Furley argued that this atomism presupposes a fairly precise knowledge of Aristotle, it is nonetheless true that Epicurus' theory of knowledge is rather primitive and indicates a lack of elementary philosophical training. Secondly, if the Epicurean philosophy of nature was very closely connected with practical life, it should be remembered that the many-sided and scholarly Democritus held the same view in a period that somewhat antedates the expansion of the influence of Socrates and Plato.

I would suggest that at heart Epicurus was interested in physics because of its bearing on a certain attitude towards life which included primarily liberation from fear of the gods and of death. Yet this attitude was dominated by a cosmic vision, founded on pure theory and of supreme importance to the philosopher; so much so that his whole theory of life and his practical attitude would have been inconceivable and untenable without this theory of nature as its foundation. So while Epicurus may have cultivated physics in function of ethics, I should not like to conclude that "therefore" pure theory itself was a fundamentally indifferent matter to him. On the contrary, physical theory was of supreme importance to the philosopher himself, and it was presupposed in his ethics.

In what then did "the philosophical attitude towards life" consist for Epicurus? Of course, Epicureanism was in principle a form of hedonism; but in this case the very principle of hedonism was worked out in the sense of a definite asceticism. It could already be found more or less clearly in Democritus and was reinforced by Epicurus who, having proposed his first principle of pleasure as the supreme good, continued to prescribe that desires should be limited to the strictest minimum of physical necessity, declaring that, if only this minimum is fulfilled, supreme pleasure is attained. To this he added that, though bodily pleasure is the starting point and undeniable basis, yet the pleasure of the mind is of greater import since it takes in both the future and the past as well as the present. Thus, however paradoxical it may seem, an accurate description of the view of life of Epicurus as well as of Democritus *must balance the egocentric striving for happiness with a clear tinge of ascetical spiritualism*. The point is well made then, if it is acknowledged that these two philosophers are by no means so far removed from the Stoa as has usually been thought, nor even, practically speaking, from such a high-minded spiritualist as Plato.

Passing on to the Stoa, the same point may be made regarding the relation between *theoria* and *praxis*, but with one reservation. From the beginning Stoic philosophy exhibited a more learned character than one could find among Epicurus and his pupils. To a greater extent than modern observers are aware, the Stoics, for all their unmistakable interest in practical life, were theoretical philosophers whose view of life was determined by a physico-metaphysical explanation of the cosmos. They too were philosophers in the Greek sense of the word. This means that for them philosophy was theoretical insight implying a certain manner of life that was ascetical and spiritual in character. The difference between Epicurus and the Stoa does not lie in the fact that for the latter philosophy implied an attitude of abnegation regarding externals, while for the former it did not; nor does it mean that the one practised a *strict* abnegation while the other had only a touch of it. The difference lies elsewhere. Epicurus holds that man is by nature an a-social being, inclined to harm his fellow-man[1]. He advised his followers "to release themselves from the prison of affairs and politics"[2] and "to live unknown"[3]. The Stoa, on the the other hand, discovers a natural link between man and man and, as a consequence, has a much higher opinion of social life and its duties. Thus, while all Greek philosophers entertained an ideal of autarchy, the Stoa proposed a philosophy that was essentially social, in sharp contrast to the Epicurean a-social view.

ARISTOTLE

With this much as background, let us now turn to that most theoretical philosopher of all, Aristotle, who deemed a branch of learning the more "scientific" to the extent that it had less to do with praxis and with that underlying principle of physical objects which he

---

[1] Epicurus, *Kyriai doxai* 31-34; cf. also 6-7.
[2] *Sententiae Vaticanae* 58.
[3] The famous words Λάθε βιώσας are commented on by Plutarch, p. 1128-1130. For further texts see my *Greek Philosophy* III, nr. 879.

called "matter". Here, if anywhere, our thesis that for the ancient Greeks philosophy never meant theory in the exclusively intellectual sense would seem in danger of being overthrown.

First of all, it must be observed that the "contemplative life", though its method was always intellectual, had an obviously ethical and religious character for Plato, the Pythagoreans, and the later Platonists, whereas it was more specifically intellectual for Aristotle and was practised in a somewhat different frame of mind. For Plato, the ideal of the philosopher's life was the contemplation of transcendent, purely intelligible Reality (true Being), and the elevation of the mind to the supreme principle, the Good, which is beyond all Being. This contemplation was felt by him as the experience of a divine and overpowering Reality and of its ultimate Ground. Once granted, it imposed on the philosopher stern and exacting duties on behalf of his less-gifted fellow men. For Aristotle, on the other hand, the philosopher's life was that of the scholar and researcher who, whether his investigations concern the physical world, mathematics, or a purely noetic reality, rejoices in the research itself and in the acquired knowledge. His outlook does not have any specifically religious tone or content, and, notwithstanding his assumption of the existence of transcendent, purely spiritual beings, it is not apparent that Aristotle was inspired in his personal life by the thought of a divine and perfect reality; nor was he impelled to feel any sense of duty towards other, less-privileged fellow-men. And its top his ethics exhibits that peculiarly egocentric feature already noted in Democritus and Epicurus[1].

It would be an error, however, to conclude that we have found in Aristotle a doctrine of pure theory which, by definition, excludes praxis and has no implications for practical life. It was Aristotle who drew up the very definition of the "contemplative life"[2] in contradistinction both to the life of pleasure in which money and external goods are pursued, and to the life which seeks honour, power, and glory. Thus, Aristotle's ideal for the philosophical life presupposes not only detachment from the things that engage the intense interest of the crowd, but an equal detachment from the more refined object of interest to which the educated and accomplished[3] aspire. This means that for Aristotle the philosophical life implies *a certain ascetical*

---

[1] I am thinking here in particular of the picture of the μεγαλόψυχος, *E.N.* IV 3, 1123a34-1125a16.
[2] *E.N.* I 5, 1095b14-1096a10.
[3] οἱ χαρίεντες, 1095a17, b22.

attitude of mind, just as it did for Plato and Socrates. Though not too absolute in his assertions, even Aristotle underscores the comparative independence of the philosophical life with respect to material conditions[1].

Such a view would appear at first glance to be rather naive. Did not Aristotle's ideal of the contemplative life presuppose the leisure that depends on the institution of slavery, which in its turn depends on political power and is caused by the desire of material ease? And did it not presuppose such a measure of health as would enable a man to exercise that faculty which Aristotle calls supreme? That is quite true. And it is just for this reason that the Stoa, keenly aware of the unstable and transitory character of external things, cultivated the ascetical element.

PLOTINUS

It was for the same reason that Plotinus, too, that most contemplative and spiritual thinker of late Antiquity, adopted the whole Stoic practice of ascesis along with the contemplative ideal. The inner independence ("autarchy") of the wise man is strongly emphasized[2], detachment from the things of the world becomes the absolute and primary condition for the life of the spirit, which for Plotinus is the only "life" in the full sense of the word, and most essentially a "human" life. As with Aristotle and Seneca[3], to be a man is not to be man-in-a-body with the usual desires and strivings, nor is man essentially a composed being. His real self is spirit, and as such he is not accessible to any of the influences from below[4].

To one who would object that human thinking depends on certain physical conditions, Plotinus would reply that this only *seems* to be so, but it cannot possibly be true. For suppose that a man be struck by illness or suffer an accident so that his mental faculties are troubled or destroyed; in such a case, the true life of the spirit would not be disturbed or hampered, though it would be no more perceptible to us.

---

[1] Autarchy as a characteristic of the contemplative life is repeatedly mentioned by Aristotle. See in particular *E.N.* X 7, 1177 a 27 - b 1.

[2] *Enn.* I 4, 14-16.

[3] For Aristotle, see *E.N.* X 7,1178 a 2; cf. Cicero *De re publ.* VI 26 (De Vogel, *Greek Phil.* III, nr. 959 b): "Nec enim tu is es quem forma ista declarat, sed mens cuiusque, is est quisque". Seneca, *Epist.* 121, 14 (De Vogel, *Greek Phil.* III, nr. 1002).

[4] E.g. *Enn.* I 1, 7 and 10.

ON THE TERM ΦΙΛΟΣΟΦΙΑ

The self-consciousness of the soul is a kind of mirror in which the higher life of the spirit is reflected. The mirror may go to pieces, but the life of the spirit goes on[1]. Thus, the wise man is beyond magical influences, beyond the effect of herbs or drugs, in short, beyond any influence of the sensible world[2]. Here, with Plotinus, we find Greek spiritualism in its most refined and mature form: philosophy is a way of life, an attitude towards life, or what is nowadays called a *spirituality*. However, this does not in the least detract from the fact that the method is an intellectual one: for Plotinus, "the life of the spirit" is a life of thinking. Just as in Plato, and in a way in Aristotle, purely speculative and abstract thought is ranked above "discursive" thinking which always "runs from one thing to the other", whereas the higher kind of abstract thinking is "intuitive", that is to say that it finds its object within itself.

It is true that at the top Plotinus knew about a direct contact with, or contemplation of, that supreme Principle which is the ultimate Source of everything. It transcends intellectual knowledge and reveals itself only to the man who, living the life of the spirit, is in a "purified" condition (purified, viz. from the desires of the body and from all vices that spring from them). Thus, Plotinus' philosophy, though it ends in mysticism, was thoroughly a way of Greek dialectic, as intellectual as any Greek philosophy ever was.

EARLY CHRISTIAN WRITERS

The prevailing spiritualist character of Greek philosophy and the fact that, as a rule, it was actually a way of life explains why ancient Christian writers from St. Justin to St. John Chrysostom were wont to call the Christian life and faith "philosophia", a usage which was adopted by Erasmus in the early sixteenth century and should be taken there much more as a continuation of the early Christian tradition than as an abrupt return to paganism[3]. When St. Justin, a pagan living in the city of Flavia Neapolis (the old Sichem in Samaria) in the middle of the second century, tells the story of his life, he recounts his experiences with representatives of the various schools of philo-

---

[1] *Enn.* I 4, 10.
[2] IV 4, 43; cf. I 1, 3 and 6; III 6, 1-6.
[3] Erasmus, as St. Justin and Clement of Alexandria did before him, recognized the working of the Logos in some of the Greek philosophers and was struck by the Christian character of their style of living. Hence the famous word in one of his *Colloquies*, the *Convivium religiosum*: "Sancte Socrates, ora pro nobis".

sophy. Disappointed by a Stoic philosopher who was unable to teach him anything about God, he turned to a Peripatetic, an "acute spirit". But on the very first day the philosopher asked Justin to fix an honorarium for him "that the teaching might not be without fruit". "And for that reason I left him", says Justin, "in the opinion that he was no philosopher at all"[1].

A perfectly Greek reaction. For the Greeks *required* of the philosopher that he should be detached from external things, admiring and having confidence in him when he showed this attitude. When he did not, they would not acknowledge him as a philosopher at all. On the other hand, their respect for the true philosopher is confirmed by many examples. Impressed by his total disinterestedness, the people of Elis honoured their fellow-citizen Pyrrho by exempting all philosophers from taxes, for his sake[2]. As for Cleanthes, who was poor and had to earn his own livelihood while a student, the Athenians responded to him with enthusiasm. Thus, they applauded him one day when he was walking in the streets of Athens and the wind blew his cloak aside showing that he wore no shirt[3].

To return to St. Justin, he declares, when beginning the story of his life, that "philosophy is a great good, and of great value in the eyes of God" because it leads us to Him and unites us to Him. Later on, after he had learned of the revelation of God in the Jewish prophets and finally in Christ, he concludes that "this philosophy alone was found by him to be a solid basis for life". Now can we say that this view of philosophy is also Greek? Did the Greeks regard it as the task of philosophy to lead men to God?

This is not a question that can be answered in a single word, whether in the affirmative or in the negative. Certainly, from its beginning, Greek philosophy raised the question of the First Cause, and from Thales to Plotinus it was the philosopher's task to give a rational explanation of the whole of things. Greek thought always understood that this meant ascending to the supreme Being and to the First Principle of all. And if some regarded this Source as transcendent, even those who, like the Stoics, were immanentists sought for God with increasing awareness and intensity. Justin, therefore, could rightly say that for him Christian revelation satisfied that deepest longing for certitude, for the metaphysical knowledge and real contact

---

[1] *Dialogus c. Tryphone*, c. 2-8.
[2] Diog. Laert. IX 64.
[3] Diog. Laert. VII 169.

with God which he had always sought in the philosopher's schools.

Sought for – but not attained. For as St. Augustine writes in his *Confessions:* "Seeing your peaceful home from a mountain top without finding a way to it is quite different from being on a highroad leading there, made by the care of the divine Emperor"[1]. And in still another work, St. Augustine writes:

> If the ancient philosophers... were to come back to life again and find the Christian churches filled, the pagan temples empty, the human race summoned to desire not temporal and transitory goods but spiritual and intellectual goods in the hope of life eternal, and responding eagerly to this summons, they would say perhaps (if indeed they were such men as history records them to have been): "This is the ideal that we did not dare preach to the people. We have yielded to the current of their habits rather than drawn them to our own belief and commitment"[2].

We have here a contrast between the esoteric character of most of the Greek philosopher's Schools, in particular of Platonism, and on the other hand the call of Christianity to all men to abandon temporal pursuits and embrace the life of the spirit. There is an implied criticism here of Porphyry and Iamblichus, the direct successors of Plotinus, with their defense of paganism. Plato too is included in this criticism. Not that he made any concessions to the crowd, but he tried in vain to lead them according to the standards of his own philosophy. He was unable to communicate to the masses the truth which he knew himself. In brief, the Christian faith is the fulfilment of what philosophy sought.

In this connection, the distinction between philosophy and theology made by St. Thomas Aquinas is of a considerable importance. Both are concerned with the same things but they proceed according to different means and methods, philosophy operating exclusively by natural reason, theology standing on the firm base of Christian revelation. The latter not only starts from a certitude which philosophy can only seek as its final term, but it also possesses an ampler knowledge.

St. Thomas held the human intellect in high esteem. Indeed, he was convinced that by itself reason is capable of coming to a knowledge of

---

[1] *Confess.* VII, 21, in fine.
[2] *De vera relig.* 4, 6.

God's existence and, within certain limits, of His nature. But he also knew that man is weak and that, practically speaking, he all too frequently fails to acquire that knowledge of God which in principle he can attain by the use of natural reason.

This being so, we must be careful to make the proper reservations when St. Justin says, without qualification, that "philosophy leads man to God", and that "she alone unites us to Him"[1]. This much, however, is true: Greek philosophy did seek God and its quest became increasingly more intense and self-conscious with the passage of time.

SUMMARY OF THE GREEK CONCEPTION

In treating of what philosophy meant to the Greeks, we had to touch on the metaphysical side of the problem, while dealing with contemplation and its object. But we also found that contemplation implied or presupposed a certain attitude towards life since, for the Greeks, pure theory was never pure theory alone. This generally neglected aspect of the question seemed to us no less important than the metaphysical one, in as much as there was a necessary link between the two aspects in the Greek mind. It became urgent, then, to correct what has almost become the traditional view of modern interpreters: I mean the tendency to hold up someone like Socrates as an admirable person without observing that in the philosopher's own mind his moral attitude and behaviour were essentially bound up with his philosophy, and that this was not an exceptional case, since the normal Greek view included both aspects.

To say that "philosophy" for the Greeks meant "rational reflection on the whole of things", is correct enough as far as it goes. But if we are to complete the definition, we must add that "by virtue of the loftiness of its object, this reflection implied a very definite moral attitude and way of life which were held to be essential both by the philosophers themselves and by their contemporaries". This simply means that philosophy was never merely an intellectual affair. It is just as great an error to hold that in the classical period the manner of life had no bearing on philosophy, as to maintain that in the later

---

[1] Miss A. M. Malingrey, *"Philosophia"*, Étude d'un groupe de mots dans la littérature grecque, des Présocratiques au IVe siècle après J. Chr., Paris 1961 (a work which appeared after the present paper had been written) puts it in this way: when Christian writers started using the word φιλοσοφία for the contents of revealed truth, they gave to the term a new connotation, covering much more than it ever did before (Malingrey p. 127 f.; 292-300).

ON THE TERM ΦΙΛΟΣΟΦΙΑ

Hellenistic-Roman period *theoria* yielded to *praxis*. This much can be admitted: there is a certain shift of emphasis in the later period from the theoretical to the practical aspects of philosophy, not by everyone, but at least in some cases. Thus, while the philosophy of nature was still of the greatest importance for Epicurus, he did lay a great deal of stress on philosophy as an attitude towards life. In the Stoa, on the other hand, we find a few important thinkers, and in their surroundings quite a number of more or less important scholars, who were intensely interested in theory for its own sake[1], while others clearly transferred the emphasis to morals[2]. In the case of the Sceptics it would hardly be correct to speak of a transfer of accent, since they were usually theoretical thinkers with intellectual interests. Finally, at the end of the epoch, we have Plotinus and Porphyry who, though philosophy implied to them as categorically as possible a style of living, remained in the theoretical tradition of Plato and Aristotle.

We may now draw together the conclusions of our investigation as follows: In older Greek philosophy we find a *theoria* which necessarily implies a certain moral attitude and style of life; in later Greek philosophy we find, not always but more often than not, a moral attitude and style of life which necessarily supposes *theoria*.

CONCLUSION

To conclude. While for many modern philosophers philosophy reaches its goal when every non-rational element is eliminated, so that

---

[1] While distinguishing between "scholars" and "thinkers", I do not intend to separate these qualifications from one another. The Stoa, like several other Greek schools of philosophy, offers the example of scholarly thinkers and of "thinking" scholars! Of "important thinkers", however, there have always been only a few. But it might be a sign of the theoretical interest found in this school that, in several of its chief representatives and among their followers, scholarly research in various fields of science flourished.

[2] It should be noticed here that in the comparison made by the Stoics in illustration of the division of philosophy the order of the three parts is not always the same. According to the current idea of what Stoic philosophy was most interested in, one might expect that in the comparison with a living being physics would be compared with the flesh, while ethics would correspond by analogy to the soul. Yet according to Diogenes Laertius (VII, 40) the sequence is as follows: Logic corresponds to the bones and sinews, ethics to the fleshly parts, and physics to the soul. Once again, in the simile of the egg, the yolk in the center is not ethics but physics, to which it is added that the sequence of the last two parts was subject to variation (see De Vogel, *Gr. Phil.*, III, n. 898).

a purely intellectual way of thinking has been reached, while any concern about practical living or of attaining to a kind of Reality which is said to be beyond reason is excluded, the Greek view of philosophy either may appear as impracticable and undesired, or as an ideal, worthy to be striven after in our days. The fact that in the Greek idea of philosophy the very life of reason is so to speak personalized or "moralized", must appear attractive and even exemplary to some modern men who feel that the ancient idea of philosophy implying a way of life, far from being inferior to a mere intellectual cleverness, was in fact much more. These persons will be most faithful to the Greek ideal, when they understand philosophy as an appeal to the person as a whole to place himself under the direction of reason and, while living on the level of pure theory, practise a theoretically founded morality.

PYTHAGORICA

CHAPTER II

LES FRAGMENTS DITS DE PHILOLAUS[1]

I.

En 1922, Monsieur Armand Delatte, professeur à l'université de Liège, publia son *Étude sur la politique pythagoricienne* – dans ce temps-là un sujet assez nouveau et une étude vraiment révolutionnaire –. Une vingtaine d'années après, aux États Unis, M. Von Fritz et, un peu après lui, M. L. Minar ont repris le même sujet. M. Von Fritz en a fait un très bel ouvrage, solidement fondé sur une analyse impeccable des sources. Aux sources écrites il a ajouté le témoignage des monnaies auquel on ne saurait guère se dérober.

Quelques années après, M. Van der Waerden a traité les mathématiques et l'astronomie pythagoriciennes dans toute une série d'études. Récemment, en 1963, les travaux combinés de ces deux savants ont produit une étude d'ensemble sur la personne et l'œuvre de Pythagore qu'on peut lire dans le vol. XXIV de la *Realencyclopädie* de Pauly-Wissowa.

Un peu avant la publication de l'article mentionné ci-dessus, une autre étude d'ensemble a paru sur Pythagore et l'ancien pythagorisme: celle de M. Guthrie dans le premier volume de son *History of Greek Philosophy* (Cambr. 1962). Après avoir toujours entendu dire que, sur la personne de Pythagore, point n'est possible de savoir rien de précis, excepté qu'il croyait à la métempsychose, cela fait vraiment du bien de voir un homme intelligent occupé à reconstruire la philosophie qui puisse remonter à Pythagore lui-même, et cela en partant de principes parfaitement raisonnables.

Cependant, dans la même année qui a vu paraître le premier volume du *History* de M. Guthrie un autre livre important a paru sur Pythagore et sur l'ancien Pythagorisme: c'était le volume intitulé *Weisheit und Wissenschaft* par M. Walter Burkert, étude très substantielle qui

[1] Cette étude sur les textes de Philolaus date de janvier 1968. Elle est inédite. Le texte fut lu en grande partie pour la Faculté des Lettres à Liège, le 20 et 22 mars 1968.

renouvelle essentiellement la thèse allemande bien connue que, pour Aristote déjà, il n'y avait pas de philosophe Pythagore. M. Burkert, bien entendu, croit à l'existence d'un pythagorisme philosophique avant Platon. C'est qu'il défend très nettement l'authenticité d'un nombre de textes de Philolaus. Mais, à son avis, c'est là le début du pythagorisme philosophique et, à un degré assez modeste, scientifique. En somme, Philolaus ne s'occupait guère de problèmes mathématiques. C'était Archytas qui dans le cercle des pythagoriciens s'en occupait le premier, – toujours si l'on veut faire exception pour Hippasos qui était expulsé de l'École. Avant Philolaus, d'après M. Burkert, pas de trace d'un pythagorisme philosophique ou scientifique. Tous les textes qui en témoignent sont d'une époque beaucoup plus tardive. On ne s'y trouve nullement sur une base ferme. A cause de cela, mieux vaut ne pas s'y fier. Il y a les textes de Philolaus – non pas tous ceux qui sont imprimés chez Diels-Kranz comme fragments authentiques, mais un certain nombre en tout cas – et voilà le commencement. Philolaus fait de la philosophie, non pas d'une manière bien originale, bien sûr, mais enfin il en fait. Il fait la philosophie comme on peut s'y attendre dans l'époque où il vivait, c'est-à-dire la seconde partie du cinquième siècle: il le fait un peu en eclectique, sous l'influence des courants philosophiques et scientifiques de son temps. Ce n'était pas très original, mais dans l'École pythagoricienne de son temps c'était une chose absolument nouvelle.

Alors, que penser du pythagorisme plus ancien et de son fondateur? C'est parfaitement clair, nous dit M. Burkert: le sage de Crotone n'était nullement philosophe dans le sens des Milésiens ou de Parménide, c'était un «sage» d'un style plus ancien et pré-philosophique, admiré par ses contemporains pour ses dons surnaturels et cette espèce de «sagesse» qui est propre au schamanisme. A ses élèves il donnait des préscriptions de vie (les ἀκούσματα) d'un caractère nettement primitif, tels que: s'abstenir de haricots, défense de ramasser ce qui est tombé, pas toucher un coq blanc, pas enjamber une barrière, etc. – et voilà tout. C'était les «acousmatiques» qui étaient les pythagoriciens de marque ancienne: les «mathématiques» (μαθηματικοί) étaient de date plus récente – pas antérieurs au 5ième siècle bien sûr, et même probablement pas antérieurs à Philolaus.

C'est donc avec Philolaus que le pythagorisme fait son entrée dans l'histoire de la philosophie et de la science. Cette thèse, évidemment, implique bien des problèmes. Je me propose d'examiner l'ensemble de cette théorie, particulièrement les problèmes relatifs à une philosophie et à une science mathématique pythagoriciennes antérieures à Philolaus, dans un autre chapitre[1]. Dans l'exposé suivant je veux me limiter aux problèmes autour des textes de Philolaus, leur authenticité, leur contenu, leur valeur philosophique. M. Burkert a traité ces textes dans un chapitre important qui est un des plus intéressants de son ouvrage. L'approche nouvelle qu'il y a faite est pour nous une raison d'étudier ces textes avec une attention spéciale et intensifiée.

La controverse sur l'authenticité des fragments de Philolaus a commencé par l'excellente étude de August Boeckh, 1819. Boeckh acceptait tous les fragments actuellement rassemblés dans le paragraphe 44 B de Diels-Kranz, comme authentiques, même le num. 21, dont l'inauthenticité a été facilement reconnu et démontré par Zeller. Cependant, en Angleterre, les fragments étaient rejetés en bloc par Bywater (*Journal of Philology* 1868). Bywater fut suivi par Burnet in *Early Gr. Phil.* (1892, [4]1945); plus tard par Erich Frank qui, dans son fameux livre *Plato und die sogenannten Pythagoreer* (1923), défendit la thèse que tous les soi-disant fragments de Philolaus étaient un produit de l'Académie, dans la première génération après Platon: ce sont Speusippe et Xénocrate qui en étaient les auteurs. – Le livre de Frank, dans ces années-là, a fait une assez grande impression. La défense des fragments, habilement faite par M. Mondolfo dans la *Rivista di Filologia* de 1937, n'était qu'une *vox clamantis in deserto:* la confiance en l'authenticité de ces fragments avait été assez profondément ébranlée. En Angleterre, M. J. E. Raven a encore exprimé ses doutes dans son livre *Pythagoreans and Eleatics*, Cambridge 1948. Quelques années plus tard, dans le volume *The Presocratic Philosophers*, composé par MM. Kirk et Raven, Cambridge 1957, les fragments attribués à Philolaus sont rejetés, non pas comme un produit de l'Académie immédiatement après Platon cette fois-ci, mais essentiellement à cause d'une ressemblance supposée de ses fragments à certains textes d'Aristote. C'est cette ressemblance en premier lieu qui fait dire les auteurs du volume cité: «Les fragments attribués à Philolaus peuvent être rejetés, avec regret mais avec peu d'hésitation, comme faisant partie d'une falsification post-aristotélicienne, assez adroitement basés sur les exposés qu'Aristote lui-même a donnés du système pythagoricien».

Après cette assertion c'est une surprise agréable de lire dans le beau volume de M. Guthrie, *A History of Greek Philosophy* I (Cambridge

[1] Voir le ch. III.

1962), que l'auteur s'est laissé convaincre par Mondolfo et que, ne trouvant rien dans les fragments qui ne saurait être écrit par Philolaus, il ne voit pas de raisons suffisantes pour rejeter ces fragments.

M. Burkert prend une position un peu différente de ses prédécesseurs: il remarque que, après tout, il n'y a pas lieu d'en faire une alternative, comme s'il faudrait ou bien accepter tous ces fragments, ou bien les rejeter en bloc. Lui, il accepte les numéros 1-7, 13 et 17 comme fragments authentiques du livre de Philolaus, et cela non seulement pour des raisons négatives telles que « il n'y a rien là que Philolaus n'aurait su écrire», mais pour la raison positive que ces textes sont de style ancien et présocratique. A son avis on ne saurait en dire autant des autres.

Quant au principe, évidemment, la remarque de M. Burkert est fort juste: personne n'aimerait plus défendre l'authenticité du fragment 21 qui contient des termes et des idées nettement stoïciens, aristotéliciens et platoniciens; mais alors, ne faut-il pas étendre son doute aux fragments dix et douze, sans que tous les autres fragments ne partagent la même suspicion? Moi, il me faut avouer que la formule élégante pour ἁρμονία comme πολυμιγέων ἕνωσις καὶ δίχα φρονεόντων συμφρόνησις (fr. 10), bien qu'on ne saurait exclure que Philolaus l'ait écrite, me paraît assez suspecte, et il en est de même pour le πέμπτον σῶμα, dit ὁ τᾶς σφαίρας ὁλκάς, du fr. 12.

Mais il est temps de laisser toute polémique et d'examiner les textes tels qu'ils nous parlent eux-mêmes. Je veux commencer par poser quatre questions.

1. *Philolaus peut-il avoir écrit ces textes*? Cela veut dire: n'y a-t-il rien là qui ne suppose une date ultérieure? (De tels indices sont, e.a., des termes ou des idées platoniciens, aristotéliciens ou stoïciens, ou encore, plus généralement parlant, un langage d'une époque ultérieure au 5ième siècle).

2. *Y a-t-il des indications positives* qui imposent une date assez haute, disons antérieure au 4ième siècle?

3. En cas que Philolaus soit l'auteur de ces textes, faut-il admettre qu'il fût l'auteur des théories et principes explicitement ou implicitement contenus dans ces lignes, ou faut-il plutôt voir en lui le porte-parole de théories et d'idées bien antérieures? (Cela veut dire: y a-t-il des parallèles plus anciens?)

4. Quel est le rapport de ces textes à l'exposé d'Aristote dans *Métaph.* A 5? Avons-nous ici la source, ou au moins la source prin-

cipale, de cet exposé, ou faut-il constater l'existence de différences assez considérables?

En vue de ces quatre questions mais sans essayer de donner une réponse directe, examinons les textes.

Fr. 1. Diog. Laerce VIII 85. Περὶ φύσεως ὧν ἀρχὴ ἥδε· «ἀ φύσις δ'ἐν τῷ κόσμῳ ἁρμόχθη ἐξ ἀπείρων τε καὶ περαινόντων, καὶ ὅλος (ὁ) κόσμος καὶ τὰ ἐν αὐτῷ πάντα.»

Voici le commencement du livre »Sur la nature«,
Et, à l'arrangement du monde, la Nature fut composée de choses illimitées et de choses limitantes, le monde dans sa totalité ainsi que tout ce qui est en lui.

Dans le fragm. 1 il faut prêter quelque attention à la particule δέ. Boeckh l'a très bien remarquée. C'est à cause de sa présence qu'il a cru que, malgré ce qu'en dit Diogène Laerce, notre fragm. 1 ne saurait avoir été le début du livre de Philolaus. Remarque fort raisonnable – autant qu'on ne se souvient du fait que la même particule se trouve dans la première ligne du fragm. 1 d'Héraclite[1], – fragment étrange, lui aussi, pour former le début d'un livre, mais dont, tout de même, cette place est bien attestée. Il faut se rappeler, en outre, qu'on trouve la particule δέ dans le fragm. 1 de Ion de Chios[2], et au début de plusieurs traités du Corpus Hippocraticum[3]. Il me semble que, dans ce cas, M. Burkert a vu bien quand il a trouvé dans l'usage de la particule δέ de notre fragment le signe d'un style archaïque. Voilà donc une première indication pour attribuer à notre fragment une date assez haute.

Boeckh qui n'était nullement dépourvu de sens critique, a trouvé que la particule δέ n'était pas l'unique difficulté de notre fragment: pour lui, il s'agissait du sens même. «*La nature dans le cosmos* est composée de choses illimitées et de choses qui limitent, le cosmos dans son ensemble et tout ce qui est en lui.» Qu'est-ce que cela veut dire? En quoi *la nature* du cosmos se distingue t-elle du cosmos lui-même? «La nature», est-ce les choses qui sont dans le cosmos? Elle serait alors identique à τὰ ἐν αὐτῷ πάντα. Et sinon, que pourrait-elle être qui ne serait pas le cosmos lui-même?

---

[1] Diels VS 22, τοῦ δὲ λόγου τοῦδε ἐόντος ἀεὶ ἀξύνετοι γίνονται ἄνθρωποι -
[2] Diels VS 36, ἀρχὴ δέ μοι τοῦ λόγου· πάντα τρία καὶ οὐδὲν πλέον ἢ ἔλασσον τούτων τῶν τριῶν.
[3] Voir Burkert, *W.u.W.* p. 234, n. 73.

On ne manquera pas d'observer que la traduction proposée par moi différait un peu de celle de Boeckh. En mettant que «à l'arrangement du monde, la Nature *fut composée* de choses illimitées et de choses limitantes», je n'ai pas voulu suggérer que ἐν κόσμῳ soit pour ainsi dire une apposition adverbiale qui indique le temps, mais j'ai rendu l'aoriste ἁρμόχθη. En effet, on ne saurait traduire «La nature dans le cosmos est composée de» –. Boeckh s'est créé des difficultés un peu plus que réelles en écrivant: «Die Natur im Kosmos, heisst es, *ist aus Unbegrenztem und Begrenzendem gefügt*»[1]. Ce n'est pas cela que le texte dit. Il dit:

La nature dans le cosmos fut jointe *de choses illimitées et de choses limitantes*.

Ce n'est pas un état de choses, c'est un procès réalisé dans le passé, qui est exprimé par le verbe ἁρμόχθη. C'est pourquoi on peut traduire:

A l'arrangement du monde, la Nature dans l'univers fut composée de –

Le procès a pu durer quelque temps, mais en tout cas il s'agit d'un procès qui s'est réalisé dans le passé.

Boeckh avait raison, d'ailleurs, de remarquer que l'expression du texte est un peu vague. De ce fait il a voulu conclure que, premièrement, *il faut corriger le texte* («Die Stelle muss verderbt sein»!) et, deuxièmement, qu'il est impossible qu'il ait été écrit en tête du livre. Disons plutôt que cette phrase un peu maladroite et un peu vague a pu en effet avoir été écrite, telle que nous la lisons, au commencement du livre d'un philosophe assez ancien, qui cherchait à s'exprimer avec un peu de peine. Tout ce qu'il faut admettre est que, peutêtre, Philolaus n'ait pas disposé immédiatement de cette clarté exemplaire que Boeckh a voulu lui attribuer. Et voilà donc un autre argument en faveur d'une date assez haute à attribuer à notre texte.

Fr. 2. Ἐκ τοῦ Φιλολάου περὶ κόσμου. ἀνάγκα τὰ ἐόντα εἶμεν πάντα ἢ περαίνοντα ἢ ἄπειρα ἢ περαίνοντά τε καὶ ἄπειρα· ἄπειρα δὲ μόνον ⟨ἢ περαίνοντα μόνον⟩ οὔ κα εἴη. ἐπεὶ τοίνυν φαίνεται οὔτ' ἐκ περαινόντων πάντων ἐόντα οὔτ' ἐξ ἀπείρων πάντων, δῆλον τἆρα ὅτι ἐκ περαινόντων τε καὶ ἀπείρων ὅ τε κόσμος καὶ τὰ ἐν αὐτῷ συναρμόχθη. δηλοῖ δὲ καὶ τὰ ἐν τοῖς ἔργοις. τὰ μὲν γὰρ αὐτῶν ἐκ περαινόντων περαίνοντι, τὰ δ' ἐκ περαινόντων τε καὶ ἀπείρων περαίνοντί τε καὶ οὐ περαίνοντι, τὰ δὲ ἐξ ἀπείρων ἄπειρα φανέονται.

Extrait du livre de Philolaus *«Sur le monde»*.

[1] Boeckh, *Philolaus* p. 46.

Il est nécessaire que les choses qui existent soient ou bien toutes limitantes ou illimitées, ou qu'elles soient à la fois limitantes et illimitées. Or, qu'elles soient exclusivement illimitées ou exclusivement limitantes, ce n'est pas possible. Donc, puisqu'il ne paraît consister uniquement en choses limitantes ni uniquement en choses illimitées, il est évident que le monde et ce qui est en lui est composé de choses limitantes autant que de choses illimitées. C'est clair aussi par ce qu'on voit dans les travaux des hommes: leurs matériaux qui consistent en choses limitantes limitent, ceux qui consistent à la fois en choses limitantes et illimitées limitent et ne limitent pas, tandis que ceux qui ne consistent qu'en choses illimitées paraîtront illimitées.

Dans les fragments 1 et 2 il est question de «choses qui limitent» et de «choses illimitées»: περαίνοντα et ἄπειρα. M. Burkert trouve dans ces termes une autre indication pour une date assez ancienne. C'est que περαίνοντα et ἄπειρα sont beaucoup plus concrets que des formes abstraites telles que πέρας et ἄπειρον. Tandis que les dernières évoquent chez lui un peu trop vivement certaines réminiscences platoniciennes, avec περαίνοντα et ἄπειρα il se sent bel et bien au 5ième siècle: c'est l'authentique Philolaus qui a dû écrire cela.

Mon commentaire à moi serait un peu différent. Ma première remarque serait plutôt que, avec ces textes, apparemment nous ne sommes pas à la base même du pythagorisme philosophique, et cela parce que, d'après ce que nous en savons, la forme originelle du dualisme pythagoricien n'était pas περαίνοντα - ἄπειρα mais πέρας - ἄπειρον. C'est en tout cas ce qu'en pensait Aristote qui dit à propos de la συστοιχία (*Metaph.* A 5, 986a 22-29) que Alcméon de Crotone déjà avait cette théorie, et peutêtre l'eût-il empruntée «à eux» – ce serait alors la toute première génération de l'École pythagoricienne à laquelle remontait cette doctrine –, ou peutêtre «eux» l'eussent-ils empruntée à lui.

Et pourquoi les principes de πέρας - ἄπειρον seraient-ils postplatoniciens? Le principe du ἄπειρον était introduit par Anaximandre. Était-il impossible qu'un philosophe d'une génération plus jeune, instruit aussi bien par les Milésiens que par les mathématiciens de Babylon, eût ajouté à ce principe unique en contre-partie un principe déterminant, qu'il eût introduit sous le nom de πέρας? Ce n'est que quand on a une certaine thèse à défendre qu'on peut soutenir que point ne fût possible de parler de πέρας au 6ième siècle. Comme si le grand Parménide n'ait pas parlé du ἐόν et du μὴ ἐόν, termes abstraits et mis au singulier, et encore, comme si cet ἐόν formidable – un, total et indivisible – ne fût pensé pour exclure le dualisme pythagoricien. Ce ne sont là, enfin, pas des fables. Ce sont ou bien des faits indéniables – l'ἄπειρον d'Anaximandre et le ἐόν de Parménide –, ou des choses aussi vraisemblables qu'il est tout à fait raisonnable de les accepter (il est attesté que Parménide était de formation pythagoricienne et que, plus tard, il s'est séparé de cette École).

Que Philolaus ait parlé de περαίνοντα et ἄπειρα, c'est là exactement la signature d'un siècle postérieur où dominait la pensée pluraliste. M. Burkert a absolument raison quand il dit que Philolaus n'était pas très original. Mais cela ne signifie nullement qu'il n'ait pas exposé une doctrine ancienne, dont les principes remontent au fondateur de l'École. Au contraire, s'il n'en avait pas été ainsi, il faudrait reconnaître qu'il fût un philosophe de grande allure, un innovateur fort important, auquel il faudrait assigner dans l'histoire de la philosophie une place de premier ordre, à côté d'un Parménide et d'un Héraclite. Et dans ce cas, on peut être certain qu'Aristote l'aurait mentionné. S'il ne l'a pas fait, cela ne prouve pas qu'il n'ait pas connu son livre (sur ce point-ci, encore, je suis d'accord avec M. Burkert): c'était qu'il ne le considérait nullement comme un grand fondateur (ce qu'il serait, en effet, d'après la thèse de M. Burkert) mais essentiellement comme exposant d'une tradition philosophique très ancienne. Et c'est cela ce qui explique le silence d'Aristote.

D'autre part, tout en admettant que Philolaus exposait essentiellement la doctrine dualiste de l'ancien pythagorisme, nous ne nions nullement qu'il ait subi quelque influence de son propre siècle, en particulier quand il parlait de περαίνοντα καὶ ἄπειρα au lieu de πέρας - ἄπειρον. Zénon, quand il déduisait les conséquences de l'hypothèse que l'être soit multiple, disait[1]: dans ce cas, il faut ou bien que les choses existantes soient limitées en nombre – πεπερασμένα – (s'il y en a exactement autant qu'il existe), ou qu'elles soient illimitées en nombre – ἄπειρα – (parce qu'il y a toujours quelque autre chose entre les choses existantes, et de nouveau d'autres entre celles-ci). Philolaus qui écrit peu de temps après Zénon, préfère le terme περαίνοντα à celui de πεπερασμένα. Il adopte en même temps les termes pluralistes de Zénon et les altère selon ses propres vues.

En ce qui concerne le style de notre fragment, M. Burkert a fait une autre remarque fort juste: la répétition fréquente des mêmes termes

---

[1] Diels-Kranz 29 B 3.

fait l'impression d'une certaine rigidité de forme, d'un manque de souplesse qui est certainement un trait archaïque.

Que signifient les mots: δηλοῖ δὲ καὶ τὰ ἐν τοῖς ἔργοις (l. 5-6)? Kranz traduit: «Das beweist auch die Beobachtung in der Wirklichkeit». Dans une édition antérieure des Fragments des Présocratiques Diels avait rendu τὰ ἔργα par «les champs»[1]. Avant lui, Boeckh avait supposé que l'auteur a pensé à des «constructions»: la signification de «bâtiments» se trouve fréquemment chez les auteurs grecs, et c'est là, expliquait-il, la comparaison la plus naturelle pour illustrer la construction du monde[2]. Diels, apparemment, a remarqué que c'est plutôt aux champs cultivés que l'ancien Grec associait le mot ἔργα. On ne saurait lui contredire. Pourtant, ce ne sont ni les champs cultivés seuls ni les bâtiments seuls qui sont désignés par le mot ἔργα. Ce mot désigne, généralement parlant, *le travail des hommes et son produit concret*. Dans notre fragment de Philolaus l'expression τὰ ἐν τοῖς ἔργοις ne veut pas dire «la réalité», comme parfois le Grec oppose ἔργῳ à λόγῳ, mais elle désigne le travail humain et ses produits comme phénomène analogue qui éclaircit les procès de la Nature qu'on voit dans l'univers: c'est qu'il y a la même loi sur les deux terrains, – celle du nombre. Nous trouverons les deux terrains mentionnés l'un à côté de l'autre dans le fragm. 11, les lignes 16-20 (11-13).

Fr. 3. ἀρχὰν γὰρ οὐδὲ τὸ γνωσούμενον ἐσσεῖται πάντων ἀπείρων ἐόντων (κατὰ τὸν Φιλόλαον).

C'est qu'il n'y aura pas d'objet de connaissance du tout, si toute chose est illimitée.

Ce fragment ne nous pose pas de problèmes particuliers. Il faut seulement remarquer qu'il s'agit ici du problème de la connaissance: aucune chose ne saurait être connue[3], nous dit l'auteur, si tout était illimité. Cela veut dire: si l'on n'admet pas le principe du πέρας, pas moyen de connaître aucune chose.

Fr. 4. καὶ πάντα γα μὰν τὰ γιγνωσκόμενα ἀριθμὸν ἔχοντι· οὐ γὰρ οἷόν τε οὐδὲν οὔτε νοηθῆμεν οὔτε γνωσθῆμεν ἄνευ τούτου.

---

[1] «Die Äcker», VS 2. Aufl.
[2] «die natürlichste Vergleichung zu dem Weltbau». Boeckh, *Philolaus* p. 50.
[3] τὸ γνωσούμενον comme forme, sans doute pourrait être le sujet de la phrase. Il est plus probable, tout de même, que l'auteur a pensé à l'objet.

Et en effet, tout ce qui est connu contient le nombre; car sans cela, pas moyen de rien penser ou de rien connaître.

Encore une fois, c'est du problème de la connaissance qu'il s'agit; mais la façon de poser ce problème est de signature post-anaximandrienne. C'était après Anaximandre qu'un philosophe contemporain un peu plus jeune se voyait contraint de constater: il nous faut absolument introduire un second principe, celui du πέρας, sous peine de ne pouvoir rien penser et rien connaître.

Il fallait un vrai philosophe pour poser le problème ainsi dans la seconde partie du 6ième siècle, d'accord. Mais saurait-on dire qu'il fût impossible de poser ce problème avant la seconde partie du 5ième? – Si l'on parle ἐξ ὑποθέσεως, sans doute on le dira. Sinon, il faudra se souvenir du fait que, peu de temps après Pythagore, encore au 6ième siècle, Parménide aussi s'occupait du problème de la connaissance. D'une manière bien différente, bien entendu. – C'est qu'il était Parménide, et non pas Pythagore. Mais il faudra reconnaître que, après tout, il n'y a aucune raison pour dénier *a priori* que Pythagore ait pu poser le problème de la connaissance.

Fr. 5. ὅ γα μὰν ἀριθμὸς ἔχει δύο μὲν ἴδια εἴδη, περισσὸν καὶ ἄρτιον, τρίτον δὲ ἐπ' ἀμφοτέρων μειχθέντων ἀρτιοπέριττον· ἑκατέρω δὲ τῶ εἴδεος πολλαὶ μορφαί, ἃς ἕκαστον αὐταυτὸ σημαίνει.

Le nombre a deux espèces propres, le pair et l'impair, et un troisième qui est un mélange des deux, le pair-impair. Et chacune de ces espèces a beaucoup de formes, que chacune fait paraître elle-même[1].

Il est très possible que la troisième espèce soit introduite par Philolaus, mais on ne peut guère douter que la distinction entre le pair et l'impair remonte à la première génération de l'École et au fondateur lui-même. Elle se trouve nettement chez Épicharme, fr. 2.

Quant à l'ἀρτιοπέριττον, si quelqu'un remarque que cette notion ne saurait être très ancienne, parce qu'elle comprend en premier lieu le ἕν et pour cette raison se range au-dessus des opposés ἕν - πολλά, et même des opposés ἄρτιον - περιττόν, on pourrait répondre par les réflections suivantes. (1) Que le concept d'ἀρτιοπέριττον implique la tendance de se ranger au-dessus des opposés mentionnés, il n'y a point de doute. (2) Que pour cette raison-même la conception ultérieure qui fait du ἕν le principe suprême et absolu, est un développement assez

[1] ἕκαστον, sc. εἶδος.

logique et compréhensible, ce n'est pas moins clair. (3) Cela ne veut pas dire, tout de même, que le concept d'ἀρτιοπέριττον ne puisse avoir été pensé longtemps avant. On aurait tort, sans doute, de vouloir imposer aux penseurs d'un siècle archaïque les exigences logiques d'une période bien ultérieure. Pour eux l'ἀρτιοπέριττον n'était, certes, pas incompatible avec le caractère fondamental des opposés ἄρτιον - περιττόν. (4) Quant au pair d'opposés ἕν - πολλά, je ne suis pas sûre qu'il fît partie de la συστοιχία originelle. Je pense plutôt qu'il fut ajouté après Parménide.

En somme, ce que nous trouvons dans le fragm. 5 de Philolaus peut très bien avoir été écrit par lui, tout en reproduisant une doctrine bien plus ancienne.

Nous en arrivons au long fragment 6[1]. Il consiste en deux parties: dans la première il s'agit des principes généraux de l'univers – dits «des choses» –, dans la seconde des intervaux de la musique. C'est surtout la première partie qui n'est pas tellement claire.

Fr. 6, 1-9. περὶ δὲ φύσιος καὶ ἁρμονίας ὧδε ἔχει· ἁ μὲν ἐστὼ τῶν πραγμάτων ἀίδιος ἔσσα καὶ αὐτὰ μὲν ἁ φύσις θείαν γα καὶ οὐκ ἀνθρωπίνην ἐνδέχεται γνῶσιν πλέον γα ἢ ὅτι οὐχ οἷόν τ' ἦν οὐθὲν τῶν ἐόντων καὶ γιγνωσκομένων ὑφ' ἁμῶν γα γενέσθαι[2] μὴ ὑπαρχούσας τᾶς ἐστοῦς τῶν πραγμάτων, ἐξ ὧν συνέστα ὁ κόσμος, καὶ τῶν περαινόντων καὶ τῶν ἀπείρων. ἐπεὶ δὲ ταὶ ἀρχαὶ ὑπᾶρχον οὐχ ὁμοῖαι οὐδ' ὁμόφυλοι ἔσσαι, ἤδη ἀδύνατον ἦς κα 5 αὐταῖς κοσμηθῆναι, εἰ μὴ ἁρμονία ἐπεγένετο, ᾧτινιῶν ἄδε τρόπῳ ἐγένετο. τὰ μὲν ὦν ὁμοῖα καὶ ὁμόφυλα ἁρμονίας οὐδὲν ἐπεδέοντο, τὰ δὲ ἀνόμοια μηδὲ ὁμόφυλα μηδὲ ἰσοταγῆ ἀνάγκα τᾷ τοιαύτᾳ ἁρμονίᾳ συγκεκλεῖσθαι, οἵα μέλλοντι ἐν τῷ κόσμῳ κατέχεσθαι. 10

Essayons de traduire.
Quant à la nature et l'harmonie il en est ainsi. L'être des choses qui est éternel et la nature elle-même permet une connaissance divine et non seulement humaine, —

D'habitude on rend le mot ἐνδέχεται par «suppose» ou «exige». Or, cette traduction est un peu adaptée au contexte, c'est à dire, d'après les idées des éditeurs modernes. Pourtant, le mot ἐνδέχεται signifie «permet», et il est plus correct de s'en tenir là. Un peu plus loin

---
[1] Je cite les textes de quelque longueur d'abord avec les numéros des lignes selon l'édition de Diels-Kranz. J'ajouterai entre parenthèses les numéros des lignes de mon propre texte.
[2] Voir n. 2 de la page suivante.

l'auteur lui-même nous expliquera pourquoi il dit que la Nature nous «permet» une connaissance divine et non seulement humaine (fr. 11, l. 16-20 = 12-15 dans mon propre texte, infra, p. 50 ff.).

Quant au terme «la ἐστώ des choses», il ne présuppose pas nécessairement l'οὐσία d'Aristote, bien que pour l'interprétateur moderne il soit bien séduisant de se servir du terme «substance». Mieux vaut peutêtre, pour éviter une terminologie par trop technique, parler simplement de *l'être des choses*. C'est un peu vague, bien entendu. Mais la formule ne précise pas davantage. Elle n'indique ni spécialement «l'essence», ni exclusivement «l'existence» des choses. Elle dit tout simplement l'être, ou l'être-là[1].»

«L'être des choses» est identifié un peu vaguement à «la nature ellemême» qui est apparemment la totalité des «choses». Quelques lignes plus loin (4-5) il est dit que «le cosmos consiste en choses qui sont, en choses limitantes ainsi qu'en celles qui sont illimitées».

Donc, «les choses», c'est bien les περαίνοντα et les ἄπειρα qui ensemble forment le cosmos. Or, nous dira l'auteur dans les lignes suivantes (6-7), ce serait là chose impossible (ἀδύνατον ἦς κα αὐταῖς κοσμηθῆναι), si l'harmonie ne s'était ajoutée à ces principes (les «choses qui sont là» sont appelées ἀρχαί) puisqu' elles ne se ressemblaient pas et n'étaient point de la même espèce (οὐχ ὁμοῖαι οὐδ' ὁμόφυλοι ἔσσαι).

Tout cela se comprend assez bien. Cependant, nous avons sauté deux lignes: après «permet une connaissance divine et non seulement humaine» le texte continue (3-4):

«sauf qu'il serait parfaitement impossible que rien des choses qui sont et sont connues par nous ne soit devenu, si l'être des choses n'eût été là.»

J'ai dû me décider pour certaines solutions un peu incertaines et de caractère conjectural. Mais en somme, il me semble que c'est ainsi que le texte se comprend le mieux, tandis qu'on reste fidèle à la tradition des manuscrits autant que possible[2].

---

[1] M. Burkert, *W.u.W.* p. 238 n. 96, a remarqué à juste titre que le terme n'est pas propre au dialecte dorien, mais au dialecte ionien. On trouve le composé εὐεστώ non seulement chez Démocrite (fr. 2), mais chez Hérodote (I 85) qui se sert aussi des mots ἀπεστώ (IX 85) et συνεστώ (XI 128).

[2] Malgré l'explication de Mme Timpanaro, il me faut avouer que je ne comprends pas bien le πλέον γα ἤ. D'ailleurs, si l'on veut prendre le πλέον ἢ ὅτι dans le sens de «de plus» ou «en outre», il faut changer γιγνωσκομένων (ce qui est probablement correct) en lisant γιγνωσκόμενον et ensuite il faut lire γα γενέσθαι, tout en supposant que γιγνωσκόμενον γενέσθαι soit dit pour «puisse être connu». Il est bien plus probable que la forme γεγνέσθαι qui se trouve dans les Mss. provient d'un γεγενῆσθαι.

Achevons la traduction de la première partie du fragment (4-10).

– (l'être des choses) qui sont les parties constituantes du monde, choses limitantes ainsi que choses illimitées. Mais, puisque les principes qui étaient là ne se ressemblaient pas et n'étaient point de la même espèce, il serait impossible de former avec eux un univers organisé, – si l'harmonie ne s'était adjointe à eux, de quelque manière que se soit. Or, les choses pareilles et homogènes n'avaient nullement besoin de l'harmonie; mais les choses non-semblables et hétérogènes, qui ne s'arrangent pas dans le même ordre, ces choses-là avaient besoin d'être enfermées ensemble par une pareille harmonie qui les retiendra avec force dans un ordre établi.

Le sens du passage est suffisamment clair et logique: l'auteur veut dire que les περαίνοντα καὶ ἄπειρα qui sont les parties constituantes et pour ainsi dire les éléments du monde, sont vraiment des «principes»: ils devaient être là pour qu'aucune chose existante et connue par nous puisse naître ou «devenir».

Bien qu'on puisse se flatter d'avoir interprété le texte correctement, on ne saurait se dissimuler qu'il reste des questions plus précises et assez difficiles à répondre. On pourrait se demander, par exemple: Mais qu'est-ce que c'est que ces «choses limitantes et illimitées» qui pré-existent à tout devenir et à toute formation d'un cosmos? Nous ne saurions dire, il me semble, ce que Philolaus s'est imaginé. Peut-être des corps géométriques élémentaires, tels que Platon s'est figuré les triangles dont sont constitués les corps des éléments. Ce serait là donc une pensée pythagoricienne que Platon aurait repris dans son *Timée*[1] en parlant de la constitution des éléments terrestres, ainsi qu'il a repris la théorie pythagoricienne des intervaux de la musique pour expliquer les mouvements des corps célestes[2].

Quoiqu'il en soit, il faut constater que la connotation de «essence» ou «substance» est certainement impliquée dans «l'être» des principes qui sont les περαίνοντα καὶ ἄπειρα.

Pour Philolaus, la ἁρμονία est nettement un troisième principe qui s'ajoute nécessairement à ces deux ἀρχαί pour les rendre capables de se joindre dans un ordre qui est celui du cosmos universel.

La partie musicologique de notre fragment (l. 11-17) nous oriente plutôt vers une date assez ancienne, parce que c'est par des noms archaïques que l'auteur désigne l'octave, la quarte et la quinte: il se

---
[1] 53 c ss.
[2] *Timée* 35 b ss.

sert du terme ἁρμονία au lieu de διὰ πασῶν, de συλλαβή au lieu de διὰ τεσσάρων, et de δι' ὀξειᾶν au lieu de διὰ πέντε.

ἁρμονίας δὲ μέγεθός ἐστι συλλαβὰ καὶ δι' ὀξειᾶν· τὸ δὲ δι' ὀξειᾶν μεῖζον τᾶς συλλαβᾶς ἐπογδόῳ. ἔστι γὰρ ἀπὸ ὑπάτας ἐπὶ μέσσαν συλλαβά, ἀπὸ δὲ μέσσας ἐπὶ νεάταν δι' ὀξειᾶν, ἀπὸ δὲ νεάτας ἐς τρίταν συλλαβά, ἀπὸ δὲ τρίτας ἐς ὑπάταν δι' ὀξειᾶν· τὸ δ' ἐν μέσῳ μέσσας καὶ τρίτας ἐπόγδοον· ἁ
15 δὲ συλλαβὰ ἐπίτριτον, τὸ δὲ δι' ὀξειᾶν ἡμιόλιον, τὸ δὲ διὰ πασᾶν δὲ διπλόον. οὕτως ἁρμονία πέντε ἐπόγδοα καὶ δύο διέσιες, δι' ὀξειᾶν δὲ τρία ἐπόγδοα καὶ δίεσις, συλλαβὰ δὲ δυ' ἐπόγδοα καὶ δίεσις.

La grandeur de l'octave (ἁρμονία) contient la quarte (συλλαβή) et la quinte (δι' ὀξειᾶν) et la quinte est d'un ton (ἐπόγδοον) plus grande que la quarte. C'est que de la corde suprême (hypatè) jusqu'à celle du milieu l'interval est une quarte, de la corde du milieu jusqu'à l'ultime (la nètè) l'interval est une quinte; de l'ultime à la troisième (tritè) l'interval est une quarte, de la troisième à la suprême c'est une quinte. L'interval entre la corde du milieu et la troisième est d'un ton, la quarte a la proportion de 4 : 3 (ἐπίτριτον), la quinte celle de 3 : 2 (ἡμιόλιον), l'octave celle du double (2 : 1) (διπλόον). Ainsi, l'octave consiste en cinq tons entiers et de deux demi-tons (διέσεις), la quinte de trois tons entiers plus un demi-ton, la quarte de deux tons entiers plus un demi-ton.

Fr. 7. Stob. *Ecl.* I 21,8: τὸ πρᾶτον ἁρμοσθέν, τὸ ἕν, ἐν μέσῳ τᾶς σφαίρας ἑστία καλεῖται.

La première chose arrangée, l'un, qui se trouve au milieu du globe (de l'univers), s'appelle le Foyer.

τὸ πρᾶτον ἁρμοσθέν, τὸ ἕν – il est séduisant de rayer τὸ ἕν, si non comme une simple dittographie (ce qui n'est pas impossible, bien entendu, mais toujours un peu improbable), comme une glose. Si l'on barre τὸ ἕν, on obtient un texte qui se lit parfaitement bien et ne donne lieu à aucune suspicion. «La première chose arrangée, au milieu du globe, s'appelle le Foyer.» Or, rien de plus vraisemblable que l'insertion du ἕν par une main ultérieure.

Celui qui parle ainsi pense à la position absolument dominante du *Un* dans le pythagorisme de l'époque romaine, et c'est là un fait indéniable. Quand même on aurait tort de suivre la suggestion faite. C'est que l'idée de l'Un telle que nous la trouvons dans le pythagorisme depuis le premier siècle av. J.C.[1], est totalement différente de, et même

[1] Pour la première fois dans l'extrait d'Alexandre Polyhistor chez Diogène

incompatible avec, celle d'un *un* qui résulte d'un procès d'harmonisation de principes contraires: cet Un-là est au-dessus des opposés, il en est la source-même. A cause de cela l'argument se laisse renverser: puisque, dans notre fragment, le Un ne précède pas les opposés fondamentaux πέρας - ἄπειρον mais résulte d'une espèce de mixtion de ces deux, ce fragment paraît provenir d'un pythagorisme plus ancien que celui des premiers siècles avant notre ère.

Quant à l'idée même d'un ἓν πρῶτον ἁρμοσθέν, son caractère légitimement pythagoricien-de-date-ancienne nous est confirmé par Aristote dans deux passages de la *Métaphysique*.

Dans les lignes qui précèdent N 3, 1091 a 13, il s'agit de la génération des nombres, doctrine platonicienne opposée par Aristote. « Quant aux Pythagoriciens », poursuit-il, « la question de savoir s'ils admettent une telle génération oui ou non, est parfaitement claire. Car ils disent explicitement que, l'Un une fois constitué, fût-il de surfaces, de plans, de semences ou d'éléments qu'ils ne savaient préciser, immédiatement la partie la plus voisine de l'Illimité commença à être entraînée et limitée par le principe limitant. » C'est à dire, pour eux il s'agissait de l'origine de l'ordre universel, dit du cosmos, et l'arrangement de cet ordre a commencé par la constitution de l'Un.

L'autre passage se trouve dans M 6, 1080 b 20 ss. Dans les lignes précédentes l'auteur a parlé de la distinction faite par certains philosophes (qu'il ne nomme pas) entre deux espèces de nombres: le nombre idéal et le nombre mathématique. Les Pythagoriciens sont rangés parmi ceux qui n'admettent que le nombre mathématique. Ce qui est propre à leur École, c'est qu'ils ne séparent pas le nombre des choses, mais disent que les choses sensibles consistent en nombres. « Ils construisent, en effet, le ciel entier de nombres – non pas de nombres composés d'unités; les unités, d'après eux, sont des grandeurs extensives. Mais comment s'est constitué l'Un premier ayant de l'étendue, c'est ce qu'ils ne peuvent expliquer. »

Dans les deux cas il s'agit non pas tant de mathématiques ou de méta-mathématiques que de l'origine des « choses » et de l'univers. C'est-là un procès qui, d'après les Pythagoriciens, a commencé par la constittuion de l'Un. Aristote dit que le mode de cette constitution n'était pas précisé. Il est clair, en tout cas, que dans aucun de ces passages Aristote ne confondit la théorie pythagoricienne avec celle de Platon ou des platoniciens. La théorie qu'il a en vue était une théorie pré-platonicienne, plus primitive dans son identification du

Laerce VIII 25. On admet généralement que les « Livres pythagoriciens » excerpés par Alexandre dataient du 2ième siècle av. J.C.

nombre avec les choses sensibles, et indépendante de Platon dans sa conception de l'Un. L'Un y est présent, cependant: il est à la base de la formation de l'ordre cosmique.

Revenant à notre fragment 7 il nous faut conclure que le texte est acceptable tel qu'il nous a été conservé par la tradition, et tel qu'il a été accepté comme authentique par example par Diels.

II.

Après avoir examiné les sept premiers fragments de Philolaus qui ont trouvé grâce même aux yeux sévères de M. Burkert, passons maintenant aux fragments qui suivent dans l'édition des Présocratiques de Diels.

Fr. 8. Iambl. in Nic. p. 77: ἡ μὲν μονὰς ὡς ἂν ἀρχὴ οὖσα κατὰ τὸν Φιλόλαον (οὐ γὰρ ἕν φησιν ἀρχὰ πάντων;) κτλ.

Fr. 9. Iambl. in Nic. p. 19, 21: «φύσει καὶ οὐ νόμῳ», ὥς φησί που Φ.

La monade qui est le principe de toutes choses (d'après Philolaus. Car il ne dit pas que le principe de tout soit le un).

Une fois qu'on a accepté le fragment 7 (avec le ἓν πρῶτον ἁρμοσθέν), il est difficile à voir pourquoi il faudrait rejeter le fragm. 8, comme le propose M. Burkert: Philolaus, en effet, paraît avoir pris la monade comme ἀρχή de toutes choses[1].

Il n'est pas clair non plus pourquoi Philolaus, qui vivait dans le seconde partie du 5ième siècle et venait du pays où vivaient de fameux Sophistes, ne saurait s'être servi de l'opposition φύσει - νόμῳ, comme le dit notre fragment 9. On ne saurait en dire autant du fragm. 10.

Fr. 10. Nicom. *Arithm.* II 19 p. 115,2: ἁρμονία δὲ πάντως ἐξ ἐναντίων γίνεται· ἔστι γὰρ ἁρμονία πολυμιγέων ἕνωσις καὶ δίχα φρονεόντων συμφρόνησις.

καὶ οἱ Πυθαγορικοὶ δέ, οἷς πολλαχῇ ἕπεται Πλάτων, τὴν μουσικήν φασιν ἐναντίων συναρμογὴν καὶ τῶν πολλῶν ἕνωσιν καὶ τῶν δίχα φρονούντων συμφρόνησιν.

L'harmonie est l'unification d'une multiplicité de choses qui se mélangent, et la concordance de choses qui sont en discorde.

[1] Iambl. in Nicom. p. 77, 9f. dit que Philolaus parlait de μονάς au lieu de ἕν. Nous possédons aussi le témoignage de Théon de Smyrne qui dit que Philolaus et Archytas employaient les termes ἕν et μονάς sans distinction. Voir mon livre *Pythagoras and Early Pythagoreanism*, p. 207f.

Sans doute, la définition de ἁρμονία comme πολυμιγέων ἕνωσις καὶ δίχα φρονεόντων συμφρόνησις peut se défendre – une pareille antithèse n'était nullement impossible dans la seconde moitié du 5ième siècle, et le terme ἕνωσις se trouve chez Aristote dans une formule plus ou moins semblable[1]; pourquoi donc serait elle impossible pour Philolaus? – Ces arguments sont raisonnables; et pourtant la formule de πολυμιγέων ἕνωσις me semble suspecte. Évidemment elle est fort possible après Anaxagore, – mais c'est cela même qui la rend moins acceptable pour moi. Bien sûr, δίχα φρονεόντων συμφρόνησις est une formule joliment pythagoricienne, si l'on croit à l'existence d'une philosophie sociale chez les pythagoriciens de date ancienne, – une théorie de ὁμόνοια et de φιλία qui comprend l'univers et l'homme, l'homme physique ainsi que l'homme moral et intellectuel; théorie qui s'accorde merveilleusement avec l'image politique d'une συμφρόνησις τῶν δίχα φρονεόντων dans la nature. Alcméon n'en faisait-il pas autant quand il parlait de l'ἰσονομία des qualités opposées dans le corps humain, ou de la μοναρχία de certaines d'elles, dont la première est cause de la santé, la seconde de maladie[2]? Et n'est-ce pas là une trace visible d'une philosophie à la fois cosmique et sociale chez les Pythagoriciens de date bien antérieure à Philolaus? En lisant le *Gorgias* de Platon, les pages 504 b (la définition de la santé comme un état d'équilibre résultant de τάξις et de κόσμος[3]) et 507 e-508 a (la doctrine de κοινωνία καὶ φιλία καὶ κοσμιότης, attribuée à des σοφοὶ ἄνδρες qui ne sont pas nommés mais dont l'identité ne laisse pas de doute[4]), on ne saurait en douter. Moi, je n'en doute aucunement. Bien que le mot de συμφρόνησις ne se lise pas avant Polybe, je sais bien qu'un pareil langage est tout à fait de style pythagoricien. Pourtant, ce point positif ne peut m'aider dans mes doutes concernant la πολυμιγέων ἕνωσις. En somme, δίχα φρονεόντων peut se référer exactement aux περαίνοντα καὶ ἄπειρα; quant à πολυμιγέων, je n'en vois pas la possibilité.

Voilà mes raisons pour ne pas croire à l'authenticité du fragm. 10.

Fr. 11. Theo Smyrn. 106, 10 περὶ ἧς (on the Dekas) καὶ Ἀρχύτας ἐν τῷ Περὶ δεκάδος καὶ Φ. ἐν τῷ Περὶ φύσιος πολλὰ διεξίασιν. Stob. *Ecl.* prooem. cor.

---

[1] Je pense à *De gener. et corr.* I 328 b 22: ἡ δὲ μῖξις τῶν μικτῶν ἀλλοιωθέντων ἕνωσις. Autre part Aristote se sert du terme ἕνωσις comme opposé à διαίρεσις, e.g. dans *Phys.* IV 13, 222 a 30.
[2] Alcméon, Diels VS 24, B 4.
[3] Voir mon *Pythagoras* p. 244.   [4] Ibid., p. 83, 103 ss.

1   Φιλολάου. θεωρεῖν δεῖ τὰ ἔργα καὶ τὴν οὐσίαν τῶ ἀριθμῶ καττὰν
δύναμιν ἅτις ἐστιν ἐν τᾷ δεκάδι· μεγάλα καὶ παντελὴς καὶ παντοεργὸς καὶ
θείω καὶ οὐρανίω βίω καὶ ἀνθρωπίνω ἀρχὰ καὶ ἁγεμὼν κοινωνοῦσα ***
δύναμις καὶ τᾶς δεκάδος. ἄνευ δὲ τούτας πάντ' ἄπειρα καὶ ἄδηλα καὶ ἀφανῆ.
5   γνωμικὰ γὰρ ἁ φύσις ἁ τῶ ἀριθμῶ καὶ ἡγεμονικὰ καὶ διδασκαλικὰ τῶ
ἀπορουμένω παντὸς καὶ ἀγνοουμένω παντί. οὐ γὰρ ἦς δῆλον οὐδενὶ οὐδὲν
τῶν πραγμάτων οὔτε αὐτῶν ποθ' αὑτὰ οὔτε ἄλλω πρὸς ἄλλο, εἰ μὴ ἦς
ἀριθμὸς καὶ ἁ τούτω οὐσία.

l. 1-6 (= 1-4) *Il faut contempler les œuvres et l'essence du nombre selon la force qui est en la décade. C'est qu'elle est grande et complète et cause de tout, principe et guide autant de la vie divine et céleste que de la vie humaine. Elle prend part à ..... la force de la décade elle-aussi. Et sans elle tout est illimitée, vague et obscure.*

l. 7-11 (= 5-8) *Car la nature du nombre nous rend capables de connaître les choses, nous guide et nous instruit de tout ce dont on est incertain et ce qu'on ne sait pas. Car rien ne serait clair à personne, ni des choses elles-mêmes ni de l'une en relation à l'autre, s'il n'y avait le nombre et son essence.*

Le fragm. 11 dans son ensemble me paraît indubitablement pythagoricien. Il s'agit de la fonction et de la nature du nombre: il faut la contempler dans la décade, nous dit l'auteur. C'est là qu'on la voit dans sa plénitude. Le nombre est essentiellement source de connaissance, source unique et indispensable. Car sans lui rien ne saurait être connu, par lui tout devient accessible à la connaissance.

Comment cela se fait-il? L'auteur va nous l'expliquer.

8   νῦν δὲ οὗτος καττὰν ψυχὰν ἁρμόζων αἰσθήσει πάντα γνωστὰ καὶ ποτά-
γορα ἀλλάλοις κατὰ γνώμονος φύσιν ἀπεργάζεται σωμάτων καὶ σχίζων
10   τοὺς λόγους χωρὶς ἑκάστους τῶν πραγμάτων τῶν τε ἀπείρων καὶ τῶν
περαινόντων.

l. 11-15 (= 8-11) *C'est que dans l'âme, lui, le nombre, adapte toutes les choses aux sens et par là les rend connaissables et «abordables» entre elles selon la nature du gnomon, en faisant prendre corps aux proportions des choses – de celles qui sont illimitées et de celles qui sont limitantes – et en les fendant, de sorte qu'elles sont séparées les unes des autres. –*

Ces quatre lignes évoquent déjà tout un nombre de questions. Je préfère les discuter avant de poursuivre la lecture. Qu'il s'agisse ici du problème de la connaissance, ce n'est là en tout cas pas une raison pour jeter aucune suspicion sur notre fragment: si l'on accepte les fragments 3 et 4, il ne faut pas s'étonner de trouver les mêmes idées ici. Que l'auteur trouve «la nature du nombre» avec une clarté particulière dans la décade, cela encore n'offre sûrement aucune raison pour rendre le texte suspect. Au contraire, on pourrait plutôt y trouver une confirmation de la date ancienne de notre fragment: l'idée de la décade comme comprenant en elle d'un mode intensifié toutes les qualités «dirigeantes» du nombre, est archaïque: le serment par la tétractys, bien que le texte n'en soit conservé que dans les *Vers d'Or*, n'est guère une construction du premier siècle. Il remonte sûrement à l'époque archaïque.

On a trouvé des difficultés dans le terme φύσις. M. Burkert n'a pas manqué de signaler une différence entre l'emploi de ce terme dans les fragm. 1 et 6 d'une part, et celui de notre fragment de l'autre: dans les premiers fragments φύσις signifiait la totalité des choses de la nature, non pas *l'essence* des choses individuelles. Ce serait là, d'après lui, une signification de date plus récente. Or, si l'on se rend compte de l'emploi du terme φύσις chez les présocratiques en général et chez Philolaus en particulier, il faut observer deux choses: (1) En général, chez les présocratiques le terme de φύσις se trouve dans cinq ou six significations plus ou moins différentes. (2) Si dans les textes dits de Philolaus on trouve le mot φύσις dans deux ou trois significations différentes qui ont des parallèles exactes chez d'autres auteurs de la même époque, il n'y a là rien qui ne saurait nous étonner, voire rendre ces textes suspects à nos yeux.

Envisageons les faits.

1. La «nature», c'est pour les Grecs de cette époque avant tout la force créatrice d'où proviennent toutes les choses qui sont au monde, la force cachée et silencieuse qui est la cause de leur être, telles qu'elles sont, et de leur comportement. C'est dans ce sens-là que, au début du 5ième siècle, le poète Épicharme, après avoir constaté que les poules ne produisent pas de petits vivants mais les font vivre en les couvant, ajoute: «Or, c'est la Nature seule qui connaît le secret de cette sagesse; car elle sait ce qu'elle sait entièrement par elle-même».

C'est dans le même sens que Philolaus dit (d'après une citation par Nicomaque) que «la Nature démontre la ποιότης et la couleur des choses dans la pentade». Et l'auteur du traité Περὶ τροφῆς: φύσις ἐξαρκεῖ πάντα πᾶσι[1], et Démocrite dans le fragm. 176: «La fortune

---

[1] Hippocr. Π. τροφῆς 15.

(τύχη) accorde de grands dons, mais elle est instable; la Nature suffit à elle-même».

2. Deuxièmement, la Nature, c'est la totalité des choses elles-mêmes qui sont issues de la force créatrice que je viens de mentionner. Le titre Περὶ φύσεως qui était d'un usage courant chez les présocratiques, peut comprendre les deux aspects. Dans le fragm. 1 de Philolaus nous trouvons φύσις signifiant nettement la totalité des choses.

3. Troisièmement, la «nature» signifie la *disposition naturelle*, opposée à ce qu'on apprend par l'instruction (μάθησις) ou par la pratique (μελέτη, ἄσκησις), les dons naturels de l'esprit (Épicharme, fragm. 33[1] et 40[2], Protagoras fr. 3[3], Critias fr. 9, Démocrite fr. 242[4]).

4. Quatrièmement, la «nature» veut dire «la nature des choses prises dans leur ensemble». La «nature» des choses, c'est leur vrai caractère, c'est leur essence – si l'on veut se servir d'un terme aristotélicien; et puisqu'il s'agit des choses prises dans leur ensemble, c'est de la totalité de l'être qu'il s'agit.

C'est ainsi qu'Héraclite a dit que «la Nature aime se cacher» (φύσις κρύπτεσθαι φιλεῖ, fr. 123). Ce n'est là, certes, ni de «la totalité des choses, ni de leur «simple être naturel» (l'être-là) qu'il s'agit[5], c'est de leur «vrai caractère» qui est plus réel que l'apparence, mais ne saute pas aux yeux.

Ici, il me semble, nous nous trouvons le plus près de la «nature» dans le fragm. 6 de Philolaus: «*L'être* des choses (ἁ ἐστὼ τῶν πραγμάτων) qui est éternel, et la Nature elle-même permet une science divine et non pas humaine» .... Ce n'est sûrement pas la nature visible, pas «l'être naturel» des choses dont il s'agit ici. C'est le «vrai caractère» des choses, leur nature cachée, leur sens métaphysique, – si l'on veut, leur essence.

Dans ce contexte il faut se rappeler aussi du premier fragment d'Archytas: après avoir loué la connaissance des mathématiciens, il dit qu'il ne faut pas s'étonner si les mêmes personnes paraissent avoir

---

[1] Diels VS 23, B 33: ἁ δὲ μελέτα φύσιος ἀγαθᾶς πλέονα δωρεῖται, φίλοι. («L'exercice donne plus qu'une bonne disposition naturelle»).

[2] B 40: φύσιν ἔχειν ἄριστόν ἐστι, δεύτερον δὲ ⟨μανθάνειν⟩. («Avoir du talent, c'est la première condition, la seconde est d'apprendre»).

[3] Diels VS 80 B 3: φύσεως καὶ ἀσκήσεως διδασκαλία δεῖται. «Pour apprendre il faut des dons naturels et de l'exercice».

[4] Diels VS 88, B 9: ἐκ μελέτης πλείους ἢ φύσεως ἀγαθοί. – Democr.: πλέονες ἐξ ἀσκήσεως ἀγαθοὶ γίνονται ἢ ἀπὸ φύσιος. Diels VS 68, B 242.

[5] Burkert, *W.u.W.* p. 254: «Inbegriff alles Seienden – wie in (Philolaus) B1 und B6 – (oder auch) das naturhafte Sein eines bestimmten Dinges».

des idées exactes sur les choses particulières: «car si l'on a des connaissances exactes sur la nature des choses dans leur ensemble (περὶ τᾶς τῶν ὅλων φύσεως), il fallait bien qu'on eût – c'est à dire, que les mêmes personnes eussent – des idées exactes sur les choses particulières aussi».

Le texte est intéressant, parce qu'on passe de la φύσις τῶν ὅλων à la connaissance des choses particulières, τῶν κατὰ μέρος, οἷά ἐντι, c'est-à dire: à leur φύσις, leur «comme elles sont», leurs qualités, leur propre caractère. Or, c'est cela précisément ce que nous appelons «l'essence».

Nous en arrivons ici à ce qu'on peut distinguer comme cinquième signification. Mais avant de passer à notre numéro 5, je veux mentionner encore le texte suivant de Sextus Empiricus qui cite Philolaus comme témoin de la doctrine pythagoricienne que le λόγος qui provient ἀπὸ τῶν μαθημάτων soit «critère», c'est-à dire: moyen, ou instrument, de connaissance. «Philolaus disait que le λόγος qui contemple *la nature de l'univers* – la nature de toutes les choses dans leur ensemble (τῆς τῶν ὅλων φύσεως) – a une affinité avec elles.»

Ce texte aussi implique le passage de «la nature des choses prises dans leur ensemble» à celle qui est propre à chacune de ces choses qui sont comprises dans la totalité. C'est bien ainsi que «la raison qui provient des mathématiques» est «instrument de connaissance» tout-court: ayant une affinité avec les choses elles-mêmes, elle peut les connaître, autant dans leur ensemble qu'individuellement.

5. «La nature», cela signifie aussi chez les philosophes de cette époque: *l'être qualifié des choses individuelles*, leur caractère propre, leur «essence». Quand Héraclite dit, par exemple, que tout se passe selon un λόγος éternel, mais que les hommes ne le comprennent pas – «Ils n'ont aucune idée des paroles et des faits tels que je les expose, en distinguant et expliquant la nature de chaque chose" (κατὰ φύσιν διαιρέων ἕκαστον καὶ φράζων ὅκως ἔχει), – il s'agit là aussi de «l'être naturel» des choses individuelles, mais de leur *être qualifié*, de leur *caractère propre*. Or, c'est exactement ainsi que Gorgias dit dans sa *Louange d'Hélène*, 15: «C'est que les choses que nous voyons n'ont pas la nature que nous voulons, mais *celle qui est propre à chacune d'elles*»[1].

Les parallèles ne manquent pas. Je cite quelques exemples.
Parménide, fr. 10,1: αἰθερίαν τε φύσιν τά τ' ἐν αἰθέρι πάντα.
Empédocle, fr. 110,5: ὅπη φύσις ἐστιν ἑκάστῃ.

---

[1] Gorgias, fr. 11, 15 chez Diels (VS II, p. 293): ἃ γὰρ ὁρῶμεν, ἔχει φύσιν οὐχ ἣν ἡμεῖς θέλομεν, ἀλλ' ἣν ἕκαστον ἔτυχε.

Diogène d'Apollonie, fr. 2,5 : ἕτερον ὂν τῇ ἰδίᾳ φύσει.

Hippocrate, Π. τροφῆς 17 : μία φύσις ἐστὶ πάντα ταῦτα καὶ οὐ μία· πολλαὶ φύσιές εἰσι πάντα μίαν οὖσαν.

Cette dernière phrase rappelle Héraclite, dont le fragm. 106 est particulièrement intéressant dans notre contexte. Il parle de φύσιν ἡμέρας ἁπάσης μίαν οὖσαν. C'est-à dire, il désapprouve Hésiode qui nomme certains jours «bons» et d'autres mauvais, comme s'il ignorait que «la nature de chaque jour est une et la même.»

Pareillement nous trouvons dans le traité hippocratique Π. διαίτης I 24 (à la fin) : οὕτω μὲν αἱ τέχναι πᾶσαι τῇ ἀνθρωπίνῃ φύσει ἐπικοινέουσιν. «Ainsi tout les arts s'accordent avec la nature de l'homme.»

6. Nous voilà à la sixième signification, ou plutôt le sixième mode d'emploi de notre terme : il joint immédiatement celui du numéro précédent.

La formule Περὶ φύσεως ἀνθρώπου nous est bien connue : c'est le titre d'au moins deux traités sur l'homme, écrits tous les deux vers la fin du 5ième siècle ou un peu antérieurement, le traité hippocratique et celui de Prodicus de Ceos[1]. On pourrait traduire ce titre simplement par : «Sur l'homme».

Cela veut dire que les Grecs de cette époque emploient de pareilles formules comme une sorte de périphrase pour indiquer telle ou telle chose.

Les exemples abondent. En voici quelques uns.

Parménide fragm. 16, 3 : φύσις μελέων («les membres»).

Empédocle fragm. 63 : ἀλλὰ διέσπασται μελέων φύσις (les membres, sc. de l'homme et de la femme, sont différents).

Gorgias, *Helena* 14 (Diels fr. 11, p. 292) : πρὸς τὴν τῶν σωμάτων φύσιν.

Cp. Empédocle A 34 (Galenus in Hippocr. *De nat. hom.* 15, p. 32 K.) : τὴν τῶν συνθέτων σωμάτων φύσιν.

C'est ici qu'il faut placer Philolaus fragm. 11 avec les expressions ἁ τῶ ἀριθμῶ φύσις et (un peu plus loin) κατὰ γνώμονος φύσιν : dans la première il y a encore plus ou moins clairement la notion de «caractère propre» ou «essence», dans la seconde la formule est presque purement périphrastique.

Nous nous sommes arrêtés un peu longuement à cette expression de ἁ φύσις ἁ τῶ ἀριθμῶ. Il fallait ce petit détour pour retrouver du terrain solide. Il est clair maintenant que la signification de «caractère propre»

---

[1] Voir Prodicus chez Diels VS 84, B 4.

pour le mot φύσις ne saurait jeter pas le moindre doute sur l'authenticité de notre texte. Quant à οὐσία (ce qui se lit dans la première ligne), c'est là évidemment un terme aristotélicien. Nul part on ne le trouve dans ce sens avant Aristote. Il y a donc sûrement lieu de se demander si Philolaus a pu écrire cela.

Ce qui est certain, c'est que la teneur de tout ce passage est pythagoricienne, pas moins que, par exemple, les fragments 4-6. Si le fragm. 11 contient quelques difficultés dans les lignes 11-15 (= l. 8-11 dans mon texte ci-dessus), il faut constater que le fragm. 6 n'en offre pas moins; et si le terme d'οὐσία est aristotélicien, il faut reconnaître que celui de ἐστώ dans le fragm. 6 implique au moins le même sens. Ce sont là des faits qu'on ne saurait nier.

Examinons maintenant les lignes 11-15 (= 8-11). Voici encore une fois le texte.

8   νῦν δὲ οὗτος καττὰν ψυχὰν ἁρμόζων αἰσθήσει πάντα γνωστὰ καὶ
    ποτάγορα ἀλλάλοις κατὰ γνώμονος φύσιν ἀπεργάζεται σωμάτων καὶ
10 σχίζων τοὺς λόγους χωρὶς ἑκάστους τῶν πραγμάτων τῶν τε ἀπείρων
    καὶ τῶν περαινόντων.

Comment se fait-il que le nombre est instrument de connaissance par rapport à toute chose? Voilà la question. L'auteur répond: c'est que, dans notre âme, le nombre adapte toutes les choses aux sens, et par là les rend connaissables et «abordables» (προσήγορα) les unes aux autres.

On comprend mieux cette explication en se rappelant que dans le fragm. 13 (qui est assez généralement accepté comme authentique) le cœur est qualifié de «principe de la ψυχή et de l'αἴσθησις», tandis que la fonction intellectuelle a son principe dans le cerveau. Or, nous savons par Théophraste, *De sensibus* 25 s., que c'était Alcméon qui distinguait la faculté intellectuelle de la faculté sensitive, mais que, tout en plaçant la première dans le cerveau, il enseignait que, indirectement, c'est du cerveau que les sens dépendent eux aussi. Si l'on compare ce que le Socrate de Platon dit dans le *Phédon*, 96b4-8, il est extrêmement probable que c'est Alcméon qui a vu le procès de la connaissance de cette manière, qu'elle commence par les sens et, par l'intermédiaire de la μνήμη et de la δόξα, λαβούσης τὸ ἠρεμεῖν, en arrive à l'ἐπιστήμη.

Si ce n'était pas dans le *Phédon*, certainement, personne n'aurait cru que ces lignes-là puissent avoir été écrites une génération avant *Analyt. post.* II 19! Le cas est intéressant. C'est qu'il nous avertit de ne pas être trop catégorique dans des énonciations telles que «une telle expression» ou «une telle phrase ne saurait avoir été écrite avant Aristote». Peutêtre faut-il appliquer cette leçon au fait de la présence du terme οὐσία dans le fragm. 11 de Philolaus...

Quoi qu'il en soit, il est clair que l'auteur de notre fragment voit le nombre comme principe qui, en rendent les choses accessibles aux sens par un procès d'assimilation (ἁρμόζων αἰσθήσει), les rend «communicables» entre elles en y mettant de la mesure précise (κατὰ γνώμονος φύσιν).

Le participe σωματῶν qui suit (correction de Böckh pour σωμάτων) n'a pas manqué d'effrayer les philologues modernes – pas tous, évidemment, mais quand même plusieurs d'un nom illustre. Quant à la pensée, rappelons le fragm. 126 d'Empédocle, qui se lit: σαρκῶν ἀλλογνῶτι περιστέλλουσα χιτῶνι, «couvrant les âmes d'un corps, comme d'un habit qui ne leur est pas propre».

On ne saurait dire que le verbe σωματοῦν soit de basse époque: on le trouve chez Aristote et chez Théophraste. Le cas est donc pareil à celui de ἕνωσις: on ne saurait dénier a priori qu'un terme que nous lisons pour la première fois dans un texte du 4ième siècle, ait été employé par Philolaus un siècle auparavant. En soi, ce n'est pas là un argument absolu contre l'authenticité du texte. En principe, il est possible que Philolaus se soit servi du mot σωματῶν pour exprimer que le nombre qui rend les choses connaissables, pour ainsi dire «*donne un corps aux* λόγοι *des choses*», et d'autre part, «les fend en deux».

Manière bizarre de s'exprimer? – Peutêtre. Mais nullement étranger au climat de la pensée pythagoricienne. Pour les membres de cette École, en effet, c'était le nombre qui faisait les choses ce qu'elles sont, qui leur rend leur grandeur extensive et leur détermination, aussi bien quantitative que qualitative; c'est-à-dire, c'était le nombre qui leur donnait leur substantialité, ou disons, leur «corps». D'autre part, en fendant leurs λόγοι, le nombre les faisait périr, en faisant naître d'autres choses. C'était là la théorie pythagoricienne de la ἐστώ éternelle des choses, tant limitantes que illimitées.

12-15: ἰδίοις δέ κα οὐ μόνον ἐν τοῖς δαιμονίοις καὶ θείοις πράγμασι τὰν τῶ ἀριθμῶ φύσιν καὶ τὰν δύναμιν ἰσχύουσαν, ἀλλὰ καὶ ἐν τοῖς ἀνθρωπικοῖς ἔργοις καὶ λόγοις πᾶσι παντᾶ καὶ κατὰ τὰς δημιουργίας τὰς τεχνικὰς
15 πάσας καὶ κατὰ τὰν μουσικάν.

1. 16-20 (= 12-15) *Or, tu peux voir la nature et la force puissante du nombre non seulement dans les choses mi-divines et divines, mais dans*

les travaux humains aussi, et dans les paroles humaines, dans toutes et partout, ainsi que dans tous les ouvrages des arts et dans la musique.

Cette section ne présente pas de graves difficultés. La distinction entre les δαιμόνια καὶ θεῖα πράγματα et les ἀνθρωπικὰ ἔργα qui, tous, sont pénétrés de la force du nombre, ne saurait guère nous étonner. Pour l'auteur, sans doute, les «choses démoniques», c'est-à dire mi-divines, et «divines», mentionnées ensemble, indiquent l'ordre *de l'univers* ou *de la Nature* qui, comme telle, n'est pas le produit de l'activité humaine et dépasse nos forces. En somme, c'est la même idée que nous trouvons chez le Socrate de Xénophon (*Memor.* I, 1, 15): lui aussi, il oppose aux «choses humaines» (τἀνθρώπεια) qu'il faut apprendre pour les reproduire à son gré, les «choses divines» (τὰ θεῖα): «les vents, les eaux, les saisons» et toutes ces choses que, apparemment, on ne saurait comprendre, puisqu'on n'est jamais capable de les reproduire[1]. Ce n'est là, sûrement, pas tellement l'esprit Ionien qui parle, mais c'est bien certainement l'esprit pythagoricien.

Or, c'est cette vue de la Nature qui nous explique la signification d'un mot qui, au premier moment, devait nous étonner: c'était le mot ἐνδέχεται au début du fragment 6. Voici le texte encore une fois: ἁ μὲν ἐστὼ τῶν πραγμάτων ἀίδιος ἔσσα καὶ αὐτὰ μὲν ἁ φύσις θείαν γα καὶ οὐκ ἀνθρωπίνην ἐνδέχεται γνῶσιν.

«L'être des choses qui est éternel, et la Nature elle-même *permet* une connaissance divine et non (seulement) humaine» –.

Les traducteurs modernes, en mettant «exige», altèrent le sens du mot ἐνδέχεται, – d'après les exigences du contexte, à ce qu'il leur semble. C'est qu'ils n'étaient pas suffisamment entrés dans le monde de la pensée pythagoricienne pour partager les vues de ces anciens penseurs et par là pour comprendre le sens exact d'un pareil terme. En somme, la pensée pythagoricienne est un monde étrange pour nous autres, à la distance énorme où nous nous trouvons. Or, voici ce qu'ils nous expliquent eux-mêmes. La Nature qui est la totalité de l'Être, consiste en choses non seulement «humaines», c'est-à dire produites par l'homme, mais elle consiste en grande partie en choses *divines* – choses qui dépassent l'intellect humain parce qu'elles ne sont ni produites par nous ni ne sauraient être jamais produites par la force humaine. Or, bien que, dans un sens, ces choses nous dépassent, elles sont accessibles à notre intellect en tant que le nombre est présent en elles et nous les fait connaître. Donc, c'est bien ainsi que la Nature qui

---

[1] Xen. *Mem* I, 1, 15.

en grande partie est divine, nous *permet* une connaissance divine et non seulement humaine. – Pour eux, la Nature ne l'«exige» pas – cela n'aurait pas de sens –, elle le *permet*.

Les δαίμονες comme intermédiaire entre les dieux et l'homme nous rappellent le premier discours de Pythagore, aux jeunes de Croton, chez Iamblique V.P. 37[1], où l'on trouve l'ordre suivant: les dieux – les démons – les héros – les hommes, et de ceux-ci en premier lieu les parents. Il est fort improbable que l'origine de cette hiérarchie soit chez Platon. J'ai démontré ailleurs que les lignes des *Lois* (717b) où ces quatre groupes sont mentionnées, sont précédées par quelques préscriptions sur les sacrifices à faire aux dieux chthoniques tant qu'aux dieux olympiens, – préscriptions qui sont d'un caractère nettement pythagoricien et archaïque. Je ne m'étonnerais pas, d'ailleurs, si dans cette matière Pythagore joignît l'ancienne sagesse populaire (comme il l'a souvent fait), tout en lui prêtant un caractère plus rationel et d'ordre moral[2].

l. 16-20: ψεῦδος δὲ οὐδὲν δέχεται ἁ τῶ ἀριθμῶ φύσις οὐδὲ ἁρμονία· οὐ γὰρ οἰκεῖον αὐτοῖς ἐστι. τᾶς τῶ ἀπείρω καὶ ἀνοήτω καὶ ἀλόγω φύσιος τὸ ψεῦδος καὶ ὁ φθόνος ἐστι. ψεῦδος δὲ οὐδαμῶς ἐς ἀριθμὸν ἐπιπνεῖ· πολέμιον γὰρ καὶ ἐχθρὸν τᾷ φύσει τὸ ψεῦδος, ἁ δ'ἀλήθεια οἰκεῖον καὶ σύμφυτον τᾷ
20 τῶ ἀριθμῶ γενᾷ.

(l. 21-26 = 16-20) *Et la nature du nombre, tout comme l'harmonie, repousse fermement tout ce qui n'est pas vrai; car le mensonge leur est étranger. Le mensonge et la jalousie sont plutôt propres à la nature de l'illimité, de ce qui est dépourvu d'esprit et de raison.*

Le mensonge ne souffle nullement sur le nombre. C'est qu'il est hostile à sa nature, tandis que la vérité est propre et alliée au genre du nombre.

Comment on juge ces lignes du point de vue de l'authenticité, dépend largement de l'idée qu'on se fait de l'emploi du terme φύσις chez les présocratiques. Si l'on a l'idée que des expressions telles que ἁ τῶ ἀριθμῶ φύσις ou ἁ τῶ ἀπείρω φύσις étaient étrangères au 5ième siècle – comme le suppose M. Burkert –, alors, évidemment, on trouvera

---

[1] Iambl. *V.P.* 37: (Il faut honorer ce qui est plus ancien plus que ce qui est postérieur, p.e. le lever du soleil plus que le coucher, l'aube plus que le soir, le commencement plus que la fin, etc.) «les dieux plus que les démons, les démons plus que les sémi-dieux (= les héros), ceux-ci plus que les hommes.» – Sur ce passage voir mon «*Pythag.*», pp. 70-74.

[2] Voir à ce propos mon *Pythag.* sur le thème de «Reform-movement», pp. **126, 133, 139.**

dans notre texte des arguments décisifs contre l'authenticité. Seulement, l'idée qu'on se faisait ne tient pas debout. Nous avons vu que, depuis Parménide et Héraclite jusqu'aux traités hippocratiques, aux Sophistes et à Démocrite il existe de nombreux exemples, à la fois de la φύσις comme «nature individuelle ou spécifique», «vrai caractère», «essence», et de l'usage périphrastique. Avec ces parallèles dans notre esprit, les lignes 21-23 (dans mon texte 16-18) de notre fragment ne nous présenteront pas la moindre difficulté. Au contraire, leur langage paraît s'accorder parfaitement à celui de leur époque.

M. Burkert y voit une autre difficulté; c'est que ἁρμονία, au lieu d'être ajouté aux περαίνοντα καὶ ἄπειρα comme un troisième principe qui vient pour ainsi dire du dehors, dans notre fragment paraît à peu près synonyme du nombre: ψεῦδος δὲ οὐδὲν δέχεται ἁ τῶ ἀριθμῶ φύσις οὐδὲ ἁρμονία. Or c'est incompatible avec la ἁρμονία comme troisième principe, surajouté aux deux autres, comme nous l'avons trouvé dans le fragm. 6. Dans notre fragment, par contre, le nombre et l'harmonie s'opposent ensemble à «la nature de l'ἄπειρον qui est non-pensable et déraisonnable».

Certes, il semble bien qu'il y a là une certaine différence. Pourtant, il faut se demander: «Mais où dans la συστοιχία faut il placer le nombre?» Du côté du πέρας, puisqu'il s'oppose à l'ἄπειρον? – Si l'on répond par l'affirmative, je crains qu'il en résulte des conséquences désastreuses: c'est que le nombre se rangerait du même côté que le περισσόν (l'impair) et serait opposé à l'autre, celui de l'ἄρτιον (le pair). Or, nous voilà pour le nombre dans exactement la même position qui paraissait impossible en vue de l'harmonie. Mais, après tout, le nombre ne fonctionnait pas du tout dans la συστοιχία, telle que nous le connaissons par Aristote.... Et cela, comme on voit, pour de bonnes raisons.

En somme, ni le nombre ni l'harmonie n'avait leur place dans la συστοιχία originelle. Étaient-ils considérés comme une espèce de «mélange», – un moyen terme entre le πέρας et l'ἄπειρον, entre ἕν et πολλά? Ou faut-il plutôt dire que le nombre comme tel *devait* se ranger du côté du πέρας puisque, essentiellement, il s'identifie à lui?

On peut le dire. Mais alors, que penser de l'harmonie? N'est-elle pas la juste proportion, – donc, une chose bien déterminée?

Mieux vaut ne pas nier ces apories. Ce qu'il faudra en conclure, ce n'est tout de même pas autre chose que la leçon suivante: *que la logique même des principes pythagoriciens les pousse vers la conséquence que le nombre lui-même et l'harmonie comme juste proportion s'identifient au péras, en s'opposant à l'apeiron.*

Voilà la conséquence qui s'est présentée à l'esprit de notre auteur. Au lieu de crier à l'incompatibilité, mieux vaut reconnaître les problèmes réels qu'il avait à résoudre.

Les trois dernières lignes (dans mon texte les l. 18-20) n'offrent pas de problèmes plus difficiles que celles qui précèdent. L'auteur se répète. C'est ce qu'il a fait également dans d'autres parties des fragments.

«Le mensonge ne souffle nullement sur le nombre. C'est que le mensonge est hostile à sa nature. La vérité, par contre, est familière et apparentée au genre du nombre.»

τᾷ φύσει (l. 19), sc. τῷ ἀριθμῷ. Au lieu de φύσις l'auteur parle aussi de γενεά. On ne saurait dire que rien de tout cela soit étranger à son style ou à celui de son siècle.

En somme, l'unique exception à cette règle que nous avons trouvée dans notre fragment, c'était le terme d'οὐσία dans la première ligne. Faut-il conclure à l'inauthenticité du fragment dans son ensemble?

Moi, j'aimerais répondre: tout au plus pour la forme. Il est fort invraisemblable, en effet, que Philolaus ait parlé d'οὐσία pour dénoter le caractère propre d'une chose. Mais que cette notion-même lui ait été familière, on ne saurait le dénier. Enfin, toute la teneur de notre fragment est si indubitablement pythagoricienne, tellement remplie des mêmes idées que les textes précédents, qu'il faut bien reconnaître que la provenance de notre texte ne diffère pas de celle des autres. Peutêtre est-ce là une petitite retouche d'une main post-aristotélicienne. Moi, je veux faire quelque réserve sur ce point, mais je ne suis guère disposée à rejeter tout le fragment 11.

Nous en arrivons au fragm. 12, où il s'agit des πέντε σώματα dont le cinquième – après les quatre éléments d'Empédocle – est nommé ὁ τᾶς σφαίρας ὁλκάς.

Fr. 12. Theo Smyrn., p. 18. 5 W.: καὶ τὰ μὲν τᾶς σφαίρας σώματα πέντε ἐντι, τὰ ἐν τᾷ σφαίρᾳ πῦρ (καὶ) ὕδωρ καὶ γᾶ καὶ ἀήρ, καὶ ὁ τᾶς σφαίρας ὁλκάς (?) πέμπτον.

Et les corps du globe sont cinq: le feu et l'eau, la terre et l'air qui sont dans le globe, et (ensuite) le bateau de transport du globe qui est le cinquième.

Ce «bateau de transport» a trouvé des avocats parmi les philologues modernes. On pouvait dire que le αἰθήρ comme une espèce de cinquième élément, air supérieur et très légèr, distinct selon sa place naturelle et selon sa qualité, de l'air épais et ordinaire que nous respirons, était une notion très ancienne en Grèce, connue depuis Homère. C'est vrai. Et quand même, l'αἰθήρ n'était pas parmi les ῥιζώματα d'Empédocle. Ce serait donc Philolaus qui, après lui, aurait innové. Évidemment, ce n'était pas impossible. Il est vrai, encore, que la géométrie grecque connaissait les «cinq corps» longtemps avant que Théétète inventât la construction du dodécaèdre. *Mais* – et voici notre objection principale – ce serait là attribuer à Philolaus au 5ième siècle une doctrine qui de la manière la plus nette est attribuée à Aristote par toutes nos sources antiques.

Mais peut-être y a-t-il une autre solution: ne pourrait-on pas prendre τᾶς σφαίρας dans le sens d'un génitif explicatif? Alors, ce serait le globe lui-même de l'univers qui est considéré comme le «bateau de transport» qui porte les autres éléments[1]. On pensera à l'Être complèt de Parménide, εὐκύκλου σφαίρης ἐναλίγκιον ὄγκῳ/μεσσόθεν ἰσοπαλὲς πάντῃ[2], et au σφαῖρος κυκλοτερής d'Empédocle[3]. Chez ce dernier, dans un autre fragment[4], le procès de l'univers est expliqué comme un double mouvement:

> τοτὲ μὲν γὰρ ἓν ηὐξήθη μόνον εἶναι
> ἐκ πλεόνων, τοτὲ δ' αὖ διέφυ πλέον ἐξ ἑνὸς εἶναι,
> πῦρ καὶ ὕδωρ καὶ γαῖα καὶ ἠέρος ἄπλετον ὕψος.

«Tantôt il s'est développé une chose une, pour subsister seule au lieu d'une multiplicité, tantôt, par contre, c'est les choses multiples qui se produisent pour exister au lieu de l'un: le Feu et l'Eau, la Terre et l'immense hauteur de l'Air.»

On peut conclure de ces textes qu'Empédocle concevait son σφαῖρος comme une totalité non-différenciée, mais qui comprenait en elle potentiellement l'existence des quatre éléments et toute la multiplicité des choses qui en proviennent. Ce n'est, en tout cas, ni une espèce de cinquième élément, ni une espèce de *sphère matérielle* consistant en une substance différente des quatre éléments terrestres et qu'on pourrait caractériser comme mi-céleste; une *sphère «éthérée»*, en somme, qui fonctionnerait comme ὄχημα ou véhicule, portant toute autre chose, ou, disons, portant l'univers. Ce n'est pas cela, il me

---

[1] Dans mon séminaire de l'hiver de 1967 où nous avons discuté sur les textes de Philolaus, c'était M. J. Mansfeld qui a proposé cette solution.
[2] Diels VS 28, B 8, 42-44.
[3] Diels VS 31, B 27 et 28.
[4] fr. 17, v. 16-18.

semble, ce qu'Empédocle avait en vue en parlant de son σφαῖρος.

Philolaus, ou l'auteur de notre fragment, a-t-il pu s'inspirer de la conception du σφαῖρος d'Empédocle? Il me semble que non. Les deux idées sont trop différentes.

Du point de vue construction grammaticale, sans doute, l'explication proposée est parfaitement possible. Je crois seulement qu'elle ne rend pas l'idée de l'auteur. Voilà pourquoi je n'accepte pas la solution proposée.

L'argument le plus solide en faveur du ὁλκάς est à mon avis celui qui remarque que l'image du bateau de transport pour dénoter le cinquième élément est trop bizarre pour avoir été inventé par un falsificateur. C'est là une espèce d'extension du principe de *lectio difficilior anteferenda* qui, en tout cas, n'est pas négligeable. Il faut envisager cet argument, il faut le peser.

Je l'ai essayé, et je l'ai trouvé trop léger.

Ma conclusion: on ne saurait accepter le fragm. 12. Certes, il vaut mieux ne pas trop dogmatiser sur le point de l'inauthenticité. Mais il faut dire que ce fragment reste suspect, tout comme le num. 10.

Fr. 13. Theol. arithm. p. 25, 17 de Falco.

καὶ τέσσαρες ἀρχαὶ τοῦ ζῴου τοῦ λογικοῦ, ὥσπερ καὶ Φ. ἐν τῷ Περὶ φύσιως λέγει, ἐγκέφαλος, καρδία, ὀμφαλός, αἰδοῖον· 'κεφαλὰ μὲν νόου, καρδία δὲ ψυχᾶς καὶ αἰσθήσιος, ὀμφαλὸς δὲ ῥιζώσιος καὶ ἀναφύσιος τοῦ πρώτου, αἰδοῖον δὲ σπέρματος (καὶ) καταβολᾶς τε καὶ γεννήσιος. ἐγκέ-
5 φαλος δὲ <σαμαίνει> τὰν ἀνθρώπω ἀρχάν, καρδία δὲ τὰν ζῴου, ὀμφαλὸς δὲ τὰν φυτοῦ, αἰδοῖον δὲ τὰν ξυναπάντων· πάντα γὰρ ἀπὸ σπέρματος καὶ θάλλοντι καὶ βλαστάνοντι'.

(Il y a quatre principes de l'être vivant doué de raison, comme le dit aussi Philolaus dans son livre *De la nature:* le cerveau, le cœur, le nombril, la partie génitale.) *La tête est le lieu propre de la pensée, le cœur celui de l'âme et des sens, le nombril celui où l'embryon prend ses racines et l'origine de sa croissance, la partie génitale du sperme, de l'éjaculation et de la génération. Or, le cerveau dénote le principe de l'homme, le cœur celui de l'animal, le nombril celui de la plante, et la partie génitale celui de tous. Car tous les êtres vivants germent et poussent par la semence.*

Avec le fragm. 13 nous nous sentons sur un fond plus solide. C'est un des fragments, d'ailleurs, sur lesquels l'accord des philologues est le plus général. L'anthropologie esquissée ici possède nettement un caractère archaïque: on y reconnaît facilement la théorie d'Alcméon de la primauté du cerveau; d'autre part, on ne manquera pas de remarquer que cette anthropologie diffère de celle de Platon.

Dans les numéros 14 et 15 de Diels il s'agit de la doctrine orphico-pythagoricienne de l'âme «incarcérée», pour ainsi dire, dans le corps, de la vie terrestre comme moyen d'expiation, et de la défense de mettre fin à sa vie par ses propres moyens et par son propre choix. Ce sont là des doctrines d'origine indubitablement orphico-pythagoricienne, bien connues comme telles par quelques passages célèbres du *Phédon* de Platon, confirmés par un autre passage non moins intéressant qui se lit dans le *Cratyle*, 400c. Ce dernier passage commente sur l'adage de σῶμα σῆμα d'une manière fort originale, en expliquant le corps, premièrement, comme l'instrument par lequel l'âme «indique» (σημαίνει) ce qu'elle veut indiquer; ensuite, (ce qui est plus surprenant encore) comme l'instrument par lequel elle est sauvée (σῶμα - σῴζειν), et c'est en vue de cette fonction que le corps entoure l'âme pour ainsi dire comme une barrière. Cela veut dire: pour la garder (σῴζειν) l'âme a comme enceinte le corps (περίβολον - φρουρά, δεσμωτήριον). Le nom de Philolaus n'est pas mentionné. «*Certains gens disent* (τινές φασιν) que le corps est le σῆμα de l'âme parce que»... etc. «Mais il me semble surtout que οἱ ἀμφὶ Ὀρφέα lui ont donné ce nom» – etc.

Le plus ancien témoignage de Platon sur cette doctrine se trouve dans le *Gorgias*, 493a. Socrate y dit: «Mais peut-être en réalité sommes-nous morts. C'est ce que, un jour, j'ai entendu dire à des hommes sages» (ἤκουσα τῶν σοφῶν). Suit le σῶμα σῆμα, et ensuite la jolie comparaison de l'âme des gens qui ne sont pas maîtres de leurs passions à un crible (κόσκινος), «parce qu'elle était (selon l'informateur de Socrate) percée de trous, laissant tout fuir par aveuglement et par oubli». L'auteur de cette dernière comparaison n'est pas nommé non plus: elle a été inventée, comme dit Socrate, par «quelque spirituel conteur de mythes (τις μυθολογῶν κομψὸς ἀνήρ), peut-être un Sicilien ou un Italien». Rien ne nous autorise à attribuer à Philolaus l'un ou l'autre de ces adages.

Le texte du *Phédon* plaide plutôt contre[1]. Socrate a dit que, bien que la mort soit chose souhaitable pour un philosophe, il n'est pas permis de se faire violence à soi-même. Simmias et Cébès, les deux élèves de Philolaus, s'étonnent de ces paroles qui leur semblent contradictoires.

---

[1] *Phédon* 61d-62b.

Ils demandent que Socrate s'explique. Socrate: «Comment? Vous autres, Simmias et Cébès, qui étiez à l'École de Philolaus, vous n'avez pas entendu parler de ces choses?» – «Rien de précis du moins», répondent les deux jeunes gens. Un peu plus loin Cébès reprend que lui, en tout cas, il a entendu dire à Philolaus, *et à certains autres aussi*, qu'il n'est pas permis de mettre fin à sa propre vie. Mais la raison de cette interdiction lui a échappé complètement, à ce qu'il paraît. – Alors, Socrate de lui expliquer que, dans cette vie, l'homme est, pour ainsi dire, placé à un poste (ἔν τινι φρουρᾷ ἐσμεν). Or, il n'a pas le droit de quitter ce poste sans avoir reçu un ordre explicite du commandant, c'est-à dire, du Dieu qui surveille notre vie et auquel nous appartenons (ἡμᾶς τοὺς ἀνθρώπους ἓν τῶν κτημάτων τοῖς θεοῖς εἶναι).

C'est là à ce qu'il paraît un point de vue nouveau pour les deux anciens élèves de Philolaus. Socrate, lui, introduit son explication en disant que *c'est là ce qu'on raconte dans les Mystères* (ὁ ἐν ἀπορρήτοις λεγόμενος περὶ αὐτῶν λόγος).

Il me semble qu'il faut conclure de ces textes que ni le σῶμα σῆμα, ni le ἐν φρουρᾷ τινί ἐσμεν ne paraissent avoir été des adages spécialement propres à Philolaus. Au contraire, il semble plutôt qu'il ne s'en est pas servi de préférence. Sans doute ces adages faisaient partie d'une doctrine orphico-pythagoricienne qu'il connaissait bien et qu'il acceptait.

Il y a quelques autres témoins de date postérieure qui mentionnent la même doctrine. Le plus ancien d'eux est *Cléarque*, élève d'Aristote et membre de l'École péripatéticienne, à peu près de la même géneration que Théophraste et Aristoxène. Cléarque était admirateur de Platon et faisait l'exégèse de la *République*. Les fragments de son ouvrage Περὶ ὕπνου[1] montrent qu'il partageait les idées de Platon sur l'âme: son fragm. 8 raconte une belle histoire «schamaniste», de la même espèce que le mythe de Er. Cléarque a dû s'intéresser vivement à la doctrine orphico-pythagoricienne de l'âme; il a dû connaître la littérature et les opinions existantes à ce propos. Il est donc raisonnable d'attacher une valeur particulière à son témoignage quand il parle de la doctrine pythagoricienne de l'âme enchaînée dans le corps et vivant ici-bas une vie de pénitance, τιμωρίας χάριν. Or, il ajoutait que, selon cette doctrine, si l'on ne restait dans cette condition jusqu'à ce qu'on soit libéré par le Dieu, les épreuves par où il fallait passer seraient augmentées. Comme auteur, ou informateur, Cléarque men-

---

[1] Fr. 5-10 Wehrli.

tionne: non pas Philolaus, mais «le pythagoricien Euxitheus»[1]. — Nom inconnu pour nous, mais information importante, pourtant, puisque ce n'est pas Philolaus qui est nommé.

Le témoin suivant est *Clément d'Alexandrie, Strom.* III 17 (Stählin II, 203, 11). Ici pour la première fois le nom de Philolaus est mentionné.

Fr. 14. Clem. *Strom.* III 17: μαρτυρέονται δὲ καὶ οἱ παλαιοὶ θεολόγοι τε καὶ μάντιες, ὡς διά τινας τιμωρίας ἁ ψυχὰ τῷ σώματι συνέζευκται καὶ καθάπερ ἐν σήματι τούτῳ τέθαπται.

«Il vaut la peine aussi de mentionner ce qui est dit par Philolaus. Le pythagoricien parle ainsi» (suivent les lignes qui, avec le σῶμα σῆμα et le κόσκινος, sont enregistrées par Diels comme fragm. 14 de Philolaus):

Les anciens théologiens et profètes eux-aussi témoignent que l'âme est jointe au corps à cause de certaines punitions, et qu'elle est ensevelie en lui comme dans un tombeau.

Ce sont exactement ces lignes qui se retrouvent chez Théodoret, *Thérapeutique* V 14. Or, Théodoret, sans doute, n'est pas un témoin indépendant. Il a lu Clément, et c'est là la source de son information.

Et Clément? Est-il un témoin de premier ordre, lui? Faut-il s'imaginer qu'il ait jamais vu le livre de Philolaus, ou qu'il possède une connaissance directe de la tradition religieuse des pythagoriciens, telle que nous l'avons trouvée chez Platon et chez Cléarque? Je ne crois pas. Clément qui vécut quatre à cinq siècles après Cléarque, n'a sûrement pas vu de livre de Philolaus. Il a lu Platon, et c'est par lui qu'il connaît les idées pythagoriciennes sur l'âme et l'au-delà. C'est par la lecture du *Phédon* qu'il connaît le nom de Philolaus, qu'il associe un peu librement à la tradition de ces «anciens théologiens et prophètes» qu'il a trouvés cités chez Platon avec tant de respect et de sympathie. A côté de Cléarque Clément, certes, n'est pas un témoin de valeur égale. On a donc tort de le citer comme tel. Ce qui est clair, c'est que Cléarque nomme explicitement un autre pythagoricien comme auteur du σῶμα σῆμα et de la théorie de l'expiation, tandis que Platon, lui, connaît ces idées comme pythagoriciennes mais fait plutôt paraître qu'elles n'étaient pas particulièrement propres à Philolaus.

Il faut dire la même chose à propos de la φρουρά (le fragm. 15 chez

---

[1] Fr. 38 Wehrli, provenant de l'ouvrage Π. Βίων de Cléarque et conservé chez Athénée IV 157c.

Diels). Ici également nous avons un témoignage chrétien: c'est *Athénagore* qui dit[1]:

Fr. 15. Athenag. 6 p. 6,13 Schw.: καὶ Φ. ὥσπερ ἐν φρουρᾷ...
Plato, *Phaedo* 62 B: ὡς ἔν τινι φρουρᾷ... τοὺς ἀνθρώπους ἓν τῶν κτημάτων τοῖς θεοῖς εἶναι.

Et Philolaus aussi, qui dit que toutes les choses sont retenues par Dieu comme en dépôt, montre par là d'une part que Dieu est un, d'autre part qu'il est au-dessus de la matière.

C'est-à dire, Athénagore cite la doctrine pythagoricienne que «toute chose est retenue par Dieu comme en dépôt» en témoignage préchrétien pour l'unité et pour la transcendance de Dieu. En oûtre, il attribue cette doctrine à Philolaus. Mme Timpanaro cite ce témoignage en premier lieu. Évidemment, c'est le seul texte sur la φρουρά où Philolaus est nommé. Mais est-ce là un témoignage de premier ordre? Nullement. Il en est exactement comme chez Clément: Athénagore a lu le *Phédon;* c'est par là qu'il connaît la doctrine pythagoricienne de ἐν φρουρᾷ ἐσμεν et en même temps le nom de Philolaus. C'est lui qui joint les deux.

Or, ce serait un peu naif d'en appeler à lui pour corriger Platon.

Le fragm. 16 provient d'Aristote, *Ethica Eudemia* II 8, 1225a30, qui cite Philolaus explicitement, comme témoin de la non-responsabilité de l'homme pour certaines de ses pensées, pour certains de ses sentiments et pour certaines actions qui en sont la conséquence; «C'est que», Philolaus dit, «il y a certain λόγοι qui sont plus forts que nous».

Fr. 16. Eth. Eud. B 8 1225a 30: ὥστε καὶ διάνοιαί τινες καὶ πάθη οὐκ ἐφ' ἡμῖν εἰσιν, ἢ πράξεις αἱ κατὰ τὰς τοιαύτας διανοίας καὶ λογισμούς, ἀλλ' ὥσπερ Φ. ἔφη 'εἶναί τινας λόγους κρείττους ἡμῶν.'

Kranz traduit: «Es gibt gewisse *Gedanken*, die stärker sind als wir».
J. Solomon (Oxford transl.): «Some *arguments* are too strong for us».
Dirlmeier, dans sa traduction de la *E.E.* suit Kranz. Dans son commentaire il remarque: «Was das für λόγοι sein könnten, darüber ist keine Vermutung erlaubt». Il est permis, pourtant, de remarquer que λόγοι ne signifie pas nécessairement «pensées» ou «arguments». Ce

---
[1] Athenagoras, *Presbeia* 6, p. 6, 13 Schwartz.

terme peut signifier aussi: *proportions numériques*, et c'est même là une chose très familière à la pensée pythagoricienne. Ce qu'*Aristote* a voulu dire dans notre passage, c'est parfaitement clair. Dans le passage précédent il a parlé d'actions qu'on ne saurait appeler entièrement libres, parce qu'elles ont été faites, par exemple, pour échapper à la mort ou à de violentes souffrances. Enfin, il y a ceux qui parlent en trance et qui agissent en trance (ἐνθουσιῶντες καὶ προλέγοντες). On ne saurait dire que, eux, ils sont maîtres de leurs paroles et de leurs actions. Il paraît donc qu'il existe des activités de l'esprit (διάνοιαι) aussi qui ne sont pas en notre pouvoir, «*mais, comme disait Philolaus, il y a certaines raisons qui sont plus fortes que nous*».

J'ai traduit λόγοι par «des raisons» – terme qui, certainement, embrasse plus que les arguments de l'intellect; «le cœur a ses raisons» lui-aussi, comme l'a dit Pascal, – et j'ai rendu διάνοιαι par le terme général qui comprend non seulement les activités intellectuelles, la parole et la pensée, mais l'action morale et la production aussi[1].

Je n'ai pas voulu dire par là que Philolaus ait voulu dire simplement que, parfois, *les passions* sont plus fortes que nous. D'ailleurs, ce n'était pas là le contexte chez Aristote non plus.

Philolaus qu'a-t-il voulu dire? Certainement il *faut* poser cette question, Mme Timpanaro[2] a eu parfaitement raison d'y voir un problème et de chercher une interprétation telle qu'elle s'accorde avec ce que nous savons de la morale pythagoricienne. Or, cette morale, dit elle, n'est aucunement telle qu'on puisse s'attendre à trouver chez Philolaus un argument en faveur de l'ἀκρασία. Il est donc probable qu'Aristote a détaché ces paroles de leur contexte originel et par là en a altéré la tendance.

Mon commentaire sera un peu différent. Si l'on veut avoir une idée de ce que Philolaus peut avoir voulu dire avec sa sentence sur les λόγοι qui sont plus forts que nous, il faut relire quelques pages du *Timée* de Platon, 82a-89c. Platon, lui aussi, considère la santé physique et morale de l'homme comme conditionnée par un certain équilibre des éléments physiques qui composent son corps. Or, cet équilibre n'est pas autre chose que la juste proportion numérique de ces éléments. Et c'est là exactement ce qu'en pensaient les pythagoriciens.

Cela ne veut pas dire, ni pour les pythagoriciens ni pour Platon,

---

[1] Aristote, *Métaph.* E 1, 1025b25: Πᾶσα διάνοια ἢ πρακτικὴ ἢ ποιητικὴ ἢ θεωρητική.

[2] *Pitagorici*, Testimonianze e frammenti II, p. 234.

qu'ils aient cru que le caractère et le comportement de l'homme, enfin son état intérieur, soit entièrement déterminé par la constitution physique, à tel point qu'il soit impossible de l'influencer, soit par la volonté rationnelle, soit par des influences extérieures. Loin de là, on voit Platon toujours préoccupé des problèmes de l'éducation, c'est-à dire de la formation du caractère, et Aristoxène nous cite de nombreux exemples de la technique *pythagoricienne* qui vise à dominer les passions. C'étaient sans doute en premier lieu les pythagoriciens qui se servaient méthodiquement de la musique pour influencer certaines passions violentes, telles que la colère. Avec combien de succès ils pratiquaient cette méthode, c'est ce qu'on peut voir dans les examples cités par Jamblique, V.P. 112-113[1]. Mais ce n'était non seulement la thérapie par une méthode non-rationnelle que les pythagoriciens pratiquaient, c'était celle par la persuasion aussi. Nous le savons par les mêmes sources. Dès qu'un pythagoricien se sentait en proie à la colère, il sortait de la compagnie où il se trouvait pour regagner son équilibre intérieur avant de parler à qui que ce soit[2].

Il ne faut donc certainement pas s'imaginer que Philolaus ait plaidé la cause de l'ἀκρασία, tout court. Mais, tout comme Platon, il a su que l'état intérieur de l'homme et son comportement dépendent en grande partie de sa constitution physique, et que la ἕξις de l'un est beaucoup plus heureuse que celle de l'autre. Sans qu'il ait jamais pensé que, en général, ce fait dispense l'homme de la lutte contre le vice, il a certainement pu dire qu'il y a «des λόγοι qui sont plus forts que nous». La traduction de «raisons» n'est pas mauvaise. Il est même possible qu'elle soit exacte; c'est-à dire, l'auteur a pu s'exprimer avec une certaine ambiguité voulue, laissant à ses auditeurs (ou ses lecteurs) la tâche de préciser quelle est la fonction particulière des dits λόγοι.

Ici se termine la série des fragments du Περὶ φύσιος de Philolaus.

---

[1] Les principes chez Iambl. *V.P.* 64 et 110s. Voir mon *Pythag.* pp. 162-166; pour les textes, pp. 261 ss.
[2] Diog. Laerce VIII 20; Iambl. *V.P.* 196-197; Diod. X 7. Mon *Pythag.* pp. 161s., 178s., 258.

III.

LES BAKCHAI DE PHILOLAUS

Fr. 17. Stob. *Ecl.* I 15, 7: Φιλολάου Βάκχαι. ὁ κόσμος εἷς ἐστιν, ἤρξατο δὲ γίγνεσθαι ἀπὸ τοῦ μέσου, καὶ ἀπὸ τοῦ μέσου εἰς τὸ ἄνω διὰ τῶν αὐτῶν τοῖς κάτω. ἔστι (γὰρ) τὰ ἄνω τοῦ μέσου ὑπεναντίως κείμενα τοῖς κάτω. πρὸς γὰρ τὸ μέσον κατὰ ταὐτά ἐστιν ἑκάτερα, ὅσα μὴ μετενήνεκται.

Le cosmos est un, et il a commencé à devenir à partir du centre; c'est-à dire, montant du centre en haut par la même distance qu'il descend en bas.-

Fr. 18. - - I 25, 8 Φιλολάου ἐκ Βακχῶν. Zitat (περὶ ἡλίου) ausgefallen.

Les numéros 17-19 chez Diels nous parlent d'un ouvrage de Philolaus intitulé Βάκχαι. Il n'y a pas de quoi douter de l'authenticité de ce titre[1]. D'après les extraits de Stobée l'auteur y traitait des problèmes cosmologiques. Sans doute on peut avoir l'impression que ce sujet ne cadre pas très bien avec le titre. Il me semble que c'est là en tout cas un argument en faveur de son authenticité: «Βάκχαι», ce n'était sûrement pas l'espèce d'étiquette qu'un éditeur postérieur aurait pu inventer pour un livre de cosmologie.

Les idées sur l'origine du cosmos, exposées par Philolaus dans cet ouvrage selon Stobée, cadrent parfaitement avec le fragm. 7: l'arrangement de l'ordre cosmique prenait son commencement au centre, et s'étendait en haut par la même distance qu'en bas. D'après le fragm. 7 il y a «le foyer» au centre du cosmos: il est le πρῶτον ἁρμοσθέν, et il est le un. Puisqu'il est «au centre *du globe*» (ἐν τῷ μέσῳ τῆς σφαίρας), il est clair que le fragm. 7 présuppose exactement les mêmes proportions du cosmos qui sont décrites dans notre passage de Stobée:

Car il y a un parallélisme précis entre ce qui est au-dessus et ce qui est en-dessous du centre. C'est que pour ce qui est en-dessous ce qui se trouve au centre est chose suprême, tandis que pour ce qui est au-dessus ce qui se trouve au centre est chose infime. C'est-à dire: pour les deux les distances sont identiques; les directions seules sont inverses.

Burkert a bien vu que ce parallélisme et cet échange de choses d'«en haut» et de celles d'«en bas» se trouve également dans la cosmologie du Περὶ ἑβδομάδων [2]. C'est une conception archaïque et préplatonicienne.

[1] Diels croyait qu'il est de provenance alexandrine.

Le fragm. 19 cite les *Bakchai* de Philolaus, en même temps que le Ἱερὸς λόγος dans son ensemble et «l'explication de Pythagore sur les dieux», en exemple de théologie qui se sert du symbolisme des nombres.

Fr. 19. Procl. in Eucl. p. 22, 9 Friedl.: διὸ καὶ ὁ Πλάτων πολλὰ καὶ θαυμαστὰ δόγματα περὶ θεῶν διὰ τῶν μαθηματικῶν εἰδῶν ἡμᾶς ἀναδιδάσκει καὶ ἡ τῶν Πυθαγορείων φιλοσοφία παραπετάσματι τούτοις χρωμένη τὴν μυσταγωγίαν κατακρύπτει τῶν θείων δογμάτων. τοιοῦτος γὰρ καὶ ὁ Ἱερὸς σύμπας λόγος καὶ ὁ Φιλόλαος ἐν ταῖς Βάκχαις καὶ ὅλος ὁ τρόπος τῆς Πυθαγόρου περὶ θεῶν ὑφηγήσεως.

«Platon nous enseigne toute une théologie par l'intermédiaire des formes mathématiques, et la philosophie des Pythagoriciens se sert de ces mêmes formes comme d'une espèce de voile qui couvre les divins mystères. Car telle est toute la *«Doctrine sacrée»* (Ἱερὸς λόγος), *et celle de Philolaus dans les Bacchai et enfin tout l'enseignement de Pythagore dans son explication sur les dieux».*

Celui qui a lu et étudié l'ouvrage de M. A. Delatte sur la littérature pythagoricienne[1] sait bien de quoi il s'agit. Delatte a décrit toute cette littérature dite «arithmologique» et en a analysé les restes. C'est par les Θεολογούμενα ἀριθμητικῆς, ouvrage de basse époque, que nous connaissons les identifications des dieux avec les nombres de 1 à 10[2]. Les identifications sont faites d'après les attributs de ces dieux qui semblaient aux pythagoriciens correspondre le plus à certains nombres. Or, quelle est la base de ces speculations assez bizarres? Sont-ce là des produits de la fantaisie des épigones des premiers siècles de notre ère, ou faut-il admettre que, à la base de leurs écrits, il y a une tradition ancienne qui remonte au fondateur-même de la secte pythagoricienne?

Delatte croit, en effet, que Nicomaque a connu, et puisé dans, le Ἱερὸς λόγος attribué à Pythagore lui-même. Il a trouvé des traces de cet écrit – qui, bien sûr, n'est pas de la main du fondateur-même, mais pourtant remonte à ses successeurs immédiats[3], – des traces multiples qui se retrouvent dans les trois *Vies de Pythagore* que nous possédons: il y a des termes très spéciaux, des adages d'un caractère très particulier qui par les sources ultimes de ces trois biographies étaient attribués

[1] A. Delatte, *Études sur la littérature pythagoricienne*, Paris 1915.
[2] Les *Theologoumena arithmetikes* de Nicomaque de Gérasa n'existent plus. L'ouvrage que nous possédons sous le même titre nous est parvenu sous le nom de Iamblique. On sait qu'Anatolius, évêque de Laodicée en 280, était l'auteur d'un livre Περὶ δεκάδος, et d'un autre ouvrage intitulé Ἀριθμητικαὶ εἰσαγωγαί

unanimement à Pythagore lui-même. Or, ces «sources ultimes» étaient: *Aristoxène* et *Timée*, le premier issu de l'École pythagoricienne du 4ᵉ siècle, le dernier historien de l'Italie méridionale et de la Sicile à la même époque. Les deux devaient être bien au courant de la tradition pythagoricienne, telle qu'elle vivait dans l'École-même (Aristoxène) et, en un sens plus général, dans les milieux où le Maître et ses disciples ont vécu et travaillé. Plus récemment M. Guthrie, dans le premier volume de son *History of Greek Philosophy*, a allégué que, dans une École comme celle de Pythagore, qui avait nettement le caractère d'une communauté religieuse, la tradition a dû être particulièrement stable et tenace. C'est là à son avis un argument en faveur d'une grande continuité de doctrine dans l'École pythagoricienne.

Or, le principe de ce qu'on appelle «l'arithmologie» faisait-il partie du pythagorisme ancien, ou faut-il reconnaître que c'était là une espèce de produit bâtard d'un esprit plutôt fantaisiste que profond, plutôt dégénéré qu'archaïque? Question difficile, à ce qu'il paraît, parce que toutes nos sources pour la méthode arithmologique d'identifier les dieux et les nombres sont de basse époque. Il y a Iamblique qui cite plusieurs fois un λόγος περὶ θεῶν de Pythagore ou de son fils Tèlaugès; il y a Proclus et Syrian qui citent le même ouvrage. Nicomaque mentionne un σύγγραμμα περὶ θεῶν de Pythagore, et Moderatus de Gadès lui attribue exactement cette espèce d'identification des dieux et des nombres que nous trouvons dans les Θεολογούμενα dits de Iamblique. Il est vrai, comme l'a observé M. Delatte, que les mêmes identifications sont citées par Porphyre, *De abstinentia* II 36, et par Plutarque, *De Iside* 10, comme d'origine pythagoricienne. Mais cela peut-il nous garantir l'ancienneté de cette origine?

Il y a pas mal d'arithmologie chez Lydus, *De mensibus*. C'est un auteur qui vécut au 6ⁱᵉᵐᵉ siècle. Or, chez lui on trouve l'identification de la monade à «Hyperionides»: Helios, nous dit l'auteur, se réfère à la monade comme son εἰκών. L'identification directe se trouve dans un traité anonyme d'arithmologie, cité par Delatte, *Litt. pythag.* p. 197. Pourtant, même si l'on admet qu'il y a des choses pareilles chez Hippolyte et dans la *Cohortatio* de ps. Justin, tout en concédant le

---

dont on trouve des fragments chez Eusèbe, *Hist. eccl.* VII 32, 14-19. Ces fragments d'Anatolius contiennent de l'arithmologie pythagoricienne.

[3] Voir Delatte, *Litt. pythag.* pp. 19-29. Sa conclusion (p. 27): «Je ne vois pas qu'on puisse y voir autre chose qu'une composition orale que le Maître confiait à la mémoire de ses disciples.»

caractère très spécial de l'identification du Soleil et de la Monade, ce n'est toujours pas plus près qu'au deuxième siècle qu'on en arrive, – et c'est toujours bien loin de l'époque archaïque[1].

Le λόγος περὶ θεῶν, référé par Iamblique, était un ἱερὸς λόγος écrit en dialecte dorique, qui date du premier siècle de notre ère ou un peu plus tard. C'est de la même époque que date le Ὕμνος εἰς ἀριθμόν, un autre document arithmologique, dont nous trouvons les traces chez Proclus et Syrian. Ce sont donc là des falsifications de basse époque. Cela n'empêche pas que la doctrine des nombres des anciens pythagoriciens n'était nullement une pure arithmétique au sens moderne mais fortement mêlée de symbolisme. Et c'est là certainement un trait archaïque qui date des origines. Si l'identification des dieux avec des nombres était déjà faite au cinquième siècle av. J. Chr., on ne saurait le dire. Il est possible que ce soit là une application postérieure du principe de l'arithmologie. Mais le principe lui-même remonte aux origines. Speusippe qui a rassemblé tout le matériel sur les nombres pythagoriciens dans son ouvrage Περὶ Πυθαγορικῶν ἀριθμῶν, loin d'être le fondateur d'une discipline archaïsante, était en effet l'héritier d'une longue tradition.

Après lui, les alexandrins se sont occupés de cette matière, et c'est leur travail qui est la source de la littérature arithmologique pythagoricienne des premiers siècles de notre ère.

Qu'il y ait eu de l'arithmologie dans les *Bacchai* de Philolaus, je le crois bien, si l'on prend le terme au sens large de *symbolisme des nombres*. Quant à l'identification des nombres avec des dieux, je n'en suis pas sûre. Les indications nous manquent.

Passons au fragm. 20 qui par Diels est qualifié de «zweifelhaft». Le fragment nous est parvenu dans trois sources, dont la plus ancienne est Philon d'Alexandrie dans son traité *De opificio mundi*. Les deux autres sont Anatolius dans le *De decade*, et Lydus, *De mensibus*. Nous connaissons déjà les deux derniers auteurs et l'intérêt qu'ils portaient à l'arithmologie. Quant à Philon, l'étude plus ou moins approfondie de ses ouvrages nous apprend qu'il connaissait bien la tradition pythagoricienne, qu'il s'y intéressait et en nourrissait son esprit.

---

[1] L'identification de la monade à Hyperionides etc. se trouve chez Lydus, *De mensibus* II 6. Cp. Hippolytus, *Ref.* VI 23; ps. Justinus, *Cohortatio* 19. Voir Delatte, *Litt. pythag.*, p. 197ss.

Sur le nombre sept chez Philon voir aussi le *De opif. mundi* 36 et 40ss.; Varro ap. Gellium, *N.A.* III 10, 12; Censorinus, *De die nat.* 7, 2.

LES TEXTES DITS DE PHILOLAUS

Les trois sources nous disent que Philolaus qualifiait le nombre sept de ἀμήτωρ et de παρθένος: c'est le seul des dix premiers nombres, disait-il, *qui n'engendre ni n'est engendré*. Que, pour cette raison, il l'ait qualifié d'ἀκίνητος, cela ne me semble pas invraisemblable. Enfin tous les trois citent la ligne suivante:

Fr. 20. ἔστι γὰρ ἡγεμὼν καὶ ἄρχων ἁπάντων, θεός, εἷς, ἀεὶ ὤν, μόνιμος, ἀκίνητος, αὐτὸς ἑαυτῷ ὅμοιος, ἕτερος τῶν ἄλλων.

Car il est guide et gouverneur de tout ce qui existe, dieu, un, éternel, permanent, immuable, se ressemblant à lui-même et différent des autres choses.

Sont-ce là des choses que Philolaus a pu écrire? Peutêtre sommes nous un peu trop inclinés à réprouver un tel texte ou au moins à le déclarer suspect. Tout d'abord, il faut savoir que la place prépondérante accordée au nombre sept remonte à une haute antiquité et précède celle de la décade[1]. On la trouve dans le traité *De hebdomadibus* et dans plusieurs autres traités hippocratiques. Le prédicat de παρθένος pour la heptade se trouve dans un petit traité pythagoricien sur le nombre, traité par M. Delatte dans la section sur les *Anecdota arithmologica*[2], et daté dans l'époque alexandrine. Il n'y a aucune raison de supposer que la vénération pour la heptade soit de date postplatonicienne; au contraire, c'est plutôt une indication qui nous oriente vers l'époque archaïque.

Quant aux autres prédicats attribués à la heptade dans notre fragm. 20, – concédons que pour un philologue moderne c'est chose normale et une attitude propre à sa méthode de travail que de commencer par des doutes radicaux et de supposer comme au moins le plus vraisemblable que tout cela soient des produits de falsificateurs postérieurs. Peutêtre est-ce bien la tâche de notre génération de nous approcher d'un texte pareil avec un esprit plus ouvert, et de faire abstraction de tous les préjugés du 19ième siècle et de ses successeurs. En somme, y a-t-il dans notre texte des choses que Philolaus ne pourrait avoir écrites? Y a-t-il, par exemple, des termes ou des idées nettement

---

[1] Voir les études de N. Roscher, cités dans mon *Pythag.* p. 169 n. 1. Voir aussi J. Hehn, *Siebenzahl u. Sabbath bei den Babyloniern u. im A.T.* (Leipz. Sem. Studien II 5, 1907) et quelques autres études, mentionnées dans mon *Pythag.*, p. 174 n. 1. J'ai traité moi-même la question du nombre sept chez les pythagoriciens, dans les pp. 169-174 de mon *Pythag.*

[2] Delatte, *Litt. pythag.* p. 167 ss.

platoniciens ou aristotéliciens? Je n'en trouve pas. Après tout, on ne saurait dire que la formule de αὐτὸς ἑαυτῷ ὅμοιος ou ἕτερος τῶν ἄλλων soit particulièrement platonicienne, ni que le mot ἀκίνητος, si l'on veut dire qu'une chose apparemment ne se meut pas, soit particulièrement aristotélicien.

Ma conclusion: il me semble parfaitement possible, même probable, qu'il y a eu de l'arithmologie dans les *Bacchai* de Philolaus, et au moins possible que les textes allégués par Philon et par quelques autres auteurs proviennent de lui.

Considérons aussi le fragm. 21, non pas pour en défendre l'authenticité, mais pour voir en quoi il diffère des autres fragments et quels sont les arguments pour le rejeter.

Le fragment nous est parvenu par Stobée, comme plusieurs autres des fragments de Philolaus. Il est cité comme provenant de son livre Π. ψυχῆς et contient des arguments pour la thèse de l'éternité du monde – doctrine bien connue depuis Aristote, fréquemment discutée à l'époque hellénistique et exposée dans un traité spécial, conservé sous le nom de Philon. Ce qui rend notre fragment suspect, c'est donc en premier lieu le thème lui-même, ensuite les arguments, enfin quelques termes et idées qui sont nettement platoniciennes ou post-platoniciennes. Suivons le texte.

Fr. 21. Stob. *Ecl.* I 20, 2 p. 172, 9: Φιλολάου Πυθαγορείου ἐκ τοῦ Περὶ ψυχῆς. Φ. ἄφθαρτον τὸν κόσμον εἶναι. λέγει γοῦν οὕτως ἐν τῷ Περὶ ψυχῆς. — l. 1-3. παρὸ καὶ ἄφθαρτος καὶ ἀκαταπόνατος διαμένει τὸν ἄπειρον αἰῶνα· οὔτε γὰρ ἔντοσθεν ἄλλα τις αἰτία δυναμικωτέρα αὐτᾶς εὑρεθήσεται οὔτ' ἔκτοσθεν φθεῖραι αὐτὸν δυναμένα.

Pour cela le monde reste impérissable et infatigable pour toute éternité; car ni à l'intérieur de lui, ni à l'extérieur on ne trouvera jamais d'autre cause plus forte que lui qui pourrait le détruire.

C'est là un argument stoïcien et qui présuppose la conception stoïcienne du cosmos comme totalité de l'être, parfait, et par là divin. C'est la conception du monde que nous connaissons bien par Cicéron, *De natura deorum* II – cela veut dire par Posidonius –, mais déjà par le traité Περὶ κόσμου qui nous est parvenu dans le Corpus Aristotelicum, le chapitre 5.

l. 3-5. ἀλλ' ἦν ὅδε ὁ κόσμος ἐξ αἰῶνος καὶ εἰς αἰῶνα διαμενεῖ, εἷς ὑπὸ ἑνὸς τῶ συγγενέος καὶ κρατίστω καὶ ἀνυπερθέτω κυβερνώμενος.

Mais ce monde existait de toute éternité, et durera jusque dans l'éternité, un, gouverné par Un qui lui est apparenté, très fort et invincible.

L'éternité et l'unité du monde sont des doctrines aristotéliciennes. Mais par le ἑνὸς τῶ συγγενέος κυβερνώμενος elles apparaissent ici dans une transposition stoïcienne qui fait du Gouverneur du cosmos un être «de la même famille» que le cosmos lui-même.

l. 5-7: ἔχει δὲ καὶ τὰν ἀρχὰν τᾶς κινήσιός τε καὶ μεταβολᾶς ὁ κόσμος εἷς ἐὼν καὶ συνεχὴς καὶ φύσει διαπνεόμενος καὶ περιαγεόμενος ἐξ ἀρχιδίου·

Le cosmos possède aussi le principe du mouvement et du changement (en lui-même), puisqu'il est un et continu, pénétré du souffle par la nature (φύσει διαπνεόμενος) *et tournant autour de son centre* (περιαγεόμενος) *depuis le commencement.*

Jusqu'à la dernière ligne nous nous trouvons entièrement dans le climat de la pensée stoïcienne: le cosmos qui est la totalité de l'être, auquel rien ne manque, doit évidemment avoir le principe de son mouvement en lui-même; l'unité et la continuité, le souffle du πνεῦμα qui le pénètre φύσει, ce sont tous des traits stoïciens très nets. Enfin la rotation du monde. Sans doute il faut penser à l'univers et aux mouvements cycliques des sphères célestes, non pas à la rotation de la terre autour de son axe. C'est-là une doctrine relativement jeune. Elle était enseignée par Hicétas et Ecphantus, des pythagoriciens du 4ième siècle. Ils étaient des innovateurs qui dans leurs temps prenaient une place isolée. Platon, probablement[1], n'a pas accepté leur théorie. Elle était étrangère à Aristote et aux premiers stoïciens (p.e. à Cléanthe dans son Hymne à Zeus). Le mouvement cyclique du ciel, par contre, des planètes et de leurs sphères, c'est à dire de l'univers dans son ensemble, c'était une conception connue, en principe au moins, depuis Anaximandre et élaborée au 4ième siècle par Eudoxe, Callippe et Aristote. Comparé à leurs théories le système dit de Philolaus qui fait danser δέκα σώματα autour du feu central, appelé le Foyer[2], fait une

---

[1] Il s'agit de l'interprétation de *Timée* 40b: Γῆν δὲ... εἰλλομένην τὴν περὶ τὸν διὰ παντὸς πόλον τεταμένον – Burnet (*Early Gr. Phil.*³ pp. 302s.) qui lisait ἰλλομένην, suivi par Cornford (*Plato's Cosmology* pp. 120ss.), croyaient que Platon a adopté la théorie de la rotation de la terre autour de son axe; Rivaud, par contre, démontre que Platon a cru à l'immobilité de la Terre qui occupe la position centrale dans l'univers et par là se trouve en parfait équilibre: toute l'explication des phénomènes célestes dans le *Timée* est fondée sur cette hypothèse (voir Rivaud, éd. du *Timée* dans la Coll. Budé, Introd. pp. 59-63).

[2] Diels-Kranz 44 A 16; cp. notre fragm. 7.

impression plutôt primitive. Mais, enfin, l'idée d'un mouvement cyclique ne manque pas. La ligne que je viens de citer n'est donc pas nécessairement d'une date postérieure à Philolaus, comme c'est le cas pour la dernière ligne du fragment, où nous trouverons le «Démiurge».

l. 7-10: καὶ τὸ μὲν ἀμετάβλατον αὐτοῦ, τὸ δὲ μεταβάλλον ἐστί· καὶ τὸ μὲν ἀμετάβολον ἀπὸ τᾶς τὸ ὅλον περιεχούσας ψυχᾶς μέχρι σελήνας περαιοῦται, τὸ δὲ μεταβάλλον ἀπὸ τᾶς σελήνας μέχρι τᾶς γᾶς.

Et une partie de lui (sc. du cosmos) *est invariable, l'autre partie change toujours. Or, la partie invariable, en partant de l'Âme qui embrasse l'univers, s'étend jusqu'à la lune, et la partie changeante de la lune jusqu'à la terre.*

Il y a quelques difficultés dans ce texte. Du point de vue de langue c'est la forme περαιοῦται qui est étrange. Nous connaissons bien ce verbe dans le sens de «traverser», traverser une rivière, par exemple. Pour «s'étendre» le Grec pouvait dire περαίνειν.

Quant à la pensée, il y a d'abord la distinction entre ce qui est invariable et ce qui change toujours. Est-ce là une conception pythagoricienne? Boeckh n'en doutait pas. Moi, j'en doute. Je ne vois pas que cette distinction cadre bien avec l'idée fondamentale de la philosophie pythagoricienne: l'identification des choses avec les nombres. Par là le pythagorisme est à mon avis une métaphysique de l'immanent. Non pas l'immanence d'une «Âme du monde», comme l'a cru Boeckh, mais l'immanence du nombre qui était divin. C'est dans cette tendance à l'identification directe, dans cet immanentisme métaphysique que je vois la différence entre les pythagoriciens et Platon[1].

Deuxième point: la doctrine de l'âme du monde. Quels étaient les arguments pourquoi on a pu trouver là une doctrine pythagoricienne du 5ième siècle? Tout ce que nous pouvons dire, c'est que les anciens pythagoriciens avaient l'idée du monde respirant. Cette idée semble impliquer celle d'un ζῷον, et l'idée d'un ζῷον présuppose une âme.

C'est là une séquence d'idées qui est logique. Mais peutêtre l'est-elle un peu trop pour correspondre à la réalité de la pensée pythagoricienne. En tant que nous la connaissons, il faut constater que la notion du cosmos comme ζῷον non seulement n'y domine pas, mais qu'elle n'apparaît même point du tout. Ce qui domine, c'est la présence du nombre. Or, le nombre est certainement regardé comme une force divine ou un principe divin. Il est possible que, à l'époque archaïque

---

[1] Voir mon *Pythag.* p. 197, 200ss.

déjà, les pythagoriciens ont identifié certains nombres avec certains des dieux traditionnels. Mais il n'y a aucune indication pour croire que les pythagoriciens du 5ième siècle, ou même du 4ième, aient développé une doctrine d'une Âme du monde, pénétrant le cosmos et l'entourant.

C'est là exactement l'Âme du monde telle qu'elle a été conçue et décrite par Platon dans le *Timée*[1]. Par contre, pas de trace de cette conception dans l'aperçu de la philosophie pythagoricienne présenté par Aristote dans *Métaph.* A 5.

Troisième point: la division de l'univers en une partie non-changeante située au-dessus de la lune, et une partie sublunaire qui est celle de la nature changeante, est aristotélicienne.

«Mais», dira-t-on, «n'avez-vous donc pas remarqué que la même distinction se trouve aussi dans la cosmologie de Philolaus, référée dans Stobée[2], cette cosmologie dont vous venez de reconnaître le caractère archaïque?»

C'est vrai. Mais c'est là exactement un point qui, après la danse archaïque des dix corps, nous fait supposer le travail additionel d'une main postérieure.

l. 10-16: ἐπεὶ δέ γε καὶ τὸ κινέον ἐξ αἰῶνος ἐς αἰῶνα περιπολεῖ, τὸ δὲ κινεόμενον ὡς τὸ κινέον ἄγει, οὕτως διατίθεται, ἀνάγκη τὸ μὲν ἀεικίνατον τὸ δὲ ἀειπαθὲς εἶμεν· καὶ τὸ μὲν νῶ καὶ ψυχᾶς * ἀνάκωμα πᾶν, τὸ δὲ γενέσιος καὶ μεταβολᾶς· καὶ τὸ μὲν πρᾶτόν τε δυνάμει καὶ ὑπερέχον, τὸ δὲ ὕστερον καὶ καθυπερεχόμενον· τὸ δὲ ἐξ ἀμφοτέρων τούτων, τοῦ μὲν ἀεὶ θέοντος θείου τοῦ δὲ ἀεὶ μεταβάλλοντος γενατοῦ, κόσμος.

Et puisque la force motrice (τὸ κινέον) circule (περιπολεῖ) d'éternité, tandis que ce qui est mû est mis dans une disposition telle que la force motrice le mène, il est nécessaire que la force motrice soit toujours en mouvement, tandis que ce qui est mû soit toujours passif. Il est également nécessaire que la première soit toute entière le terrain de la pensée et de l'âme, le dernier celui de la naissance et du changement; que la première excelle par sa force, et que l'autre soit dépassé. Or, ce qui est composé de ces deux, du divin qui court toujours et du naissant qui toujours change, c'est le cosmos.

Boeckh a très bien vu qu'il manque quelque chose dans la logique de ce passage. C'est qu'il commence par une division en deux parties

---
[1] *Timée* 34 b.
[2] DK 44 A 16.

qui semblent embrasser la totalité, et qu'il finit par une division en trois. Constatons que la première division est celle de la Stoa, qui distingue un aspect actif et un aspect passif dans la Nature qui est la totalité de l'être[1]. Et en effet, pour les Stoïciens «ce qui meut» (τὸ κινοῦν) est toujours en mouvement, tandis que l'autre chose est toujours passive. Ni Platon ni Aristote n'aurait pu faire cette distinction, elle est essentiellement stoïcienne. Par contre, l'explication qui suit – celle qui oppose la pensée et l'âme à l'ensemble de ce qui naît et change – c'est du stoïcisme platonisé.

Enfin, dans les dernières lignes, notre fragment en arrive à la conception que nous connaissons par le passage de Stobée sur la cosmologie de Philolaus[2]: dans ce passage la partie supérieure – ou, disons, la zône supérieure – du globe de l'univers est appelé ὄλυμπος, la partie sublunaire qui entoure la terre s'appelle l'οὐρανός. La dernière est le terrain de la naissance et du changement. Dans ce passage elle s'oppose comme telle aux τεταγμένα τῶν μετεώρων, aux «phénomènes célestes qui sont bien ordonnés»: ce sont «les cinq planètes, le soleil et la lune», enfin, tout ce qui se trouve entre «l'olympe» et «le ciel», et c'est là ce qui s'appelle le *cosmos*.

Or, si l'on se rappelle que dans la zône supérieure (l'olympe) il y a «pureté des éléments» (εἰλικρίνειαν τῶν στοιχείων), c'est-à dire qu'il y a là l'élément le plus pur que les Anciens appelaient l'*éther;* si l'on voit ensuite que, d'après l'auteur du fragm. 21, la zône supérieure est en éternel mouvement et qu'elle est même décrite comme «le divin qui court toujours», – alors, il faut bien constater que tout cela évoque un peu trop vivement ces lignes d'Aristote dans le *De Caelo* I où il dit que «le lieu suprême» est appelé par le nom de αἰθήρ, ἀπὸ τοῦ θεῖν ἀεὶ τὸν ἀΐδιον χρόνον θέμενοι τὴν ἐπωνυμίαν αὐτῷ[3].

Boeckh croyait qu'il s'agissait de l'Âme du monde; c'est elle, pense-t-il, qui est toujours en mouvement et qui exerce une influence directe sur les mouvements des astres. La différence entre leurs movements et ceux du monde sublunaire est que ces derniers ne dépendent pas directement de l'Âme du monde, mais suivent le mouvement des corps célestes; et c'est pour cela que l'auteur de notre fragment appelait ces choses «passives».

Ce que Boeckh n'a pas vu, c'est, premièrement, que l'idée d'une

---

[1] Diog. Laert. VII 134; Aet. I 3, 25 (*Doxogr.* 289); Seneca, *Ep.* 65, 2. De Vogel, *Greek Phil.* III, nr. 899.
[2] DK 44 A 16.
[3] *De caelo* I 3, 270b22s.

Âme du monde n'est pas d'origine pythagoricienne. Par cette erreur fondamentale il pouvait croire à l'authenticité de notre fragment et expliquer notre passage comme exprimant les idées de Philolaus sous une forme un peu incomplète. Il est remarquable, pourtant, que même la formule du «divin qui court toujours» n'a pas éveillé ses soupçons.

l. 17-22 : διὸ καὶ καλῶς ἔχειν ἔλεγε, κόσμον ἦμεν ἐνέργειαν ἀίδιον θεῷ τε καὶ γενέσιος κατὰ συνακολουθίαν τᾶς μεταβλατικᾶς φύσιος. καὶ ὁ μὲν ⟨εἷς⟩ ἐς ἀεὶ διαμένει κατὰ τὸ αὐτὸ καὶ ὡσαύτως ἔχων, τὰ δὲ καὶ γινόμενα καὶ φθειρόμενα πολλά. καὶ τὰ μὲν (ἐν) φθορᾷ ὄντα καὶ φύσεις καὶ μορφὰς σῴζοντι καὶ γονῇ πάλιν τὰν αὐτὰν μορφὰν ἀποκαθιστάντι τῷ γεννήσαντι πατέρι καὶ δημιουργῷ...

A cause de cela il disait: *Il est correct que le cosmos est une éternelle activité de Dieu et du Devenir, d'après l'accompagnement de la nature changeante. Et lui (le cosmos) dure éternellement, un et toujours identique à lui-même; les choses sublunaires, par contre, naissent et périssent, et sont multiples. Mais les choses qui périssent conservent néanmoins leur nature et leur forme, et par la génération elles reproduisent la même forme pour le Père qui les a engendrées, le Démiurge.*

Ces derniers mots «sind vom Berichterstatter zugesetzt», déclare Boeckh. La formule κατὰ τὸ αὐτὸ καὶ ὡσαύτως ἔχων, bien que toute aussi platonicienne que le Démiurge, ne le dérange pas. Pour nous, il y a déjà un problème dans la première ligne de cette section; le cosmos est une ἐνέργεια ἀίδιος de Dieu et du Devenir. Il faut une large mesure de confiance pour croire que Philolaüs ait écrit des choses pareilles. Moi, je n'en ai pas tant. Au contraire, cette ἐνέργεια éternelle de Dieu et du Devenir me met immédiatement en plein climat stoïcien et post-aristotélicien, où des termes spécifiquement aristotéliciens se retrouvent dans une ambiance nouvelle: celle d'un immanentisme où «Dieu» est toujours en mouvement et lié à l'éternel Devenir.

Cette revue des textes nous a retenu un peu longtemps, mais elle était nécessaire pour avoir une base solide. Une fois faite, elle nous permettra de répondre sans délai aux quatre questions posées au début de cette étude.

La première était celle de savoir s'il n'y a dans ces textes rien qui ne suppose une date plus récente. Après notre examen nous pouvons répondre: en somme, il y en a peu; si l'on fait abstraction du fragm. 21, il y en a très peu.

Résumons.

Dans les fragm. 1-7 il n'y a rien qui ne nous oriente décidément vers une date postérieure au 5ième siècle. Il y a sûrement certaines choses plus ou moins remarquables, telles que le τὸ γνωσούμενον (fr. 3), ἁ ἐστώ (fr. 6), τὸ ἓν πρᾶτον ἁρμοσθέν (fr. 7) et la ἑστία au milieu de la σφαῖρα, ce qui suppose la cosmologie attribuée à Philolaus, mais qui reste toujours un peu problématique.

Ce qui est le plus remarquable de tout, c'est peutêtre l'emploi du dialecte dorien. Car, enfin, Philolaus était Crotonien, et Crotone n'était *pas une ville dorienne. C'était une colonie d'origine achaïque. Pythagore, lui, parlait l'ionien.* C'étaient les pythagoriciens du 4ième siècle qui parlaient le dorien, langue d'Archytas de Tarente. Mais il y a quelques indications pour soutenir que, vers la fin du 5ième siècle déjà, une espèce de κοινή dorique était en formation ou s'était déjà formée.

Dans les fragm. 8-16 il y a quelques expressions un peu douteuses – telles que πολυμιγέων ἕνωσις (fr. 10), σωμάτων (fr. 11), le fameux ὁλκάς comme πέμπτον σῶμα (fr. 12) – et un seul terme qui est nettement aristotélicien (οὐσία, fr. 11). Pour les fragm. 14 et 15 il y a le contexte chez Platon qui plaide plutôt contre l'attribution de ces adages à Philolaus en particulier.

Dans les fragm. 17-20 les deux derniers contiennent certaines choses qui nous orientent plutôt vers un siècle postérieur à Philolaus: je veux dire la référence à un ἱερὸς λόγος ou à un λόγος περὶ θεῶν de Pythagore, où les dieux seraient expliqués selon la méthode de l'arithmologie. Tout comme le navire de transport et les cinq corps du fr. 12, on ne saurait rejeter l'explication arithmologique des dieux bien catégoriquement par rapport au 5ième siècle, mais c'est un point douteux.

Il faut en dire autant à propos des deux dernières lignes sur la heptade, citées par Diels sous le num. 20.

Dans le fragm. 21, enfin, les idées et les termes postplatoniciens abondent. Ils sont là avec une telle clarté qu'ils ne nous laissent pas le moindre doute.

Deuxième question: Y a-t-il dans ces fragments des indications positives qui nous orientent vers le 5ième siècle?

Pour tout un nombre de fragments il faut répondre par l'affirmative. M. Burkert l'a fait pour les num. 1-7, 13 et 17. Nous y ajouterons quelques uns. Résumons encore une fois.

1. Une indication très positive est la particule δέ au début du fr. 1;

2. le style très circonspect qui répète plusieurs fois les idées dominantes dans le fragm. 2;
3. le pluriel περαίνοντα - ἄπειρα au lieu de πέρας - ἄπειρον (fr. 2);
4. les termes archaïques pour les intervalles de la musique (fr. 6);
5. «la force de la décade» (fr. 11);
6. le nombre comme principe de connaissance (fr. 3, 4,11);
7. les deux espèces du nombre (fr. 5);
8. le «foyer» au centre de l'univers (fr. 7);
9. les quatre principes de l'homme (fr. 13);
10. les λόγοι (μαθηματικοί) qui dominent (fr. 16);
11. l'arrangement du cosmos qui commence au centre (fr. 17);
12. le nombre 7 comme ἀμήτωρ et παρθένος (fr. 20).

Troisième question: Philolaus était-il l'auteur des théories exposées dans ces fragments, ou était-il le porte-parole de théories et d'idées qui en grande partie vivaient dans l'École pythagoricienne depuis deux ou trois générations?

La question s'impose par la théorie récemment défendue par M. Burkert, qui trouve en Philolaus le commencement de la philosophie pythagoricienne: avant lui, rien n'aurait existé qui soit digne de ce nom. Il est clair que, s'il en est ainsi, Philolaus était une des grandes figures de l'histoire de la philosophie: un vrai fondateur, philosophe de grande allure qu'il faudrait placer au niveau de Parménide, d'Empédocle, d'Anaxagore. Or, dans ce cas, on peut être sûr que, dans son aperçu de la philosophie précédente dans le livre A de la *Métaph.*, Aristote n'aurait pas manqué de le nommer. Le fait qu'il ne le nomme pas dans cet aperçu – il le connaît et le cite ailleurs, comme nous avons vu (fragm. 16) – s'explique parce qu'il ne le regarde nullement comme un fondateur, mais comme représentant une tradition honorable et déjà ancienne de son temps. Qu'Aristote lui-même fût loin de penser que la philosophie pythagoricienne commença par Philolaus, c'est hors de doute: on n'a qu'à relire le chapitre 5 de *Métaph.* A où, e.a., la συστοιχία est attribuée ou bien à Alcméon ou aux pythagoriciens de son temps, c'est-à-dire à la génération qui succédait immédiatement au fondateur de l'École.

Cela ne veut pas dire, évidemment, qu'il n'y ait rien de personnel dans l'œuvre de Philolaus. Il y a, sûrement, des choses particulières à lui, e.a. l'emploi du pluriel dans l'antithèse de περαίνοντα καὶ ἄπειρα. Ce qui importe, c'est que l'essentiel de ses idées est un fond traditionnel qui remonte aux origines de l'École.

Notre quatrième question concernait la relation des textes de Philolaus à l'exposé d'Aristote dans *Métaph.* A 5. Une comparaison attentive nous démontre que les textes de Philolaus, loin d'être la base de l'aperçu d'Aristote, ont certainement une affinité à la doctrine décrite par lui, telle qu'on peut retrouver dans ces textes les traits essentiels de la philosophie pythagoricienne d'après l'esquisse d'Aristote, sans qu'il y ait correspondance exacte pour tous les détails. Au lieu d'avoir l'impression que les textes de Philolaus ont été la source principale d'Aristote, j'ai plutôt l'impression qu'il disposait d'une information plus large qui ne consistait pas nécessairement en traités écrits.

Question finale: que faut-il penser de l'authenticité de ces textes?
1. Des dix-neuf numéros acceptés comme authentiques par Diels-Kranz il y en a quelques uns que, à mon avis, il faudrait placer dans la catégorie des *dubia*, et quelques autres qu'il vaut mieux ne pas compter parmi les fragments de Philolaus du tout. Parmi les *dubia* il faudrait placer les numéros 10 et 12. Moi, personnellement, j'ai des doutes très forts par rapport au fragm. 10, à tel point que je suis inclinée à le rejeter. Mes doutes sont moins forts envers le fragm. 12 («das verdammte Lastschiff», pour citer Burkert). Là, je vois au moins la *possibilité* que ce soit authentique.

Malgré l'οὐσία (essence) dans la première ligne, je ne doute pas de l'authenticité du fragm. 11. D'après son contenu, ça cadre trop bien avec les autres fragments, et avec ce que nous savons de la doctrine pythagoricienne en général.

Les num. 14 et 15 contiennent de la doctrine pythagoricienne, même des citations précises. Mais il paraît que les formules et adages cités n'étaient pas propres à Philolaus. Il ne faudrait donc pas les placer parmi les fragments, mais tout au plus dans la catégorie de «related texts».

Quant aux num. 17-19, si on limite les «fragments» à proprement parler au titre Βάκχαι, évidemment, ces fragments sont authentiques. L'intention de Diels-Kranz allait un peu plus loin: sans vouloir dire que les textes imprimés sous 17 et 19 soient des citations directes, les éditeurs allemands étaient d'avis que ces textes référaient une partie du contenu de ce livre de Philolaus; c'est-à-dire, ils acceptaient que dans ce livre Philolaus traitait des problèmes cosmologiques (num. 17-18) et, en outre, des problèmes d'«arithmologie», et cela dans ce sens que l'auteur a appliqué le symbolisme des nombres à l'explication de la nature des dieux (num. 19). Par rapport à ce dernier point, je ne veux pas en dénier la possibilité; mais on ne saurait dire que ce soit certain. Moi, j'aimerais donc mieux placer le num. 19 parmi les *dubia*.

2. Dans le num. 20 de Diels-Kranz, par contre, je trouve des choses que je peux accepter comme authentiques sans aucune difficulté. Ce sont les prédicats de ἀμήτωρ et de παρθένος pour la heptade. Quant aux deux dernières lignes, je les rangerais parmi les *dubia*, laissant la possibilité qu'elles soient authentiques.

Il en est ainsi pour le num. 20a aussi: c'est la qualification de la dyade comme «épouse de Zeus». On ne saurait en dire beaucoup plus. Il est possible que ce texte soit authentique, mais on ne saurait en être certain.

3. A propos du fragm. 21, par contre, aucun doute n'est possible: il a été placé parmi les *spuria* pour des raisons parfaitement solides.

CHAPTER III

AN IMPORTANT GERMAN WORK ON PYTHAGORAS AND THE PYTHAGOREAN TRADITION[1]

In his Erlangen "Habilitationsschrift" the young scholar Walter Burkert took up the heritage of Zeller and a few other German scholars concerning Pythagoras and the Pythagorean tradition. It is certainly a very able work that lies before us in the big volume *Weisheit und Wissenschaft, Studien zu Pythagoras, Philolaos und Platon*, published in Nürnberg in 1962. The problems confronting the author when starting from Zeller and those who came after him, were the following.

First, in Zeller's account, the figure of Pythagoras disappeared in the mist of legend. Next, the Pythagorean philosophy as described by Aristotle and confirmed by the Philolaus fragments was not exactly situated: it remained anonymous and chronologically undetermined. Zeller did not doubt the basic importance of the Pythagoreans for Greek mathematics, astronomy and musicology, though in fact the ground might appear not to be solid at all. Later research has led to different results. Scholars have not been able to agree. As to the person of Pythagoras, several attempts have been made to come to a more positive reconstruction; but, for lack of real evidence, no agreement could be reached here either.

The results our author arrived at himself are, briefly speaking, the following.

1. A distinction must be made between post- and praeplatonic tradition on what is called the Pythagoreans. Plato's immediate successors Speusippus and Xenocrates created that which is later called Pythagorean philosophy by interpreting as Pythagorean philosophy Plato's doctrine in the *Timaeus* and the metaphysics of numbers and of two ultimate principles taught by Plato in his later years. Another well-known member of the Early Academy, Heraclides

[1] This chapter was written recently, March-April 1969.

Ponticus, attributed to Pythagoras the introduction of the term philosophy in Plato's sense, together with the view that "the knowledge of the perfection of numbers is the soul's beatitude". All this has been taken over by later doxography: "the Pythagoras tradition is the Plato interpretation of the Early Academy". To this whole complex of ideas belongs that of κάθαρσις by the study of mathematics and mathematical disciplines: this is not originally a Pythagorean thought; it stems from Plato, for it presupposes the doctrine of transcendent Ideas.

2. Aristotle, in his description of the Pythagorean philosophy, is quite free from this Platonic influence: what he depicts is in fact pre-platonic Pythagoreanism. That in this description the name of Pythagoras is never mentioned, cannot be fortuitous; Aristotle apparently thought that no philosophical doctrine could be attributed to Pythagoras with any certitude.

3. Who, then, was the author of this anonymous Pythagorean philosophy? This question is answered by Burkert quite categorically: the author of this philosophy was Philolaus. It is a kind of philosophy which, though number does play a role in it, cannot be characterised as mathematical. The extant fragments of Philolaus' book confirm that this was exactly the way of thinking of this 5th century Pythagorean. No doubt his book was known to Aristotle: he must have used it as his primary source for early Pythagorean philosophy.

4. From this inference – for such it is – another inference is drawn: if Philolaus was the author of this philosophy, there apparently did not exist anything like a Pythagorean philosophy before him. Moreover, there did not exist anything like early Pythagorean mathematics. Musicology and cosmology started with Philolaus, Pythagorean mathematics with Archytas. This is our earliest evidence. All further evidence concerning Pythagorean science is of a much later date: the Neopythagoreans of the first centuries A.D. and after them the Neoplatonists attributed to Pythagoras and to his early disciples what is in fact considerably later.

5. Thus, the whole image of Pythagoras as a man of science and a rational philosopher turns out to be a construction due to the projections of later centuries. What he must actually have been is: a man who in his day impressed people by a peculiar kind of "knowledge", – the knowledge that is proper to the "shaman", the man of supernatural gifts, who must have his place in the history of religion and that kind of wisdom which preceded scientific thinking. Therefore,

Pythagoras' name is to be deleted both from the history of science and of philosophy.

It is certainly discouraging to hear an intelligent man say such things as those in section (4), when such good arguments have been advanced on the topic of Pythagorean mathematics by B. L. van der Waerden and K. von Fritz, – both of whom probably understand more of mathematics than does Burkert. However, in his opinion the historians of science are apparently unable to decide this matter: they have *proved* that they cannot, since they do not agree, – but the philologist can decide, for he can prove that there is no evidence.

I repeat, it is discouraging to hear such things from an intelligent man, the more so when one sees that in this case the philologist's decisive argument is obviously the result of incorrect reasoning. I do not think for a moment that Von Fritz – who is a philologist – will change his opinion on Pythagorean mathematics by reason of Burkert's argument. Van der Waerden, I am sorry to say, did, – doubtless because he is not a philologist.

But, however unattractive it may be, let us take up the matter at the beginning and – granted that there are many valuable things in Burkert's work – see where and in what he is more or less seriously mistaken.

Ad 1. It is a well-known fact that, not so long after Plato, a certain fusion took place of Plato's later doctrine of two ultimate principles with Pythagoreanism. We find this as an accomplished fact in the Πυθαγορικὰ ὑπομνήματα referred to by Alexander Polyhistor in Diogenes Laertius VIII 24-35, and dated in the 2nd cent. B.C. Similarly we find Plato's later doctrine labelled "Pythagorean philosophy" in Sextus Empiricus, *Adv. math.* X 248-282. With regard to the first section of Alexander Polyhistor's account (c. 25, on First principles) Festugière[1] remarked that this part might be the oldest and, as its earliest possible date, might go back to Speusippus, who was always eager to bring his theories under the banner of early Pythagoreanism. I dealt with this subject in ch. VI of my own book on Pythagoras and Early Pythagoreanism. Burkert is rather more precise when positing categorically that Speusippus and Xenocrates were the first to label Plato's doctrine of First principles and the successive deduction of

---

[1] *Les "Memoires pythagoriques" cités par Alexandre Polyhistor* in *Revue des Etudes grecques* 1945, p. 1-65.

numbers, geometrical figures and bodies from these principles: "Pythagoreanism". This far I think he is right. There are texts to confirm this. Yet, is it not making too general a statement to say as Burkert does that Plato's immediate successors "created" later Pythagorean philosophy by interpreting Plato's doctrine in the *Timaeus* etc. as Pythagorean philosophy? We must distinguish, we must express ourselves in a more modest, more limited form. It must be stated, no doubt, that the philosophers of the Early Academy, in particular Speusippus and Xenocrates, very probably gave a peculiarly Platonic tinge to the Pythagorean doctrine of πέρας - ἄπειρον. But this does not take away from the fact that it was originally a Pythagorean doctrine, adopted and worked out in a special way by Plato. That there was not a part of Pythagorean doctrine in the *Timaeus*, cannot be inferred from it. There are certainly indications that there was.

That Pythagoras called himself a φιλόσοφος and his kind of wisdom φιλοσοφία, is mentioned in a story which Cicero read in Heraclides Ponticus. Of course it cannot be inferred from this fact that Heraclides simply *invented* the story, including the use of the terms φιλόσοφος and φιλοσοφία by Pythagoras. That he used them "in Plato's sense", is not said by Heraclides. From other sources[1] going back to the 4th cent. Sicilian historian Timaeus we learn that Pythagoras called himself by that name in opposition to the so-called "Seven Sages". That this is probably true, is confirmed by Heraclitus, fr. 35. When the solitary philosopher of Ephesus, who elsewhere speaks with contempt of the πολυμαθία of some people of famous name – Hesiodus, Pythagoras, Xenophanes, Hecataeus – assures that certainly φιλόσοφοι ἄνδρες must know many things, we find here an early use of the term φιλόσοφος which is all the more striking since in those days it was not common. Is it hazardous to say that it must refer to some famous contemporary, whose "knowledge of many things" is referred to by the author not appreciatively but ironically? Now Pythagoras was of the above-mentioned "knowers of many things" perhaps the most famous for his learning – and moreover the most detested by Heraclitus (cf. fr. 129)! J. A. Philip[2] recently explained this as a kind of "jalousie de métier". I think fr. 35 can be fully understood only if it is assumed that – according to our best tradition (not only Heraclides Ponticus, but also Timaeus of Tauromenium) – Pythagoras called

---

[1] Diodorus X 10.
[2] *Pythagoras and Early Pythagoreanism*, Toronto 1966, p. 178.

himself by that name, that he did so rather emphatically and that at the beginning of the 5th century this was a well-known fact.

Elsewhere I dealt in more detail with the problems associated with the terms φιλόσοφος and φιλοσοφία[1], and I do not intend to repeat myself. I must, however, explain where Burkert's method of approach is faulty. The point is this that, when in some passage of Iamblichus – *in casu* V.P. 59 – the term in question is explained in a purely Platonic and Neoplatonic wording, B. concludes that, ergo, the whole testimony loses its value and cannot be used as evidence concerning early Pythagoreanism. *In casu*, Iamblichus V.P. 58 says that Pythagoras was the first to call himself φιλόσοφος; next (c. 59), the contents of φιλοσοφία is described in clearly Neoplatonic and Platonic terms. No wonder, of course, that Iamblichus describes it in these terms, which were familiar to him and to his age. But one cannot infer from this that *Pythagoras* did not refer to himself and to his wisdom by that term. It must be stated that our first explicit evidence does not only come from Heraclides Ponticus, that Diodorus' text does have some positive value, and that Heraclitus' fragments 35, 40 and 129 are of considerable importance.

Next, the idea of κάθαρσις by the study of mathematical sciences, included music. First, we have to distinguish: there is κάθαρσις by music, and there is κάθαρσις by mathematical science (including musicology). The former is a harmonizing influence of sound and rhythm on the feelings – even on the most violent passions – of man. It is difficult to see why this could not be an originally Pythagorean practice. There is nothing particularly Platonic about it – unless one starts with the idea that the early Pythagoreans, up to Philolaus, cannot have had any concern with music at all and that everything in this field must come from Plato. But that is an approach ἐξ ὑποθέσεως.

The other kind of κάθαρσις is very different: it works through the intellect, by means of the "contemplation" of numbers, of geometrical bodies, of the regular motions of the heavenly bodies and of musical intervals. Plato, no doubt, knew this kind of κάθαρσις. But does it necessarily presuppose the doctrine of transcendent Ideas? – Of course it does in Plato's *Phaedo*[2], where Socrates describes the philosopher's life as a search for Truth – "Truth" being the knowledge of pure νοητά – and this is called a κάθαρσις, i.e. a "purification" from the

---
[1] In my *Pythagoras* etc., p. 96-102.
[2] 65a-68b.

desires of the body. But it is Plato who is speaking here, and this is not Pythagoreanism. It is different to say that to the Pythagoreans – let us suppose for a moment to the *early* Pythagoreans (just as a hypothesis to be checked) – the "contemplation of numbers" and their laws was a kind of sacred mystery, a study of things Divine, and therefore an initiation of the mind into an order which, though it was immanent in the cosmos, ruled and dominated that cosmos in its entirety, including man and the human world. No theory of transcendent Ideas is needed or implied here. It can be said to be a more or less primitive view or belief, – but it cannot be said that such a view of the universe and of man was either impossible or unfitting to a man like Pythagoras and to his early followers.

We have to remark that precisely this kind of view of numbers and mathematical theory was not Plato's: it is here that he separates himself from the Pythagoreans and blames them, either implicitly or explicitly, for having stopped too soon. For him the place of mathematical studies was a different one: taken in themselves they were not to him an initiation into the Divine: they were *a preparation of the mind*, in order to detach it more and more from sense-perception and to train it in abstract thinking, so that it would be able to "contemplate" those pure νοητά which to him were true and perfect Being.

Here we are exactly at the point where Plato and the Pythagoreans diverged. Wherever later Pythagoreans speak of νοητά as a transcendent order, we have to do with a Platonized form of Pythagoreanism. Making abstraction of this later kind, we have to point out that Plato and Aristotle knew a different kind of Pythagoreanism, and that Plato in particular, though he took over their curriculum of four mathematical disciplines, gave to it in his system of παιδεία a place different from that which it had with them, a place subordinate to philosophy-itself. In the VIIIth chapter of my book on Pythagoras and early Pythagoreanism I explained this in broader outline and pointed out that even as late as the 2nd cent. A.D. a Pythagorean text is found which still shows traces of the original immanentism of Pythagorean philosophy[1].

On the whole, Burkert apparently has the impression that the impact of Pythagorean philosophy on Plato's thought was not important, at least not in the greater part of his life and work. It comes in only in a fairly late period of his life, in the *Philebus,* and in the theory

[1] My *Pythagoras* etc. p. 201 f.

of First principles and ideal Numbers of which we have some knowledge from Aristotle and a few other texts. I must say that I had the same impression in an earlier period of my life, and I think I can explain fairly well why this was so. It was because I had grown up with the idea that of Pythagoras as a philosopher or mathematician nothing can be known for certain, that of course in his myths about the life hereafter Plato was strongly influenced by Orphico-Pythagorean doctrine, and that the leading principles of Pythagorean philosophy were adopted by him only rather late, as appears in the *Philebus* and in the ἄγραφα. It is rather curious that I was not struck by a passage like the *Gorgias* 507e-508a until much later, after having repeatedly been confronted with fairly clear indications that something more can be known about early Pythagoreanism than I had dreamt of before.

Burkert, of course, knows the *Gorgias* passage very well. It would be strange, indeed, and hardly understandable that he should not recognize its Pythagorean character – until one realises that this author's mind is apparently entirely dominated by a certain preconceived idea. That the notion of ἰσότης γεωμετρική comes right down from Archytas, is evidently known to him as well as to anybody. And of course we need not tell him how important this notion was to Plato in his political thought, from the *Gorgias* through the *Republic* and the *Statesman* up to the *Laws*. Nor do we need to tell him about the κόσμος- and τάξις-principle in the *Gorgias*, about κοινωνία, φιλία and κοσμιότης as ruling principles both in the cosmos and in the life of men. He thinks that "Anklänge an Empedokles und Euripides" (Empedocles' cosmic power φιλότης, and Eur. *Phoen.* 535ff. on ἰσότης) are sufficient proof that these terms and principles are not specifically Pythagorean.

Ad 2 and 3. Aristotle's account of Pythagorean philosophy is, of course, of basic importance. Now let us suppose for argument's sake that Philolaus was the author of this philosophy. In that case, he must have been a very important philosopher, a thinker of the level of a Parmenides, Empedocles or Democritus. That Aristotle did attach considerable value to this Pythagorean philosophy, appears clearly from the fact that he dedicated a whole chapter to it. But if he had considered Philolaus as its author, we may be sure that he would have mentioned him. The fact that he did not mention his name certainly does not mean that he did not know Philolaus' book (B. is quite right in this), but it does mean that he did not consider him as the author of the Pythagorean philosophy nor regard him as a first rank philosopher. He must have seen in him the exponent of a much earlier tradition. This, and only this, provides an adequate explanation for his silence concerning Philolaus in *Metaph*. A 5, while the names of Parmenides, Anaxagoras, Empedocles and Democritus are repeatedly mentioned.

Let us now start from the opposite hypothesis, supposing, again for argument's sake, that Philolaus was not the author but the exponent of this philosophy, and assume that its origin lies much further back, in the second part of the 6th cent. In this case not only Aristotle's silence about Philolaus has been adequately explained, but there is another still more important consequence: the Pythagorean philosophy itself, as described by Aristotle, fits much better into the framework of the 6th century than it would do into that of the 5th. Philosophically speaking one can say: it is in this early period, immediately after the Milesians and in reaction to them, that this dualist explanation of the cosmos must have originated. It is there that, as a counterpart of Anaximander's ἄπειρον, a principle of limitation called πέρας was postulated by the creative mind of a true philosopher. If then those who carried on this philosophical tradition were called Pythagoreans, the creative philosopher himself must have been Pythagoras.

We shall check this conclusion when dealing with point 5. At present we have to point to one other inconvenience that follows from Burkert's hypothesis of Philolaus as the creator of Pythagorean philosophy. "If that philosophy started with Philolaus, this means that before Philolaus no Pythagorean philosophy existed." So we are told. Well, the man who asserts this seems to forget that Aristotle clearly took the opposite view. For, after having mentioned the table of opposites he concludes: "In this way also Alcmaeon of Croton conceived it, and either he took it over from them, or they took this theory over from him."[1] Now Alcmaeon must have been a younger contemporary of Pythagoras. He was not a member of the School, but he "heard" Pythagoras and lived in friendly relations with him and his followers. Whatever one wishes to think of this, this much is clear from Aristotle's text that, without the slightest doubt, Aristotle believed in the existence of a Pythagorean school of philosophy in the days of Alcmaeon and in the generation preceding him.

[1] *Metaph*. A 5, 968 a 15 ff.

Ad 4. "There is no early evidence that points to either a rational philosophy or to mathematical science practised by Pythagoras. A Pythagorean mathematics did not exist before Archytas; Pythagorean musicology and cosmology started with Philolaus." That is Burkert's thesis. I take the first proposition, concerning Pythagoras himself. We have to contradict Burkert on this point: both Heraclitus, fr. 40 and 129, and Herodotus IV 95 clearly point to a vivid and many-sided intellectual interest of the Ionian "sophist" Pythagoras. In Herodotus' Salmoxis story we do not read that the Greek Pythagoras learnt his "shamanist" wisdom from the Thracian Salmoxis, but the other way round, that the Thracian had learnt the Ionian way of life from the Greeks he had been familiar with, in particular from the "not so trifling sophist Pythagoras". P. M. Schuhl pointed this out already many years ago in his excellent *Essai sur la formation de la pensée grecque* (1934). More recently J. A. Philip rightly emphasized the importance of Heraclitus' above-mentioned fragments as a testimony to the fact that in those days Pythagoras was considered first and foremost a thinker: "if he had been known as a "shaman" Heraclitus would not have spoken of him in the terms in which he did".[1]

So much for the supposed lack of evidence on Pythagoras as a philosopher. Let us now consider Burkert's argument about the non-existence of an early Pythagorean system of mathematics. I begin by stating that I am not an historian of mathematics and do not pretend to be so. But I can see where and what exactly is Burkert's mistake when he asserts that there is no earlier evidence on Pythagorean mathematics than that of Neopythagorean and Neoplatonic writers. The crucial point is: Eudemus' well-known testimony about Pythagoras having turned the study of geometry from practical use into the form of "liberal education", i.e., the form of a theoretical discipline. Here is the text, found in Proclus in Euclid. p. 65, 15 Friedl.:

Ἐπὶ δὲ τούτοις (sc. Thales, Mamercus, Hippias) Πυθαγόρας τὴν περὶ αὐτὴν (sc. τ. γεωμετρίαν) φιλοσοφίαν εἰς σχῆμα παιδείας ἐλευθέρου μετέστησεν, –[2].

It is generally admitted that Proclus took his information from Eudemus' History of geometry, which was an excellent source. We have a similar testimony to Pythagoras as having brought the study of arithmetic from commercial use to the more advanced status of theoretical thought. It is taken by Stobaeus from Aristoxenus,

[1] J. A. Philip, *Pythagoras and Early Pythagoreanism*, Toronto 1966, p. 178.
[2] M. Timpanaro-Cardini, *Pitagorici* III, p. 48, sub 1.

Περὶ ἀριθμητικῆς. The text runs as follows (Stobaeus I, pr. 6, p. 20. 1 W.)[1]:

'Εκ τῶν 'Αριστοξένου Περὶ ἀριθμητικῆς. Τὴν δὲ περὶ τοὺς ἀριθμοὺς πραγματείαν μάλιστα πάντων τιμῆσαι δοκεῖ Πυθαγόρας καὶ προαγαγεῖν εἰς τὸ πρόσθεν ἀπαγαγὼν ἀπὸ τῆς τῶν ἐμπόρων χρείας, πάντα τὰ πράγματα ἀπεικάζων τοῖς ἀριθμοῖς.

Certainly the account does not mean that nothing like early Pythagorean arithmetic existed. It does mean that for Pythagoras reflection on numbers led to a theory on the cosmos and the nature of physical things.

A third testimony must be added: that of Aristotle in *Metaph.* A 5, 985 b 23. He says that, among those philosophers who introduced another cause next to Matter (mentioned by him in the preceding chapter, 984 b 23) *and before them*, the Pythagoreans were the first to undertake the study of mathematics (τῶν μαθημάτων ἀψάμενοι πρῶτοι) and advanced it (ταῦτα προήγαγον). Having been brought up in it (ἐντραφέντες ἐν αὐτοῖς) they came to the opinion that the principles of mathematics are the principles of all things. Now in mathematics numbers are naturally first and they had the impression of seeing in the numbers quite a few similarities with things being and becoming, rather than in Fire and Earth and Water. Thus, they came to their conception that the other things are similar to Numbers, and that the elements of Numbers are the elements of all things[2].

Now this is the Pythagorean philosophy which is attributed by Burkert to Philolaus and emphatically denied to any earlier Pythagoreans. However, it must be noted that in Aristoxenus' above-cited text, in which the same kind of philosophy is referred to, the name of Pythagoras is mentioned. Moreover, in Aristotle's text "the Pythagoreans" are said *to have been the first to undertake the study of mathematics*, and it is said that they did so *before others* who introduced something like a formal cause.

But let us return to the first-cited text, that of Proclus in his commentary on Euclides, quoted by Wehrli as part of a rather long fragment from Eudemus' Γεωμετρικὴ ἱστορία and let us consider it somewhat more closely. Eudemus says that geometry was first discovered in Egypt, where it took its origin from practical use. Thales

[1] Ibid., sub 2.
[2] M. Timpanaro-Cardini, *Pitagorici* III, p. 56 ff., sub 4. Mrs. Timpanaro comments well on the words ἐν δὲ τούτοις καὶ πρὸ τούτων. On the formula οἱ καλούμενοι Πυθαγόρειοι see her Introduction to that volume, p. 7 ff.

was the first to bring it to Greece. He found out many things himself and laid a foundation for those who came after him to build on. Here first Mamercus, the brother of the poet Stesichorus is mentioned, next Hippias of Elis. Next, Pythagoras is mentioned, ἐπὶ τούτοις – which obviously does not mean "after these" but "besides them". And Pythagoras is mentioned "besides them" because there is something peculiar about the way in which he tackled these studies. This is what the author explains in the following lines. I shall quote them in full, because the problem is: were these lines actually written by Eudemus, or only a part of them, or nothing at all. The text reads:

Ἐπὶ δὲ τούτοις Πυθαγόρας τὴν περὶ αὐτὴν φιλοσοφίαν εἰς σχῆμα παιδείας ἐλευθέρου μετέστησεν, ἄνωθεν τὰς ἀρχὰς αὐτῆς ἐπισκοπούμενος καὶ ἀΰλως καὶ νοερῶς τὰ θεωρήματα διερευνώμενος, ὃς δὴ καὶ τὴν τῶν ἀλόγων πραγματείαν καὶ τὴν τῶν κοσμικῶν σχημάτων σύστασιν ἀνεῦρεν.

It is evident that the terms ἀΰλως καὶ νοερῶς are Neoplatonic, and specifically Proclus' terminology. The sentence as it stands gives the impression that Eudemus' statement runs up to μετέστησεν, and that the rest is Proclus' comment, or at least that in that part of the sentence he renders in his own words some explanation given by Eudemus, in which something may have been said similar to that which we found in the above-cited texts of both Aristoxenus and Aristotle, viz. that Pythagoras made what we are inclined to call a "speculative" use of geometry, using it to explain the world and all kinds of things.

Now let us see how Burkert comments on it. He begins, of course, by stating that such terms as ἀΰλως and νοερῶς are Proclus' terminology. Next, he points out that, according to Aristotle's explicit statement, the Pythagoreans did exactly the opposite of what is ascribed to them in our text: far from considering the geometrical theses "without matter", they connected them with bodies – τὰ γοῦν θεωρήματα προσάπτουσι τοῖς σώμασι –, a procedure which marks them off from Plato and all his true followers. Further, did not Eudemus always speak of οἱ Πυθαγόρειοι, just as Aristotle did, and not of Pythagoras? –

But in this case we are not left with some more or less well-founded suspicions: fortunately there is a text which raises these suspicions to the level of certitude. It is in Iamblichus, *De communi mathematica scientia*[1]. Here we can see that the questionable sentence does not

[1] Cmsc. 22, p. 69 ff.

come from Eudemus at all: *Proclus took it literally from Iamblichus.*
Conclusion: *Eudemus did not record anything about Pythagoras.* Of Eudemus' supposed testimony to the basic contribution of Pythagoras to the study of mathematics nothing remains.

This is indeed a somewhat startling conclusion. But let us read the text of Iamblicus. He begins by telling us that, if we wish to practise mathematics in the way of the Pythagoreans, we have to follow their way, so full of the Divine, a way that leads upward, purifies the heart and brings one to perfection. Then follows the sentence to which Burkert alludes. It runs as follows:

"Ότι τοίνυν οὐδὲ εἰκῇ Πυθαγόρας τὴν περὶ τὰ μαθήματα φιλοσοφίαν εἰς σχῆμα παιδείας ἐλευθέρου μετέστησεν, καὶ τῷ πλήθει τῶν δεικνυμένων πολὺ προῆγεν αὐτὰ καὶ τῇ τῶν ἀποδείξεων ἀκριβείᾳ τῆς τε ἀναγκαίας χρήσεως πρὸς τὸν βίον περιττότερον αὐτὰ ἤρκεσεν, ἐντεῦθεν ῥᾴδιον καταμαθεῖν·

(Then follows a new chapter, in which the significance of mathematics for practical life as well as for its own sake is shown).

Now, what proves to be "literally" the same? Just that part of the sentence in which it is stated that Pythagoras turned the study of mathematics into the form of a liberal παιδεία: exactly this statement, from τὴν περὶ τὰ μαθήματα φιλοσοφίαν up to and including μετέστησε is almost the same, the only difference being that Iamblichus writes παιδείας ἐλευθερίου while Proclus had ἐλευθέρου. That part of the sentence which I supposed to be either Proclus' comments or his way of rendering some further explanation of Eudemus, runs quite differently in Iamblichus.

What can we reasonably conclude? Not, anyhow, that Eudemus did not say a word about Pythagoras and that, ergo, his supposed testimony to early Pythagorean mathematics vanishes into the winds, but rather that both Iamblichus and Proclus read the same statement in Eudemus' well-known work, – that perhaps they quoted that statement by heart, whence a slight difference in form, and lastly, that they commented on it each in his own way.

This is what seems reasonable to me. In Iamblichus we found the same procedure in V.P. 58-59, with reference to Pythagoras calling himself a φιλόσοφος. As to the contents of our present passage, I find it not too hard to understand Proclus' explanation ἄνωθεν τὰς ἀρχὰς αὐτῆς ἐπισκοπούμενος καὶ ἀΰλως καὶ νοερῶς τὰ θεωρήματα διερευνώμενος. In fact, the Pythagoreans considered Numbers and their laws as a divine order, and we have no reason to doubt that Pythagoras did so. That is what Proclus could express in the words ἄνωθεν τὰς ἀρχὰς αὐτῆς ἐπισκοπούμενος. The identification of things and numbers mentioned by Aristotle can be approached from two sides: either one can take it in the sense that "numbers were connected with bodies", i.e. that numbers were understood as having extension, or one can take it in this way that "things were connected with numbers", number being so to speak their "essence", i.e. their intelligible aspect. If one takes the first approach, the modern interpreter will say that the Pythagoreans "materialized Number"; when taking the other approach he has to do the opposite and state that, however primitively it may have been expressed, in fact the Pythagorean philosophy did not tend to materialize Number, but rather to introduce into philosophy something like a "formal cause". And this is the way in which Aristotle regarded Pythagorean philosophy. Proclus followed this approach, which is why one had better not say that by the expressions ἀΰλως καὶ νοερῶς he goes against Aristotle's testimony.

I think it unnecessary to follow Burkert on his way of eliminating all further relatively early evidence: Eudemus was the "Kronzeuge" of Pythagorean mathematics; once he has been discarded, little trouble will remain about any other witnesses, such as Aristoxenus and Aristotle. The former compromised himself by telling the story that Pythagoras introduced measure and weight, and as to the latter – well, it is obvious that he thought the Pythagoreans were intensely concerned with the study of mathematics before coming to that kind of para-mathematical philosophy which he describes as theirs. But in Burkert's opinion mathematical studies had not necessarily to precede, which is why he declares Aristotle's testimony as "unverbindlich", including the fr. 191 in Aristotle's name, in which it is said that *Pythagoras* – in this case the name is mentioned – was at first intensely concerned with the study of mathematics and numbers, and only later on did not refrain from Pherecydes' τερατοποιΐα. Of course that is only consistent on Burkert's part: if Aristotle's testimony on these things is not trustworthy, why should it not be discarded?

Thus the way is free for stating that there is no earlier evidence than that of many centuries later, of people like Iamblichus and Proclus.

In fact, Eudemus, the "Kronzeuge", was discarded by a faulty method, and I am afraid the others fared no better.

Ad 5. To Burkert's shamanist thesis objections were recently made by J. A. Philip[1]. The author, as we shall see in a succeeding chapter, is not at all inclined to ascribe to Pythagoras anything that is not solidly founded. He not only follows Burkert in denying the existence of an early Pythagorean mathematics, previous to Philolaus, but even goes so far as to deny that Pythagoras founded something like a "brotherhood". That he taught a doctrine of metempsychosis, is a fact so solidly attested that it cannot be denied. However, there must have been a fundamental difference between Pythagoreanism and similar religious movements. For "all beliefs somehow merged in the main stream of Greek religion – Pythagoreanism, how ever curious its origins, became not a religious creed but a philosophy". The author asks why this was so. He finds Heraclitus' testimony helpful in explaining it.

Now Heraclitus' fragments 129, 81 and 40 definitely point to a Pythagoras who read, studied and used as a basis for his own thought all writings available to him. This is not the "shamanist" type of man; it is that of a man of learning and intellectual interest.

This is perfectly correct, but it is not the only point. Philip himself, who endeavours to deny that Pythagoras founded a Society (a "brotherhood", if one wishes to use that term), has to grant that "of those who called themselves Pythagoreans during Pythagoras' life and in the half-century after his death, most will have been his political partisans, sympathizers in his moral reforms".

Well, if Pythagoras was a *moral reformer*, moreover, if he behaved *in politics* so as to have given rise to political clubs of so-called Pythagoreans until at least half a century after his death, – one does not see very well that all that was in Philip's premises; on the contrary, it rather seemed not – but *if* he was all that, then, certainly, he was not a mere primitive such as Burkert depicts him. A *moral reformer* is something different from a shaman giving taboo prescripts to his followers; and a political leader, how ever one views him, is something different again.

To conclude, – I do not imagine that it is easy, or even possible, to convince a man like Burkert, unless perhaps after some ten or twenty years. But I might convince a few others who initially were too readily inclined to believe that he had proved his case. Anyhow, although I did not really like it, these pages had to be written.

[1] *Pythagoras and early Pythagoreanism*, p. 177 f.

CHAPTER IV - VIERTES KAPITEL

NOCHMALS DIE PYTHAGOREERFRAGE:

J. A. Philip, Pythagoras and Early Pythagoreanism[1]

Zu Anfang des Jahres 1966 erschien in der von der Universität Utrecht herausgegebenen Reihe *Philosophical Texts and Studies* mein Buch *Pythagoras and Early Pythagoreanism*. Einige Monate später wurde in einem andern Weltteil ein Werk veröffentlicht unter genau demselben Titel. Der Verfasser ist J. A. Philip, associate professor of Classics in the University of Toronto. Das Buch erschien als Supplementband VII zum *Phoenix*, Journal of the Classical Association von Canada. Der Verfasser war seit Jahren mit der Pythagoreerfrage beschäftigt. Es geht ihm nicht um irgendwelche spezielle Seite dieser Frage (wie es bei mir der Fall war), sondern um das Ganze. So ist denn sein Werk zu einer eingehenden Untersuchung geworden, in welcher, praktisch gesprochen, sowohl Guthries wie Burkerts Ansichten über die Pythagoreer nachgeprüft werden. Zwar war dies nicht die eigentliche Absicht des Verfassers – er war ja schon mehrere Jahre vor dem Erscheinen dieser beiden wichtigen Arbeiten über die Pythagoreer mit dieser Frage beschäftigt –, aber tatsächlich wird für uns sein Werk zu einer post-Guthrie und post-Burkert Studie über das Ganze der Pythagoreerfrage; ein Werk, das zwar nicht an erster Stelle polemisch ist, aber einen durchaus selbständigen Charakter hat, in welchem aber – mit Recht – zu Guthrie und zu Burkerts Positionen Stellung genommen wird.

Der Verfasser hat die Absicht gehabt, alles Polemische in den am Ende eines jeden Kapitels hinzugefügten Notizen unterzubringen. Diese Methode gibt ihm Gelegenheit, neben den unabhängig behandelten Hauptthemen des Problems, eine Menge spezieller Fragen mehr oder weniger eingehend zu erörtern. So findet sich bisweilen in diesen Notizen recht Wertvolles und Neues, welches der vollen Aufmerksamkeit würdig ist. Es ist nicht immer polemischer Art was sich

---

[1] Dieses Kapitel wurde neulich geschrieben, April 1969.

da findet; oft ist es einfach eine eingehende und recht interessante Erörterung von gewissen Detailfragen.

Die befolgte Methode bringt aber auch einen Nachteil mit sich. Man hat den Eindruck, dass der Verfasser öfters, nachdem er zuerst seine eigenen Ansichte auseinandergesetzt hat, nachträglich in den Notizen zu nicht unwichtigen Konzessionen gebracht wird, welche seinen ursprünglichen Gedanken über dieselben Probleme schnurstracks zuwiderlaufen. Diese Widersprüche finden sich sogar nicht nur zwischen dem eigentlichen Text und den Notizen, sondern auch zwischen den vorhergehenden Kapiteln und der Schlussfolgerung im letzten Kapitel; das heisst also, zwischen den Prämissen und der Konklusion. Um des sachlichen Interesses willen möchte ich das Ganze etwas näher betrachten.

Philip fängt mit einer Erörterung der zu folgenden Methode an. Er unterscheidet drei Möglichkeiten. Die erste ist die, welche von der Erkenntnis der Geschichte und Literatur der betreffenden Periode im weitesten Sinne ausgeht, und in Übereinstimmung damit Elemente zur Rekonstruktion aus der Überlieferung herauswählt. Er nennt diese Methode *intuitiv*. Obwohl er zugibt, dass sie in den besten Händen zu wichtigen Ergebnissen geführt hat, wählt er dennoch nicht diese, sondern die dritte. Doch werden wir sehen, dass er sich in seinem Schlusskapitel weitgehend dieser „intuitiven" Methode bedient.

Die zweite Methode, welche gleichfalls abgelehnt wird, ist die der Quellenkritik. Sie hat in fast jeder Hinsicht zu den meist verschiedenen Ergebnissen geführt, und scheint somit nicht geeignet zu objektiven Einsichten zu gelangen.

Die dritte schliesslich ist die, welche von Aristoteles ausgeht. Das erscheint ihm eine gänzlich verantwortete Wahl, denn Aristoteles ist, so meint er, unser frühester Zeuge, der philosophisch einigermassen wichtig sei; und zwar ist er ein sehr zuverlässiger Zeuge, denn er verfügte über adäquate Quellen – so versichert uns Ph. –, welche er mit dem grössten Scharfsinn und Unparteilichkeit benutzte.

Da könnten wir doch ein bisschen staunen, sowohl um was gesagt wie um was nicht erwähnt wurde. „Ältere Zeugnisse, so weit es solche gibt, habe ich freilich in Betracht gezogen", sagt uns Herr Ph. – „aber sie sind eben ganz wenige." Und er nennt sie: ein paar Fragmente Heraklits (die sich übrigens im Schlusskapitel als ganz wichtig bewähren werden), eines von Xenophanes, eines von Demokritos. Platon? Nein, er ist nicht dabei, und soll, dem Urteil des Verfassers nach, auch nicht dabei sein. „Man muss ja zuerst einigermassen darüber Bescheid wissen, was der ältere Pythagoreismus war, bevor man über dessen Einfluss bei Platon urteilen kann." Und diese notwendige Orientierung muss ja von Aristoteles kommen. „Der Einfluss der pythagoreischen Philosophie auf Platon war im ganzen gering", heisst es sodann. „Er lässt sich erst ziemlich spät spüren: im *Philebos*, im *Timaios*, und in der ungeschriebenen Lehre."

Der *Timaios* ist wenigstens da, so bemerken wir mit Freude. (Bei Burkert wurde die Sache ja umgekehrt: was im *Timaios* steht, war *Platons* Lehre, und diese wurde in der frühen Akademie als Pythagoreismus gedeutet.) Das ist also ein Plus. Aber der *Gorgias* fehlt, und sogar *Staat* 600 a-b. Letztere Stelle wird zwar später erwähnt, wenn die „Bruderschaft" erörtert wird; zunächst aber ist diese Stelle nicht beim Verzeichnis der „wirklich wichtigen" Quellen, – und *Gorgias* 507e-508a fehlt gänzlich. Was die Bruderschaft anbetrifft, diese wird zwar später behandelt, wird aber a priori als legendarisch ausgeschlossen.

Und das versteht sich: es steht ja kein Wort darüber bei Aristoteles, und sein Zeugnis hiess ja „adäquat", d.h. genügend breit um eine repräsentative Vorstellung zu geben von dem, was der Pythagoreismus tatsächlich war.

Es ist klar, dass es hier an ein paar festgewurzelten Aprioris nicht mangelt. Bemerken wir nur noch, dass im Verzeichnis der vor-aristotelischen Zeugnisse, die einigermassen wichtig seien, auch die Philolaostexte fehlen, und gleichfalls Archytas. Man soll sich da nur nicht wundern, wenn später irgendwo in einer Notiz anerkannt wird, dass zwar von den Philolaostexten verschiedene sehr gut echt sein könnten – „aber", so werden wir da erfahren, „sie waren philosophisch ja durchaus nicht wichtig". Philolaos war, so werden wir da weiter vernehmen, überhaupt kein Philosoph: in Theben hat er wahrscheinlich Musikunterricht gegeben, und an der pythagoreischen Philosophie hatte er von seiner Jugend her nur so ein paar vage Erinnerungen.

In einem folgenden Kapitel wird „die Tradition" erörtert. Ph. meint damit: nicht eine gelehrte Tradition, welche das geschriebene Werk der Philosophen – Platon und Aristoteles z.B. – erklärt, sondern eine Tradition, die aus dem mündlichen Unterricht erwächst und um den Meister herum eine Legende schafft, welche durch Jahrhunderte hindurch fortbesteht und ihre Wiedergeburte und wiederholtes Aufleben hat. Gegen den Hintergrund einer solchen Tradition – der des Pythagoreismus in der Geschichte – will er Aristoteles' Berichte über die Pythagoreische Lehre verstehen. Die Tradition hatte ihren Ursprung im 6. Jahrh., zog sich durch das 5. hindurch, um erst im 4. geschriebene Form anzunehmen, und lebte weiter bis zum Ende des Altertums und darüber hinaus bis in unsre Tage.

D.h., es hat wiederholt Gruppen von Menschen gegeben, welche sich Pythagoreer nannten und in ihrer Weise das Denken des Pythagoras auf der Grundlage der bestehenden Tradition interpretierten. Eine richtige „Schule", eine Kontinuität hat es nicht gegeben, meint Ph. (die famose „Bruderschaft" sei eben nur spätere Konstruktion).

Die Platonisierung der Pythagoreischen Lehre geschah in der alten Akademie und setzte sich in der späteren Überlieferung fort; die biographische Tradition war literarisch und fing mit Herakleides Pontikos an. Dieser schuf das Bild des religiösen und okkult-begabten Pythagoras und einer Pythagoreischen Lebensart streng ethischen Charakters.

Auch Aristoxenos hat manches zur Pythagorastradition beigetragen: er geht nur teilweise auf Aristoteles zurück, manches hat er selbst erfunden.

Der Verf. erwähnt dann in hellenistischer Zeit (2. Jahrh. v. Chr.) das Entstehen eines Corpus Pythagoricum nach Archytas in Süd-Italien, und die Epitome des Alexander Polyhistor. Das waren aber Ausnahmen. Eine richtige Wiederbelebung erfolgte nur im 1. Jahrh. v. Chr. in Rom, und dann auch in Alexandrien; und diese wurde sehr wichtig für spätere Jahrhunderte.

Er spricht dann von der neupythagoreischen Zahlenlehre und Metaphysik des Moderatus von Gades und Nikomachos von Gerasa; er erwähnt Apollonios von Tyana, dessen βίος von Pythagoras, meint er, vielleicht viel weniger überschwenglich war als später Iamblichos; – der ältere Neupythagoreismus war ja durchaus keine populäre Religion, sondern eine streng intellektuelle Lehre wissenschaftlicher Form, welche nur für die philosophisch gebildeten zugänglich war.

Später findet dann eine gewisse Vermischung mit dem „Mittel"- und Neuplatonismus statt: Numenios war daran beteiligt; Porphyrios und Iamblichos kamen erst spät. Ihre Βίοι des Pythagoras sind aber für uns wichtig.

Wenn er diese ganze Geschichte überblickt, so kann der Verf. feststellen, dass nur Aristoteles der früheren Tradition selbstständig-kritisch gegenüberstand. Und damit bekommt dann die von ihm gewählte Methode ihre Rechtfertigung.

Wir machen am Ende dieses zweiten Kapitels ein paar Bemerkungen:

(1) die „politischen Reaktionen", welche es im 5. Jahrh. notorisch gab, werden durchaus nicht erklärt; (2) Philolaos und Archytas wurden nicht erwähnt; (3) die historische Tradition des Timaios von Tauromenium und seiner Nachfolger fehlt. – Zwar werden wir später erfahren, dass Timaios kein unabhängiger Zeuge war: er kam ja erst ziemlich spät nach Athen, gegen Ende des 4. Jahrh., nachdem Dikaiarch und Aristoxenos schon geschrieben hatten, und er besuchte nicht einmal die süditalischen Städte. Übrigens – was hätte er da über Pythagoras erfahren können? Es gab ja nichts als Legende.

Das sind bekannte Klänge. Überzeugend sind sie eben nicht[1].

Das nächste Kapitel behandelt das 5. Jahrhundert. Hier wird nochmals gesagt, dass es keine Spuren gibt, welche uns Anlass geben die Existenz einer religiös-philosophischen Bruderschaft in diesem Jahrhundert anzunehmen. Ph. meint, dass es dergleiche Gemeinschaften im frühen Griechenland, und sogar im ganzen Altertum bis auf die Zeit nach Christo, nicht gegeben hat. Das ist nun offenbar ein Irrtum. Es könnte vielmehr für das alte Griechenland bezeichnend sein, dass die Philosophen dort Schulen gründeten, in welchen zusammen gelebt und gearbeitet wurde. Nur ausnahmsweise waren die griechischen Philosophen einsame Figuren, und sicher war die Akademie eine Art Kultgemeinschaft und Lebensgemeinschaft. Ein schönes Beispiel bietet die hippokratische Medizinerschule auf Kos mit ihrem ausgesprochen paternalistischen Karakter. Man hat daraus sogar beweisen wollen, dass der hippokratische Eid ein pythagoreisches Dokument sei[2]. Dem gegenüber habe ich nachgewiesen, dass es durchaus nichts spezifisch pythagoreisch war, den Meister als Vater zu betrachten und zu ehren: auch im sokratischen Kreis, bei Platon und in der Akademie (Arkesilas), bei den Eleaten und bei Epikur lässt sich das aufweisen[3].

Es ist merkwürdig, in diesem Kapitel, wo denn endlich neben Hippasos auch Philolaos erwähnt wird, ganz nachdrücklich die These zu finden: *all our evidence is post-aristotelian,* – um so merkwürdiger, weil in einer Notiz zum selbigen Kapitel zugegeben wird, dass die Fragmente ganz gut echt sein können[4]. Was Hippasos anbetrifft, so wird gesagt (entgegen Von Fritzens schönem Artikel über „die Ent-

---

[1] Meine Gründe werde ich später angeben (unten, S. 102f.).
[2] Edelstein, *The Hippocratic Oath*, Baltimore 1943.
[3] Näheres hierüber in meinem Buch *Pythagoras* etc., p. 240f.
[4] p. 41, N. 9.

deckung der Inkommensurabilität durch Hippasos von Metapont"[1], er könne die Irrationalität nicht entdeckt haben, weil es eben keine früh-pythagoreische Mathematik gegeben habe. Davon ist der Verf. offenbar vonvornherein überzeugt. Das alles kommt ja nur aus ganz späten Quellen. – Burkerts Ausschaltung von „Eudem als Kronzeuge der pythagoreischen Mathematik" war diesem Autor zweifellos willkommen. Man darf aber nicht vergessen dass Von Fritz, wie Van der Waerden, gute sachlichen Gründe hatte, um das Bestehen einer pythagoreischen Mathematik vor Hippokrates von Chios und Diodor anzunehmen. Die (neuere) These von Szabó, der älteste mathematische Beweis sei nicht pythagoreisch, sondern eleatisch gewesen, ist eben auch nicht mehr als eine Hypothese. Zweifelsohne ist es ganz gut möglich, dass die Pythagoreer *direkte* Beweise gegeben haben bevor die Eleaten die indirekte Beweismethode eingeführt haben[2].

Obwohl unser Autor allem, was nicht aus Aristoteles stammt, grundsätzlich ablehnend gegenübersteht, trifft man hie und da bei ihm Sachen an, die man kaum erwarten könnte. So heisst es z.B. gleich im Anfang unsres Kapitels[3]: "Es war unwahrscheinlich, dass Pythagoras, als er nach Kroton kam, da ein günstiges Klima für philosophische und sonstige wissenschaftliche Forschungen vorgefunden habe; er fand aber bestimmt einen fruchtbaren Boden um *seine politische und moralische Ideen, welche mit seinen philosophischen Theorien übereinkamen*, einzupflanzen."

Das ist geradezu überraschend. Man fragt sich nur: woher kommen denn diese politischen und moralischen Ideen des Pythagoras, von denen man ja bei Aristoteles nichts hört? Und woher eine *Philosophie* des Pythagoras, – der ja, wie man gewöhnt ist zu hören, bei Aristoteles systematisch nie genannt wird? Das könnte sodann eine glückliche Inkonsequenz sein. Zunächst wirkt sie etwas sonderbar.

Gegen Ende unsres Kapitels wird die Frage gestellt: *Wer waren denn die Pythagoreer des Aristoteles?* Waren es Pythagoreer aus dem 4. Jahrh., etwa Archytas und seine Schule, wie es Frank in einem berühmten Buch behauptet hat? – Mitnichten. – Pythagoreer aus dem 5. Jahrh. also, Philolaos etwa, wie es neulich Burkert verteidigt hat? – Auch das nicht, sagt unser Autor. Wirklich grosse Gestalten hat es eben im 5. Jahrh. nicht gegeben. Hippasos war nicht der Mann, der

---

[1] In: *Zur Geschichte der griechischen Mathematik*, Darmstadt 1965, Ss. 271-307.
[2] Vergl. M. Timpanaro-Cardini, *I Pitagorici* III, Ss. 272-36.
[3] S. 25.

der Urheber dieser von Aristoteles beschriebenen Philosophie sein könnte; Philolaos auch nicht. Er war keine Figur von Format. Das kann man ja aus den Fragmenten erkennen. Nur eine Möglichkeit bleibt übrig: *diese Philosophie muss auf Pythagoras selbst zurückgehen.* Er, und kein anderer, muss ihr Urheber sein.

Sieh da. Das ist überraschend, aber man muss sagen, dass es ganz und gar redlich und überzeugend ist. Der Autor hat durchaus recht: es gibt im 5. Jahrh. keinen pythagorischen Denker, dem man die Erfindung dieser Philosophie zuschreiben könnte.

Es folgen noch ein paar bemerkenswerte Sachen. Zuerst stellt es sich heraus, dass es sogar im 4. Jahrh. noch ein „body of Pythagorean doctrine" gab, welches (obwohl es der Meinung unsres Verf. nach keine richtige pythagoreische Schule gab) dennoch treu bewahrt blieb. In seinem Schlusskapitel sagt Ph., die meisten derjenigen, die sich Pythagoreer nannten im 6. sowie im 5. Jahrh. seien wohl politische Parteigänger des Pythagoras gewesen und Sympathisanten mit seiner sozialen Reform. Einige von diesen werden Pythagoras' Lehre über die Seele angenommen haben. Nur ganz wenige werden sich für seine physische Theorien und für seine Zahlenlehre interessiert haben. „Aber seine Autorität war genügend um die Bewahrung und Übertragung seiner Gedanken in ihren Hauptzügen sicherzustellen."

Da könnte man staunen und sich fragen, ob nicht vielleicht doch zuviel verworfen wurde; ob es nicht doch eine pythagoreische Schule gegeben habe. Ich glaube – es sei nur nebenbei bemerkt –, dass Ph. das intellektuelle Interesse und die intellektuelle Fassungskraft der damaligen Griechen stark unterschätzt hat. Aber Ph. gibt nicht nach: es gibt keine Hinweise auf eine früh-pythagoreische Schule, und dabei muss man es bewenden lassen.

Der zweite bemerkenswerte Punkt bei Ph. ist, dass jetzt hervorgehoben wird, Parmenides' Philosophie sei undenkbar, wenn nicht eine pythagoreische Philosophie vorausgegangen wäre, – eine Lehre, die er bestreitet und die offenbar für ihn eine hohe Autorität besass. Denn die Autorität, die er ihr gegenüberstellt, ist nicht weniger als eine göttliche Offenbarung.

In diesem Kontext wird auch pythagoreischer Einfluss auf Demokritos erwähnt. Was Platon anbelangt, er musste natürlich hier genannt werden. Es geschieht aber in sehr beschränktem Masse: weder *Gorgias* 507/8 noch die eschatologischen Mythen sind dabei. „Die deutlichste Stelle ist im *Philebos*" (16c); es werden weiter die geometrischen Elemente im *Timaios*, die numerischen Verhältnisse in der

Weltseele und – merkwürdig genug – die Lehre von der ὁμοίωσις θεῷ erwähnt.
Und damit kann man dann zu Aristoteles herübergehen.

Es folgt ein Kapitel über die Gegensätze, zunächst eines über die Kosmologie. Die πέρας - ἄπειρον Lehre, sowie was weiter aus ihr abgeleitet ist, muss alt sein: sie passt gut ins 6. Jahrh., wo sie unmittelbar bei Anaximandros anschliesst. Die Identifikation von Zahlen und Dingen mutet gleichfalls archaisch an: sie muss auf die erste Generation zurückgehen. Ph. macht an dieser Stelle eine interessante Bemerkung: auch die Tatsache, dass die Pythagoreer durchaus keine Erklärung von der Bewegung und dem stetigen Wechsel der Dinge bieten, weist in diese Richtung. Denn es ist eine primitive Vorstellung, dass die Welt selbst lebendig sei und die Ursache der Bewegung und des Wechsels in sich hat.

Schliesslich kann er folgendes feststellen: die Herleitung der Zahlen aus Geradem und Ungeradem, welche wieder auf πέρας - ἄπειρον zurückgeführt werden, und der Aufbau des Kosmos aus Zahlen, sodass letzlich πέρας - ἄπειρον die Grundprinzipien des ganzen Kosmos seien, das ist eine primitive Lehre, welche deutlich präplatonisch ist. Im 5. Jahrh. gibt es keine Gestalt von einigem Format, dem man diese Lehre zuschreiben könnte. Sie muss also auf Pythagoras selbst zurückgehen. Auch die Tatsache, dass diese Theorie keinen Einfluss zeigt von der eleatischen, heraklitischen, oder sonstigen Philosophie des 5. Jahrh., bezeugt ihr hohes Alter. Schliesslich, schreibt man sie nicht dem Pythagoras zu, so sei man gezwungen zu verneinen, dass Pythagoras überhaupt ein Philosoph gewesen sei. Und dann wird es schwer zu erklären, dass seine Gestalt einen so langen Schatten hinter sich gezogen hat.

Sehr Wichtiges findet sich in einer Notiz zum 5. Kapitel[1]. Es handelt sich um die Lehre von der zyklischen Wiederkehr historischer Ereignisse. Gewöhnlich wird das auf Grund von Eudem, Fr. 88 W., ohne weiteres als feststehend angenommen. Ph. aber hat sich die Sache einmal genau angesehen, und ist zum Ergebnis gelangt, Eudems Zeugnis könne nicht als Beweis, dass die Pythagoreer etwas Ähnliches gelehrt haben, zitiert werden, und zwar aus folgenden Gründen. Eudem kritisiert hier den pythagoreischen Begriff der Zeit: die Py-

---

[1] S. 75, N. 12, sub 3.

thagoreer, so bemerkt er, versuchten die Zeit in Termini der Zahlen zu fassen; das war aber unmöglich, denn in den Zahlen gebe es kein „Früheres" und „Späteres". In dieser Weise könne man also zu keiner richtigen Theorie der Zeit gelangen. „Wir können zwar sagen, dass dieselben Jahreszeiten zurückkehren, dieselben Äquinoxen, Solstitia etc. Diese sind *der Gattung nach* identisch. So bald wir aber sagen, dass sie *der Zahl nach* zurückkehren, sowie die Pythagoreer es tun, dann werde ich einmal in einer zukünftigen Stunde mit meinem Stock zum Anweisen in der Hand zu Ihnen reden, und Sie werden da genau so sitzen, es wird alles genau so sein, und es wird geschehen zu derselben Zeit."

Aber — so wird es eben *nicht* sein, denn die Sachen wiederholen sich nicht ἀριθμῷ.

Das ist eine sehr interessante Bemerkung. Sie steht da so bescheiden in einer Notiz, verdient aber unsre volle Aufmerksamkeit. Nicht, dass die periodische Wiederholung alles reellen Geschehens nicht aus der pythagoreischen Ansicht der Zeit folge. Das tut sie eben tatsächlich schon, und Eudem gebraucht das zur Reductio ad absurdum. Es ist aber, erstens, möglich, dass die Pythagoreer selbst diese Folgerung nicht gezogen haben; und zweitens, es ist *sicher*, dass der Peripatetiker Eudem sie abgelehnt hat. Und das ist wichtig. Viel zu leicht nimmt man es ja als feststehend an, dass die Griechen „die lineare Zeit" nicht gekannt hätten, sondern nur „die zyklische Zeit", in der sich nie etwas Neues ereignet, sondern immerzu dasselbe sich wiederholt. Ph. hat einen wichtigen Beitrag zum Bestreiten dieser famosen These geliefert. Ich hoffe einmal darauf zurückzukommen.

Im nächsten Kapitel wird die Zahlentheorie erörtert. Ph. korrigiert Aristoteles, wenn dieser sagt, die Pythagoreer seien die ersten gewesen, welche sich mit mathematischen Studien beschäftigten, und hätten diese Studien in hohem Masse weitergeführt: da ist Aristoteles irregegangen, meint unser Autor; es lässt sich ja keine Spur einer pythagoreischen Mathematik vor Archytas aufweisen. Aristoteles' eigne Beschreibung des pythagoreischen Denkens widerspiegelt auch durchaus kein Interesse an Arithmetik oder Geometrie. Das pythagoreische Interesse an Zahlen war ausgesprochen einer anderen Art, näml. jener spekulativen Natur, welche man *arithmologisch* nennt. Und das war dann gerade ein primitiver Zug. Es handelt sich um solche Sachen

[1] Sie stammt vom Theologen Oscar Cullmann, in einem berühmten Buch: *Christus und die Zeit*. Eine interessante These, aber viel zu leicht geglaubt!

wie sie sich in der Einleitung zum 7. Buch des Eukleides finden: die Zahlen werden da wie Träger eines eignen Charakters mit spezifischen Eigenschaften betrachtet; sie lassen bestimmte Kombinationen zu, sind quadratisch oder länglich, „prim", freundschaftlich, u.d. Das war die Art des altpythagoreischen Denkens über die Zahl.

Aus πέρας und ἄπειρον wurde von den Pythagoreern ein ἕν hergeleitet, welches der Kosmos war. Wenn dieses ἕν in der umgebenden Leere zu atmen anfängt, entstehen aus den Zahlen die vielen Dinge. Eine weitere Erklärung der Vielheit wird nicht gegeben. Das ist gleichfalls ein primitiver Zug. Platon hatte eine Theorie über die Ableitung der Zahlen aus den Prinzipien, die Pythagoreer besassen keine solche Theorie. Sie lehrten ohne weiteres, dass die Dinge Zahlen sind.

Aristoteles' Beschreibung dieser pythagoreischen Theorie ist korrekt, obwohl unsympatisch. Er hatte eben keine mathematische Phantasie und fand somit in diesen Gedanken nur logischen und physikalischen Unsinn. Ph. selbst stellt die pythagoreische Welterklärung, qua Konstruktion einer „dritten Welt" neben der reellen und derjenigen der Sinneswahrnehmung, der Welterklärung der modernen Physik an die Seite.

Am Ende seines 6. Kapitels fasst er nochmals die Gründe zusammen, welche ihn veranlasst haben, die von Aristoteles beschriebene pythagoreische Philosophie dem Pythagoras zuzuschreiben. Diese Gründe sind durchaus stichhaltig.

Im 7. Kapitel (über Astronomie und Harmonie) ist von der sog. Kosmologie des Philolaos die Rede. Ph. charakterisiert sie als ein nichtmathematisches, verhältnismässig primitives System, in welchem ein gewisser Widerspruch enthalten ist, dass nämlich das Feuer das zentrale Element ist, während andererseits „Zeus" und „Olympos" an der Aussenseite ihren Sitz haben. In diesem Kontext spricht Ph. von Philolaos als Philosophen: man solle bedenken, dass er als sehr junger Mann aus Süditalien weggegangen sei um sich in Theben anzusiedeln. Das erkläre, dass er keine einigermassen wichtige Philosophie gelehrt habe. Er habe wohl Musikunterricht gegeben.

Die Theorie von der Harmonie der Sphären (im 8. Kap. behandelt) könnte qua poetische Vorstellung auf Pythagoras selbst zurückgehen, obwohl sie qua astronomisch-mathematische Theorie ans Ende des 5. Jahrh. passt. Als ältestes Zeugnis für diese Theorie wählt Ph. den Mythos von Er. Dass sich eine ähnliche Theorie schon früher bei den Assyriern findet, wird von ihm nicht erwähnt. Er blickt ja nicht in diese Richtung: dass etwa Pythagoras tatsächlich Mesopotamien besucht und da längere Zeit verbracht haben könnte, kommt bei ihm nicht ernstlich in Betracht.

Dass Pythagoras die Lehre von den musikalischen Intervallen entdeckt habe, bestreitet er. Die Vorstellung von der Sphärenharmonie brauche ursprünglich keine mathematische Grundlage gehabt zu haben.

Im 9. Kapitel, anlässlich der *Symbola* wird endlich die Frage des vonvornherein verworfenen pythagoreischen Bundes – der „Bruderschaft" – näher betrachtet. Es gibt ja da ein paar Probleme. Zunächst gibt es Platons Zeugnis im *Staat*[1] über eine spezifisch pythagoreische Lebensart. Was bedeutet denn das? „Schulen", wo man in organisierten Gemeinschaften zusammenlebte, gab es ja im Altertum gar nicht[2]. Doch haben, wie es scheint, sowohl Dikaiarchos wie Timaios von der Gründung einer Bruderschaft durch Pythagoras gesprochen. Porphyrios' Beschreibung der Ankunft und des Vorgehens des Pythagoras in Kroton (V.P. 18ff.) stammt ja aus Dikaiarchos, und Timaios hat ganz sicher an die Existenz religiös-politischer, von Pythagoras gegründeten Gemeinschaften, in denen der Besitz gemeinschaftlich war, geglaubt. Was soll man dazu sagen?

Ph. bemerkt zuerst, dass zwar in Porphyrios, V.P. 18, Dikaiarch als Quelle genannt wird, dass aber später, gerade wo von der Gründung der Bruderschaft die Rede ist, Nikomachos erwähnt wird. Und so müsse es eben sein; denn, weil es ja im 4. Jahrh. durchaus keine dergleichen Gemeinschaften gegeben habe, so könnte Dikaiarch schwerlich die Gründung einer solchen Bruderschaft dem Pythagoras zugeschrieben haben.

Etwas schwieriger wird es bei Timaios. Zwar meint Ph. behaupten zu können, dass der Spruch des κοινὰ τὰ τῶν φίλων nicht spezifisch pythagoreisch sei; aber dennoch bleibt die Tatsache, dass dieser Historiker des 4. Jahrhunderts die Existenz einer pythagoreischen Bruderschaft ganz deutlich erwähnt hat. Ph. erklärt, wir wissen um politische Klubs (ἑταιρεῖαι) und sonstige Vereine im 4. Jahrh. Das seien zwar keine religiösen Gemeinschaften, aber Timaios habe sie offenbar so gedeutet. Politische ἑταιρεῖαι habe es jedenfalls im 5. Jahrh. gegeben. Das habe dann Timaios ins 6. projiziert, und so hätten wir dann die Geschichte von der Gründung der Bruderschaft durch Pythagoras bekommen.

---
[1] 600b.
[2] Meine Gegenargumente habe ich schon oben gegeben.

Ganz überzeugend ist das, freilich, nicht. Was Nikomachos anbelangt, Ph. irrt sich wenn er meint, dass um 100 n. Chr. organisierte religiöse Gemeinschaften – „mit einer Regel, Hierarchie und Orthodoxie" (!) – eine frequente Erscheinung gewesen seien. Die Gründung derartiger Gemeinschaften datiert erst vom 4. Jahrh. Timaios' Zeugnis kann man schwerlich wegerklären. Dass er nicht in Süditalien und Sizilien gewesen sei, ist kaum glaublich, und dass die in jenen Gegenden noch lebende Legende über diese Sachen nichts mehr wissen könne, ist eine Aussage welche die Leugnung der Kontinuität zu ihrem hypothetischen Ausgangspunkt genommen hat. Quod erat demonstrandum...

In seinem vorletzten Kapitel (über die Seelenwanderung) kritisiert Ph. die von Burkert vertretene Schamanenthese. Hat es überhaupt in der alt-griechischen Welt so etwas wie den Schamanismus gegeben? Ph. bestreites das. In arktischen Ländern war der Schamanismus eine Institution, welche eine Zentrale Stelle im öffentlichen Leben einnahm. Der Schaman unternimmt seine Seelenreise im Auftrag der Gemeinschaft. Bei seiner Rückkehr bringt er eine Botschaft für diese Gemeinschaft mit. Nichts dergleichen findet sich bei den sog. griechischen „Schamanen": sie machten ihre Seelenreisen nur als Privatsache. Von einer Botschaft ist nie die Rede. Es müsse daher vielmehr der Unterschied als die Ähnlichkeit zwischen den nordischen Schamanen und solchen Gestalten wie den Griechen Aristeas und Hermotimos betont werden. Die Frage, ob Pythagoras ein „Schaman" gewesen sei, wird von Ph. in negativem Sinne beantwortet. Das Bild von Pythagoras, das man z.B. aus Herakleitos' oben genannten Fragmenten gewinnt, ist bestimmt nicht das eines Menschen der dem intellektuellen Leben seiner Zeit fremd gegenüberstand; im Gegenteil, es ist ganz deutlich das Bild eines Forschers. Die Tatsache, dass dieser selbe Mensch auch bestimmte religiöse Überzeugungen gehabt hat und Ansichten über die Seele, welche wir religionsgeschichtlich bei den Orphikern unterzubringen gewohnt sind, darf uns nicht dazu bringen, den Charakter des Pythagoras als Denker und Philosoph zu verneinen.

Man soll eben, so mahnt uns Philip – und mit dem grössten Recht –, den Begriff der Philosophie an ihren Anfängen nicht zu eng nehmen. Fasst man diesen Begriff etwas weiter, so dass alles Nicht-rationale nicht per se ausgeschlossen ist, so wird für die Gestalt des Pythagoras Platz sein.

In seinem Schlusswort geht Philip weitgehend nach der von ihm anfänglich verworfenen intuitiven Methode vor. Er spricht ausführlich über das kulturelle *Milieu* in dem Pythagoras nicht nur seine Jugend, sondern auch seine reifen Jahre verbracht hat: es war die hochgebildete Kultur von Samos um die Mitte des 6. Jahrhunderts, in nächster Nähe von Milet. Es ist einfach undenkbar, dass ein intellektuell begabter Mensch der aus dieser aufgeklärten Umgebung stammte, ein Obskurantist gewesen sei, und dann von Herakleitos als Vielwisser charakterisiert werden könnte und die Autorität erworben hätte, die er sich offenbar erworben hat.

Es bestand offenbar, so führt Philip weiter aus, im Griechenland des 6. Jahrh. eine religiöse Bewegung, welche an ein mehr persönliches Fortbestehen der individuellen Seele als die schattenhafte Hades-Existenz bei Homer glaubte. In der weiteren Geschichte des Denkens ist aber der Pythagoreismus nicht in irgendwelcher religiöse Bewegung aufgegangen: er unterschied sich davon deutlich durch seinen intellektuellen und ethischen Charakter. –

Hier müssen wir als Zuhörer interrumpieren um eine kritische Frage zu stellen; nicht was den intellektuellen Charakter des weiteren Pythagoreismus anbetrifft – es ist ja klar, dass unser Autor das mit seinen Voraussetzungen behaupten kann –. Es ist vielmehr diese These vom ethischen Charakter des weiteren Pythagoreismus, die bei uns eine Frage hervorruft. Wir verstehen zwar ganz gut, worauf der Autor hinaus will: er behauptet, der Pythagoreismus sei von der Orphik in diesem Punkt verschieden, dass die Orphik amoralisch-ritualistisch, der Pythagoreismus hingegen ethisch orientiert war. Wir fragen nur: woher kommt denn das? Steht das etwa bei Aristoteles? – Es will uns nicht einleuchten.

Philip erklärt es uns vom pythagoreischen Glauben an die Zukunft der Seele aus: wenn du glaubst, dass deine Seele im Laufe einer Reihe von Inkarnationen schliesslich als letztes Ziel einen göttlichen Zustand erreichen kann, so wirst du dich sorgfältig um deine Seele kümmern. Und hier redet dann unser Autor ganz von der von ihm wie es schien anfänglich verneinten Kontinuität aus: es muss, so stellt es sich nun heraus, doch eine Kontinuität bestanden haben. Denn „dieser göttliche Zustand muss für Pythagoras genau dasselbe bedeutet haben, als er später für die Pythagoreer, Platoniker, Neupythagoreer und Neuplatoniker bedeutet hat. Die göttliche Fähigkeit ist die intellektuelle Fassungskraft, die in die Geheimnisse des Universums durchzudringen und die verborgene Natur des Sichtbaren zu ergründen vermag." Diese intellektuelle Fassungskraft setzt eine geistige und moralische Reinigung voraus oder schliesst sie ein: die Sorge für die Seele war eine intellektuelle und zugleicher Zeit ethische Disziplin des ganzen Menschen.

Auf diesem Grunde kann dann Philip schliesslich sagen, die mächtige Bedeutung des Pythagoras in der Philosophie liege teilweise in seiner Theorie der numerischen Fassbarkeit der physischen Struktur und in seiner Vorwegnahme der quantitativen Analyse; aber nur teilweise. Wie wichtig auch diese Einsichten für das weitere Denken gewesen seien, viel wichtiger noch sei das folgende gewesen: die Auffassung der Philosophie als eines Lebensstils, eines τρόπος τοῦ βίου (!), einer intellektuellen und geistigen Disziplin, durch welche die Seele zur Aktualisierung ihrer göttlichen Natur und zur Erkenntnis fortschreitet. „Und dadurch machen wir unsselbst dann dem Göttlichen ähnlich."

So ist dann am Ende bei diesem höchst skeptischen, viel verneinenden Professor Philip, der uns sagte, nur von Aristoteles ausgehen zu wollen, ein recht klassisch-platonischer Pythagoras zustande gekommen. Das ist immerhin sehr interessant. Er hat es sich eben überhaupt nicht leicht gemacht. Nachdem er am Anfang so vieles verneint hat, hätte er auch am Ende viel mehr verneinen können. Das wäre leichter gewesen – aber, wie er selbst sehr gut gesehen hat, weniger befriedigend qua Erklärung des ganzen Phänomens des Pythagoreismus. Zwar sind die Verneinungen, mit denen er angefangen hat, lange nicht alle aufrechtzuerhalten. Einigen davon hat er selbst in seinen Notizen explizite, oder auch in seinem Schlusskapitel implizite, widersprochen. Wie dem auch sei, unter den schweren Bedingungen, die er sich am Anfang gestellt hat, hat er eine sehr eindringende Forschung in positivem Sinne zu Ende geführt. Dabei ist er einen sehr selbständigen Weg gegangen, und hat sich am Ende keineswegs von einem engen Rationalismus beherrschen lassen.

Die kritische Frage, welche man bei seinen „Schlussfolgerungen" stellen muss, ist diese: wenn dann für Pythagoras die Philosophie von Anfang an diesen Charakter einer ethisch-asketischen Disziplin hatte, war dann für ihn die Gründung einer Schule nicht geradezu eine Notwendigkeit?

Aber – es gibt eben für die Existenz eines ethisch-sozialen Pythagoreismus unleugbare Zeugnisse, die voraristotelisch sind. Platons Text über den Πυθαγόρειος τρόπος βτίοῦου hat Ph. nachträglich anerkannt. Die Gorgiasstelle über φιλία und κοσμιότης aber ist ein fester Grund. Die Bedeutung der geometrischen ἰσότης für Platons politisches Denken weist auf etwas ganz anderes hin als nur eine späte Adaptation der pythagoreischen Zahlenmetaphysik bei Platon. Das ganze Problem aber der ethisch-sozialen Philosophie des Pythagoras, obwohl Ph. es am Ende mit der *intuitiven* Methode bis zu einem gewissen Grade anerkannt und gelöst hat, fordert tatsächlich eine andere Behandlung. Das würde aber eine Untersuchung an sich erfordert haben, und diese ist zufälligerweise gleichzeitig in einem andern Teil der Welt durchgeführt worden und in einem gleichnamigen Werk ungefähr gleichzeitig mit Philips Schrift veröffentlicht.

SOCRATICA

CHAPTER V

WHO WAS SOCRATES?[1]

I consider it to be quite a privilege to speak of Socrates, not only because of the wonderful picture drawn by Plato of his master in what we call the Socratic dialogues, but perhaps mostly because there is a real challenge in the difference of opinion among modern scholars on the question of "Who was Socrates?" I have solid grounds for being convinced that we *can* answer that question in a positive manner; that is, I think I can explain, first, that it is not true (as some modern scholars hold) that we are unable to grasp the historical reality that stands behind the name of Socrates; second, that there are a few modern interpretations of Socrates which are suggestive but false; third, that one and only one interpretation is well founded and correct. I think it is worthwhile to spend an hour considering these points.

Socrates is one of those four famous Greek philosophers who did not leave any written works. The other three are: Pythagoras, who in Aristotle's day already seemed to disappear in the mist of a remote past; Pyrrho, the founder of the Sceptic School, and Carneades, that famous dialectician who was the head of the New Academy in the second century. On none of these so much as on Socrates have modern critics endeavoured to demonstrate that he never existed[2]. The most refined representative of the nineteenth-century style of criticism is O. Gigon, who modified Dupréel's thesis insofar as he does not deny explicitly that there existed an Athenian called Socrates, and even that he may have been an important personality. But he does hold that we cannot know of what importance was Socrates. To prove his

---

[1] Copyright by the Regents of the University of California. Adapted from ,,Who was Socrates?" *Journal of the History of Philosophy*, Vol. 1, No. 2, pp. 143-161, by permission of the Regents.
[2] E. Dupréel, *La légende de Socrate et les sources de Platon* (Brux. 1921); O. Gigon, *Sokrates* (Bern, 1947; Samml. Dalp). (See my review in *Mnemosyne* (1950); see also *Phronesis* (1955), 1.) A. H. Chroust, Socrates, *Man and Myth* (London, 1957), adopts essentially Gigon's thesis.

thesis Gigon deals first with the tradition about the indictment, the litigation and condemnation of Socrates; next with the story about the Delphic oracle and Socrates' calling to philosophy; then with his marriage and family life, and last, with his relation to the city of Athens. It is not too difficult to cite divergent and even contradictory information on all these points.

As to Plato's dialogues, in which the philosopher Socrates is pictured – to the life, as it might seem to us – according to Gigon the historical value of these writings is by no means greater than that of any other of our sources. Why should they be more trustworthy? Because the image they present is beautiful? That would be a deceptive ground, for Plato may have invented freely, and we have good reason to believe he did.

In fact, if anybody holds that we do not know anything for certain about Socrates, he must begin by disparaging Plato's testimony altogether. Next, he must deny that Aristotle said a word of truth about what was the *proprium* of Socrates as a philosopher, and in what Plato differed from him. Third, he must assert that there is a complete disagreement between Plato and Xenophon as to the personality of Socrates, not to mention the fifth-century comedian Aristophanes (who, as a matter of fact, drew a fairly strange portrait of the philosopher). After having thus rejected the testimony of contemporaries and their direct successors, he may turn to the gossip of those later authors who have no authority at all: Aristoxenus, a furious anti-Socratic, who is cited by Plutarch as a classical instance of malignity; Diogenes Laertius, that late writer (3rd century A.D.) who tells us the strangest stories about all Greek philosophers; Athenaeus, Herodicus, Aelianus, and so on – and find there divergent and contradictory information about Socrates' life and behaviour.

Let us begin by stating that we must not follow this procedure. Moreover, let us state that it is not interesting to us that, while Plato and Xenophon say Socrates was married to Xanthippe, Aristotle says he was married to Aristides' daughter Myrto, and Aristoxenus declares he was married to both at the same time. It is of no importance either that, while we know from good sources that Socrates took part in the campaign to Potidaea (432/1) and in the battle of Delion (424/3) and behaved bravely, later authors differ in certain details from what is found both in Plato and in Xenophon. Nor should it shock us to find in different authors different information about that inner voice which Socrates called his *daimonion*. What we deny is that such divergencies should throw a radical doubt on what we may call our classical tradition of the *philosopher* Socrates and should compel us to cease from any historical approach to this philosopher. Against this we maintain that the doubt thrown by certain modern critics on Plato's testimony is insufficiently founded – partly improbable (I am thinking of Gigon's late dating of the Socratic dialogues), partly untrue (for instance, that a dialogue like the *Protagoras* would be spurious), and that therefore, the very basis of the agnostic thesis on Socrates proves to be unstable.

As to the superstructure, Gigon and his followers who *practically* deny the historicity of the philosopher Socrates, have to reconstruct the history of Greek thought without him. That is what Gigon did: the writers of the Socratic dialogues (not only Plato and Xenophon, but Antisthenes, Aeschines and Aristippus as well) borrowed their subjects simply from the sophists. And why they all had the strange hobby of taking a certain Socrates, the son of Sophroniscus, as the protagonist of their "conversations", and why they all chose conversation as the form of their literary products, are questions which obviously are not answered by this hypothesis, and according to its authors, may not even be asked.

To this procedure we oppose our view and state, first, that the influence of the *thinker* Socrates on Greek thought is undeniable; second, holding that there surely existed an Athenian Socrates, son of Sophroniscus, brought to death by drinking hemlock in the year 399, and possibly – or even probably – an important personality, only unknown to us, and next to sit down and construct the history of Greek thought without him is, if not entirely contradictory, surely not quite reasonable. What would be reasonable to do, and evidently *should* be done is to collect carefully the testimonies of post-Socratics on the *thinker* Socrates, to compare them and find out what we learn from them concerning the philosophical method and "views" (eventually "doctrine") of Socrates. That this is not impossible nor unfruitful is what I hope to show in the following pages[1].

---

[1] It should be mentioned here, that, in the years after his "Socrates", Gigon himself gave a contribution to this task by his Commentaries on the *Memorabilia* of Xenophon. His interpretations, however, show a certain inability to see the common elements between Socrates and Plato, or, when he sees them, to value them positively. See my review in *Erasmus* (1957). Some valuable material and good judgment can be found in Paul Rabbow's posthumous work, *Paidagogia* (Göttingen, 1960), in particular pp. 107-125, with notes and appendices. See my review of this work in *Mnemosyne* (1963).

What are the essential features of Socrates according to Plato's Socratic dialogues? First of all, Socrates is represented here as the untiring inquirer, discussing with everybody who is willing to answer his questions; inquiring into the sense of ethical concepts in particular; encouraging people to formulate a definition, considering and refuting proposed definitions again and again, trying a new one; and finally, concluding the conversation by stating that we do not yet know what virtue is and have to begin anew. This procedure, as it is practised by Socrates, is impressive enough. We feel a mighty intellect behind these discussions, a fervent and tenacious desire for intellectual clarity, an unshakable belief in Reason as the ruling force of human life, and a dominating will, leading other people on the way of seeking the truth untiringly and living up to the standard imposed on us by reason.

This is impressive, both from the intellectual and from the moral point of view; first, because we feel that what is happening in the Socratic dialogues – e.g., in the *Laches*, the *Phaedo*, the *Republic* (b. I) – is a great thing in that phase of the history of the human mind, something entirely new; moreover, a thing which, in a sense, is still of an exemplary value to us in our striving after a reasonable and justified view of life. Or, in case we should lack such a desire and for ourselves should not care for such discussions as Socrates used to carry on with his fellow-citizens in the market place and in the sporting schools of Athens, we might feel as if Socrates speaks to us when he addresses his fellow-citizens as follows:

> "My dear friend, you who are an Athenian, a citizen of the most famous city in wisdom and in strength, don't you feel ashamed of caring so much for making money and striving after honour and glory, while you are not interested at all in wisdom and in truth, nor in the well-being of your soul and in moral progress?" (Plato, *Apol.* 29d-e).

It is with these words that in the *Apology* Plato makes Socrates answer the suggestion of his judges that he stop his habitual search for truth and his usual discussions with the people of Athens. Socrates thanks them politely for being willing to free him, but he declines the condition of stopping what he considers to be his peculiar task. "Gentlemen, I thank you very much, but I shall obey God more than you, and as long as I have breath and strength, I shall never cease to philosophize and to exhort everyone of you I meet, speaking to him as I used to do, and saying..." (the words cited above).

WHO WAS SOCRATES?

That is Socrates according to Plato: an indefatigable inquirer, a man who by the intellect appeals to the intellect, but through the intellect seeks to form and educate the inner man. As it is said by Nicias in Plato's *Laches* (187e):

> "You seem to me not to know that whosoever comes near Socrates, even if he first begins to talk about something else, will be absolutely led on by him to render an account of himself and his own life, both at present and in the past; and next, once he has come so far, that Socrates will not let him go before he has considered all that with the greatest care."

Compare Alcibiades' testimony in Plato's *Symposium* (215d-216c): he declares that, though it never occurs to him to feel ashamed before anybody, Socrates alone makes him feel profoundly troubled and ashamed of himself and his usual life.

Heinrich Maier[1], therefore, rejected Aristotle's testimony[2] that Socrates was essentially a dialectician, whose personal contribution to the history of human thought consisted of these two things: (1) what Aristotle called *the method of inductive reasoning*; (2) *the search for definition*. Aristotle was not a contemporary of Socrates; his testimony, therefore, is not of the same value as Plato's. And in Plato's dialogues Socrates appears not to have been primarily concerned with any purely intellectual problem. What he was really interested in was not definitions – it should be observed that he did not succeed in making any![3] – but the *soul of concrete man*. And caring for the souls of his fellow-men, first of all his fellow-citizens of Athens, was felt by Socrates to be a religious duty, a task imposed on him and to be fulfilled in service of "the God" (*Apol.* 30a, 31a). This means, according to H. Maier, that Socrates was essentially what we could call *a missionary or a pastor*, not a logician or "philosopher of concepts" (Begriffsphilosoph).

Though Maier was quite right in observing the essentially ethical character of Socrates' philosophy and its religious ground, he was radically mistaken in opposing this to the intellectual business of criticizing and analyzing proposed definitions and seeking for right ones – as if such a business was not really what Socrates was interested

---

[1] *Sokrates* (Tübingen, 1913).
[2] *Metaph.* A 6, 987b1-10; M 4, 1078b23-30.
[3] The same remark was made by G. Bastide, *Le moment historique de Socrate* (Paris, 1939).

in and what he thought to be his moral duty, imposed on him by a God. The whole matter is that for us, modern men, the search for intellectual clearness, even analyzing moral concepts such as "virtue", is not at all identical with moral life itself. For us, being able to *define* "courage" or "justice" is not even essentially connected with *being* courageous or just, so that intellectual clearness would bring men necessarily to the practice of virtue. For Socrates, however, these two things were essentially linked up with one another. Therefore, his intellectual task of interrogating people on their ideas about moral values, his tireless endeavour of refuting false views and his search for correct definitions was in itself his method of moral education and of "caring for the soul"[1]. This may seem strange to us – but any other interpretation would misconceive what Socrates in fact was aiming at.

Usually we are told that this connection, or even identification, of intellectual insight and moral behaviour was a sample of "Greek intellectualism". I think by this qualification we do not gain a real insight into the grounds of Socrates' thought. We should penetrate into it more profoundly. Let us then listen again to Socrates in the Platonic dialogues and see how their testimony is confirmed by Xenophon on several important points. Perhaps by doing so we shall come to a deeper understanding of that famous statement which is unanimously ascribed to Socrates by all our best sources[2], the doctrine that "nobody sins willingly".

Let us take the Crito. Socrates is condemned to death. He is in prison, waiting for execution. His friend and pupil Crito comes to him and proposes to him a possible escape: in Thessaly he will be well

---

[1] I did not read P. Rabbow's work, *Paidagogia*, before writing the present study for the University of California, Berkeley. I am glad to say I find in Rabbow's posthumous work a clear understanding of the above mentioned point (p. 121 f.). His description of Socratic education as given in pp. 110-120 is really excellent. Only, when turning to Plato for better understanding the total character of Socratic Reason, he proves to be unable to understand the inner experience which he feels must be at the bottom of this kind of "intellectualism". See my review in *Mnemosyne* (1963).

[2] Plato, *Protag.* 345 d; Aristotle, *Nic. Eth.* VII 3, 1145 b 21-27. Cf. the main thesis of Socrates in the Platonic dialogues, such as *Laches, Hippias Minor, Protagoras, Gorgias* and *Meno*: that virtue is knowledge. Also in Xenophon, *Mem.* III 9, 5; Aristotle, *Eth. Eud.* I, 1, 1216 b 6-8, "Socrates held that all virtues are knowledge, so that it is the same to know what is justice and to be just".

received by Crito's friends and could spend the rest of his days in peace. Socrates thanks Crito for his benevolence and zeal, but declines the proposal. *Why*? Because accepting it would imply abandoning all those basic principles whose validity he had established throughout his lifelong discussions with his friends. What principles? They are mentioned explicitly:

1. Not to care for everybody's opinion but only for that of those who have a precise knowledge about the subject-matter in question.

2. That Soul is superior to Body.

3. That the important thing is not merely to live, but to live well – i.e., as good men.

4. That good means just or righteous.

5. That *just* or *righteous* means never to do wrong to anybody, even if one has suffered injustice.

> "Did we agree about this or not? Consider whether you still share my view or whether we must start the discussion anew. To me it seems that the same principles are still valid. Do you accept that or not?" "I do", says Crito. "Well, then", says Socrates, "on these grounds I cannot do what you suggest. I cannot fly from here, for by doing so I would do wrong to my greatest benefactors, namely, the laws of the city which protected me throughout my life. And what then could I answer if in the life hereafter I should come before those righteous Gods who rule yonder? What could I say to them? How could I bear to look into their faces, I who had violated the principles of justice here?"

Now let us observe what Socrates is doing here. He submits strictly to the rule of law and order in the city, so strictly that he submits freely and deliberately to undergo the execution of an unjust condemnation. This he does as quite a natural thing and without a word of complaint. It seems to me that this acceptance of law and justice under an unreasonable and unjust verdict is of a tremendous grandeur. For the rest, this scene of the *Crito* confirms a number of positive features in Socrates' teaching which we come across again and again in Plato's dialogues. First, there is the respect of precise knowledge about any subject-matter. The point is of basic import both to Socrates and to Plato. It brings them in opposition to the sophists, who take a pride in discoursing on any subject and outwitting the experts by a show of well-chosen words. To this art of rhetoric Socrates opposes philosophy, as the service of truth standing against the service of untruth and delusion[1]. Moreover, philosophy cares for the souls of the people whom it addresses, rhetoric never does[2]. Thus, in this point we find directly that close connection of intellectual knowledge and moral behaviour which appears to us to be characteristic of Socrates in the *Apology*.

Next, there is the thesis that Soul is of an order superior to that of the body. This too is a fundamental thesis in Plato's thought and work, from the *Apology* and *Crito* to the *Timaeus* and *Laws*. No doubt it was a Socratic principle. It should be noticed here that the thesis of the superiority of Soul to body does not at all imply a contempt of the body, as is often attributed to Plato by modern authors who like to oppose what they call "Greek" to "Christian" thought. There was no contempt of the body either in Socrates or Plato. On the contrary, in that same *Crito* where we find the superiority of the soul mentioned among the basic principles of Socrates, the argument runs:

"Would it be worth-while to you to live with a bad and disordered body?" And after the interlocutor answered, "No, of course not", Socrates continues that, therefore, just as the body needs a careful and correct treatment, so the soul, which is of so much higher value – should be cared for and treated well, according to the advice not of anybody, but of those who are able to judge and give good advice about it.

That is what is found throughout Plato's works, in the great discussions with the sophists (*Protag., Gorg., Meno, Republic*). It is the basis of Plato's own educational system, planned in the bb. II-IIIff. of the *Republic*, where the greatest care is bestowed on the physical training of those who are to be philosophers and leaders of the state. We should notice again that according to Xenophon's *Memorabilia*[3], Socrates showed the greatest interest in the due care of the body. The point is sometimes noticed as a discrepancy between Plato's and Xenophon's Socrates[4], and it is usually suggested that Xenophon

---

[1] *Gorg.* 463 a-c.
[2] *Gorg.* 502 d - 503 a. On expert knowledge being required for anything, cf. e.g., *Protag.* 318-319. It should be noticed that "the talk about cobblers, builders, smiths, etc." is also mentioned by Xen., *Mem.* IV 4, 6, as peculiar to Socrates. See also *Mem.* I 2, 9; III 6, 7; IV 2. In Plato also *Laches* 184 de; *Gorg.* 451 aff.
[3] *Mem.* I 2, 4; IV 7, 9.
[4] O. Gigon, in his commentary on the *Mem.* I, p. 32, states "a general agreement" between Plato and Xenophon on this point.

attributed his own views to the master whom he wished to defend. But let us observe that there is no opposition between Xenophon's and Plato's Socrates on the point in question: in both we find the body trained and cultivated in service of the soul. This is Socratic, and it is Platonic too. One has only to read the *Republic* and (if one wishes to know Plato's later views) the *Timaeus*[1] and the *Laws* to be convinced of this.

The third point, that mere living does not matter, but to live as a good and righteous man is important, could be illustrated by quite a number of passages, both in Plato and in Xenophon. There is the Socrates who, when being a member of the Council, is charged with bringing a certain Leon of Salamis to the City for execution. But Socrates, who thinks the matter unjust, goes calmly home, not worried at all about his personal safety. This happened under the rule of the so-called thirty tyrants, and would probably have cost him his life had not that régime fallen shortly thereafter[2]. Then, there is the Socrates who, according to Alcibiades' testimony in Plato's *Symposium*[3], behaved bravely in the battle of Delium, in particular in the dangerous retreat after the battle. Third, there is his refusal to Crito, when a safe escape is offered to him from prison and from death[4]. What Xenophon, who was a soldier, admired first of all in Socrates was doubtless his bravery and firmness, together with his extreme sobriety and hardiness against all kinds of privations[5]. The same qualities are attested to us by Alcibiades in Plato's *Symposium* (219e-220b).

Fourth, that "living morally well" is identical with justice, is a Socratic thesis which can be illustrated, e.g., by the discussions in the *Gorgias* and the first book of the *Republic*. In both the just man is called the person who lives morally well and is happy, while the unjust lives badly and is always unhappy. In *Republic* I[6] justice is defined as the specific "virtue of the soul" which, as such, warrants that a man lives well and is happy. In Xenophon compare, for instance, *Memorabilia*, III 9.5.

---

[1] The second part (59c-90d).
[2] *Apol.* 32cd.
[3] *Symp.* 220e-221c.
[4] *Crito* 46b ff.
[5] Xenophon speaks repeatedly of Socrates' ἐγκράτεια, αὐτάρκεια and καρτερία. *Mem.* I 2, 1; I 3, 5-15; I 6, 3; and the whole treatises I 5, II 1, and IV 5 (on ἐγκράτεια).
[6] 353d-354a.

Fifth, that the just man never will do wrong to anybody is opposed by Socrates to the popular view of Polemarchus (in *Rep.* I 335d) that justice consists of helping one's friends and harming one's enemies. Against Thrasymachus, who calls him silly and defends the view that justice is the right of the strongest, Socrates maintains the same position as he did against Polos, that defender of tyranny in the *Gorgias*: the man who disposes at random of other people and enriches himself at their expense is not just. He is far from living well and can never be happy. He will be in a most miserable state even if he escapes punishment. For in that case his soul will not be cured of evil and will have to meet its Judges in the life hereafter in a state of deformity and ugliness, full of wounds and bruises from the evil done to fellow-men[1]. The just man, on the contrary, who never harmed another person, lives in inner happiness and peace. Full of confidence, he may believe that in the life hereafter he will meet benevolent and righteous gods and that a better life is in store for him yonder. Exactly this appears to be the belief of Socrates who, at the end of his *Apology* speaks to his judges as follows:

> "But you also, judges, must regard death hopefully and must bear in mind this one truth, that no evil can come to a good man either in life or after death, and God does not neglect him. So, too, this which has come to me has not come by chance, but I see plainly that it was better for me to be dead now and be freed from troubles" (*Apol.* 31 cd).

It is a consistent portrait we have before us. Moreover, it is not only Plato's testimony, but in most features it is that of Xenophon's Socrates too. There is one important difference between the Socrates of the one and of the other: Plato's Socrates is an ironist, who always plays the role of knowing nothing and not being able to teach any positive wisdom to anybody. He compares his function to his mother's art of assisting in the birth of children; the only difference is that she assists in the bringing forth of physical offspring, while he, who lacks the gift of producing himself fruits of wisdom, assists others in producing intellectual fruits[2]. Or also: the Platonic Socrates is a master in the art of bringing people to a state of embarrassment and perplexity[3]. This character of irony, which is essential in the Socrates of

[1] *Gorg.* 524e-525a; cf. the myth of Er in *Rep.* X.
[2] *Theaet.* 149a-151b.
[3] *Meno* 80a.

Plato, is lacking almost entirely in Xenophon's portrait of the philosopher. But how could it be otherwise? The good Xenophon was not a man to appreciate irony. He portrays for us a Socrates who is a man of piety and of the strictest justice, extremely sober, self-controlled and hardened; moreover, a man who is used to questioning other people in search of a definition; who in his discussions likes to speak of cobblers, carpenters and other craftsmen; in short, a man who shares the character and hobbies of the Platonic Socrates – only *not* an ironist. Xenophon represents him as giving good advice in all kinds of situations and never makes him the strange fellow he is in Plato's dialogues.

Should the difference cause us any trouble? I do not think so. On the contrary, nothing could be more surely expected. And let us observe: if one knows how to read between the lines, here and there one will recognize a trace of the ironical Socrates. Take for instance *Mem.* I 1.15:

> "Concerning the philosophers of nature, Socrates used to consider also this point. Those who are learning about human things expect to be able to reproduce that which they are learning both for themselves and for whomsoever they like. Is it in the same way that those who are inquiring into divine things expect they will be able, once they have understood how all things (in nature) happen, to reproduce these things whenever they like: winds, waters, seasons and whatever they need of such like things; or do they not expect anything of the kind but is it enough to them just to understand how each of these phenomena happens?"

Surely the good Xenophon did not mean this passage as a sample of Socratic irony. In fact, it is. For to Socrates, "knowing" is taken in the strictest sense: the man who "knows" a thing because he understands both the "what" and the "how" *must* be able to reproduce that thing at random. Therefore, Socrates ironizes the pretension of those who presume to know what is "divine", namely, natural phenomena, which he thinks are beyond our understanding.

One other instance. In *Mem.* I 4, Socrates is introduced talking with a certain Aristodemus, surnamed "the little". This little man was known as neither sacrificing to the gods nor consulting oracles. He was in those days what the Athenians called an atheist. Socrates makes him first grant that he who makes living beings, endowed with intellect and motion, is more admirable than the man who makes lifeless images, devoid of intellect and motion; second, that things that are useful to some purpose are always the product of intelligence, while those things which have no rule or order and do not serve any purpose are the product of chance; third, that if one considers the human body from this point of view, and the natural drift of procreation inborn in man and of feeding and rearing the children that are born, of striving for life and fleeing death, man appears rather to be the work of a wise creator who loves and wishes to preserve the human race. Then Socrates asks the little man:

> "And do you think yourself to possess some intelligence?" "I should think so!" replies the little man. "And that other beings do not possess any, but that all intellect existing is concentrated in your own little body? And then, what about those huge and innumerable (heavenly) bodies, which move through the universe in such a perfect order? Do you think they do so by lack of intelligence?" "Yes, for I do not see anybody who could direct them, as I see the craftsmen that make everything that is produced." "You don't see your own soul either, which directs and governs your body. So, according to your principles you may say that you don't do anything by reason but everything by chance" (*Mem.* I 4. 4-9).

This curious piece of conversation not only shows us quite a bit of Socratic irony but we also find in it the argument of teleology in nature, used as a proof of the existence of a transcendent Reason, creative of and dominating physical reality, which means to Socrates a proof of the existence of God. Now this is, once more, not just an invention of the good Xenophon, who desires to exculpate his master from the charge of atheism. It corresponds exactly to that passage in the *Phaedo* where Plato introduces Socrates telling his intellectual life story, and where Socrates gives witness that in his younger years he was keenly interested in natural philosophy, eager to learn the causes of physical things, how they come into being and exist and pass away. He says that he was not satisfied at all with the materialistic theories offered to him by most of the Greek philosophers of nature, and was delighted upon hearing of Anaxagoras' principle that a *Nous* is at the origin of all life and motion in the universe. He expected that this philosopher would explain to him in a really satisfactory way *why* everything is at it is, namely, because it is *best* for it to be as it is. But the young Socrates was soon disappointed, finding that, in fact,

Anaxagoras made little use of his excellent principle of *Nous* for the explanation of the world, but endeavoured to explain things by exactly the same kind of material causes alleged by all other philosophers before him[1].

I think we should not neglect the agreement of our two most important contemporary witnesses, nor is it reasonable to declare that Xenophon simply took his material from the Platonic dialogues. Xenophon, surely, was not a philosopher. But he did know about what subjects Socrates used to talk with the Athenians and what was his usual tone and method. We do have to consider Plato and Xenophon as two witnesses who both have known the man of whom they speak. Therefore, we must state that the (probable) fact that Socrates believed in the existence of a good and righteous God, caring for and exercising providence on our world, is well attested, as well as his belief in a life hereafter ("the immortality of the soul") and in the foundation of our moral order on a transcendent ground.

Let us go back for one moment to the *Crito* and state the main tendency of Socrates' argument in that dialogue. It was exactly this, that Socrates was convinced on reasonable grounds that our moral values – the notions of "good" and "just" – are not just human laws, invented by our own reason, but have their roots in a transcendent, suprahuman order. Everybody would grant without any hesitation that such was Plato's doctrine. For this very reason, however, they would hesitate to concede that it was Socrates who already firmly held this view. They would be rather generally inclined to think that Plato in his dialogues ascribed his own convictions to his master, and that in fact the Socrates of history was least of all such a convinced metaphysician as Plato was. Now evidently this holds good in part. That is to say, Socrates was not the author of such a developed metaphysical doctrine as Plato's theory of the Ideas. But that Socrates *did* hold that our moral values are not just human inventions but are objective realities rooted in a transcendent order is well attested, not by Plato only, but by Xenophon as well. I think of *Mem.* IV 4: a dialogue between Socrates and the sophist Hippias on the question of whether what is according to the law (νόμιμον) is identical to what is just (δίκαιον)[2]. But before citing that conversation more explicitly, let us observe that what Plato attributes to Socrates in the *Apology* and *Crito*, and even in the *Gorgias*, is not the theory of Ideas – say, the

---

[1] Plato, *Phaedo* 98b; cf. Aristotle, *Metaph.* A 4, 985a18.
[2] *Mem.* IV 4, 12-25.

existence of Justice-itself in a transcendent order – but simply that our moral behaviour is observed by righteous gods who in the world hereafter have it either punished or remunerated. Hence it may be said, indeed, that for Socrates our moral concepts were not just productions of the human mind but were rooted in a divine and transcendent order; or, as Xenophon put it: were valid for the gods as well. Moreover, let us add this general remark: that a doctrine is obviously held by Plato – e.g., that the stars are living beings endowed with a superior kind of soul and intellect and as such, divine[1] – is not *per se* a reason to deny that is was explicitly a Socratic doctrine before him. We have undeniable evidence, e.g., that Socrates adored the sun as a god[2] and attributed a soul and intellect to the stars on the same grounds as Plato did[3].

Let us now consider *Mem.* IV 4.12ff. Socrates holds that what is according to the law is what is just. Hippias opposes him: the laws of cities are made by men and are often changed. How then can you take them so seriously? Socrates replies that as long as a law is valid it should be obeyed, just as the fact that peace comes after war is no reason for insubordination in battle. Next, Socrates asks Hippias whether he admits the existence of any unwritten laws. Hippias answers in the affirmative. "Can you say these laws were made by men?" "Hardly", replies Hippias, "since unwritten laws are accepted in any country, while the people living all over the world could neither come together nor agree." "Who, then, made these laws?" Hippias thinks they were made by the gods, attesting this by the fact that the first law accepted everywhere is that the gods should be worshipped. But there are other generally accepted unwritten laws too. E.g., the law that forbids sexual intercourse between parents and children, or marriage between brothers and sisters. Now, do you think the gods prescribe what is just, or anything that is not just? Hippias agrees with Socrates that the gods can only prescribe what is just. Socrates concludes that for the gods also "what is according to law" appears to be just.

What is contained in this passage is, in fact, that an analogy is admitted between human law and divine law. The authority of the first is founded on the latter by analogy. "Justice" is not confined to the sphere of human interests, but extends to and is rooted in the

---

[1] Plato, *Tim.* 40; *Nom.* X 898d-e, 899a-c.
[2] Plato, *Symp.* 220d.
[3] Xen., *Mem.* I 4, 8.

divine order. The testimony is important, since it attests that Socrates, though not a "developed metaphysician" as Plato was, did accept what must be called *a transcendent or metaphysical basis of our moral principles*. What he called "knowledge" in that field was exactly this: the insight that our moral principles are not just productions of our own mind but have an objective reality rooted in a divine and transcendent order.

Let us turn now to that famous Socratic maxim that *"nobody sins willingly"*. *Why* is it that for Socrates *knowing* what is just was identical to *doing* it? How could he believe that in his practical life *man cannot do else than be totally dominated by intellectual insight*, and this while everybody can see with his eyes that only too frequently men act against their better insight and choose deliberately to do wrong?

We know what Socrates replied to this: he said that in fact those people choose what *seems* good to them, erring in their judgment of what is good and bad. For if they *knew* really what is good and just, they could only do that[1].

In order to understand this one should first of all realize that for Socrates *knowledge* has a strict sense: *knowing* is being dominated by the Truth one "sees". Why? Because *Truth* is something transcending our physical reality, something divine, imposing on us an absolute claim. Hence, obedience to moral laws or principles is directly a matter of "saving our souls". And a first Socratic principle was that the soul is far more precious than the body.

E.g., "knowing what is just" means, *knowing* one could never do any harm to anybody without violating a divine and sacred order; that is, without harming and damaging one's soul, which is the most precious thing we possess. Now, *knowing* that, i.e., *seeing* the *reality* of the transcendent order, implies *acting* according to it. Or, if anybody goes against this vision, it can only be by compulsion. For nobody would choose deliberately to damage one's own most precious good.

Take, for instance, bravery in war. We "know" the principle that one must defend one's city at the cost of physical life; that physical life is not of first interest, but to live and act according to law and justice (which are the same) is; that forsaking these principles is transgressing not only the civic law, but a divine order represented by

---

[1] The distinction between δοκεῖν and βούλεσθαι in the *Gorgias*.

the gods themselves, who are the embodiment of goodness and of justice in the most perfect sense. Seeing that, man cannot choose to act against it.

This, then, was Socrates' so-called intellectualism: a most vivid and direct consciousness of the reality of a transcendent world. This "knowledge" is, for him, *rational;* it is founded on intellectual research and reflection, on mutual agreement in discussion, which he is ready to start again as soon as anybody should declare that he was no longer convinced. I think we should not hesitate to conclude that, for Socrates, knowledge of the good is rational, but it is much more indeed than what *we* mean by purely intellectual understanding. It is *categorical* in life because it implies both *accepting* and *spiritually realizing the existence of a transcendent order*, from the claims of which no reasonable man can wish to withdraw.

Let us summarize and conclude. *What do we know about Socrates?*

1. Of the four sources that should be considered, we have left Aristophanes on one side. Elsewhere I have dealt explicitly with the historical problems evoked by that strange portrait of Socrates which the ancient comedian offered to the citizens of Athens in his *Clouds* (423). We could then state that the portrait of a Socrates who is the director of a kind of research institute for natural sciences had a limited foundation of truth: that in his younger years Socrates was, in fact, very interested in the philosophy of nature[1]; that he had, in fact, a circle of special pupils, and that a kind of school teaching is attributed to him by Xenophon as well[2].

2. We did not deal at length with Aristotle's testimony either, but limited ourselves to a short reference to it. In fact, Aristotle's testimony that it was Plato who introduced the theory of the Ideas, whereas Socrates just sought for definitions, is a most precious indication about the character of the Platonic dialogues. We must admit that Aristotle knew the school tradition well enough to inform us properly about the question of whether Plato's Socrates was a historical portrait without more ado, or a kind of *transposition*, in which Plato's own thoughts were attributed to the historical person of his master; a procedure which, evidently, does not imply that those "Socratic dialogues" which seem to have been written with the purpose of giving an essential picture of the Master and which, in fact,

[1] Plato *Phaedo* 96a ff.; cf. Xen. *Mem.* IV 7.
[2] *Mem.* I 6, 14.

correspond well to Aristotle's indications, would lack any historical value.

3. In considering the essential features of Socrates according to the Socratic dialogues of Plato, we found a remarkable correspondence between Plato's description and Xenophon's testimony in the *Memorabilia*. Observing that the note of irony, not-knowing and embarrassment, though not absent from Xenophon if one knows how to read him, was much more strongly stressed by Plato, we found a Socrates discussing the same kind of subjects and in the same manner in both authors. The features of soberness and hardiness which are so prominent in the Socrates of Xenophon appeared to be not lacking in Plato's Socrates either; so that, on the whole, we could state that our most important contemporary sources do not contradict but confirm one another.

4. From Aristotle we learn that Socrates was not a full-grown metaphysician as Plato was. Though a careful study of the use of the terms ἰδέα and εἶδος in Greek writers of the fifth century, in particular in the medical literature, makes it quite possible and even probable that Socrates, who sought for one "kind" that is common to the many phenomena of virtue, used the term of μία ἰδέα or ἓν εἶδος, I do not insist on that[1]. But what I hope to have established and made clear in the preceding pages is that Socrates was far from being either an agnostic (as some moderns use to think) or a man who did not admit of anything beyond our individual human intellect. I hope to have proved on sufficient grounds that Socrates firmly believed in the existence of a transcendent (metaphysical) reality, that he believed firmly in the life of the soul hereafter, in the existence of good and righteous gods, and in the validity of our moral principles for the gods as well. Or, to put it in other words, that he based moral values on a transcendent order.

Rejection of false interpretations. We came across or left behind us quite a number of more or less important one-sided accounts, misunderstandings and misinterpretations of the man and philosopher Socrates.

1. One-sided and therefore false was H. Maier's account which denied that Socrates would have been a dialectician interested in making

---

[1] I dealt with that side of the Socratic problem in the first part of my work, *"Een keerpunt in Plato's denken"*, and summarized it in my *Greek Philosophy*, pp. 224-228.

definitions, and made of him a kind of missionary and pastor, only interested in the "souls" of his fellow-men. We had to state that the essential point was that Socrates' mission was performed by intellectual methods, and that rational reflection itself was considered by him as the only and legitimate way to virtue and to "saving one's soul".

2. We left behind us A. E. Taylor's interpretation of Socrates as an ascetic and a mystic, who is repeatedly found in "trance". We corrected: first, Socrates was not an *ascetic* (in the usual sense of this term). We found him to be extremely sober and hardened, having very few physical needs. But that is a different thing. Second, when it was observed in the camp near Potidaea that Socrates stood *thinking* during a whole night, this might be an example of an unusual concentration of the intellect rather than an instance of a kind of mystic trance. Taylor's arguments did not hold true. Also, his view of Socrates "always talking of the immortality of the soul" must be tempered and reduced to other proportions. That is what we did, in stating that Socrates believed firmly and on rational grounds both in the existence of good and righteous gods and in a life hereafter.

3. Also, Taylor's portrait of a Socrates who was "the director of a Research Institute of Science" seems to be more of a parody than an historical account. It was surely paying too much honour to the funny play of Aristophanes.

4. J. Burnet, who, together with Taylor, attributed to Socrates the whole theory of the Ideas as it is expounded, e.g. in Plato's *Phaedo* and *Republic*, made another profound mistake. It is only too much renewed by Dr. V. de Magelhaes-Vilhena in his important study on the Socratic problem, *Le problème de Socrate* (Paris, 1951).

These were the misinterpretations of the first part of this century. At this moment the most important errors about Socrates seem to be the following:

5. Socrates is often represented as the *founder of an autonomous ethic*, since for him human reason had to find out what is good and evil. Obviously this was not for him a "law" imposed from outside (what is called by Kant "heteronomy").

The concept of "autonomy" comes from Kant, who opposed it to the biblical and Christian notion of a divine "law" imposed on man by God (which, according to Kant, is a case of heteronomy). To find in Socrates the founder of moral autonomy, since he was the first to form the moral values in himself and recognized no authority whatsoever beyond his own individual reason, is not a new interpretation at all. On the contrary, the whole view is rather an old-fashioned one, dating from nineteenth-century rationalism. It was advocated *in optima forma* by Karl Joël[1] and repeated after him by numerous others, of whom I mentioned two more or less illustrious representatives: F. M. Cornford (author of numerous and important works in the field of Greek philosophy) and K. R. Popper, who, in his work, *The Open Society and its Enemies*, Vol. I, opposed Socrates as the *individual rationalist* to the "totalitarian" philosopher who was Plato. With Popper the thesis of Socrates' *individualistic rationalism* gets a *pointe* against any system of collectivism, in which the law of a group is imposed on everybody. All those, however, who advocate the thesis of *Socrates as the founder of moral autonomy* agree in this, that they see in Socrates a man who did not accept any authority except his own individual reason.

I hope to have made clear that this view is based on error. It is even a tragic error, since it would bring Socrates together with the sophists whom he opposed with all his forces and intelligence. For what else does it mean to say there is no authority but our own individual reason? It is exactly what Protagoras defended: *"As it seems to me, so it is to me, and as it seems to you, so it is to you"*.

What, then, is the difference? For this much is clear: that in fact Socrates appeals to reason and follows what he thinks to be just.

The difference is that Socrates did admit an authority, not *besides* but *beyond* his own intellect and that of any man, namely, that of "the God" to whose service he had dedicated his life; and in general, that of the divine order which is behind our moral concepts. It is going against the most explicit testimony of our two contemporary witnesses

---

[1] *Geschichte d. ant. Phil.* I (1921), 832ff.: Socrates was accused of corrupting young people. In the *Clouds* he was represented as undermining a father's authority, and in general as degrading tradition into "opinion" (lacking authority). This was essentially right. "For Socrates was the first wholly free man on earth, the first entirely independent character, not because he would have torn himself away from all moral bonds and, like the sophists, would have despised all laws and values, but because he shaped these values into a new form in his own mind, because he wore the law within himself and *in autonomy created personality*. Yes, the true emancipation of the individual, its spiritualisation into personality, was achieved in the hour of Socrates' death, which by this very fact became the hour of birth of a new humanity."

who knew and loved the man, to eliminate this element from Socrates' life and work.

Where the thesis of "individual rationalism" is leading to, may be seen in our day in Jean Paul Sartre. He is the man who proclaims (as Joël did concerning Socrates) that man is *completely free and independent of all authority*, since *he has the law within himself*, i.e., since he himself determines what is good and evil. That is, that *man* (individual man!) *creates the moral principles. C'est l'homme qui crée les valeurs.*

And here we find ourselves again in the company of Protagoras, "As it seems to me, so it is with me, and as it seems to you, so it is for you".

There is no "justice", no good and evil, right and wrong *in itself*. It is *we* who make these notions according to our own standard.

Socrates was very far from that. For him, justice existed in an objective sense. It was, in fact, a transcendent reality, founded on a divine order. Thus far Socrates was indeed a metaphysical thinker: for him man is not an isolated being detached from that transcendent reality which alone is the real basis of our moral principles. Socrates, on the contrary, was a man who could neither understand nature and physical things nor ourselves and human soul without God.

In this he was quite different from some of his contemporaries and very far indeed from those who in our day proclaim themselves completely free and independent since they and they alone "make" or "produce" the moral values.

6. I come to the sixth and last erroneous interpretation. It is that of those who make of Socrates an *agnostic* and say he acted in practical life merely by a kind of instinct[1]. He who wishes to defend this view can obviously refer to Socrates' own emphatic proclamation that he did not know anything. One could argue that this confession of ignorance should be taken strictly; Socrates declared again and again that he was totally ignorant. Well then, we have no right to say that this was not true.

Socrates, then, was a true agnostic. He did not know, literally, what justice and what virtue is. He did not see or acknowledge any general ground of our moral actions. How then did he act in practice?

---

[1] The view was advocated eloquently by the regretted Dutch philosopher, H. J. Pos, in a remarkable article in the *Revue internationale de philosophie* (Brussels, July, 1949) entitled "L'existentialisme dans la perspective de l'Histoire". *Keur uit de verspreide geschriften van Dr. H. J. Pos*, Assen 1958, dl. II, p. 224-237.

Merely by some kind of intuition, and this is not to be taken in an intellectual sense but rather as a kind of instinct then, it seems.

Thus, the eloquent advocate of this interpretation, H. J. Pos, concluded: "The *seeming* intellectualist Socrates turns out to have been an *intuitive*, whose moral certainty left no place for any other justification of moral action but that which lies in the deeds themselves."

That is to say: (1) that Socrates did not admit of any transcendent ground for moral principles; (2) that he did not even believe in the positive value of rational thought with regard to morals; (3) that instead of it he placed a direct moral intuition and confided in the rightness of that.

This, too, is a curious instance of self-projection of the modern agnostic thinker, who himself does not believe in any transcendent ground of our moral principles; who is a "nominalist" as to the sense of human concepts and thinks that consequently human action can never be founded on general principles. In fact, we are here very far from the Socrates of Plato's Socratic dialogues and of Xenophon's. Both of them attested to us that Socrates was a deeply religious man who believed as firmly in the existence of a transcendent order as he believed in the sense of our moral reflection. Very far from denying the value of rational thinking with regard to moral action, Socrates says repeatedly that those who act well on the ground of "true opinion" – which is still more "intellectual" than the "moral instinct" advocated by Pos! – are only good in the popular sense of virtue, but that philosophical reflection only (by which the soul raises itself to the level of transcendent reality) makes man virtuous in the higher or philosophical sense[1]. The Socrates of our unanimous tradition taught as a basic principle that virtue is essentially knowledge. It is true that he tried in vain to define it, but he *did* admit that "justice" is an objective reality which is beyond our visible world and to which we have to conform[2]. The Socrates of Plato and of Xenophon was a Socrates who felt responsible for the souls of others. Far from taking from them all moral ground by leading them into the void of meaninglessness (as

---

[1] *Phaedo* 82 a-c (on δημοτικὴ ἀρετή); cf. *Meno* 97 a-98 a. In practice, right opinion may bring us to the place where we wish to arrive as well as knowledge does. But right opinions resemble the images of Daedalus: if you don't bind them fast they run away! So you must tie them up by a rational ground. That is what gives them stability and transforms them into *knowledge*, which, evidently is of a higher level.

[2] *Apol., Crito, Gorg., Meno, Rep.* I; also Xenophon in *Mem.* I, 4.

Pos thinks he did), the Socrates of Plato and of Xenophon sought in discussion to establish a common insight and thus to reach a supra-individual level. Moreover, he believed that "virtue" and "justice" are valid also for the gods, and that a better life is in store hereafter for the man who lived in justice.

The true reason, finally, why Socrates was not able to define that "knowledge" which is virtue was, no doubt, that the supreme Good is not a *genus*. It is, as will be said later by Plato, *the deepest foundation of all knowledge and all being*. Plato will say also that the insight in the supreme Good is not a kind of knowledge you can "teach" another like any other discipline. It is a matter of a long spiritual preparation, and an insight by which a man is inwardly transformed.

This is, I think, the kind of "intuition" that was in fact behind the questions of Socrates. He was not a sceptic or agnostic, and least of all an anti-intellectualist. He believed in reason and in argument, but both Plato and Xenophon point out again and again that he considered our moral concepts as anchored in a metaphysical reality. For this interpretation I gave you the evidence. If you test it carefully, I think you will acknowledge its truth.

CHAPTER VI

WAS SOCRATES A RATIONALIST?

In the city of Yokohama near the beautiful Sankeien Garden there is the Hasseiden, the "Hall of eight Sages". This hall, erected by a well-known Japanese statesman, houses the images of Gautama, Confucius, Socrates and Christ, of Prince Shotoku and of three Buddhist priests. To the Western visitor the place given to Socrates in this company may provide a subject of meditation. First, he will be struck by the fact that to the Japanese statesman who built this hall – a man of the 20th century – the name of Socrates meant so much, that he ranked him among the greatest spiritual leaders of humanity. That is to say, to Mr. Kenzo Adachi Socrates was not just a remarkable intellect, say the founder of a scientific form of logic (as he was, more or less, to Aristotle), or a man who taught his contemporaries an attitude of perpetual criticism – criticism of traditional forms of thinking (which, of course, might be considered as a great danger by those who are "traditionalists", as it was in the city of Athens in Socrates' own days) –; nor just as a school-philosopher (as he is considered nowadays in many English speaking universities). Obviously, to the Japanese statesman Adachi the name of Socrates meant much more. He saw in him a spiritual leader in the full sense, i.e. a guide *in a way of life, a guide to virtue, to wisdom and to happiness*, which obviously is much more than just a teacher of correct thinking. Now, anticipating my own interpretation I wish to declare that in this Mr. Adachi was entirely right. This is what I hope to explain and confirm by reference to the sources.

In Western Europe scholars have called Socrates "the founder of autonomous ethics". It was expressed in this form by the Basle Professor Karl Joël in the first part of this century, and a few years

[1] This chapter was written in English in the summer of 1966, and read as a seminar lecture to Sophia University, Tokyo, Nov. 1966. It appeared in Japanese in a volume entitled "Greek philosophy and Religion", Tokyo 1969.

later by the well-known Professor Cornford of Cambridge (England)[1]. The term "autonomous ethics" comes from Kant. It was used by him as the opposite of "theonomous" ethics, in which the Divinity is supposed to prescribe to man what is good and evil. According to autonomous ethics it is man himself who by his own reason has to decide what is right and wrong in the field of human action. In our own generation it is said by Sartre: *It is man who creates the values.* Exactly in this sense according to these scholars Socrates taught people that *there is no authority beyond human reason.*

If this were true, then as a matter of fact Socrates would have been the founder of autonomous ethics. That is to say, he would have been a true rationalist. He is regarded as such, for example, by the well-known logician and philosopher of scientific method K. R. Popper, who in his work *The open Society and its enemies* opposes Socrates to Plato as an "individual rationalist" who does not admit any authority above his own individual reason, to what he calls a "naturalist", i.e. a metaphysical thinker who founds our moral principles and concepts on an objective and transcendent order[2].

What I wish to establish in this conference is: that this view of Socrates is erroneous; that as a matter of fact Socrates was not at all an "individual rationalist", who would not have accepted any authority above his own individual reason. On the contrary, we shall find Socrates a man who not only in many circumstances of life consulted the Gods about what to do and told others to do so, but found the very basis of our moral principles in a divine order existing beyond and independent of man. On the other hand, Socrates' behaviour was by no means "autonomous" with regard to the laws of the community in which he lived. On the contrary, he felt himself bound by these laws which had protected him throughout his life, so much that he deliberately chose to undergo an unjust condemnation, prison and death, instead of accepting a safe and easy proposal of escape offered to him by his friends[3].

Moreover, Socrates will be found by us not to have been a "humanist" in that sense which nowadays is often attached to this term. I mean, he was not a person who believed in man and human possibilities but

---

[1] Karl Joël, *Geschichte der Antiken Philosophie* I, Tübingen 1921, p. 832. F. M. Cornford, *Before and after Socrates*, Cambridge 1958, p. 46ff. Cf. p. 126.
[2] K. R. Popper, *The open Society and its Enemies*, London 1945, ³1949, vol. I, ch. 5 and 10.
[3] Plato, *Crito* 50a-54e.

not in God. Far from that, he considered man as a being which is strictly limited in its powers of understanding things, whereas God, or the Gods, are beings who possess both an unlimited power of understanding and an unlimited power of helping man and sustaining the world-order. He considered man as virtually able to realise justice in his life on earth but in practice very frequently deficient, the Gods, however, as beings that possess an absolute justice and maintain this in their care for man, both in this life and in the life beyond.

But let us now return to the sources. It is not only Plato's earlier dialogues that supply us with the material to reconstruct a historical picture of Socrates. No doubt Plato's Socratic dialogues *do* furnish us quite important material, but they are by no means our only source. Without Xenophon and Aristotle's important testimony they would certainly leave us in a much greater uncertainty than we are now in. Sometimes, it is true, Plato's testimony speaks for itself. I am thinking, for example, of that passage in the *Symposion* in which a portrait of Socrates is drawn by the young Alcibiades[1]. The speaker begins by comparing Socrates to certain wood-cut images of Silens, ugly as to their outward appearance, which when opened appear to bear the image of a God within them. They are represented as flute-players, such as the satyr Marsyas, who played wonderful melodies, fascinating to his hearers. And does not Socrates do the same by means of his spoken words and arguments? Next, Alcibiades speaks of Socrates' moral strictness, of his incredible endurance in the hardships of military expeditions. Lastly, he tells this remarkable story. In the Athenian expedition to Potidaea in the Thracian Chersonesus it happened one day in the camp that Socrates was observed to have been standing from daybreak until the evening, obviously thinking on something and completely absorbed in thought. The soldiers came to look at him with a certain curiosity and surprise, and when he did not move, some of them brought their beds out and slept in the open, just to see whether he would go on standing there throughout the night. This was in fact what happened: Socrates stood there till daybreak. Then he said a prayer to the sun and went off.

All this, certainly, is drawn from life. And many a modern reader of the Socratic dialogues might feel inclined to say the same of so many other scenes depicted by Plato, where we find Socrates discussing about the question of what one or another particular virtue is, say piety or

---

[1] Plato, *Symposion* 215a-220d; *Greek Phil.* nr. 208a-c.

justice, courage or selfrestraint, with any person he would meet and who happened to be willing to reply to his often so puzzling questions. But we have to be cautious. It should be borne in mind that Plato was a *literary* author, who deals with the characters and subjects of his dialogues with a considerable liberty. Others among his contemporaries acted similarly: there were Socratic dialogues written by Antisthenes, by Aeschines, by Xenophon, and probably by a few others who belonged to the circle of Socrates' friends. None of these pictures was historical in the sense we usually assign to this term. It is for this reason that some modern philologists and historians have observed that we know only a *Socratic literature*, but that we do not have any strictly historical portrait of Socrates[1]. In a sense this is true. Not in the sense that we do not possess any strictly historical data about Socrates. We do. But it is true in this sense, that not any dialogue, either of Plato or of Xenophon, is a historical document in the modern sense of the term.

This does not mean that Plato's Socratic dialogues are of no value from the point of view of history. On the contrary, they are highly valuable to the historian. But he has to use them with certain reservations, knowing that the scenery may have been arranged by Plato with great liberty, and that the words attributed to each of the speakers were not literally spoken by them. What is true is evidently that *similar talks* were frequently held by Socrates, that such were the kind of subjects he used to deal with, and such the kind of arguments brought forward by him.

For example, a discussion on the concept of "bravery" as it is found in Plato's *Laches* is certainly typical of what a Socratic discussion was. This does not mean, however, that on a certain day in history precisely these few persons met somewhere in the city of Athens and discussed with Socrates about the education of their sons, of what the boys should be taught and what not. The scenery may have been freely invented by Plato; but the kind of discussion, the method of inquiring into the meaning of some particular ethical concept, the way of attempting a definition, refuting it, attempting another which is refuted again, a third and a fourth, and finally ending with the statement that one does not yet know what bravery is and has to start again, – all this, no doubt, is truly typical of a Socratic discussion.

---

[1] This is the thesis which was advocated most impressively by the Swiss scholar O. Gigon: *Sokrates*, Sammlung Dalp, Bern 1947. I replied to this book in Mnemosyne 1951, pp. 30-39: *Une nouvelle interprétation du problème socratique*.

Plato offers us a number of other examples, e.g. that conversation of Socrates and the famous sophist Protagoras about the question of "Whether virtue can be taught". The strange result of this talk is: that Protagoras who was not willing to agree with Socrates that virtue is knowledge, is found at the end defending the thesis that virtue can be taught, while Socrates, who always asserted that virtue is knowledge, at the end finds himself defending the thesis that virtue cannot be taught...

Such ironical situations, too, are characteristic of Socrates' way of handling moral problems.

It is important for modern criticism that the portrait of Socrates in Plato's dialogues is essentially confirmed by Xenophon: in Xenophon's *Memorabilia* too we find a Socrates who tirelessly discusses about virtue with all kinds of people, who makes them try to find a definition, who always speaks about craftsmen and their craftmanship, and by his arguments tries to win his partners over to his own favourite view that virtue is knowledge. It is interesting to find the following description in Xenophon:

> Hippias, who had not been in Athens for a considerable time, found Socrates talking: he was saying that if you want to have a man taught cobbling or building or smithing or riding, you know where to send him to learn the craft. But if you want to learn justice either yourself or to have your son or servant taught it, you do not know where to go for a teacher. When Hippias heard this, he cried in a tone of raillery:
>
> "Well, Socrates, are you still saying those same things that I heard from you so long ago?" – To which Socrates replies: "Yes, Hippias, always the same; and – what is more amazing – on the same topics too! You have such a vast knowledge that perhaps you never say the same thing on the same subjects"...[1]

Memorabilia IV 4, 5-6. I followed the translation of E. C. Marchant (Loeb) with a certain liberty.

The subjects on which Socrates used to discuss are also mentioned in *Memorabilia* I 1, 16. Next to such virtues as piety, justice, self-restraint, bravery and their opposites we find here such subjects as *What is a state, What is a statesman, What is government* and *What is a governor*.

On the topic of "craftmanship" cf. I 2, 9: Socrates was against the Athenian custom of appointing officials by drawing of lots. After all, you do not assign a steersman, a carpenter or a flute-player by lot! Cp. *Memor.* III 6. In Plato: *Crito* 47 b ff.; *Laches* 184 de; *Protagoras* 319 b ff.; *Gorgias* 451 a ff., 463 a-c. Diogenes Laertius VI 8 mentions the story that Antisthenes advised the Athenians to appoint mules by vote to be horses...

It has been said by some modern critics that the Socratic irony, so dominant a feature in Plato's dialogues, is altogether lacking in the good Xenophon's Socratic talks. This is, however, saying too much. Though this peculiarity of Socrates was certainly not so much in line with Xenophon's character as, for instance, his endurance and self-restraint (which are strongly emphasized by this author[1]), for the careful reader the irony is present there as well. We shall come across another instance in a moment.

It has been often said that Xenophon used to attribute his own preferences to Socrates. One instance is the emphasis laid on the care of the body. This might seem to be correct. Yet, it must be observed that in Plato's *Crito*[2] the care of the body is mentioned as one of the basic principles, preached by Socrates throughout his life and never to be abandoned. It is said in that passage that, when the body is in a bad condition and muddled by ill treatment, life is no longer worth living for a man.

Of how great an interest Aristotle's testimony on Socrates is, will be seen clearly in such dialogues as the *Phaedo* and the *Republic*. Of the *Phaedo* in particular a considerable part is to be considered as first rate historical evidence about Socrates. I wish to extend this to the autobiographical account given in the pages 96 a ff.[3]. The Socrates who was not satisfied with the theories of earlier philosophers of nature, who at first sight welcomed Anaxagoras' *Noûs* with the warmest enthusiasm but next is bitterly disappointed because this philosopher too explains natural phenomena much more by material causes than by that Spirit which was said to move and govern everything, – this is, no doubt, the Socrates of history. But a few pages further on we find the same Socrates expounding the theory of the Ideas, which we are used to attributing to Plato. On what grounds? What is our criterion for making the distinction between the Socrates of history and the Socrates whom Plato made the spokesman of his own metaphysical theory?

---

[1] On self-restraint: Xenophon, *Memor.* I 2, 1; I 6, 2-3; IV 5. On endurance: I 6, 7; I 2, 1. On having no wants (τὸ μηδενὸς δεῖσθαι): *Memor.* I 6, 10; De Vogel, *Greek phil.* 222.

[2] 47 b-e.

[3] In my *Greek Phil.* I, this passage is reproduced under nr. 216. On p. 145, n. 1, the reader finds the parallel of Xenophon, *Memor.* I 4, 4-9, by which it is confirmed that Socrates believed firmly in divine Providence and based this conviction on the teleological order of nature, in particular in living beings and in man.

It is Aristotle who enables us to make this distinction. He procures us the criterion we needed by stating that Socrates was concerned with the search for definitions, but Plato was the first to attribute to such concepts the ontological status which is meant in the theory of the Ideas[1].

Even Aristophanes has something to contribute to the picture of the historical Socrates[2]. When he makes fun of Socrates by putting him upon the stage as the Director of an "Institute for advanced Studies of Nature", he confirms what Plato has Socrates tell in the *Phaedo*, viz., that in his younger days he was full of enthusiasm for the philosophy of nature, but later, disappointed by the explanations of earlier philosophers, he abandoned this kind of research and turned into another method.

After these preliminary questions let us turn to some particular problem. What was Socrates' attitude towards Divinity, towards religious tradition, towards Nature and man? We shall start from a passage in Xenophon, not in the *Memorabilia*, but in the *Anabasis*. It is in the beginning of book III, where Xenophon speaks about himself for the first time and tells about how he came to join the expedition of Cyrus. Xenophon had been invited in a letter by a friend who begged him to come over to Sardes and promised him to introduce him to Cyrus. Now Xenophon desired very much to go, but since it was an important decision, he asked Socrates for advice. It was towards the end of the Peloponnesian war, and everybody knew that Cyrus was a friend of the Spartans. Socrates is afraid of favouring the enemies of his native city and tells Xenophon to consult the Delphic God. Xenophon then goes to Delphi and asks the God the following question: "To which of the Gods have I to sacrifice and to whom shall I pray, that the journey which I wish to make may be successful and that I may return safely?"

---

[1] Aristotle, *Metaphysics* A 6, 987b1-10; M 4, 1078b23-30; *Greek Phil.*, nr. 204.
[2] I have discussed Aristophanes' testimony about Socrates in one chapter of my book *Een keerpunt in Plato's denken* (A crisis in Plato's thought), Amsterdam 1936, and argued that the apparant contradiction between Aristophanes' comedy "The Clouds" and Plato's *Apology* 19cd, in which Socrates denied categorically that he was ever concerned with the study of nature, can be solved when one considers the considerable space of time which lies between the performance of "The Clouds" (423) and Socrates' discussions in the days when Plato and Xenophon used to hear them. Cp. also Wolfgang Schmid, *Das Sokratesbild der Wolken*, Philologus 97 (1948), pp. 209-228.

And the God replied to him, telling to whom he should make his sacrifices.

Then, Xenophon goes to see Socrates and reports to him what the oracle replied. But Socrates rebukes him for having asked the oracle as he had done: he should have asked the God whether it was better for him to go or not. Instead of this he had decided himself, and afterwards asked the God to give his sanction. "But", Socrates went on, "having asked your question in this form, you have to do what the God told you"[1].

As to the historicity of this story, there cannot be the slightest doubt. For us the story is extremely interesting. It shows us Socrates as a *traditionalist* in matters of religion, but at the same time as a man who gave a very personal and profound meaning to the traditional forms. This is what we shall find in a number of other texts, both of Plato and of Xenophon.

It was a tradition among the Greeks to consult the Delphic oracle in great undertakings of which, humanly speaking, the end could not be foreseen, e.g. the founding of a colony. Thus, in his advice to the young Xenophon Socrates followed a very old national tradition. He did so from conviction, not incidentally, but as a general rule of conduct. We learn the background from another passage in Xenophon[2]. Here Socrates says that there are many things in life the consequences of which we cannot foresee. Man can learn and master certain arts and crafts, and this he *must* do in order to fulfil certain human tasks. But the power of human knowledge is limited, many things are hidden from us. For instance, you may plant a field well, but you know not who shall gather the fruits, you may build a house well, but you know not who shall dwell in it; you may marry a pretty girl, but you cannot know whether she will bring you sorrow. In all such things man needs the help of divination; for to those who are in their grace the Gods grant a sign.

This is not exactly the attitude of what we usually call a "rationalist". Socrates who, it seems, had immense confidence in reason, – since he was convinced that he contributed essentially to the training of men in virtue by teaching them to think correctly on moral concepts –, this Socrates was profoundly aware of the limits of human understanding: in the most ordinary, and in the most elementary

---

[1] Xenophon, *Anabasis* III 1, 4-7.
[2] Xenophon, *Memor.* I 1, 6-9; *Greek phil.* nr. 217c.

things of life we are at the limits of our comprehension; we do not know things, and we cannot know. God knows them.

On Socrates' belief in Providence Xenophon says:

> "He believed indeed that the Gods care for man, but not in the way most men believe this. For they think the Gods know certain things, while ignoring certain others. Socrates however thought that they knew everything, our words and deeds and secret purposes; that they are present everywhere, and give signs to men about everything that concerns man"[1].

Somewhat earlier in the same treatise[2] Xenophon observed that Socrates believed in signs given by the Gods to man, "like everybody who believes in mantic and makes use of the flight of birds, of prophetic words[3], coincidences and sacrifices". But, Xenophon continues, these men do not believe that it is the birds or the people met by accident who know what profits those who ask for a sign, but that they are the instruments by which the Gods make something known to men; and that was also Socrates' belief. The only difference was that most men say the birds or the people they meet dissuade or encourage them, while Socrates said that the deity gave him a sign.

This is Xenophon's explanation of that inner voice which Socrates says he used to hear from boyhood on certain occasions, which always turned him away from doing certain things but never positively impelled him to do a thing[4]. Socrates called this the *daimonion*. We hear[5] from others in his circle, who understood this as some special favour granted by the Gods to Socrates, and in fact, it rather makes the impression of some particular gift. Anyhow, this inner voice mentioned by Socrates in Plato's *Apology* in a sober form, obviously enlarged and exaggerated by later authors, was not a phenomenon such as would suit a rationalist who is supposed not to have accepted any authority above his own individual reason.

There is another remarkable passage in Xenophon[6] which is revealing

---

[1] Xenophon, *Memor.* I 1, 19; *Greek phil.* nr. 217b.
[2] Xenophon, *Memor.* I 1, 3-4; *Greek phil.* nr. 217a.
[3] A φήμη, as it occurs, for instance, in the *Odyssea* XX 100ff., might be any chance utterance, conceived as prompted by the Gods and hence significant and prophetic.
[4] Plato, *Apology* 31d; *Greek phil.* nr. 220a.
[5] E.g. in Plato's *Euthyphro* 3b. See also Xenophon, *Memor.* IV 3, 12, *Apol.* 14. *Greek Phil.* 220c-e.
[6] *Memor.* I 1, 11ff., in particular 15. I pointed to this passage also in the preceding chapter.

with regard to Socrates' attitude towards Nature and the philosophy of nature of his day. This is what Xenophon says:

> "Socrates did not, as most philosophers do, speak about the nature of the universe, the origin of the cosmos, and about the laws by which the phenomena of the heavens are governed. – First, he would consider whether those who were concerned with such problems thought to have acquired a sufficient knowledge of human things, so that now they could concentrate on this field; or did they think that it was their duty to neglect human affairs and consider only things divine? – He used to ask also the following question concerning these philosophers. Those who have learned human things believe that they will be able to reproduce that which they have learned, both for themselves and for whomsoever they like. Is it the same with those who inquire into divine things? Do they imagine that, once they have discovered the laws by which the heavenly phenomena are produced, they will be able to create whenever they like winds, waters, seasons and whatever they need of such things? Or do they not expect anything of that kind but *are they satisfied with just knowing the causes of these various phenomena?*"

The last part of this passage was probably not meant to be ironical. Its unmistakable irony about that discipline which pretends to be the *science* of nature, is the more precious to us. Strictly speaking, "science" is something absolute: it implies a complete control of its subject. But if that is so, is it not a tremendous presumption to speak of any *science* of nature? Do we ever possess any adequate knowledge of the causes of natural phenomena? If we actually did, we would be able to reproduce them whenever we liked and for whomsoever we liked. But that is exactly what we are not able to do.

For Socrates nature is full of mysteries. Can we explain life adequately? Do we understand the reason why things in nature are as they are? Apparently Socrates believed that the efficient structure of natural organisms points to a divine Intellect as its cause. In his opinion neither the "purposiveness" of nature nor the phenomena of life and motion can be explained by material causes. That is why he was not satisfied with the natural philosophy of his day[1].

Without any doubt he believed that the heavenly bodies possess

---

[1] Plato, *Phaedo* 96a-99c; Xenophon, *Memor.* I 4, 4-9; *Greek phil.* 216.

souls, for it seemed to him impossible to explain the regular movement of such large bodies unless they were ruled by a mighty intellect. This is the argument he used, according to Xenophon[1], in his talk with Aristodemus, that small man who was known as an atheist, who never sacrificed nor consulted an oracle. If we might feel inclined to think that it may well have been Xenophon who attributed this argument to Socrates, we have to remember Alcibiades' speech in Plato's *Symposion* and the description of Socrates' behaviour in the camp near Potidaea, where he stood thinking throughout a day and a night, and at sunrise he went off "after having said a prayer to the sun"[2].

The last words, written without any purpose but that of giving a true account of that remarkable event – which evidently must have been known in Athens in those days to all those who participated in that expedition –, these words reveal to us just one point which otherwise we could never be certain of, viz. that the argument used by Socrates in his talk with Aristodemus according to Xenophon's *Memorabilia*, which in a general sense was confirmed for us in the autobiographical passage of Socrates in the *Phaedo*, actually was the conviction of the historical Socrates, also on the point of the celestial bodies having souls.

There are a few passages in Plato's dialogues in which – not systematically but incidentally – Socrates appears as a traditionalist in matters of religion. But behind the traditional forms these passages reveal to us a very profound and personal religious belief. Let us consider a few of these texts.

1. *Apology* 41 a-d. Socrates expects to find "yonder" the "true" judges who are much more just than the judges here. For this conviction he refers to a certain religious tradition[3] which he does not mention by name; but it is known to us as the Orphic-Pythagorean tradition concerning what happens to souls after death. That is what Plato's Socrates describes in the myth at the end of the *Gorgias*. He introduces it in the following words:

> "Now listen to a very beautiful tale. You will think, I suppose, it is not a true story, but I think it is. For what I am going to tell you, I shall tell you as the truth."

---
[1] The above-cited passage in *Memor.* I 4.
[2] *Symposium* 220d; *Greek phil.* 208c.
[3] He refers to it as λεγόμενα, "things that are told".

There follows a description of the judgment passed on the souls after death[1].

It is often said that in the *Apology* Socrates – who on this point has frequently been opposed to Plato – is sceptical about the life hereafter. Those who say so[2] obviously refer to that passage in which Socrates, explaining to his judges that there is no reason for fearing death, says that there are two possibilities: either death is something like a deep and dreamless sleep, or it is a moving from here into another, better kind of life. He goes on as follows:

> "But you too, Sirs, may be full of hope with regard to death, and one thing in particular you may accept as an indubitable truth, namely, that for a good man there is no evil, neither in his life here nor after death, and certainly the interests of such a man are not neglected by the Gods. Also this what now happens to me does not happen by chance, but this is perfectly clear to me, that at present it is better for me to be dead and freed of all kind of troubles."

Then he recommends his sons to the care of the judges and concludes his speech with these words:

> "But now it is time to go, for me to die, for you to live. Which of us will go to a better lot, this is hidden from everyone, except God."

Is this the word of a sceptic? – I do not think so, I think these are the words of a man who was very well aware of the limits of human knowledge, but knew that his lot was in the hand of God and trusted that in his hands it was safe. With Socrates the last word was not that of a rationalist, this term being taken in the sense of a man who wants to explain everything by reason, and beyond his individual human reason does not admit any source of certainty, either in the field of theoretical speculation or in the field of action. All this proves to have been far from Socrates: he knew the *limits* of the human intellect. But at the same time he felt *certain* of some things which are not given to man to know. He recognized the mystery and trusted in God.

---

[1] *Gorgias* 523 a ff.; cp. also *Phaedo* 107 d 5 - e 2.
[2] I think in particular of the well-known handbooks of Zeller and Überweg. They were followed by many others, so that this view has become more or less a school-dogma. It has been opposed with good arguments by E. de Strycker, S.J., *Socrate et l'au-delà d'après l'Apologie platonicienne*, in *Les Études Classiques* 18 (1950), pp. 269-284.

This is the attitude which appears also in *Phaedo* 62b. In the preceding lines it has been stated that sometimes it is better for a man to be dead than to live, but nonetheless in such a case it is not permissible to "do good to oneself": one has to wait for another "benefactor". Socrates says to his young friend Cebes:

> "This may seem absurd to you, but perhaps it makes a good sense. For what is said on it in the Mysteries[1], I mean that man is placed on a watchpost and is not allowed to dismiss himself and run away, that seems quite a great thing to me and not easy to fathom. But anyhow this much seems true to me, Cebes, that the Gods care for us and that we men are one of the possessions of the Gods. — Well then, what would you do if a slave of yours was going to kill himself without having received your order? Would you not be angry and punish him if you could?" — "No doubt, I would", he said.
> And Socrates: "Well, perhaps that shows that it isn't unreasonable that a man ought not to put an end to himself unless God brings constraint upon him, as he does now upon me"[2].

2. *Phaedo* 60c-61b. While being in prison Socrates composed a hymn to Apollo. When his friends asked him, somewhat surprised, why he did this, he gave the following explanation. In his dreams he had repeatedly received an order to "make music". At first he had interpreted this in such a sense, that he was told just to go on with doing what he did, since philosophy was the highest kind of music and this was what he was practising. But, as the order was repeated, it seemed safer to him to take it to the letter and obey the order in the most obvious sense. For it seemed safer to him not to pass away until he had fulfilled a sacred obligation. So then he composed the hymn to the god and, moreover, put into verse a few of Aesop's fables which he knew by heart.

3. *Phaedo* 118de. Socrates has drunk the poison and now lies down, waiting for the end. He is covered by a cloak. His legs have become cold and rigid. By the time the cold reached about his stomach, he removed the cloak he had put over his face and said: "Crito, we owe a cock to Asclepius; pray do not forget to pay the debt."

A few moments later he died.

---

[1] Here too the Orphic-Pythagorean rites and doctrines are referred to.
[2] In the last sentence I have followed Hackforth's elegant translation.

It was usual in Greece to sacrifice a cock to Asclepius as a thanksgiving for recovered health. It cannot be doubted, then, why Socrates said to Crito "We owe a cock to Asclepius": obviously he took death as an awakening to a better and more normal life. Since we have found Socrates repeatedly expressing his respect for the Orphic-Pythagorean tradition and even expressing his agreement with the doctrines of that circle, we shall not be shocked by the thought that is obviously implied in Socrates' last words. Nor shall we feel inclined to deny the obvious meaning of these words, though of course we know that some scholars have done so[1]. We only wish to observe that just a moment earlier in the scene described by Plato on the last page of the *Phaedo*, when one man of the group of friends was weeping aloud and the others, too, could hardly refrain from weeping, Socrates rebuked them saying:

> "What are you doing, you odd fellows! That is precisely why I sent the women away, that they might not misbehave like that. For I have always heard that one should die in silence"[2].

Now this is a Pythagorean principle[3].

4. *Phaedrus* 279 bc. Socrates and Phaedrus have been discussing in the heat of the afternoon in a lovely shady spot on the bank of the Ilissus under a large plane-tree. When it is time to leave, Socrates prays to the gods who dwell in that place. This is what he prays:

> "Dear Pan and you other gods who dwell in this place, give me beauty in the inward soul. And may all the outward things I have be in perfect agreement with the inward man. May I reckon the wise to be wealthy, and of gold may I have no more than a temperate man can carry with him. –
>
> "Do we ask anything more, Phaedrus? For me, I think, this is enough."
>
> *Phaedrus*. "Ask the same for me. For friends have all things in common."

---

[1] I am thinking first of all of Wilamowitz, who declared in a most categorical tone that of course it is impossible that Socrates would have meant such a thing. For many years scholars have been far too much impressed by this opinion.

[2] *Phaedo* 117 de.

[3] Cp. Iamblichus, *Life of Pythagoras* 257, discussed in my book *Pythagoras and Early Pythagoreanism*, p. 185. The text of Iamblichus is printed on p. 273, nr. 43.

The last words are a famous Pythagorean adage[1].

Here too Socrates' attitude is traditionalistic. The contents of the prayer, however, show a profoundly religious attitude, probably with an Orphic-Pythagorean tinge.

Another prayer approved by Socrates is mentioned in the pseudo-Platonic dialogue *Alcibiades* II, 142e-143a. Here Socrates quotes an anonymous poet who wrote the following prayer:

> "King Zeus, give us what is good, whether we pray for it or not,
> and protect us against evil, even when we pray for it".

This poet was a wise man, Socrates says, and apparently he had friends who were not wise: they asked from the gods what was not good for them. Therefore he wrote this prayer on their behalf, teaching them that it is enough to pray for the good. No need of any specification, for the gods know much better than we know what is good for us.

In a later author we find this prayer cited as a Pythagorean prayer[2].

Next we have to consider more closely Socrates' life-work which, according to Plato, he called "a service to the God"[3].

Socrates was a passionate educator, and an educator of outstanding qualities and with a very peculiar method; an educator of the people, one should say, for in fact he used to discuss things with anybody who was willing to reply to his questions, and according to his own words in the *Apology* he extended his care to everyone, but to his fellow-citizens in particular[4]. His method was an intellectual one. Xenophon says in one of his Socratic conversations: "Socrates made those who were in regular contact with him more able in discussion"[5]. He explains that by the following words:

---

[1] The Pythagorean adage κοινὰ τὰ τῶν φίλων is quoted from Timaeus in Diogenes Laertius VIII 10. It is also referred to in a scholion on our *Phaedrus* passage (ed. Hermann VI, p. 275) and in Photius' *Lexicon* 129. See my *Pythagoras*, p. 281, nr. 13.
[2] Orion, *Anthologia* V 17. Cf. also *Anthologia Palatina* X 108. Earlier traces of this Pythagorean tradition in Diodorus X 9, 7-8 and Diogenes Laertius VIII 9 (probably from Timaeus). See my book *Pythagoras and Early Pythagoreanism* pp. 182ff. (It must be observed that on p. 182 the *Alcibiades* II is erroneously cited as *Alcib. Mai.* This should be, of course, *Alcib. Mi.*).
[3] *Apology* 23bc, 28e, 29b-30a, 30de.
[4] *Apology* 30a.
[5] *Memorabilia* IV 6, 1.

> "For Socrates held that those who know what any given thing is will also be able to explain it to others. It is no wonder, however, he said, that those who do not know are uncertain themselves and bring others into uncertainty. For this reason he never gave up considering with his companions what any given thing is"[1].

Xenophon then mentions a few examples. What is pious, what is just, what is wise, what is good, what is beautiful? What is courage, what is kingship, what despotism? And what is a good citizen? Socrates never gives his companions any direct answer. Even according to Xenophon's records he did not just tell people what the thing was they were inquiring into. "I never teach them anything", he would say according to Plato, "for I am not wise; I am ignorant. I can only ask questions, and by these questions make people conscious of the difficulties of the subject and of their own ignorance"[2]. He *does* claim to have the peculiar gift of "rousing" others[3], of stimulating their own intellectual activity, of leading them on the way to finding a solution of certain problems by their own thinking power. This is what he calls his obstetric art: the art of assisting others in bringing forth intellectual fruits, while he is unable to produce anything himself.

After all, we can agree with Xenophon that Socrates made his companions "better dialecticians". Such must have been the result of his discussions, even if they never resulted in a satisfactory definition of the subject. Socrates' questions will have contributed considerably to intellectual clarity, to correct distinctions, clearer concepts. But the strange thing is: *Socrates claims to have been educating people in the moral sense.* What he mentions as the real purpose of his activity is: "to care for the souls" of his fellow-citizens and of anybody, and make them better men[4]. And in this we must take him literally, for in his discussion with the sophist Gorgias it is in this that he opposes philosophy to rhetoric, that the latter does not care for the souls of the hearers, nor does it ever make them better men, while philosophy cares for their souls, for virtue and for justice, and claims to lead people on that way[5].

---

[1] In my translation I have partly followed Marchant.
[2] See *Theaetetus* 149a-151b and *Meno* 80a. *Greek Phil.* nr. 209. Cp. also the *Apology* 21b-d.
[3] *Apology* 30e: he has been given to the Athenians by the Deity as a gad-fly to a great and noble horse.
[4] *Apology* 29e, 31b.   [5] *Gorgias* 502b10-503d; 515a-517b; 519c-e.

WAS SOCRATES A RATIONALIST?

Our problem is: *how could Socrates imagine it was possible to make people virtuous by mere intellectual discussions on moral concepts?* Does one get to the bottom of this problem by answering that Socrates was an intellectualist? – I rather think this answer would increase the existing difficulties and misunderstanding.

The problem is connected with another one. *Is it true that Socrates who most emphatically declares to be ignorant and hence to be unable to teach his companions any positive doctrine, was fundamentally a sceptic, having no certitude on anything?* – He proves not to be so. For why did he reject the plan of escape proposed to him when he was in prison waiting for death? Because of a number of firm convictions, formulated in clear words and founded on mutual agreement in discussion with his friends. "*We*, you and I, *agreed* that certain things are so and so. To me the same principles seem to be always valid, exactly as I have defended them throughout my life. But if you have anything to say against them, just say it. We shall consider the point anew"[1].

Then follow those principles of which Socrates says that he is certain; but nonetheless he is willing to bring them again into discussion as soon as anybody says he has anything to object.
1. Not to care for the opinion of the crowd, but only for the opinion of those who can judge about the matter on the basis of precise knowledge.
2. The soul is of higher value than the body.
3. Physical life is not of primary importance; what is of primary importance is to live a morally good life.
4. Good, beautiful and righteous are identical.
5. One must never do wrong, and in no respect,
6. Nor return wrong, if anyone has wronged us.

One by one Socrates re-examines these principles. He asks Crito whether he still agrees with him or has anything to object. Crito has not.

Then, and only then, does Socrates declare that the same principles are still valid and hence the consequences have to be accepted: he will not run away, but undergo the judgment passed on him by the state whose laws he has always accepted.

Socrates accepts, and asks others to accept with him, that which follows from "what was agreed"[2]. Thus, this "rationalistic individualist", as he has been called, is found constantly occupied with es-

[1] *Crito* 46 c ff.
[2] ἐκ τῶν ὁμολογουμένων. *Crito* 48 b 11.

tablishing and consolidating inter-individual communication and agreement. He does not stand isolated with his moral convictions, on some inaccessible island of a personal intuition. He is always engaged in breaking through the isolation of the individual by striving for some mutual agreement in the discussion with others.

In fact, agreement was attained in Socrates' circle, and that on basic principles. Not that Socrates ever imposed these things on others. He never did. But in a common search he and his companions came to a common result. It is this process of searching together with others which Socrates indicated by the words "caring for your soul".

Was it then so certain that this kind of discussions had the power of forming the moral character? Apparently this is what Socrates expected from his method. How could he think so? How could he believe that he could make men morally better by means of mere intellectual reflexion? Is not this a strange conviction? How could he maintain that virtue is knowledge and that nobody sins willingly?[1] After all, the tragic situation of a man who, overpowered by his desires, chooses not the right thing which he knows he should do, but the wrong thing which he knows he should reject, – this situation was well known in the world of Socrates[2]. How then could he deny that?

He could do that exactly as, for instance, Karl Barth could deny that any man who once has believed in Christ could ever lose his faith. If someone should object to this that it is proved by fact that some people who once were believers have now lost their faith, the theologian would say: "Those people have never actually believed." Exactly in this way Socrates says: when people do what is evil,

---

[1] The definition that virtue is knowledge is found in many of Plato's Socratic dialogues, e.g. the *Laches, Hippias Minor, Protagoras, Gorgias, Meno*. In Xenophons's *Memorabilia* it is found, for instance, in III 9, 5. Aristotle mentions it explicitly in the *Eudemian Ethics* I 5, 1216b6-8. *Greek Phil.* 204c.

The thesis that nobody sins willingly (οὐδεὶς ἑκὼν ἁμαρτάνει) is found, e.g. in Plato's *Protagoras* 345d. It is quoted by Aristotle in the *Nicomachean Ethics* VII 3, 1145b21-27. *Greek phil.* 204d.

[2] The Athenians could see it on the stage in the person of Medea: Euripides, *Medea* 1078ff., has her speak the words

> "Yes, I know what evil things I shall dare, –
> But passion is stronger than my decisions.
> And this is what causes the greatest evil to mortal men".

It is highly probable, as has been suggested by Bruno Snell in *Philologus* 97 (1948), pp. 125ff., that in these verses the poet protested against Socrates' maxim.

knowing that it is such but, as it is said, "overpowered by their desires", they do not actually know what is the right thing.

There are two aspects to this matter: knowing and its object. Now, for Socrates "knowing" was something mighty; it was *dominating* its object and getting to the bottom of it. Let us remember the passage in Xenophon on natural science. And what about the object, that which is right?

Socrates has never been able to define it, though he always discussed it and maintained at the cost of his life that one must do what is right and just, and not the opposite. If he had been an intellectualist – as he is frequently said to have been –, he would have said according to strict logic: "I do not know what is right and just, and if I do not know what it is, I can neither do it myself nor teach others to do it."

But he did not say that, and that was not at all what he meant. On the contrary, though he could not define it, he was very positive about what was right and just in practice, and he did not hesitate a moment about what to do under certain difficult circumstances. Moreover, he was sincerely convinced that by his discussions about virtue he taught men to do what is right, to "know" about what is right and just, and hence to practise it.

If this should seem contradictory and confused, Socrates himself explains it when he says that he does not possess any knowledge which he could teach others, but that he has the gift of rousing something in others, something by which those others come to produce spiritual fruits and find in themselves what they would not have found without his help. Apparently Socrates roused something in different kinds of people. This we can see when observing the very different positions of those who are known to us as Socratics: an Antisthenes, an Aristippus, an Euclides of Megara, Stilpo, Plato...

However amazing it may seem, it appears to have been true: Socrates was not able to teach his companions *what* they had to think about what is right and good. But he did *rouse* something in them.

What was the right and the good in his own eyes? Of course we shall not answer this question by giving a definition. But we had to ask it, for it leads us to a better understanding of that famous Socratic maxim that no man sins willingly.

"If anybody actually *knows* what is right, he cannot act against it. Whenever men do wrong, they actually do not *know* what they are doing." That is what Socrates says. It is no intellectualism. It is the word of a man who knows that "what is right" in its roots transcends the sphere of human things; in other words, *that the right and the good are rooted in a divine order.*

There are a number of texts that point in this direction. We found Socrates saying that a good man is never abandoned by the Gods, neither in this life nor in the life hereafter[1]. We found him saying that God cares for man, that we are his property and therefore are not allowed to run away from the post that has been assigned to us[2]. We found him speaking of the righteous judges "yonder"[3] and of the laws he expected to find in Hades[4]. In a talk with the sophist Hippias, reported by Xenophon, he says that what is lawful (νόμιμον) and what is just (δίκαιον) are the same, and in their identity are maintained by the Gods[5].

I do not think that Socrates taught a metaphysic of the transcendent, such as J. Burnet and A. E. Taylor thought he did. They attributed to him the whole theory of the Ideas known to us from Plato's classical works. Against this theory stands Aristotle's testimony. On the other hand, a Socrates such as I have described here is testified to us by his contemporaries. This is what follows from that picture.

1. He was not a rationalist of the type of, for instance, John Toland, who held that everything can be explained by reason and, hence, that there are no mysteries either in nature or in religion or in human life.

2. He was not an individualistic rationalist in the sense of K. R. Popper either; that is to say, not a man who did not accept any authority above his own individual reason and would not have acknowledged the existence of a divine and transcendent order in which our moral principles are founded.

3. Neither was he a "humanist" in that modern sense of the term which would mean that he considered man as independent of God, left to himself and detached from any metaphysical background.

4. The Socrates we find in the testimonies of his contemporaries certainly put an enormous trust in reason. He found in the intellect the way and means to educate man to lead a moral life of obedience and service to God. But at the same time he was very well aware of

[1] Plato, *Apology* 41 d.
[2] Plato, *Phaedo* 62 d.
[3] Plato, *Apology* 41 a.
[4] Plato, *Crito* 54 c.
[5] Xenophon, *Memorabilia* IV 4, 25; *Greek Phil.* nr. 223.

the limits of the human intellect. He was intensely interested in individual men and constantly made an appeal to the thinking-power of those with whom he came into contact. As a religious traditionalist he reminds one of Pythagoras who, according to a tradition which I have found to be trustworthy, was also a great educator of the people[1]. Socrates, however, differed from Pythagoras in the method he used. For Pythagoras, besides the work in his School which was a closed community, educated the people of Croton as such, and this he did by repeatedly addressing the whole population, divided according to age and social position into four large sections. Socrates on the other hand, worked by means of personal conversations of a strictly intellectual character, which nonetheless were considered by him as means to lead people to self-reflexion, and by self-reflexion to raise them to a higher moral level. When comparing him with Pythagoras, such as we know the latter from his speeches to the people as they are recorded in Iamblichus' *Life of Pythagoras*, one must conclude that in his religious traditionalism Socrates gave a similar kind of personal character and spiritual depth to the traditional forms as we find them in the speeches of the philosopher of Croton.

---

[1] The arguments for this view are given in my book *Pythagoras and Early Pythagoreanism* (Phil. Texts and Studies 12, Assen 1966).

PLATONICA

CHAPITRE VII

EXAMEN CRITIQUE DE L'INTERPRETATION TRADITIONNELLE DE LA PHILOSOPHIE DE PLATON[1]

Il existe, à ce qu'il me semble, une image pour ainsi dire classique du Platonisme.

Commençons par en déterminer les traits essentiels.

Notre premier point est ce que je voudrais nommer la position métaphysique fondamentale. Platon a accordé aux universaux une valeur ontologique. Le monde suprasensible, constitué ainsi par les Idées (Formes) érigées en hypostases, était pour lui l'exemple éternel, parfait et immuable des choses finies et périssables, imparfaites et toujours changeantes.

Le second point est une conséquence qui en résulte pour la théorie de la connaissance. La connaissance a pour objet l'être éternel et immuable, non l'être transitoire et toujours variable du monde sensible. Or, l'Être éternel n'est atteint que par la pensée pure. Il en résulte que l'homme, s'il veut parvenir à une vraie connaissance, doit se détacher des sens autant que possible et chercher l'être même par la pensée elle-même.

Troisième point: conséquence pour la psychologie et pour l'anthropologie. Le corps est un obstacle pour l'âme qui l'empêche de parvenir à la contemplation du véritable être. Σῶμα σῆμα.

Quatrième point: conséquence pour la manière d'apprécier le monde visible. Le philosophe vit dans le monde visible comme un étranger. Il s'efforce constamment de le fuir autant que possible et de s'élever par l'esprit vers la Réalité éternelle.

Loin de nous de vouloir nier que cette image classique du Platonisme ait son fondement dans l'œuvre littéraire de Platon. Sa base métaphysique est esquissée aussi clairement que possible dans le *Phédon*,

[1] La base de ce chapitre est une conférence faite au Collège de M. Jean Wahl à Paris, 1949. Le texte en a paru dans la *Revue de Métaphysique et de Morale* 1951. Du présent chapitre plusieurs pages ont été écrites récemment pour remplacer des passages qui ne me plaisaient plus.

dans le *Banquet* et dans la *République;* et nous la trouvons encore à la fin du *Philèbe*, dans le *Timée* et même dans les *Lois*. Qu'il me soit permis de rappeler ces choses brièvement.

Dans un passage bien connu du *Phédon*[1], Platon a exposé sa théorie des deux mondes: d'une part le monde visible qui se transforme sans cesse, d'autre part le monde invisible toujours identique à lui-même. Or, c'est une hypothèse nécessaire, nous dit Platon dans le même dialogue[2], que d'admettre l'existence de ce monde invisible: sans elle, il ne voit pas moyen d'expliquer vraiment le monde visible et ses phénomènes.

Auquel de ces deux mondes l'âme appartient-elle? – Et Platon de répondre[3]: l'âme appartient plutôt au monde invisible. Elle est, en tout cas, apparentée à ce monde-là, tandis que le corps appartient au monde visible. Le philosophe s'efforcera donc de détacher son âme autant que possible de toute communication avec le corps; autant qu'il peut, il cherchera l'être éternel avec son âme, – c'est-à-dire, avec sa pensée pure et en soi[4].

Platon nous fait connaître le même fond de sa pensée dans le fameux discours de Diotima au *Banquet*[5]: le vrai amour s'élève du beau concret et particulier à la Beauté elle-même, qui est absolue; qui ne connaît ni devenir, ni périr, ni croissance, ni déclin; qui n'existe pas par intervalles, ni n'existe pour certaines personnes et non pour certaines autres, ni à cet endroit-ci et non à tel autre. La Beauté même n'a pas de forme qu'on saurait percevoir ou toucher à l'aide des sens; elle ne possède ni corps ni couleur. S'il est donné à l'homme de jouir de la contemplation de cette beauté parfaite, – non pas à l'aide des yeux du corps, bien entendu, mais par cette faculté qui permet de contempler le Beau lui-même – si, donc, il est donné à quelque personne de contempler cette Beauté, alors, et alors seulement la vie de l'homme sera digne d'être vécue. Alors aussi, il produira des fruits de vraie vertu, non pas d'une vertu d'apparence, parce qu'il est en contact avec la vraie Réalité[6].

Conformément à ces idées, Platon déclare dans sa *République*[7] que

---

[1] *Ph.*, 79a.
[2] 100a-101e.
[3] *Ph.* 79b et suiv.
[4] *Ib.*, 64d-66a.
[5] *Symp.*, 211bc.
[6] 212a.
[7] *Rép.* V, 479e.

"ceux qui contemplent la multitude des belles choses, mais qui ne voient pas la Beauté en elle-même, et qui ne sont pas capables non plus de suivre une autre personne qui essaie de les conduire à la contemplation de cette Beauté là, et que ceux qui voient la multitude des choses justes, mais non pas la Justice en elle-même", – Platon déclare que tous ceux-là n'ont que *des opinions* sur toutes choses, non de la vraie connaissance. Par contre, ceux qui contemplent constamment «les choses en elles-mêmes», ces choses «qui sont toujours de la même manière et identiques», ceux-là ont la connaissance et non pas des opinions.

C'est alors[1] que suit la définition des philosophes: «ceux qui sont capables d'atteindre à ce qui existe toujours d'une manière immuable». Tous les autres sont comme des aveugles qui ne voient pas la vraie Réalité, et par là même, ils ne sont pas compétents pour gouverner une communauté.

La contemplation de la réalité véritable est donc le but que se propose toute l'éducation des philosophes futurs; et c'est de leur contemplation de l'Être éternel que dépend le salut du monde, de l'individu tout autant que de la communauté.

Voilà ce qu'on pourrait nommer l'apogée du Platonisme classique. La ligne se continue: on retrouvera les mêmes pensées dans les dialogues d'une période ultérieure et même dans ceux de la dernière phase de la pensée de Platon.

Qu'on se rappelle tout d'abord l'intermezzo du *Théétète*. Le mal rôde fatalement autour de la nature mortelle; c'est le monde d'ici-bas qu'il hante toujours. Il faut donc s'évader au plus vite d'ici-bas vers là-haut. Et cette évasion consiste à s'assimiler à Dieu dans la mesure du possible. Or, on s'assimile en devenant juste et saint, tout en possédant l'esprit philosophique[2].

Dans le *Politique*[3], Platon déclare: «Conserver toujours le même état, les mêmes manières d'être et de rester éternellement identique, cela ne convient qu'à ce qu'il y a de plus divin, et la nature corporelle n'est point de cet ordre.»

Il faut se rappeler ici ce passage vers la fin du *Philèbe*[4], un dialogue qui appartient à la dernière phase du Platonisme, où l'auteur a dit encore une fois, et à ce qu'il semble définitivement, son opinion sur la

[1] VI, 484b.
[2] *Th.*, 176a.
[3] 269d.
[4] *Phil.*, 59ab.

possibilité d'une science de la nature, et sur la connaissance en général. Voici ce qu'il dit: «Celui qui s'adonne à l'étude de la nature n'est pas occupé de ce qui est toujours. C'est à ce qui devient, deviendra et devint, qu'un tel homme applique son labeur. Eh bien, saurions-nous affirmer que, des choses pareilles, aucune puisse jamais devenir sûre au sens de la plus exacte vérité, puisqu'aucune d'elles jamais ne fut ni ne sera ni n'est actuellement dans le même état?» – Et l'interlocuteur de répondre: «Comment l'affirmer?» – On conclut que, sur des choses qui n'ont aucune espèce de fermeté, on ne saurait acquérir quoi que ce soit de ferme, et que, par conséquent, aucune science au sens strict du mot ne sera possible à leur sujet.

Quant au *Timée*, avant de commencer son exposé sur la création du monde, l'auteur nous donne toujours la même déclaration de principes métaphysiques[1]. «Tout d'abord il faut», dit-il, «à mon avis, faire la division suivante. Quel est l'être éternel, qui ne naît point, et quel est celui qui naît toujours et n'existe jamais? Le premier est appréhendé par l'intellection et par le raisonnement, car il est constamment identique. Quant au second, il est l'objet de l'opinion jointe à la sensation irraisonnée, car il naît et meurt, mais n'existe jamais réellement.»

Or, le premier, c'est-à-dire l'être éternel et immuable, est l'archétype d'après lequel le monde visible a été formé par le Démiurge, et si notre cosmos est bien ordonné et bon, c'est qu'il a été fait par une intelligence, d'après l'exemple de l'Être parfait et éternel.

Tout cela montre clairement la même position fondamentale. On sera donc à peine surpris de trouver la même théorie métaphysique à l'arrière-fond du dernier grand ouvrage de Platon, les *Lois*. Elle y figure, en effet, dans une des dernières pages[2], où il s'agit d'établir un comité de surveillance qui devra maintenir les lois de la seconde cité de Platon. Pour ceux qui seront membres de ce collège, il faudra évidemment une éducation spéciale. Laquelle? – Platon répond: celle qui dirige l'esprit vers l'Idée, qui, étant une, est à la base des choses multiples et inégales. Car celui-là, en tout cas, sera l'homme de métier et le gardien des qualités exigées, qui n'est pas seulement capable de contempler les choses multiples, mais qui se précipite vers l'Un et sera capable de le connaître. Les yeux fixés sur l'Un, il établira de l'ordre dans toutes les choses concrètes.

Voilà, encore une fois, l'idée fondamentale de toute la philosophie

---
[1] *Tim.*, 27d-28a.
[2] 964e-965c.

de Platon. Loin de nous l'idée de vouloir prétendre que cette interprétation manque de fondement. Ce que nous voulons dire et ce que j'espère démontrer, c'est que: 1º dès les premiers ouvrages, on trouve d'autres aspects du Platonisme à côté de celui que nous venons de décrire; 2º que, dans une phase ultérieure de la pensée de Platon, ces autres éléments se sont accentués davantage, en sorte que l'image traditionnelle du Platonisme s'en trouve plus ou moins modifiée.

Examinons d'abord la thèse métaphysique de l'existence d'une réalité éternelle et immuable, «qui garde toujours la même manière d'être et qui reste éternellement identique à elle-même». Posons la question: cette invariabilité n'exclut-elle pas nécessairement le mouvement? – Et voilà ce que nous trouvons confirmé par Aristote, qui écrit dans le premier livre de sa *Métaphysique*[1]: «Quant au mouvement, si l'on veut que ces déterminations soient mouvement» (par «ces déterminations» il veut dire: l'Excès et le Défaut, ὑπεροχὴ καὶ ἔλλειψις, dont le Grand-et-petit n'est qu'un aspect), – si l'on veut, donc, que l'Excès et le Défaut soient mouvement, il est évident que les Idées seront mues. Sinon, d'où le mouvement est-il venu? C'est l'étude tout entière de la nature qui en est ruinée.»

Il s'agit ici de la doctrine des premiers principes, qui appartient à la dernière phase de la philosophie de Platon. En dehors du témoignage de Platon lui-même dans le *Philèbe* et d'un certain nombre de textes d'Aristote qui sont assez difficiles à expliquer, nous sommes renseignés sur cette doctrine par deux exposés un peu plus amples, dont l'un est fait par Hermodore, élève direct de Platon, et conservé chez Simplicius, tandis que l'autre se trouve dans l'*Adv. Math.* X de Sextus Empiricus. Grâce à ces deux passages, nous pouvons assez bien comprendre comment Aristote peut dire que le Grand-et-petit de Platon, qui n'est qu'un aspect de l'Excès et du Défaut, soit identique au mouvement. C'est que, dans la dernière période de la pensée de Platon, le Grand-et-petit était une qualification de l'Infini (l'apeiron), ce que Platon précise ainsi[1]: «tout ce qui contient en soi un plus ou un moins» (μᾶλλον καὶ ἧττον); c'est-à-dire, comme l'a si bien expliqué M. Robin, *tout ce qui oscille entre deux extrêmes*, un excès et un défaut (ὑπεροχὴ καὶ ἔλλειψις). Comme tel le Grand-et-petit c'est l'instable, l'ἄστατον (d'après Hermodore) qui ne trouve point de repos; enfin, c'est le mouvement. C'est l'opposé de ce qui a trouvé la juste mesure, l'opposé du *métrion* et de *l'ison*, et par là c'est ce qu'on qualifie d'*irrégulier* et

---
[1] A 9, 992b, 7-9 (traduction de J. Tricot).
[2] *Phil.*, 24a-d.

d'*inégal.* Or, Eudème, l'élève d'Aristote, qui a fait une étude spéciale du Platonisme, nous dit[1] que Platon enseignait que *l'inégal et l'irrégulier et le non-être sont identiques au mouvement;* ce qui est, une fois de plus, confirmé par un texte dans les *Physiques* d'Aristote.

Vu les témoignages d'Hermodore et de Sextus, nous avons le droit de conclure – en dépit des protestations de M. Cherniss – que telle a été vraiment la doctrine de Platon[2].

Or, le Grand-et-petit formait avec l'Un les premiers principes auxquels Platon a réduit et les Idées et le monde sensible. Aristote en conclut que, le Grand-et-petit étant mouvement, les Idées qui en dérivent doivent être mobiles. Ce qui serait, d'après son opinion à lui, contraire à la thèse fondamentale du Platonisme.

Il appert néanmoins que Platon lui-même n'en a pas jugé ainsi. Lui-même le premier, et non pas seulement Aristote, s'est posé la question de savoir s'il est possible d'expliquer l'existence d'une multiplicité de choses, en partant de l'hypothèse des Éléates; et ensuite, si l'on peut jamais parvenir à quelque connaissance en partant de cette hypothèse-là. Il y a répondu par la négative. Plusieurs fois, d'abord dans le *Parménide*[3], ensuite dans le *Sophiste*[4], il a démontré l'être du non-être. Il a déterminé le non-être comme *Autre*, et il a introduit le mouvement dans la théorie des Idées[5]. A partir du *Parménide* et du *Sophiste* – M. Wahl l'a bien remarqué dans son *Étude sur le Parménide,* – le monde platonicien des Idées n'est plus l'être rigide des Éléates comme le croyait Aristote. Qu'on se souvienne de cet endroit dans le *Sophiste*[6] où Platon attribue à son παντελῶς ὄν *la pensée et la vie, l'âme* (c'est-a-dire la conscience) et *le mouvement,* puisque, le mouvement manquant, aucune intelligence ni aucune compréhension ne serait possible.

On ne saurait conclure autrement: c'est Platon lui-même qui, en principe, consciemment et explicitement, a vaincu la thèse de Parménide.

On objectera peut-être que, tout de même, Platon n'a pas osé

[1] Ap. Simpl., 431. Cp. Ar., *Phys.* III, 2, 201 b 20.
[2] Voir *infra*, le ch. XII (= *Problems concerning later Platonism* dans *Mnemosyne*, 1949). On trouvera les textes relatifs à cette question dans mon *Greek Philosophy* I, Brill, Leyden (1950), ³1963, ⁴1969.
[3] 161 e - 162 b.
[4] *Soph.*, 257 a-b.
[5] *Ib.*, 249 a et suiv.
[6] 248 e - 249 b.

assumer les conséquences de cette victoire, puisque, à la fin du *Philèbe*, il a rejeté la possibilité d'une véritable science de la nature, et cela en partant toujours de la thèse bien connue des Éléates que, de ce qui change constamment, aucune science n'est possible, faute de stabilité.

Natorp a considéré ledit passage du *Philèbe* comme un retour en arrière – on pourrait même dire comme une récidive. En effet, Platon lui-même, dans ses dialogues d'une période ultérieure, nous donne plus d'une fois des raisons d'admettre qu'il était, en fait, plus «avancé» qu'il ne paraît ici. Par exemple, le mouvement régulier des corps célestes, dont il parle si souvent et avec une admiration si vive, n'est-il pas le résultat d'une participation à ce même principe d'identité qui est Idée, d'après Platon, et base de la connaissance? Ensuite, dire que, par là même, cette partie du monde, tout en se mouvant, porte en soi un principe de stabilité, qui, de lui-même, en garantit le caractère connaissable, serait-ce là une conclusion trop téméraire?

C'est ici, sans doute, que, selon les principes de la philosophie de Platon se présente la possibilité d'une véritable connaissance du monde sensible. Mais le problème est plus compliqué qu'il n'en a l'air. C'est que, pour Platon, le monde des corps célestes était d'un ordre supérieur à notre monde: les astres, tout visibles qu'ils sont, n'étaient nullement pour lui des αἰσθητά tels que les choses périssables d'ici-bas. Il les regardait comme des êtres divins et éternels. Dans un sens il en était encore ainsi pour Aristote: lui, il considérait les corps célestes comme une classe à part, τὰ ἀΐδια τῶν αἰσθητῶν, qui comme tels étaient séparés des αἰσθητά καὶ φθαρτά. Comme *êtres éternels et nécessaires* (ἀΐδια καὶ ἀναγκαῖα) les astres pouvaient être objet d'une science stricte (ἐπιστήμη), ce qui n'était pas possible pour les choses sensibles et concrètes en tant que telles. Ce qu'on peut connaître des choses sensibles, c'était pour Aristote leur aspect intelligible, leur *forme* (εἶδος) qui est leur essence (τὸ τί ἐστιν). Or, pour Platon la Forme était transcendante. Donc, la connaissance des objets physiques était-elle entièrement impossible?

Il semble que non. Mais Platon s'approche de ce problème d'une manière bien différente de celle d'Aristote. Pour Platon, c'est grâce à la contemplation des corps célestes et de leur mouvement régulier que l'homme en arrive à la connaissance du nombre, et c'est par le nombre et par certaines figures géométriques que la structure des choses visibles est déterminée. C'est donc par là que les phénomènes de notre monde deviennent accessibles à notre intellect, – en tout cas *plus ou moins* accessibles. Que pourtant Platon n'a pas osé parler d'une science stricte de la nature, s'explique 1º par les exigences rigoureuses qu'il impose à la connaissance ; 2º par la précarité de la physique de son temps, qui n'était pas suffisamment développée pour satisfaire à ces exigences.

En principe, il est certain que la thèse fondamentale de Parménide a été vaincue par Platon, et que la théorie des Idées postérieure à cette crise n'a forcément plus le caractère parménidien du *Phédon*, du *Banquet* et de la *République*.

Notre contradicteur n'est peut-être pas encore satisfait. Il pourrait dire: Soit, j'accorde que Platon a réfuté en principe la thèse de Parménide, dans son dialogue du même nom et dans son *Sophiste*; – ne reste-t-il pas que, pratiquement, dans ses derniers ouvrages (le *Politique*, le *Philèbe*, le *Timée* et les *Lois*), il garde exactement la même position des problèmes et les mêmes solutions que dans les dialogues antérieurs? Ne trouvons-nous pas toujours dans ces dialogues postérieurs l'opposition fondamentale entre un monde éternel et immuable, toujours identique, et d'autre part le monde des choses visibles, qui naissent et périssent et qui changent constamment? Et n'est-il pas vrai que, de cette position fondamentale, l'auteur tire jusqu'à la fin les mêmes conséquences, tant pour la connaissance humaine que pour la relation entre le corps et l'âme, et finalement pour l'appréciation de la réalité visible?

A cette dernière question, nous répondons par un *non* résolu et énergique. En effet, il y a une distance remarquable entre les idées sur l'homme – corps et âme –, entre l'appréciation du monde visible qu'on trouve dans le *Phédon* ainsi que dans l'intermezzo du *Théétète*, et d'autre part, ce qu'on en trouve dans le *Timée*. Et j'oserais même dire que, bien qu'il ait nié jusqu'au bout la possibilité d'une science de la nature dans le sens rigoureux, Platon a cependant modifié son attitude, quant à la théorie de la connaissance.

Envisageons d'abord les problèmes de l'âme et du cosmos.

1. C'est un principe indiscutable dans tout le Platonisme, y compris la dernière période, que *l'âme est supérieure au corps*. Il s'en suit directement qu'on ne saurait expliquer le monde physique uniquement par la physique, mais que, finalement, ce monde ne s'explique que par ce qui est supérieur, c'est-à-dire par l'esprit et l'âme. Nous connaissons cette conviction de Platon par le *Phédon* (la doctrine des deux mondes, l'âme étant apparentée à l'Invisible, tandis que le corps appartient au visible, et le passage sur l'origine de la théorie des Idées); mais elle est tout aussi ferme et décidée dans le *Timée*. Car, dans ce dialogue,

c'est le Démiurge lui-même qui crée les âmes individuelles; mais, quant à la tâche de fabriquer pour ces âmes des corps, il la confie aux «dieux visibles», c'est-à-dire aux âmes des astres qui ont été créées par lui[1]. Et c'est peut-être dans le dixième livre des *Lois* que la supériorité de l'âme est enseignée avec le plus d'emphase.

On a remarqué à plusieurs reprises que c'est dans le *Phèdre* que Platon a, pour la première fois, défini l'âme comme *ce qui porte en soi-même le principe de son mouvement*[2]. L'âme a, comme telle, une valeur causale, donc explicative, par rapport au monde physique. Voilà le principe qu'on retrouve dans le dixième livre des *Lois*[3], où l'auteur démontre que, en tout cas, une âme doit être cause autant du mal que du bien physique.

On a parfois cru que Platon enseigne ici une autre philosophie qu'auparavant; qu'il a abandonné la théorie des Idées afin de la remplacer par une théorie de l'âme ou d'âmes individuelles[4]. C'est évidemment, une erreur. Le *Timée* nous apprend avec une clarté suffisante que le monde de l'Être immuable est l'archétype du monde qui est créé par le Démiurge et par les dieux visibles (qui sont les âmes des astres). L'âme du monde, ou plutôt les âmes du monde, dont il est question dans le dixième livre des *Lois*[5], sont des êtres créés, qui ont manifestement leur place entre le monde des Idées et le monde visible. On ne saurait en douter. – Mais, s'il en est ainsi, il semble bien qu'il y a une certaine différence avec ce que nous avons trouvé dans le *Phédon* : là, les deux mondes, l'un visible, l'autre invisible, et l'âme qui appartient au dernier, ou qui y est en tout cas apparentée – Platon reste un peu dans le vague; – ici, entre les deux mondes, l'un éternel et immuable, l'autre plein de mouvement et de changement, l'âme qui est la cause du mouvement.

Certes, on peut objecter que, dans le *Phédon* non plus, l'âme n'est pas une Idée. C'est exact. Ce qui est clair et sûr, c'est que l'âme y est tout de même plus près de l'Être éternel et immuable; puisqu'il fallait choisir entre les deux, elle appartient à l'invisible. Si l'on avait inter-

---

[1] *Tim.*, 41 a-d.
[2] *Phèdre*, 245 c - 246 a.
[3] 895 et suiv.
[4] C'est l'opinion de Fr. Solmsen, dans son ouvrage intitulé *Plato's theology* (Ithaca, 1942), et celle de M. Lutoslawsky, d'après un mémoire dans les *Proceedings* du Xe Congrès International de Philosophie, à Amsterdam, 1948, pp. 1076-1080 (malheureusement l'auteur n'a pas eu l'occasion de prononcer ce discours au Congrès).
[5] 896-897.

rogé Platon à ce sujet, il n'aurait sûrement pas affirmé que l'âme est une Idée. Si l'on avait insisté en disant que, dans ce cas, il fallait bien qu'elle fût un être intermédiaire, je crois qu'il l'aurait concédé. Après tout, ce qu'il faut reconnaître, c'est que ce qui était un peu caché et implicite dans le dialogue antérieur, s'est développé en théorie explicite dans les derniers écrits du maître. Or, c'est là précisément ce qu'on nomme une évolution.

Passons au second point. L'âme est, d'après la description du *Phédon*, quelque chose d'absolument supérieur au corps, puisqu'elle est du côté de l'Invisible. Elle est immortelle, tandis que le corps est périssable. Sans doute, il faut donc, en se servant de la terminologie d'Aristote, nommer l'âme une substance, c'est-à-dire un être qui existe par soi, et qui est d'une nature supérieure au corps. – Mais, s'il en est ainsi, la question se pose de savoir s'il est possible que l'âme subisse des influences du corps: ce qui est supérieur peut-il être influencé par l'inférieur? – Saint Augustin a très bien vu[1] qu'à cette question, on ne peut répondre que par la négative.

Or si l'on ouvre le *Timée* dans les dernières pages[2], on fait une découverte assez surprenante. Car ce que nous trouvons ici, ce n'est pas autre chose qu'un exposé assez détaillé *des influences du corps sur l'âme*. La débauche, nous dit Platon, provient en grande partie d'une disposition mauvaise du corps. Pareillement, presque tout ce que l'on met sur le compte de l'impuissance à dominer la volupté, tout ce que l'on reproche aux gens vicieux, on leur en fait grief injustement. C'est, encore une fois, en grande partie d'une disposition maligne du corps que ces vices proviennent. Quant aux douleurs, pareillement, l'âme peut avoir beaucoup de misères par le fait du corps. La mélancolie et la mauvaise humeur, toutes sortes d'audaces et de lâchetés; la mauvaise mémoire et la lenteur d'esprit, c'est encore d'une disposition défavorable du corps qu'ils résultent.

Les remarques qui suivent ne sont pas moins intéressantes. La symétrie la plus souhaitable, voire la plus précieuse, c'est celle du corps et de l'âme. Car, à supposer qu'une âme forte et grande habite un corps trop faible et trop petit, il y a toujours disproportion, et, dans ce cas, «l'animal tout entier» (ὅλον τὸ ζῷον) n'est pas beau. Comment pourrait-il l'être, puisqu'une disproportion existe là où une bonne pro-

---

[1] Voir *De musica*, VI, 8; cf. *Conf.*, X, 6, 9 et *Enarratio* in Ps. CXLVI, éd. Paris altera, Tom. IV, 2, p. 2344 A.
[2] 86 b - 88 c.
[3] 87 e - 88 a.

portion était exigée? Pareillement un corps trop grand est toujours laid, outre qu'il est fatiguant et encombrant pour le sujet qui le porte.

On lit alors: «*De même faut-il en juger pour ce composé de corps et d'âme que nous appelons un vivant.* Si, en lui, l'âme, plus forte que le corps, s'exaspère, elle l'agite violemment et tout entier par le dedans: elle l'emplit de maladies et le consume», etc.

«Le composé de corps et d'âme que nous appelons un vivant». τὸ συναμφότερον, qui s'appelle chez Aristote τὸ σύνολον. Les deux conceptions, toutes voisines qu'elles semblent, ne sont pas les mêmes. C'est que des deux termes, bien qu'ils se rapportent à la même chose, l'une, le συναμφότερον, signifie la cohabitation de deux éléments hétérogènes, tandis que l'autre, le σύνολον, exprime l'union naturelle constituée par ces deux éléments. Pour Platon, dans un sens l'union de l'âme et du corps n'était pas naturelle, puisque les deux parties appartiennent à des ordres différents. Pourtant, il s'agit d'une véritable union, qui même paraît être naturelle en tant qu'elle s'est constituée d'après les lois divines de la Nature. C'est l'Esprit divin qui les inspire, qui a confié à l'âme la tâche de gouverner, de dominer et de conduire un corps matériel qui, sans elle, serait dépourvu de vie, de mouvement et de la faculté rationnelle. Pour Platon, c'est l'intellect qui domine l'être humain. Il *faut* qu'il le domine pour que cet être soit vraiment humain, et il ne *peut* accomplir cette tâche que parce qu'il y a union véritable. Dans cette union, l'âme rationnelle n'est aucunement forcée de perdre son caractère divin: elle le gardera intact si elle se comporte dignement. Alors, après avoir accompli sa tâche ici-bas, elle s'en ira aux régions pures du νοητόν, où elle vivra éternellement sa vie de pur esprit[1]. Par contre, si elle ne se comporte pas dignement, une autre vie et de nouvelles épreuves l'attendent.

Platon rejoint ici les vues de son Socrate dans le *Phédon:* dans le *Timée* ses convictions sur le destin de l'âme ne sont pas changées. Ce qui est différent, c'est son point de vue, c'est les problèmes qu'il se pose; là, il s'agissait de la vie du philosophe, ici de la vie de l'homme en tant que tel, c'est-à-dire des problèmes de l'âme unie à un corps humain. Dans un sens Platon se trouve ici tout près d'Aristote dans le *De anima.* Ce qui est curieux, c'est que le disciple – qui a le nom d'être beaucoup moins «spiritualiste» que le maître – en effet l'était davantage. C'est que, enfin, Aristote met son νοῦς actif tout à fait à part du σύνθετον. Celui-ci, composé de l'âme et du corps, forme une unité

---

[1] *Phédon* 80e-81a, 114c. Dans le *Timée* cp. 41e-42d; 90e-92c.

essentielle dont les deux éléments naissent et périssent ensemble. Chez Platon, l'interpénétration de ces deux éléments, tout différents qu'ils sont, est plus intime et plus complète. C'est pourquoi il est difficile pour l'âme divine – la «partie» supérieure de l'âme – de se maintenir dans son caractère propre, difficile, mais non pas impossible, – tandis que pour Aristote la supériorité du νοῦς est telle que cette faculté purement intellectuelle conçue en substance tout à fait autonome et indépendante, soit entièrement exempte d'influences d'en bas: le νοῦς qui est venu θύραθεν, s'en ira après la mort du σύνθετον humain vers des régions plus élevées.

Dans un sens Aristote dans le *De anima* est tout près du *Timée*, mais après tout, ses solutions sont différentes. Son σύνολον est d'une nature autre que celle du συναμφότερον, et son νοῦς qui est χωριστός par nature, est par là-même plus «séparé» que ne l'était l'âme divine et supérieure chez Platon.

Parfois, on s'est étonné qu'Aristote ait commencé, dans la première période de son travail[1], par suivre la doctrine du *Phédon*, et non, à ce qu'il semblait, les idées sur l'homme qui étaient celles de son maître pendant le temps qu'il passa lui-même dans son École. Il me semble que cette observation n'était pas entièrement dépourvu de fondement. Certes, Aristote était fortement «influencé» par les vues exposées dans le *Timée*, autant par rapport à la cosmologie qu'aux théories physiques, en particulier à celle du devenir. C'est en vue de ces idées, ou plutôt de ces suggestions, que ses propres théories se sont formées. Quant à la théorie de l'âme, il semble bien qu'Aristote s'est orienté tout d'abord au *Phédon*, et qu'il lui a fallu toute une vie avant d'arriver, consciemment et explicitement, à une idée de l'âme et de sa relation au corps non pas identique mais pourtant pareille à celle que Platon avait déjà atteinte dans le *Timée*.

Le fait mérite d'être noté. Il nous offre un parallèle pour cet autre fait que nous avons déjà constaté: à en croire Aristote, le mouvement était exclu du monde platonicien des Idées, tandis que nous savons directement par le *Sophiste* que Platon admet le mouvement comme un des cinq genres les plus élevés, qui appartiennent au monde des Idées. Il semble que, dans les deux cas, le jeune Aristote était complètement fasciné par l'image spirituelle du Platonisme classique. C'est avec ce Platonisme-là qu'il a lutté; il en a triomphé à sa façon, –

---

[1] Qu'on se rappelle le dialogue *Eudème*, écrit par Aristote pendant son séjour à l'Académie, avant le milieu du 4ième siècle.

par une victoire qui, sur presque tous les points essentiels, avait été anticipée par Platon.

2. Après la question de l'âme c'est celle de l'appréciation du monde visible qui requiert notre attention. Ici également, nous nous trouvons devant un dogme fondamental du Platonisme; un dogme qui, du commencement jusqu'à la fin, reste inébranlable: l'opposition d'un monde supérieur et invisible, éternel et immuable, au monde du devenir, visible, variable et transitoire. C'est l'opposition que nous trouvons dans le *Politique*[1] et le *Philèbe*[2], dans le *Timée*[3] et dans les *Lois*[4], aussi bien que dans le *Phédon*, le *Banquet* et la *République*. Or, si l'on ouvre le *Timée* à la page 47 d'H. Etienne, on constatera un changement tout à fait remarquable qui s'est produit dans l'appréciation du monde visible par Platon. Voici ce qu'on y lit[5]:

«De fait, la vue, selon mon raisonnement, a été créée pour être, à notre profit, le principe de la plus grande utilité. Car de tous les discours qu'on peut faire maintenant sur le monde, nul n'aurait oncques pu être tenu, si les hommes n'avaient jamais pu voir, ni les astres, ni le soleil, ni le ciel. Mais dans l'état actuel, ce sont le jour et la nuit, les mois, les périodes régulières des saisons, les équinoxes, les solstices, toutes choses que nous voyons, qui nous ont procuré l'invention du nombre, fourni la connaissance du temps, et permis de spéculer sur la nature de l'univers. Par là, nous nous sommes élevés à une certaine philosophie[6], telle que nul bien plus grand ne fut jamais accordé, ni ne le sera jamais par les dieux à la race des mortels. Voilà, dis-je, le bienfait le plus considérable que nous apportent les yeux; tout ce qu'il y a de bienfaits inférieurs, pourquoi les célébrer? Et quant à ceux-là, si l'on devient aveugle, il faut n'être point philosophe pour verser sur leur perte des larmes inutiles. Pour nous, nous dirons que la cause en vertu de laquelle Dieu a inventé la vision et nous en a fait présent est la suivante et toujours la même. Ayant contemplé les mouvements périodiques de l'intelligence dans le ciel, nous les utiliserons, en les transportant aux mouvements de notre propre pensée, lesquels sont de même nature, mais troublés, alors que les mouvements célestes ne connaissent pas de trouble. Ayant étudié à fond ces mouvements

[1] 269 d.
[2] 59 c.
[3] 27 d -28 a.
[4] XII, 965 bc.
[5] Traduction de A. Rivaud.
[6] ἐπορισάμεθα φιλοσοφίας γένος. Je m'écarte ici de la traduction de Rivaud.

célestes, participant à la rectitude naturelle des raisonnements, imitant les mouvements divins qui ne comportent absolument aucune erreur, nous pourrons stabiliser les nôtres, qui ne cessent point d'errer.

«Pour la voix et l'audition, notre raisonnement sera encore le même: les dieux nous en ont fait présent pour la même cause et en vue de la même fin.»

Voici donc le même Platon – qui a écrit dans le *Phédon* que, pour atteindre à la vérité, il faut que l'âme se détache du corps autant que possible (là, il n'était question des sens que sous l'aspect de l'entrave qu'ils sont pour l'âme), faisant ici l'éloge des sens pour le secours inestimable et indispensable qu'ils nous donnent. Nous reviendrons sur cette question du point de vue de la théorie de la connaissance. Quant à l'appréciation du monde sensible, on objectera peut-être que, dans le passage cité du *Timée*, il ne s'agit pas de la valeur de notre cosmos, qui, d'après un autre passage de ce même dialogue[1], est seul de son espèce. Ce dont il s'agit, c'est du mouvement des corps célestes qu'il a nommés des dieux visibles. – Cette remarque est juste; cependant, il faut se rappeler que notre cosmos, lui aussi, est qualifié par l'auteur de notre dialogue de «dieu créé», dieu «qui devait naître un jour», un ποτὲ ἐσόμενος θεός[2]; être vivant, doué d'âme et d'esprit. Il est impossible de méconnaître que, dans les pages qui précèdent[3], Platon a parlé de ce cosmos et de sa perfection avec un accent nettement religieux. Autant que possible ce monde-ci est semblable à son Créateur: dans sa bonté, le Dieu a voulu que toutes choses fussent bonnes; il a fait du Monde un être vivant, doué d'intelligence et pourvu d'une âme[4], puisque l'exemple éternel, le monde des Idées, est un être vivant[5]. Enfin, l'ayant façonné ainsi, image magnifique des dieux éternels, le Démiurge se réjouit, et, pour le faire ressembler encore davantage à l'archétype éternel, il crée le temps, «image mobile de l'éternité».

Peut-on dire que tout cela n'est que de la mythologie, un jeu de métaphores poétiques, dont la vérité même reste entièrement problématique pour l'auteur? – Certes, Platon était trop exigeant envers ce qu'il appelait *science*, pour offrir les théories du *Timée* au lecteur avec une pareille prétention. Cela n'empêche pas que les images mêmes dont il se sert, nous donnent des indices suffisants pour pouvoir

[1] *Tim.*, 31b.
[2] 34ab.
[3] *Tim.*, 29e-30c; 31b.
[4] 30a-c.
[5] ζῷον ἀΐδιον, 37d.

affirmer certaines vérités. Ce qui est vrai, c'est que, depuis le *Phédon* et la *République*, l'attitude du philosophe envers le monde sensible s'est nettement modifiée. Beaucoup plus que dans la période antérieure, l'intérêt est tourné vers le monde d'ici-bas. C'était le caractère d'imperfection des choses concrètes, comparées à leur exemple éternel, qui était souligné dans les dialogues antérieurs; à présent, c'est la ressemblance, aussi parfaite que possible, qui est accentuée. Dans la période antérieure, c'était la fuite d'ici-bas qui était prêchée aussi radicalement que possible, tandis que maintenant l'homme est averti de conformer sa pensée au cours régulier des corps célestes. C'est donc l'ordre cosmique *visible* qui, dès lors, est devenu pour lui la règle pour l'élévation de l'esprit.

On remarquera peut-être qu'il n'y a point là d'élément nouveau: à quoi, autrement, servirait-il que, dans la *République*, les futurs philosophes dussent s'occuper de mathématiques et d'astronomie pendant dix ans? – Sans doute, a-t-on raison. Pour notre part, nous ne voulons pas prétendre qu'il y ait une différence *absolue* entre le Platon du *Phédon* ou de la *République* et celui du *Timée*. Ce que nous voulons dire, c'est que, chez Platon, une modification s'est accomplie; partant de sa position métaphysique fondamentale, il s'approche de l'homme et du monde, et enfin de la connaissance humaine d'une manière différente d'autrefois.

C'est ce dernier point qui nous reste à démontrer. Qu'on nous permette, avant de passer à ce dernier sujet, de faire une remarque sur un passage du *Politique*[1], qui peut illustrer excellemment sur quel point précis et en quelle mesure un élément nouveau est apparu dans l'appréciation du monde visible chez Platon[2].

«Conserver toujours le même état, les mêmes manières d'être, et rester éternellement identique, cela ne convient qu'à ce qu'il y a de plus éminemment divin, et la nature corporelle n'est pas de cet ordre. Or, l'être que nous appelons Ciel et Monde, tout comblé qu'il ait été de dons bienheureux par celui qui l'engendra, ne laisse point de participer au corps. Il ne saurait donc être entièrement exempt de changement, mais, en revanche, dans la mesure de ses forces, il se meut sur place, du mouvement le plus identique et le plus un qu'il puisse avoir».

Ce passage, lui aussi, ouvre une nouvelle perspective pour la théorie de la connaissance. En ce qui concerne l'appréciation du monde sensible, il me semble qu'elle s'est modifiée plus ou moins depuis le

---
[1] 269 d-e.
[2] Je cite la traduction de A. Diès.

Théétète et le *Parménide*. On a parlé avec enthousiasme d'un «nouveau sentiment pour le monde», *ein neues Weltgefühl*[1], qui serait né avec la transposition de l'allégorie de la caverne par Aristote, dans son dialogue Περὶ φιλοσοφίας. Ce qui est nouveau dans cette transposition, c'est que l'idée d'un exemple transcendant a complètement disparu; c'est notre monde à nous qui est devenu la réalité véritable. L'ordre qu'on y constate était, pour le jeune Aristote, signe de l'existence des Dieux, qui devaient en être les créateurs. Plus tard, cette idée a disparu de son esprit. Dès lors, le monde visible existe en soi. Est-ce là un progrès, par rapport à la vérité? Franchement parlant, je crois que non. Je crois que, chez Aristote, ce qu'on perd est plus important que ce qu'on gagne. Mais le «nouveau sentiment pour le monde», salué avec tant d'enthousiasme par Jaeger dans le Περὶ φιλοσοφίας d'Aristote, il est présent croyons-nous, dans le *Timée* de Platon. Dans cet ouvrage de Platon, le monde visible est apprécié comme un chef d'œuvre de la plus haute perfection. Se servant de la terminologie employée plus tard par Saint Athanase[2], on pourrait dire qu'«une image du Logos», – c'est-à-dire du monde éternel des Idées – a été créée en lui, et que, par conséquent, l'homme qui contemple l'ordre cosmique, y voit, comme dans un miroir, l'image de la Réalité transcendante et invisible.

3. Nous voilà parvenus à notre dernier point: la théorie de la connaissance. Est-ce que, chez Platon, quelque changement s'est accompli dans la théorie de la connaissance depuis sa réfutation de la thèse de Parménide?

Nous avons commencé par constater sur ce point une identité de position quasi fondamentale. La connaissance n'est possible que de ce qui est toujours identique à lui-même, non pas de ce qui change constamment et ne possède aucune stabilité, – voilà la thèse de Platon jusque dans le *Philèbe*, où il a rejeté encore une fois et explicitement la possibilité d'une science de la nature. Puisqu'il en est ainsi, n'est-il pas paradoxal de vouloir prétendre que, depuis le *Théétète* et le *Parménide*, un changement assez important se soit accompli chez Platon dans son attitude envers la question de la connaissance? C'est pourtant là la thèse que nous voulons défendre.

Remarquons dès l'abord qu'un changement de position en métaphysique, telle que l'introduction de l'idée de mouvement et du

---

[1] W. Jaeger, *Aristoteles*, p. 167-168; la traduction anglaise de R. Robinson parle de «a new attitude towards the world» (p. 164).
[2] *Contra Arianos*, Or. II, cc. 79-81.

μὴ ὄν dans la théorie des Idées, crée en principe la possibilité d'un changement dans la théorie de la connaissance. Ensuite, il faut signaler un point de la doctrine de Platon que, d'habitude, on fait trop peu ressortir; c'est que, dans ce système, la perception a eu toujours une fonction positive. N'est-ce pas, selon un passage bien connu du *Phédon*[1], à propos de quelque observation que je me rappelle l'Idée? comme je me rappelle Simmias, quand je vois le portrait de Simmias; ou même à propos de choses tout à fait différentes, par exemple, je me rappelle Simmias, quand je vois l'habit de Simmias. C'est cette même fonction positive de la perception qui est confirmée explicitement dans le *Théétète:* ce ne sont point les sens qui perçoivent, nous dit l'auteur[2], c'est l'âme qui perçoit par le moyen des sens. Et ce n'est point dans les impressions que réside la science, mais dans le raisonnement sur les impressions. Il est vrai que l'auteur poursuit: «Car l'être et la vérité, ici, ce semble-t-il, se laissent atteindre, et là, c'est impossible». Cela ne doit pas, tout de même, nous faire fermer les yeux sur le fait que c'est sur les impressions que le raisonnement s'exerce. Qu'est-ce à dire sinon que la sensation est le point de départ, nécessaire et indispensable, de toute connaissance humaine?

Il existe pourtant, semble-t-il, une certaine distance entre le point de vue de Platon dans le *Phédon* et celui du *Théétète*. Dans le *Phédon*, les sens sont considérés essentiellement comme une entrave pour l'âme qui veut atteindre à la connaissance de la vérité, tandis que, dans le *Théétète*, ils sont appréciés plutôt positivement, comme un moyen pour faire parvenir l'âme à la connaissance de la vérité.

L'ultime problème demeure: l'objet de la connaissance, pour Platon, peut-il être jamais le monde sensible? Vu le passage précité du Philèbe[3], ne faut-il pas répondre à cette question que, pour Platon, l'objet de la connaissance ne saurait être que le monde intelligible, qui est transcendant?

Telle est la question décisive. Pourrait-on répondre que, dans un passage précité du *Politique*[4], Platon ait reconnu un élément de stabilité dans le monde sensible? Le Ciel *et le Monde*, y dit-il, puisqu'ils participent au corps, ne sauraient être entièrement exempts de changement. Ils ont néanmoins autant de stabilité que possible: ils se meuvent sur place, et de la même manière, par une seule sorte de mouvement. –

---

[1] 73e-75b.
[2] *Th.*, 184b-186d.
[3] 59a-c.
[4] 269de.

S'il en est ainsi, l'argument par lequel Platon a rejeté la possibilité de la connaissance du monde sensible dans le *Philèbe*, d'après ce qu'il semble n'existe plus: dès qu'il y a de la stabilité, ce monde est connaissable, et dans la même mesure. –

Voilà ce qui est bien séduisant pour un lecteur moderne. Mais – il ne faut toujours pas oublier que le cosmos dont il s'agit ici, c'est le monde des corps célestes, c'est l'univers dans son ensemble, et que cet univers, bien que visible pour nous à un certain degré, pour Platon n'était pas du même niveau que notre monde sensible: pour lui, il était d'un ordre supérieur, divin et éternel.

Quand même on ne saurait nier que le monde des astres forme pour ainsi dire un intermédiaire entre le pur Intelligible et les αἰσθητά: de la façon que nous avons décrite ce monde supérieur par ses mouvements réguliers nous procure la connaissance du nombre et par là nous offre une voie d'accès à une certaine mesure de connaissance de notre monde visible.

Voilà ce qu'il faut conclure. C'est un résultat modeste, mais tout de même pas négligeable. Qu'on relise la page du *Timée* sur la fonction de la vue. On y trouve constaté en mots directs que «ce sont le jour et la nuit, les mois, les périodes régulières des saisons, les équinoxes, les solstices, toutes choses que nous voyons, *qui nous ont conduits à l'invention du nombre*, qui nous ont fourni *la connaissance du temps*, et enfin, qui nous ont permis de faire *des recherches sur la nature de l'univers*»[1].

Sans doute, cette περὶ τῆς τοῦ παντὸς φύσεως ζήτησις s'exerce-t-elle au moyen de la connaissance du nombre. N'est-ce pas cela même qui nous est dit au début du *Philèbe*, qu'il ne faut pas passer directement de l'Un à l'infini, mais que, ce dont il s'agit, c'est la détermination précise des degrés intermédiaires? Or, le «genre mixte», entre l'Un et l'Infini, c'est, d'après l'auteur du dialogue le monde visible.

Ce qui importe ici, c'est encore *la troisième hypothèse du Parménide*, si l'on veut s'en tenir à la dénomination employée par M. Wahl. Il s'agit de la troisième déduction, où l'on tire de l'hypothèse ἕν εἰ ἔστιν les conséquences pour «l'autre», c'est-à-dire pour le monde des choses

---

[1] Rivaud traduit: «qui nous ont permis de *spéculer* sur la nature de l'univers». Nous préférons un autre terme pour qualifier cette περὶ τῆς τοῦ παντὸς φύσεως ζήτησις, parce que, même si l'on a raison de dire que, pour Platon, il s'agissait bien d'une philosophie spéculative sur la nature de l'univers, le principe de l'application du nombre aux étages intermédiaires entre l'un et l'apeiron donne au moins la perspective d'une physique à l'aide des mathématiques.

multiples, ce qui est le monde visible, en ne prenant pas l'idée de l'Un dans le sens absolu. C'est dans ce cas que la possibilité de toute sorte de combinaisons de notions s'ouvre, et par là la possibilité d'un certain travail d'intellection et de connaissance.

Finalement, il y a le terrain de la morale et de la société humaine qui appartient au domaine de la connaissance humaine, prise dans le sens large d'expérience. On a remarqué que l'*Ethique à Nicomaque* et les *Politiká* d'Aristote se distinguent par un esprit largement ouvert à la pratique de l'expérience humaine. W. Jaeger[1] mentionne comme une chose nouvelle l'étude historique sur cent cinquante-huit *politeiai*, qui formait le fondement des *Politikà*. Mais on a tort d'opposer la morale du *Gorgias* et de la *République* à celle de l'*Ethique à Nicomaque*, et tout autant d'opposer la méthode de traiter les questions sociales qu'on trouve dans la *République* à celle des *Politikà*. C'est que, dans les deux cas, il y a un degré intermédiaire: dans la morale, c'est le *Philèbe*, dans la science politique, ce sont les *Lois*. Or, dans le *Philèbe*, Platon a cédé un peu de sa position antérieure dans la question de l'ἡδονή: l'ayant rejeté de toutes ses forces dans son *Gorgias* et dans la *République*, il a refondu ses idées plus tard, et a fini par céder une certaine place légitime au plaisir dans la meilleure vie qui existe pour l'homme et qu'il appela la vie mixte. Sans doute, il a montré par là un esprit très ouvert à un point de vue entièrement opposé au sien: l'argumentation d'Eudoxe de Cnide en faveur de l'ἡδονή. Nous connaissons l'argument d'Eudoxe par Aristote, dans le dixième livre de son *Éthique à Nicomaque*: tout être vivant cherche le plaisir par nature et instinctivement, tandis qu'il évite son contraire. Il faut donc bien que le plaisir soit un bien, et même le bien supérieur à tous les autres. – Certes, Platon n'accepte pas cette thèse-là. Mais le fait que la théorie d'Eudoxe l'a forcé à refondre ses propres idées sur le plaisir, est significatif pour l'esprit même de la pensée de Platon dans sa dernière phase: ce n'est pas là le dogmatisme clos que plusieurs auteurs récents supposent. C'est plutôt une philosophie de plus en plus ouverte à l'expérience humaine, morale et sociale.

Le dernier grand ouvrage de Platon, les *Lois*, est un témoignage indiscutable de ce même esprit: Aristote, certainement, n'était pas le premier à faire une étude historique des législations existantes. Sur cette voie, Platon l'a précédé: c'est par une semblable étude que Platon a préparé ses *Lois*, ouvrage fait pour la pratique et qui a porté

---

[1] *Aristoteles*, pp. 264 et suiv.; 339-340 et 402.

des fruits pour la vie pratique pendant l'époque de l'hellénisme[1]. Méthodiquement, le dernier dialogue de Platon prend une position intermédiaire entre la *République* et les *Politikà* d'Aristote.

Ce ne sont là que quelques indications. Notons le fait que, dans la dernière période de sa vie, Platon était plutôt tourné vers l'expérience. Ce fait nous paraît indiscutable. En ce qui concerne la théorie, il me semble qu'il faut constater que Platon était plus avancé qu'il n'en a l'air dans le passage plusieurs fois cité de la fin du *Philèbe*. A. Mansion, dans son excellente *Introduction à la Physique aristotélicienne*, a parlé du passage en question comme du dernier mot de Platon sur la possibilité d'une science de la nature. Il a exposé que Platon est allé aussi loin que possible de son point de départ métaphysique: il n'aurait pu admettre la possibilité d'une science du monde visible au sens strict sans rejeter la base même de sa philosophie, la théorie des Idées.

Dans un sens Mansion avait raison: l'objet de la connaissance, prise au sens strict du terme ἐπιστήμη, c'était le νοητόν, et le νοητόν était transcendant. Et pourtant, ce n'est pas là la seule chose à dire. Il y a, en effet, pour Platon une voie d'accès à une certaine mesure de connaissance du monde sensible. Ce n'est pas une voie directe, mais c'est une voie réelle et praticable. Elle prenait son point de départ dans l'observation des mouvements célestes par le moyen des yeux. Ainsi, elle présupposait le corps humain et la perception.

Tout ceci prouve que Platon, dans la dernière phase de sa pensée, se rapproche davantage d'Aristote qu'on ne le croit d'habitude. Sa doctrine de l'homme et du cosmos, sa théorie de la connaissance même, paraissent, dans la dernière période de sa pensée, être assez proches de celles qu'on trouve plus tard chez le disciple qui a rejeté la théorie des Idées. Mais sur tous les points mentionnés il y a des différences entre les positions des deux philosophes. Or, ce qu'il y a là de plus intéressant, c'est que dans ces différences-mêmes c'est Platon qui nous paraît le plus «moderne». Dans ses vues de l'homme incarné c'est lui qui nous a paru moins «spiritualiste» qu'il n'en a le nom, – moins spiritualiste, en somme, que l'auteur du *De anima*. Quant à la connaissance du monde visible, il nous faut constater que la voie indirecte de Platon – celle qui s'approche des phénomènes visibles par l'intermédiaire du nombre et des figures géométriques – est en somme bien plus près de la science moderne que celle d'Aristote qui, faisant abstraction de la matière,

---

[1] Voir Burnet, *Greek Philosophy*, vol. I, p. 304; Glenn R. Morrow, *Plato's Cretan City*, Princeton 1960, p. 5s. Voir aussi l'introduction de M. L. Grenet à l'édition Budé des *Lois*, vol. I, Paris 1951.

prétend connaître les choses en saisissant leur «forme» ou essence qualitative par un acte direct de l'intelligence.

En métaphysique, bien entendu, la doctrine d'Aristote se sépare nettement de celle de Platon. Mais c'est toujours un fait assez significatif que la métaphysique chrétienne de Saint Thomas d'Aquin, bien que son auteur s'inspire d'Aristote dans presque tout son système, n'ait su que rétablir les Idées de Platon dans leur caractère d'archétypes transcendants qui se trouvent dans le Logos divin.

En suivant l'évolution de la pensée grecque dans l'Antiquité, il nous faut remarquer, pour conclure notre exposé, que le Platon du *Timée* n'est pas tellement éloigné de l'idée de Loi cosmique (κοινὸς νόμος) des Stoïciens malgré l'hypothèse platonicienne des Idées transcendantes.

CHAPITRE VIII

PLATON A-T-IL OU N'A-T-IL PAS INTRODUIT LE MOUVEMENT DANS SON MONDE INTELLIGIBLE ?[1]

(Critique des interprétations modernes de Soph. 249a et de Tim. 31b)

Depuis que Mgr. A. Diès, dans son édition du *Sophiste* (1925), a proposé de traduire le παντελῶς ὄν de *Soph.* 249a par la formule de *l'être universel* et qu'il a expliqué cette formule en disant que «l'être en sa plénitude est *la somme de toutes les formes ou espèces de l'être*»[2], il semble bien que cette interprétation a été acceptée assez généralement: Cornford l'a adoptée dans son Plato's *Theory of Knowledge*[3], et finalement on la retrouve dans l'ouvrage important de Sir David Ross[4] qui a repris l'interprétation de Cornford d'un ton bien catégorique. On pourrait avoir l'impression que, à propos de ce texte si important pour comprendre le sens de la théorie des Idées dans la dernière phase de la pensée de son auteur, un *consensus* s'est établi qui repose sur une base solide.

C'est encore Mgr. Diès qui, parallèlement à son interprétation de *Soph.* 249a, interprète le παντελὲς ζῷον de *Tim.* 31b par: *le Vivant en sa plénitude*, ce qui veut dire: *la somme de tous les vivants intelligibles*. Et sur ce point encore il est suivi par Cornford[5], par M. Harold Cherniss[6] et par Sir David Ross[7]. En effet, l'interprétation des deux textes est intimement liée: dès qu'on explique le παντελὲς ζῷον du *Timée* non comme l'idée de *Vivant* mais comme *le Monde intelligible* dans son ensemble, conçu comme un Être vivant, doué d'une Âme et de la faculté de penser (*Nous*), une autre interprétation du παντελῶς ὄν du *Sophiste* devient possible, sinon nécessaire. D'autre part, dès qu'on

---
[1] Le présent chapitre reproduit ma contribution au Congrès International de Bruxelles, 1953 (Actes, vol. XII, pp. 61-67). J'ai repris le problème dont il s'agit dans le ch. IX de ce volume.
[2] Platon, *Oeuvres Complètes*, VIII 3, Notice p. 289.
[3] London, 1935, p. 244-247.
[4] *Plato's Theory of Ideas*, Oxford 1951, p. 44, 108-111.
[5] *Plato's Cosmology*, London 1937, p. 39-42.
[6] *Aristotle's criticism of Plato and the Academy*, Baltimore 1944, App. IX.
[7] O.c., p. 212.

admet que le παντελῶς ὄν du *Sophiste* signifie *le Monde intelligible*, vu dans son ensemble comme *un Vivant*, doué d'âme et de pensée, voilà qu'une autre interprétation du παντελὲς ζῷον du *Timée* se présente: comme modèle du monde sensible ce sera, non plus une seule Idée, celle du Vivant qui contient en soi tous les vivants intelligibles, mais plutôt *l'ensemble des Idées*, formant *le Monde Intelligible*, vu comme un Ζῷον, doué de vie, d'âme et de pensée.

Voici les raisons pour lesquelles la plupart des interprètes modernes ont adopté l'explication proposée par Mgr. Diès dans son édition de 1925.

1. Il est impossible que Platon ait introduit le mouvement dans son monde Intelligible, l'immutabilité des Idées restant la condition première et indispensable de toute la théorie des Idées: c'est par elle seule qu'il peut expliquer la possibilité de la connaissance et de toute compréhension. (Cornford: «there can be no intelligence without unchanging objects».)

2. Platon ne parle jamais de ses Idées comme d'activités conscientes, de forces vivantes, d'esprits. (Cornford: «The Forms are never represented as living and thinking beings».)

3. Quand donc Platon dit (*Soph.* 249d) que τὸ ὄν τε καὶ τὸ πᾶν comprend les deux: ὅσα ἀκίνητα καὶ κεκινημένα, il faut en conclure que *non seulement les Idées* («tout ce qui est immobile») *méritent le prédicat d'être, mais aussi tout ce qui se meut.*

Or, il me semble que cette conclusion n'est pas impeccable, et cela pour deux raisons. (1) Si l'on entend par tout ce qui se meut: *le monde visible*, les mêmes textes qui s'opposent à admettre que Platon ait introduit le mouvement dans son monde des Idées sont là pour nous empêcher absolument de dire qu'il ait voulu attribuer l'être au monde des γιγνόμενα qui, d'après *Tim.* 27d-28a et *Phil.* 59a-c, changent toujours, naissent et périssent, ὄντως δὲ οὐδέποτε ὄν(τα). (2) Si, par conséquent, la formule de ὅσα κεκινημένα ne signifie pas le monde visible, c'est-à-dire *les corps* et tout ce qui est corporel, il nous restent deux possibilités: ou bien il a voulu indiquer par cette formule *l'âme et la pensée*, en les regardant comme un μεταξύ entre le monde visible et celui des Idées; ou bien il a en effet, dans un certain sens, voulu introduire le mouvement dans son Monde intelligible, mais d'une telle façon que cela ne détruise pas l'immutabilité des Idées.

Interrogeons d'abord ceux qui, parmi les interprètes modernes, ont expliqué le παντελῶς ὄν de *Soph.* 249a comme l'être universel. Ce qu'ils ont voulu dire par cette formule, c'est en tout cas que, dans ce passage du *Sophiste*, Platon a élargi son idée d'être. En y admettant le monde corporel? – A première vue, je ne trouve cette thèse ni chez Mgr. Diès dans sa *Notice* de 1925, ni chez Cornford. Il me semble plutôt qu'ils ont voulu l'éviter. Le premier dit[1], en citant Brochard: «*le mouvement, l'intelligence, l'âme et la pensée* ne sont pas exclus de l'être total». L'autre[2]: «The world of real being, in fact, does not consist solely of the unchanging Forms, ...but must contain as well *life, soul, intelligence and such change as they imply*».

Cependant, en examinant la question de plus près, on trouvera que Mgr. Diès, en tout cas, n'a pas évité l'écueil signalé ci-dessus: selon lui, c'est bien au monde visible que, dans son *Sophiste*, Platon a voulu attribuer l'être. Dans sa thèse en 1909[3], Diès a commencé par distinguer l'οὐσία (qui signifie les Idées) du παντελῶς ὄν qui, d'après lui, signifie le Monde visible, être animé d'après le *Philèbe* et le *Timée*. En 1925 Diès écrit[4]: «J'avais le tort en 1909 (*Définition de l'Etre*, p. 87 et n. 215), de vouloir distinguer le παντελῶς ὄν de cette totalité de l'être et de n'y voir que le monde animé et intelligent du *Philèbe* et du *Timée*». Or, cela ne veut pas dire qu'il abandonne complètement son interprétation antérieure; cela signifie seulement qu'il la complète: loin de nier que le monde visible appartienne au παντελῶς ὄν, il ajoute simplement que les Idées y appartiennent aussi.

Dans ce cas, donc, c'est bien le monde corporel qui est devenu un ὄν. C'est tout à fait l'avis de Sir David Ross qui, à la fin de son interprétation de notre passage du *Sophiste*, déclare en termes clairs[5]: «Finally, summing up the argument, he says that reality must include all things immovable and movable; the immovable Forms which alone the Friends of Forms admit to be real, *the movable bodies which alone the materialists admit to be real*, and the souls which have «movements of their own». »

Une telle interprétation pourrait nous sembler évidente à nous autres, lecteurs modernes qui sommes habitués à regarder le monde visible comme une réalité indubitable. Il en était autrement de Platon, qui, jusque dans ses derniers écrits, a toujours opposé les γιγνόμενα aux

---

[1] *Notice*, p. 289, n.
[2] *Plato's Theory of Knowledge*, p. 245.
[3] *La définition de l'Etre et la nature des Idées dans le Sophiste de Platon*.
[4] *Notice*, p. 289, n.
[5] *Plato's Theory of Ideas*, p. 111.

ὄντα et s'est refusé absolument à appeler ὄν ce qui change et, comme tel, ne possède aucune fermeté[1].

Quant à Cornford, il me semble qu'il a voulu éviter cette conclusion en déclarant que l'espèce de mouvement à laquelle Platon, dans son *Sophiste*, a voulu attribuer la réalité, c'est *le mouvement spirituel*: «the real includes spiritual motion, as well as the unchanging Forms» (p. 247). Sans doute, il a raison. La seule question qui se pose alors, c'est de savoir si «le mouvement spirituel» auquel Platon a pensé ici, c'est celui de l'Âme du Monde et de l'âme humaine, formant une espèce de μεταξύ entre les Idées et l'ordre du corporel, – ou, d'autre part, si c'est dans son Monde intelligible-même que Platon a admis ce mouvement. Cornford, sans doute, a exclu la dernière possibilité, croyant qu'une telle conception est incompatible avec l'immutabilité des Idées. Quant à moi, je n'en suis pas sûre. Et cela pour les raisons suivantes:

a. *Il est certain qu'il a admis un noûs transcendant.*

b. *Il est du moins probable que, en rapport avec ce noûs transcendant, il a parlé d'une âme, l'une et l'autre étant pour lui inséparablement liés.*

Le premier point (a) a été bien établi par M. R. Hackforth, dans un article court, mais important[2]. Il nous renvoie à *Phil.* 23c-30e: dans ce passage la Cause du mélange est un Noûs, indubitablement distingué de celui du monde; et je crois qu'il a eu raison de rapprocher ce texte de *Tim.* 29a, où le Démiurge est appelé ὁ ἄριστος τῶν αἰτιῶν.

---

[1] Voir toujours *Tim.* 27d-28a et *Phil.* 59a-c, cité sous (I). N. R. Murphy, dans son *Interpretation of Plato's Republic*, Oxford 1951, s'efforce de démontrer que Platon n'a pas admis des «degrés d'Etre», qu'il n'a jamais regardé les objets naturels comme non-réels et que la «non-réalité» chez lui est une question d'opinions fausses de notre part, non d'un certain défaut de la part des objets (voir les pages 126-129, 150, 200). Je crains que M. Murphy ne se trompe assez gravement. Ce qui est vrai, c'est que Platon attribue *un certain degré* de réalité aux objets naturels, en tant qu'ils participent aux Idées. Et si l'on n'est pas content de cela, il faut dire, comme M. Ross l'a dit (*Plato's Theory of Ideas*, p. 39): «from now on he (Plato) is committed, until in the *Sophistes* he sees a better way, to a false and dangerous disparagement of all particulars, in the supposed interest of Forms» – «from now on» signifiant que, selon M. Ross, Platon a commencé par parler de la relation des Idées aux choses concrètes comme d'une simple relation d'universel au particulier, n'impliquant aucun «disparagement» du dernier, et que ce n'est que plus tard que, par la terminologie de «ressemblance», l'idée d'un défaut des «particuliers» s'est introduite. La question qui m'occupe ici, c'est de savoir en quel sens Platon *a vu un meilleur chemin* dans le *Sophiste*. Qu'il n'a pas choisi le chemin de M. Ross, c'est clair par les textes cités ci-dessus. Il l'a même rejeté avec toute son énergie.

[2] *Plato's Theism*, in Class. Quarterly 1936, p. 4-9.

En Hollande, M. H. J. M. Loenen[1] s'est prononcé pour la thèse que Platon n'a pas admis l'existence d'un Noûs transcendant, parce que ce serait là «un dédoublement inutile»: c'est le noûs du Monde visible qui exerce sa providence sur notre cosmos. Point n'est besoin d'admettre, en outre, un Noûs transcendant; et même il est impossible de l'admettre, parce que, d'après Platon[2], le noûs n'existe que dans une âme, tandis que l'âme est toujours liée à un corps.

Quant au premier argument, il se comprend fort bien que pour M. Loenen le noûs immanent suffit pour expliquer l'ordre cosmique; mais, encore une fois, pour Platon il n'en était pas ainsi. Car, pour lui, c'est le Démiurge qui a formé l'Âme du monde, Âme raisonnable, douée d'un noûs. Or, le Démiurge comment pourrait-il former une Âme raisonnable, comment créer un système d'*ordre*, s'Il n'était pas lui-même un Être rationnel? Pour Platon, c'était complètement exclu. Selon lui, l'existence d'un noûs immanent présuppose un Noûs transcendant. M. Loenen a donc tort de vouloir identifier le Démiurge au premier Principe ineffable et surrationnel et de nier l'existence d'un Noûs dans l'ordre intelligible de Platon. D'ailleurs, des textes comme *Soph.* 265c et *Polit.* 273ab s'y opposent.

Cependant, le deuxième argument de M. Loenen mérite notre attention: c'est que Platon dit à plusieurs reprises que le noûs ne peut exister que dans une âme, tandis que l'âme est toujours liée à un corps. Or, la dernière partie de cette assertion repose sur une erreur: Platon ne dit nulle part que l'âme ne saurait exister que dans un corps. Tout ce qu'il a dit (*Tim.* 30b) c'est que le Démiurge a mis l'Intellect dans l'âme et l'âme dans le corps, parce qu'il s'est aperçu que «de choses visibles dans leur nature, ne pourrait jamais sortir un Tout dépourvu d'intelligence qui fût plus beau qu'un Tout intelligent».

Il n'en suit pas, certainement, que l'âme et le noûs ne puissent subsister que dans un corps. Loin de là, le *Timée* exclut même nettement cette thèse. Car le Démiurge, voulant façonner le monde d'une telle manière qu'il fût une œuvre aussi parfaite que possible, le forma d'après un Modèle éternel. Or, comme le cosmos formé d'après ce Modèle est un vivant, doué d'âme et de noûs, il faut bien admettre que, en tout cas, le Modèle lui-même est un vivant qui, de quelque façon supérieure, possède – peut-être faut-il dire: est – une Âme et un Intellect.

---

[1] *De Nous in het systeem van Plato's philosophie.* (Thèse de l'Université d'Amsterdam, 1951).
[2] *Soph.* 249a, *Phil.* 30c, *Tim.* 30b, 37c, 46d.

Ici deux questions se posent.

I. Ayant posé la question: «A la ressemblance de quoi entre les vivants l'Ordonnateur a-t-il ordonné le monde?» (30c), Platon a répondu: «Pas, en tout cas, à la ressemblance d'un être concret, parce que ceux-là sont tous imparfaits; mais, ce dont font partie tous les autres vivants, soit considérés isolément, soit pris ensemble, posons que c'est à cela qu'il doit ressembler le plus.» – Quelle est l'Idée dont font partie tous les autres vivants (sc. intelligibles)? On a répondu: c'est l'αὐτόζῳον, le Vivant en soi.

Si je veux quand même défendre que, à cet endroit, il ne s'agit pas d'une seule Idée, mais de l'ensemble des Idées, nommé le cosmos intelligible, envisagé comme un Tout, vivant et intelligent, c'est que la logique de toute la conception de Platon l'exige: s'il y a un cosmos, c'est-à-dire un système d'ordre, c'est que la multiplicité (sc. des différentes Idées) est gouvernée par des suprêmes Principes d'ordre. Or, nous savons[1] que Platon a considéré comme tels les Nombres et les Figures idéales. C'est donc là que nous nous trouvons en réfléchissant sur le Noûs du Cosmos Intelligible.

II. Voici l'autre question: Peut-on dire que, pour Platon, le Cosmos Intelligible était *un Vivant, douée d'Âme et d'Intellect*? N'est-ce pas plutôt que ce que nous nommons (en termes platoniciens, d'ailleurs) le Cosmos Intelligible *est*, par sa nature même, un Noûs transcendant et qu'il ne convient pas de parler, par rapport à ces hautes régions d'être, de ψυχή? – Tel était, en effet, l'avis de M. Hackforth dans l'article cité plus haut: il croit que, dans les cinq passages où Platon dit que le noûs ne peut exister que dans une âme, il s'agit toujours d'un cosmos qui *possède* un noûs, non de *ce que c'est que le Noûs en lui-même;* et donc qu'on n'a pas le droit de conclure de ces passages que le Noûs *qui est la Cause* et *qui est Dieu* existe dans une âme.

Diès, *La Définition de l'Être*, n. 280, p. 80, est incliné au même avis: «L'âme ne peut habiter, semble-t-il, que les existences concrètes et visibles», dit-il en nous renvoyant à *Tim.* 30b. Mais, comme nous l'avons remarqué, de cet endroit on ne saurait tirer cette conclusion. D'autre part, que, d'après Platon, le noûs soit toujours dans une âme, voilà ce qui me semble bien difficile à nier. En effet, ceux qui le font, le font malgré les cinq textes cités plus haut, et parce qu'il partent d'une certaine théorie préétablie. Moi, pour ma part, j'aimerais avancer les points suivants:

[1] Voir les textes dans mon *Greek philosophy* I, le paragraphe sur les Idées Nombres, spécialement les numéros 372, 373.

1. Dans *Soph.* 249a, le sens naturel du παντελῶς ὄν est toujours celui qu'on y a trouvé assez généralement avant la Thèse de M. Diès: c'est de l'Intelligible que parlaient les Amis des Idées, c'est donc à ce même Intelligible que Platon dit qu'on ne saurait refuser la vie et le mouvement, l'âme et l'intellect.

2. En traduisant le terme παντελῶς ὄν par *l'Être absolu* ou l'Être parfait, on suit l'usage général de la langue grecque et spécialement celui de Platon[1], tandis que la traduction d'*Être universel* ou de *la somme totale de l'être* présuppose une signification extensive du mot παντελῶς que, de fait, cet adverbe ne possède guère.

3. En attribuant ainsi une espèce de mouvement – bien entendu, un mouvement spirituel – au Monde intelligible, Platon n'a ni représenté les Idées individuelles comme des êtres vivants qui seraient une espèce d'Esprits, ni détruit le caractère d'immutabilité des Idées.

4. Si l'on trouve cette conception trop étrange pour être acceptée, il faut qu'on se rappelle l'idée chrétienne de Dieu telle qu'on la trouve p.e. chez S. Thomas d'Aquin: là aussi on admet que l'Esprit divin est immuable, que cet Esprit contient des Idées immuables tout comme les Idées platoniciennes, et néanmoins on attribue à Dieu et la Pensée et la Volonté, donc le «mouvement spirituel» qu'elles impliquent.

Qu'on juge de cette conception comme on veut, – ce qui me semble certain, c'est qu'il faut interpréter la théorie des Idées de Platon, du moins depuis le *Sophiste*, dans le sens indiqué ici. Ce faisant, on suivra essentiellement la trace de Léon Robin.

---

[1] Cp. *Rép.* V 477a, *Soph.* 245a.

CHAPITRE IX

SOME CONTROVERSIAL POINTS OF PLATO INTERPRETATION RECONSIDERED[1]

It is certainly a widely held view that nothing like a "hierarchy of being" was taught by Plato. I place the term "hierarchy of being" between quotation marks, because it is an almost technical expression, used with reference to the view of reality held by Plotinus and those who followed him. With reference to Plotinus the meaning of the term is indeed quite clear. Now, since the days of Zeller and Praechter all of us have learned to start with the idea that the theory of the three hypostases, though it may have been foreshadowed in the preceding centuries, was essentially a new development. In Plato, so we thought, things were different. First, you could not say that for him all Being sprang from one Principle which itself was beyond being and intelligence. Next, though of course Plato had his two world-theory, you could not say that he clearly taught a hierarchical order of three levels of reality. Nor did he conceive of the intelligible world (τὸ νοητόν or τὰ νοητά) as an Intellect (νοῦς), from which the Soul originated, which in its turn is the cause of the material world.

Obviously all this has not primarily to do with Plotinus. It has to do with Plato, and I wish to approach it entirely from that angle. My question is: does the underlying Plato-interpretation hold good or not?

I. Let us begin by considering the first point involved in the above statement and ask: *What about the ἀγαθόν in Rep. VI* 508c-509c? Is this actually a principle from which all being springs, while it is itself above Being and intellectual understanding?

To this question one answer only can be given, for Plato's text is quite explicit: it says, in fact, that the Good is cause both of "knowledge" and of "truth", ἐπιστήμη being the human knowledge of intelligible Being, and ἀλήθεια its object, which is intelligible Being

[1] This chapter was written recently, June 1969.

itself. This is very carefully distinguished from its cause, the ἀγαθόν. It is *not separated* from it, as if there were no connection; but it is definitely distinguished from it, in the same way as in the visible world the sun, which is cause both of the light through which we see and of our faculty of seeing, is not identical with either, though they do resemble it. Moreover, the sun is for the visible things not only the cause that they are seen, but also of their existence, of their coming into being and their growth, while it does not come into being itself. Likewise in the intelligible order the Good is cause both of our knowledge of intelligible Being and of its Being itself, while the Good itself is beyond Being, surpassing it in dignity and power.

This is clear language. Can it be argued against this that, nonetheless, the Good is introduced as ἡ τοῦ ἀγαθοῦ ἰδέα (508e2), and ergo is something entirely different from Plotinus' ἕν which is no "form"? – This would be nothing else than going against Plato's own explicit words: while he repeatedly explains that "the Good" – at first introduced by him as ἡ τοῦ ἀγαθοῦ ἰδέα – does *not* belong to intelligible Being but surpasses it, it is urging against him: "But by calling it yourself an *idea*, you classed it in fact as an *intelligible Being* amongst intelligible Beings, and consequently, since intelligible Being can be known by the intellect, it is clear that it can be known by the intellect."

This might seem correct when taken by itself. When read in the context however, it turns out not to be correct. One must remember that ἰδέα is a very general term, which by Plato could be used in a far less "technical" sense than we are accustomed to take it. It is a term like φύσις in Philolaus[1]. When Plato begins by speaking of "the Good" as ἡ τοῦ ἀγαθοῦ ἰδέα and next explains that it does not belong to intelligible Being but surpasses this "in dignity and power", we must follow him and acknowledge that apparently he did not intend to say that the Good is "an Idea".

Very characteristic is the way in which, immediately after the ἐπέκεινα lines, Socrates replies to Glauco who asks for a more detailed explanation of the simile of the sun. "Go through this again from the beginning to the end, and please don't omit anything."

SOCR. "Well, certainly, I do omit many things."

GL. "Please don't, not even a small point."

SOCR. "I think I shall do, and even much; but nonetheless, I shall do my best,"

---

[1] Cf. above, ch. II, on the Philolaus texts, pp. 45-48.

Then follows the passage of the divided line[1], in which "being" is divided into two main sections, νοητόν and ὁρατόν, each of which is subdivided into two sections, the first of which is a pure νοητόν subs. ὁρατόν, the other indirectly so, while in both sections "images" are introduced. We shall come back to this passage when dealing with our second main point, the "hierarchy of being". At present, while dealing with the First Principle, we have to note that, in discussing the section of the νοητόν, Plato does mention that dialectic has to rise above the assumed ὑποθέσεις – cp. *Phaedo* 100a-b, where the "idea" is explained as a "hypothesis", necessary as a basis for knowledge – to the ἀνυπόθετον, the ultimate Principle of all.

In book VII of the *Republic* a further explanation follows. From the simile of the cave he draws the consequence with reference to education. Education appears not to be what it is usually supposed to be: it is not bringing knowledge into a soul which is deprived of it – like bringing light into blind eyes; it is rather turning round the body together with the soul from the world of becoming towards Being, "that it may become able to stand the contemplation of Being and of that which is most shining, compared to it; and that is: *the Good*"[2].

The words εἰς τὸ ὂν καὶ τοῦ ὄντος τὸ φανότατον θεωμένη are usually taken as "looking at Being and the most shining of Being", which is the Good. I.e.: τοῦ ὄντος is usually understood as a *genitivus partitivus*. However, it is quite a frequent usage in Greek that the noun on which the genitive depends does not indicate a thing *belonging to* that which stands in the genitive but, the genitive having a comparative meaning, a thing which does *not* belong to that which is expressed in the genitive. Thus it is said in the *Ilaid*, when Hecube takes some precious garment out of a chest, as a gift for a visitor:

ἔκειτο δὲ νείατος ἄλλων.[3]

"And it lay at the bottom of the chest", underneath the other garments, but not belonging to the others.

For this reason the above mentioned text of the *Republic*[4] can not be alleged to prove that Plato, after having rather emphatically placed the ἀγαθόν *above* Being, nonetheless, in a further explanation,

[1] *Rep.* VI 509d-511e.
[2] 518c/d.
[3] Il. VI, 295; cp. *infra*, p. 230.
[4] 518 c/d.

spoke of it as being. Nor can it be said, as it is sometimes done[1], that the passage on the Good in the *Republic* is "just an isolated passage". It is as "isolated" as those on the line and the cave. That is to say, it dominates the whole metaphysical theory that is behind the education of the philosopher in the *Republic*. It is on the vision of this supreme Principle that the well-being of humanity ultimately depends.

Moreover, one must not forget that the passage on the Supreme Principle from which all Being springs has its organic place in Plato's theory of knowledge and in his metaphysics not in the *Republic* only, but that it is taken up in the philosopher's later doctrine of the One. We know from explicit and clear texts[2] that in his later years Plato identified the Ἀγαθόν with the one, and that he lectured "on the Good" in this sense.

Sometimes the argument is heard that, though in the *Republic* the Good is said to be "above Being", it is not said to be above the intellect[3]: in fact, these opponents argue, this was not what Plato meant. They assert that in Plato's view the Good could be known by the intellect: it is not at all that unpredicable Subject which is Plotinus' ἕν, nor the ἄρρητον of his successors. That is to irrationalize Plato's thought at the top, whereas in fact, it remained rational up till the ultimate ground.

There is some fundamental misunderstanding in this argument. First, one must realize that for a Greek philosopher, from Parmenides up to the later Neoplatonists, the ἐπέκεινα τῆς οὐσίας *implied* a being beyond intellectual apprehension. For Plato in particular "true Being" was correlative with "true knowledge", while the derived and secondary "being" of things visible was correlative with some lower and secondary form of knowledge. This is expressed at the end of the passage of the divided line[4]; it is again expressed in the *Timaeus*[5]. When in the latter dialogue a third principle is introduced which is neither "being" nor "becoming", an indefinite principle of space which is the framework within which things becoming come to be, it is

[1] E.g. by Ph. Merlan in his chapter on Plato in the Cambridge *History of Later Greek and Early Medieval Philosophy*, 1967.
[2] Aristoxenus, *Harm. elem.* II, p. 30 Meibom. Cf. Aristotle in *Metaph.* N 4, 1091b13-14; *Eth. Eud.* I 8, 1218a24-28. De Vogel, *Greek Phil.* I, nr. 364; Gaiser, *Platons ungeschriebene Lehre*, p. 452f., nr. 7.
[3] The argument was used by one of the participants in the *Colloque international sur le néoplatonisme*, held at Royaumont (France), June 1969.
[4] 511c-e.
[5] 29b-d.

because of its very character of indefiniteness, spoken of[1] as a "difficult and vague kind of thing" (χαλεπὸν καὶ ἄμυδρον εἶδος) that can hardly be explained in words. Because it does not formally share the intelligible – the Forms do not enter it as such, it is only μιμήματα that enter[2] – it evades, so to speak, the grip of the intellect[3]. Again it is said that, since it is neither an ὄν nor a γιγνόμενον, it can neither be grasped by the intellect nor by sense-perception. It can be touched only by some kind of bastard reasoning, λογισμῷ τινι νόθῳ[4].

Since, then, for Plato there was this strict correlation between the kind of being and the kind of knowledge, both existing at different levels, moreover, since ὄν in the strict sense is νοητόν, it is clear that for him what was beyond Being was as such beyond the grip of the intellect. The ἀγαθόν is a Subject, not a predicate, just as the ἕν was a Subject, not a predicate. It was impossible to explain or define it further. It was ἀνυπόθετον, and of this no further account can be given. The intellect must "postulate" it. It must be assumed, on penalty that thinking and reasoning would become impossible. But it cannot be described in any rational terms.

This is Plato's doctrine of the Good, later also called the One. It was the one ultimate Principle *above* Being, the Principle from which intelligible Being springs. What could be remarked with regard to this is: that it is impossible to derive the multiplicity of Being – the many Forms – from a unique Principle which was strictly one. In order to explain the variety of Forms Plato needed another Principle, that could account for indefiniteness. Now, is not this in fact what he assumed in his ἄπειρον principle? At the level of the ὄν he distinguished as basic *genera* both identity (ταυτότης), and difference (ἕτερον). Once the latter is admitted, an indefinite multiplicity will arise. And that is what had to be explained. In this sense then it must be said that for Plato the indefinite principle or ἄπειρον had its function not only with reference to the sensible world, as it appears in the *Timaeus*, where we hear about it as a "third" principle to be assumed next to "being" and "becoming". Apparently it also had its function at the level of intelligible Being, since the ἕτερον which is given together with the ὄν, gives rise to an infinite multiplicity.

---

[1] *Timaeus* 49 a.
[2] *Timaeus* 50 b-c.
[3] *Timaeus* 51 a/b: μεταλαμβάνον δὲ ἀπορώτατά πη τοῦ νοητοῦ καὶ δυσαλωτότατον αὐτὸ λέγοντες οὐ ψευσόμεθα.
[4] 52 b.

Since this was Plato's doctrine – as was seen very well by Sir David Ross[1] –, we can understand that not so long after Plato a monistic interpretation of the doctrine of the two ultimate principles arose, in such a way that the "other" or indefinite principle is subordinated to the first. This is what we find in Alexander Polyhistor's *Pythagorica hypomnemata*[2], which must be dated not later than the second century B.C.

The same interpretation is found in Sextus Empiricus, *Adv. math.* X (= *Against the Physicists* II, section 267 of the chapter on what is called there "Pythagorean doctrine" (248-282). It is rather curious that this passage on what was actually Plato's doctrine ends in a definitely dualist rendering of the doctrine of first Principles (275-276), though the monistic interpretation was given at the beginning[3]. From Alexander Polyhistor's account we must conclude that the monistic interpretation prevailed at least as early as the 2nd century B.C. Festugière tried to trace it back to the 3rd century[4]. In fact, it may have sprung up quite shortly after Plato or even in his immediate surroundings, since the tendency was present in his conception.

II. But let us now proceed to the next point, which is: whether a "hierarchy of being" was taught by Plato. Enough has been said about the Principle that ranks above eternal Being. But what about being itself, taken in the broad sense? In the *Phaedo*[5] Plato speaks about "two kinds of being", the visible and the invisible, the latter always in the same condition, while the former is ever changing. These two classes are usually opposed the one to the other as ὄντα (in the strict sense) to γιγνόμενα. The ὄντα, also called ὄντως ὄντα, are qualified as "the things-themselves" – αὐτὰ ἕκαστα, αὐτὸ τὸ καλὸν καὶ ἀγαθὸν καὶ μέγα etc.[6] – and as such opposed to the καλὰ πράγματα whose beauty is neither stable nor identical with itself[7]. They are πολλὰ καὶ καλά,

---

[1] In: *Plato's Theory of Ideas*, Oxford 1951, the chapter on the ideal numbers (ch. XII).
[2] Diog. Laert. VIII 25. De Vogel, *Greek Phil.* III, nr. 1279.
[3] See the text of Sextus in *Greek Phil.* I, nr. 371 b (given there as a parallel to Hermodorus in Simpl.). On the presence of both the monistic and the dualist version of the theory in Sextus see my *Pythagoras and early Pythagoreanism*, 202-207.
[4] In: *Hermès Trismégiste* IV, pp. 43-51, referring to an Orphic text on the μονὰς ἀρρενόθηλυς.
[5] 79 a.
[6] *Phaedo* 100 b, *Rep.* 476 b-d, 479 e.
[7] Next to the above mentioned passage of *Rep.* V see also *Symp.* 211 a-b.

an ever changing variety, whereas the καλὸν αὐτό is a unity, always identical with itself. Of the concrete things it is said that they "come into being and perish again, but never ARE in the full sense of the term"[1].

Nonetheless, *in a sense* they *are*. Plato does not altogether deny them the εἶναι. He does not refer to them as non-being. If they were, no form of knowledge of them would be possible. But we do know them, in a way. Sense-perception in itself is not ἐπιστήμη, but "sensing" does have some meaning, and for Plato δόξα is not concerned – as it was for Parmenides – with non-being as such. Δόξα, so it is established in *Rep.* V[2] – must refer to some definite object, which is a unity (ἕν τι) and, though it is not "being", cannot be non-being either. For non-being is not a definite object (ἕν τι), it is just nothing. Thus δόξα, which is more obscure than knowledge but more clear than ignorance, must refer to *something between being and non-being*, something that partakes of both.

In this way Plato determines the place of sensible reality in his scala of being, and parallel to this the place of the kind of knowledge we can have of this reality in his scale of kinds of knowledge. The sensible world is not non-being; it is real, though it is not ὄντως ὄν, and qua reality it must partake of being.

Exactly the same is expressed in the word εἰκών which is so often used in the *Timaeus*. For Plato an "image" does not mean something non-real. It is a reality, but a reality of a secondary order. Primary reality is the ὄντως ὄν. The image depends on it, both in its existence and in its quality. It is, therefore, "secondary", if this term be taken in the general sense of "indirect" or "derived". Perhaps at a closer inspection we shall prefer to call it "third" instead of "second". At the present stage of our inquiry let us notice that it is essential to the image that it resembles the original. This is the ground of Plato's actual valuation of the visible world: though it is not primary Reality (the ὄντως ὄν), it is full of order and of beauty, since it "partakes" of it, i.e. actually resembles it.

Let us also observe in this context that in Plato's view no "rehabilitation" of sensible "being" was needed after the *Phaedo* and the *Republic*. In those dialogues he had determined very precisely what the place of that kind of being was. He had neither denied its reality nor despised its value. He had just taxed it according to its level. It

---
[1] *Timaeus* 28a: γιγνόμενον καὶ ἀπολλύμενον, ὄντως δὲ οὐδέποτε ὄν.
[2] 478b-e.

is quite true to say that in those works – which certainly represent a certain period of his life – his inner eye is turned towards the ὄντως ὄν and that he is continually trying to make others turn that way. Later he will show some more detachment: his inner certainty will be firm enough to be able to look again at what was called the "shadows" of the cave: At first, it was their "shadow" character that had to be emphasized in order to make clear that they were not Reality itself; next, the stress will be on their *resemblance* to primary Reality. That is their character of εἰκόνες.

In the *Philebus* (59a-c) it is said again that of things ever changing no knowledge in the strict sense is possible. Yet, in the same dialogue it is pointed out that the philosopher's task is to see that, in the mixture of πέρας and ἄπειρον, the precise number can and should be found: for this is the task of scientific reasoning, not to pass on immediately from the one to the infinite, but to find out by careful inquiry the precise number that lies in between[1].

Thus, Plato's position in metaphysics is not essentially changed, nor is his theory of knowledge. There is certainly a new approach, both to the doctrine of being and to that of knowledge, in the dialogues from the *Theaetetus* and *Parmenides* onwards. New views will be introduced, but they do not overturn the doctrine of primary and secondary Reality on the one hand, and that of primary and secondary knowledge on the other.

It seems useful to stress this, because in the last decades voices have been heard again and again telling us that Plato did change his metaphysics, that in his later years he abandoned the theory of Forms and "rehabilitated" the visible world by recognizing it as fully being[2].

---

[1] *Phil.* 16c-17a.

[2] P. Wilpert, *Zwei aristotelische Frühschriften*, 1949, thinks that Plato abandoned the theory of Ideas in his later years and instead of it taught the doctrine of two ultimate principles. To this view it must be said that the doctrine of First Principles (which certainly was held by Plato in his later years) is not at all incompatible with the theory of Ideas. Sir David Ross, *Plato's Theory of Ideas*, 1951, who understood this perfectly well, did think that in the *Sophistes* (248e-249a) Plato "rehabilitated" sensible reality and recognized it as "being" without any restriction. G. E. L. Owen was so much convinced that this rehabilitation was made, that he felt the need of dating the *Timaeus* immediately after the *Republic*, since it seemed to him impossible that such a passage as *Tim.* 27d-28a would have been written after the *Sophistes* (Class. Quart. 1953). – To this we must reply (1) that the opposition of τὸ ὄν ἀεί which is always the same, to the γιγνόμενον which comes to be and perishes, is on no account restricted to the *Timaeus* in what is usually considered as Plato's later work. It

Having thus re-established that the two world theory is basic Platonic doctrine, without any restriction of periods, let us now raise the question of whether for Plato there was, ontologically speaking, something between Primary and "secondary" reality, some kind of being which does not belong to the νοητά but is definitely inferior to them, while at the same time it is clearly superior to anything corporeal. To this question we can answer first of all: yes, indeed, this description applies precisely to the Soul. In fact, the Soul is not a νοητόν; she does not form part of the intelligible order, but is related to it, – even closely related. On the other hand, she is clearly of an order superior to anything corporeal, since she alone is a self-moving being and as such can be a cause, while material things cannot.

However, another answer to the same question is possible as well: we could say that for Plato mathematical objects constitute an intermediate sphere between the νοητά and the αἰσθητά. When saying so we should repeat what Aristotle says in *Metaph.* A 6, 987b10-11. I venture to suppose that, had Aristotle not written that line or had we never read it, we might not have given this reply. It is true, of course, that in the passage of the divided line the objects of mathematical thought do take some kind of intermediate place between pure νοητά and the objects of sense perception. They are a kind of semi-νοητά, conceived with the help of visible figures though they are not to be identified with these. The fact that in Plato's scheme of the line the mathematical objects are one part of the section of νοητά, and on the other hand that in the other section of the line, representing the αἰσθητά, they are parallelled by the images or imitations of physical

is present in the *Philebus* as well, where we read that of ever changing things no adequate knowledge is possible (59a-c). Similar things are found in the *Politicus* 269d. Moreover, in the XIIth book of the *Laws* (965c) it is stated that those who have to keep the order of the Laws will not be able to do so, unless they are trained in tracing the variety of the manifold things back to the unity (sc. of the Form). (2) What Owen failed to see is, that on the whole the *Timaeus* is characteristic of Plato's later period (the subject of the origin of the visible world, the emphasis on its beauty and order, the faculty of seeing praised as the greatest benefit given by the Gods to men, the author's intense interest in the problems of man living in a body – all this is peculiar to Plato in his later years).

Nor can we share the opinion of W. Kamlah (*Platons Selbstkritik im Sophistes*, 1963) who thinks that, though Plato did not abandon the theory of the Ideas, he did change his basic conception, since he abandoned the view that concrete things are "images" (imitations) of an archetypal exemplum. See my review in *Gymnasium* 1966, p. 301 f.

objects might be not the main reason why we might not have come to the idea of mentioning the mathematical objects as an intermediate class of beings between intelligible and sensible reality. In fact, the true reason might rather have been that it is strange to us to consider the objects of mathematical thinking as a class of *being* at all. However, Plato did consider them as such, and so the second answer was perfectly correct.

Does it follow from this that for Plato the soul was identical with the objects of mathematics? – It is hard to answer this question, either in the affirmative or in the negative since, put in this general form, it is not clear what it means. This much is clear, (1) that for Plato the soul was a kind of being intermediate between the intelligible and the sensible world, (2) that he held the objects of mathematics to be so as well. We can explain the first statement somewhat further. In what sense precisely was soul thought to be "between" the so-called two worlds? This question can be answered as follows.

Throughout his written works Plato laid a heavy stress on the superiority of the soul with regard to the body and anything corporeal. It is one of the basic convictions of his Socrates in the *Apology*[1] and in the *Crito*[2]. Because of this conviction he thinks it his first and most important task to teach his fellow-men and -citizens to care for their souls much more than for anything in the world. In the *Phaedo* again it is the essential superiority of the soul that underlies the whole argument for immortality: the Soul in itself is not of the order of perishable things, she is of a superior order. She can and must free herself from the desires and aspirations of the body in order to be truly what she is. And this detachment from the body – which is called a purification and is felt as a liberation – is achieved by steadfastly concentrating the attention on that which is above sensible things and is their archetype and ground[3]. The soul can perform this task of "striving for true insight" ($\varphi\rho\acute{o}\nu\eta\sigma\iota\varsigma$) because she is naturally akin to intelligible being. She does not belong to it herself[4], but she is related to it, while the body is of a different nature, lower, and for that very reason dependant on the soul. It is the soul which, by guiding and governing the body, gives it harmony and beauty, but also life and motion[5].

[1] *Apol.* 29 d-e.
[2] *Crito* 47 c-48 a.
[3] *Phaedo* 65 a-67 b.   [4] *Phaedo* 79 b 8-c 1.
[5] *Phaedo* 105 d 1-2; cf. *Phaedr.* 245 c-246 a; *Nom.* X 895 e-897 d.

SOME CONTROVERSIAL POINTS

This is the view of the soul which we find in the earlier Socratic dialogues, fully in the *Phaedo*, which is underlying in the body-and-soul training of the philosopher in the *Republic*, and is expressed anew in the *Phaedrus* doctrine of soul as a self-moving principle which as such has to take care of a body. Next, we can follow the line through *Philebus* and *Timaeus*, where the World-soul is introduced as the immediate cause of life and order of the cosmos[1], and lastly we find the doctrine in *Laws* X[2]. In the last mentioned book it is argued against the older philosophers of nature that Matter cannot be the first cause of things: Matter in itself cannot be a cause at all. Only Soul can, and she is "older" than the body. That is to say, soul *precedes* any corporeal existence. She is a kind of being of a more fundamental order: the priority in time implies an ontological superiority[3].

This doctrine of the priority of Soul to Body in *Laws* X is not at all a new doctrine, introduced in Plato's last great work. Exactly the same view of nature was expressed by Socrates in the *Phaedo* where he tells his intellectual life story[4], and we may be sure that the writer of the *Phaedo* was as certain of the soul's ontological superiority to corporeal being as the author of the *Timaeus* was.

Approaching the problem from this angle we can ask the question: Is it true, after all, that for Plato the Soul was second in the order of being, and that in his view sensible things were third?

I think we must answer this question in the affirmative. The term "hierarchy of being" is just a formula. But its meaning is sufficiently clear. Can it be legitimately applied to Plato's view of the order of things? – I think it can. We have really not to pass by Plotinus in order to arrive at such an interpretation. It is Plato's own text that imposes it on us.

Now what about the relationship of the Soul to the objects of mathematics? Plato's description of the composition of the World-soul in the *Timaeus*[5] shows us a little bit how closely in his view the two "intermediates" were related. There is another text which reveals to us something of Plato's thought on this topic. It is in Aristotle, *De anima* I 404b18-27. Here we learn that Plato, doubtless in his

---

[1] *Philebus* 28e-30d. In the *Timaeus* see in particular 34b-c.
[2] 891c-899b.
[3] 892a-c.
[4] 96a-c.
[5] 35b-36d.

193

later years, equated νοῦς to the one, ἐπιστήμη to two, δόξα to three and αἴσθησις to four. Now these were the numbers which in the Academy were used as symbolizing the point, line, plane and solid. "In his latest phase, then, Plato established a correlation between four faculties of the soul and four types of geometrical objects". Thus Sir David Ross concluded his comments on the above-cited passage[1].

This much, then, can be said by way of explanation of the two "intermediates". That the second of them, the objects of mathematics, were for Plato essentially nearer to the νοητά than to the αἰσθητά, will be perfectly clear to all those who remember the divided line, for there in fact the mathematical objects formed part of the section of νοητά according to the main division. We found the same with reference to the Soul: she, too, appeared to be essentially much closer to intelligible things than to the world of natural objects.

III. The third controversial point we have to consider is: whether there is any evidence that Plato ever regarded the intelligible world as a νοῦς. At the first glance it might seem obvious that the equation Νοῦς = τὰ νοητά is Plotinian, but not Platonic. So it must seem at least to those who are familiar with what is rightly considered as Plato's classical dialogues: such dialogues as the *Phaedo*, the *Symposium*, the *Republic*, the *Phaedrus*. In these works, no doubt, there is not a trace of the above mentioned equation. However, it is different in the *Sophistes* and the *Timaeus*. In the *Sophistes* we find a passage that urges us to ask the above question. It is 248e-249a. I dealt with this text and the related passage in the *Timaeus* 31b in the XIth International Congress of Philosophy held in Brussels in 1953. For the reader's convenience I have had that paper reprinted in the preceding chapter of the present volume. It was read in Brussels to a numerous audience and there was plenty of time for discussion. However, I do not remember having heard any serious arguments against it. Nonetheless, I do not have the impression that most scholars share my interpretation. On the contrary, most of them seem to be rather reluctant to follow my suggestion. For that reason I think it useful to consider the matter anew.

[1] *Plato's Theory of Ideas*, p. 215. The text is in my *Greek Phil.* I, nr. 372; Gaiser, *Platons ungeschriebene Lehre*, nr. 25A. I commented on the text in *Problems concerning later Platonism*, *Mnemosyne* 1949, pp. 299-318; *infra*, ch. XII, pp. 277-281. A few years later the same text was commented on in a broader study by H. D. Saffrey, *Le Περὶ φιλοσοφίας d'Aristote et la théorie platonicienne des Idées Nombres*, Leiden 1955. See also Gaiser's above cited work, p. 45.

SOME CONTROVERSIAL POINTS

In the preceding pages of the *Sophistes* the "friends of the Ideas" have been introduced. They were said to defend themselves very cautiously, from some high place, invisible, and to maintain almost by force "that some intelligible and incorporeal forms are true being". They oppose coming-to-be (γένεσις) to "true being" (ἡ ὄντως οὐσία), of which the former is ever changing and perceived by the senses, while the latter is always the same and known by the soul through reasoning.

All this sounds perfectly Platonical. However, the position of these philosophers is carried ad absurdum, because they are said to deny that ποιεῖν and πάσχειν belong to being. Now, since of knowing and being known the former is an activity, while the latter is passive, it follows that true being cannot be known.

This conclusion certainly does not render Plato's opinion in any period of his life. But we do have the impression that in the preceding passage the position of the "Friends of the Ideas" is deliberately depicted in such a way that the above consequence must follow.

It is further explained that, according to this argument, Being in so far as it is known by knowledge, is moved – because "being known" is undergoing an activity – and this, we said, could not happen to that which is in eternal rest.

THEAET. Rightly so.

The Eleatic Stranger then goes on: "But, good heavens, what about this? Shall we be easily convinced that in fact motion and life, soul and insight are not proper to the perfectly Being, and that it neither lives nor thinks, but solemn and holy, deprived of thinking, deprived of motion, is in perpetual rest?"

THEAET. "That would be a terrible concession."

STR. "Shall we then say that it does possess thinking, but not life?"

THEAET. "How could we?"

STR. "Do we confirm then that both of these are in it, but shall we deny that it has them in a soul?"

THEAET. "How could it possess them in another way?"

STR. "But are we going to say then that it does possess thinking, life and soul, but is totally unmoving, though possessing a soul?"

THEAET. "That seems completely absurd to me!"

STR. "We must concede then, that also what moves and motion belong to Being."

What is established here concerning the ὄντως ὄν? Does the author intend to say that motion and life, soul and insight must be attributed to it? And what, then, does this mean? Are we to believe that Plato *somehow* wished to introduce motion – the motion of thinking and of being known – into his intelligible world, – that world which hitherto was always particularly distinguished by the feature of the ἀεὶ ὡσαύτως καὶ κατὰ τὸ αὐτὸ ἔχειν?

Modern scholars have mostly thought that this cannot have been intended by Plato, since it would affect the Ideas in their most essential character. A different interpretation had to be found, such as would do justice to the text and yet not destroy Plato's most essential teaching on the Ideas. In the beginning of this century Mgr. A. Diès proposed the following solution[1].

The παντελῶς ὄν of 248c does not so much mean "perfect being": it refers rather to *being in its completeness*. Hitherto Plato had called "being" in the full sense: intelligible being only; now he is *extending* that concept. From now on the soul and animate beings too will be counted among the ὄντα.

What Plato is doing here, far from declaring the Ideas to be "moving" – which was impossible *per definitionem* – is simply to place the Soul and animate beings in the second part of the first main section of the divided line, that part of νοητά which in *Rep.* VI was assigned to the objects of mathematics. Thus, Soul and animate beings are recognized as fully ὄντα, while the character of the Ideas qua unchangeable entities is not interfered with.

This interpretation of Diès was quite generally accepted, a.o. by Cornford in *Plato's Theory of Knowledge*, 1935[2].

How ever attractive this interpretation might seem since it does not affect the essential character of the Ideas, a major difficulty remains, viz. it does not actually do justice to Plato's text. For, after all, the Stranger from Elea did not say that something had to be *added* to that solemn and holy world of "that which perfectly IS" – a moving kind of being to that which by its very nature was unmoving –, but his problem was: how that which IS in a perfect way (τὸ παντελῶς ὄν, not παντελές!), could itself be deprived of life and thinking. This problem could not be solved by *adding* to it a different kind of being

---

[1] *La définition de l'être et la nature des Idées dans le Sophiste de Platon*, (thèse), Paris 1909.

[2] Repr. 1946. Cherniss adopts the same interpretation, and so did E. de Strycker S.J., who still thinks that this is actually what Plato intended.

which does possess life and thinking. Though in fact by such an addition the concept of "being" and of νοητόν would be extended, that which is νοητόν *properly speaking* would remain as "solemn and holy" as ever: no life and motion, no soul and thinking would be proper to it.

I think we have simply to follow the text as it stands. We then have to make the statement that the question asked by the Stranger from Elea "Shall we be easily convinced" had the character of a reductio ad absurdum. It means that it is absurd to deny motion and life, soul and insight to that which IS in a perfect way. Τὸ παντελῶς ὄν, it must be remarked, cannot mean "*complete* being". Since the adverb is used, ὄν is to be taken as "existential *being*", and παντελῶς means "in an absolute way". The rendering "perfect Being" or "absolute Being" is correct.

This much is sure, then, that the Stranger from Elea, who plays the leading part in the *Sophistes*, thinks it essential to intelligible Being qua *perfect* Being that it is living and thinking. It is to be observed here, by the way, that the same Stranger is speaking when the doctrine of the five most important kinds is expounded and that of the κοινωνία τῶν γενῶν. These doctrines are usually accepted as Plato's. It does not seem to be hazardous, then, to suppose that it was actually Plato's thought which is expressed in the Stranger's view of intelligible Being qua perfect Being.

Having established this point we must ask next: What does this mean with reference to the intelligible World as it was originally conceived by Plato?

I mean this: If it is established now that the intelligible order qua perfect Being cannot be deprived of a soul and must be "thinking", what is implied in this as to the nature of the individual Ideas? Does the newly expressed view actually say that the Ideas, each of them in particular, are living beings, moving and thinking? Is that what Plato meant?

I think not. What the discussion was about was: the intelligible order as a whole. This is what was called παντελῶς ὄν. When it is said that this, qua *perfect* Being, must be living and thinking, no statement is made about the nature of individual Ideas, at least not directly so. Individual Ideas are identic with themselves and different the one from the other. But they can be inter-connected, not all of them with all, nor in an arbitrary way, but some of them with certain others, and in a certain way[1]. This is what is done by the act of thinking. And

[1] *Sophistes* 251d-253e.

with reference to this operation of connecting and separating, applied by the intellect to intelligible Being, it is said that Perfect Being "undergoes something" and thus, in a sense, "moves".

But "being known" and "thought" is not the only thing which in our text is attributed to intelligible Being. *Life, thinking* and *insight* are also attributed to it. Now what does this mean? Not, anyhow, that individual Ideas are changing. As it is said in the text, it has to be referred to the totality of intelligible Being. To Plato this totality appeared as an *articulate unity,* as is brought out by his method of diaeresis. But does not this presuppose an *organic unity?* And is not this precisely what the Greek called a ζῷον? How ever strange it might seem to us to regard the intelligible World in this way, when we approach the matter on this side, following the lead of Plato himself in his reflections on the structure of Being, we can see the meaning of that strange conception.

Once we see that an articulate multiplicity presupposes an organic unity, that in the Greek view an organic unity presupposes a soul and implies the idea of a living being, we are not far from understanding what Plato meant by the statement that to the παντελῶς ὄν life and motion, soul and thinking could not be denied.

That a living being, endowed with soul and reason, is always superior to things deprived of these, is a thought that plays a leading part in the *Timaeus*. But it must have been one of the basic convictions of Socrates, as appears from the autobiographical passage in the *Phaedo*[1]. As a parallel we have in Xenophon's *Memorabilia* the dialogue of Socrates with Aristodemus, that small man in Athens who did not believe in the Gods: here Socrates begins with the question "Which people seem to you more worthy of our admiration, those who make images that cannot think or move, or those who make living beings endowed with reason and fully active?"[2]. Plato thinks in the same line when he concludes from the very perfection of Being, that Soul and thinking cannot be denied to it.

In the *Timaeus* 30b-c, it is said that of visible things nothing can be best unless it possesses soul and thinking. That is why the Demiurge made the visible world a ζῷον ἔμψυχον ἔννουν τε τῇ ἀληθείᾳ.

But this visible world was made after an eternal pattern. What else could this be but a ζῷον παντελές? If Plato had not explicitly said so, we might have inferred this from his preceding words. But he does

[1] 96a-99b.
[2] Xenophon, *Memor.* I 4, 4.

say it explicitly, even more than once: the παράδειγμα of the visible world is referred to as a ζῷον παντελές or ἀίδιον¹, or also as the τέλεον καὶ νοητὸν ζῷον².

A word by way of explanation of these texts. In the *Timaeus*, 30c-31b, after having declared that the Demiurge made the visible world a living being with a soul and thinking, the author raises the question of "which kind of living Being" could have been the pattern after which the world-ζῷον was made. This pattern, he says, has within itself all intelligible living beings; it is a παντελὲς ζῷον, an absolute Living Being.

What does he mean? Is it just one Idea, that of ζῷον? Or must we assume that the archetype of the visible world qua ζῷον is the intelligible order in its totality, conceived as a Living Being? In this context we must say that logic definitely points to the latter meaning. But there are two or three other passages to be compared.

37c-d. When the Father who had created it saw that the world he had made had become a moving and living being, he rejoiced and in his satisfaction reflected on how he could make it still more resemble the pattern. "Now, since that pattern was an eternal living Being (ζῷον ἀίδιον), he endeavoured to make this All too resemble it as much as possible." Here the emphasis is on the eternity of the pattern. To make his created world resemble it as much as possible the Demiurge created Time, "a moving image of Eternity".

39d-e. Next, after describing the planets and in particular sun and moon which, so to speak, are the clock of the universe, the author says that they were made to the purpose that "this here" would be as similar as possible to "the perfect and intelligible Living Being", "to the imitation of the eternal Nature". "This here" means, no doubt, the visible world. It has to imitate the eternal Nature of the τέλεον καὶ νοητὸν ζῷον, and to achieve this the regular revolutions of the heavenly bodies are a mighty help³.

Again, what is this "perfect and intelligible Living Being"? – I think, indeed, that the only fitting answer we can give is: *the intelligible world* which in its totality is the παράδειγμα to this our visible world.

We possess a text of Aristotle which corroborates this interpretation. It is in the *De anima*, I 2, 404b18, on which I commented more

---

[1] *Timaeus* 31b, 37c8-d2.
[2] *Ib.* 39d7-e2.
[3] Cf. *Timaeus* 47a-c.

explicitly elsewhere[1]. In fact the αὐτόζῳον referred to in this text which is said to have sprung "from the Idea-itself of the One, and from the first length, breadth and depth", can be hardly anything but the whole of the intelligible world. I think this point cannot be seriously doubted.

However, two objections can be raised with reference to the preceding argument. First. When considering *Soph.* 248e-249a where life, thinking and insight were attributed to Being in its perfection, I asked: what does this mean with regard to the individual Ideas, and answered: not, anyhow, that they are changing. The text refers to the totality of Being. This totality appeared to Plato as an articulate unity. Now an articulate unity presupposes an organic unity, and an organic unity either is or presupposes a living being. – So we said. There is a difficulty in this. It is the following.

"The totality of Being appeared to Plato as an articulate unity." I could point here to the method of diaeresis and recall the words of *Phaedrus* 265e: κατ' εἴδη δύνασθαι διατέμνειν κατ' ἄρθρα ᾗ πέφυκεν. Now this refers to the repeated splitting up of a conceptual unity – μία ἰδέα – which we know so well from the different instances given in the opening section of the *Sophistes*. The objection could be raised here in this form.

"In saying that to Plato the totality of Being appeared as an articulate unity – a thesis which I am not going to attack – you referred to the method of diaeresis. But you must know that this method consists of an analysis of individual "forms" or "ideas" by splitting them up repeatedly. Thus, this method is particularly concerned with *single* Ideas which, in fact, appear not to be "individual" in so far as this term implies indivisibility. However, you wished to establish that Plato's new view of intelligible Being as a thinking ζῷον did not interfere with the character of individual Ideas, and look here, – it is precisely the individual Ideas that appear to be each of them *an articulate unity*. My problem is, then: if an articulate unity is an organic unity, and an organic unity either *is* or is part of a living being, are you then going to tell us that also the individual Ideas are living beings, having a soul and the faculty of thinking? Or what would you say to this?"

To this argument I am not going to concede immediately that the

---

[1] *Problems concerning later Platonism* II, *Mnemosyne* 1949, p. 299-318; *infra*, ch. XII p. 277ff.; Sir David Ross refers to the text in *Plato's Theory of Ideas* p. 214f.; H. D. Saffrey O.P. deals with it at length in his above cited study.

ζῷον view of intelligible Being leads of necessity into a βυθὸς φλυαρίας. But let us see whether in fact any reality that is found to be an *articulate unity* must be as such a living being. It seems to me that this is not so. First, the expression "articulate unity" can be used metaphorically. In that case no further conclusion can be drawn. The metaphora is not meant to imply that there is actually a living being behind the "articulate" structure of the subject. – Second, if the subject referred to, is actually meant to be an *articulate* unity, it would be in fact an organic unity. However, this is not always a living being. It may be a part of it. Now it seems likely to me that Plato's view of reality was like this. Since he conceived the physical universe as a ζῷον, all things within it acquired the character of organic parts of the living whole. And since this visible world was an εἰκών of an eternal archetype, that eternal παράδειγμα itself had to be a perfect Living Being, of which the particular Forms were so to speak the living members. Indeed they might be in themselves an articulate unity, this being not a separate Living Being, but an organic part of a greater whole.

In this way, I think, the ζῷον conception does not lead to nonsense. However queer it might seem to a modern mind, we can grasp its meaning if we take the trouble to follow Plato's lead.

The other objection that can be made to my argument is the following.

"Plato concludes from the very perfection of Being, that soul and thinking cannot be denied to it." So you say. Then, you go on to make the statement: "In the *Timaeus*, 30b-c, it is said that of visible things nothing can be best, unless it possesses a soul and thinking. For that reason the Demiurge made the visible world a living being with a soul and thinking mind." Your further argument is: but this visible world is made after an eternal pattern. *Ergo*, the pattern a fortiori must be a living Being with a soul and thinking mind. – What you failed to see is: that *Timaeus* 30b speaks against this inference. For it is established there with a certain emphasis that *of things visible* nothing without a thinking mind can ever be more beautiful than a being with a thinking mind. And concerning *things visible* it is added that a thinking mind can only exist in a soul. "And that is why He placed the thinking mind in a soul, and soul in a body when He built the universe." That is then precisely what you should not project on the "eternal pattern"! –

This too is an interesting argument. The late Professor Hackforth of Cambridge used the text *Tim.* 30b in a paper on *Plato's Theism*[1] to prove that Plato does leave room for a transcendent Noûs that is not in a soul; e.g. the Demiurge in the *Timaeus*, who is to be identified with the fourth principle or αἴτιον in the *Philebus*[2], is a transcendent Noûs.

I think, indeed, that Hackforth was nearer the truth than those who assert that the Demiurge in the *Timaeus* was a soul "because in Plato's view noûs could only exist in a soul". In fact, nowhere does Plato say that the Demiurge was a soul. He does say that the Demiurge *created* the soul, and that he established the order in the cosmos as a reasonable Cause, κατὰ νοῦν. It is justified, then, to identify the Demiurge with the fourth Principle or αἴτιον of the *Philebus*, which is νοῦς.

However, one should not forget that Plato's terminology with reference to soul and thinking is not yet fixed in the way we know from Plotinus, which was, generally speaking, the way of all post-Aristotelian authors. In the *Phaedo* Plato speaks of a cosmic noûs in the sense of Anaxagoras, but to design human thinking, the intellect which alone is capable of grasping the ἀλήθεια, he speaks of αὐτὴ ἡ ψυχή or ἡ ψυχὴ αὐτὴ καθ' αὑτήν[3], that is to say the "pure" soul, detached from the body as much as possible. He also says that that man will best approach the knowledge of things being, who goes to them as much as possible αὐτῇ τῇ διανοίᾳ, or also αὐτῇ καθ' αὑτὴν εἰλικρινεῖ τῇ διανοίᾳ[4]. In the *Theaetetus* he says in the same way: not the senses are capable of perceiving the κοινά (those general predicates that are not the object of one particular sense organ), but αὐτὴ δι' αὑτῆς ἡ ψυχή alone is capable of doing that[5]. In the *Phaedo* again it was "the soul-itself" which was capable of possessing φρόνησις[6], in the *Sophistes* however, it is νοῦς καὶ φρόνησις that are mentioned together[7]. Further, in the *Philebus*[8], the *Timaeus* and *Laws* X soul is the principle of life and motion; when she is good, she is endowed with noûs[9], and noûs

[1] Class. Quart. 1936, pp. 4-9.
[2] 26e; cf. 30a-e.
[3] *Phaedo* 65c, 66c1, 67a1.
[4] *Ib.* 65e7, 66a1-2.
[5] 185d.
[6] 65a7ff.
[7] 249a.
[8] 30c5-e1.
[9] *Timaeus* 30a-c, 47e-48; *Laws* 896d-897d.

is really the divine in us[1] and most properly speaking ourselves, just as in the cosmos noûs is the cause of order[2].

In this context it is interesting to re-read *Timaeus*, p. 90. The author is concerned here with what is referred to in this dialogue as the divine soul[3] or simply as τὸ θεῖον[4] – the intellect, placed in the head and separated from the soul of the passions by the "isthmus" of the neck. In our passage (90a) it is introduced as τὸ κυριώτατον παρ' ἡμῖν ψυχῆς εἶδος: with regard to this part of the soul it is remarked that "the God gave it to each of us as a kind of δαίμων", and the man who honours this divine genius that dwells in him by exercising his thinking faculty, that man is really εὐδαίμων. It is worth noticing the terms the author uses here: φρονεῖν μὲν ἀγαθὰ καὶ θεῖα, ... καθ' ὅσον δ'αὖ μετασχεῖν ἀνθρωπίνῃ φύσει ἀθανασίας ἐνδέχεται, τούτου μηδὲν μέρος ἀπολείπειν.

These words remind us very strongly of some well-known passages in Aristotle[5], in particular the following lines from *Eth. Nic.* X 7: Εἰ δὴ θεῖον ὁ νοῦς πρὸς τὸν ἄνθρωπον, καὶ ὁ κατὰ τοῦτον βίος θεῖος πρὸς τὸν ἀνθρώπινον βίον. Οὐ χρὴ δὲ κατὰ τοὺς παραινοῦντας ἀνθρώπινα φρονεῖν ἄνθρωπον ὄντα οὐδὲ θνητὰ τὸν θνητόν, ἀλλ' ἐφ' ὅσον ἐνδέχεται ἀθανατίζειν καὶ πάντα ποιεῖν πρὸς τὸ ζῆν κατὰ τὸ κράτιστον τῶν ἐν αὐτῷ[6].

To this one must not object that in our passage of the *Timaeus* "the divine in us"[7] is not referred to by the term νοῦς, making the suggestion that Plato had not used that word to denote the κυριώτατον of the soul[8]. Those who speak in this way seem to forget that the pages of the *Timaeus* abound with periphrastic expressions, even to such a degree that only by way of exception are things directly mentioned by their names. Nonetheless, there is not the slightest doubt that the thinking part of the soul of man was called νοῦς in the *Timaeus*, as may be seen e.g. in the description of the liver which in its shining surface reflects as a looking-glass the impressions and images of the thoughts (διανοήματα) effected on it by the power of νοῦς[9].

We can conclude that neither Aristotle's way of speaking with

---

[1] *Timaeus* 69d6-7 (νοῦς), 90a (τὸ κυριώτατον παρ' ἡμῖν ψυχῆς εἶδος), 90c7-8 (τὸ ἐν ἡμῖν θεῖον).
[2] See *Timaeus* 47e, *Laws* 897b-c.
[3] *Timaeus* 41c.
[4] *Timaeus* 69d7-8.
[5] *E.N.* X 7, 1177b26-1178a7; *Metaph.* A 2, 982b28ff.
[6] 1177b29-1178a1.
[7] τὸ ἐν ἡμῖν θεῖον, *Timaeus* 90c7-8.
[8] τὸ κυριώτατον παρ' ἡμῖν ψυχῆς εἶδος, 90a.
[9] *Timaeus* 71b7.

reference to noûs nor Plotinus's are alien to Plato's in the works of his later years. On the other hand, it is clear that Plato could speak of "soul" at the level of intelligible Being: since for him νοῦς was the best and most proper part of soul, the conception of a Soul that is essentially νοῦς and exists in the order of intelligible Being is in no way absurd. Speaking Plotinian language we could say: at that level soul is "noïfied". However, one must realize that this was exactly Plato's thought, as appears e.g. in *Phaedo* 82b/c (the "deification" of the philosophos) and 114b/c (the philosophoi will live here-after as pure spirits); cf. also *Timaeus* 90c-d: by making τὸ ἐν ἡμῖν θεῖον resemble the regular motions of the Universe the spiritualized man will thus attain the best life proposed by the Gods to man for now and for the time to come.

Without any doubt Plato regards Noûs as θεῖος. It is in man as a little part of immortality, so it is said in *Nom.* IV[1]. "For it does not suit that Noûs is subordinate to anything: it must rule all, since it is truly what it is and is truly free according to its nature", so he says elsewhere in the *Laws*, and he goes on to say: "For now it is absolutely nowhere, except for a modest degree of it"[2].

The words νῦν δὲ οὐ γάρ – a beautiful Greek ellips – mean: "But now, if it does not appear that Noûs rules all, the reason is" –

The reason is: that it is not anywhere, ἀλλ' ἢ κατὰ βραχύ – "except for a small measure of it". The expression reminds the reader of *Tim.* 51e, where it is said that of true opinion every man gets his share, "but of Noûs the Gods only, and human kind only in a small measure."

Lastly, what to think of the ἀληθινὸς καὶ θεῖος νοῦς, which in *Phil.* 22c is opposed to the νοῦς of an individual man, even of Socrates? The ideal Noûs which alone is above any ἐγκλήματα, where is it to be situated? Surely the World-soul's νοῦς is of a greater perfection than the νοῦς of any individual man. But Noûs is not exhausted, so to speak, with the World-soul's νοῦς. There are a number of divine Souls, created by the Demiurge, which most certainly in Plato's view had thinking minds: the Souls of the celestial bodies, whose νοῦς was certainly not inferior to the World-soul's νοῦς. But after all, all of them were "created Gods", and their Creator most certainly was a Noûs himself, a Noûs of the transcendent level.

Now I am not going to say that the Demiurge, being a transcendent Noûs, was "God" in such a sense as Christians or, generally speaking,

---
[1] 713e-714a.
[2] *Laws* IX 875c-d.

"theists" use the term. Plato, no doubt, called his Demiurge a God. But definitely we are not here on the level of the First and ultimate Principle.

It is Plato's way of thinking, no doubt, to assume that the many created thinking minds have their ground in an eternal and intelligible Mind. And this then must be the Demiurge.

This much seems sure to me. It is the way of Plato's fundamental hypothesis. I do not see that we can go much further. Is the Demiurge to be identified with the intelligible World? We can find an argument in the fact that, in the *Timaeus*, where the Demiurge makes the visible world resemble as much as possible the eternal pattern, he is also said to make it as much as possible like himself. Yet, let us not dogmatize on this point and not yield to the temptation of urging the logical consequences of a way of speaking which, at least in part, was mythologizing, and no doubt deliberately so. On Plato's part this means: making some reservations. From us it requires that we do the same.

In reply, then, to the above formulated objection with regard to *Timaeus* 30a-b, I think we could make the following statements.

1. The text of the *Timaeus* (31b, 39e) does point clearly to an intelligible archetype of the visible world, conceived as a ζῷον. In this conception a perfect, i.e. *thinking* soul is certainly implied. In Plato's way of speaking both the terms ψυχή and νοῦς could be used here.

2. The Demiurge was a transcendent Noûs, to be situated at the level of intelligible Being. However, this is not sufficient ground for identifying him with the intelligible order as such. Some more reservation is needed.

3. It does seem so that in *Tim.* 37c the Ideas are referred to as ἀίδιοι θεοί. It is true, of course, that elsewhere Plato does not call them by that name. However, Cornford's interpretation ("a *shrine* for the eternal gods", sc. for the celestial bodies)[1], made for the purpose of escaping the conclusion that in this case indeed the Ideas were referred to as θεοί, is artificial and, all things well considered, does not fit the context. For in Plato's view the visible world was not made by the Demiurge as a shrine for the heavenly bodies: the heavenly bodies are not "in it", but are considered as an order superior to it. The visible world is nothing but this our world here, governed and held together by its own Soul, the World-soul, created by the Demiurge. The stars too have their souls and as such are "visible Gods". But they

[1] F. M. Cornford, *Plato's Cosmology*, London 1937, ³1952, p. 97ff.

constitute an order definitely superior to our world. Plato does speak of τὰ πάντα, when referring to the Universe. He does so, e.g., in *Tim.* 90c/d. But this is not our visible world, constituted of the earthly elements. This world, indeed, made as a ζῷον by the Demiurge, is an "image" of the "eternal ζῷον" (39e) which is the intelligible order. It can be called an εἰκών, but also the term ἄγαλμα is quite an appropriate term for it.

Lastly, we should not wonder too much, that in the *Timaeus* the intelligible Forms are referred to as "eternal Gods". It is fitting in the style of this dialogue.

This, then, just as a remark made "by the way". After all *Tim.* 37c too belongs to the controversial points of Plato interpretation.

Returning to *Soph.* 248e-249a, I should like to consider a few other objections that have been, and are now and then brought forward with reference to the ζῷον interpretation.

The first is, e.g., found in Crombie's *Plato*[1]. He qualifies this interpretation as an anachronism, since it would imply a *subjectivation of being*, – and this, he says, is of a much later date: it does not occur before Plotinus.

Now first, those who use this argument are mistaken in their Plotinus interpretation. In fact, the ἀρχηγός of Neoplatonism does not "subjectivate" Being at all. On the contrary, he repeatedly posits with a certain emphasis, though Νοῦς = τὰ νοητά and τὰ ὄντα = τὰ νοητά, that the intelligible order is *primarily* Being[2] and that the identification of νοητά with Νοῦς does not at all imply that the intelligible "objects" (as we are accustomed to say) were "produced" by the divine Intellect in such a way that they would not have existed before. Of course, this makes no sense, since Being is *eternal* Being in which all things are ever present in an eternal NOW. In Plato, there is not the slightest doubt about this, νοητά are BEING, primary (archetypal) Being. Moreover, in Plato's text there is no direct reference to a divine Mind thinking the νοητά. Neither in the *Timaeus* nor in our passage of the *Sophist* does Plato start from such a concept. What he does start from is: the concept of Being in its perfection. And this, he says, implies Soul and Motion, Thinking and Wisdom[3].

Thus, as an implication of the perfection of Being, the notion of a

[1] I. M. Crombie, *An examination of Plato's doctrines*, London 1962-63.
[2] *Enn.* V 9, 7-8; cf. VI 2, 21.
[3] φρόνησις.

thinking Mind arises. But, both in our *Sophistes* passage and in the *Timaeus*, Plato speaks rather of a *perfect Living Being* – which for him implies thinking. Nowhere does he speak of a divine Noûs thinking on itself. All we can say is that, logically speaking, at the level of intelligible Being the "perfect Living Being" can be nothing but a Divine Mind. And "thinking" at this level is intuitive thinking, i.e. a thought that finds its object within itself. In that sense, then, the equation: Noûs = τὰ νοητά is Platonic.

Secondly, there is a whole set of arguments that were at my request put forward by Professor E. de Strycker (Antwerpen) in a discussion that took place in my own Institute at Utrecht, March 1969. The essential points were the following.

1. In Plato's dialogues there are many things that must not be taken as the author's opinion. In each particular case the context has to be carefully considered. Now in *Soph.* 248e-249aff. the problem is: If all motion, including both ποιεῖν and πάσχειν, is denied to the παντελῶς ὄν – as in fact it is by the "Friends of the Ideas" –, intelligible Being cannot be known. However, knowledge of intelligible Being must be possible. Therefore, *some* kind of motion must be attributed to "perfect Being".

Which kind of motion? – Obviously the passive one of being known, which qua πάσχειν is a κινεῖσθαι.

This point being established, the Stranger from Elea (say, Plato) has got what he wanted: the conclusion is

"Καὶ τὸ κινούμενον δὴ καὶ κίνησιν συγχωρητέον ὡς ὄντα."

That is to say, "motion" in the passive sense of being known is attributed to intelligible Being. That this and nothing but this was actually what Plato wished to argue, can be seen in what follows: the doctrine of the five supreme kinds is concerned with the intelligibility of being, and so is that of the κοινωνία τῶν γενῶν.

2. In Plato the term νοῦς does not have the character it has in Plotinus: it is not a "hypostasis", not a kind of substance; it is just a function or activity of the soul.

3. Granted that the ζῷον interpretation of the *Sophistes* passage is not an anachronism qua subjectivation of Being, yet in a sense it is an anachronism. For the concept of God as a thinking Mind that thinks on itself is Aristotle's and not Plato's.

Of these three objections the first is by far the most important.

Here an interpretation of the *Sophistes* passage is proposed, which might seem acceptable – were it not that a whole part of Plato's text is simply passed over. For it is not so that our passage only argues that Being must be known and *ergo,* since being known implies a passive motion, motion in the passive sense must be admitted. It says explicitly and with a certain emphasis that *Life* and motion, *Thinking* and wisdom cannot be denied to that which perfectly IS. Can we say to that: "Well, yes, that is what Plato says here, but it is not what he *intends* to say. What he intends to establish is that Being is known and thus, in a sense, a passive motion is to be admitted."

I ask: Does he make fun then, in this passage? Does the Eleatic Stranger make fun, here in this dialogue where – after a long hesitation – he sets out to attack the august wisdom of his venerable Father Parmenides, not without excusing himself for appearing to behave as a murderer of his own father?

Surely, there is a good part of humour in the description of the "Sons of the earth" and the "Friends of the Ideas". But in answering the problem raised by the latter in their radical denial of any kind of motion, any ποιεῖν or πάσχειν, to that which perfectly IS, I rather have the impression that he is in dead earnest. I really do not see we have the right to say here: "O yes, of course, he says that, but that is not what he **means".**

The argument that the text stands quite alone in Plato's work does not hold good. It is true that the *Sophistes* goes on to follow the line of the intelligibility of Being in the passive sense. But in the *Timaeus* we are confronted with the reality of a transcendent archetype of the visible world which by the Demiurge was made a living being. Now it is not so that the Idea of ζῷον, containing the pattern of all kinds of living beings, will do as a pattern of this visible world. It is obviously the intelligible order as such that is referred to in these passages. Moreover, we have the passage in Aristotle's *De anima* I 2 concerning αὐτὸ τὸ ζῷον, which can only be understood in this sense[1].

As to the meaning of νοῦς in Plato, I have said a word on that.

Lastly then, there is the point that Aristotle, and not Plato, is to be credited with the concept of "God as a Mind that thinks on itself". This is a strange argument indeed. As if, because Aristotle describes his Prime Mover as νόησις νοήσεως, Plato could not have conceived of his perfect Being as living, and "moving" with the motion of a thinking

---

[1] Above, p. 200, with n. 1.

SOME CONTROVERSIAL POINTS

mind. To this I can only repeat: *but he says it*! And I am not satisfied with the reply: "Oh, he says so much!"

These then are a few points involved in the three major controversial questions of Plato interpretation mentioned in the beginning of this chapter. I think it was worth-while to consider them afresh.

CHAPTER X

WHAT WAS GOD FOR PLATO?[1]

1. *The problem, in the judgment of Ancients and Moderns*

"Plato's theology" is a subject which has been much discussed, both in Antiquity and in the modern era, particularly in the last century. In Antiquity it was, no doubt, because again and again philosophically minded people found a religious inspiration in Plato's thought and handed his philosophy on to their pupils exactly in this sense. In the modern era the approach to Plato has been very different: historic-philological interpretation found a "problem" in Plato's theology because it could be tackled from different angles and hence gave rise to very different results. Modern investigation has discovered a conflict in Plato: the conflict between philosophical thought on the one hand, and "religion" in the traditional sense on the other. It has found in him all kinds of difficulties which we are not able to solve adequately, because Plato himself, it has been said, never made any systematic theology. If anybody who had not read his Plato but studied the modern scholarly literature on the subject, should try to arrive at a true understanding of what Plato thought about God, I am afraid he would get the impression that this is rather an obscure subject, full of uncertainties and subjective interpretation. He would think that it is hardly possible to find the truth about this matter. What is remarkable is, that in later and late Antiquity such a difficulty was not felt.

In later Antiquity Schools of Platonism existed in which the philosophy of Plato was understood and lived in a religious sense. This does not begin as late as the so-called Neo-platonist School, say with Plotinus, in the 3rd century A.D., in Alexandria and in Rome; we find it in Plutarch in the early 2nd century and in the very heart of

---

[1] This chapter goes back to a lecture given in Dutch and followed by further explanations. It dates from March 1963. The text was first published in the South African *Acta classica* of 1964-65, afterwards in my book *Theoria* (1967). A Japanese translation appeared in the above-mentioned volume "Greek philosophy and Religion", Tokyo 1969. This is the first English edition.

ancient Greece. Plutarch lived not far from Delphi and was a pious believer in the Gods of Greek tradition. We find it also in the *Epitome* of Albinus, in the popular preacher and writer Maximus of Tyrus, and in the work of that strange fellow who was the African Apuleius. They all give a precise answer to the question of *"What was God according to Plato"*[1].

Plutarch's answer is very clearly expressed in the treatise on the E in Delphi[2]. It is a discussion between six persons on the meaning of the big letter E which was written on the wall of the Delphic temple. Different explanations are proposed. The last speaker, Plutarch's master Ammonius, rejects them all and declares: This letter signifies the answer of man given to God. For to everyone who approaches this place the God says: *Know yourself*[3]. To this command we for our part reply: *EI*: *Thou art*. You, God, are; you alone exist, in the full sense of the term. All the other things and beings, including ourselves, *are* not really: all mortal beings are between coming-into-being and passing away. They are unstable, vague and somehow unreal. You cannot catch hold of them if you try to grasp them: like water they run through your fingers. True being, on the other hand, is eternal, it has no beginning and no end. It does not change, it is beyond time, it has neither past nor future. For that would mean being-not-yet or being-no-more. God only IS simply and without any restriction: not in time, but in eternity, which is beyond motion, time and change. Nothing is before Him, nothing after Him, nothing is older, nothing younger; being one in the "now" which is one, he has completed the "always". Hence, only this eternal Being IS in the full meaning of the term.

Therefore He has to be addressed in veneration with this word: *Thou art*, or also like some of our forefathers used to say: *Thou art one*. For the divinity[4] is not many, just as everyone of us consists of innumerable elements or properties, a manifold mixture, consisting of all kinds of things. That which IS must be one, just as the One must *be*. For "otherness" which as a principle of distinction[5] separates

---

[1] Τίς ὁ θεὸς κατὰ Πλάτωνα was the title of one treatise of the philosopher-preacher Maximus of Tyrus. Apuleius, too, wrote a special treatise on Plato's theology.
[2] *De E apud Delphos*, ch. 17-20.
[3] The Γνῶθι σαυτόν which also was written on the Delphic wall.
[4] τὸ θεῖον.
[5] He refers to the ἕτερον, which in Plato's *Sophistes* was assumed as one of the five supreme kinds.

itself from being, ends in coming-to-be, that is, in not-being in the full sense. −

That was Plutarch. Maximus of Tyrus in his treatise *What was God according to Plato* argues as follows.

The world around us is full of strife, discord and disharmony. But in all this strife you can see that the world is ruled by one uniform Law which is reasonable, one *Logos*[1]. For one God is the King and Father of all. There are many gods, sons of God, who are subordinate to Him and assist Him in ruling. All agree on this, Greeks and non-Greeks, inland- and coast-inhabitants, wise men and not-wise.

The world is a stream of continually changing things. Hence, if we want to find the one God who is always identical with himself, we have to climb up by means of our reason as to an akropolis and place Him there on the level of Noûs itself which is the supreme Ruler.

Maximus explains further: I do not mean that noûs which in principle is able to think but actually does not always do so, but the actually thinking Noûs which is always thinking, without release and without any limitation. *Absolute* thought. "The messenger[2] from the Academy gives us Him as our Father and declares Him to be the generator of the universe"[3]. He does not call Him by name, for he does not know any; he neither speaks of colour nor of size, for he did not see nor touch Him.

> "The Divinity itself[4] cannot be seen by the eyes, not expressed in spoken words, not touched by the body, nor heard by the bodily sense of hearing. Only by what is most noble, most pure and most spiritual, by what is lightest and most precious of the soul can it be seen through a simile and heard by a kindred spirit. It comes present to us wholly and at once by a total understanding[5].
>
> "Perfectly to comprehend its Nature has not yet been granted us here. But if you wish to hear at least something about it, well then, let us say that God is *beauty, radiant beauty*, − not of the body, but He is the Source from which all corporeal beauty

---

[1] It is interesting to find such a Stoic-Heraclitean description of the universe in this second century Platonist.

[2] ἄγγελος.

[3] γεννητὴν τοῦ ξύμπαντος.

[4] τὸ θεῖον αὐτό.

[5] ἀθρόᾳ συνέσει.

springs. If this is sufficient, then you have now seen God; if it is not enough, how shall we denote Him then?"

It is clear what was for these authors the answer to the question of what was Plato's God: they teach us without any hesitation that for Plato God was *intelligible Being*, which is *perfect Being*; that Being which must be assumed as existing in a transcendent order, if we want to explain the presence of sensible things in their manifold and ever changing appearance. For their very change implies a certain harmony and order. And how to account for this otherwise than by referring back to that perfect Being which is an ever thinking Noûs?

It is clear that in distinguishing a noûs which by nature is such that it can think but does not actually think, and another Noûs which is always actually thinking, Maximus follows Aristotle, though from a considerable distance. That he was not alone in this, will appear in Albinus' *Epitome* X 2-3, in which not only the distinction between a potential noûs and an always actually thinking Noûs is made, but also the latter is transcended by a "first Noûs" which acts as the unmoved Mover of the always thinking noûs of the universe, while it is described itself as "thinking of itself". Apparently Platonism of the second century A.D. passed both through the Stoic doctrine of the cosmic order and through Aristotle's Prime Mover theory. Nonetheless, it is a kind of Platonism. That God is described here by preference as archetypal Beauty, will not be too strange to the readers of Plato's *Symposium*: it is interesting, however, because modern interpreters of Plato have often objected to this identification.

After all, both Plutarch and Maximus are speaking about intelligible, perfect Being which, as is said in the *Phaedo*, is accessible only "to the Soul-itself", detached from the body and its desires as much as possible. Under these conditions, however, it was believed to be accessible, up to a certain degree at least.

In fact, this was Plato's doctrine in the most classical accounts he gave of the concept of *philosophy* and the task of the *philosophos*. First, in the *Phaedo*. Here philosophy is defined as an exercise in dying; for it is striving after φρόνησις, i.e. after knowledge of intelligible Reality which can be attained only when the soul is "in itself" and "pure" as much as possible, detached from the body and its desires[1]. That is why the philosopher will always be glad to go "yonder", for he has good grounds for hoping that there he will find what he has

---

[1] 67c-68b.

longed for throughout his life. The object of that longing, φρόνησις, includes for Socrates *true virtue*: self-restraint (σωφροσύνη), courage (ἀνδρεία) and justice (δικαιοσύνη), for these presuppose exactly a complete detachment from bodily desires[1]. Thus, philosophical insight proves to be a kind of purification, and true virtue appears to be impossible without it.

"Let us posit two kinds of being, the visible and the invisible", Socrates goes on[2]. "To which of these two is the soul most akin?" — It is obvious that she is most akin to the invisible. In contradistinction to the ever changing visible world the invisible is described as always the same[3]. Now, when the soul considers anything with the help of the body (which belongs to the world of visible things), she is dragged off to that which is always changing and always eluding the grasp of the intellect. Hence, she is troubled and feels dizzy and uncertain. On the other hand, when she investigates anything by herself, she leaves things here, passing on to things yonder, "to what is pure and always-being, immortal and always identic with itself". And since she is akin to that, she is always together with those things whenever she is living to herself. That is the end of erring: she is "always in the same way and identic with herself". The body, however, is most like what is human and mortal, non-intelligible, multiple: it falls asunder and is never identic with itself.

Therefore, the soul will aspire to go yonder, to that divine Reality to which she is related. Yonder she will be at home and feel happy.

The man who has these aspirations is called φιλόσοφος by Plato. In the *Phaedo* the "lover of wisdom" is opposed to the "lover of the body" (φιλοσώματος), who will appear to be also a "lover of money" (φιλοχρήματος) and often a lover of honour (φιλότιμος) too[4].

Thus far the *Phaedo*. The soul *resembles* that which is divine: she bears *a close resemblance* to it (is ὁμοιότατον), she is *akin* to it (συγγενής), and she is *assimilated* to it by detaching itself from the body and by itself searching after that superior *Reality* which is yonder. Thus, she passes into the same nature: always identic with itself, eternal and immortal. The word θεῖον is repeatedly used here to indicate intelligible Reality.

This is what we find in the *Republic* as well. In b. V[5] a definition of the *philosophos* is sought for. *Philosophoi* are people who both like to learn and learn easily. They are insatiable in their hunger for knowl-

[1] 69b.   [2] 79a.   [3] 80ab.   [4] 68bc.
[5] 474d-480a; *Greek Phil.* nr. 289ab.

edge. But here a distinction must be made: there is true knowledge, and there is a kind of half-knowledge. The first is concerned with an ὄν, the latter with a μὴ ὄν. The great majority of those who like to learn, however, are not interested in "things-themselves", which is the intelligible object, but in things concrete, which is a kind of imperfect image of them. Men like to *see*: they are φιλοθεάμονες. That is to say, they like to see *things* of beauty. But Beauty-itself, the intelligible Source of all visible things of beauty, is beyond their understanding. They are not able to see it at all.

This means: they do not achieve any *true* knowledge but stop at that kind of half-knowledge which Plato, following in the footsteps of Parmenides, called δόξα. "Lovers of wisdom" (philosophoi), however, are those who search for Being-itself, the only object which can be truly known. They do not stop at the many beautiful things – those things that from certain points of view or after a certain lapse of time will appear ugly –, they are able to raise their spirit to Beauty-itself, Greatness-itself, Justice-itself, and so on.

Here, then, follows the definition of *philosophoi*[1].

"*Philosophers are those who are able to live in contact with that which is always in the same way and identic with itself*".

φιλόσοφοι μὲν οἱ τοῦ ἀεὶ κατὰ ταὐτὰ ὡσαύτως ἔχοντος δυνάμενοι ἐφάπτεσθαι.

That is, those who are able to live in perpetual or repeated contact with eternal, perfect Being, the present infinitive (ἐφάπτεσθαι) expressing either a continual or a repeated action.

Towards the end of Book VI a similar division of reality is given as in the *Phaedo*: the realms of the visible and the invisible are now opposed the one to the other as αἰσθητά to νοητά, objects of sense-perception to objects of thinking[2]. What is meant by this opposition is expressed in the simile of the cave[3]: it is meant in such a sense that there is one reality only, which is both "real" and "true", the ὄντως ὄν, intelligible Being. Both its transcendent character and its dazzling beauty are strongly emphasized in the simile.

The ultimate ground of intelligible Being is the Idea of the Good. In the intelligible order it takes a similar place as the sun in the visible world: it is both the cause of being and of its being known. Plato does not call it an ὄν. As the ultimate ground of being it transcends being:

[1] At the beginning of Book VI, 484 b; *Greek Phil.* nr. 289 c.
[2] 509 d - 511 e; *Greek Phil.* nr. 294.
[3] VII 514 a - 517 c; *Greek Phil.* nr. 295.

it is ἐπέκεινα τῆς οὐσίας, superior to it both in dignity and power[1].

Pressed by Glauco to explain precisely what is meant by the analogy with the sun Socrates answers more or less evasively: he will certainly omit many things, not deliberately, but because he is not able to give a complete account. Anyhow, he will do his best. There follows at the end of Book VI that passage in which the intelligible is spoken of as "hypotheses" serving as "steps", by means of which one can ascend to the last and absolute Ground, the ἀνυπόθετον. Thus, at the end of the simile of the cave it is said that the soul, once she has ascended the way up to the νοητὸς τόπος, at the end will see the Idea of the Good. She will see it – though "hardly"[2], and this sight is necessary for anybody who wishes to act wisely, either in private or in public life.

Here, then, is the calling of the philosophos for human society: he who alone knows Reality and Truth, and has seen something of its deepest ground, he alone is able to lead other men on to a life in accordance with this norm. As to himself, he will not desire to return to the world of those who do not know Reality and Truth, "from divine sights to human things", as Plato says[3]. But he *has* to go back for the sake of the others, who live in darkness and never have seen Light.

We can quote other parallels. There is the ascent from visible beauty to spiritual beauty, culminating in the contemplation of Beauty-itself, in the speech of Diotima[4]. Here too, the sight of Beauty-itself is described as an inner experience which grants to man the complete realization of all his aspirations and desires. It is also said that the man who has attained to this sight cannot fail to produce fruits of true virtue, because he has come into contact with Truth itself[5].

Then, there is the ascent of the soul in the *Phaedrus*[6]: the upward ride to the "place above the heavens", where those souls that are able to follow the Gods will enjoy the sight of eternal Truth. "It has neither colour nor form, it cannot be touched, it can be contemplated only by

---

[1] 509b; *Greek Phil.* nr. 292, at the end.
[2] VII 517b: τελευταία ἡ τοῦ ἀγαθοῦ ἰδέα καὶ μόγις ὁρᾶσθαι. *Greek Phil.* 295, at the end.
[3] ἀπὸ θείων θεωριῶν ἐπὶ τὰ ἀνθρώπεια.
[4] *Symposion* 210a-212b; *Greek Phil.* 273.
[5] ἅτε τοῦ ἀληθοῦς ἐφαπτομένῳ (212a).
[6] 246a-248e; *Greek Phil.* 272.

the spirit, which is the governing part of the soul." Soul is described here as a charioteer guiding a horse team, one horse of which symbolizes the human passions: it pulls downward to the earth and is reluctant to go upwards. Hence a violent struggle: many of the souls are not able to follow the lead of "the Gods" (that is, the perfect souls) who ride upward easily and undisturbed. They stay behind and loose their wings, they fall back on the earth and remain in the semi-knowledge of "opinion". The purified souls, however, ride upward and attain to the divine Reality of "things-themselves", the sight of which they enjoy with great delight and satisfaction.

Now shall we say that such a "place beyond the heavens" is a mere product of fantasy, that it cannot exist and that, even *if* it existed, man could not profit by it because it would be separated from the world in which he lives?

That is what Aristotle said. Platonists in later Antiquity judged differently. To them that language about an ὄντως ὄν which is beyond the visible world and in which this world is founded, was not so strange. They did not feel it as a difficulty that, for instance, Socrates says in the *Phaedo*[1] that the soul, which is invisible and goes to a place of the same nature – "noble, pure and invisible" – will find in Hades "the good and wise God"[2], and that he himself, when it is God's will, will have to go there in a moment. They were far from drawing the conclusion that, *ergo*, for Plato God was something different from that impersonal world of Ideas which was a mere abstraction. To them the ὄντως ὄν, very far from being a mere extract from things here and resulting from a certain operation of the human mind, was *primary Being*, ontologically prior both to the visible world (of which it is the cause) and to human knowledge. Plato called it τὸ θεῖον. He *lived* the contemplation of it clearly as the fulfilment of his most profound aspirations. It is here that we moderns utter the word "God". The Platonists of later Antiquity did so, too. That is what we found in Plutarch and in Maximus of Tyrus. It is interesting to see how Plato's doctrine was understood by St. Justin who lived in Palestine in the middle of the second century and followed the teaching of a Platonist before coming into contact with Christianity. Justin describes it himself in the opening section of his *Dialogus*, in which he tells the story of his life[3].

[1] 80 d.
[2] τὸν ἀγαθὸν καὶ φρόνιμον θεόν. [3] *Dialogus cum Tryphone* 2-8.

One day he had retired to a solitary region to be alone with his own thoughts. At that time he had been in the School of Plato for some time – perhaps for several years. He had gone there after having been disappointed in the masters of several other schools of philosophy which he had tried successively. He had left them in the end, because they did not teach him anything about God. In the School of Plato he felt more at home.

> "I was fascinated by incorporeal things", he says. "The contemplation of the Ideas gave wings to my intellect, and I thought I had become wise in a short time. I even was so stupid as to hope I would see God directly. For that is the goal of Plato's philosophy."

Apparently he means that the contemplation of the ὄντως ὄν and of its ultimate ground, the Idea of the Good, was "the goal of Plato's philosophy". And that much would have been granted by Plato himself, I suppose.

Justin, then, is walking there in his self-chosen place of retreat, not expecting to find any human being there. He is surprised at seeing in that place a dignified old man who follows him at some distance. Justin turns round to him and starts a conversation. The other asks him what he has come to that solitary spot for. "I like to converse with myself without being troubled," replies Justin, "and nothing is as important as philosophy."

"What is philosophy", the other asks, "and what happiness does it bring?" To this question Justin gives the following explanation.

„Philosophy is the science of Being and science of the Truth, and happiness is the reward for this science and wisdom."

"And what do you call God?" the other asks.

Justin replies promptly:

> "That which is always in the same way and identic with itself, which is the cause of the existence of all other things, that is God. He is not to be seen with the eyes, as other living beings, but can be grasped by the spirit only. The eye of the spirit is such as to be able to see Being-itself which is the cause of all that is intelligible. This Being-itself, which is beyond all being, unutterable and ineffable, is the only true Beauty and the true Good. Well then, this springs up suddenly in well-endowed souls, by congeniality and by the love of contemplation."

This is the Platonism of Justin, before he had come into contact with Christianity. Certain solutions have been found here, and identifications made, which modern interpreters often make great difficulties of. First, the Good, which according to *Republic* VI was ἐπέκεινα τῆς οὐσίας, is called by Justin "Being-itself which is beyond all being". Second, this is said to be unutterable and ineffable – indeed not a bad rendering of what Plato meant –, thirdly, this is identified with αὐτὸ τὸ καλόν, fourthly, this is called *God*. Plutarch and Maximus of Tyrus did not find any difficulties in such identifications either. And were they wrong, after all? What else was intended by Plato in that supreme principle which he called the Good? Ranking it beyond Being, he might have called it unutterable and ineffable, as he did in fact by having his Socrates declare himself unable to give any adequate account of it. And was not this Principle to him the Source of all beauty, and in so far Beauty-itself?

According to the testimony of his own students, Plato identified his Idea of the Good with the One[1]. It must be accepted that he did so, at least in his later years. But is there any indication that he ever called the Good "Beauty-itself"? – "In the *Symposion*," it might be answered, "he did, at least implicitely." I think so. Yet, Plotinus, that most congenial interpreter of Plato's philosophy, did not make that identification. He placed Beauty on the level of intelligible Being, not on the level of the One. Yet, in the contemplation of Beauty he enjoys something of the presence of God. He *does* call it "God" – as he did concerning intelligible Being as a whole.

Here we touch upon another difficulty to modern thought: the ancient Greeks – not Plato only but, for instance, Aristotle and later Platonists as well – thought it quite a normal thing to speak of "God" and "the Divine" on different levels. To them it was not so that, if the One or the Good is God, *ergo* intelligible Being which springs from it is *not* God. Platonists feel very strongly the transcendency of that Being, its perfection, its character of a norm. To them it was as it were that side of the supreme Divinity which is turned to man. In itself, the Divinity is "unutterable", that is, beyond thinking just as it is beyond being, even intelligible being. What man can understand by his reason is: that such an ultimate principle, which is absolutely one, *must* be assumed. But he cannot describe it, nor give any rational account of it. Plato, and also Plotinus, call it "the Good", but in doing

[1] Aristotle, *Metaph.* N 4, 1091b13-14; Aristoxenus, *Harmonices elementa* II, p. 30 Meibom. *Greek Phil.* nr. 364; Gaiser, *Ungeschriebene Lehre*, nr. 7.

so they were clearly conscious of the fact that in this case "good" is not a predicate which as such could be distinguished from its subject. It is the subject itself. "God *is* his essence, he *is* his goodness", St. Thomas says[1], and in this he follows the Platonists, in particular Plotinus[2]. Certainly in this sense God could be called "Beauty" as well, and Plotinus did not deny this, though as a rule he preferred to call the One "the Good".

There is one other thing in Plato's thought on the Divine which is alien to the modern mind. It is the fact that purified souls, that is those who live up to the standard of philosophy, are called "gods"[3]. This does not mean that these souls are identified with intelligible being. It *does* mean that they are related to it, rather than to material things, including the body. Hence the "flight from here" and the "assimilation to God as far as possible" (*Theaetetus* 176ab): the soul has to make herself resemble God as much as possible, if she wishes to be "divine". It is not said in this passage that man must be ἴσον to God, which would mean "identic with", but ὅμοιον, which indicates resemblance. And the ὁμοίωσις θεῷ is defined as "becoming just and pious with the help of philosophical insight"[4]. That is to say, it is not possible to come up to that level without "philosophy" – which means: without detaching oneself from the body and searching for transcendent Truth by that faculty by which alone it can be found.

Again, that souls living on this level are called "gods" does not mean that Plato when writing this, say in the *Phaedo* or the *Phaedrus*, would not have regarded intelligible Being or the Idea of the Good as God. That is a modern kind of misunderstanding, which is very far from Plato indeed. Our passage of the *Theaetetus* says exactly the opposite. For what is meant by "God" in that famous formula of ὁμοίωσις θεῷ? "That man who wishes to be happy must fly from here to yonder and make himself resemble God as much as possible." One answer only can be given here: "God", that is *the intelligible order*, the Ideas, including the Good. This transcendent order in its totality

---

[1] Thomas Aquinas, *S. Th.* I 3, a. 3: Deus est idem quod sua essentia vel natura;
 S. Th. I 19, a. 1, ad 3 m: Voluntas Dei est eius essentia. – Objectum divinae voluntatis est bonitas sua, quae est eius essentia.
 S. Th. I 40, a. 1, ad 1 m: Quia vero divina simplicitas excludit compositionem subjecti et accidentis, sequitur quod quidquid attribuitur Deo, est eius essentia.
[2] Plotinus, *Enneades* VI 8, 12.1-15; VI 8, 13.5-8, 27-33; V 5, 13.1-11. *Greek Phil.* III, nr. 1393.
[3] E.g. in the *Phaedrus* myth, and in *Phaedo* 82b-c.
[4] δίκαιον καὶ ὅσιον μετὰ φρονήσεως γενέσθαι (*Theaet.* 176b).

was to Plato "God", and he even said so explicitly in the above-quoted lines.

Whatever may be further said about second century Platonism, this much is certain, that these Platonists understood much better about what Plato was actually concerned[1] than many of his 19th and 20th century interpreters. For on this very point, which for Plato was most essential, modern Plato interpretation made its gravest errors.

The first was this: that, since for Plato only souls are gods and he never called the Ideas by that name, we have to construct Plato's theology without speaking about the theory of the Ideas[2]. A very strange interpretation, which testifies to its author's inability to understand the meaning of Plato's philosophy. Since Burnet it has almost become an Anglo-Saxon tradition that Plato called only souls gods, and never called Ideas by that name. Because it may seem to be correct in the most literal sense, I wish to observe, first, that the intelligible world is often referred to by Plato as a θεῖον, second, that the word θεός is used in the ὁμοίωσις passage of the *Theaetetus* with a clear reference to the intelligible world, third, that from the *Phaedo* up to the *Timaeus* and the *Nomoi* Soul is considered as superior to the order of the body and *akin* to the intelligible order, but is never identified with the latter or ranked on a level superior to it. In the *Phaedo* and the *Phaedrus*, in both of which perfect souls are called "gods", it is indirectly, in virtue of the contemplation of the intelligible Truth, that Soul has her divine character. In the *Timaeus* it is no different: the souls of the stars, which as such are perfect, are called "gods" – but they are "created gods", gods of a secondary order, far from being superior to the intelligible world. That it was no different in the *Laws*, should not be too hard to understand for anybody to whom Plato's thought it at all congenial.

The second major error of modern Plato interpretation has been: that a contradiction, or at least an incongruity was found between his philosophic thought and his religious belief: the one and the other were supposed to have "coexisted" in his mind, if "peacefully" yet not in logical harmony. That is to say, modern thought has not been able to integrate what Plato said about "God" and "Gods" into the frame-

---

[1] *Epist.* VII 341 c: περὶ ὧν ἐγὼ σπουδάζω.
[2] This strange thesis was defended, for instance, by F. Solmsen, *Plato's Theology*, Ithaca, N.Y., 1942. The work was sharply but rightly criticized by E. de Strycker.

work of his philosophy, – a thing the Ancients did without any difficulty or hesitation. What is worse is that a solution of the "problem" was forced by separating the one element from the other by a division into periods: in the first half of his life and work, say the "classical" period, Plato is supposed to have had "philosophy without religion", while in the later works he is found to have rather "religion without philosophy"[1].

This is amazing *qua* misunderstanding. The first part of the interpretation shows a total lack of understanding as to the meaning of transcendent Reality to Plato, while in the second part the peculiar character of certain later works of Plato has not been taken into the account. No attention has been paid to the fact that in the *Timaeus* there is a good deal of mythology, applied not naively but quite deliberately. In the *Nomoi* rules are given for a population as a whole, while in the *Republic* the author was concerned with educating a small circle of carefully selected, particularly well-endowed persons. It was suggested that in the *Laws* the theory of the Ideas was superseded by a doctrine of "souls"[2]. For in the 10th book of the *Laws* souls are taught to be the cause of motion and, hence, the rulers of the universe – which, of course, is not to be denied; it is only to be completed. Soul as a cause of motion rules the universe. But it is on no account the *ultimate* cause of things, – it is just the *nearest* cause.

A similar mistake is made by those who think that, since in *Laws* X the belief in the star-souls as gods is strictly prescribed, this was in his later years the true "religion of Plato"[3]. A typical mistake of those moderns for whom the word "God" has one single meaning, and hence they are blind to the fact that for instance for Plato this was not so. The point was better understood, e.g., by Mgr. A. Diès. In his Introduction to the *Laws*[4] he observed quite rightly that in this work

---

[1] Thus P. Bovet, *Le Dieu de Platon d'après l'ordre chronologique des dialogues*, Genève 1902. Bovet followed Lutoslavsky's views expounded at the end of his famous work *The origin and growth of Plato's logic*, London 1897, ²1905. At present, some authors are still impressed by these theories, e.g. the Dutch Jesuit fr. H. Robbers in his work on Greek influences on Christian thought (1959), a book which shows a remarkable lack of congeniality with Plato's philosophy.
[2] This is what Lutoslavsky proposed in his above-cited work. The thesis was adopted, for instance, by Burnet (*Greek Philosophy* I, Thales to Plato, London 1914, ²1928) and hence got rather a strong hold on Anglo-Saxon minds.
[3] This is what H. Robbers wrote in his above-cited work, (*supra*, n. 1).
[4] Platon, *Oeuvres Complètes*, t. XI, 1ière partie, Introduction I, Plan et intention générale des Lois, p. XC f.

which was written "for everybody", Plato deliberately did not go up to the higher and the highest level, that of transcendent Being and its ultimate Cause: he thought it neither necessary nor suitable in this work to go higher than to the *first* level of divinity seen from the point of view of man. On this level it is possible to give a proof of the existence of the divinity which can be understood by the masses, and that is what Plato is doing here. Of course this does not mean that for himself there was nothing beyond that level. Far from it. A passage such as *Laws* XII 965bc, in which it is demanded from the guardians in the state of the laws, just as it was demanded from the rulers in Plato's first state, that they should be able to see the one Idea in the many and different things, such a passage proves that for Plato the background has not changed.

It is time to conclude. The question as to "What was God for Plato" proves to be more difficult, and at the same time easier than it would seem to be at the first glance. It is more difficult, because the right answer presupposes a true understanding of Plato's philosophy – and many were not able to come to such an understanding according to Plato's judgment. But that is not all. It presupposes also a certain understanding of the syncretism inherent in Greek religious tradition; I mean that kind of religious thought which is always able to give to the many gods of popular belief their place within the framework of philosophical thought. One should not think that this is a peculiarity of Plato and that, for instance, Aristotle used the word "God" in one meaning only[1]. Far from it. Aristotle, too, integrated traditional polytheism into his philosophical system. He even did so with a certain emphasis and satisfaction[2]. When reading ch. 7 of Book Λ of the *Metaphysics*, the modern reader might get the impression that to Aristotle "God" was the Prime Mover, and the Prime Mover alone. But it is not so. The First Mover proves to be at the top of a whole series, and after having determined the precise number of these unmoved Principles, Aristotle states with an unmistakable satisfaction that this strictly scientific doctrine tallies perfectly with the tradition of popular religion: quite rightly our forefathers thought that "primary substances" (αἱ πρῶται οὐσίαι) were gods. It is true that "for the persuasion of the masses" they attributed to these substances the

---

[1] Fr. Robbers in the above-cited work (*supra*, p. 222 n. 1) thinks this is so.
[2] Aristotle, *Metaph.* Λ 8, 1074a38-b13 (the last page of his chapter on the multiplicity of unmoved Movers).

mythical form of men. But nonetheless, their basic thought was right.

This is what Aristotle said with regard to the unmoved Movers of the celestial spheres: he thinks it right to call them gods. But also the higher intellect in man is somewhat emphatically called by that name in one of his relatively early works[1]. And lastly, let us not forget that in his will he ordered the dedicating of a statue of his mother in the sanctuary of Demeter, and to erect two life-size marble statues, one for Zeus Soter (*Redemptor*) and another for Athena Soteira (*Redemptrix*) both in his native town of Stagira[2].

For us all this is perhaps very difficult to understand, for the Greek it was just a normal thing. The Stoics and later Platonists continued the tradition of Plato and Aristotle in this respect: they are monotheists in their own way, that is, their monotheism does not exclude the many gods, but integrates them by subordination, either allegorized and rationalized or not.

When coming from Platonism to faith in Christ, Justin had to correct and to complete certain things. That which was completely new to him was the same as what is still new to anybody of our own days who comes from any kind of philosophy or rational belief to the revelation of God working in history, sending his prophets and in the fulness of time coming to man in a human body. For Justin this was a thing totally unheard of. And so it is for us.

This does not mean, however, that what we learned from Plato on the highest level of νοῦς, no longer counts. We should be bad philosophers if we thought so. For Justin, just as a few centuries later for St. Augustine, the Christian revelation did not cancel the Platonic doctrine of transcendent Being, it confirmed it. They learned from it that the rational thought of an intelligible order, which was the archetype of visible things, was not a dream or fantasy, and that, when the ancient Greek philosophers arrived at conceiving that primary and archetypal Reality as Life and Spirit[3], they actually saw something of eternal Truth.

[1] *Protrepticus*, fr. 10c Ross (Düring B 108-110): ὁ νοῦς γὰρ ἡμῶν ὁ θεός.
[2] *Diogenes Laertius* V 1, 16.
[3] It was Plato who, at a certain moment of critical reflection on his own metaphysics, said that life and spirit cannot be denied to that perfect and eternal Reality of his noetic world: *Sophistes* 249a. In Middle Platonism (Albinus and Maximus of Tyrus) there is a certain fusion of Plato's intelligible world with Aristotle's concept of the Noûs which eternally thinks of itself, and similarly Plotinus conceived the intelligible world as a Noûs containing the intelligible objects within itself.

It has been often said that to Plato and his followers divine Being was impersonal. This can hardly be said to be a reproach. For evidently they could not *know* that absolute Being is "personal". *We* can know, because it has been *said* to us, – because we have *seen* it in Christ. But from ourselves, by the mere power of human thinking, we could never be sure.

On the other hand, for us who have the certitude we have, Plato's reflection on eternal Being can only deepen our thoughts on God and increase our reverence and gratitude. For eternal Being is the Logos, and we know that the Logos is God.

2. *The Demiurge and the good World-Soul*

We found that in such dialogues as the *Phaedo*, the *Symposium*, the *Republic* and the *Phaedrus* Plato spoke about knowledge of the ὄντως ὄν as a kind of heavenly vision, granted only to the purified soul and raising man to a higher spiritual and moral level. Hence, Greek authors of the first centuries of our era, both non-Christians and Christians, found in this Plato's lived experience of the Divinity: eternal and unchanging Being became to them the definition of God, in so far as it is possible to "define" a Being which, as they knew quite well, is beyond our understanding. And doubtless, they were right in this, though of course a number of questions still have to be raised.

The first question to be asked is obviously: *And what about the Demiurge?* For does it not seem so that in the *Timaeus*, where Plato is constantly speaking about "God" (ὁ θεός) in the personal form, calling him "Father" and "Creator" of the soul and of the visible world in its beautiful order, – does it not seem so that here we come much nearer to the notion of a personal God who cares for man and can hear his prayer?

Asked in this form the question implies a few other problems, which in modern minds may naturally spring from a certain religious conviction. The implications are: (1) Since God is a personal God who cares for man and hears his prayers, it is in the *Timaeus* we find what actually can be called Plato's God, not so where he speaks of the Ideas, including the Good. (2) Is it perhaps true that for Plato the belief in a personal God sprung up only in his later years, after the classical dialogues? (3) If that is so, God-the-Demiurge in the *Timaeus* and God-the-good-World-Soul in *Laws* X might actually have taken the place of the Ideas and the Good. Or what else can we think?

Let us first consider the question of *What was the Demiurge*. In itself this question has a certain implication. It implies that, since in the *Timaeus* Plato is dealing with a subject he cannot deal with in terms of strict science, he speaks in a somewhat vealed form; hence, the figure of the Demiurge *signifies* something. Therefore, it is not sufficient to say, for instance: "The Demiurge was the Creator of the world and of the soul; he realized the visible world after the eternal pattern of the Ideas". This is just repeating Plato's consciously symbolic language. We *must* venture to ask the question of *What does it mean*.

I dare to reply: *the Demiurge was a transcendent Noûs*.

Does this appear in the text of Plato? I think it does. Firstly, because the Demiurge creates Soul. He creates "divine", i.e. perfect souls, that which encircles and pervades the world, and those who penetrate and rule the heavenly bodies. He also creates the bodies of the seven planets which are the "visible gods". Lastly he creates human souls. But he does not create any bodies for men. He could not do that, for if he did, they would be like the gods: immortal. That is why he charges the "created gods" to make mortal bodies for the human souls made by himself. From this account we have to conclude in any case that the Demiurge "was" or denoted a Being which ontologically was of a level superior to Soul. When using a philosophical term which Plato used himself we must say, then, that apparently the Demiurge was of the level of intelligible Being, the νοητόν, as it is called collectively by Plato in *Republic* VI 509d ff., denoting the same as "the invisible" in *Phaedo* 79a, which is opposed to the ὁρατόν.

Now from that passage of the *Phaedo* we learn that Soul "resembles more" and is "more akin" to the invisible. The latter is "that which is always in the same way", eternal and immutable Being which according to *Symposium* 212a and *Republic* V 475e ff. is the ἀλήθεια, after which the philosopher aspires and of which he alone is said to attain to the vision. Apparently the Demiurge belongs to this level of Plato's hierarchy of being. We have to remember *Philebus* 22c, where Plato's Socrates opposes "the true and divine Noûs" as a being of a higher kind to the noûs of the individual man. The terms "true" or "real" (ἀληθής and ἀληθινός) are used by Plato when he speaks about the intelligible world which is the archetype of visible things. Therefore it is almost certain that the ἀληθινὸς ἅμα καὶ θεῖος νοῦς of

Philebus 22c was the transcendent Spirit which as the Demiurge in the *Timaeus* was the Creator of the Soul.

In *Philebus* 28c is written that all wise men agree that Noûs is the king of the heavens and the earth: Noûs is said to govern and order all things, the cosmos, sun, moon and stars. A little further on, in *Philebus* 30cd, it becomes clear that in this case no transcendent Noûs was meant, but the World-Soul's intellect. The same might be true of *Timaeus* 47e, where τὰ διὰ νοῦ δεδημιουργημένα is opposed to τὰ δι' ἀνάγκης γιγνόμενα[1]. Neither this text of the *Philebus*, however, nor such passages as *Timaeus* 30b and 46d (where it is said that noûs is always in a soul) can prove that Plato did not assume the existence of a transcendent Noûs. Those who drew that inference[2] did not notice that in the above-cited passages of the *Timaeus* the visible world only is referred to. It is different in *Sophistes* 248e-249a: here the intelligible world is meant. It is of this Reality that Plato says: to this Being, which is perfect and divine, life and motion, soul and insight cannot be denied. For it is not possible to say that it does not live and think but exists, honourable and holy, without noûs, in eternal rest.

The fact that movement, be it the movement of thinking, seems to be introduced here into the realm of eternal Being, which by definition was "always the same and identic with itself", troubled modern interpreters greatly[3]. It was A. Diès who, first in his thesis of 1909, later in his edition of the *Sophistes*, proposed an interpretation which offered an escape from that inacceptable consequence: instead of motion being introduced into the intelligible world he suggested that the notion of "being" was extended, so as to include the soul[4]. Others

---

[1] This interpretation was advocated by J. H. Loenen, *De Noûs in het systeem van Plato's philosophie*, thesis, Amsterdam 1951. I wish to observe that the term δεδημιουργημένα rather obviously points to the Demiurge as Cause of the cosmic order. But of course I am willing to agree that the Demiurge made the World-Soul as his instrument.

[2] I think in particular of J. H. Loenen in the above-cited work.

[3] The interpretation expounded in the following pages, dated 1966, does not differ from that of the preceding chapter (1969). However, the latter was inspired by recent discussions, which made clear to the author how much a thorough discussion of the underlying texts was still needed.

[4] A. Diès, *La définition de l'être et la nature des Idées dans le Sophiste de Platon*, thèse Paris 1909. Cf. the *Introduction* to the Budé edition of the *Sophistes* by the same author. The interpretation of the παντελὲς ὄν of the *Sophistes* as meaning an extension of "being" was adopted by F. M. Cornford, *Plato's theory of knowledge*, Cambridge 1935, ²London 1946. It has been rather generally accepted in the Anglo-Saxon world.

went as far as to declare that from the *Sophistes* onward material things as such would have been acknowledged as ὄντα[1]. The latter interpretation is clearly erroneous; for both in the *Timaeus*[2] and in the *Philebus*[3] Being as immutable is very emphatically opposed to the ever changing world of things that come-to-be. An earlier dating of the *Timaeus*, such as was suggested by G. E. L. Owen[4], cannot save the interpretation; for it is not the *Timaeus* only, it is the *Philebus*, too, that stands against it.

The interpretation suggested by Diès and adopted by Cornford, was certainly more subtle. Yet it does not do justice to the fact that Plato emphatically declared not to be able to deny motion, life and thought to that realm of being of which he was speaking at that moment, viz. *intelligible* Being. After his introduction in which it was declared necessary to attack the thesis of Parmenides of the one and immutable Being, after the obviously ironical description of the position of the "friends of the Ideas", we must be prepared for some essential change. It is *not* that to intelligible Being which as such is and must be immovable and immutable, Soul is added as a different kind, now accepted as "being", in order to make "being" complete. That is not what Plato says. What he does say is simply *that to intelligible Being itself, of which he is speaking, motion, life and thinking cannot be denied*.

Somehow this must be understood as Plato's thought. And let he himself explain to us in what sense this is possible.

He does not do so directly, but he does more or less implicitly in the *Timaeus*, when describing the visible world made by the Demiurge as *a living and moving being* – κινηθὲν καὶ ζῶν (37c) –, made so after an eternal pattern. This παράδειγμα then is called explicitly a ζῷον ἀΐδιον, *an eternal living Being*; and since the Demiurge, who wishes to make his creation resemble the example as much as possible, cannot make it eternal, he creates Time as "a moving likeness of eternity".

Now let us consider this for a moment. The visible world, which has been described in the preceding pages as wholly permeated and ruled by a soul, was what the Greek called a ζῷον: an organic living being. It had been made so by the Demiurge after an eternal pattern, which was: the intelligible world. Now, if the likeness (εἰκών) is a ζῷον, then of course the example or παράδειγμα was. If it had not been

---

[1] This is the opinion of Sir David Ross, expressed in *Plato's Theory of the Ideas*, Oxford 1951.
[2] 27d-28a.   [3] 59a-c.   [4] Class. Quart. 1953, p. 79-95.

said by Plato, the inference should have been drawn by us. But it stands there in clear words: "Since αὐτό (the archetype) was an eternal living being, he undertook also to make this universe like it as much as he could."

That is to say, intelligible Being as a whole is conceived not only as an ordered whole, a cosmos, but as an articulated and organic unity: and that is exactly what the Greek called a ζῷον. For an organic unity is such by virtue of a soul; and since it is an ensouled being, it is a living and a moving being, moving by the motion of a thinking mind.

That is Plato's new conception of intelligible Being, and that is exactly what was expressed in *Sophistes* 249a. Modern interpreters rejected it, because to them it was an altogether strange idea. Nonetheless, this is what Plato meant[1].

Now, how was the Demiurge related to this intelligible world which was a thinking living being? It is said that in creating the world the Demiurge looked to the eternal pattern[2]. A little further on in the same passage[3] it is also said that, since the Demiurge was good, he wished that everything should be as far as possible like himself. This suggests that, in fact, for Plato the Demiurge and the eternal pattern were not separate entities but the same: the reasonable Cause called the Demiurge, who at first, while being represented as "looking to" the eternal pattern, seemed to be ranked on a level inferior to intelligible Being, now appears to be no different from it[4]. He *is*, so to speak, the intelligible order turned towards creation and personified into a creating God and Father.

Modern readers, whose mind is formed by a strictly monotheistic idea of God, might feel tempted here to conclude that, *ergo*, the Demiurge had taken the place of the Supreme Principle of Plato's metaphysics and as such has to be identified with the Good. In fact, this conclusion has been drawn again and again[5]. Plato, however, pointed in another direction. He ranked the Good *beyond* intelligible

---

[1] I expounded this view in the Brussels International Congress of Philosophy 1953: *Platon a-t-il ou n'a-t-il pas introduit le mouvement dans son monde intelligible?* (Actes du XIième Congrès de Phil., Bruxelles 1953, vol. XII, pp. 61-67).
[2] *Timaeus* 29a.
[3] 29e.
[4] This was rightly observed by P. van Litsenburg, S.J., in his thesis on *God and the Divine in Plato's dialogues,* Nijmegen 1955 (written in Dutch).
[5] Both J. H. Loenen and P. van Litsenburg in their above-mentioned works tended this way.

Being, of which it is the ultimate Cause. In the passage of *Republic* VI[1] in which he speaks about the Good and its relation to intelligible Being he is not concerned with the problem of the origin of the visible world. The latter is only referred to in a simile which shows that the function of the sun both with regard to physical things and to our knowledge of them is *analogous* to that of the Good with regard to intelligible Being and our knowledge of that. There is obviously a difference of level. The analogy, moreover, is worked out in this sense that, just as in the visible world both light and sight can be rightly called *similar* to the sun but *not identical* with it, thus in the region of the invisible, Reality and Science must be judged to be *akin* to the Good but not identical with it.

Thus, in this passage the transcendency of the First Principle to intelligible Being is clearly marked, while at the same time the difference of level between the intelligible order and visible things is unmistakebly brought out. All this is confused by modern interpretation when it suggests that the Good as the Creator of all Being must be identified with the Demiurge.

On the other hand, the Demiurge is clearly an intelligent Cause. It is a Noûs, superior to the souls created by it. But, since the intelligible world as a whole appeared to be conceived by Plato as the organic unity of a thinking mind, it is not so strange that it appears to be no different from the "eternal pattern" of the world to be created. When then the Demiurge is said to have "looked up" to that pattern, this is obviously due to the mythologizing form.

As to the identification of the Good with intelligible Being, which is advocated by those who wish to identify the Demiurge with the Good, modern interpreters[2] have pointed to such texts as *Republic* 518c8, where the Good is referred to as τοῦ ὄντος τὸ φανότατον and 526e4, where it is called τὸ εὐδαιμονέστατον τοῦ ὄντος. These texts, however, are not conclusive. For the genetive τοῦ ὄντος need not be partitive. It may be used in such a sense as, for instance, in that verse of the *Iliad* where it is said of some lovely garment:

ἔκειτο δὲ νείατος ἄλλων.[3]

"And it lay right at the bottom of the chest".

Neither is τοῦ ὄντος τε καὶ νοητοῦ (511c) conclusive in such a sense,

---

[1] 508c-509c; *Greek Phil.* nr. 292.
[2] E.g. Van Litsenburg, *op. cit.*
[3] *Iliad* VI 295.

that by these terms two different realms would have been denoted, the first of which would have been meant as superior to the latter[1]. It is much more natural to understand the two as denoting one and the same reality: Being which is intelligible. And this is certainly what Plato meant.

There are a few other problems about the Demiurge. For instance: *Was he actually a Creator?* Is it not rather that he just *arranged* some kind of eternal and pre-existing matter into the state of a cosmos?

This is an old problem. The Christian apologists of the 2nd century, for instance, blamed Plato for having assumed some matter "as old as God", or, somewhat less primitively expressed, "co-eternal". It can be questioned whether Plato meant this at all. The crucial point is how we have to understand a few lines of the *Timaeus* in which, first, some pre-existing chaos is mentioned which by the Demiurge is brought from disorder into order; next, the elements used by "the God" to construct the world are not said to have been made by him but somehow seem to be presupposed. The texts referred to are the following.

> *Timaeus* 30a. "Desiring, then, that all things should be good and, so far as might be, nothing imperfect, the god took over all that is visible – not at rest, but in discordant and disordered motion – and brought it from disorder into order, since he judged that order was in every way the better."
>
> *Timaeus* 31b-32b. "Now that which comes to be must be bodily, and so visible and tangible; and nothing can be visible without fire, or tangible without something solid, and nothing is solid without earth. Hence the god, when he began to put together the body of the universe, set about making it of fire and earth. But two things cannot be satisfactorily united without a third; for there must be some bond between them drawing them together. – Accordingly the god set water and air between fire and earth, and made them, so far as was possible, proportional to one another."[2]

If this must be taken literally, then, evidently, Plato taught that the Demiurge worked on some pre-existent material. According to a

---

[1] This is, again, suggested by Van Litsenburg.
[2] The translation is Cornford's in *Plato's Cosmology*.

more precise description, given further on in the *Timaeus*, before "creation" the elements were not yet what they are now, but "they did possess some vestiges of their own nature" (53b). When starting to describe the order of the universe, Timaeus went back to the very beginning of his discourse where the distinction was made between the two orders of existence, the intelligible and unchanging Being, and on the other hand Becoming, i.e. that which always changes. To these two a third principle is now added, which is called the Receptacle or nurse of things that come to be[1]. It is also simply called space[2]. It is said that this "Recipient" has no qualities; it is not a substantial being, but "a nature invisible and characterless, all-receiving, partaking in some very puzzling way of the intelligible, and very hard to apprehend"[3]. It provides a situation for all things that come into being, but it is apprehended itself not by the senses, but "by a sort of bastard reasoning", and is "hardly an object of belief"[4]. Now this Recipient is said to receive "the characters of earth and air" and to be filled with powers that were neither alike nor evenly balanced. By a kind of winnowing movement "the four kinds" are said to be shaken by the Recipient, so that the most unlike kinds are separated from one another, while the most like ones were thrust closest together; "whereby the different kinds came to have different regions, even before the ordered whole consisting of them came to be. Before that, all these kinds were without proportion or measure[5]".

Such, then, was the condition of the elements when the ordering of the universe was taken in hand. The god then began by giving them a distinct configuration by means of shapes and numbers.

To this description it must be observed, (1) that according to Plato's own views movement always presupposes a soul, (2) that time is created only together with the order of the cosmos. Apparently, then, we are not on the right track when taking the account of a pre-existing chaos given in the *Timaeus* to the letter. We must agree, as, for example, Cornford did in his excellent commentary on the *Timaeus*[6],

[1] *Timaeus* 48 c ff.
[2] *Timaeus* 52 ab.
[3] Ib., 51 ab.
[4] 52 b.
[5] 52 d - 53 b.
[6] *Plato's Cosmology*, p. 203 ff. Also P. J. van Litsenburg, *God en het goddelijke in de dialogen van Plato*, pp. 85 ff., argued rightly that in speaking of a "pre-existing chaos" in the *Timaeus*, one gives as it were a substantial existence to something which for Plato was not a "something" at all.

that neither the shaking movement of the Recipient nor the existence of some disordered and unformed elements at a time before order was introduced are thinkable according to Plato's own principles. But Cornford was also perfectly right when stating that, just as the figure of the Demiurge *symbolized* a transcendent and creative Spirit, the "pre-existing chaos" too must *mean* something which to Plato was quite real. Obviously he meant that there is some irrational factor by which the ordering power of the creating Spirit is limited up to a certain extent. This is brought out elsewhere in the *Timaeus* in the conception of Necessity, which is also denoted as "the erring cause".

When summarizing his preceding account Plato's *Timaeus* says again that, since at the outset things were in disorder and without any harmonious proportion, "there was not anything deserving to be called by the names we use now – fire, water, and the rest"[1]. It is somewhat abusing the text of the *Timaeus*, then, to say that Plato's Demiurge put the world together from pre-existing material or pre-existing elements. Nor should we follow the early Christian Apologists who attributed to Plato the doctrine of a "matter" that was "coeval" with God or coeternal. What Plato *did* assume in his *Timaeus* besides "Being" and "Coming-to-be" as a third principle necessary to explain the genesis of the cosmos, certainly could be called a "material principle" in the abstract sense this term had for Aristotle; but it must be borne in mind that this principle had no substantiality and was not tangible either by the senses or by the intellect.

What, after all, is *creation*? If it means that relative and finite being both in its coming-to-be and in its permanence is totally dependent on perfect and absolute Being, then it must be granted that this was exactly the meaning of Plato's theory of the Ideas. That he expressed this eternal relation in the myth of the Demiurge-Creator of the world, is a symbol full of meaning which for the author, doubtless, contained a profound truth.

After these preliminary questions let us now try to give an answer to the problems mentioned at the beginning.

1. *Is the Demiurge to be considered as Plato's true God because he has a personal character?*

This form of the problem is clearly a result of a "theist" approach: it is presupposed that "God" must be spoken of only when a personal Being is meant. Then in any case the Demiurge is "God", and the

[1] *Timaeus* 69b.

Idea of the Good is not. That is why Bovet, for instance, came to his distinction between a philosopher Plato who was "not religious", and a later Plato who was "religious" and much less of a philosopher. The Jesuit father Van Litsenburg wishes to save the religious meaning of the Idea of the Good. In this he is certainly quite right. It would be unfair to him to say that he just starts from the theist concept of God and hence, wishing to attribute a personal character to the Idea of the Good, comes to identify it with the Demiurge. Van Litsenburg emphasizes that in Plato's "classical" works the concept of a personal God is not absent at all: in *Republic* II 379 a-c Plato expressed what he thought essential to the concept of God. Now according to this passage God is essentially good and Cause of good to man. But that is to say, he is essentially Providence. Therefore, when granting that to Plato the transcendent Good was God, it is implied that he was Providence. Otherwise he could not be God. It is not alien to Plato's thought, then, to say that the Good is the same as the Creator of the cosmic order, called the Demiurge in the *Timaeus*.

This argument might seem to hold good. Yet it does not. What is wrong with it? There is one important point the author did not observe: it is the fact that Plato speaks of "God" on different ontological levels. It is true, no doubt, that Plato often spoke about "providence". From the *Apology* onwards to the *Laws* we find with him a strong belief in the care of God for man. And so essential was the belief in divine Providence to him, that in the 10th Book of the *Laws*, when framing his code with regard to religion, he treated as unbelievers not only those who denied the *existence* of God or the gods, but those who denied their providence as well. But it does not follow from this that he conceived divine Providence as a care for man and the cosmos exercised directly at the supreme level, by the Idea of the Good. This is *not* found in Plato, and it was definitely not what he meant. He taught that the Idea of the Good is the direct cause of *intelligible* Being. *Indirectly*, no doubt, it is by that very first causality the cause of *all* good, in the visible world as well. This world, however, is brought into being on a lower metaphysical level. The proof of this is, as we found, not that the Demiurge seems to be ranked under the Ideas – this *seems* to be the case at first sight, but on a closer inspection he appears to be of the level of intelligible Being itself –; rather it appears from the fact that the Good is beyond the intelligible world. And this is indeed an established fact.

But there is some more to be said about providence according to

Plato. For him the care for the cosmos and for man (in this sequence: first the cosmos, next man!) is exercised on two levels: primarily by the Demiurge who creates the Soul – the world-soul, star-souls and also human souls – and does so obviously on a level which transcends the Soul as such, secondarily by the reasonable Soul which encircles and pervades the visible world, and by the other created souls. Neither is it so that the Demiurge who is often denoted as ὁ θεός by Plato, comes to take the place of the Idea of the Good, nor does the World-soul – which is denoted as "god" and "noûs" as well – take the place of the Demiurge.

Since, then, the Idea of the Good occupies the highest level in Plato's hierarchy of being, it is against the spirit of Plato's thought to give preference to the Demiurge as a personal God over the Good which for Plato was obviously supreme, and not in the *Republic* only but up to his latest years[1].

2. *Did Plato only in his later years, after having written his classical dialogues, come to the belief in a personal God?*

Van Litsenburg, of course, tends to deny this, not only on the ground of the above-quoted passage of *Republic* II where providence appeared to be essential to Plato's concept of God, but also because the concept of a Demiurge is not confined to the *Timaeus* alone. With a certain emphasis he points out that it is found as early as in *Republic* X, where God is said to be the Demiurge of the Ideas[2]; next, it is present both in the *Sophist* and in the *Politicus*. In the *Sophist* he refers to that passage where a distinction is made between human and divine "making", in order to state that divine making is of a definitely superior character[3], in the *Politicus* the myth of the world-periods is referred to, in which is spoken of a "divine cause" (θεία αἰτία), repeatedly called Demiurge, who is said to rule the world which he has made[4].

The passage from *Republic* X is of particular interest in view of Van Litsenburg's thesis. Now is it true that in *Republic* X the Demiurge-Creator of the world is mentioned? The answer to this question must be in the negative: nothing like the Demiurge of the *Timaeus* is found

---

[1] That this was so, can be inferred with certainty from the identification with the One mentioned both by Aristotle and by Aristoxenus (*Greek Phil.* nr. 364).
[2] *Republic* X 595a-597e.
[3] *Sophistes* 265b-266d.
[4] *Politicus* 268d-275c. On this passage Van Litsenburg pp. 43-52.

in *Republic* X. There it is said that God makes the Idea of the bed, just as the craftsman (δημιουργός) makes a concrete bed by his craftsmanship. The analogy with the human craftsman does not go so far, however, that the terms of δημιουργός or δημιουργεῖν are applied to God and his activity. In this passage God is *not* called δημιουργός but simply "God", and his creative activity is not denoted by the verb δημιουργεῖν but is simply denoted by the verb ποιεῖν. Moreover, it is not the creation of the world that Plato is concerned with in this passage. All that can be inferred from it is: that "God" is said to "make" the Ideas, i.e. intelligible Being or Truth.

Van Litsenburg tells us to take the analogy with the human craftsman strictly to the letter: God is a divine Demiurge who "creates the Ideas". A powerful argument indeed on behalf of the identification of the Demiurge with the Idea of the Good. For nobody can deny that the Idea of the Good is the Cause of intelligible Being... Yet, it is better in this case not to follow Van Litsenburg's advice. We should rather follow Plato himself who, when speaking about the Good as the Cause of Being, introduced quite a different analogy: not that of a human craftsman, but that of the sun. The creative activity of the Good is compared to the radiation of light – which is the least material symbol that could be found – rather than to the production of concrete objects. And rightly so, for the symbol of the craftsman which could be used with regard to the creation of the visible world, was certainly less appropriate in this case.

For the identification, then, of the Demiurge of the *Timaeus* with the Idea of the Good, *Republic* X does not offer us a sufficient ground. It is true, of course, that causality was attributed to the Good, but on a level beyond the intelligible. Our passage of *Republic* X offers at most an *analogy* to the creative work of the Demiurge in the *Timaeus*. In the *Republic* Plato is not concerned with the problem of the origin of the visible world. That is something new in the *Philebus* and the *Timaeus*. I do not hesitate to say that both the figure of the Demiurge and of the world-soul (which appears also in *Philebus* 30c) make their appearance only relatively late in Plato's works. I do not wish to conclude from this, however, that Plato came to believe in a "personal God" only in that later period. What can be said is this: that in a sense the problems of the world and of man came only late into the centre of Plato's interest, and with them the problems of creation and of providence. That does not mean, however, that he did not believe in it before.

3. The third and last question to be answered ran as follows.

Is it so that God-the-Demiurge of the Timaeus and God-the-good-World-soul of Laws X have taken the place of the Ideas and the Good, or what else should we think?

The first part of this question has been answered by me in the negative: the Demiurge of the *Timaeus* and the good World-soul of *Laws* X have *not* taken the place of the Ideas and the Good. Behind this answer is the conviction that Plato never abandoned the theory of the Ideas. I wish to maintain this, though I have been among the first to state that the *Parmenides* and *Sophistes* mark a crisis in Plato's thought[1]. A crisis, however, does not necessarily mean an break. It *does* mean that the theory of the Ideas passed through a very severe self-criticism by its author, and that under this criticism certain things have changed. We came across a few of them: (1) Parmenides' doctrine of Being, not yet attacked in the *Theaetetus* by some deliberate hesitation[2], is criticized in the *Sophistes*; (2) motion is introduced into the intelligible world: it is one of the five "supreme kinds"[3]; (3) motion, life and thinking are attributed to intelligible Being as such[4]. To these three points I add as a fourth: the fact that from now on Plato turned his interest to a different field, to the visible world and its genesis (the *Timaeus*), to the problems of man as a soul united to a body (the second part of the *Timaeus*), to that of a certain legitimate place of ἡδονή in human life (the *Philebus*), and to the enormous task of serving human society by legislation. All this does not imply, however, that he abandoned the theory of the Ideas.

In the last twenty years it has been advocated from different sides that he did. The refutation of Parmenides' thesis in the *Sophistes* has been understood in such a sense that from now on the visible world would have been accepted as "being", this term being no longer, as it was previously, restricted to the intelligible world. Thus, for instance, Sir David Ross in his work on the theory of the Ideas[5]. He was followed by G. E. L. Owen[6]. To those who advocate this view an obvious difficulty is that in the first part of the *Timaeus* most emphatically the

---

[1] I have dealt with this crisis in my work *Een keerpunt in Plato's denken*, Amsterdam 1936.
[2] *Theaetetus* 183e-184a; *Greek Phil.* nr. 313.
[3] *Soph.* 250a-c; *Greek Phil.* nr. 339.
[4] *Soph.* 248e-249a; *Greek Phil.* 315c.
[5] *Plato's Theory of the Ideas*, Oxford 1951.
[6] *The place of the Timaeus in Plato's dialogues*, in *Classical Quart.* 1953, p. 79ff.

classical division is made between eternal and immutable Being, and on the other hand the always changing world of coming-to-be. That is why Owen proposed a much earlier dating of the *Timaeus*: does not the very introduction to this dialogue point out that it was written immediately after the *Republic*, so that it is anterior to the crisis?

What Owen failed to see is that the whole spirit of the *Timaeus*, its main problem, the appreciation of the visible world and the way in which the problems of man are treated, show clear signs of a changed interest. Moreover, with the earlier dating of the *Timaeus* all difficulties are not removed. We found the classical opposition of Being to Becoming once more in the *Philebus*[1], while the Ideas reappear towards the end of the *Laws*[2].

The thesis of the abandoning of the theory of the Ideas in its classical form also found adherents in Germany. After Wilpert who, coming from the ἄγραφα, held that the theory of *ultima principia* attributed to Plato by Aristotle and a few others was incompatible with that of the Ideas and hence must have superseded it[3], a somewhat more conservative interpretation was recently proposed by Wilhelm Kamlah[4]. He thinks that from the *Sophistes* onward the Idea is no longer represented as the archetype of things here, and these things no longer as "imitations" of the archetype. As for the *Timaeus*, Kamlah does not take the way of dating it early. He recognizes perfectly the later character of this dialogue. The fact that the Demiurge in creating the world is said to have looked to an eternal pattern (παράδειγμα) does not confuse him at all. True, the world is called an εἰκών, he says, but the stress is on the *likeness*, not on the unreality ("Scheinhaftigkeit") of visible things. The eternal pattern is the example, – it is no longer the archetype. In the *Timaeus* the visible world is no longer to be despised, it is of a lower value than the eternal which is perfect, – and that is all.

Kamlah has an open eye for the change of Plato's interest: it is perfectly right that in the *Timaeus* the approach to the visible world and man is different from what it was, for instance, in the *Phaedo* and the *Republic*. But does that mean that the theory of the Ideas in its classical form has been abandoned, so that no longer a transcendent

---

[1] 59 a-c.
[2] *Laws* XII 965 bc. Owen's dating of the *Timaeus* has been treated elaborately and has been duly criticized by H. Cherniss, *Amer. Journal of Phil.* 1957, pp. 225-266.
[3] P. Wilpert, *Zwei aristotelische Frühschriften über die Ideenlehre*, Regensburg 1949.
[4] *Platons Selbstkritik im Sophistes* (Zetemata 33), München 1963.

archetype of sensible things is assumed? In this the interpretation is mistaken. For if the Demiurge in creating the world followed an eternal pattern, which is conceived as a transcendent Reality, what else could this be but the "archetype" of visible things? And that which by K. is agreed to be an "image" (εἰκών), how would it for a Greek not be an "imitation", a μίμημα produced by the divine Craftsman after the eternal Example?

After all, it is, I think, a sign of spiritual maturity when the philosopher whose first concern was almost exclusively for the ascent of the soul to the world beyond, is now able to return to things here and is willing to occupy himself intensely with the problem of the genesis of this world and with the life of man as it is according to experience.

I now pass on to the second part of the question under discussion: if then Plato stuck to the same metaphysical conception, if the philosophical "belief" in the Ideas is not to be separated from that in a personal God-Creator and Providence as belonging to a different period of his life, how then are the two to be connected? Or did they simply coexist in his mind?

It has been observed again and again that Plato himself did not make any coherent system of "theology" in which the different aspects of his thoughts on God and the Divine would have been duly integrated and made into an ordered whole. So it seems left to us either to find connections between those different religious elements in Plato's works which to our eyes appear to stand unconnected the one next to the other, or, if we think that for himself they were actually unconnected, to opt for the thesis of a peaceful coexistence. Different ways of synthesis have been tried. Van Litsenburg added a very audacious one to them by identifying the Demiurge with the Good and reckoning the Good to intelligible Being. Even the World-soul of *Laws* X must then be ranked on the same level. This is, of course, not so simple. Van Litsenburg tries to solve this problem by suggesting that the proof of the existence of God offered by Plato in *Laws* X, was "adapted to the understanding of the masses". He does not mean by this that in Plato's eyes the World-soul was actually of a lower level than the Demiurge and the Good – for this is exactly what he wants to deny. He suggests that the proof was "metaphysically incomplete", because adapted to a lower *psychological* level.

What *should* be said in order to explain the relation between the Good, the Demiurge and the World-soul is that Plato used the term θεός *on different ontological levels.* In his metaphysics the Soul had the first degree of transcendency, seen from the material world. Soul which according to *Laws* X is of an order superior to Body[1], takes an intermediate position between αἰσθητά and νοητά, in such a way, however, that it is more akin to the latter. Plotinus was, indeed, not the first to say this. It is in Plato's *Phaedo* where the division between visible and invisible reality is made, while soul, without being reckoned as belonging to the invisible world, is said to be more akin to it[2]. Plato's doctrine of the soul as a self-moving principle is to be placed in this framework.

That the Demiurge who creates the Soul is ontologically of a superior level, i.e. of that of the intelligible, is not hard to understand. And that the Idea of the Good as the ultimate ground of intelligible being, ranks above that level, has been clearly said by Plato. It is hard to deny that the conception of a hierarchical order of being was essential to Plato's philosophy.

But this is, exactly, what explains to us why Plato speaks so differently about God and the Divine. It explains to us how the philosopher who as an educator in his great work on the best form of the state criticized the poets in their way of representing God and prescribes how they should speak about him, for himself searched for the last ground of all things by that faculty which he felt to be supreme, and in the contemplation of perfect Being and its ultimate principle lived by experience something of the fulfilment of the deepest craving of his soul, and that the same philosopher, when he had arrived at a certain degree of spiritual maturity, turns back from that height to things here below and, attempting to explain the dependence of this world on that which he knew to be primary Reality, speaks of a God-Creator who after the intelligible pattern forms the cosmos as an ensouled living being.

One must not think that to us modern men, and to us Christians, this part of Plato's thought is easily accessible, or more so than what is called his classical philosophy. In fact, the spiritual world of the *Timaeus* is to us a strange world and hard to understand, – if at least one takes it as it is. What we can say with certainty is, that the Demiurge is a transcendent Cause and a Noûs which, as the cause of Soul and of the visible world, has its place on a level inferior to the Good. I do not think we betray Plato's thought when saying: *the supreme Principle*

---
[1] 892a-c: πρεσβυτέρα τοῦ σώματος.
[2] 79a-d.

which is the Good manifests itself on a lower level, which is that of intelligible Being, in that transcendent Spirit which creates Soul. In this sense there is a coherence in Plato's thought on the Divine.

Not easy to understand, for the Christian in particular, is Plato's doctrine of the soul. The ensouled universe, the World-soul and the star-souls, they are not at all such acceptable, or even accessible conceptions to us. As it is, it is to us a strange doctrine. That the World-soul represents in the visible world the supreme Principle which is the Good[1], is perfectly true. But this fact does not give us any right to identify the one with the other. A minister "represents" the King, an ambassador, a sheriff's officer and a police-man represent the King. They do so on a different level. None of them *is* the King. But there is a connection. This is what Plato expresses in the symbol of the fathership of the Demiurge: the Demiurge *creates*, or "makes", perfect souls, including those that are to be united with a human body. That is to say, the soul depends directly on the transcendent Noûs-God which is of the level of intelligible Being, just as intelligible Being depends directly on the Good.

It must be stated again that Plotinus was not the first to say this. This doctrine is present in Plato, and this is the only way to understand the coherency of his doctrine on God and the Divine. How strange and difficult this doctrine is to a Christian, can be seen, for instance, in the case of Van Litsenburg. He is quite indignant when reading Festugière who in *L'idéal religieux des Grecs et l'Évangile* says that in Plato the soul of the philosopher deifies itself. "Nowhere in Plato do we read that", is his answer; on the contrary, again and again we find Plato praying to God for help in dealing with difficult subjects. – That is true. Only, one must not think that such prayers are not found, for instance, in Plotinus, from whom Van Litsenburg wishes to separate Plato carefully. And let us reread *Phaedo* 82 a-c. Here we read in clear words that only those who have practised philosophy will arrive at the rank and order of the gods. What else is this, after all, but "the philosopher deifying himself"? It is hardly possible to deny that this is found in Plato.

Let us conclude. Is it true that there is a lack of coherence in Plato's teaching about God and the Divine? Is there "peaceful coexistence"

---

[1] Van Litsenburg, *op. cit.* p. 188, speaks of the World-soul in *Laws* X as "representing" that which was "God" for Plato in the full sense. This is correct, if taken ontologically, not psychologically only.

of essentially heterogeneous elements, philosophy and traditional religion? – Not so, for Plato they were connected. The connection, however, can be understood only when Plato's doctrine of being is considered as it was actually conceived: as a hierarchical order. It will be easy enough, then, to place both Plato's "philosophical" approach to God and his "religious" conception of the Demiurge and his doctrine of perfect souls within the frame-work of these metaphysics. By Plato himself none of the three would have been called non-philosophical, I guess. But would one of the three have been granted by him not to have been religious? – Obviously these were the difficulties of some modern interpreters who, by applying their own criteria to Plato, separated what for him was connected and hence precluded themselves from a true understanding of Plato's thought. That thought, which was always "philosophy" and always "religious", knew God and the Divine on three different levels. That is different from what the Christian calls "God". Religious inspiration, however, is not lacking in Plato, also for a Christian, if only he knows how to understand. Most probably he will then find a copious source of religious inspiration in this Greek philosopher, not particularly in the *Timaeus* and in *Nomoi* X, or at least not exclusively there, – but perhaps still more where the philosopher speaks to philosophers.

CHAPTER XI

LA DERNIÈRE PHASE DE LA PHILOSOPHIE DE PLATON ET L'INTERPRÉTATION DE LÉON ROBIN[1]

C'est un fait bien connu que la dernière phase de la philosophie de Platon nous pose des problèmes assez difficiles à résoudre. A côté des derniers dialogues nous avons le témoignage d'Aristote, et celui-ci parle d'une forme de la théorie des Idées que nous ne connaissons guère par les dialogues. Or, Aristote était sans doute un esprit tout autre que Platon; – si nous ne le savions pas, E. Frank l'a démontré une fois de plus dans ses articles sur l'opposition fondamentale entre ces deux penseurs[2]. Cela n'empêche pas qu'Aristote a connu l'enseignement de Platon à l'Académie et que, par conséquent, il dispose de certaines données dont nous ne disposons pas. On fera donc preuve de sagesse en ne négligeant pas son témoignage. Sans doute il faut s'en servir comme d'un supplément à côté des dialogues de la dernière période de la vie de Platon. Il est clair que, en faisant cela, il faut s'avancer avec beaucoup de précaution, en se rappelant toujours que, lorsque c'est Aristote qui parle, nous n'avons jamais à faire avec des données directes, mais qu'il nous faut pénétrer à travers une interprétation et en chercher une autre, plus conforme au style de Platon lui-même.

C'est Léon Robin qui, ayant fait un travail préparatoire d'une importance capitale dans son premier grand ouvrage sur les Idées et les Nombres[3], nous a donné une telle interprétation dans son volume plus récent, intitulé «Platon»; une interprétation qui, surtout puisqu'elle

---

[1] Cette étude date de 1947. Elle fut écrite pour les *Studia Vollgraff*, volume offert en 1948 au grand helléniste et archéologue Wilhelm Vollgraff, notre maître inoubliable à l'université d'Utrecht. Les problèmes dont il s'agit ont été repris dans le chapitre XVI (sur l'idée de l'ἄπειρον chez Platon etc.), en partie dans le ch. IX. Mes raisons pour en faire reproduire le texte dans ce volume ont été exposées dans la Préface. J'y ai fait quelques retouches et ajouté quelques notes.
[2] *American journal of Philology*, 1940, pp. 34-53 et 166-185.
[3] *La théorie platonicienne des Idées et des Nombres d'après Aristote*, Paris 1908.

fait comprendre d'une façon entièrement nouvelle l'unité de style du platonisme, mérite plus d'attention et plus de confiance qu'on ne lui prête d'habitude. C'est ce que je me propose d'expliquer dans les pages qui suivent.

Qu'est-ce que la théorie des Idées? Robin en donne une description à la fois succincte et précise[1]:

«Admettre l'existence de «choses» qui ne soient qu'intelligibles; donner aux qualités, et même surtout à des qualités morales, le privilège de cette existence; prétendre que, loin d'être une sorte de sédiment des expériences de notre vie, ces purs intelligibles sont au contraire le principe éternel de la présence des qualités dans les êtres que nous percevons par nos sens et de l'existence qui, pour un temps limité, appartient à ces êtres; considérer ces essences formelles comme des réalités permanentes et exemplaires, dont ce que nous représentent nos perceptions n'est qu'apparence fuyante et copie imparfaite, – voilà l'essentiel de ce que nous appelons la «théorie des Idées» ou des «Formes».»

Cette conception se trouve déjà dans l'*Euthyphron;* puis, beaucoup plus élaborée, dans le *Gorgias*, où Platon expose que c'est un principe d'ordre, un «arrangement propre» qui fait que le bon est présent dans une chose. Le devenir peut réaliser une imitation plus ou moins réussie de l'être. Il *tend* vers l'être, et cette tendance se détermine sous la forme d'une proportion mathématique. Or, ces dernières idées ne recevront leur complet développement que dans les dialogues de la dernière période, dans le *Philèbe* surtout, ou dans les doctrines de l'enseignement oral telles que nous les a fait connaître Aristote.

A la thèse de Protagoras prétendant que l'être d'une chose consiste dans la représentation que s'en fait tel sujet, Platon oppose dans le *Cratyle* l'unité et l'identité de l'objet connu. Il faut admettre l'existence de certaines «Formes» toujours semblables à elles-mêmes, sans mouvement ni changement. Sinon, la connaissance elle-même devient impossible. D'après la théorie de la réminiscence dans le *Phédon* ces «Formes» ont une antériorité réelle d'existence.

C'est dans ce dernier dialogue que Platon envisag le problème des attributs essentiels. Ici il ne s'agit plus d'une relation entre des choses sensibles, mais *d'une relation entre des «Formes»*. Il y a certaines Formes qui peuvent participer les unes aux autres, et certaines autres qui s'excluent. Ainsi donc il y a déjà dans le *Phédon* l'idée d'une

---

[1] *Platon*, Paris 1935, ch. IV, au début (p. 100). L'exposé que je fais suivre est un résumé de ce chapitre.

participation mutuelle, éternellement réglée, des essences. Or, c'est cette première participation, nécessaire et immuable, qui fonde une deuxième participation, celle des choses sensibles à ces essences synthétiques. Cette dernière est variable et fluente. Dans ces pages du *Phédon* on voit déjà l'idée que les essences forment une hiérarchie: il y a donc là une anticipation de la doctrine du *Sophiste* sur la «communication des genres».

L'idée d'une hiérarchie de l'être devient plus distincte vers la fin du sixième livre de la *République,* où nous trouvons toute une échelle de l'être et parallèlement toute une échelle du savoir. Les objets mathématiques sont placés au-dessus des choses sensibles, les Idées au-dessus des objets mathématiques, et dans le monde des Idées l'Agathon est au sommet comme source de tout être et de tout savoir. Il y a analogie entre le domaine inférieur et le domaine supérieur de l'être, il y a en outre des *degrés intermédiaires*. Nous les retrouvons dans le second discours de Socrate dans le *Phèdre.* Il y est question d'un «lieu supracéleste», où résident les purs objets de la contemplation. Mais cette seule façon de le désigner indique que le ciel, avec ses révolutions astrales qui sont mathématiquement réglées, est un lieu *moyen* entre ce lieu qui le domine et le lieu d'ici-bas où se déroule le devenir de nos existences mortelles. Or, ce lieu moyen, où triomphe la mathématique, est aussi le lieu naturel des âmes.

Pareillement dans le *Théétète* l'examen de la définition sensualiste de la connaissance et les recherches sur l'opinion vraie et l'erreur visent à nous suggérer que le devenir a sa réalité propre à côté de l'être, mais qu'il lui est subordonné. M. Robin a caractérisé la nouvelle tendance du platonisme par une analogie expressive: «Platon est en quête d'un équivalent *philosophique* de ce qu'est *mythiquement* le démonisme; d'où l'importance que prend à ses yeux le problème de l'amour.»

Le *Phèdre* et le *Théétète,* où l'auteur est préoccupé de trouver des intermédiaires entre le monde sensible et celui des Idées, forment donc une transition au point critique dans l'évolution de la pensée de Platon: le *Parménide* et le *Sophiste.* C'est dans ces dialogues que la théorie des Idées, telle que nous la connaissons par le *Banquet,* le *Phédon* et la *République,* en même temps que la thèse du Parménide historique, est soumise à une critique sévère, qui mène à une révision profonde. Dans la seconde partie du *Parménide* c'est un *Éléatisme transformé* qui se prépare. Robin le détermine comme un *relativisme ontologique:* dans le monde des Idées comme dans celui des sensibles il y a des relations, des entrelacements d'opposés; mais dans le monde intelligible les confusions et les contradictions s'effacent, parce que, parmi toutes ces relations, on a déterminé un ordre de subordination. C'est ce que Platon a élaboré dans ses derniers dialogues: le *Sophiste*, le *Politique* et le *Philèbe*.

Jusqu'à ce point nous avons suivi l'exposé de M. Robin non seulement avec un vif intérêt, mais aussi avec une adhésion personnelle. Tout en gardant l'unité de la pensée de Platon, il a très bien montré la crise par laquelle cette pensée passe dans le *Parménide* et le *Sophiste;* ensuite, en déterminant le résultat de ce revirement comme un Éléatisme transformé, il en a marqué le caractère par un terme entièrement juste.

Après son étude du *Parménide* l'auteur délaisse pour un temps les exposés de Platon lui-même: il n'est pas possible de se former une idée à peu près exacte de la dernière phase de la philosophie dePlaton sans tenir compte du témoignage d'Aristote sur les ἄγραφα dans *Metaph.* A 6 et 9; M 4, 5, 8sq.; N et *De anima* I 3. Aristote expose d'une façon correcte la genèse de la théorie des Idées: en face de l'Héraclitéisme Platon se voit forcé d'admettre l'existence de réalités universelles, permanentes, intelligibles, à part de ce qui est individuel, changeant, sensible. A l'égard des choses concrètes elles jouent le rôle de principes déterminants, tandis que celui de principe matériel appartient à l'apeiron.

Mais, à leur tour, ces «Idées» sont des réalités composées où s'unissent un principe matériel qui est le même que celui des choses sensibles et un autre principe formel, l'Un, identique à l'Être et au Bien, et peut-être nommé aussi l'Égal. Ces deux principes constituent également ce que Platon appelait les Nombres-Idées, qui sont des essences individuelles et pour cela ἀσύμβλητοι, «inadditionnables entre eux»[1]. Au-dessous de ces Nombres-Idées Platon admettait des grandeurs pareillement idéales: la Ligne, le Triangle et le Tétraèdre, dont le rapport aux grandeurs géométriques était le même que celui des nombres idéaux à l'égard des nombres arithmétiques.

Les Nombres-Idées forment donc une classe supérieure entre l'Un et les Idées proprement dites, comme les objets mathématiques ont leur place entre les Idées et les choses sensibles. Ce ne sont pas des Idées *du* nombre (puisqu'Aristote dit dans *Eth. Nic.* I 4 que Platon

---

[1] Pratiquement cette interprétation est juste, bien que Van der Wielen (*De Ideegetallen bij Plato*, Amsterdam 1941, p. 62vv.) ait raison d'établir qu'ἀσύμ-βλητοι signifie proprement «pas comparable»: du fait qu'ils ne sont pas ὁμοειδῆ suit que les Nombres-Idées ne sont pas additionnables.

n'admettait pas d'Idées des choses dans lesquelles il y a de l'Avant et de l'Après); ce sont des *types de constitution*. Si les textes d'Aristote ont quelque ambiguité à l'égard de la place des Nombres-Idées, elle est élucidée par le clair témoignage de Théophraste dans sa *Métaphysique* (fr. XII 13 Wimmer; 6 b 11 sqq. Ross-Fobes): d'après Platon, dit-il, ce qui, à partir des principes, vient en premier lieu dans la hiérarchie des êtres, ce sont les Nombres et ensuite les Idées. «Ainsi se continuerait une doctrine qui déjà se dessinait à la fin du livre VI de la *République* et dans l'allégorie de la caverne.» Les choses de l'expérience sont des composés que nous pouvons déterminer quantitativement d'après des nombres et figures mathématiques, qualitativement d'après les Idées. Si maintenant les Idées sont à leur tour conçues *comme des composés*, il faut les réduire à un ordre mathématique plus élevé, dans lequel la qualité s'unira à la quantité. Ce seront les Nombres idéaux.

Robin trouve une confirmation de cette thèse dans les derniers dialogues de Platon: dans le *Sophiste*, où il s'agit de relations dans l'être, tandis que le monde intelligible y est vu en effet comme «un grand vivant», comme un intellect, ce qui rappelle les déclarations d'Aristote dans le *De anima*. Ensuite dans le *Philèbe* avec sa doctrine sur l'«être mixte» qui, d'après Robin, n'est sûrement pas limité au domaine de l'expérience, mais s'étend aux Idées elles-mêmes, le péras et l'apeiron étant, également dans ce domaine supérieur, les éléments constituants. La «Cause» qui produit le mélange, doit être l'Un ou l'Agathon. Et comment est-ce que les Idées sont «constituées»; comment est-ce que la «mixtion» a lieu? D'après un ordre spirituel plus élevé et plus subtil, répond Robin, et il en montre les indications dans le *Philèbe* (64 b): le *logos* de la vie mixte est comparable à une sorte d'arrangement incorporel, qui devra, en belle manière, commander à un corps animé. Robin conclut: si donc le principe du bien pour la vie de l'homme ici-bas est un cosmos spirituel, cette conception doit valoir pour le macrocosme comme elle vaut pour le microcosme: le système de relations intelligibles qui est le principe du bien pour ce grand vivant qu'est le monde, sera le monde des Idées. Et si les Idées, à leur tour, forment une espèce de corps vivant, nous trouverons, pour en commander l'organisation, un autre cosmos d'une intelligibilité encore plus subtile et plus épurée: les Nombres idéaux et les Grandeurs idéales.

Cette description de la pensée de Platon dans sa dernière phase surtout, doit être assez surprenante pour la plupart de ceux qui se sont familiarisés un peu avec les dialogues de Platon. Plus encore que par l'audacieux de l'hypothèse elle est surprenante à cause de son unité de style, qui – il faut le dire après mûre réflexion – est bien celui de Platon.

Quant à l'hypothèse elle-même – la superposition des Nombres idéaux au-dessus des Idées –, elle n'est pas nouvelle pour ceux qui ont suivi le travail de Robin dès le début: longtemps auparavant l'auteur est arrivé à cette conception, dans son premier ouvrage sur les Idées et les Nombres, qui date de 1908. Mais la méthode suivie dans ce premier travail diffère de celle dont il se sert dans le présent volume. Voyant la difficulté d'arriver à un accord sur l'interprétation de la philosophie de Platon en étudiant l'œuvre de Platon lui-même, il a, dans son premier volume, voulu s'approcher du platonisme exclusivement à travers les explications qu'Aristote en a données. Or, l'analyse soigneuse de ce témoignage l'a conduit à cette même conception que nous retrouvons maintenant dans son volume *Platon:* la conception d'un ordre hiérarchique de l'être, dans lequel les Nombres-Idées, comme des types de composition, ont leur place au-dessus des Idées.

Cette première étude avait un caractère provisoire: les résultats devaient être confrontés avec ceux d'une nouvelle analyse de l'œuvre de Platon lui-même. On pouvait donc garder ses réserves, premièrement par manque de confiance dans la méthode suivie. On pouvait se dire que Platon et Aristote sont des esprits hétérogènes et que, si l'on veut s'approcher de Platon à travers Aristote, c'est prendre un point de départ bien malheureux: on ne le verra jamais qu'à travers un autre esprit; c'est-à-dire qu'on ne le verra jamais comme il est. Ensuite, le témoignage d'Aristote sur les Nombres idéaux n'est pas tellement clair qu'on puisse en disposer comme d'une simple donnée. Le principe de la superposition des Nombres-Idées au-dessus des Idées est une déduction de Robin. C'est une interprétation, pas une donnée, et en fin de compte on en trouve bien peu dans les dialogues.

C'est la première objection que j'ai moi-même fait valoir contre la thèse de Léon Robin dans une étude antérieure[1]. Pour ce qui concerne le premier ouvrage de Robin cette objection était assez justifiée. En

---

[1] *Een keerpunt in Plato's denken* (Une crise dans la philosophie de Platon), Amsterdam 1936. Cette étude était déjà achevée avant que le volume *Platon* de M. Robin eût été publié. A vrai dire ce n'était pas le problème des Idées-Nombres qui m'a préoccupée spécialement pendant ce temps-là. Au contraire, je l'ai laissé un peu de côté, puisque le sujet de mon étude – la place du *Parménide* dans la philosophie de Platon – ne me forçait pas directement à l'étudier à fond. Ce que je cherchais, c'était le sens de la théorie des Idées telle que nous la connaissons par les dialogues, surtout le sens de cette crise que le *Parménide* y marque.

face du volume plus récent elle perd son droit: ici c'est par Platon que l'auteur veut connaître Platon, et le témoignage d'Aristote n'est allégué que pour la dernière période de la doctrine du Maître et seulement pour être vérifié par ses propres dialogues.

La seconde objection concerne l'interprétation que Robin a donné du témoignage d'Aristote. C'est W. D. Ross, éditeur et interprète de la *Métaphysique*, qui sur ce dernier point a vigoureusement protesté contre la thèse de Robin: Aristote ne donne aucun droit de placer les Nombres au-dessus des Idées. Il donne le clair témoignage *que les Idées sont des nombres*[1]. C'est une identification[2].

Robin invoque le témoignage de Théophraste[3]. *Il semble bien*[4] qu'il soit question d'une réduction des choses concrètes aux Idées, et des Idées aux Nombres. *Il semble donc* qu'ici les Nombres soient un principe plus élevé que les Idées. Mais il ne nous est pas permis d'interpréter le dit texte d'une telle façon, dit M. Ross, puisque c'est Aristote lui-même qui a enseigné distinctement et plusieurs fois la simple identification. Il faut donc interpréter Théophraste de manière qu'il ne contredise pas Aristote. En effet M. Ross réussit à trouver une telle interprétation: Platon, dit-il, identifiait plusieurs Idées au même Nombre. P.e. *quatre* était le nombre qui signifiait en même temps la justesse et un corps stéréométrique. Or, cela explique que Théophraste pouvait parler d'ἀνάπτειν εἰς, tandis qu'Aristote parle d'une identification.

Il faut remarquer: si par Platon plusieurs Idées sont réduites à un seul Nombre, ce Nombre forme en effet *le principe supérieur*. Il n'est donc pas permis d'expliquer les paroles d'Aristote comme une simple identification. Que les Idées soient des Nombres, doit être dit dans le même sens selon lequel on dit qu'une espèce «est» son genre, c'est à dire qu'elle y appartient. Nous voulons expliquer ce point un peu plus largement.

---

[1] W. D. Ross, *Aristotle's Metaphysics*, Oxford 1924, I, p. LXVII. Dans un ouvrage plus récent, *Plato's Theory of Ideas*, Oxford 1951, Sir David Ross paraît avoir modifié son opinion et a voulu reconnaître que Robin a eu raison de suivre le témoignage de Théophraste concernant la relation des Idées et des Nombres. *Plato's Theory* p. 218, n. 1, l'auteur dit en renvoyant au présent article publié en 1949 dans *Studia Vollgraff*: «I now think that in my edition of the Metaphysics I took Aristotle's statement too literally, and that Robin was right in accepting Theophrastus' statement as more accurate than Aristotle's».

[2] Voir les textes dans mon *Greek Philosophy* I, les numéros 362-363.

[3] Voir le texte dans *Greek Phil.* I, nr. 373.

[4] C'est encore M. Ross qui parle, dans l'édition de la *Métaphysique* de Théophraste qu'il a faite ensemble avec F. H. Fobes, Oxford 1929, p. 58 sq.

Notre première question doit être: de quoi est-ce que Platon admettait des Idées? Nous savons tous que dans les premiers dialogues il s'agit toujours de qualités, pas seulement de qualités morales (bonté, justesse), mais aussi de qualités géométriques (grandeur, égalité) et d'autres encore. Dans le livre VI de la *République* (507b) Platon en donne une synthèse en disant: il faut admettre des Idées de tous les attributs généraux, p.e. καλόν et ἀγαθόν. C'est de ce point de vue que Robin pouvait commencer son exposé de la théorie des Idées en disant que cette théorie consiste dans l'admission de l'existence de choses intelligibles et l'attribution de cette existence aux qualités, spécialement aux qualités morales.

Néanmoins avec cela tout n'est pas dit. Dans le livre X de la *République* (596a) Platon dit: «Nous sommes habitués à admettre un eidos de tout ce qui se présente comme une pluralité d'objets (ἕκαστα τὰ πολλά) auxquels nous donnons le même nom.» P.e. il y a beaucoup de lits et de tables, et l'ouvrier qui les fabrique, les fabrique en contemplant leur «Forme».

Ce passage rappelle celui du *Cratyle*, où Platon oppose au subjectivisme de Protagoras l'unité et l'identité de l'être, en donnant l'exemple d'un ouvrier qui fait une navette d'après la «Forme» qu'il contemple mentalement (389a,b). C'est l'hypothèse des Formes que Platon oppose au Héraclitéisme qui, en détruisant la subsistance de l'être, détruisait la possibilité de la connaissance. Qu'on compare le discours au début du *Parménide* (130c), où le jeune Socrate montre son hésitation à admettre des Idées de choses communes, même futiles et dégoûtantes. Le vieillard vénérable qu'est Parménide lui répond: «C'est que tu es encore jeune. Le temps viendra que la philosophie te prendra davantage qu'au moment présent. Alors tu ne mépriseras rien de toutes ces choses.»

Nous connaissons les Idées d'homme et de cheval par les disputations des anciennes écoles. Il est incontestable que Platon a admis d'Idées pareilles. Au passage du livre X de la *République* on a opposé le témoignage d'Aristote dans la *Métaph.* A (991b6) et M (1080a6) que Platon n'admettait pas d'Idées d'*artefacta*. Or, à ces endroits Aristote essaie de montrer que les Idées ne peuvent être cause de l'existence de choses concrètes. Il serait nécessaire d'accepter une force motrice effectuant qu'il provienne des choses qui participent aux Idées. Et d'autre part, dit-il, «il existe beaucoup d'autres choses, p.e. une maison et une bague, dont nous disons qu'il n'y a pas d'Idée».

Il semble que Platon, dans l'époque où il composait le *Cratyle* et le livre X de la *République,* s'est servi de l'analogie des produits d'art, qui sont construits par un démiurge humain d'après une «Forme» qu'il contemple mentalement. Il est vrai, Platon nomme explicitement l'Idée du lit et de la table. Mais déjà les choses de la nature, faites par un Démiurge divin, se posent au-dessus des produits de l'art; et s'il est question de «Formes» pour celles-ci, combien plus ne faut-il pas admettre l'existence de Formes pour les premières? Platon s'est donc servi de ces exemples διδασκαλίας χάριν, et il ne faut pas trop s'étonner si plus tard il s'est limité à admettre des Idées pour les choses faites par le Démiurge divin. En effet les produits d'art ne paraissent plus entre les objets ou les catégories de choses nommées dans la première partie du *Parménide.*

Ce qui est certain, c'est que Platon a admis l'existence d'Idées non seulement de qualités, mais aussi de choses; non pas de choses individuelles, bien entendu, comme plus tard l'admettront les néoplatoniciens, mais de leurs genres. Robin a donc raison quand il dit en résumant vers la fin de son premier ouvrage (p. 589): «il y en a au moins autant qu'il y a des espèces de choses ou de qualités». Et encore a-t-il raison de conclure qu'il est impossible d'identifier ces Idées avec les dix Nombres idéaux: «Ces idées, ce ne sont plus les modèles très généraux et très peu nombreux comme étaient les dix Nombres idéaux ou les trois types des Grandeurs idéales. *Ce sont des modèles spécifiques.*» Ce qui veut dire qu'ils se rapportent aux Nombres idéaux *comme des espèces à leur genre*[1].

C'est en effet cette conception des Nombres idéaux vers laquelle Platon lui-même nous montre le chemin. Elle s'accorde en même temps avec le texte de Théophraste qui parle d'ἀνάπτειν εἰς, et avec ceux d'Aristote qui disent que les Idées sont des Nombres – bien entendu comme les espèces «sont» leur genre, c'est à dire qu'ils y appartiennent. Et de fait M. Ross, bien qu'il croie devoir combattre le principe hiérarchique de Robin, est arrivé lui-même à cette interprétation, en passant par Platon et Théophraste: Platon a réduit plusieurs Idées à un seul Nombre, dit-il en interprétant Théophraste. Mais s'il en est ainsi, il faut reconnaître qu'il ne s'agit pas ici d'une simple identification. Dans ce dernier cas les dites Idées devraient être identiques, p.e. un corps stéréométrique et la justesse; et ce n'est décidément pas cela que Platon veut dire. Si donc les dites Idées, en gardant leur différence spécifique, forment les espèces de leur Nombre-Idée, ce Nombre est comme un genre supérieur à ses espèces. Le principe hiérarchique est

---

[1] Cette dernière conclusion n'a pas été formulée ainsi par Robin.

donc affirmé: le Nombre n'est pas identique aux Idées, il leur est supérieur. L'hypothèse de Robin s'est trouvée être juste en principe.

Également, dans son introduction à la *Métaphysique* d'Aristote Ross admet que les Nombres forment un ordre hiérarchique, dont ceux qui sont supérieurs embrassent plus d'Idées, tandis que ceux qui tiennent des degrés inférieurs en contiennent moins. La distance qui sépare sur ce point Ross de Robin, est bien moins grande que le premier ne suppose. Qu'on se rappelle que c'est Robin qui a dit dans sa première œuvre sur les Idées et les Nombres qu'«une Idée est autant plus élevée dans la hiérarchie de l'Être, qu'elle suppose un moins grand nombre de conciliations antérieures à partir de l'Idée la plus haute, qui est l'Unité même »[1]; c'est à dire qu'une Idée est autant plus élevée qu'elle est plus proche de l'Un. Il ne faut donc pas se représenter la hiérarchie de l'Être selon l'hypothèse de Robin d'après le schéma *a*, mais plutôt d'après le schéma plus gradué marqué de la lettre *b*:

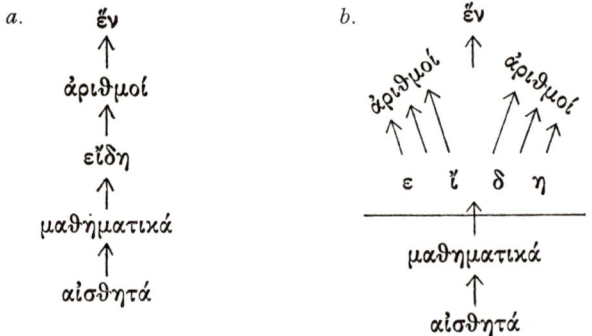

La représentation de Ross ne se distingue de celle de Robin que sur ce point que le premier se refuse à placer les Idées au-dessous des Nombres. Cette conception nous conduirait, strictement parlant, au schéma *c*, ou, puisque les nombres forment un ordre hiérarchique, plutôt au schéma *d*. (Voir la page suivante).

Mais puisque Ross reconnaît que plusieurs εἴδη, sont réduits à un seul Nombre, la partie supérieure du schéma *d* doit être corrigée de telle sorte que les Nombres, qui forment une série montante, aient chacun un certain nombres d'Idées sous eux. Selon cette représentation les Idées ne sont donc pas placées sur un même niveau, mais elles forment elles-mêmes un ordre hiérarchique, placées par groupes au-dessous des Nombres auxquels elles appartiennent.

[1] *La théorie platonicienne des Idées et des Nombres*, p. 460.

C'est peut-être cette dernière représentation (le schéma *e*) qui rend la pensée de Platon sur les Idées avec plus d'exactitude que le schéma *b*. Je n'oserais le prétendre trop catégoriquement. Dans le *Sophiste* Platon a posé l'Idée la plus générale, celle de l'Être, au sommet de l'échelle des Formes; ensuite le Mouvement et le Repos, en troisième lieu l'Identité et la Différence. Il est donc clair qu'il reconnaissait une hiérarchie entre les Formes elles-mêmes. Mais que la figure *e*, inspirée par Ross, en donne la représentation la plus heureuse, c'est une question dont on peut raisonnablement douter. Si l'on veut rendre la pensée de Platon par quelque schéma, la figure *f* vaut peut-être mieux que le schéma *e*.

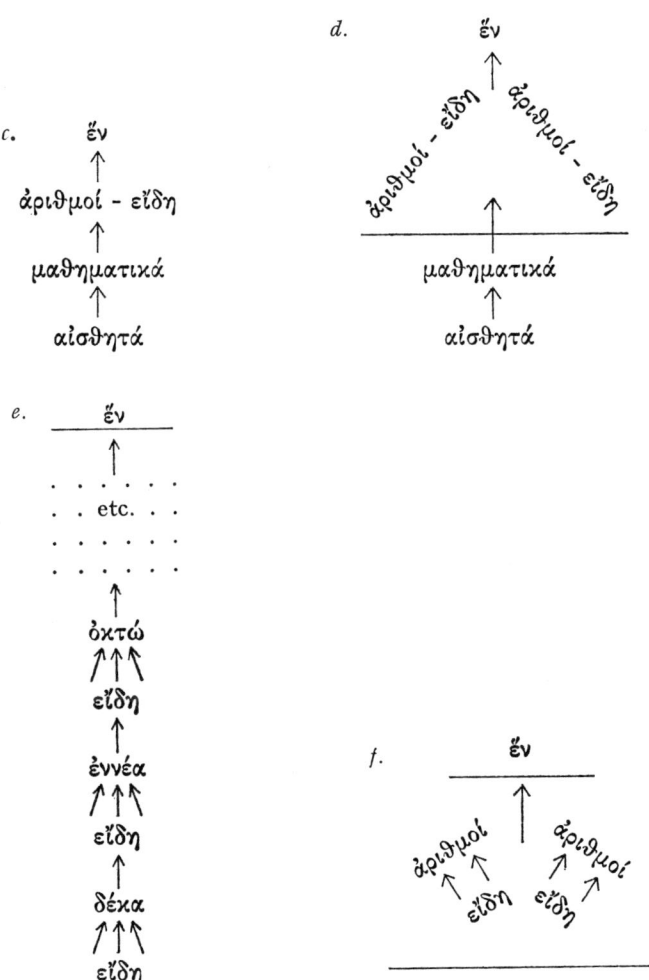

Ce qui est certain, c'est que l'hypothèse de Robin que j'ai essayé de représenter par le schéma *b*, n'est réfutée ni par la figure *e* ni par *f*. Ces divers essais de représentation n'en donnent qu'une détermination un peu plus exacte.

Il faut donc accepter le principe hiérarchique de Robin comme ὡμολογημένον. Il n'y a qu'un point sur lequel une différence d'opinion reste possible: est-il permis d'interpréter ce principe de la façon que Robin a proposée, c'est à dire que les Nombres sont les types ou modèles de l'organisation interne des Idées[1]? Ou encore[2]: «non pas des équivalents de chaque Idée, mais les types des déterminations par lesquelles chacune se trouve constituée en elle-même et dans son rapport avec les autres»; ce qui impliquerait que la fonction des Nombres idéaux par rapport aux Idées serait analogue à celle des nombres mathématiques pour la participation des choses concrètes à l'Idée[3]. C'est contre cette conception que M. Ross a dirigé sa critique. Mais il l'a fait en partant de cette thèse qu'Aristote ne nous permet pas de distinguer entre les Idées et les Nombres idéaux et de placer les derniers au-dessus des premières. Cette thèse ayant été réfutée et la dite superposition étant confirmée comme nécessaire, le reste de l'interprétation de Robin paraîtra moins étrange qu'elle ne pouvait sembler auparavant. En effet les Nombres, qui ont leur place comme des genres au-dessus de leurs εἴδη peuvent être décrits difficilement d'une autre façon que comme des «types d'organisation», des types plus élevés que les nombres mathématiques, donc «les archétypes de toute mesure», d'après l'expression de Robin.

Il peut nous sembler étrange de parler des Idées comme de «composés», qui seraient donc une multiplicité à l'intérieur. Or, ce n'est pas tout à fait cela que veut dire Robin. Il s'exprime plus prudemment. «Chaque Idée,» dit il[4], «en effet *est simple*, mais *son unité enveloppe néanmoins une certaine diversité*, qui doit être soumise à un ordre de constitution, c'est-à-dire à une loi: chaque Idée est une relation déterminée. C'est donc que toute Idée suppose des rapports avec

---

[1] *La théorie plat. des Id. et des N.*, p. 586.
[2] Ib., § 208, p. 464.
[3] Ib. p. 466: «Les choses ne peuvent imiter les Idées qu'à la condition de se soumettre à certaines formes régulières, à savoir les relations mathématiques, exactement comme les Idées elles-mêmes se constituent selon les types que leur fournissent les Nombres idéaux.» Mais ces derniers sont d'un autre caractère que les nombres mathématiques. Ceux-ci sont «des produits de la mesure», ceux-là «les archétypes de toute mesure».
[4] Ib., p. 586.

d'autres Idées. Ainsi toutes ensemble, elles forment un monde harmonieux de relations déterminées, un Cosmos; elles sont une multiplicité organisée et réglée; il faut donc un ordre de cette multiplicité, c'est-à-dire encore des lois. Ces lois, dans un cas comme dans l'autre, ce sont les Nombres. » C'est bien sur ce principe que Platon a lutté sa grande lutte dans le *Parménide* et le *Sophiste*, et c'est la conclusion de Platon lui-même que Robin a acceptée : que la multiplicité et le mouvement doivent être admis dans le domaine des Idées. Le point de départ et la méthode de son premier ouvrage ont conduit l'auteur à une attitude par trop dogmatisante et à des formules qui semblaient étranges à l'esprit de Platon. Mais dans son travail plus récent, où le témoignage d'Aristote prend une place bien plus discrète, la pensée de Platon est placée devant nos yeux, dès ses débuts jusqu'à sa dernière phase, comme une unité organique. Et dans cette unité les Nombres-Idées ont leur place d'une manière qui non seulement ne fait pas violence au *cosmos* du système, mais qui complète cette unité par un accroissement naturel. La philosophie de Platon dans sa dernière phase paraît être ici ce qu'elle est devenue dans la crise du *Parménide* et du *Sophiste:* un Éléatisme transformé. Et Robin nous a expliqué comment dans cette dernière période l'hypothèse des Nombres idéaux devenait en même temps la réfutation de la critique sur la théorie des Idées qui se levait entre la jeune génération à l'Académie de cette époque : l'argument du troisième homme, le regressus à l'infini, est exclu si l'ordre hiérarchique de l'être possède un sommet.

Concluons. C'est à tort que depuis la critique de Ross l'hypothèse de Robin sur les Nombres idéaux est considérée généralement comme périmée et réfutée[1]. Au contraire, le principe hiérarchique dans le monde des Idées doit être accepté comme certain, voire même dans un tel sens que chaque Nombre idéal est placé en genre au-dessus de plusieurs εἴδη qui lui appartiennent. Cette interprétation est nécessaire à cause des indications de Platon lui-même. En outre elle s'accorde avec le témoignage d'Aristote, et enfin avec celui de Théophraste. Elle a été affirmée du côté mathématique par l'importante étude de J. Klein[2], dont on trouve un résumé dans l'ouvrage cité de M. Van der Wielen[3].

[1] Ainsi dans la thèse déjà citée de W. van der Wielen sur les Idées-Nombres, qui, d'ailleurs, donne une excellente introduction au problème.
[2] *Die Griechische Logistik und die Entstehung der Algebra*, I, 1934, dans *Quellen und Studien zur Geschichte der Mathematik, Astronomie und Physik*, Abt. B, Band 3, p. 18-105.   [3] *De Ideegetallen van Plato*, p. 237 vv.

CHAPTER XII

PROBLEMS CONCERNING PLATO'S LATER DOCTRINE[1]

1

Since, in the first half of the nineteenth century, Trendelenburg published his work on the ideal Numbers of Plato, those who are occupied with the study of Plato's philosophy are bound to ask themselves the radical question: *do we know Plato's doctrine?* This question first of all arises from the existence of a certain discrepancy between the literary work of Plato and what Aristotle tells us about Platonism. Yet not exclusively from this. It is founded also on certain detractive utterances of Plato himself about books and the art of writing. In the first place we have to mention here the well-known passage in the *Seventh Letter*[2], where Plato says: "There is no book of mine about these things (περὶ ὧν ἐγὼ σπουδάζω), nor will there ever be. For it is not possible to speak about them as about other objects of study. But from a long intercourse with the thing itself and from a common life springs suddenly a light, kindled from a spark that leaped over, and once being lit in the soul, it feeds itself further."

Next to this the parallel-lines in *Ep.* II, 314 c: "There is no book of Plato nor will there ever be; but what is now called so is of Socrates, turned young and handsome."

Finally there is *Phaedr.* 274 e - 275 b, the answer of king Thamous to the Egyptian Theuth, who communicated to him the invention of the art of writing: "This discovery of yours will create forgetfulness in the learners' souls, because they will not use their memories; they will trust to the external written characters and not remember of themselves. The specific which you have discovered is an aid not to mem-

---

[1] This chapter contains the two papers *Problems concerning later Platonism*, previously published in *Mnemosyne* 1949. My reasons for having them reproduced in the present volume have been expounded in the Preface. The text is revised.
[2] 341 c-d.

ory, but to reminiscence, and you give your disciples not truth, but only the semblance of truth; they will be hearers of many things and will have learned nothing; they will be tiresome company, having the show of wisdom without the reality."[1]

Now, if Plato thought in this way about written books, when he, apparently, attached much more importance to the living contact of a personal intercourse, is it not plausible that for himself his most essential task was not the writing of books, but his oral teaching in the Academy? And, if so, is not the value of Plato's dialogues as a source of his doctrine strongly diminished, while that of the testimony of Aristotle and other disciples has greatly improved?

This, indeed, was the opinion of Burnet. "As we have seen"[2], he wrote[3], "he (Plato) did not choose to commit it to writing, and we are almost entirely dependent on what Aristotle tells us." Now Burnet's interpretation of Plato's philosophy as a whole has carried but little conviction in the world of Plato-scholars, principally because it was connected with an unfortunate theory about Socrates, founded on the doubtful authority of the *Second Letter* and on other wrong interpretations. Yet, as to Plato's later philosophy, many others shared Burnet's opinion and attached a great importance to the testimony of Aristotle on the doctrine of Plato in his later years. Among them the names of J. Stenzel and L. Robin may be mentioned.

On the other hand, Platonists who radically doubted of the value of what Aristotle says about Plato never have failed. We may mention in the former century Teichmüller (*Literarische Fehden*, 1881), and a generation before us P. Shorey and C. Ritter. And let us not forget those Dutch scholars who have been our masters: B. J. H. Ovink and J. D. Bierens de Haan.

Ritter says in his last greater work, *Die Kerngedanken der platonischen Philosophie* (1930): Plato continued to write until his death. So it is practically impossible that Aristotle could report anything about his oral teaching which is not to be found in the dialogues. – Ritter had, as it appears from his chronicles of Plato studies in *Bursian's Jahresberichte*, a marked aversion from those scholars who try to approach Plato through Aristotle. He read and knew the Dialogues, and the Plato he knew from them – *his* Plato – he did not find back in the works of these modern authors. In their works he felt as in a strange

[1] Translation of B. Jowett.
[2] Sc. in the Epistles VII and II.
[3] *Gr. Phil.* I, p. 312.

climate. He did not like them and he had no confidence in them. Having read a work of Stenzel for review, he sighs after fulfilling his duty: "Es durchzulesen war mir eine Qual."

Now this was exactly the attitude taken by Ovink in these questions. He did not believe in a Platonism which was not to be found in the Dialogues; and surely Aristotle was the last in whom he could have put some confidence as a witness about Plato and his doctrine, his mind and mode of thinking being contrary to Plato's mind.

As to Bierens de Haan, he was a fervent admirer of what we may call "classical Platonism", which reaches its acme in the *Republic*. He found his inspiration there, and Plato's later philosophy did not interest him, except as a confirmation of the "philosophy of life" found in the *Republic*, – and certainly he was right when finding a philosophy of life in Plato's classical dialogues, and in finding this philosophy not abandoned in the later works.

The American Platonist P. Shorey, who radically denied the value of Aristotle's testimony on Plato's later doctrine, made, in a review of Stenzel's *Zahl und Gestalt* (Class. Philol. 1924), the following important remark[1]: "We do not really know what Aristotle's testimony is. The *Metaphysics*, as it stands, is a hopeless muddle", and it is utterly impossible to decide what in his criticism refers to Plato and what to interpretations and misconceptions of Platonism in the Academy.

A new phase of these problems has lately arisen by the works of H. Cherniss[2]. What is new in his work, is not so much the author's solution of what he calls "the riddle of the early Academy" – the difficulty arising from the fact of a certain discrepancy between the contents of Plato's own literary works and the testimony of Aristotle about his doctrine –. That solution does not differ essentially from what so many older Platonists, such as Ritter and Ovink, thought about the question (which could hardly be named a problem for them). The new thing, however, is that Cherniss makes himself the interpreter of the more or less conscious feelings of aversion from Aristotle as a witness about Plato, harboured by so many readers and admirers of Plato's literary works, and that he pleads their cause with a system of

---

[1] Quoted by Cherniss in the Foreword to *Aristotle's Criticism of Plato and the Academy*, I, p. XXI.
[2] *The Riddle of the Early Academy*, first published in Berkeley and Los Angeles 1945, was reprinted in New York, 1962. Of the author's greater work *Aristotle's criticism of Plato and the Academy*, I, published at Baltimore 1944, a reprint appeared in New York 1963.

strong and precise arguments, resulting from a careful study of the whole testimony of Aristotle – his method of polemizing, of interpretation and criticism throughout his works, not only with reference to Plato, but also to the presocratic thinkers. Cherniss entertains more hopeful expectations concerning the study of Aristotle's *Metaphysics* than Shorey did. He is convinced that good results may be expected, if only all the evidence is taken into consideration; if all the material is carefully brought together, is weighed and sifted by comparing it to Plato's own testimony, being the chief means of control we have at our disposal. Till now, he argues, only part of the material has been drawn into consideration. A great and excellent part of the work has been performed by L. Robin in *La théorie platonicienne des Idées et des Nombres d'après Aristote* (1908). But 1° Robin confined his investigation to the theory of Ideas and Numbers, whereas the Aristotelian treatment of Platonic physical, psychological, ethical and political theory is equally interesting and may often illuminate obscure points in the treatment of the theory of Ideas. And 2° Robin deprived himself of the most valuable help for controlling Aristotle's testimony, by carefully refraining from making any reference to any of Plato's writings.

By his great work *Aristotle's Criticism of Plato and the Academy*, of which the first volume appeared at Baltimore, 1944, Cherniss intends to procure that solid basis which is indispensable for the forming of a tenable taxation of the value of Aristotle's testimony, and for a true solution of "the riddle of the Early Academy". In his second volume the number-theories will be more especially treated, and for the final conclusion the author's former work, *Aristotle's Criticism of Presocratic Philosophy*, will also be used.

In the meanwhile Prof. Cherniss has anticipated his own results by publishing the smaller book *The Riddle of the Early Academy* (Univ. of California Press, 1945). Here he gives his own solution for "the riddle", being a radical rejection of Aristotle's testimony, as far as it says anything about Plato and Platonism that is not to be found in the dialogues. The argumentation of the first chapter runs, shortly put, as follows.

In the discrepancy between the ideal theory of the dialogues and the doctrine which Aristotle ascribes to Plato, modern critics often showed more confidence in the account of Aristotle than in Plato's own work. Now this is an amazing fact, since these critics are almost without exception university-teachers, who must know from personal experience how mutilated and distorted their own thoughts become by passing through the notebooks of their students. Surely in the present times it would be deemed an intolerable method to accept as evidence of a philosopher's doctrine a student's or a colleague's report of his oral teaching, against the authority of the philosopher's own writings. Yet this is the procedure followed by modern Plato-critics, such as Burnet and Taylor, Robin, Stenzel, a.o.

In the passage of king Thamous' answer to the Egyptian Theuth Cherniss hears a complaint of Plato about the misunderstanding and distortion of his thoughts on the part of students. Nor does the well-known passage of the *Seventh Letter* give any credit to the testimony of Aristotle or of any other disciple. He who will be convinced of this, has only to read the text: "if any other persons write about what they heard from me and pretend to know these things (περὶ ὧν ἐγὼ σπουδάζω), I can declare this with certainty, that they in no wise understand it. And if any person would be able to write about it, it would be I" – Surely this is a testimony against Aristotle and whosoever else might pretend to teach us anything about Plato and Platonism, such as Hermodorus.

It is always said that Aristotle "used to refer to Plato's *agrapha*". These assertions give the impression that Aristotle frequently and clearly mentions lectures given by Plato. Now this is utterly untrue. There may be found just two texts in the whole Aristotelian corpus where a reference to the agrapha occurs. And by careful examination one of them (*De anima* 404 b 8-30) turns out not to be concerned with Plato at all. So there remains one single passage: *Phys.* IV 209 b 13-16. Here Aristotle says:

"This is why Plato in the *Timaeus* says that matter and space are the same; for the "participant" (τὸ μεταληπτικόν) and space (χώρα) are identical. (It is true, indeed, that the account he gives there of the "participant" is different from what he says in his so-called "unwritten teaching". Nevertheless, he did identify place (τόπος) and space)" (χώρα).[1]

Now, here we can control exactly Aristotle's interpretation by comparing it to the *Timaeus*, Cherniss remarks. And if we do that, this interpretation appears to be utterly wrong and untrustworthy: first Aristotle identifies the space of the *Timaeus* with his own conception of position, secondly he assumes that the participant there is

[1] Translation of Hardie and Gaye (Oxford Translation of the Works of Aristotle, vol. II).

the equivalent of his own "material principle", thirdly he simply states that Plato *says* that matter and space are the same. Since, then, he misinterprets and misquotes the *Timaeus*, what he says of the "unwritten teaching" may be erroneous too.

According to *Metaph.* A 6 Plato assumed the great and small (elsewhere called the indeterminate dyad) as his material principle, as well of Ideas as of sensible things. Modern scholars have discovered this doctrine in the *Philebus*, where the péras is to be identified with the One (the formal principle of Plato according to *Metaph.* A 6), and the ápeiron with the material principle, the great and small. This, again, is wrong interpretation, says Cherniss. The ápeiron in the *Philebus* simply means the phenomenal multiplicity, and the One or péras is *any* given Idea, the Ideas being called monads, and being described as eternally immutable and unmixed. That this interpretation must undoubtedly be the true one, appears clearly when we consider Plato's third class in this dialogue, being the mixture of the two: for if the péras and the ápeiron were the principles from which the Ideas are derived, then the third class must be identified with the Ideas. And this is clearly against the author's intention, for the class of the mixture is by Plato distinctly equated with the phenomenal world. Finally, of an identification of Ideas and Numbers, as it is ascribed to Plato by Aristotle, no mention whatever is made in the *Philebus*[1].

But again we can control Aristotle exactly on another point: *Phys.* I, 192a6-8. Here he says that according to Plato the great and small = the μὴ ὄν, this last term being taken in the sense which Parmenides gave to it.

Now, this assertion is utterly mistaken. For Plato did not admit the μὴ ὄν in that sense at all: he gave it a positive meaning, defining it as the ἕτερον (*Soph.* 257b-259b). The μὴ ὄν is in the *Sophist* an Idea, which pervades all the Ideas, including that of being, by which it is pervaded in turn[2]. Space, however, which is according to Aristotle identified by Plato with his material principle the great and small, does not even pervade the sensible things that come into being within it; it is no Idea, and still less does it pervade Ideas. Moreover it is utterly impossible that Plato admitted of a "material principle" with regard to the Ideas. He could admit such a principle with regard to sensible things, because of their imperfection. But that he would have accepted such a principle with reference to the Ideas, is absolutely

[1] *Riddle*, p. 18.
[2] *Soph.* 258c, 259a-b.

excluded, because it would mean the denial of their ideal character itself.

So all this is simply wrong interpretation on the side of Aristotle; wrong interpretation not of what Plato said in his oral teaching – Cherniss denies that Plato gave any regular lectures at all – but of certain points in the dialogues: the doctrine of the μὴ ὄν in the *Sophist*, that of the recipient in the *Timaeus* and that of the infinite in the *Philebus*. If, however, his interpretation is wrong on these points where we can control him, it is untrustworthy also on those questions where we cannot control him, the doctrine of the so-called ideal Numbers. On this point, too, Aristotle's statements will prove to be inconsistent with one another, and not to correspond to any doctrine in the dialogues, or even to be in contradiction to them. The only thing then we may safely conclude from this, is that the whole theory of the identification of Ideas and Numbers never has been taught by Plato; that it is merely a product of Aristotle's wrong interpretation, explained to us by his usual method of polemizing which may be found throughout his works.

Before we subject this conclusion to a closer examination, we have to consider the basis on which it is founded: the question of the testimonies about Plato's oral teaching. Cherniss says: there are – or might seem to be – just two passages in Aristotle's works, *Phys.* IV 209b 13-16 and *De anima* I 2, 404b; and of these two passages the last mentioned is not concerned with Plato at all.

Now, as to the first passage, *Phys.* IV 209b 13-16, this much is clear: Plato did not directly *say* in the *Timaeus* that matter and space are the same. He described his ἐκδεχόμενον[1] or χώρα as the space *in which* all things are formed[2], not, strictly speaking as a principle immanent in things. Yet, it cannot be denied that this description of the χώρα shows a close resemblance to what is called "matter" by Aristotle: contrary to the so-called elements, such as water, fire or air, of which the substance seems to change continually, space is something permanent[3], a pre-existing something, which has, by the very fact of its perfect indetermination, a vague and shadowy existence. Plato even calls it an ἐκμαγεῖον, a kind of plastic material for all things[4]. – Surely

---

[1] *Tim.* 50e.
[2] *Ib.* 50b-d.
[3] *Ib.* 50a: μόνον ἐκεῖνο αὖ προσαγορεύειν τῷ τε τοῦτο καὶ τῷ τόδε προσχρωμένους ὀνόματι.   [4] *Ib.* 50c.

we have no sufficient reason to conclude that at least by this term Plato proves to have thought of his third principle as "matter", i.e. as an immanent principle in sensible things. For this conclusion we have no sufficient reasons. For Plato clearly did not intend to say that his χώρα enters into things as a constituent element. This we must conclude from his comparison of the "recipient" to the mother, the forming or active principle to the father, and the intermediate nature to the offspring[1]. It is a well-known fact that the ancients had a wrong idea of the process of generation: they fancied that a human being arises from the semen, the womb being nothing more than the place in which this process is carried out. This then being so, we would certainly be wrong in concluding from the term ἐκμαγεῖον that the third principle of the *Timaeus* is meant by its author as a constituent of material things. But on the other hand we must acknowledge that just by this term Plato comes very near to the conception of Aristotelian matter. And is it quite possible that Aristotle, thinking over this passage of the *Timaeus*, was inspired to his own conception of what he called ὕλη. We can, at least, understand quite well that Aristotle who, in building his own system of philosophy, wrote about his predecessors always from the point of view of how far his own principles have been anticipated by them, said that Plato's χώρα was his own material principle.

Moreover, we can quite well understand that Aristotle, reading in the *Timaeus* that this vague and shadowy existence of the χώρα can be grasped only λογισμῷ τινι νόθῳ[2], says that Plato identifies it with the μὴ ὄν, or rather that the great-and-small and non-being are the same[3]. To this then we must say: indeed, according to the usual sense of the words Plato made his χώρα a kind of μὴ ὄν. Not, evidently in the very special and unusual sense which Plato gave to the term in his *Sophist*. Cherniss is right: in this dialogue the μὴ ὄν is the ἕτερον, and the ἕτερον is an Idea. But it must be remarked that the ἕτερον in the *Timaeus*, which is one of the constituent parts of the world-soul[4], is characterized as a principle reluctant to being mixed up with the ταὐτόν. Obviously it has a bearing om the soul's future knowledge of the sensible world. Now this presupposes *some connection with* the underlying indefinite principle. We shall consider this more closely in the second part of the present chapter[5].

[1] *Tim.* 50d: καὶ δὴ καὶ προσεικάσαι πρέπει τὸ μὲν δεχόμενον μητρί, τὸ δ' ὅθεν πατρί, τὴν δὲ μεταξὺ τούτων φύσιν ἐκγόνῳ.
[2] 52b.   [3] *Phys.* I, 192a6-8.   [4] *Tim.* 35a-b.   [5] *Infra*, p. 275ff.

Granting then that for us not everything in Aristotle's account is perfectly clear, moreover, that not always everything he says is correct, the present passage, nonetheless, gives us no reason to conclude that Aristotle's testimony on Plato is altogether untrustworthy. All we may conclude is this: that it would be neither reasonable to reject this testimony nor to accept it without any critical reserve. As to the agrapha, finally, it has no other meaning than that Plato in his unwritten teaching used to denote his δεχόμενον (Aristotle says, less correctly, his μεταληπτικόν) by another term (sc. the great-and-small).

Now we have about this unwritten teaching another important testimony of a direct disciple (ἕταιρος) of Plato: Hermodorus. The fragment is preserved by Simplicius, *Phys.* 247.30-248.15, who had it from Porphyry, who borrowed it from Dercyllides. The text runs as follows.

Ἐπειδὴ πολλαχοῦ μέμνηται τοῦ Πλάτωνος ὁ Ἀριστοτέλης ὡς τὴν ὕλην μέγα καὶ μικρὸν λέγοντος, ἰστέον ὅτι ὁ Πορφύριος ἱστορεῖ τὸν Δερκυλλίδην ἐν τῷ ια' τῆς Πλάτωνος φιλοσοφίας, ἔνθα περὶ ὕλης ποιεῖται τὸν λόγον, Ἑρμοδώρου τοῦ Πλάτωνος ἑταίρου λέξιν παραγράφειν ἐκ τῆς περὶ Πλάτωνος αὐτοῦ συγγραφῆς, ἐξ ἧς δηλοῦται, ὅτι τὴν ὕλην ὁ Πλάτων κατὰ τὸ ἄπειρον καὶ ἀόριστον ὑποτιθέμενος ἀπ' ἐκείνων αὐτὴν ἐδήλου τῶν τὸ μᾶλλον καὶ τὸ ἧττον ἐπιδεχομένων, ὧν καὶ τὸ μέγα καὶ τὸ μικρόν ἐστιν. εἰπὼν γὰρ ὅτι «τῶν ὄντων τὰ μὲν καθ' αὑτὰ εἶναι λέγει ὡς ἄνθρωπον καὶ ἵππον, τὰ δὲ πρὸς ἕτερα, καὶ τούτων τὰ μὲν ὡς πρὸς ἐναντία ὡς ἀγαθὸν κακῷ, τὰ δὲ ὡς πρός τι, καὶ τούτων τὰ μὲν ὡς ὡρισμένα, τὰ δὲ ὡς ἀόριστα»

As Aristotle often mentions that Plato called matter the great-and-small, people must know that Porphyry communicates that Dercyllides in the eleventh book of his "Philosophy of Plato", where he speaks about matter, quotes a passage of Hermodorus, the disciple of Plato's, from his book about Plato, from which appears that Plato admitted matter in the sense of the infinite and indeterminate, and that he showed with this that it belongs to things which admit of a more and less, to which belongs also the great and small. First, namely, he says: "Plato says that of all the existing things certain things exist by themselves, such as man and horse[1],

---

[1] First group (substances): A.

ἐπάγει «καὶ τὰ μὲν ὡς μέγα πρὸς μικρὸν λεγόμενα πάντα ἔχειν τὸ μᾶλλον καὶ τὸ ἧττον· ἔστι γὰρ μᾶλλον[2] εἶναι μεῖζον καὶ ἔλαττον εἰς ἄπειρον φερόμενα· ὡσαύτως δὲ καὶ πλατύτερον καὶ στενότερον καὶ βαρύτερον καὶ κουφότερον καὶ πάντα τὰ οὕτως λεγόμενα εἰς ἄπειρον οἰσθήσεται· τὰ δὲ ὡς τὸ ἴσον καὶ τὸ μένον καὶ τὸ ἡρμοσμένον λεγόμενα οὐκ ἔχειν τὸ μᾶλλον καὶ τὸ ἧττον, τὰ δὲ ἐναντία τούτων ἔχειν· ἔστι γὰρ μᾶλλον ἄνισον ἀνίσου καὶ κινούμενον κινουμένου καὶ ἀνάρμοστον ἀναρμόστου, ὥστε αὐτῶν ἀμφοτέρων τῶν συζυγιῶν πάντα πλὴν τοῦ ἑνὸς στοιχείου τὸ μᾶλλον καὶ τὸ ἧττον δέδεκται[5]. ὥστε ἄστατον καὶ ἄμορφον καὶ ἄπειρον καὶ οὐκ ὂν τὸ τοιοῦτον λέγεσθαι κατὰ ἀπόφασιν τοῦ ὄντος. τῷ τοιούτῳ δὲ οὐ προσήκειν οὔτε ἀρχῆς οὔτε οὐσίας, ἀλλ' ἐν ἀκρισίᾳ τινὶ φέρεσθαι.»

and others with a relation to other things[1]. Of this last group some have a relation to a counterpart such as good and bad, and others simply to something else. And of these some[3] are limited, others undetermined"[4]. He continues: "And all that is called great with relation to small, has the more and less in it. For it is possible to be greater and smaller ad infinitum, and in the same way also broader and narrower, heavier and lighter and all such things will go on ad infinitum. But things like the equal and the permanent and the arranged[6] do not contain the more and less; their opposites, however, do. For "unequal" admits of a difference of degree, and so does "moving" and "unarranged". Consequently of both last-mentioned groups of

---

[1] Second group: B, which is in the next sentence subdivided into two: *a.* those things which have an opposite, *b.* correlatives. In the passage of Sextus Empiricus, which will be cited *infra* (p. 267 ff.), we shall find an exact determination of the difference between those two last groups.
[2] ἔστι γὰρ μᾶλλον was printed in the edition of Aldus. The ms F shows a lacuna of three letters after ἔστιν.
[3] "Of these some are limited", sc. the group *a*, such as good and bad, in its positive part: the good, the equal, the permanent, the arranged, etc.
[4] "others undetermined", sc. the second half of group *a*: the unequal, the moving, the unarranged; and to these the whole group *b*, such as greater and smaller, longer and shorter, etc.; shortly put, all that oscillates between two extremes. According to the next sentence, "the great and small" seems to have been Plato's chief denomination of this last group, whereas it was not its single aspect.
[5] The mss. have δεδεγμένον, printed by Diels in his text. Heinze (*Xenokrates* p. 38) corrects: δέδεκται, adopted by W. van der Wielen (*De Ideegetallen van Plato*, p. 115).
[6] The positive half of the group *a*.

pairs[1] all have accepted the more and less, except the principle that is one[2]. Hence all these things (that admit of the more and less) must be called unstable, formless, unlimited and non-being, because being is denied of it. And to such things it neither belongs to have a beginning nor to have being, but it is proper to them to move without a purpose."

This passage reminds us directly of Plato's *Philebus*, where the author determines his ápeiron as "that which has a more and less within itself"[3]. While we ourselves might perhaps hesitate, and doubt whether we may connect this ápeiron in the *Philebus* with the great-and-small mentioned by Aristotle and indicated by him as the name which was given by Plato to his material principle, this identification is here directly confirmed by a first-hand witness. The great-and-small did indeed according to Plato belong to the class of the ápeiron, which is defined as "all that which has a more and less in it". One aspect of it – apparently the most prominent – was the great-and-small, and it seems that Plato by preference – but not exclusively – called it by this name. Its opposite is: the Equal, the Permanent or Unchangeable, the Arranged, which is the péras or the One[4].

Cherniss is silent on the passage of Hermodorus in the first chapter

[1] *a* and *b*.
[2] Again: the positive half of the group *a*: τὸ ἴσον, τὸ μένον, τὸ ἡρμοσμένον, apparently identified with the ἀγαθόν. Cp. Aristoxenus, *Harm. Elem.* II 30 Meibom: καὶ τὸ πέρας ὅτι ἀγαθόν ἐστιν ἕν (to be cited *infra*).
[3] *Phil.* 24 c.
[4] The difficulty of Cherniss, mentioned above (p. 261) – that, if the péras and the ápeiron in the *Phil.* were to be identified with the two ultimate principles, the One and the Great-and-small, the third class must be identified with the Ideas – cannot be solved according to his theory. It is curious that the author, who is so severe in his criticism, does not remark the contradiction in his own interpretation, according to which the apeiron would be "the phenomenal multiplicity", and the mixed genus once more the phenomenal world. And why could not the péras have the meaning which he proposes, sc. that of the Ideas, being "Monads", and the ápeiron that of the Great and small, the third class or mixed genus being the phenomenal world?

of his *Riddle* – except in a general declaration concerning the above-cited passage of the *Seventh Letter*, where Plato says about other writers whosoever pretend to know the subjects with which he is seriously concerned: it is not possible that they understand anything about the matter at all. Here, then, Cherniss declares: "Whether authentic or not, this assertion is certainly directed against such publications as those of Hermodorus and Aristotle"[1]. He does not discuss the fragment of Hermodorus in this work. The reason of this silence may be found in a long note in *Aristotle's Criticism of Plato*, p. 169ff.: the author rejects the testimony of Hermodorus as a witness about Plato's doctrine, because in the last sentence, beginning with ὥστε, the inference is drawn that, except the first principle, "which is equal and unchangeable", all things must be called unstable, formless, infinite and *non-being*, "because being is denied of it". This assertion, Cherniss states, is in direct contradiction with Plato's own teaching in the *Sophist*, where non-being is explicitly not opposed to being, but determined positively as a ἕτερον[2]. The μὴ καλόν is here said to be as well a being as the καλόν, and the μὴ μέγα as well as the μέγα. Therefore, if Hermodorus says in this passage that it is not fitting to such like things (τῷ τοιούτῳ) to participate of being, he is in flat contradiction with Plato's own words, and cannot be taken as evidence for Plato's doctrine of the "material substrate".

Here we might observe that it is quite possible – as Cherniss himself concedes – that the said conclusion has not been drawn by Hermodorus at all, but has been added by Dercyllides. But even if Hermodorus is the author, we can simply leave this inference for his account. And even if it is wrong – which we cannot yet take for granted – this does not take away the value of his whole testimony: the tripartition of being and the final reduction of these three groups to two ultimate principles, the One and that which admits of the more and less, may prove to have been Platonic teaching.

Two remarks, again, must be made here. First[3]. The testimony of Hermodorus is confirmed by a remarkable chapter of Sextus Empiricus, *Adv. Math.* X (the second *against the Physicists*), 4, 248-282[4].

---

[1] *Riddle* p. 13.
[2] *Soph.* 258b.
[3] The second follows in the second part of this chapter.
[4] The text of the paragraphs of this chapter which are cited here, can be found in my *Greek Philosophy, A collection of texts*, I, Leiden 1950, ⁴1969, sub nr. 371b. See also Gaiser, *Platons ungeschriebene Lehre*, Stuttgart 1963, p. 499ff., nr. 32.

This chapter contains the same tripartition of being as the fragments of Hermodorus: (263) Τῶν γὰρ ὄντων, φασί (sc. the Pythagoreans, to whom Sextus ascribes this doctrine), τὰ μὲν κατὰ διαφορὰν νοεῖται, τὰ δὲ κατ' ἐναντίωσιν, τὰ δὲ πρός τι. The first group, of things that are "conceived absolutely" (κατὰ διαφορὰν νοεῖται), is further determined as τὰ καθ' ἑαυτὰ καὶ κατ' ἰδίαν περιγραφὴν ὑποκείμενα, which subsist of themselves and in complete independence, such as man, horse, plant, earth, water, air, fire; for each of these is regarded absolutely and not in respect of its relation to something else[1]. The second group, κατ' ἐναντίωσιν, is described as "those (things) which are regarded in respect of their contrariety one to another, such as good and evil, just and unjust, advantageous and disadvantageous, holy and unholy, pious and impious, in motion and at rest, and all other things similar to these". The third group, finally, τὰ πρός τι, is defined as τὰ κατὰ τὴν ὡς πρὸς ἕτερον σχέσιν νοούμενα, "the things conceived as standing in a relation to something else, such as right and left, above and below, double and half", i.e. correlatives.

Sextus then explains the difference between the second and the third group by indicating two points of distinction (266-268): (1) In the second group, those of contraries, the destruction of the one is the generation of the other, as in the case of health and disease, of motion and rest, while in the third there is co-existence and co-destruction of the one and the other (τὰ δὲ πρός τι συνύπαρξίν τε καὶ συναίρεσιν ἀλλήλων περιεῖχεν), "for there is no right unless a left also exists, nor a double unless the half also, whereof it is the double, pre-exists". (2) In the second group, that of contraries, there is no intermediate stage between the two, while in the third there is: there is nothing between health and disease, life and death, motion and rest; but in the case of relatives there is a middle state, for the equal will be between the greater and the smaller, the adequate between the more and the less, and the harmonious between the high and the low.

Sextus now proceeds to show that above each of these classes there must be a certain genus: ὀφείλει κατ' ἀνάγκην καὶ τούτων αὐτῶν ἐπάνω τι γένος τετάχθαι (269). Above the first class "the sons of the Pythagoreans" postulated the one (270), above the second the equal and unequal (τὸ ἴσον καὶ ἄνισον, 271), above the third they put "excess and defect" (ὑπεροχὴ καὶ ἔλλειψις, 273). This last term reminds us of the μᾶλλον καὶ ἧττον of the *Philebus* and in the fragment of Hermodorus. The latter finally came to two principles. So does Sextus. He asks:

[1] Translation of R. G. Bury (Sextus Empiricus, vol. III, Loeb Class. Libr.).

can these genera be again reduced to others? – And he answers (275):
Yes, for equality (ἰσότης) is brought under the One (for the One first
of all is equal to itself), and inequality (ἀνισότης) is seen in excess and
defect (ὑπεροχὴ καὶ ἔλλειψις), things of which the one exceeds and the
other is exceeded being unequal. 'Ἀλλὰ καὶ ἡ ὑπεροχὴ καὶ ἡ ἔλλειψις
κατὰ τὸν τῆς ἀορίστου δυάδος λόγον τέτακται, ἐπειδήπερ ἡ πρώτη ὑπεροχὴ
καὶ ἡ ἔλλειψις ἐν δυσίν ἐστι, τῷ τε ὑπερέχοντι καὶ τῷ ὑπερεχομένῳ. 'Ἀνέκυ-
ψαν ἄρα ἀρχαὶ πάντων κατὰ τὸ ἀνωτάτω ἥ τε πρώτη μονὰς καὶ ἡ ἀόριστος
δυάς. "But both excess and defect are ranked under the head of the
Infinite Dyad, since in fact the primary excess and defect is in two
things, that which exceeds and that which is exceeded. Thus as the
highest principles of all things there have emerged the primary One
and the Infinite Dyad."

Sextus, then, relates all this as Pythagorean doctrine. But a simple
comparison of the last-cited paragraph of Sextus with what Aristotle
tells us in *Metaph.* A 6 about Plato's doctrine of the first principles[1],
if we combine it with what we learned from Hermodorus and the
Philebus, will make it clear to us that, what we have here before us,
is no Pythagorean but doubtlessly Platonic teaching. For Aristotle
here reports that Plato admitted of two highest principles: the One,
being the formal principle, and "the great-and-small", which is, according to his terminology, the material principle. Next, defining
exactly the points of agreement and the points of difference between
Plato and the Pythagoreans, he says: Plato and the Pythagoreans
agreed in this, that 1⁰ both accepted the One as a subsisting principle,
not as an attribute of something else; and 2⁰ Numbers are by both
accepted as the cause of the being of things. As to the points of
difference, he mentions three, of which the first is: instead of the
ápeiron of the Pythagoreans, which was one, Plato adopted the dyad
of the great-and-small. Since then this point is so distinctly mentioned
by Aristotle, we must conclude that, wherever is spoken of the "ápeiron"
in the sense of the *Philebus* – i.e. as something which admits of a more
and a less, be it greater and smaller, broader and narrower, longer and
shorter, or anything else of this kind –, wherever it is qualified or
described as an "indeterminate dyad", we have no Pythagorean, but
Platonic doctrine before us.

W. D. Ross, in his *Commentary on Aristotle's Metaphysics*, vol. II,
p. 434, refers to "the evidence of Hermodorus" for ascribing to Plato

---

[1] *Metaph.* A 6, 987 b 18-27.

"the infinite dyad". Cherniss[1] replies: "there is no mention of this phrase in the fragment." As to the words, this is true; as to the sense not so. For if Hermodorus finally puts the Ἕν as the one principle opposite to "all that admits of the more and the less", and if in this last qualification we find back Plato's own description of what he calls (in the *Philebus*) the ápeiron, which contains, according to Robin's right expression, "all that oscillates between two extremes", then, without any doubt, we must acknowledge that by these words a description is given of that principle which, according to the testimony of Aristotle and his commentator Alexander of Aphrodisias, was called by Plato also the *aóristos dyad*.

Ross, of course, knows this testimony. In his *Commentary on the Metaphysics*, I, p. 169, he enumerates the various denominations given to the "great-and-small", and mentions the texts where they occur in the *Metaph.* and *Physics* of Aristotle. For the expression ἀόριστος δυάς he enumerates 13 places in the *Metaph.*, and adds that this term belongs to those which require a special treatment, because concerning this expression "it is harder to make out whether it is Plato or some of his followers that used it"[2]. But as to the fact he is perfectly right in saying that Hermodorus ascribed to Plato the infinite dyad. The use of this term in the cited chapter of Sextus confirms this.

The reader might think that Cherniss does not know this passage of Sextus. To free him from this suspicion it must be said that he knows the passage perfectly well. He only expresses a doubt as to whether we are allowed to take it "as a pertinent commentary" on Hermodorus' division of being[3], "as all who interpret the fragment do take it". He even cites the excellent article of Ph. Merlan in *Philologus* 89 (1934), where, having pointed out that the author of the Aristotelian treatise on the *Categories* constantly asks whether the concerning objects have an ἐναντίον and whether they admit of a μᾶλλον καὶ ἧττον, the writer concludes that the passage of Sextus in *Adv. Math.* X, where the same expressions are used, contains no

---

[1] *Aristotle's Criticism of Plato I*, p. 171, at the end of note 96.
[2] It must be remarked here that Alexander of Aphrodisias ascribed it explicitly to Plato, *Metaph.* p. 56 H., l. 18-20: διὸ καὶ ἀόριστον αὐτὴν ἐκάλει δυάδα, ὅτι μηδέτερον, μήτε τὸ ὑπερέχον μήτε τὸ ὑπερεχόμενον, καθὰ τὸ τοιοῦτον, ὡρισμένον, ἀλλ' ἀόριστόν τε καὶ ἄπειρον. Cp. Simplicius, Phys. 151 l. 6 D.: λέγει δὲ ὁ Ἀλέξανδρος ὅτι κατὰ Πλάτωνα πάντων ἀρχαὶ καὶ αὐτῶν τῶν ἰδεῶν τό τε ἕν ἐστι καὶ ἡ ἀόριστος δυάς, ἣν μέγα καὶ μικρὸν ἔλεγεν.
[3] *Aristotle's Criticism of Plato I*, p. 286 f., note 192.

Pythagorean, but Academic doctrine, the trace of which is directly followed by the author of the *Categories*. He finds this inference confirmed by Hermodorus[1].

The passage of Sextus, together with the fragment of Hermodorus, has been treated again by P. Wilpert[2], in apparent ignorance of Merlan's article. Wilpert compares the text of Sextus, where the three groups are reduced to the two highest principles, with the short compendium which is given by Alexander of Aphrodisias, *Metaph.* 56.13-21 (Hayduck), especially in this sentence (1. 16-17): τὸ μὲν ἴσον τῇ μονάδι ἀνετίθει, τὸ δὲ ἄνισον τῇ ὑπεροχῇ καὶ ἐλλείψει. He concludes that the account of Sextus and that of Alexander apparently must be traced back to the same source: Aristotle's account of Plato's lecture περὶ τἀγαθοῦ. Sextus, however, did not use that account directly, but a source in which the doctrine was qualified as Pythagorean. As a parallel to this remarkable fact Wilpert cites the so-called *Divisiones Aristoteleae*[3], a collection of Platonic-Aristotelian diaereses, parts of which have been preserved by Diogenes Laertius. Pieces of this collection may be found in the *Florilegium* of Stobaeus under the names of various Pythagorean authors. Iamblichus, too, gives in his *Protrepticus*, ch. 5, a number of such like "Pythagorean" diaereses. Now in this work large pieces of Platonic dialogues together with the *Protrepticus* of Aristotle were adopted as Pythagorean doctrine. In the same way the Περὶ τἀγαθοῦ of Aristotle may have been annexed already in Sextus' time.

These arguments, joined to the indications of Aristotle about the difference between Plato and the Pythagoreans, might remove the doubt of Cherniss as to the passage of Sextus. But some other, still stronger arguments must be added. First. To the remark of Merlan about the occurring of the questions of ἐναντίον and of μᾶλλον καὶ ἧττον in the *Categories* we must add this point, that in the tenth chapter of the same work, which belongs to the so-called *post-praedicamenta*, 11b38-12a20, the same differences which are mentioned by Sextus as characterizing the second and the third group of beings, may be found: (1) There is a group of contraries that cannot exist together. These can never have intermediates; for example, health and disease,

---

[1] Ph. Merlan, *Beiträge zur Geschichte des antiken Platonismus*, I, *Zur Erklärung der dem Aristoteles zugeschriebenen Kategorienschrift* (Philologus 89, 1934, pp. 35-53).
[2] P. Wilpert, *Neue Fragmente aus* Περὶ τἀγαθοῦ, Hermes, 1941, pp. 225-250.
[3] Edited by H. Mutschmann, Leipzig 1906.

odd and even. (2) The second group is of those contraries which can coexist. They can have intermediates; for example black and white, good and bad (φαῦλον καὶ σπουδαῖον)[1].

On other grounds it might be proved that the chapters 10-15 of the *Categories* are an early Aristotelian work: the division in various kinds of opposites, which are enumerated in ch. 10, is used in the *Topics*[2]. But even if these chapters were not the work of Aristotle, it must be acknowledged that the tenth chapter contains the same ideas which are set forth by Sextus, *Adv. Math.* X, 266-268. And this congruity gives us sufficient reason to infer that both authors go back to the same tradition, namely that of the early Academy.

Second. We saw that Sextus reduced the third group of beings, the correlatives, to the genus ὑπεροχὴ καὶ ἔλλειψις (§ 273); and he, again, ranked this genus, ὑπεροχὴ καὶ ἔλλειψις, under the head of the indefinite dyad (§ 275). To this must be compared two passages of Aristotle's *Physics*, I. The first is *Phys.* I 4, 187 a 16-20[3]. The author is speaking here of the "physicists" who accepted one material ἀρχή, and explained the multiplicity of the phenomenal world by rarefaction and condensation. He continues:

Ταὐτὰ δ' ἐστιν ἐναντία, καθόλου δ' ὑπεροχὴ καὶ ἔλλειψις, ὥσπερ τὸ μέγα φησὶ Πλάτων καὶ τὸ μικρόν, πλὴν ὅτι ὁ μὲν ταῦτα ποιεῖ ὕλην, τὸ δὲ ἓν τὸ εἶδος, οἱ δὲ τὸ μὲν ἓν τὸ ὑποκείμενον ὕλην, τὰ δ' ἐναντία διαφορὰς καὶ εἴδη.	Now there are contraries, which may be generalized into "excess and defect". Compare Plato's "Great and Small" – except that he makes these his matter, the one his form, while the others treat the one which underlies as matter and the contraries as differentiae, i.e. forms[4].

---

[1] The text runs as follows: ὅσα δὲ τῶν ἐναντίων τοιαῦτά ἐστιν ὥστε ἐν οἷς πέφυκε γίνεσθαι ἢ ὧν κατηγορεῖται ἀναγκαῖον αὐτῶν θάτερον ὑπάρχειν, τούτων οὐδὲν ἔστιν ἀνὰ μέσον. ὧν δέ γε μὴ ἀναγκαῖον θάτερον ὑπάρχειν, τούτων ἔστι τι ἀνὰ μέσον πάντως· οἷον νόσος καὶ ὑγίεια ἐν σώματι ζῴου πέφυκε γίνεσθαι, καὶ ἀναγκαῖόν γε θάτερον ὑπάρχειν τῷ τοῦ ζῴου σώματι, ἢ νόσον ἢ ὑγίειαν. καὶ περιττὸν δὲ καὶ ἄρτιον ἀριθμοῦ κατηγορεῖται, καὶ ἀναγκαῖόν γε θάτερον τῷ ἀριθμῷ ὑπάρχειν, ἢ περιττὸν ἢ ἄρτιον. καὶ οὐκ ἔστι γε τούτων οὐδὲν ἀνὰ μέσον, οὔτε νόσου καὶ ὑγιείας οὔτε περιττοῦ καὶ ἀρτίου. ὧν δέ γε μὴ ἀναγκαῖον θάτερον ὑπάρχειν, τούτων ἔστι τι ἀνὰ μέσον, οἷον μέλαν καὶ λευκόν.... καὶ φαῦλον δὲ καὶ σπουδαῖον.
[2] On the authenticity of the *Categories*, see L. M. de Rijk in *Mnemosyne* 1951, pp. 129-159.
[3] Gaiser, *Platons ungeschriebene Lehre*, p. 522, nr. 45.
[4] Translation of R. P. Hardie, Oxford 1930.

This passage shows that at the time this book was written – probably still in the Academy – the term ὑπεροχὴ καὶ ἔλλειψις was well-known and frequently used, perhaps by Plato himself, perhaps by his followers; and that it had almost the same meaning as that other term, which was so frequently used by Plato, the "Great and Small".

The other passage from the same book is *Phys.* I 6, 189b8-16. Here also the author speaks about the same "physicists" who accepted one element as ἀρχή.

Ἀλλὰ πάντες γε τὸ ἓν τοῦτο τοῖς ἐναντίοις σχηματίζουσιν, οἷον πυκνότητι καὶ μανότητι καὶ τὸ μᾶλλον καὶ ἧττον. Ταῦτα δ' ἐστὶν ὅλως ὑπεροχὴ δηλονότι καὶ ἔλλειψις, ὥσπερ εἴρηται πρότερον. καὶ ἔοικε παλαιὰ εἶναι καὶ αὕτη ἡ δόξα, ὅτι τὸ ἓν καὶ ὑπεροχὴ καὶ ἔλλειψις ἀρχαὶ τῶν ὄντων εἰσί, πλὴν οὐ τὸν αὐτὸν τρόπον, ἀλλ' οἱ μὲν ἀρχαῖοι τὰ δύο μὲν ποιεῖν, τὸ δὲ ἓν πάσχειν, τῶν δ' ὕστερόν τινες τοὐναντίον τὸ μὲν ἓν ποιεῖν τὰ δὲ δύο πάσχειν φασὶ μᾶλλον.

All, however, agree in this, that they differentiate their One by means of the contraries, such as density and rarety, and more and less, which may of course be generalized, as has already been said, into excess and defect. Indeed this doctrine too (that the One and excess and defect are the principles of things) would appear to be of old standing, though in different forms; for the early thinkers made the two the active and the one the passive principle, whereas some of the more recent maintain the reverse.

Hence follows: there is in Aristotle's days, during his first Athenian period, a doctrine which makes *the One* and *excess and defect* the principles of being; namely in this way that the One is the active (or formal) principle, the other the passive or material principle. It would be impossible not to recognize here the two ultimate principles of Plato's later doctrine: the One or péras on the one hand, and on the other the Infinite which is called the Great and Small or also the Infinite Dyad. Aristotle finds this latter principle foreshadowed in the μανὸν καὶ πυκνόν of the older physicists. Exactly the same thought occurs in the *Metaphysics*, A 9, 992b4-7, where once more "the Great and Small" (here called by this name) are compared with the μανὸν καὶ πυκνόν of the older philosophers of nature. Ταῦτα γάρ ἐστιν ὑπεροχὴ καὶ ἔλλειψις.

Thus in *Metaph*. H 2, 1042b25 and 35 among the principles of being are enumerated: μᾶλλον καὶ ἧττον, πυκνὸν καὶ μανόν and the like. Πάντα γὰρ ταῦτα ὑπεροχὴ καὶ ἔλλειψίς ἐστιν.

How strongly Aristotle at the beginning of his own metaphysical theory was dominated by the thought of two ultimate principles, the One and the Indefinite, may also be seen by his interpretation of Anaxagoras, in *Metaph*. A 8, 989a30-b21. This philosopher, he says, had, if only we explain him well, rather modern thoughts. For finally he assumed two principles, all other things being mixed with one another and νοῦς only being unmixed and pure. "From this it follows, then, that he must say the principles are the One (for this is simple and unmixed) and the Other (τὸ ἓν καὶ θάτερον), which is of such a nature as we suppose the indefinite to be before it is defined and partakes of some form (οἷον τίθεμεν, "we in the school of Plato", τὸ ἀόριστον πρὶν ὁρισθῆναι καὶ μετασχεῖν εἴδους τινός). Therefore, while expressing himself neither rightly nor clearly, he means something like what the later thinkers say and what is now more clearly seen to be the case"[1].

From all these passages, then, we surely must infer that Sextus with his ὑπεροχὴ καὶ ἔλλειψις, like Hermodorus with his μᾶλλον καὶ ἧττον, did speak Platonic language, and that the term of θάτερον as well as that of ἄπειρον could be used to indicate the "other" principle which, according to Plato's later doctrine, stands opposite to the One.

2

We now come to our second remark relative to the thesis of Cherniss. It concerns his protest against the conclusion of Hermodorus (or Dercyllides), that things which admit of a μᾶλλον καὶ ἧττον, being unstable and infinite, would be non being: ὥστε ἄστατον καὶ ἄμορφον καὶ οὐκ ὂν τὸ τοιοῦτον λέγεσθαι κατὰ ἀπόφασιν τοῦ ὄντος.

It is clear that here is not spoken of the μὴ ὄν in the sense of the *Sophistes*. The term μὴ ὄν is not even used. But we may well think of some other passages of Plato. I then might first draw attention to *Phil*. 59a-b, where Plato asks the question whether a science of nature is possible. His answer to this question is, that concerning those things *which do not possess any stability*, nothing stable can be reached by us, so that there cannot be any insight or knowledge about them. "The

---
[1] Translation of W. D. Ross, "what is now more clearly seen to be the case", sc. by Aristotle's own theory of eidos and hyle.

stable, the pure and the true" is περὶ τὰ ἀεὶ κατὰ τὰ αὐτὰ ὡσαύτως ἀμεικτότατα ἔχοντα, or what is most akin to them. — Plato leaves us no doubt: the names of νοῦς and φρόνησις, it is said, "have their truest and most exact application"[1] ἐν ταῖς περὶ τὸ ὂν ὄντως ἐννοίαις (when the mind is engaged in the contemplation of true being).

In the *Timaeus* again[2], there is a principle called θάτερον, which is one of the constituent elements of the "mixture" from which the World-soul, star souls and the souls of men are created. It is certainly an intelligible principle and, since its nature is opposite to that of the ταὐτόν, it is incorporated in the mixture only reluctantly and by force[3]. Now, how is this principle related to the ἕτερον of the *Sophistes* on the one hand, and to the ἄπειρον as described in the Hermodorus fragment on the other?

I think there is a positive relation to both of them. First, since the ἕτερον of the *Timaeus* must be an intelligible principle, it is certainly essentially related to the ἕτερον of the *Sophistes*. On the other hand, since it is described as an element that struggles against the perfectly regular motions ruled by the ταὐτόν, moreover, since it must be a constituent part of the Soul-substance because the soul must be able to communicate with the sensible world, it is certainly related to that world too; and this relationship implies a connection with the ἄπειρον as underlying principle of sensible reality, such as it is described in the *Philebus*, 24e-25a, a description which is paralleled in the Hermodorus fragment.

In this context we must remember a passage in Aristotle's *Physics*, 201b20-21, where it is said that "some" defined "motion" as ἑτερότης καὶ ἀνισότης καὶ τὸ μὴ ὄν[4]. Simplicius in his comment on this passage cites Eudemus, who wrote before Alexander about Plato's opinion on motion and says: "Plato says that motion is the great and small and non-being and irregularity and the like"[5]. Now Plato explicitly says in his *Sophistes* that motion and rest are not identical with ἕτερον and

---

[1] *Phil.* 59d, translation of Jowett.
[2] The following passage has been entirely rewritten (1969).
[3] *Tim.* 35a7-8: τὴν θατέρου φύσιν δύσμεικτον οὖσαν εἰς ταὐτὸν συναρμόττων βίᾳ.
[4] In the light of this passage it becomes quite clear that Aristotle, in *Metaph.* A 9, 992b7, having compared the great and small to the μανὸν καὶ πυκνόν of the physiologists — ταῦτα γάρ ἐστιν ὑπεροχὴ καὶ ἔλλειψις — continues: περί τε κινήσεως, εἰ μὲν ἔσται ταῦτα (sc. the μέγα καὶ μικρόν, or ὑπεροχή τε καὶ ἔλλειψις) κίνησις, δῆλον ὅτι κινήσεται τὰ εἴδη.
[5] Simpl., *Phys.* p. 431:6-9, Πλάτων δὲ τὸ μέγα καὶ μικρὸν καὶ τὸ μὴ ὂν καὶ τὸ ἀνώμαλον καὶ ὅσα τούτοις ἐπὶ ταὐτὸ φέρει τὴν κίνησιν λέγει.

ταὐτόν. And yet in *Phil.* 59 he opposes the changing world, which is not always the same, to the ὄντως ὄν which is always κατὰ ταὐτά. Is there a contradiction here? – No, there is not. Briefly, since in the *Sophist* there is mention of motion and rest as principles inherent in *intelligible Being*, while in the *Philebus* the author speaks about the *sensible world*. Concerning motion and rest as *intelligible principles* it is said that ταὐτόν and θάτερον may be predicated of both, each being other than the other and the same with itself. Now what is predicated of both, cannot be either of them. For in that case motion would be at rest and rest in motion. Thus, on the other hand, the eternal world of the intelligible is τὰ ἀεὶ κατὰ τὰ αὐτὰ ὡσαύτως ἔχοντα, while sensible things are τὰ μὴ κεκτημένα βεβαιότητα. Could it be said that to them motion is ἑτερότης καὶ ἀνισότης? And could this be referred to as μὴ ὄν?

I think we have to answer this question in the affirmative. For the ἄπειρον described in *Phil.* 24e-25a was in fact an element essential to this changing world of ours, and might be qualified as ἑτερότης καὶ ἀνισότης, while it could certainly be referred to as μὴ ὄν.

Let us conclude. First, there are three independent witnesses, Hermodorus (Dercyllides), Aristotle and Eudemus, who attribute to Plato the use of the term μὴ ὄν for his material principle or also for movement, or who say at least that in fact this principle is οὐκ ὄν. Secondly, "movement" is mentioned by Aristotle in connection with ἑτερότης καὶ ἀνισότης, and by Eudemus on a par with the great and small, the ἀνώμαλον "and the like". We may infer that by "movement" here is not meant the moving sensible world as such, but that side of it which is to be referred to the lower or material principle, which is described as "what possesses the more and the less". We saw that to Plato its chief aspect was "the great-and-small", and since its nature is defined as *an oscillating between two extremes*, we can understand that it could be identified with movement. We find this aspect of it in Hermodorus, where he states that this whole kind which possesses the μᾶλλον καὶ ἧττον, is *unstable* (ἄστατον). Thirdly, Plato nowhere calls the sensible world a μὴ ὄν, but he does oppose it to the ὄντως ὄν. Again we infer that not the sensible world as such is meant by Plato to be non being – we all know that he argues in the *Philebus* that it must (and can) be mathematically determined –; but what he means to say is this, that sensible things have an element in them, the nature of which is "moving", fluctuating, oscillating between two extremes, and therefore unstable and opposite to true being.

This then we may acknowledge on good grounds as being Platonic doctrine. It does not compel us to athetize the testimony of Hermodorus nor that of Aristotle as being false and untrustworthy; on the contrary, their testimony enables us, when we consider it carefully, to form for ourselves a clearer, a more precise and therefore a truer image of what Plato taught.

We proceed to our next point: the other passage in Aristotle concerning Plato's unwritten teaching, *De anima* 404b[16-27].[1]
The content of this passage, with the preceding alinea, is as follows[2]:
"All those who had special regard to the fact that what has soul in it is moved, adopted the view that soul is to be identified with what is eminently originative of movement. All, on the other hand, who looked to the fact that what has soul in it knows or perceives what is, identify soul with the principle or principles of Nature, according as they admit several such principles or one only. Thus Empedocles declares that it is formed out of all his elements, each of them also being soul. – In the same way Plato in the *Timaeus* fashions the soul out of his elements; for like, he holds, is known by like, and things are formed out of the principles or elements, so that soul must be so too. Similarly also ἐν τοῖς περὶ φιλοσοφίας λεγομένοις it was set forth that the Animal-itself (αὐτὸ τὸ ζῷον) is compounded of the Idea itself of the One together with the primary length, breadth and depth, everything else, the objects of its perception, being similarly constituted. Again he puts his view in yet other terms (ἔτι δὲ καὶ ἄλλως): Mind is the monad, science of knowledge the dyad (because it goes undeviatingly from one point to another), opinion the number of the plane (3), sensation the number of the solid (4); the numbers are by him expressly identified with the Forms themselves or principles, and are formed out of the elements; now things are apprehended either by mind or science or opinion or sensation, and these same numbers (1, 2, 3, 4) are the Forms of things."
According to Cherniss two passages in the *Metaphysics* must procure the proof of this thesis, that the doctrine, which is said here to occur

---

[1] Text in *Greek Phil.* I, nr. 372; Gaiser, *Pl. ungeschriebene Lehre*, p. 485, nr. 25a. A few years after the publication of the present article in Mnemosyne 1949 H. D. Saffrey commented on the same text of Aristotle in a broader study, which appeared in 1955 (Leiden, series Philosophia antiqua) under the title: *Le Περὶ φιλοσοφίας d'Aristote et la théorie platonicienne des Idées Nombres*. See also Gaiser's above cited work, p. 45.
[2] I give the translation of J. A. Smith, Oxford 1931.

ἐν τοῖς περὶ φιλοσοφίας λεγομένοις – Smith translates, as nearly all interpreters, ancient and modern, understand these words: "in his (sc. Plato's) lectures "On Philosophy" " –, namely that "the Animal itself"[1] is compounded of the Idea itself of the One, together with the primary length, breadth and depth (i.e. the ideal Numbers, 1, 2, 3, 4), is not the doctrine of Plato at all, but of Xenocrates: *Metaph*. 1036 b 13-15 and mostly 1090 b 20-32. In the first-mentioned place a distinction is made between τὸ εἶδος τῆς γραμμῆς and the line itself (αὐτογραμμή): of those who admit Ideas some say that the eidos of the line is two, others the line itself. The problem is mentioned again in 1043 a 33. In these two passages there is no reason at all to believe that here exclusively the opinion of Xenocrates is referred to.

In 1090 b there is indeed spoken of Xenocrates. Though his name is not mentioned, it appears clearly from the expression κινεῖν τὰ μαθηματικά, by which Aristotle reproaches him with speaking unmathematically about number. In fact Xenocrates was the man who, while Speusippus accepted only the mathematical number, identified this number with the Ideas and "made" spatial magnitudes (μεγέθη) out of numbers: length out of the dyad, planes out of 3, bodies out of 4. Aristotle asks: "Will these magnitudes be Ideas, or what is their manner of existence, and what do they contribute to things?" – He answers his own question: "These contribute nothing, as the objects of mathematics contribute nothing"[2].

Next he speaks about "those who first posited two kinds of number, that of the Forms and that which is mathematical". Here Plato is meant. Against him and his followers he says: they cannot tell us how the mathematical number will exist or from what it comes. –

Now this much is clear, that in the present passage Plato and Xenocrates could not be mentioned together, because the former did not identify Ideas with the mathematical number, while the latter did. Even if the doctrine that line is 2, plane 3 and solid 4 was taught by both, it had a different meaning to each of them. That it has in fact been taught also by other Platonists than Xenocrates and probably

---

[1] In *Tim*. 30 b the visible kosmos is called by Plato a ζῷον. Themistius says rightly that αὐτὸ τὸ ζῷον is the kosmos noètós. Cp. *Soph*. 249 a, where Plato says that the παντελῶς ὄν must have motion and life, soul (or conscience) and thought (νοῦς or φρόνησις). This can hardly mean anything but that, platonically speaking, the world of Ideas is a "living being", a ζῷον which has thought and conscience. – The problem concerning the interpretation of these texts was taken up by me in the preceding ch. IX (1969).
[2] Translation of W. D. Ross, Oxford, ²1928.

by Plato himself, is likely from passages such as *Metaph.* Z, 1036b. This probability is increased by Sextus, *Adv. math.* X, 259-260, and 278-280, where, among other indisputably Platonic doctrine, this also is set forth.

But let us consider the cited passage of the *De anima* itself.
"Plato in the *Timaeus* constructs the soul out of the (sc. his) elements. – Ὁμοίως δὲ καὶ ἐν τοῖς περὶ φιλοσοφίας λεγομένοις διωρίσθη, αὐτὸ μὲν τὸ ζῷον ἐξ αὐτῆς τῆς τοῦ ἑνὸς ἰδέας καὶ τοῦ πρώτου μήκους καὶ πλάτους καὶ βάθους."

Cherniss remarks: the words ἐν τοῖς περὶ φιλοσοφίας λεγομένοις must not of necessity mean Plato's lectures on philosophy. They can just as well mean Aristotle's own dialogue entitled περὶ φιλοσοφίας. That they *can* mean this, is proved by the fact that the ancient commentator Themistius understood them so; that they *do* mean it, is proved by Aristotle himself, who ascribed in his *Metaphysics* the theory that the line is two, the plane three and solids four, clearly to Xenocrates and not to Plato.

Here, then, we must protest. Surely, in *Metaph.* 1090b 32-33 the doctrine of Plato is sharply distinguished, both from that of Xenocrates and from that of Speusippus, namely in this, that Plato assumed two kinds of numbers, the ideal Number and the mathematical, while his two disciples did not. But nowhere does Aristotle say that the theory with which we are concerned here, namely, that the line is to be referred to the number two, the plane to three and the solid to four, has been taught *exclusively* by Xenocrates, and not by Plato too.

On the other hand, when we consider the cited passage from the *De anima*, we must remark that in this very passage the doctrine of Xenocrates on the soul, namely that soul is a self-moving number, is sharply distinguished from the preceding theory, which therefore can hardly be ascribed also to Xenocrates. For directly after the passage of which we gave the translation supra, i.e. immediately after the words "εἴδη δ'οἱ ἀριθμοὶ οὗτοι τῶν πραγμάτων" ("and these numbers", sc. 1, 2, 3, 4, "are the forms of things"), Aristotle goes on: ἐπεὶ δὲ καὶ κινητικὸν ἐδόκει ἡ ψυχὴ εἶναι καὶ γνωριστικὸν οὕτως, ἔνιοι συνέπλεξαν ἐξ ἀμφοῖν, ἀποφηνάμενοι τὴν ψυχὴν ἀριθμὸν κινοῦνθ' ἑαυτόν.

Smith translates the sense of the passage very clearly: "Some thinkers, accepting both premisses, viz. that the soul is both originative of movement and cognitive, have compounded it of both and declared the soul to be a self-moving number."

This then is the doctrine of Xenocrates. We may safely infer that

279

the preceding theory, even if it is closely akin to his views – as Cherniss rightly shows it is[1] – is not set forth here by Aristotle as Xenocrates' theory, but as a piece of Platonism. As to the term αὐτὸ τὸ ζῷον, Cherniss thinks it does not mean the kosmos noètós, I think it does. And if the latter interpretation is right, it means that Plato taught that the intelligible world or the world of Ideas can be referred back to the elementary numbers 1, 2, 3 and 4, τὰ δ' ἄλλα ὁμοιοτρόπως, "and sensible things too".

Now, if we write these 1, 2, 3 and 4 in old-Pythagorean manner in the form of a tetractys, then we have the *image* of the dekas. We might ask the question whether it may not be explained thus, that Aristotle testifies that Plato did not assume more than ten ideal Numbers. This explanation may seem at first sight rather attractive. – Yet it has some serious difficulties[2].

[1] Cherniss treats our passage of the *De anima* again in *Aristotle's Criticism of Plato*, App. IX, pp. 568-580. He finds his interpretation confirmed by the fr. 15 of Xenocrates, where it is said that he called the monad νοῦς, which he identified with the "primary god"; and by the fr. 5, according to which Xenocr. adopted a triple classification of psychical faculties – ἐπιστήμη, δόξα and αἴσθησις. In the fragments of Xenocr. the identification of these three faculties with the numbers 2, 3 and 4 does not occur. But it can be found in Aëtius, attributed to Pythagoras and the Pythagoreans. We find more traces of Xenocr. there (Cherniss *o.c.*, p. 570f.) – Now it seems to me highly probable indeed that the said identification was taught by Xenocrates, just because it was Platonic doctrine. Only, that it was not this, has not been proved by Cherniss at all.

[2] W. van der Wielen, *De Ideegetallen van Plato*, p. 193, rightly remarks that, strictly speaking, to Plato the ideal Numbers two, three and four (together with the one, which was not a number) were sufficient for the explanation of the whole system of Ideas, and consequently of the sensible world. He also thinks of the tetractys. But he shrinks from attributing to Plato the addition of these four numbers to ten, an operation which would be in contradiction with the nature of the monad and of the ideal Numbers. How then can we explain that Plato assumed nine ideal Numbers besides the monad, as Aristotle says he did? – Van der Wielen proposes this solution: as in the dialogues there is a part of strict reasoning, and a part of mythical form, so in the lecture on the Good too there may have been some portion of mythology. Plato may have spoken there by the mouth of a Pythagorean, and we can ascribe to this fictitious person the adding of the 1, 2, 3 and 4 up to ten. – Now, this is a highly attractive, yet a too uncertain hypothesis. We can hardly admit that Plato in a lecture of an apparently highly esoteric character (see the testimony of Aristoxenus on the next page) had a theory of his own set forth, a theory on matters he thought of the highest importance, by a person who explained it in a way quite opposite to his own principles. Consequently we are more inclined to assume either that Plato really admitted nine ideal Numbers besides the One, or that others from

What can be inferred with certainty is this, that Plato did admit in his ideal World a restrained number of higher principles, Numbers, to which the Ideas, and indirectly sensible things, could be referred back; which means that he admitted of *a certain hierarchy in his kosmos noètós.*

This again is confirmed by the often quoted chapter of Sextus, *Adv. math.* X 258, where, in a whole setting of Platonic doctrine, the author argues that above the Ideas there must be some higher principle: Number. – We will see later that Theophrastus points in the same direction.

Besides the commentators of Aristotle, who were all of a much later period and of whom Alexander is the only who has seen Aristotle's account of the lecture Περὶ τἀγαθοῦ, we have concerning Plato's oral teaching two other testimonies. One of them is the well-known story of Aristoxenus, *Harm. Elem. II* p. 30 Meibom. Aristoxenus tells us that those who came and heard Plato's lecture on the Good, were deeply disappointed when they heard there nothing else than "about mathematics and numbers, geometry and astronomy, καὶ τὸ πέρας ὅτι ἀγαθόν ἐστιν ἕν" – which means: "and that the Finite is the Good, which is identical with the One."[1]

Cherniss asserts that it is highly improbable that in this lecture Plato would have identified Ideas and Numbers; and for this reason, that Alexander in his explanations of Aristotle's account of the lecture

---

the *image* of the tretractys, used by himself, concluded that he intended to assume ten. But the latter possibility is surely the less probable.

It might be put forward that in later Pythagorean doctrine, which was closely akin to Platonism, more than four numbers are mentioned. See for instance the scholion in Arist. *Metaph.* 985 b 29 (Brandis, *Scholia in Arist.* p. 541 a 23-26): τὸν δὲ τέσσαρα ἀριθμὸν ἔλεγεν τὸ σῶμα τὸ ἁπλῶς, τὸν δὲ πέντε τὸ φυσικὸν σῶμα, τὸν δὲ ἐξ τὸ ἔμψυχον, e.q.s.

We find, indeed, in this passage the thought that the monas is the principle of ἕνωσις, ὁμοιότης, εἰδοποιία and ταὐτότης, while the dyad is called the principle of ἑτερότης, διαίρεσις and ἀνομοιότης, – "the reason why they also called the dyad matter, because it is the cause of separation" (ib. a 29-33). Now here one may definitely speak of Platonic influence. Yet it is difficult to make out what exactly is the addition of a later generation to the Platonic doctrine of numbers, and what is to be related to himself.

The same must be said of the doctrine which is attributed to Philolaus by the author of the *Theologoumena arithm.* (Diels, V.S.[5] 44, A 12).

[1] Text in De Vogel, *Gr. Phil.* I, nr. 364c; Gaiser, *Platons ungeschriebene Lehre*, p. 452, nr. 7.

derives this identification, and the notion that the principles of number are the principles of everything, from the doctrine that points are substantially prior to lines and are "monads with position". Now this is exactly what Aristotle says that Plato denied altogether[1]: for in *Metaph.* 992a 20-24 Aristotle testifies that Plato did not attribute to points any existence at all. Hence, if we accept his evidence in this matter, it follows that Plato in his lecture on the Good did not give any account of the identification of Ideas and Numbers; for Aristotle could not have said that he gave the explanation which Alexander proposes, and if Aristotle had reported some other account, Alexander would have had no reason to propose this one.

In this case again, as in that of Hermodorus, we must state that, even if the explanation causes some difficulties, the value of the testimony itself is not taken away. It is possible, surely, that Alexander gave a wrong explanation concerning the grounds of Plato's doctrine. But even if he did, the testimony of Aristoxenus stands as it stands, and we are not allowed to deny nor to diminish the importance of it.

For the rest, Cherniss' difficulties as to the explanations of Alexander may receive some light from the above-cited passage of Sextus (*Adv. Math.* X 260). In a preceding paragraph (258) the author argued that the Ideas could not be ἀρχαί, but must be referred back to a higher genus: numbers. He then proceeds to prove that numbers once more must be referred back to two ultimate principles, the One and the indefinite dyad. His argumentation runs as follows (259ff.): Natural bodies are no primary reality. They must be referred back to geometrical forms or solids; and these again to planes, and planes to lines. "καὶ ἐπεὶ ἡ ἁπλῆ γραμμὴ οὐ χωρὶς ἀριθμοῦ νενόηται, ἀλλ' ἀπὸ σημείου ἐπὶ σημεῖον ἀγομένη ἔχεται τῶν δυοῖν, οἵ τε ἀριθμοὶ πάντες καὶ αὐτοὶ ὑπὸ τὸ ἓν πεπτώκασιν (καὶ γὰρ ἡ δυὰς μία τις ἐστὶ δυάς, καὶ ἡ τριὰς ἕν τι ἐστί, τριάς, καὶ ἡ δεκὰς ἓν ἀριθμοῦ κεφάλαιον), ἔνθεν κινηθεὶς ὁ Πυθαγόρας ἀρχὴν ἔφησεν εἶναι τῶν ὄντων τὴν μονάδα, ἧς κατὰ μετοχὴν ἕκαστον τῶν ὄντων ἓν λέγεται."

If the intention of this passage is, as Wilpert thinks, to set forth that for Plato the point had *an ontological priority* to the line, three objections must be made. First, if Plato taught that the line is not apart from number but, being drawn from a point to a point, involves the number two, and that the two once more, being a single two, presupposes the one, it might be said that in this case the one has not an ontological, but simply a logical priority. – Secondly, when the

[1] Cherniss, *Riddle*, p. 28f.

author of this passage says that *Pythagoras*, moved by these considerations, declared that the One is the principle of existing things, by participation in which each of the existing things is called one, are we then allowed to attribute this whole reasoning to Plato? Can it not be that, in fact, we have here Pythagorean doctrine before us? – Thirdly, even if the priority of the One is meant as an ontological priority, and even if the doctrine of the above passage is Platonic, then it must still be remarked that here *the point* is not spoken of as anterior to the line, but the *monad*, while the point is not mentioned as being ontologically prior at all.

To these objections may be said: First, the priority of the One must indeed be conceived as having an ontological character, just as well as the Ideas are for Plato *ontologically* prior to things (to put it in Aristotelian terms: they exist παρὰ τὰ πράγματα). According to the above passage Plato argues: if the One did not exist, there could not be a two; hence a line could not exist. But if no line could exist, then no plane, and if no plane, no solid. But if no solid, no natural bodies could possibly exist. – What is posterior, can be abolished; what is prior cannot. To this Platonic view Wilpert in the above-cited article quotes an interesting parallel from the *Divisiones Aristoteleae*, preserved in the codex Marcianus (in the edition of Mutschmann, p. 64):

φύσει δέ ἐστι πρότερον οἷον ἥ τε μονὰς τῆς δυάδος καὶ τὸ μέρος τοῦ ὅλου καὶ τὸ γένος τοῦ εἴδους, καὶ ἁπλῶς ὅσα αὐτὰ ἀλλήλοις μὴ συναιρεῖται, τούτων τὸ μὲν συναιροῦν πρότερόν ἐστι, τὸ φύσει δὲ συναιρούμενον ὕστερον· οἷον τῆς μονάδος ἀναιρεθείσης ἡ δυὰς ἀναιρεῖται.

Second, that especially these paragraphs of the chapter of Sextus do contain Platonic doctrine, may be seen directly from what follows: the doctrine of the ἀόριστος δυάς as the second principle next to the One. For this is, according to Aristotle in *Metaph.* A 6, a chief point of difference between Plato and the Pythagoreans, to whom the ἄπειρον was one.

The third objection is the most important. It contains a real difficulty. For is it not true that, according to this account of Sextus, Plato did refer the line back to the number two, and the number two, being single, to the One? The point is mentioned only incidentally. So that Wilpert says too much when he sums up the contents of this reasoning in these terms: natural bodies can be reduced to stereometrical figures, stereometrical figures to planes, planes to lines and *lines to points*. Quod est demonstrandum.

Alexander says, commenting on *Metaph.* 987b33 (p. 55, 20-26 H.):

"Plato and the Pythagoreans assumed numbers as the principles of things, because they thought that the first and the uncompounded is principle, and that of bodies planes are first (for what is simpler and is not annihilated is naturally first), of planes lines, according to the same reasoning, and of lines points (στιγμαί), which the mathematicians called σημεῖα and they themselves monads, as they are utterly uncompounded and have nothing before them; and the monads are numbers, so numbers are the first of things."

This argument differs from that of Sextus on the point in question, since Alexander refers lines back to points and identifies points with monads, while according to Sextus lines presuppose *two* points, and the number two, being single, presupposes the One.

We have another account by Alexander, which is a report of what Plato said, according to his disciples, in the lecture περὶ τἀγαθοῦ (ap. Simpl. *Phys.* p. 454, 22-29 D.). It is this passage which induces Cherniss to deny the value of this whole report, because points are here called "monads having position". The quotation of Simplicius begins as follows:

"For Plato, who sought the principles of things (τὰς ἀρχὰς τῶν ὄντων), thought, because number seemed to him naturally prior to the other things – for the limits of the line are points, and points are monads with position, and without the line there is neither a plane nor a solid, but number can exist also without these –, because then number is naturally first to the other things, he deemed that this is a principle, and that the principles of the first number are the principles of all number. And the first number is the two, and of this the principles are the One and the great-and-small." –

To this we must compare Aristotle, *Metaph.* 992a 20-24: τούτῳ μὲν οὖν τῷ γένει (sc. points) καὶ διεμάχετο Πλάτων ὡς ὄντι γεωμετρικῷ δόγματι, ἀλλ' ἐκάλει ἀρχὴν γραμμῆς – τοῦτο δὲ πολλάκις ἐτίθει – τὰς ἀτόμους γραμμάς. καίτοι ἀνάγκη τούτων εἶναί τι πέρας· ὥστ' ἐξ οὗ λόγου γραμμή ἐστι, καὶ στιγμὴ ἔστιν. –

In these lines Aristotle answers the question of how the presence of points in the line must be explained: "Plato used to object to this class of things as being a geometrical fiction." Which means: a kind of *hypothesis*, such as is meant in *Rep.* 510 c - 511 b and 533 c. So Plato "destroyed" this hypothesis. He explained the line by another, more "abstract" theory, completely without the help of the senses. "He gave the name of principle of the line – and this he often posited – to the indivisible lines." It is not strange, indeed, that Plato could explain the line by the Idea of line (if this is meant by ἄτομος γραμμή, as I think most probable it is). We could only remark that Plato then could just as well explain the plane by the Idea of plane, and the solid by the Idea of solid. – Of course he could. But the essential point is, that he tried to dispense with the point, saying: "line is two" – we complete with Sextus: "and the two being single, presupposes the One". – Now of course it may be said, with Aristotle, that Plato implicitly did admit the point by the preceding argument. Indeed he did. And that is the reason why Alexander gave of his theory the account he gave.

Can we come to a conclusion? – I answer: I hope we can. First. The theory "natural bodies from solids, solids from planes, planes from lines, and lines from points" is a rather obvious train of thought, ruled by the same law. So it might seem that he who admits the first three members, admits the fourth too. This is seen in the above-cited passage from the *Metaphysics*; it may also be seen in *De caelo* III, 300a8-10[1].

Second. It seems that Plato wished to evade the assumption of the point. Hence he explained the line by his indivisible line. The question is: how did he pass from this to his ultimate principles: the One and the infinite Dyad? – Sextus gives us the answer to this question by saying: the two, being single, presuppose the One.

We may conclude (1) that Alexander interprets Plato in Aristotelian terms when he nevertheless introduces in his account of Plato's doctrine the notion of "points" which were called monads, or even "monads with position", and (2) that the account of Sextus is more precise.

We add two remarks: first, that Alexander agrees with Sextus on this point, that he too knows that Plato considered *two* as the first number, not the monad. And secondly that, this point being an ἴδιον Πλάτωνος, it is an evidence the more for the Platonic character of the passage of Sextus.

It must be said then, that Cherniss was not right in his inference that Plato in his lecture on the Good did not give any account of his doctrine of Ideas and Numbers, because Aristotle could not have said that he gave the explanation which Alexander proposes.

Lastly we have the testimony of Theophrastus, *Metaph.* 6b11-14 Ross-Fobes, where it is said that Plato "reduced sensible things to

---

[1] εἴπερ ὁμοίως ἔχει στιγμὴ μὲν πρὸς γραμμήν, γραμμὴ δὲ πρὸς ἐπίπεδον, τοῦτο δὲ πρὸς σῶμα.

Ideas, and the Ideas to Numbers"[1]. This implies that to Plato Numbers were a higher principle. Hence it follows immediately that a hierarchy must be assumed in the intelligible world, of which the One or the Good stands highest.

Robin indeed has followed this line. His interpretation, however, has been accepted by hardly any of the Plato-scholars of our age. W. D. Ross[2] tried to show that it is in contradiction with the statements of Aristotle, who says again and again that for Plato Ideas and Numbers were simply identic[3]. Most modern critics accept this view[4]. I opposed to it[5] that Robin's interpretation is essentially right; that it is not only compatible with Aristotle's testimony, but that this testimony itself points definitely in the said direction (we shall have to explain this shortly in the following pages), and that Plato himself does so by his hierarchical conception of being, which is displayed most clearly at the end of the sixth book of his *Republic*. We might add to it: this interpretation is also confirmed by the account of Platonic doctrine which is given by Sextus, *Adv. math.* X 258 ff.

We have now come to our last point: the final conclusions of Cherniss concerning the theory of ideal Numbers, which is ascribed to Plato by Aristotle. Cherniss argues as follows: Aristotle's testimony proves to be untrustworthy where we can control it (as on the so-called "material principle"); so where we cannot control it, it is untrustworthy too. Where it does not correspond, then, to any doctrine in the dialogues, we have to confide in Plato's own writings and to reject what Aristotle says.

A simple application of these principles leads to the rejection of Aristotle's testimony on the ideal Numbers and on the doctrine of two ultimate principles, the One and the indefinite Dyad. All this is declared to be "wrong interpretation"; not of any "oral teaching" of Plato – for this is a mere hypothesis –, but (as we can see it in the question of the "material principle") of the dialogues. In fact, Plato never taught it.

[1] Text in *Greek Phil.* I, nr. 373; Gaiser, *Pl. ungeschr. Lehre* p. 494, nr. 30.
[2] *Aristotle's Metaphysics* I, Introduction LXVII-LXXI.
[3] On Ross' revised judgment of 1951 see above, p. 249, n. 1.
[4] Also Van der Wielen, although his own interpretation of *De anima* 404b points in another direction.
[5] *La dernière phase du Platonisme et l'interprétation de M. Robin* in *Studia Vollgraff*[1], Amsterdam 1948, pp. 165-178; ch. XI of the present book.
Also in *Een groot probleem uit de antieke wijsbegeerte*, Utrecht 1947, pp. 11-14.

To this we answer shortly. First, there is something wrong in the premises. When Cherniss says[1]: "Aristotle's statements concerning the nature of the so-called material principle are inconsistent with one another and not only do not correspond to any doctrine in the dialogues but are flatly contradicted by the dialogues to which they themselves refer," – we might answer: "What is said about the material principle, either by Aristotle or by Hermodorus or by Sextus, certainly does correspond to *something* in the Platonic dialogues. The fact that our three witnesses agree with each other on essential points, warns us not to reject lightly what Aristotle says. On the other hand, we know that his testimony must be handled with prudence, i.e. that its interpretation requires a good measure of critical reserve."

Second. Cherniss asserts that, as Aristotle's statements concerning "the material principle" are inconsistent with one another, so also in his evidence about Ideas and Numbers there are some obvious contradictions. He mentions two. The first is this:

1. In *Metaph.* 1084a10-17 the theory of ideal Numbers is criticized because it confines these Numbers to ten.

2. In the same work, 1073a14-23 the author complains that this theory contains no statement concerning the number of real entities, but sometimes seems to treat the Numbers as unlimited, sometimes as only ten.

3. In the same work, 1070a18-19, he ascribes to Plato the doctrine that there are as many Ideas as there are natural classes.

– To this we say: The doctrine that the ideal Numbers are restricted to ten, is by Aristotle explicitly ascribed to Plato in *Phys.* 206b23. Now in the first of the above-cited passages, 1084a12-13, the same teaching is ascribed to "some": ἀλλὰ μὴν εἰ μέχρι τῆς δεκάδος ὁ ἀριθμός, ὥσπερ τινές φασιν. – We may infer: *not all* held this theory.

This, then, agrees with what is said in the second passage, 1073a 19-21, namely, that "those who say that there exist Ideas", identifying them with numbers, speak about numbers *now* as unlimited, *now* as limited by the number ten: ἀριθμοὺς γὰρ λέγουσι τὰς ἰδέας οἱ λέγοντες ἰδέας, περὶ δὲ τῶν ἀριθμῶν ὁτὲ μὲν ὡς περὶ ἀπείρων λέγουσιν, ὁτὲ δὲ ὡς μέχρι τῆς δεκάδος ὡρισμένων. –

– Evidently *not the same persons* held "now" that they are unlimited, "now" that they are limited to ten. But as Aristotle here considers those who admitted the existence of Ideas as one group, he could say that they "now" held this, "now" that. Surely it would

[1] *Riddle*, p. 26.

have been clearer if he had written οἱ μὲν – οἱ δέ instead of ὁτὲ μὲν – ὁτὲ δέ. But he might well believe that his readers would be intelligent enough to understand this.

So between 1. and 2. there is no contradiction. Now, according to 3. Plato taught that there are as many Ideas as there are "natural classes"[1]: διὸ δὴ οὐ κακῶς Πλάτων ἔφη ὅτι εἴδη ἔστιν ὁπόσα φύσει. – It must be remarked that by these "natural classes" not only classes of what we call "natural objects" are meant. To Plato also the good, the beautiful, the equal, and many other qualities, are rooted in a suprasensible reality. This he expressed by saying that they are φύσει; which means that they belong to an objective order. In this sense then he admitted εἴδη of all that is φύσει. Therefore Robin said rightly[2] that Plato admitted Ideas "au moins autant qu'il y a d'espèces de choses ou de qualités." But, this being so, we are really forced by Aristotle's testimony to accept the interpretation of Robin, who followed Theophrastus' indication that to Plato Numbers were a higher principle, above the Ideas. This indeed, we must accept, for by this principle only it is clear that more Ideas were ranged under one ideal Number.

Now, if we try to find evidence against this view in the statements of Aristotle about Idea-Numbers, it must be said that, though at first sight Aristotle seems to speak of a simple identification, there are strictly speaking, among these rather numerous texts[3] two which may seem to be in actual contradiction with our interpretation. One of them is *Metaph.* 1090 a 5, the words εἴπερ ἕκαστος τῶν ἀριθμῶν ἰδέα τις – "Since each number is *an* Idea" –. Indeed according to this text the Idea-Numbers would not be limited to ten, but they would be *as numerous as there are natural classes and qualities...*

Only, we have to ask: *is this the doctrine of Plato?*

Can it be his? – And we must answer in the negative, because in *Phys.* 206 b Aristotle said explicitly that Plato restricted the ideal Numbers to ten, while on the last-cited place in the *Metaphysics* no name is mentioned.

And *whose*, then, is the doctrine which makes each number an

---

[1] This term is used by Cherniss, *Riddle*, p. 26.
[2] *La théorie Platonicienne des Idées et des Nombres d'après Aristote*, p. 589. Cp. also *Metaph.* A 9, 990 b 6-8: καθ' ἕκαστον γὰρ ὁμώνυμόν τι ἔστι καὶ παρὰ τὰς οὐσίας, τῶν τε ἄλλων (sc. non-substances) ἔστιν ἓν ἐπὶ πολλῶν, καὶ ἐπὶ τοῖσδε καὶ ἐπὶ τοῖς ἀϊδίοις.
[3] Van der Wielen mentions 19 places (*De Ideegetallen*, p. 54 f., notes 82-84). The principal Greek texts are given in my source-book, *Greek Philosophy*, the numbers 262-263.

Idea? – We can answer this question: we know it was Xenocrates. Xenocrates who identified the mathematical number with the Idea.

That this interpretation is right, may be seen from another passage in the *Metaphysics*, namely 1081 a 5-12. Here the question is treated whether the monads are συμβληταί or not. Aristotle says[1]: "If all units are associable[2] and without difference[3], we get mathematical number – only one kind of number, and the Ideas cannot be the numbers. For what sort of number will man-himself or animal-itself or any other Form be? There is one Idea of each thing, e.g. one of man-himself and another one of animal-itself; but the similar and undifferentiated numbers are infinitely many, so that any particular 3 is no more man-himself than any other 3."

This means: if there is only mathematical number, Ideas cannot be the numbers. – We will not be such bad logicians as to say: if there is ideal Number, they are. But we may say prudently: if there is ideal Number, at least it is not excluded that they are.

We now have come to the other passage which seems to be in contradiction with our interpretation of the ideal Numbers: *Metaph.* M 7, 1081 a 12-17, the lines which follow immediately after the above-cited passage.

εἰ δὲ μὴ εἰσὶν ἀριθμοὶ αἱ ἰδέαι, οὐδ' ὅλως οἷόν τε αὐτὰς εἶναι· ἐκ τίνων γὰρ ἔσονται ἀρχῶν αἱ ἰδέαι; ὁ γὰρ ἀριθμός ἐστιν ἐκ τοῦ ἑνὸς καὶ τῆς δυάδος τῆς ἀορίστου, καὶ αἱ ἀρχαὶ καὶ τὰ στοιχεῖα λέγονται τοῦ ἀριθμοῦ εἶναι, τάξαι τε οὔτε προτέρας ἐνδέχεται τῶν ἀριθμῶν αὐτὰς οὔθ'·ὑστέρας.	But if the Ideas are not numbers, neither can they exist at all. For from what principles will the Ideas come? It is number that comes from the One and the indefinite dyad, and the principles or elements are said to be principles and elements of number, and the Ideas cannot be ranked as either prior or posterior to the numbers.

Now, if we would be severe in our judgment, we might say: here, then, indeed there prove to be two contradictions in Aristotle's

---
[1] Translation of W. D. Ross.
[2] συμβληταί means first "comparable"; then, of numbers, it means practically speaking "addible".
[3] i.e. without quality, which means: merely quantitative. The Idea-Numbers were "uncomparable" monads, qualitatively different.

account of the doctrine of Ideas and Numbers. Not those contradictions which Cherniss finds in it, but these two: 1. Aristotle, who always tries to prove that the Ideas *cannot* be Numbers, says here: they *must* be numbers, for otherwise their existence cannot be explained at all.

2. Aristotle who, by saying that the Ideas are at least as numerous as sensible things, while on the other hand ideal Numbers were restrained to ten, in fact gave reason to our interpretation according to which Numbers are a higher principle above the Ideas, now excludes the possibility that Ideas could be ranked "either prior or posterior" to the numbers...

But I think this severity would be somewhat unjust. First, because Aristotle does not really mean to say the Ideas *must* be numbers. What he means is only this, that, if Ideas must be assumed at all – which he denies –, they must be numbers, because otherwise their existence could not be explained. And as to the second point, it is clear that we have here, strictly speaking, not an *account* of Plato's doctrine, but a judgment about its possible interpretation. When then Aristotle says that the Ideas cannot be ranked as either "prior" (i.e. ontologically prior) or "posterior" (in the same sense) to numbers (he means here: mathematical numbers), we have simply to answer: Ideas in the sense of Plato must be ranked "prior" to the mathematical number; but perhaps they might be called "posterior" to the ideal Numbers. And because in this passage Aristotle speaks of the mathematical, not of the ideal Number, no real contradiction with our interpretation of the ideal Numbers can be found here.

This far, then, about the first contradiction which Cherniss finds in the testimony of Aristotle concerning Ideas and Numbers. He finds a second. It is this:

Aristotle commonly describes the platonic Ideas not as numbers, but as a metaphysical doubling of sensible things. And this in no way agrees with the idea that they are numbers.

The argument would be right, if the doctrine of the Ideas, as it is displayed in what we might call the classical Platonic dialogues – say the *Phaedo*, the *Republic*, also *Symposion* and *Phaedrus* – did exclude implicitly the doctrine of Idea-Numbers. Cherniss supposes it does. And many Plato-readers and admirers have thought so too.

To this then we must say: the conception of Idea-Numbers may seem strange to us. But is the doctrine of the classical dialogues, if we take it as it is, without removing its historical aspect, not rather strange to us, too? Take that wonderful product of platonic thought: the *Timaeus*. It is not, sincerely speaking, strange to us? I think indeed it is. The bridge between the theory of Ideas, which is more or less familiar to us by the classical dialogues, and that of Idea-Numbers, has been made by Plato himself: as to the principle, already in the *Republic* (the hierarchical principle, at the end of book VI), next in the *Philebus* and the *Timaeus*.

Robin placed, in his work *Platon*, the theory of Idea-Numbers in the midst of the later dialogues. Thus he rightly applied his view that we can neither understand nor give a correct interpretation of Plato's later doctrine without a careful study of the testimony of Aristotle and whatever later evidence we have.

To conclude this essay we wish to express our grateful admiration for the work of Cherniss. We know that our short account of his first lecture in the *Riddle* gives of necessity a very unadequate impression of the most brilliant argumentation of this little book. Indeed, these three chapters are very rich; they are really splendid. Cherniss expresses in a consequent and thoroughly well-pondered theory those more or less conscious convictions or impressions which were fostered by so many readers and admirers of the dialogues of Plato. He does so on the large and deep foundation of a most careful study of Aristotle's manner of writing what we call the history of philosophy – which was to him equal to an inquiry into the principles of his predecessors, comparing them to his own solutions and treating them as the ὕλη which must be shaped by himself into its true form and realisation. He does it, moreover, with acuteness and penetration, with a deep and real understanding for the meaning of Plato's philosophy, and, lastly, with a vast – I should like to say a *complete* knowledge of modern literature on the subject. Yet we had to combat his conclusions. There is, especially in *Aristotle's Criticism of Plato*, not only much valuable material; there is also much good interpretation, which may be of great help to those who study these subjects. Yet, on the whole, we cannot escape the impression that the author is inspired by some ὑπόθεσις: this, that Aristotle cannot be right where he tells us things about Plato which we do not know from the dialogues. I could say it in these terms: Cherniss appears in his interpretations, and still more in his conclusions, a highly orthodox and most conservative Platonist. I am afraid far more than Plato was himself...

Yet we may not close this study without a word of sincere thanks to the man who treated these difficult questions with such a learning and acuteness, with such a daring and tenacity, and most of all, with such a measure of Platonic spirit – which means: with so much true philosophy.

ARISTOTELICA

CHAPTER XIII

DID ARISTOTLE EVER ACCEPT PLATO'S THEORY OF TRANSCENDENT IDEAS?[1]

Recent theories on Aristotle's philosophy and its development

When in 1923 Werner Jaeger first published his *Aristoteles*, an almost entirely new approach to Aristotle's writings and quite an unusual view of his philosophical development was proposed to the scholarly world. In the 19th century Valentin Rose had collected the fragments of such early "exoteric" works as the *Eudemus* and the *Protrepticus* under the title: *Aristoteles pseudepigraphus*[2]. J. Bernays, though he recognized the authenticity of the dialogues, had tried to neutralize their apparently Platonic character by making it merely a question of literary form[3]. After these beginnings Jaeger made a fresh start by taking these fragments seriously as the remainder of a certain early period in Aristotle's life and work, a period in which he still shared the most essential doctrines of his master, whence he moved gradually and formed his own convictions and solutions.

Jaeger's work, however incomplete and questionable it was on many points, made a profound impression. The until that date almost exclusively systematical approach to Aristotle yielded to a more genetical method, as had been applied since many years to Plato's works. This change of method meant nothing less than a profound change in the appreciation of Aristotle's person: for a former generation Plato more or less symbolized the mind of the eternal *seeker for wisdom*, truly *philo-sophos* more than a "possessor" of wisdom and learning, a *dynamic* thinker much more than a static one, a teacher of method

[1] The present chapter was first written in 1962, shortly after the appearance of Düring's *Protrepticus* edition. It appeared in the *Archiv für Geschichte der Philosophie* 1965, (Bd. 47, pp. 261-298). A Japanese translation appeared in the volume *"Greek Philosophy and Religion"*, Tokyo 1969. The present edition is revised.
[2] Leipzig 1863.
[3] *Die dialoge des Aristoteles in ihrem Verhältnis zu seinen übrigen Werken*. Berlin 1863.

much more than of a system, a highly personal leader much more than a doctrinary teacher; Aristotle, on the other hand, was considered as the great builder of a system. That system was considered and expounded as an objective unity, whose author then appeared to have been much more a static than a dynamic spirit, more a possessor of truth than a seeker; truly a dogmatist, – not so much a changing mind, with all the uncertainties and possible contradictions involved in that. Now since Jaeger this view of Aristotle has been radically changed. In 1924 Ernst Hoffmann wrote in the Berlin Philologische Wochenschrift that "Jaeger resuscitated the living Aristotle in the flesh".

The leading principles of Jaeger's work were rather generally accepted. Sir David Ross, whose *Aristotle* first appeared in the same year as Jaeger's *Aristoteles*, essentially adopted the latter's chronology, together with the theory of an initial platonizing period in Aristotle's life. The same was done by E. Bréhier in his *Histoire de la Philosophie*, vol. I (Paris 1926) and by Ueberweg-Praechter, *Geschichte der Philosophie* I[12] (Berlin 1926). Ernst Hoffmann, as we remarked, expressed his enthusiastic admiration for Jaeger's work in the *Berliner philologische Wochenschrift* (1924). More elaborate criticism came from the side of Thomist scholars, both from the school of Louvain and elsewhere. A. Mansion (in *Revue Néoscholastique de Louvain*, 1927) raised some more or less serious objections against Jaeger's view of the *Metaphysics*. He attacked in particular the theory that Aristotle turned from speculative metaphysics to a kind of positivism: this cannot be true, for Aristotle worked at his *Metaphysics* until his death, and left the book unfinished. Mansion also differed from Jaeger in dating book Λ, the so-called Theology, much later. Mansion's judgment on this problem was confirmed by W. K. C. Guthrie, *The development of Aristotle's theology*, in Class. Quart. 1933 and 1934. As we shall see, Düring (in his recently published book), sees in Λ a very early work.

In general, Mansion pointed out that Jaeger's chronology of Aristotle's works was on many points uncertain. His results can not at all be accepted as definitive. "En somme son travail est en grande partie à refaire."

Von Ivanka, too (in *Scholastik* 1932), and a few years later Dr. F. Nuyens[1], protested against the separation of a metaphysical and an empirical period in Aristotle. The fifth chapter of the *De part.*

---

[1] *Ontwikkelingsmomenten in de zielkunde van Aristoteles*, diss. Amsterdam 1939. French translation: *L'évolution de la psychologie d'Aristote*, Paris-Louvain 1948.

anim. I, cited by Jaeger as a programme for empirical research and instruction in the Peripatetic School, is cited by Nuyens as well, but commented on in a different way: this beautiful chapter cannot be cited as a document in illustration of a "positivistic" period in Aristotle's development; on the contrary, the text shows clearly that for Aristotle the study of natural things was never separated from searching for the causes, and distinguishing the causes or "first principles" of things was for him always essentially the work of the φύσει φιλόσοφοι.

On the other hand, Jaeger's theory of a platonizing period at the beginning of Aristotle's career was neither doubted of nor rejected by any of these scholars. It was accepted rather generally and served as a basis for further research in different fields of Aristotle's thought. Thus, Fr. Solmsen inquired into the date of the various works of the *Organon* and the rhetorical writings[1]; several others carried on the discussion on the date of the ethical works[2]; others again renewed the discussion on the theology[3]. Both Bidez and Bignone were concerned with the traces of Aristotle's early works in the footsteps of Jaeger[4]; Düring and Drossaart Lulofs worked at a more precise chronology of the biological works[5].

For some thirty years very few voices were heard protesting against the theory of a platonizing period in Aristotle's early years. Some scholars must have had their doubts. As a matter of fact, H. Gadamer who came from the Marburg School, protested against the Jaeger theory in *Hermes* 1928. A few others followed[6]. In spite of these

[1] Fr. Solmsen, *Die Entwicklung der Aristotelischen Logik u. Rhetorik*, Berlin 1929.
[2] There has been a rather violent discussion between Jaeger and Von Arnim in the years 1924-1929. R. Walzer, K. O. Brink and Theiler took their part in it during the following years.
[3] H. van Arnim dealt with this topic in the *Sitzungsberichte Wien* 1931. The most important contribution in the field was, doubtless, Guthrie's in Class. Qu. 1933/'34.
[4] J. Bidez, *Un singulier naufrage littéraire dans l'Antiquité: à la recherche des épaves de l'Aristote perdu*, Bruxelles 1938. E. Bignone, *L'Aristotele perduto e la formazione filosofica di Epicuro*, Firenze 1935.
[5] Ingemar Düring, *Aristotle's De partibus animalium*, Göteborg 1943. H. J. Drossaart Lulofs, *Aristotelis De insomniis et de divinatione per somnum*, Leiden 1947.
[6] R. Philippson in *Riv. di Fil.* 64, 1936, pp. 113-125; I. Düring, first in *Eranos* 35, 1937, pp. 120-145; E. Frank in *Am. Journ. of Philol.* 61, 1940, pp. 34-53, 166-180. Occasional remarks by E. Kapp are found in *Mnemosyne* 6, 1938, p. 188, and in K. von Fritz and E. Kapp, *Aristotle's Constitution of Athens*, N.Y. 1950, Intr. p. 35.

exceptions, there was – and stayed for several years – a consensus in favour of Jaeger's theory. It is only a recent development that the basis of that theory was made the subject of a radical doubt, and that a number of scholars sat down together in order to discuss these problems. This is what happened for the first time at Oxford in the summer of 1957. In that meeting, called together on the initiative of Ingemar Düring, this Swedish scholar proposed for discussion his view on Aristotle's development as expounded in a number of articles of the preceding years. Of these four papers two dealt with problems in the *Protrepticus*[1]; two others gave an outline of the author's ideas on Aristotle's development and his main objections against the prevailing view[2]. Düring advocates what might be called *the unity of Aristotle's thought* from the earliest years up to the end. This is what he says in the Arctos paper (p. 65):

> "Since Jaeger's well-known book of 1923 on Aristotle's development, there has been a tendency to draw a picture of the young Aristotle as entirely dependent on Plato. It is a prevalent opinion that, up to Plato's death in 347, Aristotle not only accepted but also publicly defended Plato's theory of ideas and his anti-hedonistic ethics. According to this view, he suddenly changed his opinions shortly after 347, presenting in the great dialogue *On Philosophy* a whole set of new opinions, often in outspoken opposition to what he said himself in earlier writings. This view of Aristotle's development is not tenable. It is psychologically and *a priori* very unlikely and, what is more important, it is not borne out by Aristotle's early writings or by the best ancient tradition. A penetrating analysis of Aristotle's writings from the period 360-350 shows that Aristotle never accepted the theory of ideas and that, in metaphysics, physics

[1] *Problems in Aristotle's Protrepticus*, in Eranos 52, 1954, pp. 139-171, and *Aristotle in the Protrepticus*, in *Autour d'Aristote*, Louvain 1955.
[2] *Aristotle the Scholar*, in *Arctos*, Acta philologica Fennica 1954, pp. 61-77, and *Aristotle and Plato in the Mid-Fourth Century*, in Eranos 43, 1956. The latter formula was made the title of the "Proceedings" of the First Symposium Aristotelicum, which met at Oxford, August 1957. The volume appeared at Göteborg 1960, and contained Düring's interpretation of Fr. 13 of the *Protrepticus*. Shortly after the first Symposium Düring's *magnum opus* entitled *Aristotle in the Ancient biographical tradition* appeared at Göteborg 1957. In 1961 followed a new edition of the *Protrepticus* with a commentary, in 1966 the great work *Aristoteles*, Darstellung und Interpretation seines Denkens, Heidelberg, Carl Winter Universitätsverlag.

(in the ancient meaning of the word) and ethics, at a very early stage of his development, he followed his own course."

It should be remarked, first, that the view of Aristotle's development described in this passage as "a prevalent opinion" looks more like a *parody* of Jaeger's theory than like an account of it. As a matter of fact Jaeger never suggested that during his whole stay in the Academy Aristotle would not have thought for himself but just have reproduced what Plato held. Nor did Jaeger ever suggest that, shortly after 347, Aristotle "suddenly" changed his opinions. Whether or not this strange theory is nowadays, or was perhaps a few years ago a prevalent opinion, this much is sure, that Jaeger's views about Aristotle's intellectual activity during at least the last ten years of his stay in the Academy differ *toto coelo* from what is depicted here. Jaeger did not imagine at all an Aristotle who was for twenty years a student. What he imagined is: an Aristotle having the position of an independent scholar and teacher in the Academy for at least ten years. He supposed that, during those years, Aristotle taught logic and rhetoric, and that he did so in his own style. Moreover, Jaeger supposed that, during his last years in the Academy Aristotle was intensely concerned with the problems of cosmology and of philosophy of nature, not satisfied with his master's theories offered in the *Timaeus*.

Up to this point then, Düring did not offer us any revolutionary theory. On another point – and this a very important one – he did. For Jaeger had explained the fragments of the *Eudemus* and *Protrepticus* in such a sense, that it would be sure that Aristotle accepted the theory of the ideas for quite a period of his life. And this is exactly what is denied by Düring. Of first importance are obviously his grounds. They are of four kinds:

1. psychological probability;
2. the ancient biographical tradition;
3. the fragments of the early works, in particular of the *Eudemus* and *Protrepticus*;
4. the School writings dating from the same period.

Let us consider these grounds more explicitly.

Psychological probability

Obviously Düring is right when pointing out that it is improbable that Aristotle would have simply followed his master throughout the twenty years of his stay in the Academy, and would have started thinking for himself not until after Plato's death. Only – it should be said once more that this argument does not apply to Jaeger's theory at all; perhaps to some of those who came after him.

Düring imagines the young Aristotle's mind as not different from the philosopher known to us by his school writings, of which the biological works had his particular attention. For him, Aristotle is *by nature an empiricist*, – though not, to be sure, in the modern sense. Düring knows his Aristotle too well to imagine that he would have ever been a "scientist" according to the modern standard. He does not intend at all to attribute to Aristotle a kind of empiricism separated from a philosophical inquiry into "first principles", i.e.: what for Aristotle were "causes". "The truth is that, in Aristotle's writings, we can always expect to find side by side the two dominant trends: Platonic abstraction and biological empiricism"[1]. – This applies to the biological works. But – it should be applied to the young Aristotle's mind and work from the very beginnings. The "empirical trend" is on no account a later acquirement. It is a natural turn of the mind: Aristotle was φύσει an empiricist, as he was (at the same time) φύσει φιλόσοφος. Therefore, it must be wrong to imagine that he developed "from a devoted Platonist, soaked in metaphysical and ethical speculation, through a middle period of undecided vacillation, into a scholar absorbed in empirical and factual research"[2]. He was an empiricist right from the beginning.

Further it should be borne in mind under what circumstances young Aristotle entered the Academy at the age of 18: he did not find Plato in the School at that moment. Plato was in Sicily then, and Eudoxus had taken his place. Now we know that in the Academy the theory of the ideas was not at all a generally accepted doctrine; Eudoxus, in particular, did not share Plato's theory but modified it into a theory of immanent forms. His interpretation of the doctrine, his view of the rôle of ἡδονή in human life, and on the whole, his vigorously critical mind, must have made a strong impression on the young student.

Düring imagines that, from his first years in the Academy, Aristotle took an active part in the discussions on the theory of the ideas, and a very critical part. He finds a trace of these discussions in Plato's *Parmenides*: when in this dialogue one "young Aristotle" appears, why

---

[1] Düring in *Arctos* 1954, p. 76.
[2] Düring in *Arctos*, p. 75.

should not this be the young and inquisitive student, then present in the Academy and called by Plato "the mind of the School"?[1]

This may have been shortly before or after 360. About that date, doubtless, Aristotle started teaching logic, later (as it is mentioned in Cicero, *De or.* III, 141, and in Philodemus' *Rhet.* II 65, 5) also rhetoric.

As to Aristotle's psychological development, though Düring holds that Aristotle was by nature an empiricist and as such struggled against Platonism from the beginning, he is inclined to believe that the philosopher's thinking developed in the opposite direction to what is usually believed: "in fact, he was struggling to become a Platonist and to reconcile his empirical and common-sense approach to nature with Plato's idealism"[2]. He thinks we can follow this development in the fragments of his early works, and in the school writings as well. – This touches obviously on our third and fourth point. For the moment I explain shortly. Düring dates the Περὶ ἰδεῶν round 360, in the same time as Plato's *Parmenides*; he holds that neither the *Eudemus* nor the *Protrepticus* contain any text that would prove that the author accepted the theory of the Ideas; he contrasts Aristotle's early and devastating criticism with the polite and respectful words of EN I 6, – and lastly, he finds in the νοῦς-doctrine of *De anima* III an ultimate return to Platonism[3].

These views, advocated in Düring's earlier articles, are repeated and confirmed in his recent great work *Aristoteles*.

The ancient biographical tradition

The fact that in the ancient biographical tradition nothing is found about the "two Aristotles" generally believed in since Jaeger's hypothesis conquered the world, is greatly emphasized by Düring. In certain treatises on rhetoric, as was remarked above, mention is made of a sudden change in Aristotle's teaching of logic in the Academy; at a certain moment, rhetoric was added to his program. To be sure, this was an innovation in the School. But not a word is said about his ever having accepted, and next abandoned, the theory of the ideas. What we do find is: a tradition that Plato complained about Aristotle's behaviour, saying: "he kicks me like a colt." Düring cites these words

---

[1] Düring in *Eranos* 1956, p. 112. The reference is to *Vita Marciana* 7; Düring, *Biogr. trad.* p. 98 (text) and 108f. (commentary).
[2] *Eranos*, 1956, p. 112.
[3] *Arctos*, p. 76.

repeatedly[1], and declares that, with regard to this dictum, we must say: *se non è vero è ben fatto*. He finds in it a confirmation of the "persistent", and as far as we can see reliable, ancient tradition that Aristotle always had attacked the theory of ideas, also in his dialogues and when Plato still lived.

What are precisely the texts referred to? – The biographical material on Aristotle has been laid before us by Düring himself, excellently presented and arranged, and provided with some comments[2]. This is what we find in it as a reply to the above question.

In Diogenes Laertius V ch. 2 we read: Ἀπέστη δὲ Πλάτωνος ἔτι περιόντος. Follows the story of "he kicks me like a colt" (Düring, p. 29).

Let us add immediately that of the other Lives neither Hesychius nor the Vita Marciana on which both the Vita Vulgata and the Vita Latina depend, say a word about a "secession" of Aristotle from Plato.

Next, what is meant by these words? Probably not just that Aristotle criticized Plato's philosophy, in particular the theory of the Ideas, while Plato was still alive. It is rather intended to say that, while his master was still alive, Aristotle started a school of his own. As a matter of fact, this is what Aristoxenus said *expressis verbis*, and Düring thinks that Diogenes' words come from that source[3]. – Now it should be borne in mind that Aristoxenus was well-known in Antiquity for his *malignitas*, and the story about "some of Plato's companions, and of those who had lived very long in close connexion with him" who, while he was for the third time in Sicily, set up a school near to his and against it, looks rather much like a sample of that spirit[4]. The author of the Vita Marciana recognized this very well: he rejects the story, saying that Aristoxenus πρῶτος ἐσυκοφάντησε[5]. For the rest, an echo of the story is found in St. Augustine, *De civ. Dei* VII 12[6]. But, obviously, this could not be cited as an independent testimony. – Another echo of the secession story may be found in Usaibia's Arabic version of Ptolemy's *Life of Aristotle*: here it is said that, after Plato's return from Sicily, Aristotle started a school of his own, – obviously in perfect harmony with the master who, according to this biographer, during his second stay in Sicily had left Aristotle

---

[1] In *Arctos* p. 73, 1954; in *Eranos* 1956 p. 119. The reference is to Diog. Laert. V 2; Düring, *Biog. Trad.* p. 29 (text) and p. 58 (comments).
[2] *Aristotle in the Ancient biographical tradition*, Göteborg 1957.
[3] Düring, o.c., p. 58. [4] Düring, o.c., p. 378, nr. 61a.
[5] Vita Marciana 9, Düring, o.c., p. 98.
[6] Düring, o.c., p. 231, nr. 39c.

as the head of the School... It is probable that Ptolemy thus benevolently transposed Aristoxenus' malignant account.

As to the anecdote of ἀπελάκτισε¹, Düring thinks it might be true². Obviously, we are not finding ourselves on a very solid ground here. Aelianus, *Var. hist.* IV 9, who appears to know the story³, cannot be cited as an independent witness. Nor could Theodoretus who says that, during Plato's life-time Aristotle προφανῶς ἀντετάξατο (αὐτῷ)⁴. This may come from the Aristoxenus tradition as well.

Next, there is Philoponus in his Commentary on the *Anal. post.* Commenting on 77 a 5 he says: "And look how he is displeased at the doctrine about the Ideas, so that even what one might imagine of his words to introduce the notion about Ideas, is repelled by him in advance"⁵. – And in a later passage⁶: "He always appears to fight against the doctrine openly, not against those who misunderstand it; for in his *Metaphysics* he displays quite a series of long arguments against the doctrine. – Moreover, it is said that, also while Plato was still alive, Aristotle contradicted him very violently about this doctrine."

In the first sentence of the last-cited passage the author speaks of Aristotle in his school-writings. What he adds in the last sentence is obviously not a precise reference to any text in the *Exoterica*: it looks rather like a more or less loose saying, merely from hear-say.

The most precise texts telling that Aristotle sharply criticized the theory of the Ideas, not only in his school-writings but in his Dialogues as well, are Plutarchus, *Adv. Coloten* 14, 1115 A, and Proclus ap. Philoponum, *De aetern. mundi* II 2, p. 31.7 Rabe. It was on the ground of these texts that both Jaeger and Ross assumed that in Aristotle's Περὶ φιλοσοφίας the theory of the Ideas was criticized. Anyhow, there is not a trace of such a criticism in the fragments of the *Protrepticus*, whether or not the fr. 13 should be understood in an Aristotelian rather than in a Platonic sense. On the other hand, it seems hard to hold that any explicit criticism of the theory of the Ideas was found in Π. φιλ., except of the concept of ideal numbers, since Aris-

---

¹ Diog. L. V 2; Düring p. 29.
² Düring p. 58.
³ Düring p. 320, nr. 37 a.
⁴ Düring, p. 321, nr. 39 b.
⁵ Philoponus in Arist. *An.po.*, *C.I.A.G.* XIII 3, p. 133, 30; Düring, o.c., p. 322, nr. 39 d.
⁶ 243, 18. Düring ib.

totle's own words cited by Syrianus deny the first point and confirm the latter[1].

It has been rightly remarked that Plutarch's and Proclus' reference to "the Dialogues" can, and should, be taken in the broad sense, i.e. as denoting the group of the exoteric writings as a whole. This means that the criticism referred to by these two authors may have been that of the lost treatise Περὶ ἰδεῶν. To be sure, this treatise was not a dialogue, – but Π. φιλ. was not either. Anyhow, we must follow Aristotle's own testimony first. As to the date of the Π. ἰδεῶν, nothing prevents us from placing it in approximately the same years as the first book of the *Metaphysics*, and till now I did not find any indication that would exhort me to date it considerably earlier.

Are there any other texts that speak against the theory of "the two Aristotles" (if I may for the moment call it by that name)? – I think there are not. Düring[2] cites the second century Platonist Atticus (ap. Euseb., *Praep. ev.* XV) who emphasized the difference between Plato and Aristotle, both in ethics, in the doctrine of the soul's immortality, and in metaphysics (the theory of the Ideas). A very real difference. Only, if it is asked what works or what passages of Aristotle are opposed here to Plato's classical doctrine, the answer must be: with the exception of Π. ἰδεῶν the references are all to Aristotle's school-writings. On at least two of the three problems or fields of problems referred to the doctrines here attributed to Aristotle and opposed to Plato are not only lacking in the early dialogues such as the *Eudemus* and the *Protrepticus*, but it is Plato's doctrine that is found in those writings.

Let me explain. First, Atticus observes that Plato and Aristotle had very different ideas about the goal of philosophy and the nature of happiness: for Plato, perfect justice was a guarantee for perfect happiness, for Aristotle it was not – unless certain outward conditions were fulfilled (noble birth, physical beauty, wealth). Now everybody knows that this is what Aristotle holds in the *EN*. What is less known, but as clearly testified, is that in the *Protrepticus* Aristotle spoke as Plato did[3], and on this ground could be cited among the rigorists, as

---

[1] Syrianus, in *Metaph.* p. 159, 33: ὅτι καὶ αὐτὸς ὁμολογεῖ μηδὲν εἰρηκέναι πρὸς τὰς ἐκείνων ὑποθέσεις, e.q.s. Ross, fr. 11 of Π. φιλ.
[2] *Biogr. trad.* p. 325, nr. 40cde.
[3] In *Protr.* fr. 3 Ross (in Düring's edition B2-5) it is said that happiness does not depend on possessing many things, but rather on a certain inner disposition (ἐν τῷ πως τὴν ψυχὴν διακεῖσθαι). To be sure, this is not saying that "outward

Cicero cited him in the *Tusc.*, V 31, 87. Here it is said that both Aristotle and such well-known representatives of the Early Academy as Speusippus and Polemo held that happiness will always follow virtue, even up to the bull of Phalaris[1].

Of particular interest is Cicero, *De Finibus* V 5, 12. In this passage, inspired by Antiochus of Ascalon, Theophrastus is blamed for having attributed too great a part to Fortune. "Let us, therefore, cling to Aristotle and his son Nicomachus." – Did Cicero read the *Nicomachean Ethics*? Probably not, for as a matter of fact, Aristotle is not among the rigorists in that work. Cicero must have heard about it from Antiochus, who pretended to follow most faithfully the opinion of "the Ancients" – which Cicero thinks he did –, holding that in this matter there was a perfect agreement between Aristotle and Polemon[2].

The passage is instructive with regard to the problem about Aristotle's criticism of the theory of the Ideas as well. For, when it is said in the *Acad. post.* (I 9, 33) that Aristotle was the first to shake those "species" which Plato had wonderfully "embraced", it is once more

things" are altogether worthless. But it is brought out that it depends on the disposition of the soul whether or not these things are of any use to anybody. Hence, it is said (in fr. 4 Ross; Düring, B 8-9) that, in order to make a good use of the physical things that are at our disposition, man needs the guidance of philosophy. These passages have their exact parallel in Plato, *Euthyd.* 280 d - 282 d.

Cp. also *Protr.* fr. 5a Ross (Düring B 52), where it is argued that philosophy must have a bearing on practical life; and fr. 15 Ross (= Düring B 93-96): happiness depends in the highest measure on philosophical insight: it has the same relation to wisdom, virtue and true pleasure. – Nowhere it is said that certain outward things are required in order to be happy.

[1] *Sequitur igitur horum* (i.e. Peripateticorum, praeter Theophrastum) *ratione vel ad supplicium beata vita virtutem cumque ea descendet in taurum Aristotele Speusippo, Polemone auctoribus, nec ea minis blandimentisve corrupta deseret.* Also *Tusc.* V 13, 39.

Interesting is also Calcidius in *Tim.* 208-9 (fr. 17 of the *Protr.* in Ross): Aristotle called it a childish opinion to think that injustice makes one prosper, while virtue would harm (*malitiam quidem prodesse, virtutem vero obesse*). To put it in a positive statement: according to Aristotle in the *Protr.* the wise man holds that *malitia* always harms, whereas virtue always brings profit. Now, if it be granted that *malitia* is nothing but the psychological ground of doing wrong to others, this is exactly what Socrates holds against the sophists in such early Platonic dialogues as the *Gorgias* and *Rep.* I. It is mentioned as one of his basic principles in the *Crito*, 49 a-e.

[2] *De finibus* V 5, 14: *Antiquorum autem sententiam Antiochus noster mihi videtur persequi diligentissime, quam eandem Aristotelis fuisse et Polemonis docet.*

Antiochus who is speaking through Cicero's words, and it would be rather hazardous to argue that, since Cicero knew Aristotle's exoteric writings but not his school-writings, the criticism of the Ideas appears to have been present already in the dialogues and nothing in favour of it could have been in. First, Cicero must have known about Aristotle's criticism of the theory of the Ideas by Antiochus who, no doubt, was not primarily concerned with the Exoterica but rather spoke of the school-writings. Next, it should be borne in mind that Antiochus, though he claimed to restore the doctrine of "the Ancients", did not intend at all to reintroduce the theory of *transcendent* Ideas as it was meant by Plato. On the contrary, since he was definitely disposed to a philosophy of immanentism[1], he was not the man to pay any particular attention to the belief in a transcendent world of intelligible forms as it was more or less clearly expressed in Aristotle's early dialogues, such as the *Eudemus* and possibly still Περὶ φιλοσοφίας (if I may, for argument's sake, take this for granted, merely as a hypothesis).

Can it be used as an argument against such an interpretation as that Cicero "did not know that Aristotle had defended the theory of Ideas in his early writings and later changed his ideas"[2]? – I think not. First, the adherence to that theory was not clearly expressed in those exoteric writings; it was all the while a question of interpretation. Next, in this Cicero must have been greatly influenced by Antiochus who, as I pointed out, was rather inclined to ignore such a tendency in Aristotle's early writings.

As to the third point referred to by Atticus, that of the soul's immortality, it is obvious that the reference is to the *De anima*, and neglects altogether what was written by Aristotle in the *Eudemus*, the *Protrepticus*[3] and Π. φιλ.[4]

Lastly, when Atticus exclaims that in Aristotle's ethical treatises – the *E.E.*, the *E.N.* and the *M.M.* – unlike in Plato's works, no high inspiration could be found to the persuit of virtue, is it not obvious that the critic was simply speaking of these explicitly mentioned treatises, while he did not think at all of such writings as the *Pro-*

---

[1] I may refer here to A. M. Lueder's excellent work *Die philosophische Persönlichkeit des Antiochus von Askalon*, Göttingen 1940, which gives a precise description of Antiochus' place in the history of philosophy.
[2] Düring, *Biogr. trad.* p. 322, under nr. 40a.
[3] In particular the fr. 10b and c Ross.
[4] Fr. 12a Ross.

trepticus and Περὶ φιλοσοφίας, – in which, as a matter of fact, certain well-known personalities in later Antiquity *did* find an actual inspiration to the "philosophical life"?

What else can we conclude than that the criticism of Atticus, cited by Düring to confirm his thesis that Aristotle *always* spoke against the theory of the Ideas and did not start as a Platonist, if carefully considered gives rather a strong support to the theory of the two Aristotles?

Düring says[1]: "We cannot find any single ancient writer who says that Aristotle ever defended the theory of ideas, until we come to the disciples of Ammonius Hermeiu (who wish to harmonize Plato and Aristotle), and we have no utterance or text by Aristotle, directly or indirectly transmitted, which informs us in unambiguous words that he believed in Plato's two-world doctrine."

This is what we have to consider now in the fragments of the Exoteric works, in particular of the *Eudemus*, the *Protrepticus* and Περὶ φιλοσοφίας.

The Fragments of a few "exoteric writings" of Aristotle

a. The Eudemus

In the year 354 one of Aristotle's companions in Plato's Academy, Eudemus of Cyprus, died in Sicily under the standard of Dio. The story of his death is told in Cicero, *De divinatione* I 25[2]. Eudemus of Cyprus, while on a journey to Macedonia, came to Pherae, a town in Thessalia, then ruled by the tyrant Alexandros. In that city Eudemus fell very ill, so that all doctors feared for his life. In his dreams a handsome young man appeared to him and told him that he would soon recover, that the tyrant Alexandros would perish within a few days, and that Eudemus himself would return home in the fifth year thereafter. – The first two predictions were fulfilled forthwith: Eudemus recovered and the tyrant was killed by his wife's brothers. But towards the end of the fifth year, when Eudemus hoped to return to Cyprus (he was in Sicily then), he died in the battle near Syracuse. The dream was explained in this sense that, when Eudemus' soul had left the body, then it appeared to have returned home.

On the occasion of Eudemus' death Aristotle wrote a dialogue Περὶ

---

[1] *Biogr. trad.*, p. 331.
[2] Ross, *Fragm. sel.*, *Eud.* fr. 1.

ψυχῆς which he called the *Eudemus*¹. The commentators on Aristotle's much later treatise *On the soul*, usually cited under the Latin title as the *De anima*, quote a few arguments in favour of the soul's immortality, taken from the *Eudemus*. The first argument, cited in full by Philoponus, is that the soul is not a harmony, because harmony (or attunement) has a contrary, sc. lack of attunement, whereas the soul has no contrary. – The second runs as follows. Harmony in the body is either health, strength or beauty, while disharmony is the opposite of these, that is, disease, weakness and ugliness. But disharmony of the body could not be "lack of soul", – for everyman, even the ugliest (such as Thersites!) has a soul. Therefore, the soul is not an attunement.

These arguments were quoted by Philoponus, *in Ar. de An.* literally, by others (Themistius *in de An.* and Olympiodorus *in Phaed.*) in a shorter form. But all of them mention that Aristotle dealt with the soul's immortality in the *Eudemus* and offered arguments in defence of it². Elias, *in Categ.* 114, does not mention the *Eudemus*, but speaks of τὰ διαλογικά, saying: "It is chiefly in his dialogues (a term which embraces the Περὶ φιλοσοφίας and *Protrepticus* as well) that Aristotle seems to preach (κηρύττειν) the immortality of the soul"³. And Proclus *in Tim.* 338c: in the *De anima* Aristotle treats φυσικῶς of the soul, not speaking of its κάθοδος nor about its λήξεις (i.e. the interruptions in the life-in-a-body); – but in his dialogues he dealt separately with those matters and offered arguments in favour of those views⁴.

Proclus *in Rempubl.* II, p. 349 Kroll⁵ cites the following argument from Aristotle in explanation of the fact that the soul, on coming hither from yonder, forgets the sights it saw there (τὰ ἐκεῖ θεάματα), but on going from here remembers yonder its experiences made here. Of these facts the reason is, according to Aristotle: "that life without a body, being natural to souls, is like health, while life in a body, as an unnatural kind of life, is like disease. For yonder they live according to nature, but here contrary to nature; so that it naturally results that souls that pass from yonder forget the things there

---

[1] The fact is mentioned by Plutarch, *Life of Dio* 22. Ross, *Eud.* fr. 1.
[2] Philop. ap. Ross, *Eud.* fr. 7, Them. and Olymp. ib. See also Them. in *De an.* 106-107, Ross, *Eud.* fr. 2.
[3] Ross, *Eud.* fr. 3.
[4] Ross, *Eud.* fr. 4.
[5] Ross, *Eud.* fr. 5.

— just as some people, in passing from health to disease, forget even the letters they had learned —," while souls that pass yonder from this world continue to remember the things in it[1]. Aristotle adds that, when passing from disease to health, people never forget what they knew.

This text was taken by Jaeger as a clear evidence for the fact that Aristotle, when he wrote the *Eudemus*, accepted the theory of the Ideas. For what else could be the meaning of the ἐκεῖ θεάματα? Düring, however, rejects the passage altogether as a testimony of Aristotle's so-called "Platonic period": it is Proclus who is speaking, not Aristotle, and the expression "ἐκεῖ θεάματα" is not Aristotle's, but a Neo-platonic formula[2]. No doubt the dialogue as a whole dealt with the soul's immortality; but, since it was written to give a review of different opinions, in particular of those generally accepted views which were called κοιναὶ ἔννοιαι, we are not sure at all about what was Aristotle's own conviction. Anyhow, the quotation from Aristotle consists only of the explanation offered — it begins after φησὶ μὲν οὖν καὶ αὐτός —, not of the preceding sentence with the alleged facts. "Moreover", Düring goes on, "his interpretation of Plato is questionable, for the soul, on going from here and passing the stream of Lethe, was not supposed to "remember yonder its experiences here".

Let us consider this argument. As a matter of fact, the text of Proclus admits of the interpretation that only the αἰτία, not the facts it should account for, is Aristotle's. But this is not the only interpretation possible. It can be understood quite well as Jaeger understood it, that is to say: that Aristotle himself offered that explanation as an account of the two alleged facts. It is even more natural to take the passage in this sense. Evidently this does not imply that the formula τὰ ἐκεῖ θεάματα was literally used by Aristotle. Once more, it is quite possible that the whole sentence is a literal quotation. But it is not necessary. However, if the words τῶν ἐκεῖ θεαμάτων, opposed to τῶν ἐνταῦθα παθημάτων, are Proclus's, this much should be said in his honour, that he chose them well. — And, after all, this is perhaps rather an argument in favour of a literal quotation.

But suppose the alleged facts are not Aristotle's. Then, anyhow, the explanation is. And what does it say? That life without a body is for souls a natural state and therefore like health, whereas life in a

---

[1] I followed mainly Ross' translation.
[2] Düring, in *Eranos* 1956, p. 115.

309

body, since it is unnatural, is like disease. "For yonder they live according to nature, but here contrary to nature."

It is hard indeed to attribute this explanation to Aristotle and at the same time maintain that we are not sure at all whether he shared Plato's view of the soul and its kinship with a transcendent reality, the more so since we have several other fragments in which he expresses exactly the same opinion, even in a very radical form, such as is nowhere found in Plato. I am thinking of the story of the Etruscan pirates, who used to bind their captives face to face with dead bodies, a story which is used by Aristotle as a simile to express the relation of soul and body[1]. It is exactly the drastic form which seems to be particular to the young Aristotle's mind. It is not Plato's, though the substance of the thought no doubt is. – In Aristotle, we find the same view expressed at the end of fr. 15 of the *Protrepticus* according to Ross: here the life of man is called unnatural, and the human kind itself is said to be so in a sense; hence, learning and insight are difficult for us here, but will be easy in the life hereafter. After our fragment 5 of the *Eudemus* and the story of the Etruscans there is hardly anything unacceptable in that passage. Düring, however, who a few years ago was inclined to attribute this passage to the *Eudemus*, now discovered that it is written in bad Greek, and that "what it says is strange". He declares that neither Plato nor Aristotle can have written anything like this[2].

I cite two other parallels. First, if there is a difficulty in καὶ μόλις ‹ἂν› αἰσθάνοιτο (*Protr.* fr. 15 Ross, the end), one might compare Π. φιλ. fr. 8, pag. 76,4, Ross: ἐπεὶ τοίνυν τὰ νοητὰ καὶ θεῖα, ὡς ὁ Ἀριστοτέλης φησίν, εἰ καὶ φανότατά ἐστι κατὰ τὴν ἑαυτῶν οὐσίαν, ἡμῖν διὰ τὴν ἐπικειμένην τοῦ σώματος ἀχλὺν σκοτεινὰ δοκεῖ καὶ ἀμυδρά, τὴν ταῦτα ἡμῖν εἰς φῶς ἀγοῦσαν ἐπιστήμην σοφίαν εἰκότως ὠνόμασαν.

In the preceding lines the author (Philoponus in his commentary on Nicomachus' *Isagoge* I 1) declared that σοφία is called by that name, "as being a sort of clearness" (σαφεία), since it makes all things clear. "Since then, as Aristotle says, things intelligible and divine, even if they are most clear in their own nature, seem to us dark and dim because of the mist of the body which hangs over us, men naturally gave to the knowledge which brings these things into the light for us the name of wisdom."

[1] *Protr.* fr. 10b Ross; Düring, *Protr.* B 106-107. I do not see any reason to attribute this fragment to the *Eudemus*.
[2] Düring, *Protr.*, p. 257.

Second, the expectation expressed at the end of fr. 15 of the *Protrepticus*, that in the life hereafter learning and insight will be easy to attain, is paralleled in the passage of the life that waits us in the islands of the blessed[1].

And obviously for Aristotle this life was "natural" κατ' ἐξοχήν, since the intellectual function is that by which the human nature is specified. This is not Aristotle's later doctrine, neither that of *EN* X 7-8 nor of the *De anima*. For the author of the *EN* the "contemplative life" is a scholar's life realized on earth. He does not differ from the author of the *Protrepticus* in that he considers noûs as a part of the soul, its dominant and better part, and therefore our real "self"[2]. But he does differ both from the author of the *Eudemus* and of the *Protrepticus* in that the author of the *Eudemus* definitely places the true life of the soul yonder, while in the *Protrepticus*, though he still does so, at the same time the value of sense-perception is acknowledged, and it is said repeatedly that the soul attains the truth in this life, even easily[3] and often[4]. Somehow, the author of the *Protrepticus* seems to be half-way Aristotle's later view of the βίος θεωρητικός as a particularly human ideal, which can be realized in the life on earth, an ideal which we find expressed both in the introductory chapters to the *Metaphysics* (A 1-2) and in *EN* X 7-8.

"For there (i.e. in the life hereafter) they live according to nature, but here contrary to nature; so that it naturally results that souls that pass from yonder forget the things there, while souls that pass yonder from this world continue to remember the things in it" (*Eudemus*, fr. 5).

Of these two consequences the first mentioned one is established by experience, the second is not. Is it a Neoplatonic thesis, which Proclus finds confirmed by Aristotle's argument? On the contrary, it must have been known to Proclus that Plotinus, in the first chapters of *Enn.* IV 4, deliberately denied that the soul, once she is yonder, would remember anything of what she was and used to do during her life on earth: she is in *eternity* now, – that is to say, things of this life have faded away completely. How then did Proclus come to such an interpretation? In any case not along the lines of the Neoplatonic tradition. Did he then interpret Plato on his own account? But he

---

[1] *Protr.*, fr. 12b Ross; Düring, *Protr.* B 43.
[2] *EN* X 7, 1178 a 2-3; *Protr.* fr. 6 Ross, p. 35; Düring B 62; also B 67 (Ross, p. 36).
[3] *Protr.* fr. 5 Ross, p. 34; Düring B 55-56.
[4] *Protr.* fr. 9 Ross, p. 39; Düring B 101.

quotes Aristotle. And is it not more probable that he found this interpretation in the *Eudemus* than that he invented it himself?[1]

I conclude: it is probable, after all, that the fragment 5 confers to us an almost *literal* fragment of the *Eudemus*. What can be questioned is, whether in this fragment Aristotle's own opinion was expressed. Düring is not the first to deny this: it was done by J. Bernays a century before, and obviously because he could not imagine that Aristotle ever taught a doctrine about the soul which differed essentially from that of the *De anima*. However, it must be borne in mind that the *De anima* belongs to Aristotle's latest years, while the *Eudemus* was written almost thirty years earlier. In his recent work *Aristoteles*[2] Düring argues against the view of those modern scholars who hold that in the *Protrepticus* and in his dialogues Aristotle taught a philosophy different from that of his school writings. Towards the end of this great work, when dealing with the *Eudemus*, he declares[3]: *"We must maintain that in his Dialogues and in his school writings Aristotle taught essentially the same philosophy."* – That is to say, if one condition is added. Düring adds it himself to the above cited sentence when writing: *"in gleichzeitig geschriebenen* Dialogen und Lehrschriften". – "In his Dialogues and in his school writings, *in so far as they were written in the same period."*

I agree. But if this be added, no argument against the doctrine of the soul found in some fragments of the *Eudemus* and of the *Protrepticus* (which was not a dialogue!) can be derived from the above-cited principle that in both kinds of his writings Aristotle taught essentially the same philosophy. For the *De anima* and the *Eudemus*, or also the *De anima* and the *Protrepticus*, were separated by some 25-30 years. And is it not doing violence to the texts to deny such a fragment as that on the Etruscan pirates to the *Protrepticus*, and such a passage as *Protr.* fr. 15, the end, to Aristotle at all? It is true, of course, that a fragment from the *Eudemus* does not necessarily represent

---

[1] *Rep.* X 618b-619a does imply that "yonder" souls have a memory of things here, since in principle they are supposed to be able to make the right choice of life to be lived in their next incarnation. Notice in particular the words: "Therefore, one must go to Hades in the unshakable possession of this conviction" (ἀδαμαντίνως ταύτην τὴν δόξαν ἔχοντα). According to Plato, however, such a conviction was by no means a generally occurring phenomenon in man; on the contrary, he thought it strictly limited to those who had spent their life in philosophy, – which, of course, were very few.

[2] p. 42f.

[3] p. 557.

Aristotle's own opinion. But it cannot be denied that the *Eudemus* fr. 5 stands not by itself. On the contrary, there is converging evidence which makes it highly probable that Aristotle when writing the *Eudemus* and the *Protrepticus* was still inclined to consider the life of the soul without a body as normal.

It is also interesting to see how Werner Jaeger commented on the passage[1]. "The continuity of consciousness", he says, "depends on memory. Whereas he later denies that *Noûs* possesses this, in the *Eudemus* he (Aristotle) tries to save it for the soul that has returned to the other world. He does this by enlarging Plato's recollection into a theory of the continuity of consciousness in all three phases of the soul's existence – its former existence, its life on earth, and its life after death. Alongside the Platonic view that the soul remembers the other world he sets this thesis that it remembers this one. He supports this by an analogy" (sc. that life here is like a disease, while life yonder is like health). Jaeger explains: "The validity of the proof depends on the correctness of its presupposition, that man's knowledge is a recollection of "the visions there" (τὰ ἐκεῖ θεάματα). The personal immortality that the *Eudemus* teaches necessarily stands or falls along with this Platonic dogma." At first the young Aristotle followed along the lines of Plato's myth of recollection. Later on, when he abandones the theory of Forms, he inevitably dropped recollection, and pre-existence and immortality along with it.

As a matter of fact, the argument does not hold good. For, since according to our fragment Aristotle *denied* that the soul on coming hither remembers the ἐκεῖ θεάματα, the theory of recollection would not follow. Aristotle rather makes the impression of altering the doctrine in such a sense, that "recollection" is limited to certain cases of mantic by dreams, – a theory which, after all, does not square with the health and disease simile either.

This much can be said. The general tenor of the *Eudemus* was to argue that "yonder" the soul will have its true life, which is a purely spiritual life. Though in a dialogue not every argument put forward is representative of the author's opinion, we have no reason to suppose that the main tendency of the dialogue *Eudemus* was against Aristotle's own view. On the contrary, our oldest testimonies do not point in that direction, but rather clearly suggest that, in fact, in those years Aristotle shared the above-mentioned belief, which is known as Plato's. Apparently he believed in pre-existence and offered an

[1] p. 51 of the English edition.

explanation of the psychological fact that we remember hardly anything of it. He did not define the ἐκεῖ θεάματα. But certainly the belief in the existence of a transcendent intelligible world is more or less implicitly contained in the doctrine of the soul's life hereafter as accepted and defended in this dialogue.

Let us go through the other fragments of the *Eudemus* and see whether there is any further evidence concerning Aristotle's conviction about the soul and the nature of the intelligible world.

The story of Midas and Silenus (fr. 6 Ross), though in itself not conclusive, fits well into the framework set by fr. 5.

Simplicius, commenting on the *De anima* III 5, says that in the *Eudemus* Aristotle declared that the soul is a Form (εἶδός τι). Certainly this is not saying that she is an "Idea", but the expression "a kind of Form" can hardly mean anything else than that the soul has a certain substantiality, as Plato thought it had[1].

The story of Timon's grandmother, who used to hibernate two months in each year, reminds of such a case as Hermotimos of Clazomenae, a famous case of "shamanism" (to speak with Dodds) mentioned in the *Protr.* fr. 10c Ross. No doubt such stories were meant to illustrate the super-natural character of the soul and its independence of the body.

The fragments 10 and 11 deserve some more attention. In 10 (from Plutarch, *De Iside* 382d-e) the author (Plutarch) speaks about νόησις as an immediate grasping of the intelligible object: "flashing like lightning through the soul, it grants it at times to touch and to see" (θιγεῖν καὶ προσιδεῖν). He goes on: "This is why Plato and Aristotle call this part of philosophy a mystic vision (ἐποπτικὸν τοῦτο τὸ μέρος τῆς φιλοσοφίας καλοῦσι), inasmuch as those who forsake these confused and various objects of opinion leap in thought to that primary, simple, and immaterial object, and, gaining true contact with the pure truth about it, think that, as though by initiation into the mysteries (οἷον ἐν τελετῇ), they have attained the end (τέλος) of philosophy"[2].

I do not think there is any reason to place this passage under the *Eudemus* fragments.

These are my grounds. We have a precise information about what Aristotle thought of the process of human knowledge. Now both in *Anal. Post.* II 19 and in *Metaph.* Θ 10 we find exactly that immediate "grasping" of the intelligible object by noûs which he called θιγεῖν

---
[1] *Eudemus*, fr. 8 Ross.
[2] Translation by Ross.

in 1051b24[1] and described as "the most precise kind of knowledge" in 100b8-9[2]. The final chapter of the *Analytics* is obviously of an earlier date: we can use the passage on the apprehension of ἀσύνθετα in *Metaph.* Θ 10 as a commentary on its last section. In the *Analytics* it is not actually explained *how* the universal is apprehended. Somehow it is presented to us by means of a natural process: at a certain moment the universal is "established" within the soul, whenever in the stream of experience a "stand" is made. And should we ask *how* such a thing is possible, we are told that "the soul is of such a nature that this can happen to her". But it is clear enough that the author is thinking of that "direct apprehension" which is called "touching" in *Metaph.* Θ 10, and could be called "seeing" as well. Hence, in our passage of the *Analytics* νοῦς is correctly translated by "intuition": its function is not "reasoning" or "judging", in which a subject is – either rightly or wrongly – copulated with a predicate, but simply "apprehending" a thing. In this act of simple apprehension there is no possibility of error: one either "touches" the intelligible object or not. Therefore, the author could say (100b10-12): since, on the one hand, all scientific knowledge (ἐπιστήμη) is discursive, there can be no scientific knowledge of first principles (νοῦς ἂν εἴη τῶν ἀρχῶν), – "first principles" being the νοητά or intelligible "forms" of things.

Now this direct "grasping" of the intelligible essence of things, like Plato's "seeing" or "touching" the νοητά[3], could be quite well called by Plutarch "the ἐποπτικὸν μέρος τῆς φιλοσοφίας according to Plato and Aristotle". That for the one the nature of the νοητόν was very different from what it was for the other, that for the one it was primarily the form immanent in natural objects while for the other it denoted always transcendent Being, is a fact which up till the present day may be sometimes overlooked by those who concentrate their attention on the very fact of "apprehending" the intelligible object as described by both[4]. For Aristotle, too, the "form" as such is πρῶτον καὶ ἁπλοῦν καὶ ἄυλον, – though it cannot exist "apart"; and so Plutarch could say

---

[1] See my *Greek Phil.* II, nr. 559b, and the comments given there.
[2] οὐδὲν ἐπιστήμης ἀκριβέστερον ἄλλο γένος ἢ νοῦς.
[3] For instance: *Symp.* 211d-212a, *Phaedr.* 247a-248a, *Rep.* V 476b-480a; VI 484b.
[4] Thus, for instance, Dr. W. N. A. Klever, who, in his work ΑΝΑΜΝΗΣΙΣ and ΑΝΑΓΩΓΗ, Assen 1962, tried to establish a fundamental agreement between Plato's doctrine of anamnesis and Aristotle's theory of knowledge as expressed in the *An. po.* II 19 and elswhere.

what he said without any reference to any other passage in Aristotle than those well-known to us by the school writings.

Under 11 Ross cites two fragments from Al Kindi, who refers explicitly to Aristotle, but without mentioning the *Eudemus*. The first begins as follows: "Aristotle tells of the Greek king whose soul was caught up in ecstasy, and who for many days remained neither alive nor dead. When he came to himself, he told the bystanders of various things in the invisible world, and related what he had seen – *souls, forms, and angels*"... e.q.s.

No doubt, this story fits excellently into the framework of the *Eudemus*. Only, – I am not willing to believe that the author actually read these words in any text of Aristotle, be it in any Arabic translation. Here are my grounds. Al Kindi and the Arabic philosophers who came after him were formed in the Syrian schools. Now we know that, what was presented there as "Aristotelian philosophy" and "Aristotle" was, as a matter of fact, a curious mixture of Neoplatonism and Aristotelianism. Sometimes even pure Neoplatonism was labelled "Aristotle", as it happened e.g. in the case of the so-called *Theologia Aristotelis* and of the *Liber de causis*. In this climate we should not wonder to find a story very similar to that of the Pamphylian Er[1] labelled with the name of "the philosopher" (as he was called by the Arabs), and to find the "vision of yonder" attributed to the hero of this story described in the terms *"souls, forms and angels"*. Evidently there is no guarantee at all that Al Kindi found anything like that in any text of Aristotle; it is even much more probable that he did not. For this is simply how the Arabic philosophers understood their Aristotle. One finds this pictureskly illustrated in Ibn Tofail's wonderful story of Hai ibn Jokdân, that intelligent young man who arrived as a baby on an uninhabited island and later on, bred among the animals, by the simple use of his reason, invented the whole philosophy of Aristotle...[2]. He understood the theory of "form" realizing itself in "matter" in a theistic sense: as a process dominated by a personal, deliberately working divine Intellect. And when at the age of 49 Ibn

[1] Plato, *Rep.* X 614 b.
[2] See my paper "Plato, Aristotle and the ideal of the contemplative life", which was first published in Italian in the *Giornale di Metafisica*, Genova 1961, afterwards in Dutch in the volume *Theoria*, Assen 1967, in Japanese in Tokyo 1969, and appeared in English at Manila 1967 in the theological journal *Philippiniana sacra*. Though the latter publication is hardly accessible to the European reader, I had it not reprinted in the present volume, for reasons that may be easily understood.

DID ARISTOTLE EVER ACCEPT THE IDEAS?

Jokdân withdraws into a cavern in the mountains to spend the rest of his days as much as possible in contemplation, he too sees in his ecstatic vision "the intelligible Forms of things". And evidently, purified souls were yonder, and purely spiritual beings who, from Philo and Origines up to Dionysius Areopagita, were readily identified with "angels"[1]. Really, one should not imagine that any of the Arabic philosophers read anything like that in any text of Aristotle, in the literal sense at least. They read it *into* him. That is what they did.

In the second fragment of Al Kindi cited by Ross it is said that "Aristotle asserts of the soul that it is *a simple substance whose actions are manifested in bodies*". Obviously this is not the doctrine of the *De anima*. But let us observe that the Arabic philosophers conceived the noûs of *De anima* III exactly in this sense: it is the famous *intellectus agens separatus* doctrine. Nowhere is it explicitly read in Aristotle, but it may be inferred from *De anima* III 5. Nothing is more probable than that the Arabic philosophers, who had passed through Neoplatonism and confounded this with Aristotle's doctrine of noûs and the unmoved Movers, understood the immortal soul of the *Eudemus* too in the sense of "a simple substance whose actions are manifested in bodies". This need not have been explicitly in that dialogue. It was explicitly in Plotinus! And that would do…

Lastly, as fr. 12, Ross gives a passage taken from Servius in Verg. *Aen.* VI 448: *nunc femina Caeneus*. The reference is to the story of Caeneus, who, since he was invulnerable, as a punishment was changed into a maiden. Servius comments: "hoc autem dicto ostendit Platonicum illud vel Aristotelicum, animam per μετεμψύχωσιν sexum plerumque mutare". It is almost certain, indeed, that Servius' reference to Aristotle as a witness of the theory of the transmigration of souls is based on a passage in the *Eudemus*, since we know that in that dialogue he dealt with the κάθοδος and the λήξεις of the souls.

This much, then, on the *Eudemus*.

---

[1] The identification is clearly made by Philo, e.g. in *De somniis* I 141-142 (See my *Greek Phil.* III, nr. 1306c). Proclus, at the beginning of his commentary on Plato's *Parmenides*, invokes all the gods and goddesses. After them he mentions τοὺς ἀγγελικοὺς χοροὺς, τοὺς ἀγαθοὺς δαίμονας, and lastly τοὺς ἥρωας (*Gr. phil.* III, 1472a). For the Greek background cp., for instance, Diog. Laert. VIII 32 (from Alexander Polyhistor's account of the Πυθαγορικὰ ὑπομνήματα), *Greek phil.* III, nr. 1279e, and the other passages mentioned s.v. *demon* in the Index of Concepts in *Greek Phil.* III.

b. The Protrepticus

Aristotle's *Protrepticus* was an exhortation to the philosophical life, the βίος θεωρητικός. It was addressed to Themiso, the prince of Cyprus. Against the pragmatist conception of knowledge, alive in the school of Isocrates, Aristotle defends the beauty and the happiness of the purely contemplative life, which is exercised not for the sake of something else (as in the case of other, productive, arts), but solely for its own sake.

It has been observed that the kind of life which Aristotle is defending here, was the ideal of Plato and the Academy; that the φρόνησις or "wisdom" which here is declared to be the highest good[1], is not that which in the *EN* is called by the same name, denoting there "practical wisdom"[2], but that purely theoretical wisdom which Plato called φρόνησις; moreover, that the author of the *Protrepticus*, who declares that the philosopher only contemplates "the things themselves" (αὐτά) and not imitations[3], apparently still adhered to the theory of the Ideas (*Jaeger*).

Against this others brought forward, firstly, that the author of the *Protrepticus* no longer considers the soul as antithetically opposed to the body, but as using it as its instrument[4]; second, that in the *Protrepticus* that typically Aristotelian view of the teleology in nature, which implies the notion of immanent "forms", is already clearly present[5]; lastly, since this view of Aristotle's took the place of Plato's theory of transcendent Ideas and was supposed to be incompatible with it, it was inferred that apparently the author of the *Protrepticus* no longer held that theory (*Nuyens*).

Lately it has been repeatedly argued that the "things themselves", contemplated by the philosopher according to fr. 13, did not denote any transcendent beings such as Plato's Ideas, but those intelligible objects which by Aristotle were considered as first principles, viz. the forms immanent in nature (*Düring*).

As a matter of fact, when reading the fragments of the *Protrepticus* carefully, we find there almost the essential of Aristotle's philosophy on human knowledge, philosophy of nature, metaphysics and ethics

---

[1] *Protrepticus* fr. 5, p. 33 Ross; see also fr. 6, p. 36, and fr. 13 the end (p. 49); Düring, *Protr.* B 38, B 68, B 51.
[2] *EN* VI, ch. 5 ff.
[3] Fr. 13, p. 48 Ross; Düring B 48.
[4] Fr. 6, init. (p. 34 Ross); Düring, B 59.
[5] Fr. 11, p. 43 f. Ross; Dürung B 11-21.

(including what nowadays is called "anthropology") just as all those parts are known to us from the School writings. So much so, that the *Protrepticus* may be read pretty well as an introduction into Aristotle's philosophy as a whole[1]. On the other hand, we find in these same fragments quite a part of Plato's leading doctrines, not only such views as were incorporated in Aristotle's later philosophy, but also such ones as were rejected by Aristotle in his School writings. In the *Protrepticus* "Platonism" goes side by side with "Aristotelianism", sometimes so as to contradict one another.

I could illustrate this by citing some ten or twelve passages in which we find the most classical doctrines of Aristotle, and next to these ten others in which typically Platonic views are found. I shall not enumerate all of them. I prefer to concentrate on a few cardinal topics and discuss the most controversial text of the *Protrepticus*, which formed one of the pillars on which Jaeger founded his theory of a Platonizing period in Aristotle's life.

In fr. 6 of the *Protrepticus* Aristotle's classical theory of the supreme "end" of man as defined by the specific human ἔργον – which is: exercising his supreme faculty, that of thinking – is already present in all its essential features[2]. Moreover, in fr. 5 we find the principle that the wise man must rule and that he is the standard of everything that is good. Hence, since the wise man (φρόνιμος) prefers wisdom (φρόνησις), wisdom must be the supreme good. The reasonable part of man's soul, his νοῦς, is properly speaking, his "self", and its particular ἔργον is the knowledge of truth. This is its ἀρετή, and well-being (εὐδαιμονία) either consists of it or depends on it[3].

In these thoughts we easily recognize the author of the *Nicomachean Ethics*, both in his definition of the *telos* of man's life (EN I 1-7) and in the description of virtue as a mean which has to be determined by the φρόνιμος (EN II 6)[4].

In fr. 9 Ross[5] there is the statement that wisdom (φρόνησις) is preferable (αἱρετόν) for its own sake: man prefers it even to life, for nobody would choose to live deprived of his intellect; and nobody

---

[1] Enrico Berti quite rightly emphasized this in his important work *La filosofia del primo Aristotele*, Padova 1962.
[2] *Protr.* fr. 6 Ross, pp. 34-36; Düring, *Protr.* B 59-70.
[3] *Protr.* fr. 5 Ross, pp. 33f.; Düring *Protr.* B 38-40; 54-57; fr. 6 Ross, Düring B 65-70.
[4] 1106b36-1107a3.
[5] Düring, B 98-101.

would prefer to be always drunk, or a little child, or always sleeping. For exercising a faculty is better than merely possessing it.

The passage is exactly paralleled in EN I 8 and 10[1].

Next, in fr. 11 we find Aristotle's classical theory of the teleology in nature, known to us from *Phys.* II. Thus, it could be stated by the young Italian author Enrico Berti that in the *Protrepticus* almost the whole Aristotle is present[2].

Next, in *Protr.* 13, we find the following curious argument. Philosophy has to seek truth. That is, it has to seek *first principles* or *fundamental Being* (αὐτὰ τὰ πρῶτα). In this it stands opposite to all other arts and disciplines, which are always satisfied with "second" and "third" things, also called "imitations" (μιμήματα). These are apprehended by an empirical approach, not by the intellect. On the "first things" all other things depend, not only in nature, but in the field of human action and of social life as well[3].

Is not this quite Platonical? Or what else should one say when confronted with such a text as: "The philosopher only follows the example of αὐτὰ τὰ ἀκριβῆ; αὐτῶν γάρ ἐστι θεατής, ἀλλ' οὐ μιμημάτων"?

This text seemed a solid ground for Jaeger's hypothesis. But was it actually so solid?

Let us follow the argument more precisely. In fr. 12[4] Aristotle defended pure theory against Isocrates: φρόνησις is the greatest good, not for the sake of anything else that would result from it, but for its own sake. This is not saying, however, that it is of no use for practical life. On the contrary, in more than one fragment of the *Protrepticus* the usefulness of philosophy, and even its necessity, for practical life were mentioned with the greatest emphasis[5]. In fragm. 13[6] the argument is developed from the analogy with the arts. It runs as follows.

Just as a physician must have knowledge of nature, thus – yea, much more – the lawgiver. For physicians are concerned with the excellence of the body, while the lawgiver is concerned with the soul's excellence and with the well-being of the *polis*. Now, just as the other

[1] I 8, 1098b32-1099a7; I 10, 1100a1-3.
[2] E. Berti, *Il primo Aristotele*, cited *supra*.
[3] Ross, *Protr.* fr. 13, p. 48; Düring, B 48.
[4] Düring, B 42; see also fr. 5 Ross, p. 33; Düring B 40; fr. 11, Ross, p. 45; Düring B 17 ff.
[5] Thus, fr. 4 (the κτῆσις-χρῆσις argument); fr. 5 p. 31 Ross; fr. 5 p. 33 Ross (the wise man must rule, and law, – for law is a kind of wisdom, or an expression of it); Düring B 8-9; B 38-39; B 52.
[6] Düring B 46-51.

arts, e.g. that of building, borrow their instruments from nature (the ruddled line, the rule and the lathe, by reference to which we test what is to our senses sufficiently straight or smooth, were suggested by the surface of water and by the rays of light), similarly the statesman and the lawgiver must borrow *from nature and reality* certain standards by reference to which they will judge what is just, noble or advantageous. These ὅροι, then, are the "first things", opposed to "imitations", which only the philosopher can know. For all other arts and crafts are satisfied with second things or third things. – It is added that, just as the builder of a house is not a good builder unless he uses a straight rule and other exact instruments but just compares his own building with others, thus the lawgiver will not be a good lawgiver if he just copies other existing laws and constitutions without looking to what is eternal and unchanging. The author also calls this "Nature" and "the Divine".

Now let me remark that it is quite a Platonical view to make social and political life dependent on philosophical insight; and certainly nothing would be as suitable as making justice and right action depend on the knowledge of a transcendent Reality in Plato's sense: a Justice-itself and a Good-itself. Metaphysically speaking it is not absurd at all that moral concepts would have their roots in a divine and transcendent order. On the contrary, purely rationally speaking, it is much more difficult not to accept that. Nevertheless, when asking what was the meaning of these Platonical terms to Aristotle, we have to remember *Metaph.* A 2. Here σοφία is defined as the most precise and most fundamental science because it is concerned with τὰ πρῶτα[1]; next, as the most *leading* science (ἀρχικωτάτη τῶν ἐπιστημῶν) because all other things are known through it[2], and most of all "because it knows the end, for the sake of which everything must be done[3]. And that is the good of everything, and in general, the best in nature as a whole"[4].

It is clear what Aristotle meant by "first things" in this passage: they are the intelligible forms immanent in things, by which the natural objects are what they are. According to the theory of *Physics* II – which, doubtless, is presupposed in the opening chapters of the *Metaphysics* – it is these forms that dominate the process of nature:

[1] 982 a 25 f.: ἀκριβέσταται δὲ τῶν ἐπιστημῶν αἱ μάλιστα τῶν πρώτων εἰσίν.
[2] 982 b 4.
[3] 982 b 5-6: τίνος ἕνεκέν ἐστι πρακτέον ἕκαστον.
[4] 982 b 7: τὸ ἄριστον ἐν τῇ φύσει πάσῃ.

they are the οὗ ἕνεκα and "the good" of everything, and as such they could be called "the best in Nature as a whole". Now, the resemblance of our passage of the *Protrepticus* to *Metaph.* A 2 is so close, that, seeing *Phys.* II behind the latter and *Protr.* fr. 11 behind the former, I feel almost sure that we have to understand the author in *this* sense, not in that of Plato's transcendent Ideas. The *words* used here tell us how very near the author is still to his master's spiritual world. But both the theory of the teleology in nature found in fr. 11 and that of the human ἔργον which we found in other passages of the *Protrepticus*, betray to us at the same time *how far* already Aristotle, when writing that work, was on the way of shaping his own philosophy. Therefore, as to the αὐτὰ τὰ πρῶτα and αὐτά of fr. 13, I join Ingemar Düring with a grateful acknowledgement that on this point he led the way to a better understanding[1].

c. The Περὶ φιλοσοφίας

Π. φιλοσοφίας is the third much debated early work of Aristotle's belonging to the Ἐξωτερικά, which was particularly famous in Antiquity, much read and frequently cited. It consisted of three books, the first of which seems to have dealt with the history – or rather the *pre*history – of philosophical thought, including the Orient. There is a fragment concerning the Persian dualistic religion of Ormuzd and Ahriman – well-known in the Academy and mentioned, e.g., in the *Alcib. Mai.* which was probably not a work of Plato's but did come from his School –; there is spoken of Zoroaster and the Chaldean astral religion, of Orpheus and the so-called Orphic poems, of the seven Sages and of the Delphic inscription "Know Thyself" as an inspiration to philosophy. Aristotle also developed there a theory of periodical great floods destroying the existing civilizations, so that the same arts are repeatedly discovered. That in the process of rising civilizations those arts that have practical applications always come first, and those that provide for physical needs before those that procure a kind of well-being (such as music and poetry), while pure theory comes last of all, is a theory well-known to us both from the *Protrepticus* and from

---

[1] Düring's most explicit comments on fr. 13 of the *Protr.* are found in the volume *Ar. and Plato in the Mid-fourth Century*, Göteborg 1960, pp. 35-55. Though I have some reservations to make about certain details of his argument, I do think that his interpretation of the αὐτὰ τὰ πρῶτα is essentially right. No doubt this implies an important correction of Jaeger's interpretation which, on this point at least, appears to have been accepted somewhat too easily.

Metaph. A 2. When dealing with the *Eudemus* we mentioned already the fragment 8, in which the word σοφία is connected with σαφεία, "inasmuch as it makes all things clear"[1]. Here it is said that "things intelligible and divine (τὰ νοητὰ καὶ θεῖα), even if they are most clear in their own nature, seem to us dark and dim, because of the mist of the body which hangs over us" (διὰ τὴν ἐπικειμένην τοῦ σώματος ἀχλύν). The passage offers a parallel to fr. 15 (in fine) of the *Protrepticus* for a part at least[2].

Of what kind of "philosophy" was Aristotle speaking when he wrote the dialogue Περὶ φιλοσοφίας? – No doubt, for him this science was concerned with τὰ νοητὰ καὶ θεῖα. In other words, philosophy was for him a metaphysic of the transcendent and intelligible order, of the divine Reality which is beyond the sensible world. The first book dealt with early tentatives to attain to this; the second treated of Plato's philosophy, while in the third the author proceeded to build up his own theory of τὰ θεῖα. It was P. Wilpert who recognized that such was the topic of the work Περὶ φιλοσοφίας, that the theme of the work was one, corresponding with the title, and that this conception of philosophy indicates that the author was still rather close to his master's doctrine[3]. We shall find this confirmed in studying the details of the fragments.

The first important question to be considered is: whether in the Π. φιλ. Plato's theory of the Ideas was, or was not, criticized. Syrianus *in Metaph.* 159, 33 ff.[4] says: "Aristotle himself admits that he has said nothing against the hypothesis of the Platonists, but quite fails to keep pace with the doctrine of the ideal numbers, if these are different from the mathematical"[5]. – In the first part of this sentence it is clearly brought out that, according to his own testimony, Aristotle did not raise any objections against the theory of the Ideas in its classical form (known to us e.g. from the *Phaedo* and the *Republic*);

---

[1] Philoponus *in Nicom. Isag.* I, 1, Ross fr. 8, p. 76f.
[2] It should be remembered that also in the School-writings Aristotle speaks repeatedly of "intelligible things" as being γνωριμώτερα καὶ σαφέστερα in themselves (τῇ φύσει), but not so for us. E.g. *Phys.* I 1, *Anal. po.* I 2, 71b33f. (πρότερα καὶ γνωριμώτερα); cp. *Metaph.* A 2, 982a11 (μὴ ῥᾴδια ἀνθρώπῳ γιγνώσκειν) and 982b2 (μάλιστα ἐπιστητά); *E.N.* I 4, 1095b3-4 (τὰ μὲν ἡμῖν – sc. γνώριμα, τὰ δ' ἁπλῶς). Cp. also *De part. anim.* Γ 5, 644b22-29.
[3] P. Wilpert in *Autour d'Aristote* (Mélanges Mansion), Louvain 1955, p. 115f.
[4] Ross, fr. 11 of Π. φιλ.
[5] Since there is a certain opposition between the two parts of the sentence, I prefer to translate the μηδέ by *but*.

in the second part it is said that he did reject explicitly the concept of ideal numbers, which he declared to be incomprehensible. Nothing seems as reasonable as concluding that in the Π. φιλ. Aristotle did not criticize the theory of the Ideas known to us from Plato's classical dialogues[1]. How, then, was it that Jaeger, and many others with him, held that actually in this work of Aristotle the theory of the Ideas was explicitly criticized?

It might seem improbable, but it is true, to reply: this assumption was essentially due to external evidence. Plutarch's testimony in *Adv. Coloten* and Proclus ap. Philop., *De aeternitate mundi*, where it was said that Aristotle criticized the theory of the Ideas, not only in his School writings but in his dialogues as well, led these modern scholars to their inference that this criticism must have been expressed in the present writing. As a matter of fact, the ground was not solid, since the inference goes against Aristotle's own words.

There are a few other fragments to consider more closely. Fr. 12 offers a psychological explanation of how the notion of God was first conceived by the human mind: on the one hand, it sprang from "what happens about the soul" (τὰ περὶ ψυχὴν συμβαίνοντα), – on the other hand, there were the celestial phenomena (τὰ μετέωρα). Aristotle explains: In sleep, the soul is "by itself"; it comes back to its own nature and foresees and foretells the future. This is also what happens at the moment of death, when the soul is severed from the body. – The other way is: by contemplating the regular motion of the heavenly bodies and, on the whole, the order of the universe. The argument is presented in a highly suggestive form in a passage of Sextus Empiricus, *Adv. Math.* IX 26f.[2]. Though Aristotle's name is not mentioned here, it is quite possible, and even not improbable, that the passage was taken from Π. φιλοσοφίας.

The same must be said of Cicero, *N.D.* II 37,95f.[3]: that curious transposition of Plato's simile of the cavern. Here, Aristotle's name is mentioned, the title of Π. φιλ. is not. But the attribution is probable. Both this passage and that on the mantic by dreams are of the greatest interest for our problem. From the fact that mantic by dreams is believed in by the author of Π. φιλ., while in the *Protr.*[4] it is denied

---

[1] Wilpert in *Journal of Hell. Stud.* 1957, p. 161, was certainly right in drawing this conclusion.

[2] In Ross, Π. φιλ. fr. 12b.

[3] Ross fr. 13.

[4] Protr. fr. 9 Ross (p. 38/9); Düring, B 101.

that in his sleep man would ever attain to truth, the conclusion that Π. φιλ. is anterior to the *Protrepticus* imposes itself. The dialogue (if it is one) appears to be closer to the *Eudemus*, more remote from the *Protrepticus*.

The passage from Cicero, *N.D.* II 37, gives us some more precise information about its author's metaphysical convictions: the inhabitants of Plato's cavern, bound like prisoners and looking at the shadows before them, here have become inhabitants of beautiful and comfortable underground houses, adorned by statues and pictures and furnished with all kinds of lovely things. The ideal world of transcendent Forms has disappeared: there is but one reality, the sensible world in which we live. When the underground people come to see its harmony and beauty, they are led by it to believe that there are gods. Whether or not this curious passage belonged to the Π. φιλ., this much is sure, that the religious opinion represented here tallies excellently with the mentality of a man who either abandoned the theory of transcendent Ideas or was not sure of it, while he preserved his belief (which was Plato's as well) in gods who were the cause of the cosmic order. Since this notion of creation and providence does not harmonize with the concept of the Prime Mover developed in *Metaph.* Λ 7, but harmonizes remarkably well with such expressions as in *De caelo* I 4 ("God and nature create nothing without a purpose")[1], it is almost certain that this opinion of Aristotle's is fairly early. It would fit quite well in the later years of the Academy and could better have preceded the years of Assos, in which the early books of the *Metaphysics* were written.

The fragments 16 and 17 give two proofs of the existence of God. The first is the so-called *argumentum ex gradibus perfectionis*. It runs as follows.

"In general, where there is a better, there is a best. Since, then, among existing things one is better than another, there is also something that is best, which will be the divine."

It has been pointed out that the argument presupposes a Platonical way of thinking[2]. No doubt it implies the belief that the imperfect reality of sensible things has its ground in a perfect Reality beyond. In this sense the argument is found later in Anselm of Canterbury[3], in

---

[1] 271a33. A similar expression is found in *Protr.* fr. 11 Ross, p. 44; Düring, B 18.
[2] P. Wilpert in J.H.S., 1957, pp. 155-162.
[3] Anselm in his *Monologium* (I, p. 14, 11, 9ff. Schmitt) used the argument to prove that there is *one supreme Good and Great*, i.e. one supreme Principle of

Thomas Aquinas as well as in Descartes. But can it be said to suppose Plato's theory of transcendent "forms"? — Not, at least, as it is usually understood. And there is not a trace indicating that Aristotle conceived of his god(s)-providence as a mind (or minds) containing the eternal and perfect "essences" of sensible things. It is more probable, therefore, that he used the *argumentum ex gradibus* not while believing definitely in a Platonic world of transcendent forms, but rather vaguely in a God-providence who is perfect Being. This is what corresponds well with the fragments 12 and 13. No doubt the author's thought is Platonical — up to a certain extent. That he believed in a Platonic world of transcendent Ideas, however, does not necessarily follow. The author seems nearer to the *Eudemus* than to the *Protrepticus*. That is, I think, all that can be said.

In fr. 16 it is further argued that God is immutable, in 17 that there must be one supreme Principle which is the ultimate cause of the cosmic order. It would be incorrect to say that in this fragment he proves "that God is one". Probably that was not what he meant. What he says is that the divine Beings must be hierarchically ordered, so that one of them must be supreme. This corresponds well with the use of the plural in the conclusion of fr. 13 ("et esse *deos* et haec tanta opera *deorum* esse"), and with the fragments 21-26 in which the heavenly bodies are considered as divine and living beings. Though this view in itself was Plato's in the *Timaeus*, the arguments offered here are Aristotle's.

I conclude: The work Π. φιλοσοφίας, just as the *Protrepticus*, shows both Platonical and Aristotelian characteristics. Platonical may be called: (1) the religious admiration of the cosmic order as created by a divine Demiurge[1]; (2) the celestial bodies considered as divine living beings; (3) mantic by dreams accepted; (4) the belief in God(s) as the creator(s) of the cosmos. — Typically Aristotelian might be called: (1) the criticism of the ideal numbers; (2) the psychological ex-

everything existing. It is the thought of God as perfect Being. The multiplicity of transcendent forms is not referred to. Somehow it may be said to be implicitly present. But Anselm did not speak of it.

[1] I think of Seneca, *Nat. Quaest.* VII 30, and Plut., *Mor.* 477c, both under nr. 14 of Π. φιλ. in Ross. Cp. also the passage from Cicero, *N.D.* II 37 (fr. 13 Ross). The two other passages cited by Ross under nr. 13 (Philo, *Leg. alleg.* III 32, and Philo, *De praem. et poen.* 7) contain rather Stoic conceptions (the cosmos compared with a big house or a well-governed city), so that I feel not sure about their Aristotelian origin. Neither the name of Aristotle nor the title of Π. φιλ. is mentioned.

planation of the concept of God; (3) own proofs of the existence of God (for the rest still very Platonical); (4) a transposition of Plato's allegory of the cavern, such that the Ideas have disappeared, while the belief in Gods as causes of the cosmic order is preserved; which seems to point to a period in Aristotle's thinking in which the theory of the Ideas was either doubted of or abandoned, and the theory of the Prime Mover not yet conceived.

When could this work have been written? Probably not long after the *Eudemus*, and a few years earlier than the *Protrepticus* which with a high degree of probability may be attributed to the last years of Aristotle's stay in the Academy.

Looking back on these three exoteric works, we must try and answer the question: Was Jaeger's theory of a Platonizing period in Aristotle sufficiently well-founded, or should it rather be classed henceforth among the stimulating errors?

If this question is asked in the form of an alternative, I do not hesitate to choose the first thesis, though I do wish to make some reservations about the "Platonism" of Aristotle's early years. That he accepted the theory of the Ideas for, say, some ten or fifteen years, is not explicitly testified in any of the fragments. But in a somewhat more general sense, including the belief in a transcendent world with which the soul is cognate, the thesis of a platonizing period in Aristotle is testified repeatedly and with indubitable clearness. What the fragments of the exoteric works confirm is this: that Jaeger was right in so far, that for some fifteen years Aristotle seems to have been very near to Plato's metaphysics and psychology. The fragments prove that he did not criticize the doctrine of the Ideas at a very early date; probably he had some reservations about it when writing the Περὶ φιλοσοφίας (c. 350), and came more and more to his own physical, cosmological and metaphysical theories during the last years of his stay in the Academy. His explicit criticism of the theory of the Ideas in its classical form can hardly have preceded the years of Assos.

The School writings

Since Fr. Solmsen's work on the development of Aristotle's logic and rhetoric[1] it is rather generally accepted that the *Topics* are an early work dating from the first Athenian period, while *De inter-*

---

[1] Fr. Solmsen, *Die Entwicklung der aristotelischen Logik und Rhetorik*, Berlin 1929.

pretatione and the *Analytics* are almost unanimously dated in the period of Assos[1]. Düring[2] proposes a very different chronology. Starting from the conviction that Aristotle rejected the theory of the Ideas right from the beginning and already polemized against it while being a student, he finds no reason not to date *all* the logical works, including the *Analytics*, in the years before 355. In his opinion Π. ἰδεῶν belonged to the same period: 360-355, if it was not written a few years earlier. Moreover, *Metaph.* Λ and Π. φιλ. are attributed to this period as well.

The *Physics*, *De caelo*, *De gen. et corr.* and the *Meteor.* are supposed to have been written in the next period, 355-347, together with the early books of the *Metaph.* (Δ, AB, I, M 9 and N, M 1-9), the *E.E.*, the *Eudemus* and the *Protrepticus*.

One of Düring's arguments for inverting Jaeger's views was: that the author of the *Analytics* deals not tenderly with the theory of the Ideas[3], while later, in the *E.N.*, he expresses himself respectfully and with a remarkable consideration[4]. Düring seems to be particularly impressed by the qualification of τερετίσματα. But, after all, is that a harder form of criticism than what is found in *Metaph.* A 9, where it is said that to call the Ideas patterns and say that other things share in them is to use *empty words* and poetical metaphors[5]? As to *E.N.* I 6, anyhow this book was written some 10-15 years after Aristotle's first explicit criticism of the theory of the Ideas (supposing this was done in the years of Assos). It is true that in this passage the author seems to be reluctant to enter into a discussion on the difficulties involved in that theory. Nevertheless, what he says on the Idea of the Good is absolutely devastating; – moreover, it shows a complete lack of understanding of the spiritual background of that doctrine: first, an absolute and transcendent Good cannot exist, and second, if it existed, it would be of no use for man. It is very hard to hold that the author of such a passage had come nearer to Plato than he was when calling the Ideas a twittering of strings and "participation" an empty word or a poetical metaphor. As a matter of fact, the author of *E.N.* I 6

---

[1] For instance, E. Kapp, *Greek Foundations of traditional Logic*, N. York 1942, and Sir David Ross.
[2] *Eranos* 1956, p. 114.
[3] Düring thinks in particular of *An. Post.* I 22, 83 a 33, where the Ideas are called "a twittering of strings" (τερετίσματα).
[4] I 6, 1096 a 13-17.
[5] 991 a 20-22.

was very far remote from the spiritual climate of Plato's theory of the Ideas.

Are there any particular grounds for dating the *Analytics* in such an early period as suggested by Düring? There would be, – if it had been *proved* that actually Aristotle criticized the theory of the Ideas in those early years. As a matter of fact, the evidence is lacking. So far as there is any, it rather points the other way: the dating in the years of Assos seems to be most probable and pretty well founded.

As to *Metaph.* Λ, I do believe this was a fairly early work. There are several indications that make me incline to this opinion: the highly speculative character of the work, its search for a metaphysics of purely spiritual being and for an ultimate end on which (in a sense) everything in the universe depends. It can hardly be denied that such an undertaking, in its spiritual aspirations and as a basic outlook on reality, is akin to the spirit of Plato's metaphysics. On the other hand, Aristotle's view of the transcendent world is different, his method of approach is his own, and his result is a construction in which the theory of the Ideas has no place. Would it be possible at all that the theory of the Prime Mover had been thought out in the years before 355? If abstraction is made of the problems about the theory of the Ideas, there are two other definite impediments: first, that apparently in Π. φιλ. no external force was admitted that could move the heavenly bodies[1]; second, that in *De caelo I* nothing is supposed to exist beyond aether[2]. No doubt, this is prohibitive of any earlier dating of *Metaph.* Λ than in the beginning of the years of Assos.

I am personally inclined to date Λ earlier than A, and this because of the singularly theological character of the work[3]. In my opinion

---

[1] Cicero, *N.D.* II 44 (Ross, fr. 21 Π. φιλ.): the movement of the stars is supposed to be *voluntarius* and not effected by some major force. "Quae enim potest (vis) maior esse?"

[2] *De caelo* I 9, the end: οὔτε γὰρ ἄλλο κρεῖττόν ἐστιν ὅτι κινήσει. Guthrie discussed these passages in *Class. Quart.* 1933, p. 162 ff., and concluded rightly that Aristotle's theory of the πρῶτον κινοῦν was preceded by two other theories: first, that the stars are animated living beings (in Π. φιλ., closely akin to Plato, *Laws* X); second, that aether as such moves circularly, just as the earthly elements possess each their own peculiar kind of motion. No external mover is needed. Guthrie thinks that, later on, the theory of the πρῶτον κινοῦν was added to this former view, not as overthrowing it, but as a complement.

[3] Cp. my paper on the opening chapters of *Metaph.* A in the volume *Aristote et les problèmes de méthode*, Louvain 1960, reproduced in the following chapter of the present work.

there is no sufficient ground for dogmatizing about the precise sequence of Aristotle's works; but, under due reservations I should like to suggest the following sequence: *Metaph.* Λ in the beginning of the period of Assos; next, the first books of the *Physics*; thereafter *Metaph.* A. My main ground for this suggestion is: that in *Metaph.* A the theory of the four causes is clearly presupposed and of quite a dominating character, whereas in Λ 4 it rather makes the impression of being not full-grown.

If this is correct and, as a matter of fact, the first books of the *Physics* would have been written after *Metaph.* Λ, this would explain the distance in metaphysical outlook and approach between the so-called "Theology" and *Metaph.* A. As to the date of Π. φιλ., Guthrie's remarks on the development of Aristotle's theology confirm my other arguments in favour of a fairly early date of that work: Π. φιλ. may have been written not long after the *Eudemus*, i.e., not long after 354, while the *Protrepticus* must be placed a few years later, towards the end of the first Athenian period.

To make a counter-proof of Düring's suggestion: supposed that *Metaph.* Λ is very early (before 355), – does not this lead the author of this suggestion into a strange contradiction? For he imagines that Aristotle in his early years was rather violently disposed against Platonic metaphysics and much more of an empiricist than in his later years. I find it difficult to see how *Metaph.* Λ would tally with this theory. As a matter of fact, we get a much more understandable line of development if placing the Theology early in the years of Assos, to be followed by book A, – not immediately but so that something is between.

CHAPITRE XIV

A PROPOS DES PREMIERS CHAPITRES DE LA MÉTAPHYSIQUE D'ARISTOTE[1]

Pour donner un aperçu très court du contenu du premier chapitre de la *Métaphysique* d'Aristote notons les points suivants:

980 a 21-27. Le désir de la connaissance est naturel à l'homme, et c'est pour cette raison que la sensation lui est chère.

980 a 27-981 a 7. Comment se constitue la connaissance (les quatre degrés: sensation-mémoire-expérience-art. Cf. *An. Post.* II 19).

981 a 7-b 13. L'art se distingue de l'expérience par deux caractères:
1. par ce qu'il connaît l'universel (981 a 7-27, ἀκολουθοῦσαν τὴν σοφίαν πᾶσι, où je prends πᾶσι au sens neutre et ἀκολουθεῖν dans le sens de «suivre par l'intelligence»[2]).
2. par ce qu'il connaît les causes (981 a 28, τοῦτο δέ[3], 981 b 13, ὅτι θερμόν).

981 b 13-25. Les inventeurs des arts ont toujours excité l'admiration des hommes, non seulement à cause de l'utilité de leurs inventions, mais encore à cause de leur sagesse. Cependant, ceux des arts qui ne s'appliquent ni aux nécessités ni à l'agrément de la vie mais qui sont des sciences pures étaient généralement considérés comme supérieurs. Quant au moment de leur apparition, ce sont les plus tardifs.

981 b 25-982 a 3. Dans les lignes qui suivent, on renvoie le lecteur au

---

[1] Ce chapitre se base sur ma contribution au deuxième *Symposium Aristotelicum*, fait à Louvain 1960. Le texte fut publié dans le volume *Aristote et les problèmes de méthode*, Louvain 1961.

[2] On a remarqué que les quelques passages de Platon où ἀκολουθεῖν signifie «suivre une argumentation» (*Phédon* 107 b, *Lysis* 218 e, *Gorg.* 465 bc, *Ménon* 76 c) n'offrent pas de parallèle précis. J'admets qu'il y a un certain degré de différence. Mais il faut bien dire que, en somme, de «suivre une argumentation» à «suivre tous les cas» (= comprendre l'universel) il n'y a qu'un pas. On pourrait encore comparer ce passage à celui où Aristote parle de ἀκολουθεῖν τοῖς φαινομένοις (*Metaph.* A 5, 986 b 31): tenir compte de. Cela non plus n'est pas un parallèle exact. Et pourtant, on n'en est pas loin.

[3] «et d'autre part».

ch. 3 du l. VI de l'*Eth. Nic.*, où l'auteur explique la différence entre τέχνη et ἐπιστήμη[1]. Après quelques lignes de transition il résume les arguments précédents et en conclut que la sagesse s'occupe de certains principes et de certaines causes.

(Ch. 2). De *quels* principes et de *quelles* causes s'occupe-t-elle? Pour répondre à cette question, Aristote part des idées traditionnelles (ὑπολήψεις) que nous avons du σοφός.

982a8-19. Le premier trait qui le distingue est qu'il «sait tout» – dans la mesure du possible (ὡς ἐνδέχεται). Ensuite, il sait ce qui est difficile à savoir (ce qui exclut la connaissance sensible commune à tous). Troisièmement, il possède une science plus exacte et sera plus capable que les autres d'enseigner les causes. Quatrièmement, la science qui est choisie pour elle-même est supérieure à celle qu'on choisit en vue de ses résultats; cinquièmement, la science qui est plus fondamentale est supérieure aux sciences auxiliaires. «Car il ne faut pas que le Sage se conforme à la direction d'autrui; c'est lui qui doit conduire les autres».

982a21-30. Aristote explique les premiers points en remarquant que l'exigence de «savoir tout» se réalise surtout chez celui qui possède la connaissance du καθόλου. Car *connaître l'universel*, c'est en même temps connaître tous les cas particuliers qui se rangent sous le καθόλου (πάντα τὰ ὑποκείμενα) et c'est aussi connaître ce qui est pour l'homme *le plus difficile à connaître*, c'est-à-dire le plus abstrait. Suit le troisième point: «Et les plus exactes des sciences sont celles *qui s'occupent au plus haut point des principes* (αἳ μάλιστα τῶν πρώτων εἰσίν).

Ayant expliqué ce qu'il entend par l'expression «science exacte», Aristote ajoute: «Mais la science qui considère spécialement les causes est en même temps celle qui sait enseigner» (982a28ss.); car enseigner, cela se fait essentiellement en expliquant les causes de chaque chose.

Il ne sera pas trop téméraire de conclure de ce passage que la connaissance du καθόλου = celle des πρῶτα, et que les πρῶτα sont αἴτια. Cf. *Anal. Post.* I 27[2], où l'auteur dit qu'une science plus exacte est celle qui connaît non seulement le ὅτι, mais aussi le διότι.

---

[1] On pourrait observer que, dans le passage qui précède, Aristote s'est servi du terme τέχνη dans le sens général de «science», qui comprend non seulement la «science appliquée» (dite τέχνη dans le sens limité du mot) mais aussi la science pure. Cet emploi du mot ne saurait guère nous étonner. C'est que, de temps en temps, Aristote se sert des termes τέχνη et ἐπιστήμη simplement *promiscue*. Voir mes remarques à ce propos dans *Autour d'Aristote*, Louvain, 1955, p. 315-317.

[2] 87a31s. (*Gr. Ph.* II, nr. 462).

Il faut se demander: que sont les πρῶτα? «Les choses primaires, les choses fondamentales». C'est-à-dire: ce qui explique les autres choses; ou: ce dont les autres choses dépendent (cf. 982b2: διὰ γὰρ ταῦτα καὶ ἐκ τούτων τἆλλα γνωρίζεται). – Et qu'est-ce que c'est?

Une seule réponse est possible: si «τἆλλα» sont *les choses naturelles*, les πρῶτα qui les expliquent et dont elles dépendent sont les οὐσίαι[1], qui, pour les objets sensibles, sont les «formes» par lesquelles les choses sont ce qu'elles sont, et en même temps le τέλος qui se réalise dans le procès de la nature; les «substances» donc dans le sens d'essences.

Ainsi Alexandre d'Aphrodise dit, en expliquant 982a4-6 (Hayd. 9, 8-12): il faut donc chercher la connaissance des premiers principes et des premières causes; «et celles-ci sont pour ainsi dire les principes de ce qui existe, par lesquels chacune des choses existantes est ce qu'elle est[2]. Or telles sont les substances premières et proprement dites. Car celles-ci (sc. les essences) sont les principes des substances (sc. des choses qui «subsistent»), et les substances, de toutes les autres choses, comme il montrera»[3].

A première vue, les formules d'Alexandre prêtent assez à confusion: les premiers principes et les premières causes sont les οὐσίαι, voire même les οὐσίαι πρῶται καὶ κυριώταται; car celles-ci sont les principes des οὐσίαι, lesquelles, à leur tour, sont les principes de tout le reste. Qu'est-ce que cela veut dire? Est-il possible qu'Alexandre identifie les premières causes qu'il faut chercher aux οὐσίαι que l'auteur des *Catégories* a appelées «substances au sens le plus propre et primaire»?[4] Dans ce cas, les premières causes seraient identifiées aux choses individuelles et concrètes, – ce qui serait, en effet, une thèse assez étrange. Ensuite, ces «premières substances» devraient être les principes «des substances» lesquelles, dans notre passage, ne sont pas qualifiées comme δεύτεραι, mais qu'il faudrait bien prendre dans le sens des δεύτεραι οὐσίαι du ch. 5 des *Catégories*. Ce seraient donc les espèces et les genres. Or, les «premières substances» peuvent-elles en être appelées les principes? Il faut avouer que ce n'est pas impossible: ce sont, en effet, les individus qui composent les espèces et les genres. Mais peut-

---

[1] Voir aussi *Metaph.* B 2, 996b13-14.
[2] C'est là probablement ce que le commentateur veut dire.
[3] χρὴ οὖν ἐκ τῆσδε τῆς πραγματείας ἀπαιτεῖν τὴν γνῶσιν τῶν πρώτων ἀρχῶν καὶ αἰτίων· αὗται δ' ἂν εἶεν τοῦ ὄντος οἷον ἀρχαί, δι' ἃς τῶν ὄντων ἕκαστόν ἐστιν ὧν τὸ εἶναι κατηγοροῦμεν· τοιαῦται δὲ αἱ πρῶται καὶ κυριώταται οὐσίαι· αὗται μὲν γὰρ τῶν οὐσιῶν ἀρχαί, αἱ δὲ οὐσίαι τῶν ἄλλων ἁπάντων, ὡς δείξει.
[4] *Categ.* 5, 2a11: οὐσία δέ ἐστιν ἡ κυριώτατά τε καὶ πρώτως καὶ μάλιστα λεγομένη, κτλ.

on dire, comme le fait notre commentateur, que les espèces et les genres à leur tour sont les principes de tout le reste? Certes, il est vrai qu' Aristote dit cela dans une de ses apories: les genres sont les principes des choses à définir¹. Mais ce n'était pas là son opinion propre, puisqu'il remarque un peu plus loin que les différences sont encore plus importantes que les genres².

Revenons donc aux πρῶται καὶ κυριώταται οὐσίαι de notre commentateur. Elles sont, dit-il, les principes de l'être: τοῦ ὄντος οἷον ἀρχαί. Et plus explicitement, elles sont les principes δι' ἃς τῶν ὄντων ἕκαστόν ἐστιν ὧν τὸ εἶναι κατηγοροῦμεν. La phrase est construite un peu κατὰ σύνεσιν: puisque le ἐστίν est copulatif, il paraît qu'un ταῦτα, sous-entendu avant ὧν, est le prédicat. Donc, les premières substances sont les principes «par lesquels chacune des choses existantes est ce à quoi nous attribuons l'existence», c'est-à-dire une chose subsistante.

Cela suffit: il faut conclure de la définition citée que les πρῶται καὶ κυριώταται οὐσίαι de notre commentateur ne sont nullement les «premières substances» des *Catégories*. Ce sont les «quiddités»: les *formes* qui sont les essences des choses naturelles. Car celles-là seules sont «les principes par lesquels chacune des choses existantes est ce qu'elle est».

Ensuite, ce sont les *formes* qui, en effet, sont «les principes des choses subsistantes», lesquelles, d'après *Catég.* 5, sont souvent appelées «substances». Enfin, ne peut-on pas dire que les «substances» au sens indiqué sont à leur tour le principe – si l'on veut, la base – de toutes les autres choses?

En somme, c'est l'οὐσία, dans son sens définitif, tel qu'Aristote l'a définie dans le livre Z de la *Métaph.*, ch. 17, 1041 b 4-9, qui est appelée πρώτη καὶ κυριωτάτη par notre commentateur. «Τοῦτο γὰρ αἴτιον πρῶτον τοῦ εἶναι», pourrait-il dire avec son maître³. C'est donc les essences des choses que la métaphysique («la sagesse») doit chercher, et, en fonction de cette recherche, elle doit s'occuper de tout ce qui peut contribuer à la connaissance de ces principes, conclut le commentateur⁴. Il ajoute que c'est la dernière partie de la tâche à laquelle

---

¹ *Metaph.* B 3, 998 b 4-6: εἰ δ' ἕκαστον μὲν γνωρίζομεν διὰ τῶν ὁρισμῶν, ἀρχαὶ δὲ τὰ γένη τῶν ὁρισμῶν εἰσίν, ἀνάγκη καὶ τῶν ὁριστῶν ἀρχὰς εἶναι τὰ γένη.
² 998 a 30-31. Cf. Z 12, 1038 a 16-20: φανερὸν ὅτι ἡ τελευταία διαφορὰ ἡ οὐσία τοῦ πράγματος ἔσται καὶ ὁ ὁρισμός.
³ *Metaph.* Z 17, 1041 b 28.
⁴ Τήν τε οὖν τούτων γνῶσιν ἀπαιτεῖν χρὴ ἐκ τῆσδε τῆς πραγματείας, καὶ ἔτι ὅσα εἰς τὴν τούτων γνῶσιν συντελεῖ (9, 12-14).

sera consacrée la plus grande partie du présent ouvrage d'Aristote:
«car c'était impossible d'acquérir la connaissance de ces premiers
principes d'une autre façon, sans travail préparatoire et sans déblaiement d'obstacles»[1].

Voilà quelques lignes de commentaire bien remarquables. Car on nous décrit ici la métaphysique d'Aristote en disant que cette science – qu'on déclare expressément être la science suprême – vise essentiellement à la connaissance des formes qui déterminent les choses et qui sont le τέλος immanent dans le procès éternel de la nature. Elle vise à la connaissance des formes comme principes et causes premières. *C'est dire que la méthode de la métaphysique est essentiellement une méthode d'analyse logique et non pas de synthèse spéculative.*

Nous verrons plus loin ce que cette thèse implique. Pour le moment, suivons le fil de l'argumentation d'Aristote en considérant le quatrième et le cinquième trait distinctifs de la σοφία.

(4) «La science que l'on choisit pour elle-même et à seule fin de savoir, est davantage «sagesse» que celle qu'on choisit en vue des résultats».

Quelques lignes plus loin (982a30ss.), en expliquant ses propres paroles, l'auteur dit que la science qui est choisie pour elle-même est au plus haut degré «science», et qu'elle s'occupe de ce qui est au plus haut degré connaissable (τὸ μάλιστα ἐπιστητόν). «Et au plus degré connaissables sont les choses primaires et ce qui est cause (τὰ πρῶτα καὶ τὰ αἴτια). Car c'est par eux et à partir d'eux que les autres choses sont connues, – non les principes et les causes par ce qui leur est subordonné». – Par le quatrième point l'auteur confirme donc que la «sagesse», qui est la science suprême, s'occupe des πρῶτα καὶ αἴτια.

(5) «La science la plus fondamentale est davantage «sagesse» que la science auxiliaire».

Aristote explique (982b4ss.): «Et la plus fondamentale des sciences, plus que la science auxiliaire, est celle qui connaît en vue de quoi chaque chose doit être faite. Et ce οὗ ἕνεκα est le bien de chaque chose, et, pris dans son sens total, c'est le Bien suprême dans l'ensemble de la nature». – Mais, ajoute-t-il, puisque le οὗ ἕνεκα lui aussi est une cause, ce dernier caractère de la sagesse revient au même que ceux qui précèdent; c'est-à-dire que la sagesse s'occupe des premiers principes et des premières causes (αἱ πρῶται ἀρχαὶ καὶ αἰτίαι).

---
[1] εἰς ἃ καὶ ὁ πλεῖστος αὐτῷ λόγος ἀναλίσκεται· οὐ γὰρ οἷόν τε ἦν ἐκείνων γνῶσιν ἄλλως λαβεῖν, μὴ προκαταστήσαντα καὶ προεκκαθάραντα τὰ ἐμποδών (9, 14-16).

Or, le οὗ ἕνεκα qui est l'ἀγαθόν de chaque chose dans la nature, qu'est-ce? D'après l'exposé d'Aristote dans le second livre de la *Physique*, «l'essence et la forme» sont pratiquement identiques au οὗ ἕνεκα[1] dans tous les êtres naturels – comme d'ailleurs dans les produits d'art[2]. Dans les êtres naturels ce principe est identique à la forme qui se réalise et domine le procès de leur croissance. Car la φύσις est ἕνεκά του[3]. Aristote peut même dire que la φύσις *est* fin et cause finale[4]. Car «ce n'est pas toute chose qui prétend être cause ultime, c'est le meilleur»[5].

Or n'est-ce pas là exactement ce qui est écrit dans notre passage de la *Métaphysique:* que le τίνος ἕνεκεν est l'ἀγαθόν de chaque chose, et, pris dans son sens total, ce qu'il y a de meilleur dans toute la nature? – τὸ ἄριστον ἐν τῇ φύσει πάσῃ. Tricot traduit: «d'une manière générale, c'est le souverain Bien dans l'ensemble de la nature».

Répétons-le: *c'est la forme-essence qui, prise dans son sens total, est le Bien suprême dans la nature.* Par là il est parfaitement clair qu' Aristote appelle les formes-essences πρῶτα: premiers principes et causes premières.

A n'en pas douter, il faut s'en tenir à ce qu'il dit. C'est-à-dire qu'il ne faut pas se mettre à «réduire» les formes-essences des choses physiques à d'autres causes, dites supérieures, dont la plus haute serait le πρῶτον κινοῦν ἀκίνητον, premier Principe pour Aristote, et «d'où dépendent le ciel et la nature»[6].

Plusieurs interprètes, anciens et modernes, ont cédé à la tentation de venir en aide à Aristote pour «compléter et achever sa philosophie d'après ses propres principes». C'est ce que fait par exemple le R. P. Joseph Owens dans son ouvrage intitulé *The doctrine of Being in the Aristotelian Metaphysics* (Toronto 1951). Il déclare[7] que «le bien de la

---

[1] *Phys.* II 7, 198 b 2-3: τὸ τί ἐστιν καὶ ἡ μορφή sont τέλος καὶ οὗ ἕνεκα.
[2] Cf. *Phys.* II 9, 200 a 5-7: la génération de la maison se fait οὐκ ἄνευ la matière, mais celle-ci n'en est pas la cause au sens décisif. Cela, c'est le οὗ ἕνεκα: ἕνεκα τοῦ κρύπτειν ἄττα καὶ σώζειν. Cf. aussi *Phys.* VII 3, 246 a 15.
[3] II 7, 198 b 4.
[4] II 2, 194 a 28, ἡ δὲ φύσις τέλος καὶ οὗ ἕνεκα.
[5] II 2, 194 a 32: Βούλεται γὰρ οὐ πᾶν εἶναι τὸ ἔσχατον τέλος, ἀλλὰ τὸ βέλτιστον. Cf. II 3, 195 a 24: τὸ γὰρ οὗ ἕνεκα βέλτιστον καὶ τέλος τῶν ἄλλων ἐθέλει εἶναι.
[6] *Metaph.* Λ 7, 1072 b 13-14.
[7] p. 285 s. Il faut souligner qu'il ne s'agit ici aucunement d'une vue personnelle de l'auteur J. Owens. Au contraire, celui-ci ne fait que représenter l'interprétation classique qui est généralement acceptée dans l'École thomiste et, en tant que telle, était enseignée aux séminaires catholiques jusqu' à nos jours.

nature dans son ensemble »[1] est situé dans les formes, et que celles-ci *dépendent des «Entités séparées»*, i.e. des Moteurs immobiles qui, en fin de compte, sont les causes finales vers lesquelles tout se dirige. Mais ce n'est pas tout. A propos des paroles d'Aristote: la science suprême est celle qui connaît τίνος ἕνεκέν ἐστι πρακτέον ἕκαστον[2], il fait une remarque fort importante, qui mériterait plus d'attention que je ne puis y prêter dans la présente étude. Je veux la citer au moins, ne fût-ce que pour indiquer le problème dont il s'agit ici. Il dit[3] que la «sagesse» d'Aristote n'est nullement coupée de la vie pratique: au contraire, cette science qui, dans les lignes suivantes sera décrite comme une science purement théorique, *paraît être nettement régulative par rapport à tout le domaine de l'action pratique.* Bien qu'elle ait sa fin en elle-même, elle est nécessaire pour comprendre le sens ultime de l'action humaine.

Je crois que la présente remarque est d'un très grand intérêt pour comprendre plus à fond le sens – si l'on veut, la fonction – de la métaphysique dans la pensée d'Aristote. Il s'agit ici de quelques lignes qu'on a peut-être l'habitude de négliger un peu. Mais elles sont là, et c'est bien Aristote qui a écrit que la plus fondamentale des sciences lui paraît celle qui connaît τίνος ἕνεκέν ἐστι πρακτέον ἕκαστον. Et ensuite, ce τίνος ἕνεκεν paraît être «le bien de chaque chose» – c'est-à-dire le τέλος immanent des choses physiques qui n'est autre que *la forme,* – «en somme, le bien dans toute la nature». Encore une fois, c'est des formes qu'il s'agit, et c'est donc la connaissance des formes qui, pour Aristote, doit régler l'action.

Il y aura lieu de tenir compte de ce passage pour quiconque voudra trouver dans l'*Éthique à Nicomaque* quels sont, en fin de compte, les principes de l'action morale. Notons pour le moment que ce qui résulte de notre passage n'est nullement – n'en déplaise au P. Owens – que pour Aristote l'ordre de l'action humaine est dominé, ou doit être dominé, par une métaphysique de la transcendance. Ce qui en résulte, c'est ce qu'on pourrait appeler la règle du κατὰ φύσιν ζῆν. Car c'est d'après les formes-essences des choses physiques que l'action humaine doit se régler.

Cela rappelle de façon frappante le «comportement» de Ibn Jokdân, le héros du roman arabe d'Ibn Tofail, qui, parvenu nouveau-né à une île déserte et nourri par une chèvre, après avoir inventé toute la

[1] *Metaph.* A 2, 982b7.
[2] 982b5-6.
[3] Owens, ch. V, p. 85.

philosophie d'Aristote par la simple réflexion sur la nature arrive aux règles suivantes: avant tout, il faut respecter la finalité de la nature; il faut donc mener tout ce qui vit à son plein développement: éviter de manger des herbes jeunes, se nourrir plutôt de fruits, ne manger de graines que si elles sont très abondantes. S'il voit des plantes qui se dessèchent, il les arrose, un ruisseau encombré de pierres, il enlève l'obstacle. Il ne se nourrit de chair animale pour l'entretien de son propre corps que si la chair provient d'animaux qui sont très nombreux.

Si l'on compare cela à l'*Éthique à Nicomaque,* il faut constater qu'on ne voit pas Aristote préoccupé de la sorte du sort des plantes et des animaux, ni des ruisseaux encombrés dans leur courant. Ce qu'on y trouve, c'est que le philosophe détermine l'ἀρετή spécifique de l'homme d'après son ἔργον propre, c'est-à-dire d'après la fonction spécifiquement humaine, donc selon la forme-essence de l'homme. C'est là la fonction de la métaphysique dans l'éthique d'Aristote; métaphysique de l'immanence, bien entendu. Ce sont les formes-essences des êtres physiques qui sont l'ἀγαθόν dans la nature. Il ne s'agit nullement d'«entités transcendantes», ni d'un ἀγαθόν transcendant.

Mais dans la *Métaphysique* elle-même? demanderont ceux qui partagent les vues du P. Owens. On ne saurait nier qu'Aristote admette une série d'Entités transcendantes lesquelles, comme telles, ont une priorité ontologique par rapport aux formes-essences des êtres physiques. Et au sommet de cette série il plaçait le Premier Principe, le πρῶτον κινοῦν ἀκίνητον. Évidemment, ce Principe moteur est d'un ordre qui dépasse celui de la nature[1]; mais néanmoins, le philosophe dit explicitement que l'univers entier et toute la nature dépendent de ce Principe[2]. N'est-ce donc pas le philosophe lui-même qui nous impose d'attribuer aux principes immanents de la nature une place telle dans la totalité de son système métaphysique, qu'ils soient subordonnés aux entités transcendantes et qu'ils dépendent en dernière instance de l'unique Principe Premier, appelé Dieu?

Si je m'en tiens à *Métaph.* A 1-2, il faut dire: *non.* Les οὐσίαι sont πρῶτα; or, les πρῶτα, comme tels, ne dépendent d'aucun autre principe. Il ne manque pas de textes pour confirmer que telle était en effet la pensée d'Aristote; certains sont parfaitement clairs.

(1) *Phys.* II 7, 198a35-b5:

---

[1] Voir *Phys.* II 7, 198a36.
[2] *Metaph.* Λ 7, 1072b13-14.

Διτταὶ δὲ αἱ ἀρχαὶ αἱ κινοῦσαι φυσικῶς, ὧν ἡ ἑτέρα οὐ φυσική· οὐ γὰρ ἔχει κινήσεως ἀρχὴν ἐν αὑτῇ. τοιοῦτον δ'ἐστὶν εἴ τι κινεῖ μὴ κινούμενον, ὥσπερ τό τε παντελῶς ἀκίνητον καὶ πάντων πρῶτον καὶ τὸ τί ἐστιν καὶ ἡ μορφή· τέλος γὰρ καὶ οὗ ἕνεκα· ὥστε ἐπεὶ ἡ φύσις ἕνεκά του, καὶ ταύτην εἰδέναι δεῖ.

«Les principes qui meuvent d'une façon naturelle sont doubles: l'un appartient à la nature, l'autre non. Car il n'a pas en soi un principe de mouvement. Tels sont les principes qui meuvent sans être mus, comme le Principe absolument immobile qui est le premier de tous, et aussi la quiddité et la forme. Car la forme est fin et chose qu'on a en vue. Par conséquent, parce que la nature est en vue de quelque chose, il faut connaître cette cause-là aussi».

Si je vois bien, le passage contient une difficulté logique. «Il y a deux principes qui meuvent φυσικῶς». Cela veut dire: par leur nature même, non par délibération ou par un acte de volonté. L'homme moderne dirait dans un tel cas: «ils meuvent automatiquement». Le philosophe grec s'exprime avec plus de précision: l'αὐτόματον signifie pour lui une force irrationnelle; or, les causes motrices dont il s'agit ne sont ni dépourvues de raison ni contraires à la raison. Si elles ne meuvent pas par une action délibérée et voulue, c'est qu'elles sont «raisonnables» par nature et agissent comme telles. Or, l'un de ces principes n'appartient pas à la nature. C'est bien cela le sens de la formule οὐκ ἐστὶν φυσική. Et en effet, d'après Aristote, les moteurs immobiles ne sont pas des êtres naturels, lesquels seront définis comme χωριστὰ μὲν ἀλλ' οὐκ ἀκίνητα[1]. Il s'agit nettement de χωριστὰ καὶ ἀκίνητα, lesquels, selon le même passage de la *Métaphysique*[2], sont l'objet propre de la philosophie première, non de la physique. Mais – et voici notre difficulté – dans notre passage ce ne sont pas seulement les moteurs immobiles qui appartiennent à la catégorie du εἴ τι κινεῖ μὴ κινούμενον: c'est aussi le τί ἐστιν et la forme. Car le τε après ὥσπερ τό se rapporte au καί qui précède τὸ τί ἐστιν.

En effet, la forme-essence elle aussi est un κινοῦν οὐ κινούμενον. A ce titre elle peut être nommée à côté du premier Moteur. Mais est-elle par là même transcendante à la nature? Est-elle, tout comme les moteurs immobiles, οὐ φυσική? Puisqu'Aristote explique ce terme par le οὐ γὰρ ἔχει κινήσεως ἀρχὴν ἐν αὑτῇ, il y a toute apparence que la forme-essence appartienne à la même catégorie d'ὄντα que les moteurs

---

[1] *Metaph.* E 1, 1026 a 13-14.
[2] 1026 a 16.

immobiles. Mais alors, pourquoi *deux* espèces de principes, διτταὶ ἀρχαί, qui meuvent φυσικῶς? Enfin, les formes-essences des choses naturelles ne sont pas χωριστά. Elles sont essentiellement liées à une ὕλη et par là appartiennent au domaine de la nature. Elles en constituent, pour ainsi dire, l'aspect supérieur[1]; elles sont donc φυσικαί.

Ce qui est remarquable dans notre passage, c'est qu'il fait ressortir clairement le caractère ambigu des οὐσίαι: d'une part elles sont «*dans les choses*», elles ne sont donc pas transcendantes, cela est dit de la façon la plus expresse[2]; d'autre part, prises en elles-mêmes (par abstraction), elles dépassent la nature, parce qu'elles sont immobiles. Comme telles elles sont objet de la science première, la «sagesse», et sont premiers principes et premières causes. Notre passage les place comme principes autonomes à côté du premier Moteur. Y a-t-il subordination dans l'ordre de l'οὐσία? Alors, pourquoi les formes-essences sont-elles nommées «principes premiers»?

(2) Dans toute une catégorie d'êtres on ne trouve pas toutes les espèces de causes. *Métaph.* B 2, 996 a 22-29:

Τίνα γὰρ τρόπον οἷόν τε κινήσεως ἀρχὴν εἶναι ⟨ἐν⟩ τοῖς ἀκινήτοις ἢ τὴν τἀγαθοῦ φύσιν, εἴπερ ἅπαν ὅπερ ᾖ ἀγαθὸν καθ'αὑτὸ καὶ διὰ τὴν αὑτοῦ φύσιν τέλος ἐστὶν καὶ οὕτως αἴτιον ὅτι ἐκείνου ἕνεκα καὶ γίγνεται καὶ ἔστι τἆλλα, τὸ δὲ τέλος καὶ τὸ οὗ ἕνεκα πράξεώς τινός ἐστι τέλος, αἱ δὲ πράξεις πᾶσαι μετὰ κινήσεως; ὥστ' ἐν τοῖς ἀκινήτοις οὐκ ἂν ἐνδέχοιτο ταύτην εἶναι τὴν ἀρχὴν οὐδ' εἶναί τι αὐτοαγαθόν.

«De quelle façon, en effet, un principe de mouvement ou la nature du Bien pourraient-ils exister dans les êtres immobiles, puisque absolument tout ce qui est bon en soi et en vertu de sa nature propre est une fin, et par suite une cause, parce que c'est en vue de ce bien que les autres êtres deviennent et existent, et puisque la fin, le «ce en vue de quoi», est la fin de quelque action, et que toutes les actions impliquent le mouvement? Ainsi, pour les êtres immobiles, on ne pourrait admettre l'existence, ni de ce principe du mouvement, ni du Bien en soi».

Ce passage est fort important. Aristote y nie formellement que les ἀκίνητα «aspirent» à un principe supérieur, essence parfaite qui serait leur Ἀγαθόν. C'est que les formes-essences ont leur τέλος en elles-mêmes. Il en est ainsi non seulement des êtres spirituels, les οὐσίαι transcendantes, mais aussi des formes-essences des choses physiques

---

[1] *Phys.* II 2, 194 a 12-15. Voir A. Mansion, *Introd. à la Phys. Aristot.* ², p. 102-105, 195-205.
[2] *Phys*, I 7, II 1; cf. *Metaph.* A 9.

qui, bien que liées à une ὕλη, comme formes sont ἀκίνητα. Il serait donc erroné de dire que, d'après Aristote, tous les êtres de l'univers, du bas en haut de l'échelle tendent au Premier Principe et aspirent à Lui comme à leur souverain Bien[1]. Bien au contraire, il paraît que, pour Aristote, les formes des choses sont effectivement πρῶτα. Bien entendu, elles ont besoin d'une cause motrice pour se réaliser dans une ὕλη. Mais néanmoins, dans leur essence elles sont primaires et irréductibles à des principes formels qui seraient supérieurs.

(3) *Metaph*. A 9, 991 a 8-19, le passage bien connu où Aristote dit que les Idées transcendantes de Platon ne servent à rien pour expliquer le monde sensible; elles ne sont pas causes du mouvement des choses naturelles et ne contribuent en rien ni à la connaissance de ces choses (parce qu'elles n'en sont pas l'essence), ni à leur existence (parce qu'elles ne sont pas immanentes aux choses qui y participent).

Aristote a d'autres objections contre la théorie des Idées, mais celle-ci est sans doute son objection principale[2]. Ce qu'il veut prouver – et croit avoir prouvé – est que l'hypothèse des Idées est inutile et logiquement parlant un non-sens. Il n'est donc nullement nécessaire d'admettre des Entités transcendantes qui seraient les prototypes des choses sensibles. Il faut les remplacer par des formes-essences immanentes, lesquelles, à titre d'essences, expliquent *et* l'existence des choses concrètes, *et* la connaissance que nous en avons, tandis que, comme fin, elles sont causes du mouvement.

Mais, si tel était l'avis d'Aristote, il faut bien reconnaître que les «Entités transcendantes» qu'il a admises en fin de compte, ne sauraient être conçues à la façon des Idées platoniciennes; c'est-à-dire que les formes immanentes ne sauraient être réduites à elles ou subordonnées à elles dans un ordre de dépendance ontologique. Les οὐσίαι sont πρῶτα, c'est-à-dire qu'elles sont *causes premières*.

(4) *Eth. Nic.* I 6. Aristote y traite l'ἀγαθόν de Platon comme un καθόλου qu'il faudrait «abstraire» de diverses choses concrètes. Or, puisque le bien se trouve dans plusieurs catégories, il paraît impossible de trouver un κοινόν qui serait le bien en général. «Mais peut-être faut-il laisser cela pour le moment», dit-il, «car un examen précis de ces problèmes relèverait plutôt d'une autre partie de la philosophie. Il en est de même de l'Idée. Car même s'il existe un bien qui est un et prédicable de toutes espèces de choses, ou s'il existe séparé et sub-

[1] Voir l'interprétation du P. J. Owens citée ci-dessus (p. 336 f.) et ma notice dans la n. 7, p. 336.
[2] 991 a 8-9: πάντων δὲ μάλιστα διαπορήσειεν ἄν τις –.

sistant par lui-même, il est évident qu'il serait irréalisable pour l'homme et impossible à acquérir » (οὐ πρακτὸν οὐδὲ κτητὸν ἀνθρώπῳ)[1].

Cela veut dire (un peu à la façon de Gorgias) que:
1° il ne saurait exister d'ἀγαθόν transcendant;
2° s'il existait, il n'aurait aucun sens pour nous.

Or, puisque le τίνος ἕνεκέν ἐστι πρακτέον ἕκαστον qui selon *Metaph.* A 2 est l'objet de la science suprême, dite «sagesse», est un bien qui peut diriger l'action humaine, il s'ensuit, en tout cas, que ce bien n'est pas transcendant.

Mais alors, pourraient dire ceux qui partagent les vues du P. Owens, que penser du texte de *Metaph.* Λ 7, où l'auteur dit que c'est du Premier Moteur que dépend l'univers et toute la nature? Et enfin, si le τίνος ἕνεκέν ἐστι πρακτέον ἕκαστον, ce sont les formes-essences immanentes dans la nature, prises comme fins et comme principes autonomes, de quel droit Aristote reproche-t-il à Speusippe d'admettre une pluralité de principes et de rendre «épisodique» la substance de l'univers?

οὐκ ἀγαθὸν πολυκοιρανίη· εἷς κοίρανος ἔστω.

C'est là, en effet, un argument pour le P. Owens et pour tous ceux qui veulent comprendre la métaphysique d'Aristote dans le sens d'une synthèse spéculative: les οὐσίαι dans la nature doivent se subordonner aux οὐσίαι pures et transcendantes, et à la tête de toute cette série il faut placer le πρῶτον κινοῦν, Principe suprême qui domine tout. On pourrait ajouter: même si Aristote n'a pas dit cela explicitement, il faut l'inférer. Car d'après ses propres principes il faut qu'il y ait subordination.

Évidemment, je vois fort bien la force de l'argument. Ce que je veux dire est simplement: *qu'il ne s'agit là ni de l'Aristote de Métaph. A ni (probablement) de celui de la Physique, mais d'un Aristote platonisé et théiste.*

Par cette thèse je ne veux nullement isoler le premier livre de la *Métaphysique* des autres. Au contraire, la tendance des deux chapitres introductifs s'accorde parfaitement avec les livres ΖΗΘ qui contiennent la doctrine définitive d'Aristote sur la substance et sur l'acte et la puissance. Leur méthode est celle de l'analyse logique, non de la synthèse spéculative. En somme, on arrive à la même conclusion si l'on considère l'ensemble de «la *Métaphysique* en dix livres» qui, comme Sir David Ross l'a fait observer dans l'introduction de son

---

[1] 1096 b 30-34.

édition de la *Métaphysique*, forment plus ou moins un ouvrage continu[1]. C'est le livre Λ qui prend une place un peu à part.

Mais posons la question de savoir *en quel sens* Aristote voit l'univers et toute la nature dépendre du Premier Moteur. Pas, en tout cas, dans un sens total. Plus précisément, pas dans l'ordre de la substance. *Dans un sens*, bien sûr, le Premier Moteur domine l'univers et la nature: c'est dans l'ordre du mouvement[2]. Là, il y a dépendance, bien que le Premier Moteur soit, évidemment, une cause fort indirecte et éloignée par rapport aux choses sensibles.

En somme, ce n'est pas la ligne citée de Λ 7 qui oppose de graves difficultés à ce qui me paraît être l'interprétation correcte et nécessaire de notre passage du livre A, ch. 2. Il y a, certes, plus de difficulté dans le passage remarquable qui se trouve en Λ 10, 1075a11-15[3]. Aristote y parle de τὸ ἀγαθὸν καὶ τὸ ἄριστον dans l'ensemble de la nature et se demande de quelle façon la nature «possède» ce bien: comme quelque chose de κεχωρισμένον καὶ αὐτὸ καθ'αὑτό, ou simplement comme l'ordre (τὴν τάξιν).

«Ou bien ne serait-ce pas plutôt des deux manières à la fois, telle une armée? Car d'une part le bien de l'armée est dans son ordre, d'autre part, c'est le général, et celui-ci à un plus haut degré. Car ce n'est pas le général qui existe en raison de l'ordre, mais c'est l'ordre qui existe grâce au général».

Dans ce passage en tout cas la possibilité d'un Bien transcendant est admise, bien qu'un peu vaguement. Il me semble qu'on pourrait mettre le passage cité à côté de quelques autres textes d'Aristote. Ils ne sont pas nombreux, mais il y en a deux ou trois où en tout cas la vague possibilité d'un Dieu transcendant qui exerce une providence est admise. Je pense au fameux texte: ὁ δὲ θεὸς καὶ ἡ φύσις οὐδὲν μάτην ποιοῦσι[4], à son parallèle dans le *Protrept.*, fr. 11 Ross – οὗ χάριν ἡ φύσις ἡμᾶς ἐγέννησε καὶ ὁ θεός[5], – et au fragment 13 du Περὶ φιλοσοφίας[6], la transposition de l'allégorie de la caverne, où l'auteur conclut: *quae cum viderent, profecto et esse deos et haec tanta opera deorum esse arbitrarentur.* Cf. Sextus Emp., *Adv. dogm.* III 26-27 (= fr. 12b Ross).

---

[1] Ross, *Aristotle's Metaphysics*, p. XXIII.
[2] Voir Ross, *o.c.*, p. CLIII: «It is exclusively as first mover that a god is necessary to his system».
[3] Le passage est cité et discuté par Ross, *Metaph.*, Introd. p. CL. Cf. Owens, p. 285.
[4] *De Caelo* I 4, 271a33.
[5] Ross, *Fragm.* p. 44, en bas de la page.
[6] Cic., *De Nat. deorum* II 37, 95 – voir ma notice sous le no. **427** de *Greek Philosophy*, II.

Il faut ajouter que la conclusion de ces derniers passages n'exprime pas nécessairement la conviction de l'auteur.

Le thème de la théologie d'Aristote restera toujours un thème difficile. Il faudra concéder qu'on trouve chez Aristote quelques éléments pouvant conduire à une synthèse spéculative. Comme Sir David Ross l'a très bien vu[1], il y a toute raison d'accepter qu'il croyait à une hiérarchie ontologique, s'étendant des êtres physiques d'ordre inférieur jusqu'à l'homme, aux corps célestes, aux moteurs immobiles, et enfin au Premier Moteur. Néanmoins, ce premier Principe n'est pas cause totale; sa fonction est, au contraire, très limitée. S'il κινεῖ ὡς ἐρώμενον, ce n'est pas qu'il soit un «bien» pour l'homme ou pour la nature; c'est pour le premier ciel qu'il est objet d'amour. Il faudra conclure que, *en tant qu'Aristote admettait un Bien transcendant, cause de l'ordre de la nature, ce n'était sûrement pas au Premier Moteur qu'il pensait. Il a dû penser à une Intelligence divine beaucoup plus proche de notre monde, – disons: d'un premier degré de transcendance.*

C'est à Λ 10, 1075 a 11-15, en effet, que le P. Owens s'en est rapporté pour conclure qu'Aristote a subordonné les formes-essences dans la nature aux Entités transcendantes. A cette interprétation – qui est essentiellement celle des philosophes arabes, – j'oppose pour le moment deux objections:

(1) On ne voit pas bien comment Aristote pouvait admettre une Intelligence transcendante fonctionnant comme Bien pour la nature, sans retomber dans une espèce de métaphysique platonicienne telle qu'il l'a rejetée avec énergie.

(2) Si l'intelligence divine qui agit en ἀγαθόν par rapport à la nature, n'est pas le Dieu éloigné qu'est le Premier Moteur, mais un dieu voisin de notre monde, cela implique-t-il que le Premier Moteur soit une cause totale et universelle?

La première objection vaut inévitablement contre Aristote en tant qu'il a admis la possibilité d'un Bien transcendant tel qu'il apparaît dans le passage cité de Λ 10. Observons toutefois que ce passage montre une certaine hésitation et que le fr. 13 du Περὶ φιλ. n'offre rien de concluant quant à la conviction d'Aristote. Il faut ajouter que l'expression «Dieu et la nature» n'est peut-être qu'une formule plus ou moins conventionnelle[2]. Notons enfin que les textes qui semblent admettre un Bien transcendant sont tous de date ancienne.

---

[1] *Metaph.* Introd., p. CXLVIII.
[2] Ce ne seraient pas là les seuls endroits où Aristote parle de «Dieu» dans le sens de la ὑπόληψις que, d'après lui, tous les hommes possèdent à propos des

Quant à la seconde objection, je l'ai faite sous forme de question. Si l'on y répond affirmativement, il est clair qu'on s'engage dans le chemin des commentateurs arabes, qui a été préparé plus ou moins par l'école d'Alexandrie[1] et par celles de la Syrie. Or, ce choix-là n'est aucunement nécessaire. Et pourquoi donc attribuer à Aristote une conception qui est en flagrante contradiction avec sa propre théorie du Premier Moteur? Sur ce point-ci je voudrais le défendre contre une interprétation platonisante et théiste, telle qu'elle a été donnée par Alfarabi et par Avicenne, par Ibn Tofail et par Averroès même. Certes, ceux-ci n'ont pas réintroduit les Idées archétypes des choses sensibles dans l'Esprit divin du Premier Moteur, – même Avicenne n'a pas fait cela; il a placé les Idées transcendantes et exemplaires de Platon dans l'*Intellectus agens* qu'il identifiait à l'Intelligence de la sphère lunaire. C'était là en tout cas une interprétation beaucoup plus proche de la pensée d'Aristote que celle de S. Thomas d'Aquin. Il semble qu'Avicenne pouvait se réclamer de *Metaph.* Λ 10. – Mais tous les philosophes arabes ont conçu le Premier Moteur comme Cause totale et universelle, et par là ont pas mal contribué à platoniser la théologie d'Aristote.

---

dieux (*De Caelo* I 3, 270b6). On pourrait citer toute une série de passages. Nous allons en trouver plus loin dans notre ch. 2 de *Metaph.* A.

[1] Si l'on interroge le commentaire d'Asclepius sur 982b4-7, on verra qu'il ne se pose pas le problème de savoir si le τίνος ἕνεκέν ἐστι πρακτέον ἕκαστον est un bien immanent dans la nature ou non. Il commence par citer le début de l'*Eth. Nic.* pour expliquer qu'il s'agit du τελικὸν αἴτιον. Or, cette cause finale est aussi la cause de tout ce qui existe (τῶν ὄντων ἁπάντων). «Car tout ce qui existe et devient dans la nature est ἐκείνου χάριν et est incliné vers *lui*, selon son aspiration innée». Tout cela peut bien se référer à une fin immanente dans la nature. Ensuite, quand le commentateur continue en disant qu'Aristote a voulu démontrer comment le πρῶτον αἴτιον est cause des êtres – c'est-à-dire cause comme fin, – et que la science qui connaît cette espèce de cause est plus fondamentale que la science des causes qui produisent ce qui est en vue de cette fin, il ne semble pas s'écarter de la même conception. Mais quand, dans les lignes qui suivent (p. 18, l. 5-10), notre commentateur parle de τὸ πάντων τέλος καὶ οὗ χάριν τὰ πάντα ἔστι et dit que la science qui connaît cette fin ultime sera ἀρχικωτάτη καὶ πρώτη, il me semble qu'il y a ici un glissement imperceptible du télos immanent à la nature au télos ultime et total de l'univers: τὰ γὰρ ὄντα τοῦ κυριωτάτου τῶν ἀγαθῶν ἐφίεται. Or, qu'est-ce d'autre que le premier Principe absolu de l'univers, le πρῶτον κινοῦν qui ici paraît avoir pris le caractère de Bien suprême dans un sens beaucoup plus plein et universel qu'il ne l'a chez Aristote? Si je vois bien, nous assistons donc ici au passage de la téléologie immanente d'Aristote à une métaphysique d'un Bien transcendant, dominant tout ce qui existe comme sa fin ultime. Or, c'est là vraiment un aristotélisme platonisé, précurseur de celui des Arabes et de S. Thomas.

Mais il est temps de revenir au texte d'Aristote et de suivre sa pensée dans la seconde moitié du ch. 2 de *Metaph.* A.

982b11-32. La «sagesse» n'est pas une science productrice. Cela se manifeste dès ses origines: c'est par l'étonnement que les premiers philosophes ont commencé à philosopher. Or, s'étonner veut dire: reconnaître son ignorance. C'est donc à l'ignorance qu'on cherchait à échapper; – c'est-à-dire qu'on cherchait à savoir simplement pour savoir, non pour quelque motif d'utilité. L'histoire elle-même en fournit la preuve: tous les arts qui ont une application pratique, étaient déjà connus, quand on a commencé à chercher une telle espèce de connaissance. Mais, parce qu'elle n'est pas recherchée en vue de quelque autre chose, elle seule est digne d'être appelée une science libre.

Faut-il dire à cause de cela qu'elle est d'un niveau supérieur à l'intellect humain? – Au contraire, répond Aristote, *il serait indigne de l'homme de ne pas chercher la science qui lui est appropriée*[1].

Ce qu'il y a de remarquable dans la dernière phrase, est que le philosophe *pose simplement le demonstrandum:* il décide sans discussion qu'une telle connaissance est exactement celle qui est appropriée à l'homme. C'est dire que, en vertu de sa dignité humaine, – i.e. comme être raisonnable, – l'homme doit chercher cette science suprême.

982b32-983a11. Car il ne faut pas croire que la divinité soit jalouse. – Il est vrai, d'ailleurs, que la science dont il s'agit est «divine», et cela à double titre: 1° C'est Dieu qui en premier lieu est digne de la posséder; 2° elle traite des choses divines, – car Dieu paraît bien être une des causes pour toutes les choses et un principe premier.

Notons pour le moment que Dieu paraît à l'auteur non *la* Cause et *le* Premier Principe, mais τῶν αἰτίων πᾶσι καὶ ἀρχή τις. Certes, la philosophie qui doit expliquer p. ex. le phénomène du mouvement, aboutira de ce côté au πρῶτον κινοῦν, qui, dans un sens, est αἴτιον πᾶσι. Mais nullement au sens total. Car pour expliquer *l'existence* des choses naturelles et leur *substance déterminée* c'est aux formes-essences que la raison aboutira. Cf. 983a27-29 (au début du ch. 3):

μίαν μὲν αἰτίαν φαμὲν εἶναι τὴν οὐσίαν καὶ τὸ τί ἦν εἶναι (ἀνάγεται γὰρ τὸ διὰ τί εἰς τὸν λόγον ἔσχατον, αἴτιον δὲ καὶ ἀρχὴ τὸ διὰ τί πρῶτον).

Alexandre note – à bon droit –: λόγος ἔσχατος = οὐσία ἢ τὸ τί ἦν εἶναι.

---

[1] Si Aristote dit: «mais il serait indigne de l'homme de ne pas rechercher la science appropriée à lui-même», il ne faut pas s'y méprendre. Le philosophe ne pense aucunement que «la science appropriée à l'homme» serait d'une espèce inférieure à celle dont il parle et qu'il considère comme θεία (voir les lignes suivantes).

Pour les choses naturelles, les formes-essences sont la cause essentielle et le premier principe.

983 a 11-23. La possession de cette science doit, en fin de compte, nous mettre dans un état d'esprit contraire à celui de nos premières recherches. Car nous commençons par nous étonner de tel ou tel phénomène; mais finalement, après en avoir compris les causes, rien ne nous étonnerait autant que le phénomène opposé.

Nous avons ainsi établi la nature de la sagesse, et le but de notre investigation.

Cela veut dire: cette science nous mène à comprendre que les choses sont, et se comportent, nécessairement comme elles sont et se comportent, en nous en apprenant les causes.

La dernière page d'Aristote contient quelques points très intéressants qui méritent une attention spéciale.

1. Quand l'auteur dit que c'est Dieu qui, en premier lieu, pourrait posséder la science dont il s'agit, la question se pose de savoir si le philosophe prétend attribuer à Dieu une connaissance parfaite du monde: connaissance des οὐσίαι des choses naturelles apparemment, mais également connaissance des choses particulières et concrètes, en tant qu'elle est contenue dans la «connaissance de tout» au sens général, laquelle implique celle des cas particuliers[1]. Or, la seconde espèce de connaissance est exclue du moment qu'elle s'étend à tous les phénomènes du monde sensible[2]. Mais la première – la connaissance des οὐσίαι – est implicitement exclue par la critique de la théorie des Idées. Car, supposé que l'Intellect divin qui est le principe suprême pense les οὐσίαι des choses sensibles, il s'ensuivra l'existence d'«Idées» transcendantes et exemplaires dans l'Esprit divin. Et c'est là le chemin qu'Aristote s'est interdit de la manière la plus catégorique possible.

2. Immédiatement après avoir dit, en citant Simonide, que «Dieu seul pourrait jouir de ce privilège», il déclare que c'est sans doute la tâche, et même le devoir de l'homme de chercher la connaissance dont il s'agit. Il paraît bien que l'esprit humain est placé ici pour ainsi dire à très peu de distance de l'Esprit divin.

3. Puisque la possession de cette science nous mettra dans l'état de voir en pleine clarté pourquoi les choses sont ce qu'elles sont et se comportent comme elles se comportent, elle nous fera savoir pleinement et avec une connaissance strictement scientifique «was die Welt

---

[1] 982 a 23.
[2] Voir *Metaph.* Λ 9, 1074 b 21-35.

im innersten zusammenhält». Or, n'est-ce pas là vraiment, et selon les vues de l'auteur lui-même, un *eritis sicut Deus*?

Que faut-il conclure de tout cela? Que répondre à ces questions?

J'admets, pour commencer, que notre philosophe n'était pas un esprit confus. Si l'on est d'accord sur ce point, il faudra répondre à notre première question, comme nous l'avons fait tout à l'heure en réfléchissant sur la question du Bien transcendant par rapport à la nature:

Il est impossible qu'Aristote veuille attribuer au Premier Moteur une connaissance telle que la sagesse qui vient d'être décrite.

D'autre part, c'est bien à «Dieu» que le philosophe veut en premier lieu attribuer une telle connaissance. En outre, nous avons vu que dans un des chapitres mêmes où la doctrine du Premier Moteur est exposée (*Metaph.* Λ 10), Aristote accepte, bien qu'en termes un peu vagues, l'existence d'un Bien-en-soi, supérieur à l'ordre de la nature et agissant comme Providence. Or, qu'est-ce d'autre, en fin de compte, qu'un Intellect transcendant occupé des soins de notre monde? C'est-à-dire: un Dieu-providence. Telle est en tout cas la croyance de l'auteur du troisième livre du Περὶ φιλ.; croyance qui, enfin, s'accorde assez bien avec l'expression «Dieu et la nature». Car il n'est pas nécessaire qu'une telle expression dénote l'identité des deux termes. En se servant des paroles d'Aristote on pourrait dire: le mot «Dieu» indique le général, tandis que «la nature», c'est l'ordre même.

Il me semble qu'il n'est pas justifié d'écarter ces passages en disant qu'ils ne s'accordent point avec la notion scientifique de Dieu, telle qu'elle est exposée par Aristote en *Metaph.* Λ 7, 9, 10. Évidemment, ils ne s'accordent nullement avec le concept du Premier Moteur. Mais est-il permis de conclure que, par conséquent, ils n'ont pas de sens? Aristote, répétons-le, était loin d'être un esprit confus. Et, d'autre part, on ne saurait résoudre le problème de la discordance entre ces textes en disant qu'ils datent d'une période différente de la pensée de l'auteur. Une telle dissection de l'exposé de Λ 7, 9, 10, me paraît plutôt monstrueuse. D'ailleurs, Περὶ φιλ. III n'est probablement pas tellement éloigné ni de *Metaph.* A ni de Λ.

Il faudra donc trouver une meilleure explication. Or, je crois qu'elle s'est déjà présentée à nous lors de nos réflexions sur *Metaph.* Λ 10, 1075 a 11-15. En effet, elle se présente tout naturellement à l'esprit, dès qu'on abandonne l'idée que, pour Aristote, «Dieu» serait exclusivement le Premier Moteur. Ce qui semble plutôt une conclusion nécessaire de mes trois points, c'est qu'Aristote croyait à l'existence d'un Νοῦς divin transcendant à l'ordre naturel mais en différant d'*un degré* seulement et dont l'essence devait être apparentée de très près sinon identique à celle du noûs humain. Dans la hiérarchie des purs esprits ce Noûs divin doit avoir sa place beaucoup plus proche de l'homme et du monde sensible que le Premier Moteur. Celui-ci est placé par Aristote à l'extérieur du premier ciel, c'est-à-dire: à une distance infiniment lointaine de l'homme et de notre monde. Mais l'Esprit divin qui paraît connaître au plus haut degré les formes-essences des choses naturelles, doit être pour ainsi dire voisin de nous.

Où donc faut-il le placer? Aristote n'en dit pas un mot. Mais on voit bien qu'il n'est aucunement fantastique de dire qu'il faut chercher cet Intellect près de la sphère inférieure des corps célestes: celle qui est la plus proche de la terre.

Par là on peut comprendre fort bien la théorie d'Avicenne mentionnée ci-dessus[1]: ce n'est pas là simplement un essai de synthèse spéculative à peine fondé sur les textes d'Aristote. Au contraire, si l'on se rend bien compte des textes, il faudra concéder encore une fois, comme nous l'avons fait auparavant, que telle est à *peu près* la conclusion qui s'impose.

A peu près. Car il faut faire quelques restrictions plus ou moins importantes. Ce n'est pas seulement le fait qu'Aristote n'a pas soufflé mot d'une identité de l'*intellectus agens* de l'homme avec le moteur immobile de la sphère lunaire. Il y a aussi le fait qu'Aristote a nié l'existence d'Idées transcendantes d'où il faudra déduire que le philosophe n'a point conçu la connaissance des formes-essences qu'il attribue au Dieu-providence comme une connaissance de «formes» semblables aux Idées platoniciennes, – en tout cas qu'il n'a pas *voulu* la concevoir ainsi. Mais la plus importante restriction reste à mon avis celle-ci: Aristote ne paraît pas s'être intéressé spécialement aux «entités» purement spirituelles. Quand il parle du Dieu-proche-de-l'homme, du Dieu-providence, il s'exprime d'une manière un peu vague et hésitante. Ainsi dans notre ch. 2 de *Metaph*. A, 982b30, où il s'empresse de passer à l'homme et à la nature humaine. Dans ce passage il ne s'étend aucunement sur l'affinité de l'esprit humain avec l'esprit divin. Ailleurs, bien sûr, il dit que le noûs de l'homme vient θύραθεν. Mais là aussi il ne s'arrête nullement à la question de savoir *d'où* vient cet intellect. Certes, nous avons de lui tout un livre assez élaboré sur le Premier Moteur immobile et sa nature, et un autre livre

---

[1] Voir p. 345.

entier pour prouver qu'il est nécessaire d'admettre l'existence d'un tel principe. C'est que le phénomène du mouvement se trouvait au cœur des préoccupations de notre philosophe.

Ce qui est certain, en tout cas, c'est qu'Aristote ne s'est pas du tout servi du terme «dieu» dans un sens unique[1]. Le seul fait qu'Aristote a appelé le «*noûs* en nous» θεῖον et même θεός, devrait nous prémunir contre cette erreur, d'inspiration théiste. Notons encore que l'expression citée ne se trouve pas seulement dans les fragments du *Protreptique*[2], mais encore dans un passage de l'*Eth. Nic.* X 7[3]. Quant à l'expression «Dieu et la nature», elle s'éclaire d'une lumière toute nouvelle dès qu'on a compris que pour Aristote «Dieu» ne se dit pas seulement du Premier Moteur mais dénote tout Esprit pur, supérieur au monde sensible[4], y compris le *noûs* de l'homme.

Il paraît cependant que les questions relatives aux «Entités Spirituelles» ne se trouvaient nullement dans le centre d'intérêt d'Aristote, quand il écrivait les chapitres d'introduction de la *Métaphysique* et l'ensemble de l'ouvrage même. Ce qu'il y recherche, c'est essentiellement le διὰ τί des choses naturelles. Or, ce problème nous mène aux formes-essences dans la nature. C'est elles qui sont l'objet premier de cette espèce de science. Alexandre l'a très bien reconnu: il s'agit essentiellement des οὐσίαι, et la plus grande partie de l'ouvrage se compose, en effet, de travaux préparatoires.

Comment cette recherche se réalise-t-elle? Selon la méthode de l'analyse logique. Un collègue très estimé a observé dans un ouvrage récent[5] que, tout raffinés que soient les schémas logiques d'Aristote, l'influence de la logique sur la pensée philosophique elle-même a été bien limitée. Il cite comme exemple l'*Éthique à Nicomaque*. Par contre, la *Métaphysique* d'Aristote paraît toute pénétrée de logique. La critique de ses prédécesseurs en A, celle de Platon en particulier, la liste des apories en B, la manière de traiter le thème essentiel de la métaphysique, les axiomes et les lois fondamentales de la pensée en Γ, le livre des définitions (Δ), les livres sur la substance (ZH, introduits

---

[1] Comme le pense p.e. le R.P. H. Robbers, dans un ouvrage récent intitulé *Antieke wijsgerige begrippen in het Christelijk denkleven* (Nijmegen 1959), p. 132. Owens, par contre, paraît avoir très bien compris qu'il n'en est pas ainsi.
[2] Fr. 61 Rose = *Protrept.* 10c Ross.
[3] 1177b27ss; cfr. *De Part. An.* II 10, 656a8 (τὸ τῶν ἀνθρώπων γένος μόνον μετέχει τοῦ θείου... ἢ μάλιστα); IV 10, 686a28; *Eth. Nic.* X 7, 1177a15.
[4] Voir *Metaph.* Λ 8, 1074a38 (παραδέδοται δέ) – b 14.
[5] O. Gigon, *Grundprobleme der antiken Philosophie*, Bern 1959, p. 41.

par E), celui sur la puissance et l'entéléchie (Θ), y compris le chapitre final sur la vérité, le livre I (X) dans son ensemble, ainsi que M et N, tout cela est dominé par la méthode de la logique et ne saurait être écrit ni pensé sans elle. Le besoin de synthèse spéculative, par contre, semble y être extrêmement limité ou avoir à peine été éprouvé.

PRAENEOPLATONICA

CHAPTER XV

ON THE NEOPLATONIC CHARACTER OF PLATONISM AND THE PLATONIC CHARACTER OF NEOPLATONISM[1]

Plotinus says, speaking on his three main hypostases[2]: "These theories are not new. They were professed in very ancient times, only not in such an elaborate form. And what I said now, is only an interpretation of those former doctrines, the antiquity of which is attested to us by the writings of Plato himself."

He then points first to Parmenides, who brought together Being and Mind, and separated Being from the sensible world. Though he identified Being and Thinking, he stripped his Being of all material movement, and compared it with a sphere, because it contains all within it. Plotinus remarks that Parmenides, by this way of representing things, gave rise to the objection that his one was many. The Platonic Parmenides, however, was more accurate, as he distinguished between the first and strictly One, secondly the one which is many, and thirdly the one and many. "This theory", Plotinus concludes, "agrees with mine of the three hypostases, and is identical with it."

There have been, surely, according to Plotinus, more precedents of this doctrine among the ancient Greek philosophers. He mentions Anaxagoras' theory of the noûs, which is καθαρὸς καὶ ἀμιγής; Empedocles' φιλία, which is a principle of unity. Next, there was Aristotle, who made his first principle χωριστὸν καὶ νοητόν; and finally, Pythagoreans kept firmly to intelligible being. Some of them treated it amply in their writings, others in oral teaching (ἐν ἀγράφοις συνουσίαις).

Plotinus, certainly, did not intend to say that all these thinkers flatly taught his own doctrine of the three basic hypostases. He knows too well that the philosophy of Anaxagoras and of Empedocles

---

[1] The text of this chapter goes back to 1951. It was read to the Faculty of litterae humaniores at Oxford and appeared in *Mind*, January 1953. The present edition is slightly revised.
[2] *Enn.*, V, i, 8.

355

contained also quite other elements, and he explicitly opposed Aristotle's theory of a multiplicity of unmoved Movers. Only the philosophy of Plato he calls fully and without reserve his own, and, no doubt, in his opinion his own philosophy was legitimate Platonism.

Now, practically speaking, this has been the judgment of history, up till the nineteenth century. In later antiquity Platonism was known under the form of Neoplatonism. St. Augustine, who was a Platonist, learned his philosophy from Porphyry and the Neoplatonists of his time; his was a hierarchic view of the universe, and if he, finding an intelligible world above his mind, identified that world with God, he did so only because the Christian revelation told him that "the Word" or "Wisdom" is equal to the Father[1]. When, in the sixth century, Boëthius, who spoke as a philosopher, invoked God and called Him "of threefold nature"[2], we may be sure that this "last of Romans" considered the Trinity of God as a legitimate Platonic doctrine – because the theory of the three basic hypostases was in his eyes true Platonism[3].

It was in its Neoplatonic version that Platonism entered the Middle Ages. What was known and read of Plato's works – chiefly the Timaeus – was known and read through the medium of Neoplatonic commentaries. And even after the Middle Ages Plato was interpreted in this way. The revival of Platonic studies at Florence in the fifteenth century had a Neoplatonic character: Marsilius Ficinus, who translated the works of Plato, translated those of Plotinus and later Neoplatonists too. He was the author of a *Theologia Platonica*, the title of which shows rather clearly that the author regarded Plato exactly in the same way as the Middle Ages used to do.

Cambridge knew its Platonism in the seventeenth and eighteenth centuries. Thinkers like Henry More and Ralph Cudworth lived certainly in close intellectual contact with the most modern philosophers of their age – More with Descartes and Cudworth with Locke. They modernised Platonism in the style of their time. Yet, it was still a neo-platonised Platonism which occupied their mind. A more radical change in Platonic studies took place in the nineteenth century: only then was Plato separated from Neoplatonic interpretation; Plotinus'

---

[1] *De lib. arb.*, ii, 15, 39.
[2] *Consolatio*, III, metr. IX.
[3] In the seventeenth century we shall find the Cambridge Platonist Cudworth discussing amply the value of "the Trinity of Plato" and its relation to the Christian Trinity.

doctrine of emanation and that of the three – according to certain interpreters, four – hypostases was no longer accepted as genuinely Platonic. It was considered as a new philosophy, prepared to a certain degree by thinkers such as Plutarch, Philo and Numenius, but yet essentially new, and of a character different from Platonism.

This view of Neoplatonism can still be found in a number of classical works on Greek philosophy. Zeller[1] marks two essential points of difference between Plato and Plotinus. (1) Though Plato appoints to the soul an intermediate place between the Ideas and the sensible world, he describes the genesis of the soul only in a mythical form, without trying to deduce it rationally from the essence of the ideal World. (2) He did not deduce his Ideas from one principle superior to them. His Good is no more than the highest among the Ideas; and the One, which Aristotle says he assumed as first principle, together with the Great-and-small, was an immanent principle in the Ideas, not a transcendent cause, as the One of Plotinus was.

Praechter[2] expresses a similar view, when he states that Plato made the distinction between a sensible and a supra-sensible world, while Plotinus has the ἴδια (1) of dividing the supra-sensible in more than one hierarchically ordered hypostases, and (2) of deducing the sensible world from the supra-sensible.

I have the impression that scholars like Whittaker and Inge regarded Plotinus in the same way. Both dedicate a short chapter to the forerunners of Plotinus. The former mentions Philo and Numenius as thinkers who anticipated on certain points the position of Plotinus; the latter is somewhat more explicit about Plotinus' predecessors, but it is clear that he did not attribute great importance to their ideas. And in a certain sense they were right. Neither Valentinus, nor Numenius, nor the author of the Poimandres can be called true philosophers. Yet, the system of Valentinus and the revelation of Poimandres deserve special mention, because they make it clear to us that in the second and the early third centuries, at least in certain circles, the supra-sensible world was thought of as being hierarchically ordered, and this in three degrees, from the third of which the sensible world proceeds.

To put the question generally, I think there are three points which deserved special attention, and, indeed, have been more closely regarded since the days of Überweg and Zeller, since Whittaker and

[1] *Phil. d. Gr.*, III, 2, iv., ⁴1903, pp. 529f.
[2] Überweg-Praechter, *Geschichte der Phil.*, I, xii. 1926, p. 596.

Inge. There is first the question of the direct predecessors of Plotinus, secondly that of the interpretation of later Platonism; thirdly that of the intermediate stages.

Our first point: the forerunners of Plotinus.

Between Plato and the Neoplatonism of Plotinus there is an interval of six centuries – a space of time nearly as long as that between Thomas Aquinas and the Thomists or Neo-Thomists of our day. Now, it is a curious fact that, a century before Plotinus, and perhaps a generation before him, a hierarchy of being was professed and a kind of production of the sensible world which, if not identical with that of classical Neoplatonism, was at least not far removed from it. I mean the doctrine of the gnostic Valentinus, and next to it the revelation of Poimandres, which may surely be called a more precise analogy than that which can be found in Numenius, whose works were studied in Plotinus' school and who, for this reason, can claim to be a direct forerunner of classical Neoplatonism. Going further back, we have to consider such philosophers as Philo of Alexandria and Plutarch, whose way of thinking certainly offers a more general parallel. It might even happen that, in reading Plutarch, we shall find there a closer analogy with Neoplatonism than is usually accepted.

Let us then first turn to these first century thinkers. It was Eugène de Faye who, in his great work on Origen, gave a rather impressive picture of the development of ancient philosophy in the centuries which preceded the age of Plotinus. He describes how, during the first century, the world, tired of scepticism, returned to religious aspirations; how Platonism became the dominant philosophy – or rather a certain aspect of Platonism; and how this aspect, namely the belief in a transcendent intelligible world, was combined with the Stoic doctrine of the Logos, originally an immanent cosmic law, which in the so-called Middle Platonism is to occupy the intermediate place between the transcendent Deity and man. In this function the Logos is called a "second God" (δεύτερος θεός) and is qualified as Mediator (μεσίτης).

This is indeed the place the Logos occupies in the thought of Philo of Alexandria[1]. God is called by Philo ὁ Θεός, the Logos is θεός[2].

---

[1] *Alleg.*, II, 86, M. 82: God is πρῶτος θεὸς καὶ δεύτερος ὁ θεοῦ λόγος. The word μεσίτης is used by Philo in the plural, with λόγοι: μεσίταις καὶ διαιτηταῖς λόγοις χρῆσθαι (*Somn.*, I, 142, M. 642).

[2] Thus it is stated explicitly in *Somn.*, I, 229, M. 655: τὸν μὲν ἀληθείᾳ διὰ τοῦ ἄρθρου μεμήνυκεν εἰπών· "ἐγώ εἰμι ὁ θεός", τὸν δ' ἐν καταχρήσει χωρὶς ἄρθρου

PLATONISM AND NEOPLATONISM

Philo calls it also κόσμος νοητός[1], image[2] and shadow of God[3], and says that it springs from divine Wisdom and Knowledge[4], being for men identical with it[5]. On a lower level we have the κόσμος αἰσθητός, the Logos being called υἱὸς πρεσβύτατος, who alone is judged worthy of staying with the Father, while the visible world is νεώτερος υἱὸς θεοῦ, who has gone out from Him[6]. Thus, in Philo we have a kind of anticipation of Plotinus' distinction between the highest Principle and the νοῦς or νοητά. It would be artificial to assert that we have here a division into four stages. On the other hand, it should be noticed that, according to Philo's view, the Logos communicates itself to, or rather realises itself in, the cosmos, and it exists on different levels, from rational beings down to the so-called inanimate nature. Now, surely, in this conception we are not far from Neoplatonism.

As to Plutarch, De Faye thinks the Logos occupies in his philosophy the same intermediate place as we saw it occupied in Philo. But, truly speaking, he arrived at this statement ἐξ ὑποθέσεως: eager to find in Plutarch the Logos mentioned as the son of Osiris, the highest God, he states that Horus, son of Osiris, is called by Plutarch λόγος αὐτὸς ἀμιγὴς καὶ ἀπαθής. Unfortunately these words are applied by the author[7] not to Horus, but to Osiris himself. Horus was, according to Plutarch, a personification of the sensible world, which was an image of the World Intelligible.

Now by this little error I fear the theory of De Faye on the intermediate place of the Logos in Plutarch has collapsed. And yet, the parallel with Plotinus keeps its ground rather well: Plutarch knows, certainly, a hierarchy of being; there are intermediate stages between his Osiris, or the Agathon, which is called by him "the Logos itself, un-

---

φάσκων "ὁ ὀφθείς σοι ἐν τόπῳ", οὐ "τοῦ θεοῦ", ἀλλ' αὐτὸ μόνον "θεοῦ". Καλεῖ δὲ "θεὸν" τὸν πρεσβύτατον αὐτοῦ νυνὶ λόγον.

[1] *Deus immut.*, 30-32, M. 277.
[2] εἰκών: *Confus.*, 97, M. 419; 147 f., M. 427; *Spec. leg.*, I, 81, M. 215.
[3] σκιά: *Alleg.*, III, 96, M. 106.
[4] *Somn.*, II, 242, M. 690; 275, M. 691; *Fuga et inv.*, 76, M. 557.
[5] *Alleg.*, I, 65, M. 56; *cf. Fuga et inv.*, 97, M. 560.
[6] *Deus immut.*, 31, M. 277: ὁ γὰρ κόσμος οὗτος νεώτερος υἱὸς θεοῦ, ἅτε αἰσθητὸς ὤν· τὸν γὰρ πρεσβύτερον – νοητὸς δ' ἐκεῖνος – πρεσβείων ἀξιώσας παρ' ἑαυτῷ καταμένειν διενοήθη.
[7] Plut., *De Iside et Osiride*, ch. 54, 373 B: τὸν Ὧρον, ὃν ἡ Ἶσις εἰκόνα τοῦ νοητοῦ κόσμου αἰσθητὸν ὄντα γεννᾷ. Διὸ καὶ δίκην φεύγειν λέγεται νοθείας ὑπὸ Τυφῶνος, ὡς οὐκ ὢν καθαρὸς οὐδ' εἰλικρινὴς οἷος ὁ πατήρ, λόγος αὐτὸς καθ' ἑαυτόν, ἀμιγὴς καὶ ἀπαθής, ἀλλὰ νενοθευμένος τῇ ὕλῃ διὰ τὸ σωματικόν.

mixed and impassible", and the sensible world. There is a hierarchy of gods, and, on a lower level, of daemons; and there are world-souls, at least a good and a bad one, which are to be placed between the intelligible and the sensible world. Thus, there is doubtless some kind of analogy between the thought of Plutarch and the – much clearer and richer – thought of Plotinus. The question can be only whether and how far, under the mythologising form in which he usually expressed his thoughts on the structure of the universe, a division into four stages might be found in Plutarch: is there any definite indication that he placed a noûs or intelligible World between the highest Deity and Soul? – P. Thévenaz, in his study on the world-soul in Plutarch[1], answered this question in the affirmative: with Plutarch, noûs is clearly superior to soul; soul is turned towards the body, and becomes rational only by participation in Noûs, this being the higher principle, subsisting independently, given by the highest Deity, with the purpose of saving the soul. One passage is cited by him in which this superiority of noûs is explicitly stated, namely that chapter in the *De facie in orbe lunae*[2] where Sulla declares that by the greater majority of men noûs is considered erroneously as being a part of the soul, while in fact it is superior to it, in the same measure as soul is superior to body.

When, then, Thévenaz concludes[3]: "La hiéarchie néoplatonicienne se dessine: le νοῦς est supérieur, meilleur et plus divin que l'âme", he is, in my opinion, perfectly right: in this passage indeed, the Plotinian hierarchy of being is outlined. That it is, on the whole, an outstanding doctrine in Plutarch would be certainly saying too much.

What is interesting in Numenius, is chiefly his distinction between a first God who is a "roi fainéant" (βασιλεὺς ἀργός), and a second God who is "the Craftsman" (δημιουργός). Surely this is a parallel to Plotinus' distinction between the One and the intelligible World. The next distinction of Plotinus, that between Spirit and Soul, is lacking in the system of Numenius. That he adds the sensible world as a τρίτος θεός, is a point not highly appreciated by Inge, but indeed a good Platonic qualification. And we have some reason to think that Plotinus did not find fault with him for this.

Closer, at least more obvious parallels with Plotinus' doctrine are, in my opinion, found in the speculations of the gnostic Valentinus, however fantastic they may be.

[1] *L'âme du monde, le devenir et la matière chez Plutarche*. Paris, 1938.
[2] Ch. 28, 943 A.
[3] *Op. cit.*, p. 72.

Valentinus describes his intelligible world as a *pleroma*, which contains in itself thirty eternal beings, called aeons, ranged in pairs. The highest pair is called symbolically *Bythos-Sigé*. It is followed successively by *Noûs-Alètheia, Logos-Zoè, Anthropos-Ecclesia*, of which the second pair (Logos-Zoè) engenders twelve lower aeons, and the third (Anthropos-Ecclesia) ten others. One of these last ten aeons goes astray and, turning away from the pleroma, ends by being excluded from it. From her tears and sorrow certain material elements arise, which by the Demiurge, who lives in the intermediate sphere of Soul, are formed into the material world.

The scheme offers a striking parallel with the division-into-four of Plotinus: Bythos-Sigé may be easily separated from the other aeons as a first and ineffable principle. The other aeons, then, are to be compared with the Plotinian noûs. The intermediate sphere of soul, which contains the Demiourgos, has like Plotinus' third hypostasis, partly an upward direction, turned towards the pleroma, and in this case it can be saved; partly it is directed towards matter, and then it is to perish with it. It is by this intermediate sphere that, by its turning downward, the world of material things is produced. Plotinus opposes the gnostics for their teaching that the material world as such is bad and the source of evil. Yet, it must be said that the whole scheme of the Universe of Valentinus offers a remarkable parallel to the Plotinian doctrine.

Thus, in certain gnostic circles a view of the universe was taken which, though its form was more mythological, contained a division-into-four which certainly is to be paralleled with Plotinus. The first treatise of the *Hermetica*[1] offers a similar parallel. The author tells about a revelation he received about the forming of the world, and in this description a certain hierarchy of spiritual powers is exhibited, which spring forth from the highest Deity, called Noûs. We might represent it in the following scheme:

(1) First there is *Spirit* (*Noûs*), which is God and Father. It is Light. The Word, which is shining, goes out from it, and is called its son.

(2) The Light is said to divide itself into a world of *innumerable Powers* (δυνάμεις ἀναρίθμητοι). It is described as an *infinite world* (κόσμος ἀπεριόριστος), and explained as *the exemplary Form in the Spirit*[2], which can hardly mean anything else than the archetype, after the pattern of which the sensible world is to be.

[1] *Corpus Hermeticum*, ed. Nock et Festugière, Paris, 1945, I, ch. 1-11, pp. 7-10.
[2] Εἶδες ἐν νῷ τὸ ἀρχέτυπον εἶδος (*Herm.*, I, 8).

(3) A *second spirit* (ἕτερος noûs), which is the Builder of the organic universe of living beings (δημιουργός), is engendered by the highest Noûs who is God.

(4) This Demiurge creates living beings, first those animated beings which are the celestial bodies, called "governors" (ἑπτὰ διοικητάς τινας), who encircle the sensible world; and finally, together with the Logos, which represents the lower elements (earth and water), he creates the irrational living beings (ζῷα ἄλογα).

The second part of the treatise gives an account of the creation of man. It is an interesting feature that the archetypal Man is created by the first Noûs or Father of all, Life and Light, as His own image; and that this man, having entered the sphere of the Demiurge, descends to the material world and, enamoured by his own image, reflected in the elements, unites himself with it. In spite of its mythological form this anthropology reminds us rather vividly of Plotinus.

As to the cosmogony, no doubt it offers a remarkable parallel to Plotinus' view of the universe. We do not wish to deny that Inge was right when he pointed to the mythological form, the vagueness and the inconsequences of the Hermetic writings. Yet he underrated the value of these documents for the history of ideas. The real value of the revelation of Poimandres is, that it shows us that, before the rise of Plotinus' system, in certain circles, and this not only in those of professed gnostics, a fourfold hierarchic scheme of being was accepted.

Our general conclusion is: that since the first century Platonism was apparently interpreted and generally accepted in the sense of a hierarchical order of being, in which the supreme Deity is conceived as strictly transcendent and almost supra-rational, the intelligible World of archetypal Forms being placed on the second stage, while between this world and the sensible an intermediate stage is assumed, consisting according to Plutarch of lower divine or semi-divine powers or beings, of a world-soul or a subordinate Logos; with the gnostics of soul and the Demiurge, with Poimandres again of a second noûs who is Demiurge. To put it generally: the doctrine of four stages of being has not been invented by Plotinus. In fact, it existed, though in a half-mythological form. There was only required a real *thinker* who was to give to this doctrine its scientific shape and character.

Before passing on to our second main point, we have to say a word about Albinus. Dr. Witt, in his excellent treatise on this second-century Platonist, pointed out that he may be called a forerunner of Plotinus in that he strove to make a synthesis of Plato and Aristotle.

Two other points deserve attention. First, it is somewhat misleading to state that Albinus called his first principle Noûs, and therefore to oppose him to Plotinus, who placed his supreme principle above the intelligible World[1]. Albinus namely[2], after having spoken first of the material principle, matter, assumes two other ἀρχαί, which he describes as follows: one of them is the paradigmatical principle, that of the Ideas, the other "the Father and Cause of all, God". The Ideas are thoughts of God, eternal and perfect[3]. They are the pattern or archetype of the sensible world, the determining principle (μέτρον) of matter (the Aristotelian *eidos*), and with relation to us the first object of our thinking (πρῶτον νοητόν)[4]. Albinus continues: "Next, we have to speak about the third principle, which Plato almost regards as ineffable."[5] Yet, we can come to a certain understanding of it[6], by realising that Spirit (νοῦς) is superior to soul, that actual noûs is superior to potential, and that its Cause is still of a higher rank. This, then, is the first God, who is the cause of the continuous activity of the Spirit of the Universe. He is the unmoved Mover, who moves as object of desire. His own thoughts are the objects of His thinking. Albinus adorns Him with the epithets Eternal, Ineffable, Perfect-in-Himself, *i.e.* without any need, always-Perfect, and Perfect-everywhere[7].

From this passage it is evident that Albinus, though he uses other

[1] R. E. Witt, *Albinus and the History of Middle Platonism*, Cambridge, 1937, p. 128.
[2] Ch. 9 (Herm., p. 163).
[3] The question whether or not Albinus was influenced by Stoic doctrine on this point, seems to me extremely difficult to decide. Dr. Witt is categorical in asserting that Stoic influence is excluded in Albinus. I would not go so far as that. On the other hand, Dr. Witt says that the interpretation of the Platonic ideas as existing in the divine Mind, was at any rate professed in the fourth century, in the School of Plato. He infers this from the following words of Alkimos' account of Platonism (in *Diog. Laert.*, III, 13): Ἔστι δὲ τῶν εἰδῶν ἓν ἕκαστον ἀίδιόν τε καὶ νόημα καὶ πρὸς τούτοις ἀπαθές. – "An eternal thought will most naturally imply God as its thinker," Dr. Witt concludes. This inference is somewhat misleading, in so far as modern "theists" will certainly understand by "God": the *supreme* Being, conceived as the total cause of everything. A Greek thinker, however, could use the term θεός on different levels.
[4] The text runs: Ἔστι δὲ ἡ ἰδέα ὡς μὲν πρὸς θεὸν νόησις αὐτοῦ, ὡς δὲ πρὸς ἡμᾶς νοητὸν πρῶτον, ὡς δὲ πρὸς τὴν ὕλην μέτρον, ὡς δὲ πρὸς τὸν αἰσθητὸν κόσμον παράδειγμα, ὡς δὲ πρὸς αὐτὴν ἐξεταζομένη οὐσία.
[5] Ch. 10 (p. 164 H.): (τῆς τρίτης ἀρχῆς), ἣν μικροῦ δεῖν καὶ ἄρρητον ἡγεῖται ὁ Πλάτων.
[6] ἐπαχθείημεν ἂν περὶ αὐτῆς.
[7] Καὶ μὴν ὁ πρῶτος θεὸς ἀίδιός ἐστιν, ἄρρητος, αὐτοτελής, τουτέστι πάντῃ τέλειος.

terms than those used later by Plotinus, does make a clear distinction between the intelligible world of exemplary Ideas and the supreme Principle. By no means are we allowed to say that, since the first Principle is called by him noûs, in fact no such distinction has been drawn by him.

So I think Theiler[1] was right in noting as a special characteristic of the theology of Albinus: his raising of the notion of the Deity. In this point, then, Albinus cannot be opposed to the general inclinations of his contemporaries.

Our second point might seem, at the first glance, more doubtful. We saw that, in contemporary theology, in gnostic and semignostic circles, the Demiurge or Builder of the sensible world was placed inferior to the intelligible World of Ideas, and that even the Alexandrian Jew Philo did not accept the theory that the supreme God created sensible things directly. On this point, indeed, Albinus appears to me an exception, when he states that the universe, being the most beautiful structure, must have been created *by God* after the pattern of the ideal World, and thus seems to identify the Demiurge and God. I do not think that Plato himself gives us reason to make this identification, and as no precedents of this interpretation seem to occur in the Hellenic world, I am even inclined to ask whether the author has not been influenced on this point by the Christian doctrine of creation. Though not proved, such an influence cannot be excluded *a priori*, at least in Asia Minor (Albinus lived at Smyrna) and in the second century.

However this may be, the question does not interfere with Albinus' general view of the hierarchy of being. If we put it into a scheme, four stages might be distinguished: (1) the first, ineffable Principle, God, cause of all, first Spirit; (2) His thoughts, the Ideas; (3) Soul, which, though not especially mentioned as another principle, is ranged by Albinus explicitly inferior to noûs; and (4) Matter. No doubt, there is a marked difference between Albinus' account of the creation of the sensible world, and the view Plotinus takes of its origin. But we have sufficient reason to consider the Platonism of Albinus as another example of the pre-neoplatonic view of the hierarchy of being next to the above-mentioned instances[2].

---

[1] *Die Vorbereitung des Neuplatonismus* (*Problemata*, Forschungen zur klassischen Philologie, Heft 1, Berlin, 1930), p. 56: "ein besonderes Kennzeichen der albinischen Darstellung ist die Steigerung des Gottesbegriffs".

[2] In my opinion Dr. Witt, *loc. cit.*, stated erroneously that according to Albinus

PLATONISM AND NEOPLATONISM

I come to my second main subject: Plato. Is it true that Plato merely drew the distinction between a sensible and a suprasensible world, while Plotinus – say, to a certain degree, other thinkers before him–was, strictly speaking, the author of the four-storeyed hierarchy of being and the theory of its emanation from the first principle?

I do not think this view is right. Our first point to be noted is: at the end of the sixth book of the *Republic*[1] Plato ranges mathematical objects as an intermediate sphere between the pure Intelligibles and the sensible world. That this was his doctrine, is explicitly confirmed by Aristotle in *Metaph.*, A 6[2].

Now, in the same passage, Aristotle is concerned with Plato's theory of first principles. There can be no doubt as to the point whether Plato did or did not hold such a doctrine[3]. The texts, not only of Aristotle, but also of some other independent witnesses[4], are decisive. What do they mean? I treated the question at length in my *Problems concerning later Platonism*, published in the Dutch review *Mnemosyne*, 1949. My results are the following.

(1) Plato apparently admitted a hierarchical order in his intelligible World, not only in the sense that higher Forms were to be ranged above the inferior ones, as genera above their species; but again, above the Forms ideal Numbers were placed, to which, according to Theophrastus' testimony[5], the Ideas were "reduced".

(2) At the top of this whole intelligible world Plato placed the One, which seems to have been identified by him with the Good[6].

the Celestial noûs does not "emanate" from the Transcendent. Why does it "emanate" in the later construction of Avicenna, and not in the – somewhat simpler – construction of Albinus? Dr. Witt complains that by the duplication nothing is gained. One has the impression that he would have been satisfied, if only Albinus had spoken of the One instead of the first Noûs. Now Avicenna does place the One as first Principle above the Noûs; but it is interesting to see that, nevertheless, he wants a first Noûs, which is perfectly one, above the Intelligence of the first celestial sphere. And indeed he has good reasons to do so.

[1] 509d-511e.

[2] 987 b 14-18.

[3] H. Cherniss, *The Riddle of the Early Academy*, tried to defend the opposite thesis. See my *Problems concerning later Platonism*, Mnemosyne, 1949, pp. 197-197-216, 299-318 (ch. XII of the present volume).

[4] *Hermodorus* and the so-called Pythagorean source of Sextus, *Math.* X, 363 ff. (De Vogel, *Gr. Ph.*, nr. 371 a, b).

[5] *Metaph.*, 6 b 11-14 (Ross-Fobes); DV., *Gr. Ph.*, nr. 373.

[6] The most important testimony is that of Aristoxenus, *Harm. Elem.*, II, p. 30 M. (DV., *Gr. Ph.*, 364c.).

(3) He assumed another primary principle, the polar opposite of the One, called the indefinite Dyad, or the Great-and-small, which is schematically to be placed beneath the αἰσθητά[1].

Thus we get a scheme in which both at the top and at the bottom a point is to be placed, the One and the Great-and-small both being ἄρρητα. Between these points three hierarchic spheres must be distinguished: (1) the intelligible world (Forms-Numbers); (2) the mathematical objects; (3) the sensible world.

The only point on which there could be any doubt is the question of the relation of Forms and Numbers. Is it true that Plato admitted his ideal Numbers as a principle superior to his Forms, or do we have to regard those Numbers as identical with Forms? I think there are almost categorical reasons for accepting the first thesis. Very shortly put, they are the following:

(1) All our texts that seem to speak of a simple identification of Forms and Numbers admit of my interpretation. I mean: even if Numbers are a superior principle, Forms can, in a sense, be called Numbers, and Numbers Forms.

(2) There are no texts, then, that contradict this interpretation.

(3) We have the explicit testimony of Theophrastus for it.

(4) The fact that Plato's Ideas were undeniably far more numerous than his ideal Numbers (2-10), almost excludes another explanation.

As to the place of the first principles, the One and the indefinite Dyad, no doubt is possible. Our conclusion can, then, hardly be any other than that Plato in his later years taught a system of philosophy which was marked especially by the doctrine of a hierarchy of being. By this doctrine he proves to be the legitimate ancestor of Plotinus and of Neoplatonism in general; and, because this view of the universe is generally considered as specifically Neoplatonic, we are tempted to express the situation, as we found it, in this way:

The studies of the last generations concerning the sense of later Platonism, and especially of the doctrine of ideal Numbers, has led us to the insight that Platonism must be understood in a Neoplatonic sense, and that Neoplatonism should be regarded, in its essence, as a legitimate Platonism.

In writing this, my first thought is of L. Robin, who, by his work *La théorie platonicienne des Idées et des Nombres d'après Aristote* (1908), was the first to arrive at this result. At the seventh International Congress of Philosophy, held at Oxford in 1930, H. Gomperz stated

---

[1] The reader will find the essential texts concerning the question of the Ideal Numbers and the doctrine of the first principles in my *Gr. Ph.*, nrs. 362-373.

that Platonic studies had developed in this direction. A vigorous reaction has come a few years ago from the side of Harold Cherniss. He tries to eliminate the whole doctrine of the ideal Numbers, including that of the first principles; and this by showing that there are contradictions and misunderstandings in Aristotle's account of Plato's doctrine. For this reason, he concludes, Aristotle's testimony is altogether worthless. It is clear that, even if we granted the first point (and in fact, there are contradictions and misunderstandings in Aristotle's account, though perhaps not in the measure Cherniss thinks there are), the second point does not necessarily follow. Moreover, it is confirmed by other witnesses. The efforts of Cherniss, therefore, cannot be accepted as successful[1].

Our next point is: in what do the Dialogues, especially the later ones, of Plato alter or complete the above indicated outline of Plato's doctrine. By no means do we intend to say by these words that we wish to start exclusively from texts of Aristotle and some other contemporary or even later authors in order to define Plato's doctrine. We did not make abstraction from Plato's own works. But having their contents in our mind, we found some undeniable indications coming forth from those who heard his lectures, by which certain points, only vaguely foreshadowed in the later Dialogues, were shown to us in a clearer light. So now we have to turn again to these later works of Plato. An important question which here presents itself to us, is: what is the place of the soul in Plato's hierarchy of being?

It has been remarked by several modern Plato-scholars, that the doctrine of the soul takes a more important place in the later Dialogues. In the *Phaedrus* for the first time, soul is defined by Plato as the self-moving principle. And this principle is vindicated with the utmost vigour in *Laws* X, where the existence of at least two souls is required, one of which is able to cause good things in the universe, the other to cause evil[2]. Some interpreters[3] have even inferred that, in his later years, Plato had abandoned his theory of Ideas and had replaced it by a theory of souls. Now this interpretation is definitely erroneous. First, Plato did not give up his theory of Ideas, as might be seen from

---

[1] I have been very glad to see that, in his recently published volume on Plato's Theory of the Ideas, Sir David Ross came over to Robin's interpretation of the place of Ideal Numbers, which was defended by me in *Studia Vollgraff* (1948) and in *Problems concerning later Platonism*.
[2] 896a-897a.
[3] Lutoslawsky, who is followed by Fr. Solmsen.

the beginning of the *Timaeus*[1], and again from the last pages of the *Laws*[2]. Further, granted that the definition of soul as the self-moving principle appears first in the *Phaedrus*, we should remember that it has always been a first principle of Plato's philosophy that soul is superior to body. We have only to mention the *Crito* and the *Phaedo* to be convinced of this.

So we repeat our question: where in Plato's hierarchy of being is the place of soul? One reply only seems possible, even though the author did not state it explicitly, namely that soul is to be ranked between the sensible and the intelligible World. Indeed, the inference is unavoidable, once accepted that soul is superior to body, and at the same time that it is no Idea, though more akin to the intelligible than to the material world. Now this is exactly what is said in the well-known passage concerning the division into two realms of being in the *Phaedo*[3]; and some reflection on Plato's mythos about the origin of the soul in the *Timaeus* does not allow us to say that the theory of the *Phaedo* is contradicted by this later view. On the contrary, all we can possibly infer from this account, is that it strengthens the author's position known from the *Phaedo* and from several other dialogues. For the νοητόν, as it is called in *Timaeus* 48e (a passage which summarises the division into an intelligible and a sensible world, made in 27d-28a), is clearly meant as the archetypal world, according to which the sensible cosmos is made by the Demiurge[4]. But the Demiurge, composing the elements and giving its spherical form to the cosmos, gives it a soul, doubtless to make it ὅμοιον τῷ παντελεῖ ζῴῳ[5]. For this is obviously its highest honour, since "the Father who generated it" is said to rejoice when He saw that the world had become a moving and living ἄγαλμα[6]. It is always the same principle that meets us: soul is superior to body, it is the principle of motion and the characteristic of life. As such, then, it ranks higher than matter, while the soul which is immanent in the cosmos is as such of a lower stage than the intelligible World.

A new problem might present itself here to the reader, namely: if,

---

[1] 28a.
[2] *Laws*, XII, 965 bc.
[3] 79a-d.
[4] 28c-29a.
[5] The words stand in 31b, giving the reason why the Demiurge makes one cosmos only; but they could stand here too. *Cf.* 37d.
[6] 37d.

then, the intelligible World is viewed by Plato as a living being[1], which has a soul and thinking-power (νοῦς), do we not have to infer (1) that, according to Plato, soul pervades also the intelligible World, and (2) that soul seems to be primary, while νοῦς (the power of thinking) is one of its functions?[2]

Indeed, the παντελῶς ὄν is described by Plato[3] as having motion and life, soul and insight (φρόνησις) or thinking-power (νοῦς), and it is added explicitly that, if it has thinking-power and life, it is hardly imaginable in another way than ἐν ψυχῇ.

To this point we have to observe: first, that the terminology of Plato is not fixed in the way it is in Plotinus; second, that, in spite of differences in terminology, an essential agreement in basic views between them must be stated. Let us try, then, to show what is Plato's view in the above-cited passage of the *Sophist* and how it agrees with that of the *Timaeus* and elsewhere, where the soul seemed to take an intermediate place. Two points must be noted. First: doubtless, the soul which is immanent in the sensible world, and still more that which is incorporated in man, takes, according to Plato, an intermediate place between matter (body) and the Intelligible. Second: Plato speaks also of "soul" concerning his intelligible World. He does so, exclusively when he is regarding the archetypal world of Ideas as a whole, a real *cosmos*. This archetypal World is perfect, eternal Being. Viewed as a whole it is, therefore, the παντελῶς ὄν; and as such it cannot be thought of otherwise than as a living being. Now the very characteristic of a living being is that it has a soul; and the highest function of soul is: thinking. We should not abuse this unusual terminology. Indeed, Plato's view is clear: his intelligible World is superior to what we call the world-soul and the individual soul. It is superior, therefore, at least to the lower aspect of soul in Plotinus, which is immanent. It is nearer, yet superior, too, to Plotinus' higher aspect of soul[4], which is not

---

[1] My reference is to *Tim.* 31 a 8-b 3 : ἵνα οὖν τόδε κατὰ τὴν μόνωσιν ὅμοιον ᾖ τῷ παντελεῖ ζῴῳ, διὰ ταῦτα οὔτε δύο οὔτ' ἀπείρους ἐποίησεν ὁ ποιῶν κόσμους, etc., and 37 d 1-3: καθάπερ οὖν αὐτὸ τυγχάνει ζῷον ἀΐδιον ὄν, καὶ τόδε τὸ πᾶν οὕτως εἰς δύναμιν ἐπεχείρησε τοιοῦτον ἀποτελεῖν.

[2] The last point is strongly urged by H. J. M. Loenen in a thesis on the meaning of νοῦς in Plato's philosophy, which appeared at Amsterdam, 1951.

[3] *Soph.*, 248 e - 249 b.

[4] *Enn.*, IV, 9, 1: Εἰ δὲ καὶ ἡ τοῦ παντὸς καὶ ἡ ἐμὴ ἐκ ψυχῆς μιᾶς –, and 9, 4: μίαν καὶ τὴν αὐτὴν ἐν πολλοῖς σώμασι ψυχὴν ὑπάρχειν καὶ πρὸ ταύτης τῆς μιᾶς τῆς ἐν πολλοῖς ἄλλην αὖ εἶναι μὴ ἐν πολλοῖς, ἀφ' ἧς ἡ ἐν πολλοῖς μία.

immanent but αὐτὴ ἐφ' ἑαυτῆς[1]. For this too, which is called "one" and "whole", is *soul* and as such dependent on the higher region of *noûs*, the existence of a hierarchy in the first being explained by the existence of a hierarchical order in the latter[2]. This, then, being established, we have proved enough, as to this point, for our thesis.

One other question should be raised concerning the place of soul in Plato. Mathematical objects, according to his teaching, took the intermediate place, which now seems to have been taken by soul. What, then, is the relation of the one to the other?

To this question as far as I can see Plato did not reply directly. This much, however, is sure, that his direct disciples raised the question and answered it in their own way. Their answer is for us instructive: both Speusippus and Xenocrates prove to have drawn the conclusion that soul belongs to the sphere of mathematical objects, Speusippus by defining it as space or extension (τὸ πάντῃ διαστατόν)[3], Xenocrates as self-moving number[4].

Our final question relative to Plato's conception of the hierarchy of being, concerns the first Principle: τὸ ἕν. Does our view of Platonism necessarily presuppose that interpretation of the first deduction in the second part of Plato's *Parmenides* (I Aa according to my scheme, A1M1 according to that of Professor Ryle) which is judged by Ryle as illicit? I mean: that interpretation which takes this deduction as a description of the first hypostasis of Plotinus.

It is clear that my above-expounded view of the hierarchy of being according to Plato was not based at all on this interpretation of the *Parmenides*. But I will not evade the question whether or not such an interpretation is legitimate. Well, I do not think that Plato started with the intention of describing in his first deduction that most elevated principle of being which he accepted, at least finally, himself. What he did in his *Parmenides*, was something different, and far more simple. It was nothing else than what he said it was: tracing the

---

[1] *Enn.*, IV, 3, 2 (at the end): Εἰ δὴ οὕτως ἐπὶ ψυχῆς τῆς τε ὅλης καὶ τῶν ἄλλων, οὐκ ἂν ἡ ὅλη, ἧς τὰ τοιαῦτα μέρη, ἔσται τινός, ἀλλ' αὐτὴ ἐφ' ἑαυτῆς· οὐ τοίνυν οὐδὲ τοῦ κόσμου, ἀλλά τις καὶ αὕτη τῶν ἐν μέρει.
[2] *Enn.*, IV, 3, ch. 6-8.
[3] Speusippus is mentioned by Iamblichus (ap. *Stob.*, I, 49, 32, p. 363, 26W.) among τοὺς εἰς μαθηματικὴν οὐσίαν ἐντιθέντας τὴν οὐσίαν τῆς ψυχῆς, and he adds that Speus. defined it ἐν ἰδέᾳ τοῦ πάντῃ διαστατοῦ (Speusippus, fr. 40 Lang).
[4] Plutarch, *De animi procreatione* 1, p. 1012d, says that X. declared the essence of soul to be ἀριθμὸν αὐτὸν ὑφ' ἑαυτοῦ κινούμενον (Xenocr. fr. 68 Heinze).

consequences of the hypothesis εἰ ἕν ἐστιν with regard to the one itself[1], the notion of "one" being taken in the absolute sense. Originally, and taken in its first intention, it is not a "description" of any kind of being at all.

But, as I have expounded elsewhere[2], by his merely logical deductions, Plato is led to concrete reality: as soon as τὰ ἄλλα are introduced, we begin to "see". We see "other things" opposed to "the One". And in this act of opposing the one to the other, the "other things" are thought immediately as a whole which has parts, and therefore takes part in "the one", though it is distinguished from it. Thus, many combinations of concepts have become possible. And, though in this case (I B) too the notion of "one" may be taken in an absolute sense, so that no combination with other concepts is possible, yet this antithesis belongs to a void philosophy of words, while the thesis brings us into another province: a philosophy of contents.

By this fact the notion of one taken in the absolute sense, is practically proved to be a limit: our thinking forms it necessarily, but we are not able to make any further use of it.

May we then say that it is the Plotinian One? I repeat: it was not the author's intention to give a description of anything; it was his intention to make logical deductions. But the philosophy of words led him on to a philosophy of contents: the "one" in its relative position gave rise to various combinations of concepts (I A b and I B a) and implied necessarily a link with non-being (II A a). When in the thesis of the fourth antinomy (II B a) the consequences are deduced from the hypothesis of the "one non-being" taken in the relative sense, with regard to the "other things", we observe these "other things" taking almost a concrete aspect, so much so that it is hardly possible to deny their existence in the world of human experience. But, if then in the fourth antinomy the "other things" obtain this real sense, don't we have the right, and perhaps even the duty, of turning our eyes back to the first antinomy and asking ourselves which was, in fact, the

---

[1] I maintain the translation "the one", against the somewhat too categorical assertion of Ryle that the term "unity" is the true and only equivalent of the Greek τὸ ἕν. Ryle is perfectly right in observing that Plato often speaks of τὸ δίκαιον where we should use the term "justice". Yet, it is not a question of chance that such expressions like τὸ δίκαιον, τὸ ἀγαθόν, etc., are frequently used by him. When he says, e.g. that τὸ δίκαιον really exists, could the term be exchanged for δικαιοσύνη? I do not think so.

[2] *Een keerpunt in Plato's denken (A crisis in Plato's thought)*, pp. 151-160.

meaning of "the one" in absolute, and next of the one in relative position?

I think it is legitimate to do so. Now, this is what the Neoplatonic interpreters did. Were they wrong? I do not think we have the right to answer in the affirmative.

Our third, and last, subject concerns the intermediate stages between Plato and the Platonism of the first centuries of our era. This is, again, a difficult and hotly debated question. W. Theiler defended the thesis that, in reaction to the scepticism which had penetrated into the Academy, Antiochus of Ascalon, who tried to restore the Platonism of the early Academy, resuscitated the theory of transcendent Ideas by giving them a fresh signification, namely by interpreting the Ideas as thoughts of God. According to Theiler this interpretation is found in the Stoic allegories about the gods, where the Ideas are identified with Minerva, who is born from the head of Jupiter[1]. Seneca makes it his own in one of his Letters[2], where he says, speaking of the Ideas: "Haec exemplaria omnium rerum deus inter se habet". In the second century, we find it again in Albinus.

Now it is, indeed, a highly attractive hypothesis, to make Antiochus, the man who wished to restore the Platonism of the early Academy, the author of this theory. An argument for this attribution might be found in the fact that Varro, who was acquainted with Antiochus and heard his lectures, held the same view as that which is found in the Stoic allegoric writers[3].

Theiler finds another argument in the conception of the logos as instrument (indicated by the formula δι' οὗ). Of this idea, familiar to us by Philo, he finds a trace in Seneca[4], and concludes that it must find its origin in an older Greek source. In fact, this argument is less strong than the preceding one, because, strictly speaking, the "organic cause" (δι' οὗ), which is mentioned by Porphyry and by Proclus as a

---

[1] Thus in Heraclitus' 'Ομηρικαὶ ἀλληγορίαι, a Stoic work of Augustus' era, and in the handbook of Cornutus, in which Athena is called ἡ τοῦ Διὸς σύνεσις, ἡ αὐτὴ οὖσα τῇ ἐν αὐτῷ προνοίᾳ.
[2] *Ep.* 65, 7.
[3] Varro, cited by St. Augustine, *De Civ. Dei*, VII, 28, explained Jupiter = the heavens, Juno = earth, and Minerva = the Ideas, and adds to this: "caelum *a quo* fiat aliquid (the efficient cause), terram *de qua* fiat (the material cause), exemplum *secundum quod* fiat" (exemplary cause).
[4] *Ep.* 65, 8, 13.

special cause next to the παράδειγμα (called πρὸς ὅ or δι' ὅ)¹, does not occur in the cited passage of Seneca². What is said in this place is that the "example" (the Ideas) is *not properly a cause, but only the necessary instrument of a cause.* By which the author qualifies the *id ad quod*, mentioned by him³ as one of the five causes he attributes to Plato, as a subordinate cause. He does not introduce a sixth cause, as is done later by Porphyry.

But, even if we grant that Seneca offers a parallel with Philo, who calls the logos "the instrument through which the world was made"⁴, a serious objection to Theiler's suggestion of making Antiochus the author of this view arises from what we know further concerning Antiochus' teaching about the Ideas. The essential point is: did Antiochus, or did he not re-introduce the transcendent Ideas of Plato? Is it compatible with our further evidence that he did, then Theiler may be right in holding that it was Antiochus who first explained the Ideas as the thoughts of God and the instrument by which the sensible world was made. However, if our further evidence concerning Antiochus tells us that he did not accept the existence of transcendent Ideas, then the suggestion of Theiler appears to be erroneous.

Starting, then, from Varro's account in Cicero's *Acad.* I, and that of Lucullus in *Acad.* IV (*Lucullus*), we find two main points well established. (1) Antiochus separated himself from the New Academy, which had turned to scepticism, and wished to go back to the early Academy⁵. By this return he meant explicitly to restore dogmatism⁶.

(2) He did not see the least difference between the Academy and early Peripatetics: he calls it "one form of philosophy under two names"⁷. By "Peripatetics" he means chiefly Aristotle, Theophrastus

---

¹ Porphyry, cited by Simpl., in *Ar. Phys.*, 184, 11, says: Τετραχῶς οὖν ἡ ἀρχὴ κατὰ τὸν Ἀριστοτέλην· ἢ γὰρ τὸ ἐξ οὗ ὡς ἡ ὕλη ὅλη ἢ τὸ καθ' ὃ ὡς τὸ εἶδος ἢ τὸ ὑφ' οὗ ὡς τὸ ποιοῦν ἢ τὸ δι' ὃ ὡς τὸ τέλος· κατὰ δὲ Πλάτωνα καὶ τὸ πρὸς ὃ ὡς τὸ παράδειγμα καὶ τὸ δι' οὗ ὡς τὸ ὀργανικόν. Elsewhere Simpl. calls the organikon a synaition. Proclus in *Tim.* calls the paradigma sometimes δι' ὅ (telos), sometimes δι' οὗ (organon).

² *Ep.* 65, 13: Exemplar quoque non est causa, sed instrumentum causae necessarium.

³ *Ibid.*, 8: Quinque ergo causae sunt, ut Plato dicit: id *ex quo*, id *a quo*, id *in quo*, id *ad quod*, id *propter quod*.

⁴ Philo, *Cherub.*, 125ff.: God is the αἴτιον ὑφ' οὗ, ὕλην δὲ τὰ τέσσαρα στοιχεῖα ἐξ ὧν συνεκράθη, ὄργανον δὲ λόγον θεοῦ δι' οὗ κατεσκευάσθη.

⁵ *Ac.*, I, 13.

⁶ *Luc.*, 29.

⁷ *Ac.*, I, 17: una et consentiens duobus vocabulis philosophiae forma instituta

373

only as far as he agrees with the former, and later Peripatetics, such as Strato, are by him altogether excluded[1]. Stoicism is viewed by Antiochus as a correction of the doctrine of the Academy (Zeno was a disciple of Polemo)[2].

Thus we can expect beforehand that Antiochus will try to give a "philosophy of synthesis". Evidently, our first question is: did Antiochus really restore the theory of transcendent Ideas? *Could* he even do so, according to his own principles? Was he not, by these very principles, reduced to giving a non-Platonic version of the Idea, making it an immanent eidos, immanent in our mind and in individual things (as Aristotle does), and again, immanent in the cosmos as a whole (according to Stoicism)? It is clear that, in this last sense, if the cosmos be called a god (a conception which is Stoic, and even Platonic), this god has "the ideas" in his mind. And from this view to allegorising the deities of popular religion, is but a small step: "God" – the Universe (Zeus) has the "ideas" in his mind (Athena).

Now this is exactly what we see in Antiochus. When he is describing the "Platonic philosophy", he treats nature as his second point (the first being ethics), and begins by dividing it into two parts (*res duas*): the one the active principle, the other passive, both forming an inseparable unity, which is body and a qualified substance (*quasi qualitatem quandam nominabant*). From this "quality" the five elements come forth, and from these, clinging together and forming a continuity, the Universe is made which is one and includes all being (*extra quem nulla pars materiae sit nullumque corpus*)[3]. In it is perfect Reason (*ratio perfecta*), which is eternal. It is also called world-soul (*animus mundi*), and Spirit and perfect Wisdom (*mentem sapientiamque perfectam*), which they call god, a certain rational Power which takes care first of the heavenly bodies (*quasi prudentiam quandam procurantem caelestia maxime*), next on earth those things which regard man (*deinde in terris ea quae pertineant ad homines*). Sometimes they call this Power Necessity too, because nothing could happen otherwise

est Academicorum et Peripateticorum, qui rebus congruentes nominibus differebant.

[1] *Ac.*, I, 33-34.
[2] *Ibid.*, 34-35.
[3] The whole passage, *Ac.*, I, 24-29, must be compared with Diog. Laert., VII, 134-139 (*Gr. Ph.* 899a), where nature is divided into two parts, τὸ ποιοῦν καὶ τὸ πάσχον, the first of which is called ποιόν, the latter ἄποιον. The active principle, ποιόν (*qualitas* in Cic.) is God and Spirit (νοῦς), Fate (εἱμαρμένη) and Zeus. It is eternal, and perpetually building everything (δημιουργεῖν ἕκαστα).

than was determined by this Power; and sometimes it is called Chance (*fortunam appellant*).

It can be seen at a glance that we are in pure Stoicism here. And are we not here, in fact, very near to Varro's allegory of Jupiter = the heavens, Juno = earth, and Minerva = the ideas or thoughts of God? Dr. Witt writes[1]: "Regarded as the Universe, the Deity is Zeus. Regarded as the guiding Reason of the Universe, the Deity is Athene. They are one in virtue of their corporeality." And he concludes[2]: "If, then, Antiochus retained the name Idea, it meant to him exactly what πρόνοια meant to the Stoics, and it meant no more."

But let us follow for a moment Antiochus' account of Platonism. In *Ac.* I, 30, Varro comes to the theory of knowledge. Though our knowledge begins with the senses, he states, yet judgment is a question, not of the senses, but of mind. Mind alone is the judge of things, because it only sees "what is always simple and in one way, and such as it is" ("this they called ἰδέα, by a name given to it by Plato; and we may justly call it *species*").

Now this "species", he continues somewhat further on[3], was first attacked and shaken by Aristotle. The statement is put in these words: "Aristotle was the first to shake these above-mentioned species, to which Plato had clung extraordinarily (*quas mirifice Plato erat amplexatus*), so that he saw something divine in them." Theiler[4] tries to convince us that Antiochus himself "clung" to the "species" of Plato, since in the following lines he qualifies the doctrine of Theophrast as a "further corruption" (*vehementius etiam fregit quodam modo auctoritatem veteris disciplinae*). By no means does he himself wish to break the authority of the "ancients". Doubtless, this last remark is right; but I am afraid the author forgets that, in fact, what Antiochus calls "vetus disciplina" is not the doctrine of transcendent Ideas as we know it from the Dialogues of Plato, but an Aristotelised and even stoicised Platonism. It must be said that, in this very passage of the *Acad. Pr.*, one does not get the impression that Antiochus himself was inclined "to see something divine" in the species to which Plato clung so extraordinarily.

We are strengthened in this view by the other passage in the

---

[1] *Albinus*, p. 72.
[2] *Ibid.*, 73.
[3] I, 33.
[4] In his review of Witt's *Albinus*, Gnomon XV (1939), p. 105: "Antiochus wollte die *vetus disciplina* wiederherstellen".

Academics, where an account is given of Antiochus' teaching concerning human knowledge: *Lucullus* 10, 30. This account, again, is purely Stoic. The author does not know anything about transcendent Ideas; he only knows about the κοιναὶ ἔννοιαι or προλήψεις, which, according to the Stoics, are formed in the human mind as a kind of sediment of various experiences.

On the whole, the impression of Antiochus which we obtain from these texts, agrees perfectly with the qualification of Cicero, who declares[1]: *erat quidem si perpauca mutavisset, germanissimus Stoicus*. The essential point, in which he differs from the Stoa, is obviously not the doctrine of the Ideas, but, as A. M. Lueder pointed out in her thesis on Antiochus[2], it lies in ethics and anthropology: Antiochus protested against the extreme intellectualism of the Stoa and, opposing his doctrine of the *tota natura*, he did not regard virtue as the only good.

I conclude. No doubt Antiochus marks a stage in the development of Ideas between Plato and Neoplatonism. He can be said to have prepared Neoplatonism, so far as he returned from scepticism to positive doctrine and strove to make a synthesis of Plato, Aristotle and the Stoa. On the other hand, as he did not restore the transcendent character of the Ideas, it must be stated that he was essentially a Stoic.

However, Antiochus is by no means the only person to be mentioned here. The Porch itself had, almost in the same period, a great teacher who admitted Platonic and Aristotelian elements into his doctrine: Posidonius of Apamea. That Plotinus was deeply influenced by Posidonius' doctrine of "cosmic sympathy", is a point which has been noticed by Werner Jaeger[3] and Karl Reinhardt[4]. Others tried to deny this influence[5]. Now, on this point, the argumentation of Theiler[6] is decisive: there can be no doubt about the reality of Posidonius' influence on Plotinus and on later Neoplatonic writers (Proclus, Philoponus, Simplicius, Damascius), as well as on the later Stoics: Seneca, Epictetus, and most of all Marcus Aurelius with his principle of cosmic κοινωνία.

[1] *Luc.*, 43, 132.
[2] *Die philosophische Persönlichkeit des Antiochos von Askalon*, Göttingen, 1940.
[3] *Nemesios von Emesa* (1914).
[4] *Kosmos und Sympathie* (1926).
[5] Nebel, *Plotins Kategorien der internen Welt* (Heidelb. Abhandl. zur Philos., 18, p. 23), writes: "Ich glaube nicht an die schöpferische Vermittlungsrolle des Poseidonios". Also Fr. Heinemann, *Plotin* (Leipzig, 1921).
[6] *Vorbereitung des Neuplat.*, Ch. II and III.

So we have come back to the first half of the first century in following the traces that lead from Neoplatonism back to the Platonism of the early Academy.

And this early Academy itself? The Platonism of Speusippus and Xenocrates, of Polemon and Crates? In itself it may not seem so very interesting to us, late and severe observers. Admirers of Plato, and perhaps of Plotinus too, we may have passed over these direct disciples of Plato with a certain air of superiority. But here, on our way back from Neoplatonism to Plato, here it is that they prove to be interesting. This much, in any case, is sure, that Speusippus and Xenocrates, holding the Master's doctrine of first principles, taught a certain hierarchy of being[1]. It has been the merit of the late professor Ph. Merlan, to have pointed to this in his *Beiträge zur Geschichte des antiken Platonismus*, in *Philologus*, 1934[2], an early work of the author, who later took the same subject up in his work *From Platonism to Neoplatonism*[3]. Merlan concluded his earlier study by the following words:

> "As to Neoplatonic Platonism, this is general in the second century: with Albinus, Apuleius and the writer of the commentary on the *Theaetetus*. Whether or not this is influenced by Poseidonius, this much is sure, that this was also the Platonism of the Early Academy of Speusippus and Xenocrates. Certain is also that this goes back to Plato's oral teaching, much more than to his dialogues."

I hope to have made clear in the preceding part of this paper that, in the Dialogues too, some clear and undeniable traces can be found of this "Neoplatonic Platonism".

---

[1] As to Speusippus, this may be seen in Aristotle's *Metaph.*, Z, 1028b16-24: of Xenocrates, see the fragments 5, 15 and 68 Heinze.
[2] It is the Second part of the *Beiträge*, entitled *Poseidonios über die Weltseele in Platons Timaios* (*Philologus*, 89) (1934), pp. 197-214.
[3] The Hague 1953.

CHAPITRE XVI

LA THÉORIE DE L'ἌΠΕΙΡΟΝ CHEZ PLATON ET DANS LA TRADITION PLATONICIENNE[1]

Platon a exposé sa théorie de l'ἄπειρον dans le *Philèbe*[2]: c'est le principe indéfini opposé au πέρας. C'est de la mixtion de ces deux que provient le γιγνόμενον, qui est le μεικτὸν γένος. Et comme cause de la mixtion Platon admet un quatrième principe, nommé simplement l'αἴτιον. L'ἄπειρον est expliqué de la manière suivante.

Tout ce qui possède des degrés d'intensité, du μᾶλλον καὶ ἧττον, du σφόδρα καὶ ἠρέμα, du «plus ou moins», non pas de quantité limitée, appartient à la classe de l'ἄπειρον. Ce sont des choses qui se trouvent dans un mouvement perpétuel entre deux extrêmes: le chaud et le froid, le grand et le petit, le large et l'étroit, etc., sans jamais trouver de repos. Car tout arrêt signifierait de la mesure et de la quantité limitée, le ποσόν et le μέτριον, qui appartiennent au πέρας, par exemple le principe d'égalité, l'ἴσον, et le nombre entier.

Or, si un de ces principes, soit l'ἴσον, soit le διπλάσιον, est introduit dans l'Illimité (l'ἄπειρον), il en résulte quelque chose (γενέσεις τινὰς συμβαίνειν): par exemple, dans les maladies, la juste communication des deux principes, du πέρας et de l'ἄπειρον, fait surgir la bonne santé; dans le haut et le bas, le vite et le lent, qui sont illimités, des principes de limitation introduits en juste mesure produiront de la musique; et ainsi de suite, par exemple de la beauté et de la force dans les corps et beaucoup de bonnes qualités dans les âmes.

Quelques pages plus loin[3], Platon parle de l'âme du monde visible et dit que le νοῦς, qui en gouvernant ce monde y produit et maintient l'ordre, appartient au quatrième genre qui est: la Cause. Enfin, ce qui

---

[1] Ce chapitre reproduit le texte d'un exposé fait le 2 mai 1958 au Centre de Recherches sur la Pensée antique de la Faculté des Lettres de Paris. Il fut publié dans la *Revue philosophique* de la France et de l'Étranger 1959, nr. 1, Presses Universitaires de France). Un seul passage a été entièrement ré-écrit.
[2] La théorie des quatre principes: *Phil.* 23 c - 26 c.
[3] 30 a-e.

n'est pas sans intérêt, c'est que la possibilité d'introduire un cinquième principe est admise[1].

Tout cela n'est pas encore trop difficile. Si le principe de Mesure, d'Égalité et de Nombre appartient à la nature du πέρας, il faudra conclure que ce principe déterminant n'est autre que le monde des Idées, par la participation auquel les choses concrètes sont ce qu'elles sont. Il est clair ensuite que, pour expliquer l'existence des choses concrètes, Platon a besoin d'un principe illimité, qui sera nommé par Aristote: le principe matériel. C'est l'ἄπειρον, expliqué ici comme éternel procédé sans terminus et décrit, d'après ce qu'il semble, comme principe immanent des choses. Puis, il y a l'ordre de la Cause. Elle est en tout cas supérieure à la «mixture», c'est-à-dire au monde du devenir, donc: aux choses matérielles et concrètes.

Tout cela va bien. Les difficultés surgissent dès qu'on compare les quatre principes du *Philèbe* à ceux du *Timée*. Évidemment, dans l'ὄν du *Timée* 27d-28a, qui est toujours identique à lui-même, on reconnaît le monde des idées ou les νοητά que nous venons d'identifier au πέρας du *Philèbe*, tandis que le γιγνόμενον, c'est-à-dire les αἰσθητά, ne saurait être autre chose que le μεικτὸν γένος. Dans le *Timée*, Platon parle encore d'un «troisième principe» (49a), qualifié comme une «espèce vague» et par là difficile à expliquer. En soi, ce troisième principe ne possède aucune qualité. Il est décrit comme l'espace dans lequel les choses se forment – τὸ ἐν ᾧ γίγνεται – comme δεχόμενον ou πανδεχές, et comparé à la mère. Or, cela veut dire, d'après les idées que les Grecs se font de l'origine d'un être humain, que le τρίτον γένος du *Timée* n'est nullement un principe immanent égal à l'ἄπειρον du *Philèbe*.

Il faut en rester ici: d'une part, certes, le τρίτον γένος du *Timée* doit être comparé au principe illimité du *Philèbe*. Tout comme celui-ci, il est «indéfini» dans le sens de non qualifié. D'autre part, il faut faire attention à la différence: l'ἄπειρον du *Philèbe* est un principe constituteur qui entre dans les choses qui deviennent; la χώρα du *Timée* reste un principe extérieur. Elle ne livre que le cadre dans lequel les choses se forment. Certes, on comprend bien qu'Aristote a traité les deux en «principe matériel». Qu'aurait-il dû faire autrement de son point de vue à lui? Mais cela ne change rien à l'état des choses: c'est que la description du «principe matériel» du *Philèbe* n'est point conforme à celle du principe semblable dans le *Timée*.

Quant à l'αἰτία, il y a d'autres difficultés – non insolubles, à mon avis, mais discutables en tout cas. Il s'agit de la relation du Démiurge,

[1] 23e.

qui (d'après le *Timée* 29d) est un Esprit transcendant, et, d'autre part, le νοῦς de l'âme du monde dont parle le *Philèbe* (30a-d). On a voulu[1] identifier le Démiurge au Principe suprême, nommé le Bien dans la *République*[2], qui, là aussi, est traité de Cause ultime de tout être, tandis que **le νοῦς de** l'âme du monde, lui, serait (à un niveau inférieur) la cause directe de l'ordre dans le monde visible. Inutile ainsi, nous disent ces interprétateurs, d'introduire un «Noûs transcendant» – qui serait le Démiurge du *Timée* – entre le principe suprême (l'Agathon) et le noûs de l'âme du monde, qui est un noûs immanent. Le Démiurge, c'est le bon Principe, cause suprême de tout être spirituel (âme avec son noûs) et par là de tout ordre. Donc – puisqu'il n'y a point question d'autre principe dans le *Timée* – le bon Principe nommé le Démiurge ne saurait être autre chose que le Bien de la *République*.

A cette interprétation – assez plausible en soi, surtout pour ceux qui sont habitués à l'idée d'un Dieu suprême Créateur – s'oppose seulement la formule catégorique de Platon dans le passage cité de la *République* qui dit que le Bien lui-même *n'est pas d'être*, donc pas d'être spirituel, pas de νοῦς non plus, mais ἐπέκεινα τῆς οὐσίας. Il faudra bien s'y faire: le Démiurge du *Timée*, noûs transcendant d'après la claire indication du texte, ne saurait être identique au Principe suprême de la *République*. Donc, ce ne sera pas Albinus qui aura raison en expliquant le Principe suprême comme «premier Noûs Démiurge»[3]. Ce sera plutôt Plotin. Car, si le Principe suprême est au-dessus de l'être et de la pensée, cela veut dire incontestablement que l'Être dans le sens plein, l'être parfait et spirituel, c'est les νοητά. Ensuite, il faudra nous rappeler *Soph.* 248e-249a, le passage sur le παντελῶς ὄν: l'être dans le sens plein du mot ne saurait exister sans vie spirituelle, sans âme et esprit et sans sagesse. Voilà ce que nous dit Platon. J'en ai conclu autre part[4] que l'être qui est l'objet de l'intellection, l'Être intelligible donc (dont il s'agit dans le passage cité), se trouve représenté ici comme un Esprit vivant. Et il faudra reconnaître que cela n'est pas tellement étrange, au contraire, que c'est parfaitement conforme à l'idée du *Timée* qui exige qu'il existe un monde archétype et transcendant qui soit l'exemple du cosmos visible.

[1] J.-H. Loenen dans son ouvrage sur le νοῦς dans la philosophie de Platon, thèse d'Amsterdam, 1951.
[2] 508e-509e.
[3] M. J.-H. Loenen a essayé de nous convaincre de la légitimité de l'explication du Platonisme par Albinus dans deux articles de la *Mnemosyne*, 1956-1957.
[4] Voir mon interprétation de *Soph.* 248esqq. dans les *Actes du XIe Congrès international à Bruxelles*, 1953, vol. XII, p. 61-67 (le ch. VIII du présent volume).

Or, si l'ensemble des νοητά est conçu comme un être organique et vivant, doué d'âme et d'esprit, n'est-ce pas là que surgit l'idée d'un *Noûs transcendant*? Jusqu'à un certain point nous nous rapprochons ici de Hackforth qui, dans un article sur le *Théisme de Platon*[1] a démontré que, sauf les âmes pensantes des êtres vivants dans un corps, y compris le Corps du Monde, Platon a certainement admis l'existence d'un Noûs transcendant. Ce Noûs-là, pensait Hackforth, ne supposait pas d'âme, et il faut l'identifier au Démiurge, l'Esprit divin Créateur du monde.

Je comprends fort bien cette identification et, dans un sens, je crois qu'elle est juste: c'est que, en effet, dans l'ordre ontologique conçu par Platon le Démiurge occupait le rang d'un Noûs transcendant. On ne saurait en douter. Mais la ligne de la pensée de Platon que nous venons de suivre nous-même, celle de l'*Être parfait* du *Sophiste* et celle du *Timée* à propos de *l'Exemple parfait* de notre monde qui est un ζῷον doué d'âme et de pensée, cette ligne-là est un peu différente. Bien qu'on puisse dire que Platon dit tantôt que le Démiurge crée le monde les yeux fixés sur l'Exemple éternel des Idées, tantôt que le Démiurge fait ressembler ce monde autant que possible à lui-même, – une coincidence qui, sans doute, facilite l'identification de l'Exemple éternel avec le Démiurge –, il me semble pourtant un peu trop téméraire de construire une «théologie de Platon» de telle sorte que l'Être parfait des Intelligibles soit identique au Démiurge, Esprit Créateur du monde vivant. Je préfère garder un peu de réserve sur ce point et ne pas aller plus loin que Platon lui-même nous le permet. Je me borne donc à ces deux points suffisamment clairs et solides: premièrement, que le Démiurge créateur des âmes était lui-même un Noûs transcendant, deuxièmement, que Platon paraît avoir conçu l'Être parfait des Idées dans leur ensemble comme un être vivant doué d'âme et de noûs, et que c'était apparemment là l'Être vivant parfait qui d'après lui est l'Exemple éternel du monde visible.

Si l'on me demande pourquoi j'hésite à identifier cet Être parfait au Démiurge, j'aimerais répondre que le résultat de cette identification me semble un peu trop «théiste» au sens moderne et chrétien. Après tout, le Démiurge de Platon n'est présenté que sous la réserve d'un εἰκὼς λόγος. Et c'est cela qui nous impose une certaine réserve à nous aussi[2].

Mais présentement ces problèmes-là ne font qu'un petit hors d'œuvre.

[1] *Plato's Theism*, in *Classical Quarterly* 1936, p. 4-9.
[2] Cf. le chapitre IX de ce volume.

Ce qui nous intéresse ici, c'est le principe illimité. Platon ne nous en dit plus rien dans aucun de ses dialogues. C'est Aristote qui va combler le vide. Dans les *Métaph.* A, ch. 6, nous trouvons le texte suivant :

«Parce que les Idées sont les causes des autres choses, il était d'avis que les éléments des Idées sont les éléments de tout ce qui existe. Or, comme matière, c'est le Grand et le Petit qui sont les principes, et comme essence (c'est-à-dire comme principe formel) c'est l'Un. Car c'est du Grand et Petit que les nombres proviennent, par la participation à l'Un.»

On s'est étonné de ce passage, on s'est même indigné. Quoi? Les Idées, causes transcendantes des choses sensibles, dépendraient elles-mêmes des «éléments» dont dépendent les choses matérielles? Qu'elles dépendent de l'Un, principe suprême et identique au Bien de la *République*, cela se conçoit. Mais du principe illimité, comment les Idées en dépendraient-elles? Ce n'est là, en tout cas, pas ce qu'en dit le *Philèbe*. D'après ce dialogue, c'est le μεικτὸν γένος qui provient du πέρας, c'est-à-dire des Idées, et de l'ἄπειρον. Quant aux Idées, elles y ont, comme partout, la place de Principe formel et déterminant. Comment donc, encore une fois, pourraient-elles dépendre elles-mêmes de l'ἄπειρον, notion-limite qui, dans l'échelle hiérarchique de l'être, ne pourrait avoir sa place qu'à l'autre extrémité de l'Un, c'est-à-dire : tout à fait en bas, au niveau inférieur aux choses sensibles, contrepartie de l'Un qui, lui, occupe le niveau supérieur à l'Intelligible?

Ce sont là à peu près les motifs pourquoi, par exemple, M. Cherniss rejette vivement la phrase citée d'Aristote: il s'agit là d'une erreur notoire de la part du disciple – erreur manifeste, qui ne montre qu'une fois de plus comment il faut être prudent avec ces témoignages sur Platon. Aristote, au fond, n'y a rien compris.

Il me faut avouer que j'ai longtemps partagé le point de vue de M. Cherniss quant à la phrase citée d'Aristote. Je me suis opposée, par conséquent, à l'interprétation de Sir David Ross, qui, dans son chapitre – d'ailleurs excellent – sur les Idées Nombres[1], explique le Grand et Petit comme principe du multiple indéterminé, nécessaire à Platon pour expliquer la multiplicité des νοητά et range ce principe immédiatement en dessous de l'Un. Si cette explication est juste, en effet, «les éléments des Idées» seraient en même temps les éléments de tout ce qui existe, comme le disait Aristote. Cela peut nous paraître étrange à première vue, parce que nous sommes plutôt inclinés à placer le Principe indéterminé comme tel tout à fait en bas de l'échelle

---

[1] *Plato's Theory of Ideas*, London, 1951, p. 202-205.

de l'être, au niveau inférieur aux choses sensibles. Reconnaissons pour le moment qu'il s'agit là tout aussi bien d'une interprétation. Laquelle des deux vaut mieux, cela n'est pas indiqué directement par Platon lui-même. Or, ce qui est intéressant, c'est que, dès la première génération, on ne trouve dans la tradition platonicienne que l'interprétation proposée par Sir David Ross. Et voilà qui m'a amenée à réviser mon opinion originelle.

Suivons la ligne des témoignages sur la doctrine de Platon concernant les Principes ultimes. Aristote n'est pas le seul des premiers disciples qui nous en donne un aperçu sommaire. Nous possédons aussi le témoignage d'Hermodore, conservé dans un passage de Simplicius[1], dont j'ai parlé plus longuement dans un article antérieur. On y apprend que «Platon admettait la matière dans le sens de l'ἄπειρον καὶ ἀόριστον», et qu'il l'illustrait par «les choses qui acceptent le plus et moins», auxquelles appartient aussi le Grand et le Petit. Suit une dichotomie de l'être de la façon suivante.

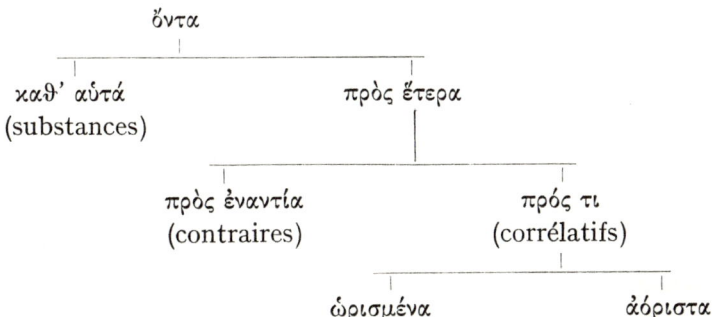

A la catégorie des ὡρισμένα appartiennent τὸ ἴσον, τὸ μένον, τὸ ἡρμοσμένον; aux ἀόριστα, tout ce qui contient le «plus ou moins», donc les notions comparatives, telles que plus large et plus étroit, plus lourd et plus léger. La dernière catégorie, c'est l'ἄστατον et l'ἄμορφον, ἄπειρον et οὐκ ὄν, parce que cette espèce reste toujours indéterminée (ἐν ἀκρισίᾳ τινι φέρεσθαι).

Dans le parallèle de ce passage chez Sextus Emp., *Adv. math.* X, 263-276, la division de l'être a la forme d'une tripartition:

1. τὰ καθ' αὑτά,   2. τὰ κατ' ἐναντίωσιν,   3. τὰ πρός τι.

---

[1] Simplic. in Ar., *Phys.* 247, l. 30-248, l. 15, cité et commenté un peu dans mon *Greek Phil.* nr. 371a, commenté plus longuement dans mes articles *Problems concerning later Platonism*, in *Mnem.*, 1949, p. 197-216, 299-318 (ch. XII du présent volume).

Le premier groupe est réduit au principe de l'Un, le troisième se trouve rangé dans la catégorie de ὑπεροχὴ καὶ ἔλλειψις, tandis que le second se partage en deux: d'une part, l'ἴσον, qui se réduit à l'Un; d'autre part, l'ἄνισον, qui appartient aux ὑπεροχὴ καὶ ἔλλειψις. Enfin, ces deux notions se réduisent au principe de la δυὰς ἀόριστος, terme qui nous est connu par l'aperçu de la doctrine platonicienne des premiers Principes chez Aristote, *Métaph.* A 6[1], qui mentionne la notion de l'Un comme commune à Platon et aux Pythagoriciens, tandis que la dénomination de dyade indéfinie au lieu d'ἄπειρον est qualifiée par lui comme ἴδιον Πλάτωνος – ce qui nous permet de reconnaître le caractère platonicien du passage cité de Sextus, lequel nous est présenté par cet auteur sous le titre de: doctrine pythagoricienne.

Nous avons ici un exemple, probablement de date assez ancienne, de cette confusion de pythagorisme et de platonisme que nous connaissons si bien, dès le 1er siècle avant notre ère, dans toute cette littérature dite pythagoricienne qui paraîtra dès lors. Est-il possible de préciser à quel moment à peu près on a commencé à confondre les deux doctrines?

Certes, le successeur immédiat de Platon, Speusippe, était un platonicien bien pythagorisant. On n'aura pas tort en disant que, dès l'Ancienne Académie, les deux doctrines se rapprochaient à tel point qu'une confusion dans la théorie des Principes ultimes était, en tout cas, bien proche. Examinons maintenant quelques textes de provenance dite pythagoricienne qui datent du 1er siècle avant J.-C.

Le premier est l'aperçu du «Pythagorisme» donné par Alexandre Polyhistor, chez Diog. Laërce, VIII, 25sqq., qui commence par un chapitre concernant les premiers Principes.

«Le principe de toutes choses est la monade. De la monade dérive la dyade indéterminée qui sert comme matière à la monade qui est cause. Ensuite, c'est de la monade et de la dyade indéterminée que dérivent les nombres, et des nombres les points. Or, c'est des points que dérivent les lignes, des lignes les surfaces, puis de celles-ci les solides, et des solides les corps sensibles»; e.q.s.

La déduction de points – lignes – surfaces – solides nous est bien connue: elle figure également dans le passage de Sextus cité tout à l'heure. En outre, elle se retrouve chez Aristote, *De anima* I 2, 404b 16-21, commenté par moi dans la seconde partie de mes *Problems concerning later Platonism* (*Mnem.*, 1949), ensuite, plus longuement,

---

[1] 987 b 26 sqq.

par le R. P. Saffrey[1]. Celui-ci s'accorde avec moi en trouvant dans le passage cité non pas la doctrine de quelque autre platonisant, disons de Xénocrate, comme l'a voulu M. Cherniss[2], mais bien de Platon lui-même.

D'ailleurs, le passage d'Alexandre commence par la théorie indubitablement platonicienne des Principes ultimes: l'Un et la dyade indéterminée. Ce qui nous intéresse en ce moment, c'est le fait qu' Alexandre paraît avoir trouvé dans les Πυθαγορικὰ ὑπομνήματα, qui sont sa source, que le principe illimité dit la dyade indéterminée provient directement de l'Un. C'est ce qui restait à deviner chez les Πυθαγορικῶν παῖδες de Sextus, qui finissaient par réduire les ὄντα aux deux Principes ultimes juxtaposés[3], tout comme la théorie de Platon était décrite soit par Aristote, soit par Hermodore.

Notons plus distinctement les écarts entre les descriptions provenant de la première génération des disciples et celle des «livres pythagoriques» dont parle Alexandre. D'après les premières, la théorie de Platon était dualiste: les ὄντα se réduisaient en dernière analyse à deux principes autonomes. Pas de trace que le second principe était rangé directement au-dessous du premier et qu'il en dépendait. Et voilà ce qui est fait chez les Pythagoriciens d'Alexandre.

Il est clair qu'il s'agit là d'*un certain mode d'interprétation* de la théorie de Platon. Il faut ajouter: de la même que chez Sir David Ross – interprétation qui, à première vue, nous a paru inacceptable. Si nous avons bien vu, Platon n'a aucunement voulu dire que le principe illimité provient de l'Un (qui est l'Agathon), ni n'a-t-il jamais pu ranger son second principe directement en dessous du premier. Ce qu'il professait, c'était, en effet, *un faible dualisme:* non pas un dualisme dans ce sens que le second principe serait du même ordre et de la même valeur ontologique que le premier. D'une telle pensée Platon était bien loin. Pour lui, le second principe, certes, était autonome et non réductible à aucun autre; mais dans l'échelle de l'être il se trouvait à l'autre bout: l'Un était un hyper-ὄν, comme l'Agathon de la *République;* la Dyade, elle, était un *infra-*ὄν, comme Hermodore le décrivait si bien.

Alors, les Pythagoriciens d'Alexandre paraissent avoir mal com-

---

[1] H. D. Saffrey, *Le* Περὶ φιλοσοφίας *d'Aristote et la théorie platonicienne des Idées Nombres*, Leiden, 1955.
[2] *The riddle of the Early Academy*, p. 14sqq.; *Aristotle's Criticism of Plato*, I, App. IX, 567-570. Voir mes notes au no. 372 de *Greek Phil.*, I. Le texte est cité là.
[3] Sextus, *Math.* X, 276.

pris la doctrine des premiers principes. Certainement la tendance moniste du pythagorisme de l'époque hellénistique y était pour quelque chose, monisme dont la première trace indubitable a été indiquée par M. Dodds chez Eudore d'Alexandrie, ca. 25 avant J.-C.[1].

Quelle était la date des livres pythagoriques dont parle Alexandre Polyhistor? L'aperçu doctrinal chez Diog. Laërce, VIII, 25-35, fut étudié plusieurs fois au courant des dernières décades. D'après Zeller, la doctrine remonte à peine plus haut que le 1er, tout au plus le second siècle. M. Wellmann, au contraire, soutenait, dans le *Hermes* de 1919[2], que le document dans son ensemble est une source légitime pour la connaissance du pythagorisme ancien. Il faisait même à peine exception pour le premier chapitre, qui est clairement postplatonicien, mais attribuait le tout à un pythagoricien du IVe siècle, contemporain de Platon, qui utiliserait lui-même des doctrines plus anciennes et propres au pythagorisme primitif. Wellmann fut suivi par Kranz, lequel, dans les cinquième et sixième éditions des *Vorsokratiker* de Diels, ajoutait l'aperçu d'Alexandre à la section des *Pythagoriciens anonymes*, ch. 58 B. Dans notre pays, ce fut M. Wiersma qui, dans un article de la *Mnémosyne* de 1941[3], prenait le parti de Wellmann et, tout en reconnaissant le caractère platonicien du chapitre sur les ἀρχαί, confirmait la thèse du savant allemand en démontrant que la plus grande partie de l'aperçu doctrinal d'Alexandre remonte à des théories cosmologiques et médicales des VIe et Ve siècles.

Moi-même, j'aurais voulu contredire la conclusion que tiraient et M. Wellmann et M. Wiersma de l'origine ancienne de ces théories. Mais le R. P. Festugière m'a prévenue. Dans son étude magistrale sur Les «*Mémoires pythagoriques*» *cités par Alexandre Polyhistor* dans la *Revue des Études grecques* de 1945, il a remarqué à bon droit que le fait que certaines théories de notre exposé remontent à Alcmaeon et à l'école médicale sicilienne ne prouve point du tout que l'ensemble de cet exposé ait été trouvé par Alexandre dans un écrit remontant

---

[1] Il s'agit d'un texte d'Alexandre d'Aphr. in Ar., *Métaph*. A 988 a 10-11. Le texte d'Aristote est: τὰ γὰρ εἴδη τοῦ τί ἐστιν αἴτια τοῖς ἄλλοις, τοῖς δ' εἴδεσιν τὸ ἕν. Or, Alexandre, p. 58, l. 31-59, l. 8, dit qu'Eudore et Euarmostus lisaient: τοῖς δ' εἴδεσιν τὸ ἓν καὶ τῇ ὕλῃ. M. Dodds suppose qu'Eudore a changé le texte d'Aristote d'après les exigences du Néopythagorisme moniste, qui dérivait l'ἄπειρον directement de l'Un (*The Parmenides of Plato and the origin of the Neoplatonic «One»*, in *Class. Quart.*, 1928, p. 129-142).

[2] *Hermes*, 54 (1919), p. 225 sqq.

[3] *Das Referat des Alexandros Polyhistor über die pythag. Phil.*, dans *Mnemosyne*, 1941, p. 97-112.

directement à la doctrine de cette époque. Au contraire, il est certain que notre aperçu ne peut servir de source pour la connaissance de l'ancien pythagorisme. Et cela pour les raisons suivantes:

1. Les ch. 25-35 de Diogène Laërce, VIII, contiennent une ἐπιτομή de l'espèce qui ne se trouve point avant l'époque hellénistique et dont le schème est déterminé par le *Timée* de Platon.

2. La première section (ch. 25, première partie, sur les premiers principes) peut être de la date la plus ancienne. Elle pourrait remonter jusqu'à Speusippe, toujours désireux de mettre ses théories sous le drapeau de l'ancien pythagorisme.

3. La section *De mundo* (ch. 25-27) contient une théorie de l'éther de forme eclectique et une théorie de l'équilibre des opposés lequel, en effet, remonte à Alcméon et à l'École médicale sicilienne, mais qui par l'auteur de notre aperçu a été emprunté probablement aux dialogues de Platon.

4. Quant à la dernière section, *de anima*, où l'on trouve une théorie du double pneuma, c'est le médecin Dioclès de Karystos qui en est la source principale.

5. L'aperçu dans son ensemble fut composé peut-être au second siècle avant notre ère, d'où date probablement l'expression εἱμαρμένη qui se trouve dans le ch. 27.

Par cette étude le point principal est solidement établi: notre passage est un document hellénistique, et l'origine plus ancienne de certaines théories qui s'y trouvent ne prouve aucunement la conclusion que, depuis Wellmann, MM. Kranz et Wiersma ont voulu en tirer.

Revenons à notre passage sur les premiers principes. Admettons, avec le P. Festugière, qu'il provient du cercle de l'Ancienne Académie et qu'il date du IIIe siècle. La différence entre les successeurs immédiats de Platon et les Pythagoriciens d'Alexandre en quoi consiste-t-elle? Les anciens Académiciens étaient-ils dualistes et s'opposent-ils par là à nos Pythagoriciens? – A peine.

La position de Xénocrate est suffisamment claire. Elle se révèle dans un curieux passage d'Aëtius[1]. «Xenocrate, fils d'Anthenor de Chalcédon», y dit-on, «faisait de la Monade et de la Dyade des Dieux, dont la première comme principe mâle occupe le rang de Père et règne au ciel. Il l'appelle aussi Zeus et impair et Intellect (νοῦς), qui est pour lui le premier Dieu. L'autre principe, comme femelle, prend la place

---

[1] Aëtius, *Plac.* I 7, 30 (Dox., p. 304 b 1); le nr. 756 dans ma *Gr. Phil.* II.

de Mère des Dieux. Elle préside au domaine au-dessous du ciel. C'est pour lui l'âme de l'univers.»

De ce passage deux choses résultent: 1) Des deux principes, la dyade est directement subordonnée à la monade. 2) Il n'est pas dit que la dyade provient de l'Un. Donc, Xénocrate a interprété la doctrine platonicienne des premiers principes dans le sens qui nous a paru évident en partant des descriptions que nous en possédons, c'est-à-dire il l'a interprété en *dualisme mitigé:* les deux principes ne se réduisent point à l'Un, mais ils ne sont pas du même rang. Ils sont irréductibles, mais le second se place au-dessous du premier.

Ce qui paraît nouveau chez les Pythagoriciens d'Alexandre, c'est qu'ils déduisent la dyade de l'Un. D'autre part, ce qui doit nous frapper chez Xénocrate, c'est qu'il considère la dyade non pas comme un principe placé à l'autre extrémité de l'échelle de l'être – au-dessous du niveau sensible, comme nous l'avons expliqué nous-même – mais qu'il le range, en effet, directement au-dessous du premier.

Quel est le cas chez Speusippe? Reçoit-on quelque lumière sur notre sujet dans les textes jamais trop clairs qu'il faut rapporter à lui? – Il me semble que si. On sait que Speusippe remplaçait les Idées par le nombre mathématique. Or, ce nombre, il l'a déduit des deux principes que voici: Ἕν et πλῆθος[1]. Et il s'est refusé à identifier le premier à l' Ἀγαθόν (comme le faisait Platon) pour ne pas être obligé à dire que la multiplicité, c'est le mal...

Ici encore, le second principe ne se réduit point au premier. Il n'en provient pas. Mais n'est-ce pas probable, enfin, qu'il se range tout de suite au-dessous de l'Un?

Ainsi, il faut bien le remarquer, on comprend mieux ce que dit Aristote au ch. 6 de *Métaph.* A[2] à propos des principes qui sont non seulement «les éléments des Idées», mais aussi «les éléments de toutes choses». Ce témoignage, en effet, ne se comprend guère tant qu'on range le second principe au-dessous du niveau sensible. Il ne se comprend que *si l'on double le principe illimité.* Car c'est cela qui s'impose, une fois qu'on reconnaît le caractère intelligible de la dyade comme στοιχεῖον des Idées: si Platon a admis sa dyade au niveau supérieur aux Idées pour en expliquer la multiplicité, c'était là, bien sûr, ce qu'on a nommé plus tard – sur la trace d'Aristote, mais dans un autre sens

---

[1] Ar., *Métaph.* N 1, 1087 b 4-9; le nr. 744 dans *Gr. Phil.* II.
[2] Ar., *Métaph.* A 6, 987 b 19-20.

que lui – ὕλη νοητή¹. Dans ce cas, on ne saurait s'étonner que, à un niveau inférieur, voire au-dessous des choses sensibles, il y a une ὕλη αἰσθητή, principe matériel pour le monde sensible qui a son archétype au niveau des νοητά.

Si l'on se rend compte de ce que cela veut dire pour expliquer Platon, il faudra se rappeler que nous avons constaté nous-même un écart indéniable entre l'ἄπειρον du *Philèbe* et le τρίτον γένος du *Timée*. Il faudra se rappeler également que, dans le *Sophiste*, Platon introduit parmi les genres suprêmes l'idée du ἕτερον, qui explique le μὴ ὄν comme réalité différente de l'ὄν. Nulle part il n'est dit dans les dialogues que le ἕτερον se confond avec l'ἄπειρον. Il est bien clair tout de même que, parce qu'il y a le ἕτερον, il y a multiplicité d'être dans le monde intelligible.

On a remarqué à juste titre² que le μὴ ὄν du *Sophiste* est du niveau intelligible. De cela, on a voulu conclure que ce μὴ ὄν ne saurait avoir rien à faire avec «le principe matériel», comme le dit Aristote. Cela peut paraître évident tant qu'on n'admet de principe matériel qu'en rapport avec le monde sensible. Dès que surgit la possibilité d'un principe pareil en vue des intelligibles, tout change. Enfin, il faut se rappeler que, dans le passage d'Hermodore, l'ἄπειρον – principe matériel concernant les choses sensibles – est expliqué comme οὐκ ὄν; non pas un μὴ ὄν, ce qui veut dire *non-être relatif* ou *réalité différente d'une autre réalité*, mais: *non-être total* «parce que l'être en est dénié».

Donc, l'ἄπειρον, principe matériel concernant le monde sensible, est non-être dans un sens plus strict, plus négatif que le μὴ ὄν du niveau intelligible, lequel, en fin de compte, paraît un être positif.

Pourquoi dire cela? – Parce que, en expliquant ce que nous savons du principe dit matériel de Platon, on est amené par les textes mêmes à distinguer ce principe à deux niveaux, dont l'ἄπειρον intelligible paraît être moins illimité que celui du monde sensible.

Or, ce qui paraît être moins connu, sauf chez ceux qui lisent Plotin, c'est que, en interprétant Platon ainsi, on se trouve sur la même voie que le grand rénovateur du Platonisme au IIIᵉ siècle: Plotin. Ce qui est intéressant, c'est qu'on y arrive en expliquant les textes de Platon et de ses disciples et successeurs immédiats.

Chez Plotin, en effet, on a une théorie claire et décidée de deux

---

¹ C'est Plotin qui, comme nous allons voir, a parlé d'une ὕλη νοητή dans le sens indiqué.
² M. Cherniss, dans son volume *Aristotle's criticism of Plato*.

matières[1], l'une intelligible (νοητή), l'autre sensible (αἰσθητή). Dans son traité Περὶ τῶν δύο ὑλῶν, il maintient l'existence d'une ὕλη νοητή contre ceux qui disent qu'il n'y a ni ἄπειρον ni ὕλη dans le monde intelligible, parce qu'il n'y a ni choses composées ni changement. Il ne faut pas toujours mépriser l'Infini, Plotin riposte; l'âme, par exemple, est dans un sens ὕλη par rapport au νοῦς. Ensuite, il existe sûrement des σύνθετα dans le monde intelligible, bien que d'une autre espèce que les corps. La matière, dans l'Intelligible, ne reçoit pas toujours une autre forme; elle possède toutes les formes à la fois. Elle n'est jamais sans forme[2]. – Pour deux raisons il faut admettre un ἄπειρον ou une ὕλη dans l'Intelligible: 1° pour expliquer l'existence d'Idées différentes (leur forme, qui diffère, suppose un ὑποκείμενον); 2° le κόσμος νοητός est l'archetypon du cosmos sensible; or, le dernier est composé de matière et de forme; donc, le premier aussi doit posséder une ὕλη[3].

Est-ce que Plotin identifie l'ἄπειρον intelligible avec le ἕτερον? – Non. L'ἄπειρον intelligible ou la ὕλη νοητή est un *produit éternel de la ἑτερότης*. Celle-ci, ainsi que le mouvement, sont ἄπειρα en eux-mêmes. C'est en se tournant vers l' Ἀγαθόν qu'ils reçoivent leur caractère défini[4].

L'ἄπειρον est donc *créé* – c'est-à-dire il n'est point du niveau de l'Un, mais du niveau directement en dessous. Il est créé *éternellement*, non identique au ἕτερον, mais son produit. Voilà exactement les choses que nous avons trouvées comme conséquences nécessaires de la conception de l'ἄπειρον décrite par Platon lui-même et illustrée par ses disciples, en cas qu'on admette un ἄπειρον archétypique. Or, dans ce cas, il faut avouer que beaucoup de choses s'éclairent. On rejoint ainsi l'explication de Sir David Ross à propos de la Dyade indéfinie: «Platon avait besoin de ce principe pour expliquer la multiplicité dans le monde intelligible. Il faut donc que la Dyade aie sa place directement au-dessous de l'Un.»

---

[1] *Enn.* II 4, Περὶ τῶν δύο ὑλῶν. Sur l'ἄπειρον dans l'Intelligible, voir aussi *Enn.* VI 2, 22 (dans le noûs), 22 s. (dans l'âme); sur le «nombre indéfini», *Enn.* VI 6, spécialement le ch. 18, au début; VI 5, ch. 4, 1. 13 sqq. (infinité de la nature de l'être total), et ch. 12, au début (force infinie de l'être total); V 8, 9, au début (Dieu, le créateur de l'Intelligible, possède une δύναμις ἄπειρος); IV 3, 8, l. 35 (l'âme est un ἄπειρον, parce que sa δύναμις est ἄπειρος); VI 7, 14 (il faut de l'ἄπειρον dans le νοῦς, pour expliquer la variété infinie des espèces). Sur ὕλη comme ἀσώματον, voir le traité 6 de l'*Enn.* III, ch. 7-19.
[2] II 4, ch. 3; aussi le ch. 5.
[3] *Ibid.*, le ch. 4.
[4] II 4, ch. 5, l. 28 sqq.: καὶ γὰρ ἡ ἑτερότης ἡ ἐκεῖ ἀεὶ τὴν ὕλην ποιεῖ.

LA THÉORIE DE L'ΑΠΕΙΡΟΝ

Le P. Festugière[1] a suivi la ligne de la pensée dite pythagoricienne. Après Xénocrate et sa théorie de deux dieux, il nous a conduits aux Pythagoriciens d'Alexandre Polyhistor; ensuite, après M. Dodds, il nous a indiqué l'interprétation d'Eudore, dans un passage de Simplicius[2]. Ici, on apprend que les «Pythagoriciens» posaient l'Un au plan tout à fait supérieur, comme principe de toutes choses; après quoi ils introduisaient au second plan l'Un qui s'oppose à la Dyade. Ces deux principes fonctionnent en tête de la συστοιχία, que nous connaissons bien depuis Arist., *Métaph*. A 5[3]: πέρας-ἄπειρον, περιττόν-ἄρτιον, ἕν-πλῆθος, δεξιόν-ἀριστερόν, ἄρρεν-θῆλυ, ἠρεμοῦν-κινούμενον, εὐθύ-καμπύλον, φῶς-σκότος, ἀγαθόν-κακόν, τετράγωνον-ἑτερόμηκες.
Aristote ajoute que la liste remonte au moins jusqu'à Alcméon.

Il faut en conclure, il me semble, que les anciens Pythagoriciens (au VIe siècle) étaient dualistes. Il est vrai, bien entendu, que, dans les lignes qui précèdent immédiatement le passage cité, Aristote a mentionné une autre théorie pythagoricienne, moniste celle-ci. On y lit que les nombres sont les principes des choses, et les éléments du nombre sont: l'ἄρτιον et le περιττόν, qui se réduisent à leur tour au πεπερασμένον et à l'ἄπειρον. Enfin, ces deux-là sont supersédés par *l'Un*, lequel contient les deux aspects, «car il est en même temps pair et impair».

Dans le chapitre cité de son *Hermès Trismégiste*[4], le P. Festugière n'a pas, à ce qu'il paraît, voulu faire attention au passage sur la συστοιχία qui suit immédiatement. Il en a parlé dans son article de 1945 (*Revue des Études grecques*, p. 32sqq.), où il nie que la table des *dix opposés* puisse être rapportée à l'ancien pythagorisme – tout en concédant que «rien n'empêche que certaines des oppositions ne leur soient dues». Cependant, il n'a nommé aucune raison pourquoi le principe dualiste lui-même n'appartiendrait pas au Pythagorisme ancien, ni même pourquoi la liste comme telle ne remonterait pas à Alcméon ou à la génération précédente, comme l'assure Aristote. Certes, il connaît un pythagorisme plus ou moins dualiste, c'est-à-dire celui qui a adopté les deux principes platoniciens. Mais, puisque cette adoption marque une phase ultérieure du pythagorisme, il a eu l'impression que le monisme y a été au début. Or, en cela, je crois qu'il

---

[1] Dans le vol. IV de son *Hermès Trism.*, ch. II.
[2] In Ar. *Phys.* I, p. 181, l. 7sqq.
[3] 986a23sqq.
[4] P. 28.

s'est trompé. Car, en effet, il n'y a aucune raison pourquoi le pythagorisme dualiste, celui de la συστοιχία, dans laquelle l'Un n'a pas de place prépondérante du tout, ne daterait du VIe siècle. Il y a, au contraire, des raisons positives pour admettre que la συστοιχία est ancienne: 1° il y a toute probabilité que Parménide a opposé son monisme radical au dualisme pythagoricien dont il est sorti; 2° la table des dix opposés, qui font un ensemble si étrangement mêlé, a bien l'apparence d'être primitive. – Il me semble qu'il faut dire que, très probablement, chez les Pythagoriciens, le dualisme a précédé la version moniste. C'est donc plus tard que l'Un a pris le premier rang, à ce qu'il semble, plutôt sous l'influence de Platon, au IVe siècle.

Après Eudore, il y a eu Moderatus au 1er, ensuite Théon de Smyrne au second siècle. Quant à Moderatus, c'est encore Simplicius[1] qui nous rapporte sa théorie de la hiérarchie des êtres: au plan supérieur, il pose l'Un qui est au-dessus de l'être; au second, le ἓν ὄν du *Parménide* de Platon, c'est-à-dire les Idées; au troisième, il y a l'Un par rapport à l'âme, Un qui participe et du Premier et des Idées, à cause de la matière (ὕλη) qui est un μὴ ὄν. *Dans les choses sensibles*, apprenons-nous ici, *ce non-être est absolu et d'un ordre inférieur à celui du* μὴ ὄν *primaire*, lequel se trouve dans le ποσόν (la quantité limitée) des nombres.

Modérat, donc, a compris la théorie platonicienne de l'ἄπειρον dans le sens qui tout à l'heure s'est imposé à nous. Très clairement, il a admis un ἄπειρον double, comme le fera plus tard Plotin.

En suivant l'exposé du R. P. Festugière[2], on retrouve l'idée d'un ἄπειρον double chez Proclus dans son commentaire sur le *Timée*, 30 a 2. «Qu'est-ce que l'illimité? Évidemment, c'est la matière que nous appellerons «illimité», la forme «limite». Si donc, comme nous l'avons dit, Dieu fait exister tout illimité (πᾶσαν ἀπειρίαν), il fait exister aussi la matière, qui est l'illimité du dernier degré. C'est cela qui est la cause toute première et ineffable de la matière. D'autre part, puisque les propriétés des sensibles étant en rapport avec leurs causes intelligibles, Platon fait dépendre partout celles-là de celle-ci, par exemple l'égal d'ici-bas de l'Égal-en-soi, et pareillement pour tous les vivants et toutes les plantes d'ici-bas, il est clair que, d'après le même procédé, il fait dépendre aussi l'illimité d'ici-bas de la Limite intelligible. Or, j'ai montré ailleurs que cet Illimité premier, qui vient avant les mixtes, Platon l'a établi au sommet des intelligibles et qu'il en fait s'étendre

---

[1] In Ar. *Phys.* I, p. 230; voir Festugière, *Hermès Trism.*, vol. IV, p. 34 sqq.
[2] Ch. III du volume cité, p. 32 sqq.

l'illumination depuis là-haut jusqu'aux degrés les plus bas[1].

Voilà ce qu'a dit Aristote dans cette ligne si obscure à première vue: «Puisque les Idées sont causes des autres choses, Platon pensait que les éléments des Idées sont en même temps les éléments de toutes choses.»

Le P. Festugière n'a pas mentionné Plotin. Pourquoi pas, je ne sais. Il passe d'Eudore et Moderatus à Proclus et son commentaire sur le *Timée*. Comme parallèle de notre passage, il nomme Jamblique, *De mysteriis*, VIII, 3[2], qui parle de «la doctrine des Égyptiens sur les principes». Là aussi, on commence par l'Un. Ensuite, on procède à la pluralité des multiples. On les trouve gouvernés par l'Un, mais «la nature indéterminée», elle aussi, y est présente. Comme on se trouve au niveau intelligible, on constate que «la nature indéterminée y est partout maîtrisée par une certaine Mesure et par la Cause suprême qui unifie toutes choses». Enfin, on en arrive à la matière. «Quant à la matière, Dieu l'a tirée de la substantialité» – ὕλην δὲ παρήγαγεν ὁ θεὸς ἀπὸ τῆς οὐσιότητος; «de la matérialité en a été retranchée par en dessous» – ὑποσχισθείσης ὑλότητος.

Pour expliquer ces derniers mots, le P. Festugière renvoie à la vision de Poimandres (I 4-6), qui, d'abord, voit «tout devenu lumière», puis du σκότος par en dessous, qui se détache du φῶς. En effet. Mais le passage de Jamblique ne se commente-t-il pas parfaitement par Plotin? C'est chez lui qu'on a explicitement cette idée d'ἄπειρον intelligible qui n'est jamais sans mesure et sans forme. Puis, quant à la ὕλη αἰσθητή, elle provient de l'οὐσιότης, en effet, c'est-à-dire de la nature intelligible. Comment? – C'est l'âme qui, pour ainsi dire, aux derniers confins du θεῖον, produit un *cercle d'obscurité* et qui ensuite, dans un second regard, l'illumine et lui donne une forme[3]. – Et comment l'âme, qui est divine dans son essence, peut-elle produire l'obscurité et le μὴ ὄν? C'est ce qui arrive, dit Plotin[4], quand elle se tourne non pas à ce qui est au-dessus d'elle – car alors elle est illuminée – mais quand elle se porte vers ce qui est au-dessous, lorsqu'elle tend vers elle-même dans son existence particulière et qu'elle veut être auprès

---

[1] Proclus, in *Tim*. B, éd. Diehl, vol. I, p. 384, l. 28 - p. 385, l. 12. Trad. du P. Festugière, avec de légères modifications.
[2] P. 264, 13sqq.; Festugière, Hermès Trism. IV, p. 38sqq.
[3] *Enn*. IV 3, 9, l. 23-26: οἷον πολὺ φῶς ἐκλάμψαν ἐπ' ἄκροις τοῖς ἐσχάτοις τοῦ πυρὸς σκότος ἐγίγνετο, ὅπερ ἰδοῦσα ἡ ψυχή, ἐπείπερ ὑπέστη, ἐμόρφωσεν αὐτό.
[4] *Enn*. III 9, 3, l. 7-16.

d'elle-même. Πρὸς αὐτὴν γὰρ βουλομένη ⟨εἶναι⟩ τὸ μεθ' αὐτὴν ποιεῖ εἴδωλον αὐτῆς, τὸ μὴ ὄν, οἷον κενεμβατοῦσα καὶ ἀοριστέρα γινομένη· καὶ τούτου τὸ εἴδωλον τὸ ἀόριστον πάντη σκοτεινόν. «Car, lorsqu'elle veut être auprès d'elle-même, elle produit au-dessous d'elle une image d'elle, qui est non-réalité. Elle-même est sans terrain solide et perd toute détermination fixe; et l'image de l'âme, qui est indéterminée, est tout à fait obscure. – Mais elle jette de nouveau un regard sur l'image et, par ce second coup d'œil, elle lui donne une forme[1].»

Que faut-il conclure de tout cela?

1. D'après Aristote, *Métaph.* A 6, 987b19sqq., c'est Aristote qui déjà a compris la théorie de Platon des Principes suprêmes d'une telle manière que le principe dit matériel n'est point restreint au niveau des choses sensibles. Donc, la théorie d'un double ἄπειρον n'a pas été inventée – disons au 1er siècle avant notre ère, dans les milieux dits pythagoriques. Elle s'est imposée tout de suite aux disciples immédiats de Platon. Probablement, ce n'était pas Aristote seul qui l'a compris ainsi. Hermodore, en décrivant l'ἄπειρον comme οὐκ ὄν, a suggéré par là même que le μὴ ὄν qui est ἕτερον est d'un autre ordre.

2. Platon admettait un Principe suprême: l'Ἀγαθόν de la *République*, plus tard nommé l'Un, posé au delà de l'être et de la pensée. Il en suit que la Dyade, principe illimité, ne saurait être placée qu'au second rang, où elle se manifeste dans la multiplicité de l'être intelligible. D'où les trois explications que nous avons trouvées: 1) celle qui dérive la Dyade directement de l'Un (les Pythagoriciens d'Alexandre Polyhistor); 2) une autre qui laisse les deux principes l'un à côté de l'autre (Sextus, *Math.* X 276); 3) une troisième qui superpose l'Un au πέρας et à l'ἄπειρον et ainsi introduit la συστοιχία pythagorique dès le second plan (Eudore et Moderatus).

3. Dans toutes ces interprétations, on trouve désignée plus ou moins une certaine solution de notre problème, sans que jamais les difficultés soient amplement discutées, les différentes possibilités envisagées, le sens de la position prise expliqué. Tout cela, d'après ce qu'il semble, a été laissé à nous. Et le résultat? Certains savants modernes ont jugé les quelques lignes d'Aristote à propos de notre question par trop obscures, voire invraisemblables[2]. On ne s'est guère intéressé pour les spéculations néopythagoriciennes. Festugière, lui, les a interprétées.

[1] Trad. Bréhier, avec de légères modifications.
[2] M. Cherniss, dans son ouvrage *Aristotle's criticism of Plato*, est bien le plus catégorique; mais il me semble qu'en général on s'est fort peu préoccupé du témoignage d'Aristote dans les lignes citées.

LA THÉORIE DE L'ΑΠΕΙΡΟΝ

Il l'a fait avec l'aide des explications plus amples de Iamblique et de Proclus. C'est bien, mais, en somme, n'est-ce pas Plotin qui le premier a vraiment expliqué la question de ὕλη et ἄπειρον, non seulement dans un, mais dans plusieurs traités philosophiques d'une grande clarté et précision?[1] Et ce sont ces idées, bien sûr, qui sont à la base des passages cités de Iamblique dans le *De myst.* et de Proclus dans son commentaire sur le *Timée*.

4. Que penser du fait que la théorie des deux ὕλαι fut en principe une théorie néopythagorique? Faut-il y trouver confirmée la thèse de M. Heinrich Dörrie, qui, dans un article sur Plotin et Ammonius Sakkas[2], a soutenu que Plotin a appris tout l'essentiel de sa philosophie de son maître alexandrin et qu'il a inventé probablement très peu de chose lui-même? – Je crains que M. Dörrie n'ait pas fait justice au génie philosophique de Plotin et, pour cette raison, je n'aimerais pas dire que sa thèse soit confirmée par l'histoire que je viens d'esquisser. Au contraire, cette histoire nous apprend tout autre chose. La théorie des deux ὕλαι ne fut pas «inventée» par les néopythagoriciens non plus. Elle faisait partie de leur tradition, c'est vrai. Mais c'est Plotin qui la première fois a traité la question d'une méthode de réflexion profonde et de critique claire et bien fondée. S'il est vrai, ce que dit Aristote, que celui seul qui possède de la connaissance scientifique est capable de l'enseigner, alors c'est Plotin qui pour la première fois paraît avoir compris notre question. Sa manière de traiter ces problèmes se distingue des trop courtes remarques ou esquisses sommaires de ses prédécesseurs par une maturité de pensée, une clarté de critique, une pénétration tout à fait remarquables.

5. Plotin se présente lui-même comme continuateur de la philosophie de Platon et comme exégète de la pensée du grand maître. Sur le point que nous avons considéré, il nous paraît être exégète de Platon beaucoup plus direct et, disons-le, beaucoup meilleur qu'on ne le croit d'habitude. La théorie du double ἄπειρον n'est pas une spéculation étrange. Elle est un problème nécessaire de l'exégèse de Platon. En outre, elle est une solution qui, après tout, rend justice autant que possible aux différents aspects de la pensée de Platon sur notre question.

---

[1] Voir plus haut, ma n. 1, à la p. 390.
[2] *Hermès* 83 (1955), p. 439-477: *Ammonios, der Lehrer Plotins*.

NEOPLATONICA

CHAPTER XVII

THE MONISM OF PLOTINUS[1]

When Plotinus proceeds to expound[2] his theory of what he terms "the three fundamental hypostases", he begins as follows:

"However does it come about that the souls have forgotten God, their Father and that, although originating from thence and belonging to Him completely, they have lost both the knowledge of themselves and the knowledge of Him?"

He replies: "The beginning of the evil is for them the temerity, coming-to-be, the first difference and the desire to be independent."

Is he here giving four different causes? No, it is one and the same cause which has made the souls forget God, their Father. It is their coming-into-existence as particular, individual beings bound in a body (ἡ γένεσις). This development is qualified (1) as "temerity" (τόλμα), (2) as caused by the first difference, the principle of all particularization and (3) by the urge towards autonomy.

In other words, particularization itself, the setting oneself up as separate, individual beings, distinct from others and detached from the one Absolute in which there is no differing, no ἑτερότης, is contrasted with the absoluteness of the One as a wantonness, a ὕβρις, a form of guilt.

This idea is already familiar to us from ancient India[3], it occurs

---

[1] This chapter contains the English translation of a paper originally written and published in the Netherlands language (*Alg. Ned. Tijdschrift v. Wijsbegeerte en psychol.* 1957; C. J. de Vogel, *Theoria* ,1967).
[2] *Enn.* V, 1, 1.
[3] The All-One as the prime source of all individual existences to which all individual souls strive to return already occurs in the earliest Upanishads (usually dated in the 6th century). Individual souls are rooted in an All-soul and can raise themselves to the all-one (brahman) by spiritual exercises. They hereby attain the state of perfection.

399

also in the young Goethe[1] and the young Schiller[2] whose minds were nourished by the Stoic pantheism of Spinoza but also by Plotinus. They read him in the Latin translation of Marsilio Ficino.

Let us now follow Plotinus' exposition further.

"Since they seemed to rejoice in their self-determination, they made frequent use of their ability to move of their own power: they went in the opposite direction and fell away from God – the greatest decline possible. And thus they also lost the awareness that they originate from yonder, just as children who immediately after their birth are snatched away from their fathers and have grown up for a long time far away no longer know themselves or their fathers."[3] They have come to love and admire the other and to despise that from which they have turned away.

Their veneration of things here and contempt for their true self is thus the origin of their total lack of knowledge of God. For whatever one strives after and admires, one regards as being higher than oneself. If, thus, one considers oneself as worse than the things which come into being and perish, one views oneself as the least valuable and most transient of all. Anyone who thinks in this way can never grasp the nature of God and his power. For this reason two kinds of argument are necessary to turn this sort of person in the opposite direction, towards the One and the First, namely :(1) one must show the worthlessness of that which they now admire, and (2) one must remind the soul of its origin and its worth. – This second argument logically precedes the first. Hence it is this, what Plotinus wishes to discuss; for, he says, it is of the greatest importance for our subject. For the *soul* after all is the subject seeking, and she must know what she is: whether she is capable of seeking such things (i.e. the highest spiritual things, the "true Being" and its last ground), whether she has eyes to

---

[1] In Goethe one finds at the end of the 8th book *Dichtung und Wahrheit* a Neoplatonic cosmogony in which the multiplicity of individual souls is produced from the divine One-ness by a sort of fragmentation process. This process, however, would finally lead to a state of nothingness if it were not counterbalanced by an 'expansion' of the infinite being. This is Goethe's youthful view of the world and is *to a certain extent* (though not entirely) Plotinic.

[2] Schiller entertains a similar concept: the divine Substance which is the All has divided itself up into an infinite number of particular beings. This *Vereinzelung*, however, cannot be the end, for it means isolation. For this reason the individual strives to return to the One-ness of the Whole. This is the movement of Love.

[3] The following is given in brief.

see this and whether it is fitting for her to seek it. For if the soul is related to it, then it is fitting for her, and if not, why should she then seek it?

Thus Plotinus takes as the first and most obvious point of departure in seeking for the first Principle which is the basis of all things: the soul's reflection on itself. This is not the only possible point of departure – one might also proceed from the beauty, order and harmony in the visible world, and Plotinus does so repeatedly[1]. Both ways lead to the same goal. For the soul finds within herself the principle which has animated everything possessing life and which is therewith origin of the cosmic order, of the movement and harmony of the All. As self-moving principle she stands above all that is physical. She penetrates this whole and governs it, both the cosmos as a whole and the individual bodies and is everywhere present, whole and undivided.

But this is not yet properly expressed. One must not imagine that a material world exists first of all, and that there are bodies which must subsequently be penetrated by the soul and turned into *living* bodies. No, without the soul there is no body at all. For the soul *makes* the visible world, she *makes* for herself a body by irradiating with her light the completely indeterminate that is called "matter" (ὕλη). Thus, through illumination, the soul "forms" for herself the visible world and is partly absorbed in individual bodies.

However, she is not an independent cause in this creation. She would not be Light if she were not illumined "from above". In other words she is herself an "image" (εἰκών): she is a mobile image of a perfect and unchangeable, purely intelligible reality: the Spirit (Noûs). This Noûs contains the eternal and unalterable Forms of things (εἴδη), the true Being in all its manifestations. The Noûs = τὰ ὄντα, the actual, original Being which contains the prime images of visible things.

The intelligible Being is a unity but not the absolute Unity which excludes multiplicity. That Unity is *above* Being, for it cannot be Being in its all-embracing multiplicity. The intelligible Being, however, is an organic, articulated unity, a unity which possesses parts and is thus a multiplicity: an ordered unity and thus a κόσμος νοητός. Plotinus was not the first to use the term – one finds it in Philo[2], but we may be almost sure that it was used earlier.

In what sense does Plotinus say that this κόσμος νοητός is a Noûs?

---

[1] E.g. in V 1, 4 and in V 9, 2.
[2] E.g. *De opif. mundi* 4 ff.

In other words: in what sense does he identify being and thought? Not, in any case, in the sense of the German idealism which posits: "Sein = Setzung des Denkens". It is not true to say, asserts Plotinus[1], that by thinking the Noûs creates its objects which did not exist before. This is the function of the soul which, in a manner of speaking, stands on the lowermost edge of the intelligible, and, bordering on darkness, shapes it into an image of herself. The Noûs, however, must contain its objects in itself. It is τὰ πρῶτα. For how should that which is thought in the primary sense obtain its objects from outside, acquiring them incidentally (ἐπικτώμενος) as a strange element and passing through them (διεξοδεύων) as does the soul to which after all that which we call "discursive thought" is proper? The Noûs is entirely different. It possesses within itself the object of its thought. It 'sees' directly what is within it: Νοῦς ἢ τὰ νοητά. In the first sense – as products of a thinking which does not possess its object in itself – the Ideas are not thoughts, but in the second sense, as content of the primary Thought that thinks of itself, they are Noûs = the collected νοητά.

This thesis is most essential for Plotinus[2]. He also arrives at it by a different road[3]. Thought is, he says, the activity (ἐνέργεια) of being. The (intelligible) being, however, is itself "activity" in the sense of "full development". Both activities thus coincide: Mind and Being have one and the same nature. They are nothing other than two aspects of the same essence, thinking and being thought, subject-object[4].

The Noûs always retains this duality and for this reason alone it cannot be the First Principle. Therefore, beyond the Noûs there must be something else which is a complete unity and for this very reason stands above thought and being. Time and again Plotinus arrives at this postulate by establishing that the Noûs after all, always comprises the duality of subject and object[5]. But the object of the Noûs is multiple. Immediately therefore there follows in these passages: the Noûs is that which is; in other words, it is τὰ πάντα. For this very reason it cannot be the One.

---

[1] Enn. V 9, 7.
[2] See also V 5, 1-2: the Noûs is the ever active, never erring thought. One must therefore situate the νοητά within the Noûs. V 6, 1: the Noûs is πρώτως νοῶν, that is, it has its object in itself. Cf. also III 9, 1.
[3] V 9, 8.   [4] V 1, 4.
[5] E.g. also VI 9, 2.

He also identifies the intelligible being with the Beautiful[1]. The Beautiful, however, is not the highest in Plotinus' hierarchy – for it always presupposes a "seeing" – albeit a *mental* seeing. The Beautiful is ἐράσμιον (an object of love). But why? – Because it bears a trace of the Good of which it is, as it were, the entrance hall[2]. The beauty of the intelligible Being induces the soul, whenever she contemplates it, to inquire after its Maker.

Thus, according to V. 1,5 the musing soul which has approached the Noûs, asks: who is it that has produced It, who is Cause of its being and of its multiplicity; who has made Numbers? – For the Number is not primary: before the duality is the One: twoness is secondary and having proceeded from the One has it as determinant. Of itself, however, it is indeterminate. And as soon as it is determined it is already a number, that is, being.

This too is a road which the soul can take in its search for the First Principle. At the beginning of his treatise on the three fundamental hypostases[3] Plotinus called that Principle "God" and "Father". Sometimes too he calls the Noûs God and Father. Quite naturally so, for the Noûs is the "Father" of the Soul, of *our* soul too which after all, in Plotinus' explicit words[4], is our true and real self. And the Noûs is a great God[5], although not the highest. There are lower gods than the Noûs: Plotinus regards the *Soul* as belonging to the *divine nature*[6]. For the latter is characterized by the fact that as primary being it has life of itself. From this it follows not alone that it is imperishable, but also that it is ἀπαθής. Now the soul possesses these qualities, at least the soul as it is according to its essential nature, purified of the "additions" (προσθῆκαι) which it all too easily acquires through the link with a body[7]. Hence the soul so long as it "looks upward", i.e. keeps its attention fixed on the Noûs, is creative. This is true of the All-soul which is "yonder" and does not enter into the physical but exercises its "providence" from a distance, but it is also true of in-

---

[1] V 8, 9; cf. IV 9, 2.
[2] IV 9, 2; cf. III 8, 11.
[3] V 1, 1.
[4] II 1, 5 (end): the higher soul is our real self. Cf. II 3, 9. Also I 1, 7. l. 14-24; 'Ourselves' i.e. our intellectual life. The πάθη form no part of this. I 1, 10: The true man is the spiritual man, ὁ ἔνδον ἄνθρωπος.
[5] V 5, 3.
[6] IV 7, 8⁵, l. 44ff - cc. 9 and 10.
[7] IV 7, 10; IV 7, 13 and 14; VI 4, 15-16. Also I 1, 12: only the soul with προσθῆκαι can sin.

dividual souls. When these contemplate the Ideas "yonder" they are called "gods"[1]. And it should not surprise us either that the Ideas themselves which after all are νοητά, that is, primary being, are sometimes called "gods" by Plotinus[2].

Below God, the Creator of the κόσμος νοητός[3], Plotinus recognizes thus a hierarchy of gods: first the Noûs and the νοητά, then the All-soul and the starry souls, the world-soul and finally the (purified) souls of individual people which are or have been linked with a body.

This, in broad outline, is Plotinus' concept of the three fundamental hypostases. Here reality in the full sense ceases. "Up to here goes the divine" declares Plotinus[4]. Whatever comes after must of necessity be of a lower order. And yet the visible world, since it was brought forth *by the soul* after the archetypal form of the νοητά, is full of beauty, indeed as perfect as possible. How could it be otherwise? It is admittedly not the actual divine Being, but is nonetheless an image which resembles it[5]. And the rising of such an image is necessary, for the soul did not signify the end of the creative power of the divine nature[6]. For every nature of necessity brings forth what comes after it. Thus "that which gives being through grace" (i.e. τὸ θεῖον or ὁ θεός) must not stop at matter: a light must radiate from the soul which illumines the darkness bordering it and thus calls into being an image of itself.

From our point of view certain important questions remain. We have first followed Plotinus on his ascending way and have seen on what grounds he assumes a first Principle of perfect unity. Time and again the important factor was that logically and ontologically unity precedes multiplicity. It is this principle which is radically thought out and applied in Plotinus. But this leads us to the question: if one proceeds from a first Principle which is perfectly one, how does one arrive from this One at the many? This is by no means easy to explain. It was not for nothing, after all, that Aristotle observed that it is impossible to explain the world with its multiplicity from one single principle.

---

[1] V 8, 5. See also IV 8, 5. 25 where the soul is called θεὸς ὁ ὕστερος.
[2] Thus in IV 3, 11: The things here are an image of 'gods'.
[3] V 8, 9.
[4] V 1, 7 (end).
[5] II 9, 8, 4, 10-20; IV 8, 6. 24. In V. 8, 12 Plotinus (like Philo) even calls the visible world 'the youngest son of God'. All the others (of the νοητά) have remained in Him (the noûs); one only has been transformed into a visible world which is an εἰκών of the Father.
[6] IV 8, 6. 9.

THE MONISM OF PLOTINUS

Plotinus was quite aware of this problem. He is constantly preoccupied with the question of how the many spring from the One[1]. Again and again he answers in the same manner, that is, by using two images: that of the over-flowing source and that of a light illumining all about it. How did the Noûs come forth from the One, he asks[2]. Or, to put it more generally: how was anything whatever, whether multiplicity, duality or number produced by the One while this did not remain in itself? His reply is: ἐξερρύη[3]; also ὑπερερρύη[4]. Its abundance was so great that it overflowed or rather constantly overflows without the spring changing or diminishing in any way. It emits a περίλαμψις as from the sun, a radiant light which continues to stream forth from it while the One itself remains what it is. Everything having an independent existence produces something which depends on it and is, as it were, an image of it. So it is with the warmth of fire and the cold of snow, and with scented objects there is the odour which they emit. Everything that has attained perfection produces something, and the ever perfect is constantly bringing forth. That which it does bring forth is eternal but of a lower order than itself. Thus the One gives birth to the Noûs and the Noûs to the soul. The Noûs is the most perfect after the One. It is, says Plotinus[5], ἄγαλμα τὸ πρῶτον ἐκφανέν, the first image (of the One) to appear. Note that he employs not εἰκών, a term which for the Greeks evoked primarily the association of "imitation" and lower order, but ἄγαλμα which rather suggests the idea of a precious jewel.

Every being of necessity brings forth what comes after it[6]: this is the dominating principle of what might be called Plotinus' doctrine of creation. This doctrine possesses two remarkable characteristics for us who are (more or less) accustomed to the Christian concept of creation: 1. Plotinus' view of creation is *impersonal* and 2, according to this theory creation occurs *by degrees*. For Plotinus "God" in the sense of the first Principle is the creator in the absolute sense, since from him proceeds the Noûs which is *everything*. To this extent one can say that the first Principle "contains everything", that, as Plotinus sometimes says[7], it is "potentially all things". The reference is also

---

[1] V 1, 6-7; V 2, 1; V 3, 12. 40-48; V 4, 1. 20-41.
[2] V 1, 6 (beginning).
[3] V 1, 6. 7.   [4] V 2, 1. 8-9.   [5] V 1, 6. 14.   [6] IV 8, 6.
[7] III, 8, 10 (beginning): δύναμις τῶν πάντων. Cf. VI 8, 21. 19-22: It contains everything within it in the sense that everything depends on it. See also VI 5, 9. 31-37: It must contain the opposite nature, i.e. multuplicity, ἐν τῇ δυνάμει.

to concrete things, for these have their prototype in the νοητά and could not develop at all if the intelligible prime image did not exist. For, according to Plotinus, nothing really new ever "becomes". The perceptible world never adds to reality anything that did not exist before[1].

Thus the first Principle, which is the Creator of the Intelligible world, is also at the same time the Creator of all things. What strikes one about Plotinus, however, is that he carefully denies his first Principle all desire to create[2]: there is no "inclination" on the part of the First towards that which might come after Him; the First remains always turned in upon itself and precisely through this being-turned-in-upon-itself, overflows in its richness, it irradiates all sides with its light which bathes all things.

The first Principle "creates" in the sense that it produces something, but it creates as it were, despite itself. It creates *as a by-product of its self-orientated, completely internal activity*. And this creation is eternal because the Cause, whose nature is ἐνέργεια, is eternal.

The same holds good, mutatis mutandis, on the plane one step lower: the Noûs is thought (not discursive but intuitive), thought that does not seek but has its object eternally and unchangeably in itself. The activity of the Noûs is: the contemplation of that eternal Being which it contemplates, says Plotinus[3], "in the light of the One." Sometimes, however, it sees that Light itself directly[4]. A double contemplation is thus proper to the Noûs: on the one hand of the νοητά within it, and on the other hand (and simultaneously) of the One above it.

This and nothing else is the function of the Noûs. The fact that it produces a third hypostasis (the soul) is a natural and not a deliberately sought for or desired consequence of this internal, purely spiritual activity. To put it succinctly: *the creation is a by-product of contemplation*.

Finally this applies without any reservation to the creation of the visible world. How did this come about? Is there a creative Spirit which consulted with itself beforehand and imagined an earth and that this had to be in the middle, and then water and that this must be on the earth, and in this manner all the other things too in sequence,

[1] VI 7, 1-3.
[2] V 1, 6. 15-27.
[3] V 5, 7.
[4] Ib., 7-10.

up to the heavens; then all living creatures, each with its own shape and parts, internal and external; and that subsequently, arranging all things in his own mind, he proceeded to carry out his plans after all these preparations?[1]

But this is impossible, says Plotinus. Even the imagining of all these things is already impossible since He (the Creator) had never seen these things. And how is one to suppose that a being turned these plans into concrete reality, who had neither hands nor tools like a human craftsman.

One possibility remains: everything must have existed in intelligible form "yonder", or rather, exist eternally. There suddenly arises then, purely through the immediate proximity ("because there is nothing between") an image and likeness of that intelligible being, either directly or through the intermediary of a soul[2].

The creation thus is not the result of reasonable deliberation, but because it is so, it is good. In this case the conclusion comes before the premises[3].

In a similar fashion the heavenly bodies – which are after all, animate beings, and thus gods – produce an effect which is impersonal, not consciously sought after. They influence the course of earthly things simply because they are exalted souls and thus powerful beings, and because everything in the All is inextricably connected. Plotinus devotes a detailed exposition to the question of how one should imagine that the influence of the gods takes place, how prayers are "granted" and "heard", how magical acts and formulas "work". All this has its basis in the cosmic inter-relation of all things which the Stoics call συμπάθεια, and must inevitably work. One must, however, beware of assuming any personal deliberation, any λογισμός, any kind of βουλεύσασθαι behind all this, any conscious preoccupation on the part of the constellations with us and our affairs, no being "influenced" by our words and deeds and no "recollection" thereof. The Gods are too exalted for this. Is not ἀπάθεια a characteristic of the divine nature? The operation of the constellations is powerful and very real and Plotinus never doubts it, but it is impersonal in character[4].

In a remarkable and very characteristic passage[5] Plotinus describes

[1] V 8, 7. 2-8.
[2] Ib. 1. 12-16.
[3] Ib., 1. 36-44.
[4] The matter is dealt with in detail in the fourth treatise of *Enn.* IV, esp. cc. 25-26 and 30-45. [5] *Enn.* IV cc. 33-35.

the movement of the All as a round-dance in which all participants spontaneously make the movements which fit in with the whole. This harmony exists because the universe is one great living being. The figures formed by the parts are as it were the proportions and distances in the living substance, its rhythms and attitudes according to an established order (κατὰ λόγον), and the parts formed by these figures are the members of the living creature. The will (προαίρεσις) remains outside these parts and does not contribute to the nature (= vegetative life) of the living being[1]. For a living creature has but one will but it has many different powers (δυνάμεις): desire, wrath, growth, birth. Thus there exists in the universe too a great diversity of forces, even in the moving, apparently lifeless things which we cannot perceive. All this indeed carries on a hidden life and supplies wonderful forces to the entire ζῷον, even though the parts may possess no will[2].

In this whole of absolute cohesion man possesses a great measure of freedom. For *spiritual* man, and this, says Plotinus, is the true man, – is, as a spiritual being, ἀπαθής: he thus stands outside or above the chain of natural causes. His soul is absorbed in the whole as an independent cause. Only to a small extent does man-as-compound undergo physical-cosmic influences at his periphery[3].

To sum up: The soul's reflection upon itself teaches it that it is exalted above all physical being as a source of movement and life; next that, progressing from one state to the other and thus being situated in time[4] it must be rooted in a higher reality which is eternal and unchanging, a spiritual world which contains within it the prime images of all things, the Noûs. Finally, since this Noûs contains the many and the all, one must assume above it a higher, absolute Principle of which nothing can be said but that it is the One.

2. How did the many come forth from the One? Answer: Automatically – through an overflow of fullness and an irradiation of splendour: not through an inclination towards the existence of something different, not through a desire to create. With the Noûs too the rise of the following (lower) hypostasis is a product of its own contemplation which remains confined to itself. The soul is the first to know

---

[1] IV 4, 35.
[2] Ib. 36.
[3] IV 4, 34, l. 1-7; cf. II 1, 5 (end); II 3, 9; I 1, 7. 14-24; I 1, 10.
[4] In III 7, 11 Plotinus defines time as: the life of the soul in a transition from one state of life to another.

a striving and thus an urge to create what is outside itself. The pure soul, however, that is the soul in its inmost being, remains in itself and is ἀπαθής.

3. The following principles form the basis of this systematic structure:
1. The One is more original than the many.
2. Every nature must of necessity give rise to what comes after it.
3. Three, and not more than three fundamental hypostases must be assumed. Stated abstractly:

Entia non sunt multiplicanda sine ratione.

Plotinus[1] emphatically supports this last principle in opposition to the so-called gnostics who, more or less mythologizing, peopled their spiritual world (πλήρωμα) with a whole series of spiritual beings, arranged in pairs. The Valentinians recognized 30. Plotinus reasons that it is essential to distinguish between the One and the Noûs, between the Noûs and the soul. No other natures can be assumed, however, in addition to these three hypostases. One cannot, for instance, split the Noûs into a "potential" and an "actual" Noûs, for according to Plotinus the Noûs is always at work. Nor can one assume a Logos proceeding from the Noûs which in its turn would give rise to the soul – in such a way that the latter would not originate directly from the Noûs. Such a possibility is excluded since it would deprive the soul of thought.

There are thus three, and no more than three fundamental hypostases – i.e. three stages in the divine nature. The lowest produces, as we saw, that reflex which is the visible world. This still possesses its own creative power, the last reflex of the soul, no longer thinking, it is true, but nonetheless "making". This is the φύσις, vegetable life with its growth force and power of procreation. This too is still "soul", albeit in the lowest degree[2]. It cannot be said to be aware, in the proper sense of the word, yet Plotinus speaks here of θεωρία: the creative activity of the φύσις merits this title because it is a *logos*, a rational principle, which creates without practical action[3].

One important problem still remains: Can Plotinus' explanation of the world, given here, in which, it would seem, everything is reduced to one principle, truly be called a *monism*? Should one not say that in the last resort it emerges as a *dualism* since, in contrast to the divine

---
[1] II 9, 1.
[2] III 8, 4. 15 ff.
[3] III 8, 3.

nature which roots and culminates in the One, we have the ὕλη as an irreducible and thus essentially independent principle. Is Plotinus' so-called monism not affected by the dualism which has been detected, not without reason, in Plato's philosophy and are not his concept of man and his view of the world, insofar as they become concrete, imbued with an unmistakable dualism?

Ultimately the answer must be: no. If one understands by dualism an interpretation of the world based on two principles, each equal and independent, then Plotinus was no dualist. One can say this with more certainty than that Plato was no dualist. And yet, on this point, there is no reason for hesitation with reference to Plato either; he too was no dualist if one defines dualism as we have done above. With regard to both thinkers one can quite simply base this statement on the fact that they expressly denied the character of being and thus independent existence to what they knew in Aristotelian terms as "the material principle": it is a shadowy thing, impossible to grasp, which can never be and has never been positively defined, a μὴ ὄν thus which is indeed nothing other than a (necessary) reflex of thought at its utmost limit. It is thus completely contrary to the line of Platonic thought to suggest that this μὴ ὄν exists as an independent being alongside and in contrast to the highest Principle which is the last basis of Thought and Being. For Plotinus – and in this he follows Plato – the highest Principle is, if not literally then certainly according to the trend of his thought, a centre of infinite power. It is the ἄπειρος δύναμις which contains everything within it, not "potentially" but *dynamically*. The ὕλη on the other hand is a powerless principle which is not even "potential" in the passive sense of being able to become something. The ὕλη is ἀπαθής, states Plotinus[1], but this has a completely different significance from that of the spirit. The apathy of the ὕλη means that it is not susceptible to influence by the moulding principle which is the Good. For this reason and to this extent it represents that which is evil[2], solely through the lack of the Good.

One of the quirks of modern thought is to link the term "matter" with the body and all things physical. For Plotinus (and here again he is following Plato) matter is in the first instance an incorporeal principle (ἀσώματον). This goes without saying. For after all, the body is something real which admits all kinds of positive modifications and

[1] III 6, 7.
[2] II 4, 16. 16ff. and III 6, 11. Cf. also I 8. The purely negative character of the ὕλη as μὴ ὄν is here strictly maintained.

various sorts of influences, while the ὕλη, precisely because it is a non-physical principle, is not susceptible to influences. It cannot be transformed into a reality by the measure of the reality which enters into it. It cannot "change", for it does not (as in Aristotle) unite with form[1]. It is, for that matter, not even Form itself which comes in the ὕλη. It is after all never more than "a shadowy image that comes in another shadowy image", "untruth in untruth" ((εἴδωλον ἐν εἰδώλῳ and ψεῦδος εἰς ψεῦδος)[2]. This is how far Plotinus is from positing "matter" as an independent and equal principle alongside and contrasted with the One. I have pointed out elsewhere that this is an erroneous concept found among the Christian Apologists of the second century, for instance Theophilus, the author of the *Cohortatio*, and many who came after them[3].

We must point out, however, that Plotinus also speaks of "matter" in a completely different manner; he acknowledges a ὕλη in the intelligible order and does not scruple to speak of an ἄπειρον in the intelligible world. For that matter, as we already saw, he calls the first Principle which is the source of the intelligible, δύναμις ἄπειρος[4].

The Noûs, that is, the intelligible, must contain infinity on account of the endless variety of sorts[5]. Is this then evil as such? Must multiplicity not be regarded as a defection from the One, and infinity – which is after all an uncountable multiplicity – absolute defection from the One?[6] No, replies Plotinus. For in the intelligible world multiplicity is always a determined multiplicity, and the ἄπειρον too is always determined in this case. If this is not so, then one descends to a lower level, to the world of becoming[7].

How then must one conceive of that ἄπειρον in the intelligible? Plotinus answers – and his reply sounds surprisingly Platonic – one must imagine two opposites at the same time and not dwell upon one of them, for instance, large-and-small[8].

This answer is so surprising because here the ἄπειρον of Plato which

[1] III 6, 10-13.
[2] III 6, 13. 31ff.
[3] C. J. de Vogel, *Het christelijk scheppingsbegrip en de antieke wijsbegeerte*, in: Tijdschr. voor Phil. 1953, pp. 409-425; *Theoria*, 1967, ch. XII.
[4] V 8, 9.
[5] VI 7, 14.
[6] VI 6, 1.
[7] VI 6, 3.
[8] VI, 6, 3.

is the Great-and-small[1] is situated in the intelligible world: "matter" has here become "intelligible matter". What has Plotinus to tell us regarding this concept? To find the answer one must consult his classic treatise on the ὕλη-concept: Enn. II 4, Περὶ τῶν δύο ὑλῶν. Here Plotinus vigorously defends the existence of intelligible matter (ὕλη νοητή). One must not, he warns us (c. 3), always despise the indeterminate. The soul is in a certain sense "matter" with regard to the Noûs, and the Noûs itself certainly contains compounds, even if not so as bodies. Matter "yonder" is of a completely different kind from the matter here in our world: matter yonder is never without form and it possesses these forms not successively, one after the other, but all at the same time. And, since it belongs to the intelligible, it is, as a matter of course, eternal. Its existence – a real existence – must be assumed since a multiplicity of individual "forms" exists in the intelligible world. For these forms must occur in a substratum (a ὑποκείμενον) which is matter. In a certain sense the intelligible world is divisible. But that which is divided is matter. Because it is a νοητόν, it is a real being, an οὐσία[2]. It is created but not therefore in time: it is eternally produced by the (intelligible) principle of difference (ἑτερότης) which belongs to the five highest genera, that is, which is on a level with the ὄν[3].

This then is Plotinus' doctrine of the ὕλη or the ἄπειρον. It is not correct to say that to him the matter of the sensible world (ὕλη αἰσθητή) is an original and independent "datum", how ever negatively conceived, yet co-eternal with the First Principle. Plotinus explicitly denies this possibility. In the treatise on the two ὕλαι[4] he employs the argument that the κόσμος νοητός, since it is the archetype of the visible world which is composed of matter and form, must of necessity possess ὕλη. This ὕλη (νοητή) exists since otherwise there could be no multiplicity (in the intelligible). But – multiplicity is already contained in principle in the One, and this is after all δύναμις ἄπειρος.

The principle of infinity in Plotinus is thus indeed rooted in the one highest Principle. This proves that his philosophical system is a strict monism, and a dynamic monism at that. The "darkness" of which he speaks, which surrounds the intelligible and, bordering on it, is il-

[1] Cf. Hermodorus ap. Simpl. 247. 30-248. 15 and Sextus Emp. *Math.* X 248-282 (De Vogel, *Greek Phil.* I nr. 371 a, b).
[2] II 4, 5. 12-23.
[3] Ib. 24-37.
[4] II 4, 4.

lumined by the soul, (for one must think of the whole of this system as a set of concentric circles around a middle point) – this darkness is no independent pre-existing being. The soul itself causes it to emerge and then shapes it. Plotinus still describes it thus in a short fragment at the end of the third Ennead[1].

With all this Plotinus sheds more light on the relationship of Plato's highest principles, the One and the indefinite duality, than Plato ever did. Plotinus has in fact already performed the "minor correction" which, as I said at the end of a previous paper on the Christian concept of creation and Greek philosophy, had to be applied from that point of view to Plato's first principles[2].

If we turn from the monism of Plotinus and glance back at preceding Greek thought we immediately see that from the very beginning the ancient Milesians were preoccupied with the question of the one ἀρχή; this is in principle the monistic problem here resolved in a somewhat primitive form. Early Pythagoreanism was most probably a dualist reaction to the monism of the Milesians. In any case the table of opposites (συστοιχία) familiar to us from Aristotle's *Metaph.* A. 5 is old and probably dates back to the sixth century. Parmenides in his turn reacts against this Pythagorean dualism with his radical thesis that only Being exists and that Being is One.

The first criticism which springs to mind is that Parmenides denies the world which we perceive, the world of multiplicity and movement. He finally allows it to remain as a μὴ ὄν alongside the ὄν, without attributing to it any reality and without deducing it from the ὄν. It is clear that this is in principle an entirely different theory regarding the visible world from that put forward by Plotinus. Plotinus' criticism, however, is not so much directed at Parmenides' teaching concerning the μὴ ὄν as against his doctrine of the ὄν: Parmenides teaches that Being is one, and this argument will not stand up. Plato's reasoning is better: he clearly situated his first Principle above the multiplicity of the intelligible Being. This criticism on the part of Plotinus is entirely correct (although incomplete).

After Parmenides come the "pluralists and atomists" as they are usually known. The latter, to whom Democritus belonged, were also pluralists according to the Greek view, for they regard a multitude of particles and the void as "beings".

[1] III 9, 3. 9-16.
[2] Tijdschr. v. Phil. 1953, p. 432; C. J. de Vogel, *Theoria*, 202.

After these comes Plato with his theory of Ideas. Was this a sort of spiritualistic pluralism? It would have been so, had not Plato in the last resort deduced his Ideas from two First Principles, that is, at least, if we can believe Aristotle's testimony in *Metaph*. A 6 as well as certain other testimonies. It has been said[1] that this is impossible. Plato cannot possibly have derived his Ideas from the two principles (the One and the Undetermined dyad or the Great-and-small) mentioned by Aristotle. For the idea that the perfect purely spiritual being of the Ideas should contain something of a material principle is in conflict with everything we know of Plato's thought, and must therefore be based upon misunderstanding and fallacy.

The remarkable thing is that it is precisely in so spiritual and so Platonic a thinker as Plotinus that we find the statement attributed by Aristotle to Plato. In my opinion this is sufficient reason for not rejecting out of hand Aristotle's testimony on the doctrine of the prima principia. But, on the other hand it also opens up to us the perspective of a derivation of the duality from the One itself since the multiplicity of Ideas already presupposes the ἄπειρον. We do not know whether Plato himself already in principle withdrew his twoness into the One, but we do know that for him the μὴ ὄν always occupies a *subordinate* place and never stood beside the One as a principle *of equal value*. To the extent, then, that some trace of dualism existed in Plato, one must say that it was a weak dualism, not a dualism in the full sense. One must say in addition that Plotinus continued strongly and faithfully the lines of Plato's thought, thereby showing clearly that the true trend of Platonic thought is monistic.

Aristotle is entirely different. He puts it first and foremost that one can never explain the world from one principle. In order to explain the act of becoming one needs three principles: matter, form and the lack of form. There are, however, many forms, and Aristotle does not enlighten us about where they come from. All we hear is that the forms are "in things". They are evidently conceived by Aristotle as real ὄντα, and this fact alone makes him a pluralist.

Apart from the immanent forms he also assumes the existence of "forms without matter", what are called by later thinkers the "intelligences" of the heavenly spheres with the Unmoved Mover at the top. This last was for Aristotle by no means the ultimate ground of being, the source of all life. He sets only the outermost heavenly sphere in motion. In any case Aristotle was a pluralist.

[1] H. Cherniss in: *The Riddle of the Early Academy* (1945).

THE MONISM OF PLOTINUS

How did matters stand with the Stoa? In spite of a certain monistic tendency what we have here is not a complete monism. Stoic physics begins with a sort of dualism: there are two ἀρχαί, the ποιοῦν and the πάσχον; the latter is the one lacking quality, the ὕλη – the first the Logos indwelling in it, the creative force, "Zeus" (Diog. Laert. VII 134). For the Stoics the ὕλη is a real being and therefore a body. It is called "substance" (οὐσία) but is, however, thought of as the material basis of all being, since everything is a transformation of the substratum which is the ὕλη. At the same time this thought has a monistic trend, since the forming power is regarded as being immanent in matter and no transcendent being is assumed. This our cosmos is the one-and-all: God and Reason, body and matter at the same time.

It is no wonder that Plotinus often polemised against this system. It was more alien to him than that of Aristotle, although in the matter of ethics he was strongly influenced by the Stoa. He repeatedly combats Stoic materialism, the Stoic doctrine of the soul, of knowledge, of perception and of feelings, and also the Stoic doctrine of categories (along with that of Aristotle). And, it must be said, his criticism is nearly always justified.

He himself imparted to the monism with which Greek thought began in its early youth, a well-considered and refined form, which to a large extent influenced Christian reflection on the concept of God.

It is not difficult to mention a couple of main points in metaphysics on which Plotinus differed from Christian thought, in particular the concept of God. We think for example of his three gradations in the Divine, and of the strictly impersonal character which he attributes to Providence. And yet it is remarkable that, when Christians come to reflect in a philosophical manner on the nature of God, Plotinus' thought has been and still is a great support to them. One can see an example of this in Thomas Aquinas' chapters in the first part of the great *Summa* on the goodness and will of God, and also when he deals with creation.

In various sorts of modern "monism" one gains the impression that the term is used much less strictly and radically than among the ancient writers, particularly Plotinus. This is not only true of Hegel and his followers but certainly also of various "psychic" or physical monisms which have arisen in the course of the last century and a half and (in most cases) disappeared again. Plotinus would certainly have proposed to Hegel and his followers that the Spirit which is "everything" and manifests itself in the endless diversity of being, cannot be the ultimate and fundamental unity. And Ostwald's theory of energy would have found an even sterner judge in this classical thinker. He would undoubtedly have pointed out that the modern philosopher neglects the most elementary distinction in concepts, since he does not distinguish the physical from the spiritual and, although combating materialism ex professo, is far from free of it himself.

It must indeed be noted that a radically thought out and consistent principle of unity is lacking in these newer forms of philosophy – since the transcendence of the first Principle has been abandoned.

Admittedly this last is not true in "monistic" Christianity. And yet Plotinus would undoubtedly have had certain reproaches to make to this religious form of thought, at least as it commonly occurs. He would have said – as he did in fact with reference to the Egyptian Sethians – that with their doctrine of creation they do not keep the spiritual purely spiritual but mingle it with the temporal, and that the God who is Spirit and Creator is not completely one and for that reason cannot be a first Principle.

The Neo-Platonists after Plotinus busied themselves with expanding and complicating the sober system of the three hypostases into a construction of various stages and intermediary stages. The Church Father Athanasius, however, recognizing in the divine Spirit which contains the All the second Person of the one God, linked that Spirit as equal with the One and thus restored the link between Christian revelation and the ripest fruit of the Greek mind.

EAST AND WEST

CHAPTER XVIII

THE MOTIVE OF ETERNAL CHANGE IN GREEK AND LATER WESTERN PHILOSOPHY COMPARED WITH INDIAN THOUGHT[1]

For many generations the early Ionian thinker Heraclitus of Ephesus has been considered as the classical philosopher of "eternal flux". "For it is impossible to step twice into the same river"[2]. "We do, and we do not step into the same rivers; we are it, and we are not it."[3]

When we step into the same river to-morrow, the river will be *seemingly* the same; yet, not actually so, for new water will be flowing between the banks. The river, therefore, will not be the same. Neither shall we ourselves be the same persons: *in a sense*, no doubt, it is *we* that shall step once more into the river. We shall be *considered as being* the same persons. But, as a matter of fact, we are not. We too have changed. We are no longer those who we were before.

The man who had this tremendous and bewildering thought did not just play with it. He was actually haunted by it. For him the ever flowing, ever changing river was a symbol of a mighty universal process: everything in nature is like the river is, and as we are ourselves: the same, and yet not the same. The physical elements turn into their opposites. "Fire lives the death of earth, air lives the death of fire, water lives the death of air, earth lives the death of water."[4] Being opposite the one to the other, they are apparently the same; for the one passes into the other and so "lives the other's death". It *is* the other, because it changes into it[5]. "The upward path and the downward path are one and the same."[6]

[1] The present chapter was written at the beginning of 1963 as a contribution to the XIIIth International Congress of Philosophy, held in Mexico City. Only a very small part of it was actually read at the Congress, since time was lacking. The text appeared in the IVth volume of the Congress Acts. I have made only a few small corrections.
[2] Fr. 91 (from Plutarch, *De E ap. Delphos* 18).
[3] Fr. 49a.   [4] Fr. 76.   [5] Fr. 88 and 67.
[6] I think it probable that by "the upward path" of Fr. 60 the author thought

What is all this tending to? Is this philosopher teaching us that, strictly speaking, *nothing at all exists* – since the next moment it will no more be what it was, nor is it now what it was the preceding moment – and that *there is, strictly speaking, no "we", no subject identical with itself, no personality*?

That is, in fact, what he *might* have said. But I do not think, he did, nor that he *intended* to do so. And that is exactly what interests me. For in another part of the world, unknown then to the Greeks, I find, almost in the same years, another man who is reflecting on himself and on the world around him, and, observing that things change and he changes too, he will *cling* to this aspect of change – of non-identity –, and will conclude exactly as I said: *Nothing at all exists; nothing is; no "I", no "we", no subject identical with itself, no person, no personality*. And he will *cling* to this thought: *that nothing is*. He will stare at it and embrace it. He feels *liberated* by it: freed from vanity, suffering and fear. He will be infinitely satisfied by this view *that nothing is*. He will accept it as truth; as the ultimate word on everything: *that nothing at all is*.

But let us go back to Ionia: to Heraclitus. His thought turned another way. From the principle of eternal flux he did not conclude the non-existence of the world and of ourselves, including the very core of our being. Under the appearance of eternal change he found rather an underlying unity[1]. In nature there is an equilibrium of opposites, a kind of elastic tension[2]; in and through the obviously existing eternal strife there is a hidden harmony[3]. And this hidden unity of Nature, he says, is what is best[4].

As to our own person, we too are changing. Yet, is there not an underlying unity? Certainly, there is some profound mystery about the "we". Its ground cannot be easily discovered: "I began to seek

of the heavier elements turning into the lighter ones, and by the downward path the reverse order.

[1] Fr. 10: "Joints: whole and not-whole, coming together and separating, harmonious and discordant; and from all things one, and out of one all things."

[2] Fr. 51: "Men do not understand how what is at variance agrees with itself. It is an attunement of opposite tensions, like that of the bow and the lyre."

[3] Fr. 8: "That which is in opposition is in concert, and from things that differ comes the most beautiful harmony."

Fr. 51, cited above, n. 7.

Fr. 54: "The hidden harmony is better than the apparent one."

Fr. 123: "Nature loves to hide."

[4] Fr. 54.

for myself", says Heraclitus[1], and: "The limits of the soul you could not find, not even if you tried every way; such a deep logos has she"[2] and: "The soul has a logos in it which increases itself"[3].

What is this principle of inner growth, inherent in ourselves? What is the ground of the hidden unity and harmony in nature? – "Everything is happening according to the logos", Heraclitus says[4]. Therefore, if any man wishes to have any real understanding, either of natural phenomena or of himself, he must "follow" the Logos, which is the "koinon"[5]: that which is common to everything, pervading the universe as a ruling force. Hence, "it is wisdom to act according to Nature, listening to her"[6].

It is certainly correct to say that for Heraclitus the Logos is a cosmic law. Moreover, for man, conforming to this Law in thought and action means virtue and wisdom. On the other hand, "the dry soul" is said to be wisest and best[7], as water is the death for souls[8]. For soul is nearest to the cosmic fire. Her very essence seems to be a fiery substance, which perishes whenever she "gets wet"[9].

Surely this is a primitive doctrine. And even it might seem to us more "modern" and more easy to understand just to deny the substantiality of the human subject, by denying its identity. For is not this a simple consequence, if one accepts the basic fact of eternal change? Soul, then, would appear to be just nothing, and there would be no "we", just as there are no natural objects.

That is the way of Buddha. It is curious that it was not Heraclitus' way. It is curious that the Ionian philosopher, who might easily have concluded the non-existence both of nature and of the human self, turned the other way round, to the eternal and *substantial* ground of everything, of nature and of human souls. "All things are given in exchange for fire, and fire for everything", says Heraclitus[10]. There is eternal change, but this does not mean that there is just nothing. It means that one thing is transformed into the other. Moreover, it is observed that this eternal process of transformation happens with a

---

[1] Fr. 101.   [2] Fr. 45.   [3] Fr. 115.   [4] Fr. 1.
[5] Fr. 1 and 2: "Therefore, one must follow that which is common [to everything]. For the Logos is in everything; but most people live as if they had their own insight."
[6] Fr. 112.   [7] Fr. 118.
[8] Fr. 36: "It is death for souls to become water, and for water it is death to become earth. For water comes to be from earth, and soul from water."
[9] Fr. 77 and 117.
[10] Fr. 90.

certain order and regularity. And the wise man, who conforms his thought to the universal Logos, will be able to understand something of the unity and harmony of all things.

In the last decennium an attempt has been made to explain the motive of eternal change away from Heraclitus' thought. The simile of the river, we are told, was not used at all to illustrate eternal change. On the contrary, its aim was nothing else than to demonstrate the identity and stability of things: though other water is ever flowing in the river, yet the river stays the same[1]. It is Plato who, by attributing to Heraclitus the doctrine of eternal flux (which, as a matter of fact, he never held), explained the river parable as a denial of the identity of things; which to him (Plato) meant: a denial of the *substantiality* of things. But this is exactly what Heraclitus did not mean.

Now certainly it should not be denied that Heraclitus taught the doctrine of eternal flux. Nor is it right to say that by the river simile he did not wish to emphasize the fact of perpetual change of everything, but the stability and permanence. However, what interests us in our present reflections is: the fact that such an interpretation could be given at all. As a matter of fact, Heraclitus did not deny the *reality*, say the *substantiality* of natural objects. He did not declare this changing world to be a μὴ ὄν, a relative non-being, nor even did he oppose it as ever-becoming to eternal Being (this far Dr. Kirk was perfectly right when separating Plato's interpretation from Heraclitus' original thought). And he was very far indeed from declaring everything, including man, to be absolutely οὐκ ὄν.

In the Greek world there was one man, some two or three generations later, who *did* declare emphatically that nothing at all *is*. It was Gorgias of Leontini. But, that was just an intellectual play. In his life Gorgias was not at all affected by this view. Plato, to be sure, considered the physical world as an imperfect image (εἰκών or "imitation") of an absolute and perfect archetype. For him the latter only was *Being*. But neither did he deny to this changing world an own, peculiar character of reality, nor did he ever sever it from that pure and perfect Being on which, according to his most clear and indubitable doctrine, it wholly depends. And this is what was held by all later Platonists, by Plutarch and Plotinus, and by the Christian Platonists as well.

Throughout his life-time Heraclitus was rather an isolated person. There were just a few who called themselves his followers – we hear of Cratylus who was Plato's master – but in the usual sense he could

[1] G. S. Kirk, *Heraclitus. The cosmic fragments*. Cambridge, 1954.

hardly be said to have had a school. Yet, throughout the history of Western thought, in Greece as well as in Western Europe, until a recent past, or even to the present day, his thought proved to be extremely fertile. It was taken over wholly and assimilated by the Stoics. They almost did what was done by Dr. Kirk: assimilating the motives of eternal change, of opposites changing the one into the other, of elastic harmony and of eternal strife. They laid a heavy emphasis on cosmic order which is dominated by a mighty universal Law, inexorable and Divine: the Logos. I cite a modern echo of this philosophical faith. It is Goethe who sang:

> *Nach ehernen, ewigen grossen Gesetzen*
> *Müssen wir alle unseres Daseins*
> *Kreise vollenden.*

In the Stoa there is not a trace of either doubt or denial of the physical universe, including ourselves as individual subjects and spiritual beings. On the contrary, this changing world is viewed as penetrated and dominated by the Divine Substance of Logos; and we ourselves in the very core of our being are recognized as literally having a share in it[1]. The divine Word which is God dwells actually in us[2]. Our innermost self, our real "we", is said to be a spark of it[3]. The Stoa teaches a philosophy of immanentism: very far from denying physical reality, it rather glorifies it by seeing it penetrated by the Divine. And human life itself in which the divine Word is particularly present is far from being destroyed in its individuality: on the contrary, it is in the Stoics that a formal theory of the "person" and what we call "personality" is developed[4]. We are very far from Buddhism here.

The history of more recent Western thought counts two extreme Heracliteans under its prominent representatives: Hegel and Bergson. Hegel declared that there was no thought in Heraclitus which he did not make his own. While doing so, anyhow he did not tend to deny either the reality or importance of the physical world; even more, by explaining it as an aspect of, or a stage in, the eternal process of self-realisation of the Divine Logos, he glorified it. Nor did he in the least tend to disparage the human personality by his adherence to the

---

[1] The soul is called by the Stoics πνεῦμά πως ἔχον and πῦρ νοερόν (Plot., *Enn.* IV, 7, 4; Porph. ap. Euseb., *Praep. Ev.* XV, p. 813c).
[2] E.g. Seneca, *Ep.* 41, 1 and 4.
[3] Epict., *Diss.* II 8, 11-12.
[4] Panaetius ap. Cic., *De off.* I 30, 107; 31, 110ff.

doctrine of eternal change. Human logos itself takes part in the movement of Divine and universal Logos; it is most literally in it and, in a sense, identical with it.

It is most curious to observe how Henri Bergson followed Heraclitus. He did it with the utmost radicalism. In our innermost life there is not a moment of identity[1]. Here, we might think, it is an unavoidable consequence to deny the human personality. Bergson did not intend to do so. On the contrary, what he says is that the continual flux of our inner life is the very condition of *duration*, and the essence of our existence as a personality.

As to the things of nature, no doubt they are in perpetual flux, even when seemingly in rest and permanence. But it is an error, declares Bergson, to think (as Plato and so many of the Ancients did) that, therefore, they are less "existent" or of a lower level than what is called eternal Being. *Why* after all, should coming-to-be be of an inferior level? Every moment new things and new situations come into being. Is not this a reality, as full and as strict as any? It is the Ancients, such as Plato and Plotinus, who made the strange mistake of declaring that everything has been from eternity, and there is never anything actually new. This is a fundamental error. And coming-to-be is as real and is of no less value than anything at all[2].

This then is the ground on which Bergson, while teaching the perpetual change of man in his interior life, could go on believing in the reality and superior value of the human person. His is a metaphysics of "creative evolution", – a *meta*physics, in which the physical process of perpetual change is raised unto the level of Being in creative motion, Being ever actively realizing itself. Thus, in the philosophy of Western Europe that same principle which led Buddha to the stern denial both of nature and of the human soul, once and again led leading spirits to a most positive and constructive philosophy, in which the sensible world as well as man in his spiritual life are fully recognized and established in their peculiar form of reality.

Now let us turn to India where, when Heraclitus was a boy, the

[1] Bergson, *L'Evolution Créatrice*, p. 4.
[2] *Bergson, L'Evolution Créatrice*, ch. IV, p. 341: "il y a *plus* dans un mouvement que dans les positions successives attribuées au mobile, *plus* dans un devenir que dans les formes traversées tour à tour, *plus* dans l'évolution de la forme que les formes réalisées l'une après l'autre". P. 372: (For modern science) "le changement n'est plus une diminution de l'essence, ni la durée un délayage de l'éternité. Le flux du temps devient ici la réalité même... un accroissement progressif de l'absolu."

young prince Gautama retired into solitude to reflect profoundly on human life. He too discovered the principle of eternal flux, – and he welcomed it and stuck to it with his whole being, so that the identity, the substantiality, and hence the reality both of the world and of individual men vanished before his eyes. *Any* reality, *any* existence vanished – including the Absolute. And this was exactly the state the Buddha wished to attain and to which he was leading the way; he was not searching for any theoretical insight for theory's sake, but what he experienced was a great and total relief by recognizing that neither the self nor anything has any substantiality in it: this insight he experienced to be the cessation of selfishness and craving, and by being the cessation of selfishness and craving to be the definitive cessation of suffering. That is why for Buddha Gautama the reflection on eternal flux, the discovery of the non-identity and non-substantiality of everything became truly *revealing*: it changed his life and, since he felt it could change the life of his fellow-men as well and deliver them from suffering, it made him a prophet and a missionary. But this is not saying enough. What should be said is that it made him the founder of a religion; a religion which throughout the centuries and up to the present day has found thousands, nay, millions of adherents, not only in India and the neighbouring island of Ceylon, but also in China and Japan, where people might seem to differ greatly from the population of India in attitude towards life.

These things are well-known facts. What interests us here is the striking difference of reaction to the same philosophical insight found in East and West. The Buddha, no doubt, was no philosopher, at least not in the usual academic sense, and he did not claim to be one. He wished to keep silent about metaphysical issues. But there has been a Buddhist philosophy. We find older Buddhism, the Hīnayāna (a school which still flourishes in Ceylon) completely dominated by the view of eternal flux, both in physical nature and in the human mind. The first Hīnayāna text cited in Radhakrishnan and Moore's *Source Book in Indian Philosophy*[1] opens by saying, first, "that all constituents of being are transitory;" next, "that all the elements of being are misery"; third, "that all the elements of being are lacking in an ego". In another representative text[2] we find "the theory of no-soul" (or no-self) expounded on the following grounds: that the body and the different

---

[1] The passage is taken from the *Anguttara-nikāya*, III, 134 (Source Book, p. 273f.).
[2] *Samyutta-nikāya*, III, 66 (Source Book, p. 280).

mental functions – feeling, perception, and even consciousness – are subject to sickness, are impermanent, and hence painful and subject to change. By these considerations the disciple is led to be disgusted at the body, etc., and hence to be freed from passion.

In the famous conversation of the venerable Nāgasena with king Milinda[1] the wise man begins by denying his own self. "There is no ego here to be found. There is no Nāgasena." Next, the wise man proceeds to demonstrate that the chariot on which the king has come to see him, does not exist. The word "chariot" is just a name, without substance. This instance serves as an analogy; exactly so it is with the human person.

The Mahāyāna, we are told[3], gives us a positive philosophy which believes in the reality of an Absolute, the essence of existence. The world of experience is phenomenal, an expression of the absolute Reality. And Nirvāna is not annihilation, but attainment. Yet, neither the Yogācāra nor the Mādhyamika, both schools that belong to the Mahāyāna, are positive philosophies in the above mentioned sense. On the contrary, what is established in the Mahāyāna, is that "the three worlds" (the phenomenal world, the ego, and the Absolute) have no objective existence. They are only "mind" (thought or consciousness). Not only the reality of external objects is denied, but that of the human self and of the Absolute as well. Thus, we read in the *Trimśika* (the Thirty Verses) of Vasubandhu, one of the founders of the Mahāyāna School (4th cent. A.D.)[3]:

> – The Enlightened One abstrusely preached
> that all *dharma's* have no entity.
> The first is the non-entity of phenomenon,
> The second is the non-entity of self-existence,
> The last is the non-entity of the ultimate existence
> of the falsely discriminative ego and *dharmas* now to be eliminated.

And in the Mahāyāna *Vimśaka* (the Twenty Verses)[4]:
"When a man perceives the true meaning of reality as it becomes, he understands that the paths of existence are empty. –

"Thus regarded, *samsāra* (i.e. the cycle of birth and death) and *nirvāna* have no real substance. –

---

[1] *Source Book*, pp. 281-84.
[2] *Source Book*, p. 273.
[3] *Source Book*, p. 336-337, nrs. 23-24.
[4] *Source Book*, pp. 338 ff.: I cite the nrs. 15, 16 and 18-20.

"The nature of all things is like things created by magic; they have no existence. They are all nothing but mind. – When the mind-wheel ceases to exist, all things indeed cease to exist."

And the great Buddhist philosopher Nāgārjuna (2nd cent. A.D.) ends his examination of Nirvāna by the following lines[1]:

> "The bliss consists in the cessation of all thought,
> In the quiescence of plurality.
> No [separate] reality was preached at all,
> Nowhere and none, by Buddha!"

When comparing the beginning of the philosophies of eternal flux in East and West, we find that they were very different. In India we find the motive of the continual change and transitoriness of all things, including the human person, essentially connected with that of human suffering, a view which is entirely lacking in the thought of the Ionian philosopher Heraclitus. Though the latter was, doubtless, interested in man and in human society, and did apply his philosophical insight to human life, he was essentially a theoretical thinker. Buddha Gautama, as we observed, was not. His inner experience of the fact of human suffering must have been singularly keen. It dominated his life and thinking. It dominated also that other primarily experienced fact – that of eternal flux, – and gave to the Buddha's reflections on this topic a singular and profound *pathos*. We find a trace of this throughout Buddhist literature. Wherever in later centuries a Buddhist philosophy arises, the doctrine of eternal flux is inculcated in the disciple's mind in order to make him realize that he himself is nothing, and that nothing is at all. And this he should realize as keenly as possible, in order to become detached from everything and by this detachment be freed from suffering.

The closest analogy to this Oriental attitude towards life is found in Greece at the beginning of the Hellenistic era, in the person of Pyrrho of Elis, who is called the founder of the Sceptic School. Pyrrho was hardly a theoretical philosopher. He neither affirmed nor denied that anything exists; things are indifferent, unstable, and such that we cannot judge them. What results when men realize this is, first, loss of speech (aphasia), next tranquillity (ataraxia)[2]. Pyrrho was described

---

[1] In: the Mādhyamika-śāstra, ch. 25, the Examination of Nirvāna, no. 24 (*Source Book*, p. 345).
[2] Aristocles in Eusebius, *Praep. evang.* XIV, 18, 2. De Vogel, *Greek phil.* III, 1087a.

by his Greek biographers as a very simple and gentle person, who by mere scepticism used to do just what everybody did, and displayed a complete indifference to everything happening around him[1], – an attitude towards life which was greatly admired by his fellow-citizens of the city of Elis. For the Greeks, however, theoretically minded they were, did appreciate, and even *required* from a philosopher, a certain detachment from outward things; and the more he proved to possess this quality, the more they trusted him[2]. But certainly, a complete indifference such as Pyrrho's, who did not even notice a precipice before his feet or cars approaching in the street, was quite unusual in Greece. One might feel inclined to ask from where it came to Pyrrho. The reply to this question is given in Diogenes Laertius' *Bios*, where we read that Pyrrho, who took part in Alexander's expedition to the Orient, met with the "gymnosophists" in India and with the so-called Magi; that he admired their way of philosophizing and following their example introduced this kind of philosophy in Greece[3].

Both of the other Hellenistic Schools that were founded shortly after the death of Alexander, that of Epicurus and the Stoa, were more or less concerned with the problem of human suffering. However, their approach to this problem was very different from the Buddhist one. The Stoics adopted Heraclitus' philosophy of eternal flux. But this philosophical theory never led them to the denial of the human self, the physical universe or the divine Spirit which was conceived as permeating and governing the universe. Moreover – the problem of suffering was never acknowledged as such! On the contrary, the Stoic philosopher *denied* the fact of suffering. And this he could do by denying that outward things meant anything to him at all. Here too we find a detachment from outward things, as complete as possible. We find an elimination of all feelings and desires. But the aim is positive. It is expressed in the formula of "how do we attain to eudaemonia" ("happiness", or rather "well-being"). The Stoic finds it in virtue, which he defined as an inner state of the soul. Outward things were said to be indifferent, not because the Stoic philosopher would consider them as unreal (because changing), – this he did not –, but

---

[1] Diog. Laert. IX, 62 (from Antigonos of Karystos); DV., *Gr. Ph.* 1082b-1083.
[2] See the Introductory chapter to this volume.
[3] Diog. Laert. IX, 61; DV., *Gr. Ph. III*, 1082a. Cp. also Plutarch, *Life of Alexander*, cc. 64-65 and 69, 3-4, where it is told how the gymnosophist Calanos burned himself on a pyre.

because these things do not depend on our will. And that which does not depend on us is not our own.

Epicurus, too, strove for eudaemonia by an extreme limitation of desires. Practically speaking, he was an ascetic in his style of life. But he never denied the reality either of the self or of outward things. And he and his disciples enjoyed profoundly such simple things as were given to them – a measure of health and physical well-being, a sober meal, and above all the company of friends. They were far from being indifferentists, and differed *toto caelo* both from Pyrrho and from the Indian Buddhists in their attitude towards life.

Frequently the Stoics engaged in social and political life, particularly the Roman Stoics. Epicureans, however, lived a retired life. Nevertheless, in both these Hellenistic schools we find an attitude towards life which, compared to the Buddhist one, shows a remarkable difference. Together with the difference of reaction to the philosophical view of eternal flux this reveals, I think, something of the divergent character of the Western and the Eastern soul. I am very well aware that in India there are other, and more positive theories on Being, on the physical world, on men and on the Absolute. Yet, Buddhism is a widespread spiritual movement. What may be said is this, I think, that on the whole the Western soul is definitely inclined to fly nonbeing and almost instinctively considers being as valuable in itself, whereas the Oriental soul rather frequently does not fly non-being, but even welcomes it and seeks it. No doubt, this divergency springs from a different psychical attitude towards life and towards the world, the Western man being more optimistic and disposed to action, while the Oriental man frequently has a profoundly pessimistic feeling about human life and the surrounding world.

We cannot close these few reflections without a word on that great 9th century interpreter of India's classical philosophical tradition: Śamkara. Just as in Greece Plato as a young man had been much impressed by the Heraclitean thought of eternal flux and from the fact that in this world there is neither stability nor identity, concluded that reality in the full sense, which is the object of knowledge, must be "yonder", so Śamkara was clearly influenced by the Buddhist philosophy of his days. Not unlike Plato he posited that there is but one "true Reality": that of eternal and invisible Being, perfect and beyond time and space. The higher soul of man, ātman, is identical with that eternal Spirit which is the Brāhman. Just as we find Plato repeatedly opposing "that which is ever changing, *comes-to-be* and perishes, but never *is*", to Being in the full sense which is always the same and identical with itself, thus Śamkara denied the reality of the phenomenal world because it is in eternal flux. What did he mean by this thesis of the non-being of the sensible world? There have been different trends of interpretation. Let me begin by saying what *Plato* meant, and did not mean, by his antithesis of *Being* to "Coming-to-be" or "becoming".

He did *not* mean to say that the sensible world is non-being or illusion (abhāva or śunya, as it is held in certain Buddhist schools). Sometimes he spoke of "two kinds of *being*, the visible and the invisible"[1], and sometimes he emphasized that *coming-to-be* is actually "coming to *be*" (γένεσις εἰς οὐσίαν)[2]. He wrote a special dialogue, the *Timaeus*, to explain that the physical world is an *image* or *representation* of the intelligible world. The word "image" (εἰκών) does not mean illusion. It contains two aspects: first, that we are concerned with a *non-primary* reality, i.e. with a secondary or dependent reality; second, it emphasizes the *resemblance* of the "image" to that which is its archetype.

As to Śamkara, he held most emphatically that there is but one reality – the Brāhman, including the ātman which in its essence is identical with it. Does this not imply that the sensible world – which according to Śamkara is not at all absorbed into the ātman, but carefully distinguished and separated from it as totally different – is non-existent and unreal? This is how many of his followers understood Śamkara, and some of his opponents as well. In our own century Śri Aurobindo understood him in this sense, and blamed him for having introduced a foreign doctrine into the classical tradition of the Upanishads. In those sacred books of ancient India, he remarked, the physical world was not said to be an illusion. This is a Buddhist doctrine which should be rejected.

Dr. Radhakrishnan went further: not only the Upanishads did not conceive the physical world as an illusion, but Śamkara did not hold this either. As a matter of fact Śamkara repudiated the Buddhist doctrine of the world as abhāva (non-existent) or śunya (void). He held that it is *dependent reality*.

Reading the text of Śamkara's Vedānta-explanations in the first

---
[1] *Phaedo*, 79a.
[2] *Philebus*, 26b.

and second book[1] will convince us directly that Radhakrishnan is right: first, we find Śamkara expounding that the world proceeds from Brāhman in whom its intelligible order – its differentiation by names and forms – has its origin. This is a perfectly Platonical doctrine. And even when Śamkara, referring to the Vedānta texts and the Bhagavadgītā, declares that for him who has reached the state of truth and reality the whole apparent world does not exist, though there is no direct parallel in Plato, there is a clear and direct parallel in Plotinus[2]. What is recognized and expressed on both sides is that, once the human self has attained to the vision of transcendent and absolute Being, the manifold appearance of this world vanishes before his eyes. What is neither expressed nor intended is: the non-existence of external things. Śamkara is explicit on this topic. "In every act of perception", he says, "we are conscious of some external thing corresponding to the idea,... and that of which we are conscious cannot but exist." And further: natural objects, perceived in the waking state, are not like those of a dream. For the latter are negated by our waking consciousness, whereas natural objects are never negated in any state. Śamkara concludes that Buddha "either was a man given to make incoherent assertions or else that hatred of all beings induced him to propound absurd doctrines".

This is perfectly clear language. However, the question might be raised of how then Śamkara's "non-dualism" could be understood as a denial of the sensible world. I think there are two grounds for this apparently erroneous interpretation: firstly, if Brāhman is said to be the only reality, and ātman is identified with Brāhman while the physical world is opposed to it as wholly different, the logical consequence seems to be that the physical world is unreal; next, when the physical world is called māyā, the ambiguity of this term could easily give rise to different interpretations. For māyā *may* denote "illusion"; but it does not necessarily do so, nor even does it primarily. Since the primary meaning of māyā is: the mysterious power of super-human beings, their marvellous skill and creative ability, the Śvetāśvatara Upanishad could call God the māyin, who by his māyā creates the world[3]. In such a passage it was certainly not intended to say that

---

[1] *Vedānta*, I 1, 2; I 4, 3; I 4, 15; II 1, 14; II 2, 28-29, and 32 (*Source Book*, pp. 511, 515ff., 530f., 534f.).
[2] *Enneads*, IV 4, 1.
[3] See on this passage (Śvet. U. 4, 9 and 10) J. Gonda, *Sense and etymology of Skt. māyā*, in: *Four Studies in the Language of the Veda*, Utrecht 1959, p. 165f.,

God is a deceiver who by some kind of trickery creates illusions. And Dr. Radhakrishnan was certainly right in rendering "māyin" by "creator" and "māyā" by "creative power". And when in the same passage the world itself is called māyā, it is certainly better not to render the term in such a context by "illusion"[1]. It should be borne in mind that in this passage as well as in Śamkara the world is considered as a self-expression of Brāhman. On the other hand, in the Vedas māyā is sometimes attributed to malignant beings. Exercised by them it takes on the character of magic art, trickery, delusion. It is true that there are passages in the Upanishads where the sensible world is described as similar to a magic illusion (indrajāla), and where māyā is explained as a dream, an appearance without substance or reality[2]. What is intended in such a passage is, if I understand it well, that man is easily inclined to take for "being" in the full sense that which, as a matter of fact, is only an *appearance* of it, – a more or less removed expression of that which in itself is Absolute and perfect and without any change[3].

After all, I think it is not saying too much even when we observe that there is a close resemblance between Platonism (including Neoplatonism) and Advaita philosophy. On both sides there is not only a positive metaphysics of transcendent Being, but also a view of the sensible world as proceeding from or dependent on that absolute Reality of which it is a – be it inadequate – expression[4].

---

and the literature mentioned there. Also J. Gonda, *Maya*, in *Tijdschrift v. Phil.* 1952.

[1] Ruth Reyna, *The concept of māyā from the Vedas to the 20th century*, London, 1962, p. 97, does translate it by that term.

[2] I am thinking of *Maitri Up.* 4,2. It may be observed, perhaps, that for ancient Indian thought a dream is not without any reality; it is just not what it *seems* to be. This much is true: even in this passage it is not meant to say that the world is just *nothing* (as it is held at least in certain Buddhist Schools).

[3] Cf. e.g., the beautiful passage on God's māyā in *Bhagavadgītā*, 4, 6, explained by Gonda in the above cited article in *Tijdschr. v. Phil.* 1952.

[4] Dr. J. F. Staal, in his work *Advaita and Neoplatonism* (Madras, 1961) concludes that of Advaita and Neoplatonism the latter is the more world-negating, the former the more world-affirming. I think there is a misinterpretation of Neoplatonism, in particular of Plotinus, behind this judgment. As a matter of fact, both Advaita and Neoplatonism (in particular Plotinus), are positive in their account of the sensible world, exactly in the above-mentioned sense.

Dr. Staal also mentions the topic of personality. He finds on both sides an impersonalism. It should be remembered here that, as a matter of fact, Plotinus created a metaphysics of the individual man (= personality) by anchoring this

THE MOTIVE OF ETERNAL CHANGE

Let me close these few pages by a word on two representative modern Indian thinkers – Śri Aurobindo and Radhakrishnan. In them we find the most radical counter-part of Buddhistic negation. For the physical fact of eternal flux does not lead these modern Indian thinkers at all to the denial of either man's individual person or of the cosmic universe. They have a strong faith in the transforming power of the Spirit; they believe in the transmutation both of the sensible world and of man's entire being, including the non-rational part of his soul and even his body. They see the physical universe as being ultimately illuminated and spiritualized, absorbed into the super-conscient Divine nature, – as man himself, who is partly a physical being, will be *wholly* (not only in part) spiritualized and made divine.

Much of this sounds very Plotinian. But does it not come close to the Christian expectation of "a new earth" and of the resurrection, – in brief, of that final state of which it is said that God will be all in all? For Christians this belief is founded on the promise of the eternal God himself. In Indian philosophers the strength and boldness of their faith and the profoundness of their spiritual life show at least that we would be very wrong when thinking that Indian philosophy would not be able to overcome that tendency towards metaphysical denial which often appears to have such a strong hold on oriental thought.

---

individuality in the intelligible order which is transcendent and divine. For him personality does not vanish on this level. Cp. my contribution on *Person and Personality in Greek and Christian thought*, to the Washington *Studies in the History of Phil.*, 1962-63.

INDEX OF NAMES

Albinus 213, 363 ff.
Alcmaeon 33, 43, 49, 387.
Alexander Polyhistor 40, 384 ff.
Antiochus 372 ff., 376.
Archytas 28, 46.
Aristophanes 124, 137.
Aristoteles 3, 4, 5, 11, 17 f., 60 f., 79, 84-86, 93, 124 f., 166, 173, 223.
  Metaph. N 3, 1091 a 15, M 6, 1080 b 20 ff.: 41; A 6, A 9, M 4, 5, 8 sq., N, *De anima* I 3: 246.
  Eth. Nic. X 7, 1177 b 26-78 a 7, *Metaph.* A 2, 982 b 28 ff.: 203.
  Phys. IV 209 b 13-16: 260, 262-264.
  Metaph. A 6: 261 f., 382-395.
  De anima I 2, 404 b 16-27: 193 f., 277-281.
  Phys. I 4, 187 a 16-20, I 6, 189 b 8-16: 272-274.
  Metaph. 1084 a 10-17, 1073 a 14-23, 1070 a 18-19: 287-289; 1090 a 5: 288 f.; M 7, 1081 a 12-17: 289-291.
  Eudemus: 307-317.
  Protrepticus: 318-322.
  Peri philosophias: 322-327.
  Metaph. Λ 10, 1075 a 11-15: 344-351.
Aristoxenus 266 n. 2, 281.
Athenagoras 60.
Atticus 304, 306 f.
Augustinus 21.
Aurobindo, Sri, 433 f.

Bailey, Cyril, 15.
Bastide, Gaston, 11.
Bergson 423 ff.

Bernays, J., 295.
Bierens de Haan 258.
Boeckh, August, 29, 31 f., 35, 50, 70-73.
Boethius 356.
Bovet 222 n.
Buddha 421, 424, 427. See also Gautama.
Burkert, Walter, 27-31, 33 f., 42, 45, 52 f., 63, 74 f., 78 f., 80-84, 86-91, 94.
Burnet, J., 29, 38 n., 126, 257.
Bywater 29.

Cherniss, Harold, 160, 176, 258 f., 262, 266 f., 270, 277-292, 385, 414 n.
Cicero, *De finibus* V 5, 12: 305 f.
Clearchus 58.
Clemens Alexandrinus 59.
Cornford 176-178, 205, 232 f.
Crates 377.
Crombie, I. M., 206.
Cudworth, Ralph, 356.

Delatte, A., 27, 64 f., 67.
Democritus 4, 15 f.
Dicaearchus 102.
Diels, H., 35.
Diès, A., 176, 178, 181 f., 196, 217, 228.
Diocles of Karystos 387.
Diogenes Laertius VIII 25 ff.: 384-388.
Dörrie, Heinrich, 395.
Düring, I., 298-330.

Ecphantus 69.
Empedocles 55 f.
Epictetus 376, 423 n. 3.

INDEX OF NAMES

Epicurus 15-17, 429.
Erasmus 20.
Eudorus, of Alexandria, 386, 392f.
Eudoxus 300.

Faye, Eugène de, 358ff.
Festugière 80, 386ff., 391ff.
Ficino, Marsilio, 356, 400.
Frank, Erich, 29, 243.
Fritz, K. von, 27, 80.
Furley 15.

Gadamer, H., 297.
Gautama 425. See also: Buddha.
Gigon, O., 109-111.
Goethe 400.
Gonda, J., 431 n.
Gorgias 422.
Guthrie 27, 29, 65.

Hackforth 181, 202, 381.
Hegel 415f., 423.
Heraclides Ponticus 78f., 81.
Heraclitus 10, 47f., 419ff., 427.
Hermodorus 272ff., 383ff.
Hicetas 69.
Hippasos 28, 96f.
Hyperionides 65f.

Inge 357f.

Jaeger, Werner, 170, 173, 295-299, 313, 324, 327, 376.
Joël, Karl, 127, 131f.
Johannes Chrysostomus 19.
Justinus 19-22, 217ff.

Kamlah, W., 191n., 238f.
Kirk, G. S., 29, 422n.
Klein, J., 255n.

Litsenburg, P. van, 229ff., 234-236, 239, 241.
Loenen, H. J. M. M., 180, 227, 269n., 380n.
Lueder, A. M., 376.
Lutoslawsky 163n., 222n., 367n.

Magelhaes, V. de-Vilhena, 126.

Maier, Heinrich, 11, 113, 125.
Malingrey, A. M., 22n.
Mansfeld, J., 55n.
Mansion, A., 174, 296.
Marcus Aurelius 376.
Maximus of Tyrus 212.
Merlan, Ph., 377.
Milinda 526.
Minar, L., 27.
Moderatus 392f.
Mondolfo 29f.
Murphy, N. R., 179.

Nāgārjuna 427.
Nāgasena 426.
Nicomachus 103.
Numenius 360.
Nuyens 296f.

Ostwald 416.
Ovink 258.
Owen, G. E. L., 190n., 237f.
Owens, J., 336f.

Panaetius 423 n. 4.
Parmenides 9f., 33, 36, 55, 413.
Philip, J. A., 81, 86, 91, 92-106.
Philo 358f., 364, 372.
Philolaos 27-77, 79, 85.
Plato 3, 5, 9, 13f., 17, 39, 57, 94, 98, 101, 102, 116-118, 134ff., 155.
  Apol. 41 a-d: 141ff.;
  Phaedo 62b, 60c-61b, 118d-e: 143.
  Ep. II 314c, *Ep.* VII, 341c-d,
  Phaedr. 274e-275b: 256f., 260.
  Phaedo 65c-67a: 202; *Phaedo* 100b,
  Rep. 476b-479e: 188-190.
  Phil. 59a-b: 157f., 161f., 274f.
  Ib. 23c-26c, 30a-e, *Tim.* 27a-28a, 49a: 378-380.
  Phil. 24a-d: 159f; *Tim.* 27d-28a: 158;
  Tim. 86b-88c: 164/5; *Tim.* 31b, 37c-d, 39d-e: 199;
  Tim. 90a,c: 203;
  Rep. VI, 508c-509c: 183-188.
  Soph. 248c-249a, *Tim.* 31b: 176-182, 194-209.

435

INDEX OF NAMES

Tim. 47: 167, 170, 199.
Plotinus 18-19, 219f., 241, 355ff., 369, 389f., 393, 395.
   Enn. V,1,1: 399ff.
Plutarchus 211f., 359f., 419 n. 2.
Polemon 377.
Popper, K. R., 127, 132.
Porphyrius 102.
Pos, H. J., 128f.
Praechter 357.
Proclus 87f., 392f.
Pyrrho 427f.
Pythagoras 3, 6-8, 27f., 36, 52, 78-106, 283.

Rabbow, Paul, 111.
Radhakrishnan 430-432.
Raven, J. E., 29.
Reinhardt, Karl, 376.
Ritter, C., 257.
Robbers, H., 222n.
Robin, Léon, 243-255, 259, 366.
Ross, Sir David, 176, 178, 194, 237, 249, 252ff., 269f., 382f.
Ryle, G., 370.
Saffrey 194, 277, 385.

Śamkara 429-432.
Sartre 128, 132.
Schiller 400.
Schuhl, P. M., 86.
Seneca 15, 372, 376.
Sextus Empiricus *Adv. Math.* X 248-282: 267-269.
Shorey, P., 258.
Simplicius *Phys.* 247.30-248.15: 264-266.
Socrates 3,8f., 11-13, 51,58, 109-151.

Solmsen, Fr., 163n., 327.
Speusippus 66, 78, 370, 377, 384.
Staal, J. F., 432n.
Strycker, E. de, 142, 207.
Szabó 97.

Taylor, A. E., 126.
Thales 4-6.
Theiler, W., 364, 372ff.
Theon of Smyrna 392.
Theophrastus *Metaph.* 6b11-19: 285f., 365f.
Thévenaz, P., 360.
Thomas Aquinas 22, 415.
Timaeus of Tauromenium 102f.
Timpanaro, Mrs. M.-Cardini, 38n. 60f.
Tofail, Ibn, 316, 337.

Valentinus 358, 361.
Vasubandhu 426.

Waerden, B. L. van der, 27, 80.
Wahl 160.
Wellmann 386ff.
Whittaker 357.
Wielen, W. van der, 256, 255, 280 n. 2, 286 n. 4, 288 n. 3.
Wiersma, W., 386ff.
Wilamowitz 144n.
Wilpert, P., 190n., 271, 323.
Witt, R. E., 362, 363n.

Xenocrates 78, 80, 278ff., 289, 370, 377, 387f., 391.
Xenophon 6, 51, 116-118, 135ff.

Zeller 78, 357.

INDEX OF SUBJECTS

Academy
  the early –: 258 ff., 377, 387 f.
  restored by Antiochus of Ascalon? 372-376.
Advaita (non-dualism) 432.
aeons 360.
agnosticism
  of Socr.? 128 ff.
agrapha
  see unwritten doctrine and ἄγραφα.
allegories
  about the gods: 372.
Anecdota arithmologica 67.
anthropologie, anthropology
  pythagoricienne: 56 ff.
  in the Hermetics: 362.
  of Plotinus: 408, 410.
Apologists 233, 411.
archetype 361 f., 363, 390, 422.
  – pal world: 369.
  – pal form: 404.
  prime image: 406.
argumentum ex gradibus 325 f.
arithmologie 64 ff., 71, 100 f.
ascetism, ascetical attitude of mind, 15 f., 18.
atheism 119 ff.
ātman 429, 431.
atomism 15.
autarchy (of the wise man) 18.
autonomy 126 ff., 131 f.

Bakchai
  les – de Philol.: 63 ff.
Beauty (itself) 13, 156, 188 f., 212 f., 216.
the Beautiful: 403.
beauty of the visible world: 404.
Being
  in Philol.: 32 ff., 37 ff.
  intelligible –: 156 ff., 163 f.
  non-b. is b.: 160 f.
  motion attributed to perfect B.: 160, 176-182, 194-209.
  hierarchy of b.: 183, *188-194*, 235, 239-242, 245; taught before Plotinus: 358 ff., 362, 363 f., 365 ff.
  intelligible B. and the Good: 184 ff., 215 ff.
  true B. correlative with true knowledge: 186 f.
  b. opposed to becoming: 186 f.; see also γιγνόμενα
  two kinds of b.: 188.
  true b. see ὄντως ὄν, under ὄν.
  visible things partake of b.: 189 f.
  b. divided into two main parts: 264 ff., 383 ff.
  tripartition of b.: 268 ff., 383 ff.
  in Śamkara: 430 ff. See also existence and entity.
body
  and soul: 54-60, 156, 162 ff.
  care of the b.: 136.
  – made by Soul: 401.
  the heavenly -ies: 407.
  in Buddhism: 426.
brotherhood (Bruderschaft)
  Pythag.: 91, 95 f., 102 f., 105 f.
brāhman 429, 431 f.
Buddhism 425-429, 433.
Bythos 361.

437

INDEX OF SUBJECTS

cause
  First C.: 21.
  the Demiurge an intelligent C.: 179 f., 231 ff., 240.
  the World-soul an intelligent C.: 180.
  the erring c.: 233.
  God the c. of good only: 234.
  the four -s: 330.
  wisdom concerned with -s: 332 ff.
  the immanent forms are first -s: 340 f.
  the prime Mover a total – ? 342 ff.
  the – of all: 363.
  four or five -s admitted: 372 f.
  the – of intelligible Being: 403, 406.
  See also αἴτιον and ἀγαθόν.
cavern
  Pl.'s simile of the – transposed by Ar.: 324 f.
change
  eternal – in East and West: 419-433.
changing and unchanging
  in Philol. fr. 21: 70 f.; in Pl.'s *Polit.*: 169, 171 ff.
chaos see matter.
chariot 426.
contemplation 406, 408.
contemplative life see theory.
cosmic order
  an argument for divine providence: 324, 325, 326.
cosmogony 362.
cosmology
  in Philol.: 37 ff., 63 f., 68-73.
  acc. to Burkert: 79 ff.; Philip: 101.
cosmos
  in Philol., see κόσμος.
  Pl.'s doctrine of the c.: see world.
creation
  in the *Tim.*: 231 ff.
  in Middle Platonism: 364.
  in Plotinus: 404 ff., 408 f.
creative evolution 424.
Creator 406, 407.
  See also Cause and Demiurge.

Daemon(s) 360.
daimonion
  of Socr.: 139.
dance, the cosmic –, 71, 408.
darkness 412 f.
  See also σκότος.
death
  Socr.' attitude towards: 142 ff.
  definition 113 f., 146, 148 n. 1, 149.
De hebdomadibus
  See ἑβδομάδες.
Demiurge
  in Philol.: 73.
  in the *Tim.*: 158, 163.
  the D. a transcendent Noûs? 179 f., 202 ff., 229 f.
  Was the D. a Creator? 231 ff.
  – Pl.'s „God"? 233 ff.
  relation to the Ideas: 229 ff., 234.
  Creator of the Ideas? 235 f.
  in Valentinus: 361 f.,
  in Albinus: 364, in the *Tim.*: 368.
  a transcendent Noûs: 379 ff.
  not identical with the Good: 380.
  See also δημιουργός.
detachment
  from outward things: 6, 8, 18, 20, 428.
Dieu(x), see God, gods.
discursive (thinking) 19.
dreams
  mantic by –: 324 f., 326.
dualisme (dualism)
  un faible – chez Platon: 385.
  – pythagoricien: 392.
  in Plotinus? 409-416.
  a certain – in the Stoa: 415.
  non -d.: 431 f.
dyad
  the indefinite –: 261, 264-274, 366, 384 ff.
  placed under the One: 384, 390; cf. 394.
  See also: indefinite and ἄπειρον.
educator
  Socr. as an –: 145 ff.

INDEX OF SUBJECTS

ego
  the –: 425 f.
  See also ,,we" and person.
elements,
  the four or five, Philol. fr. 12: 54 ff.;
  in the *Tim.*: 231 ff.
  the – of all things: 382 ff.
emanation 357; 364 n. 1.
  explained by Plotinus: 405 ff., 408 f.
entia non sunt multiplicanda, 409.
entity
  denied in Buddhism: 426 f.
Epicureanism 14-16.
eternity of the world
  Philol. fr. 21: 68 ff.
ethical
  – character of Socr.' phil.: 113 f.
ethics
  of the interior life: 11.
  background of a transcendent order: 12 ff.
  social virtue: 13, 16.
  See also morals.
  autonomous –: 126 ff., 131 f.
eudaemonia 428 f.
  See also εὐδαιμονία.
evil
  the source of –: 361, 399.
  lack of the Good: 410.
existence
  denied in Buddhism: 426 f.
  See also being and entity.
expiation (pénitance) 58 ff.
  See also τιμωρία.

Father 361, 363, 368, 399, 403.
  See also Demiurge.
fire
  the cosmic –: 421.
First principles 80 f., 159 f.
  one First p.: 183 ff.; 401 ff., 405 ff., 411. See also ἀγαθόν and ἕν.
  Pl.'s doctrine of two –: 187 f., 269 ff., 365, 383-395, 414.
  See also ἀρχαί and πρῶτα.
flux
  see change.

Forms
  conceived as living beings? 177 ff., 200 f.
  unchanging –: 178, 179, 195 ff.
  called ,,gods": 205 f.
  See also: intelligible being, under being.
  – immanent in nature: 336-341.
  the exemplary F.: 361; archetypal F.: 362.
  – and Numbers: 365 ff.

Gnostics 360 ff., 364.
God (Dieu), gods, 8, 13 f., 19 ff., 60, 64 ff., 67, 133, 137 ff., 141 ff.;
  The Ideas referred to as g.: 205 f.
  – for Plato: 210-225, 225-242.
  how man came to the notion of –: 324.
  – cause of the cosmic order: 324 ff.
  – and nature: 325, 343.
  the Logos a second –: 358 ff.
  a hierarchy of -s: 360.
  term used on different levels: 363 n. 3, 403 f.
  allegories about the –: 372.
  how souls have forgotten G.: 399 ff.
  the heavenly bodies –: 407.
  the concept of – in Plotinus: 415.
good
  the G.: see ἀγαθόν.
great-and-small 261, 264-274, 357, 366, 382 ff., 411 ff.
  See also: indefinite.
gymnosophists 428.

harmony
  in music: 39 f., 102.
  in cosmology: 37 ff., 101 f.
  celestial –: 101 f., 408.
  in nature: 421.
hedonism 10, 15 f.
heptade, la –, (Siebenzahl) 67 f.
Hermetica 361 f.
hierarchy
  of being, see being.
  in the intelligible world: 244-255, 281, 286.

439

– of gods and daemons: 360 ff.
Hīnayāna 425.
humanist
    Socr. a h.? 132f., 150f.
hypostases
    the three: 183, 355ff., 399-404, 405-409.
hypothesis
    see ὑπόθεσις.

ideal numbers (Nombres-Idées) 246-255, 261, 289-292, 323, 365 ff.
Ideas
    see Forms, and intelligible being s.v. being.
    the Idea of Good: see ἀγαθόν.
    the Demiurge and the –: 229ff., 234.
    the Demiurge creator of the –: 235f.
    the theory of – abandoned? 237ff., 367f.
    – and numbers: 246-255, 259, 261, 279, 289-292.
    friends of the –: 195ff.
    interpr. of Robin: 244ff.
    – reduced to numbers: 285-289.
    the theory of – adopted by Ar.? 295-330.
    the theory of – criticised in Π. φιλ.? 323ff., 327.
    in the *Anal.*: 328.
    – not derived from the Good? 357.
    in Albinus: 363f.
    thoughts of God? 372ff.
    transcendent – reintroduced by Antiochus of Ascalon? 373-376.
    in Plotinus: 404. A multiplicity of –: 414.
    See also νοητά and κόσμος νοητός.
image
    εἰκών: 189f., 404, 407.
indefinite
    the – principle of space: 186f.; cf. 232, 260ff.
    the ἕτερον and the – principle: 187f., 261ff.; cf. 382ff.
    See also ἄπειρον and infinite.

inductive reasoning 113.
ineffable 362.
    See also ἄρρητος.
infinite
    an – world: 361.
innumerable
    – powers: 361.
intellectualism 113f.
intellectus
    agens separatus: 317, 345.
intelligence
    attributed to perfect Being: 177-182, 194-209.
    Did Pl. assume a transcendent Noûs? 179f., 202ff.
    in Ar.: 314ff., 349f.
intelligible
    – Being, see being. Also Forms.
    the – world in Valentinus: 361.
    the – world viewed as a living being:
    See ζῷον (παντελές), αὐτόζῳον, and ὄν (τὸ παντελῶς –).
intermediate(s) 191-194, 361f., 365, 370. Cf. 407.
    See also μεταξύ, and μεσίτης.
intuitive (thinking) 19.
irony
    Socratic –: 118f., 136, 140.

knowledge
    human k. is limited: 138, 140.
    virtue is k.: 148ff.
    ruling character of k.: 149.
    – of the sensible world: 161f., 171ff., 174, 189f.
    – of existing laws: 173f.
    true Being correlative with true k.: 186f.
koinon
    the – (= the Logos): 421.

life
    phil. an attitude towards l.: 5-24.
    (zoè): 361f., 408.
    See also ζῷον.
Light 361f., 406; cf. 408.
    See also περίλαμψις and φῶς.

INDEX OF SUBJECTS

line 284 f.
living being
　See ζῷον.
logic
　the place of l. in phil.: 23 n. 2.
　in Ar.'s *Metaph.*: 350 f.
logical
　the – works of Ar.: 327 ff.
Logos
　in Middle Platonism: 358 ff.
　in Heraclitus: 421 f.
　in the Stoa: 423 f.

Mahāyāna 426.
man
　how considered by Socr.: 133, 138 f.
　a composite of soul and body: 164 ff.
　creation of – in the Hermetics: 362.
　in Plotinus: 408, 410.
　in Buddhism: 425 ff.
mantic 137.
many
　how the – springs from the one: 404 ff., 408 f.
material
　the – principle: see principle.
　the – world: see world (sensible –).
materialism
　Stoic –: 415.
mathematical objects 191 f., 370.
mathematics
　Pythagorean –: 79 f., 86-90, 97.
matter
　pre-existing – in the *Tim.*: 231 ff.
　in Valentinus: 361.
　in Plotinus: 401.
　See also ὕλη.
māyā 431 f.
Mediator 358 ff.
Middle Platonism
　see Platonism.
monade (monad)
　384 ff.
monism
　of Plotinus: 409-416.
moral reform 91, 97.
moral values 121 ff.

morals
　emphasis on m. in later Greek phil.? 23 f.
motion
　excluded from Plato's intelligible world? 159 ff.
　one of the five supreme kinds: 166.
　Soph. 249 a: 176-182; 194-209; 227 ff.
movement
　of the universe: 408.
Mover,
　unmoved – (s): 213, 224, 329 f., 342-350, 363.
　See also πρῶτον κινοῦν.
multiplicity
　See many.
musicology (musicologie)
　Philol. fr. 6, 11-17: 39 f., 79 ff.
Mystères, les –, 58.
mysticism 19.

nature
　"God and –": 325.
　teleology in –: 320.
　the supreme good in –: 336 f.
　living acc. to –: 337 f.; cf. 421.
　See also φύσις.
Neoplatonism
　a new phil.? 355-377.
　a monism? 409-416.
Nirvāna 426 f.
non-being
　proved to be being: 160 f.
non-dualism 431 f.
noûs
　See νοῦς.
number(s)
　in Philol., see ἀριθμός.
　in Plato: 249-255, 259, 261, 269, 279 ff., 284 f., 289-292.
　ideal –: see ideal –.
　self-moving –: 279 f., 367, 370.
　– derived from the first principles: 384 ff., 403.

octave
　Philol. fr. 6: 39 f.

441

INDEX OF SUBJECTS

One
    in Philol.: 40ff., 42, 55.
    in early Pythagoreanism: 101.
    in Plato: 158, 160.
    the – and Noûs: p. 364/5 n. 2.
    the – identified with the Good: 365.
    See also ἕν and ἀγαθόν.

path
    the upward and the downward –: 419.
    the –s of existence are empty: 426.
peras
    See πέρας.
periodical return of all things (zyklische Wiederkehr) 99f.
person 420, 423, 426, 433.
personality 420, 423, 424.
philosophos
    defined by Pl.: 157.
philosophy
    Greek concept of ph.: 3-24.
    term first used, see φιλοσοφία.
    Christian concept of ph.: 19ff.
    Pythag. –: 79ff., 84f., 97ff., 103ff.
    how meant by Socr.: 115ff.
    – of nature: 119, 136f., 140.
    opposed to rhetoric: 146.
Platonism
    esoteric character: 21.
    traditional view of –: 155ff.
    modified in Pl.'s later years: 162-175.
    – and Neopl.: 355-377.
    the Florentine –: 356.
    the Cambridge –: 356.
    Middle –: 358ff.
pleroma 361, 409.
pluralism 413ff.
point 284f.
power
    creative –: 409.
Powers 361.
    See also δυνάμεις.
praxis
    opposed to theory: 5-24.
prayer
    -s of Socr.: 144f.

principle(s)
    see First pr. and ἀρχαί.
    the material –: 261-277, 282-285, 378-395.
    two ultimate –: 269ff., 382ff.
    – of motion: 339f.
proportions numériques (numerical proportions) 61f.
providence
    divive – in Pl.: 234f.
    in Plotinus: 403, 415.
purification 6f., 13f.
Pythagorean books
    quoted by Alex. Polyhistor: 384ff.
Pythagoreanism 27-106.
    P. mathematics: 27ff., 79f., *86-90*, 97.
    – social theory: 84, 91, 97, 105f.
    – philosophy: 28f., 79, 97ff.
    the Philolaus texts: 29-77.

quarte
    Philol. fr. 6: 39f.
quinte
    Philol. fr. 6: 39f.

rational (explanation), rationality 4f., 11ff., 14, 23f., 79.
rationalism
    in Socr.? 137-151.
Reality
    the intelligible world called true –: 156ff., 188ff.
    sensible things partake of being: 189f.
    primary and secondary R.: 189ff.
    – of natural objects: 422f., 426f.
    – of the Absolute: 426f.
    true – in Śamkara: 429ff.
receptacle 232.
    See also space.
rehabilitation
    of sensible being: 189ff.
religious tradition
    Socr.' attitude towards –: 137ff., 141ff.
river
    symbol of eternal flux: 419ff.

INDEX OF SUBJECTS

Scepticism
    the Sceptic School: 427 f.
scholars 23, n. 1.
School 96, 102 f., 105 f.
self-consciousness 19.
    See also ego, "we" and person.
sensible things
    partake of being: 189 f.
    the s. world a "third god": 360.
    – no illusion for Śamkara: 430 ff.
"sensing" 189.
shamanism (schamanisme) 58 f., 79 f., 103 ff., 314.
sight
    how appreciated in the *Tim.*: 167 f.
sin
    nobody – s willingly: 123 f., 147 ff.
Socratic dialogues 112 ff., 133 ff.
soul
    – and body: 54-60, 147, 156, 162 ff., 192 f., 240.
    world-s.: 70 ff., 163, 180 ff.
    caring for one's s.: 114 ff., 146, 148.
    – s of the heavenly bodies: 140 f., 163.
    the – 's life after death: 142 ff.
    the – 's place in the order of Being: 156, 191-194, 357, 368, 369 f., 403 ff.
    s. attributed to perfect Being? 176-182, 194-209.
    s. as an intermediate: see intermediates and μεταξύ.
    – defined as a self-moving number: 279 f., 367.
    εἶδός τι: 314.
    in Plutarch: 360;
    in Valentinus: 361;
    the – has forgotten her Father: 399 ff.
    the – 's reflection on herself: 401 ff.
    – belongs to the divine nature: 403.
    the inner – is ἀπαθής: 409.
    in Heraclitus: 421; in Śamkara: 429 ff.
sphère éthérée 55 f.
space
    in the *Tim.*: 186 f., 232.
    defined by Speusippus: 370.

    – Xenocr.: 370.
spiritual man 408.
spiritualism 16, 19.
spiritual world
    See νοητά, κόσμος νοητός and pleroma.
Stoicism 14-16;
    in Philol. fr. 21: 68-73.
    Stoic physics: 415.
substantiality
    of things: 421 f., 425.
suffering 425, 427, 428.
symbolisme des nombres (numerical symbolism)
    Philol. fr. 19: 64 ff.

theologia
    Platonica: 356.
theology
    distinguished from phil.: 22.
    of Plato: 210-242.
    of Aristotle: 296, 329 f., 343-351.
theory
    pure th.: 7 f., 17 f.
    – ruling practical life: 8 ff., 11 ff.
    the life of the spirit: 18 f.
    th. and praxis: 23 f.
    divine th.: 216 n. 3.
thinkers
    and "scholars": 23 n. 1.
thinking
    see intelligence.
thought
    cessation of –: 427.
time
    in the *Tim.*: 232 f.
transcendent 12 ff., 20 ff.
    a metaphysic of the –: 150.

ultimate principles
    see First principles.
universality 4.
Universe, the,
    see κόσμος.
    the physical – spiritualized: 433.
unmoved Mover(s)
    see Mover and ἀκίνητα.
unwritten doctrine

of Plato: 256-292.
Upanishads 399 n. 3, 430ff.

virtue
   how considered by Socr.: 133ff,. 146ff.,
   in the *Phaedo*: 214; *Symp.*: 216.
voice
   inner v., see daimonion.

"we"
   our real self: 423; cf. 426.
wisdom
   see σοφία.
   in Heraclitus: 421.
wise man 19, 426.
world
   the two – s theory of Plato: 156ff., 167-170, 188-191.
   the visible w.: 158, 188-190.
   knowledge of the visible w.: 161f., 189f.
   the visible w. a created God: 168ff.
   the visible w. the only reality: 325.
   deduced from the intelligible? 357.
   a third god: 360.
   the source of evil: 361.
   the material w. in the Hermetics: 362.
   the intelligible w. a living being? see ζῷον (παντελές), αὐτόζῳον and being (παντελῶς).
   the visible – made by Soul: 401.
   the three – s: 426.
World-soul
   Philol. fr. 21: 70ff.
   in Plato: 179ff., 225f., 237ff.
   – s: 360.
   the – in Plutarch: 360.
writing
   the art of –: 256f., 260.

INDEX OF GREEK WORDS

'Αγαθόν
τὸ ἀ. as First principle: 183-188, 390.
ἡ τοῦ – οὗ ἰδέα: 216 n. 2; cf. 357.
identified with πέρας and ἕν: 281, 394.
criticised by Ar.: 328, 341f.
the – of each thing: 336.
– in nature: 337f.
– καθ' αὑτό: 340.
ἄγαλμα 206, 368.
– τὸ πρῶτον ἐκφανέν: 405.
ἄγραφα 238. Cf. 355.
ἀεὶ θέον, τὸ – θεῖον,
Philol. fr. 21.15f.: 71ff.
ἀεὶ κατὰ τὰ αὐτά
τὰ –: 275.
ἀεικίνατον
Philol. fr. 21.11: 71ff.
ἀΐδιος 363 n. 3, n. 7.
ἀΐδιοι θεοί 205f.
αἰσθητά
opposed to νοητά: 215, 240.
αἴτιον 202, 332ff., 378.
ἀκίνητα
τὰ –: 339ff.
ἀκρασία 61f.
ἀκρισία 265, 383.
ἀλήθεια
Philol. fr. 11.19: 52.
in Plato: 183f., 202, 216 n. 5.
ἀμετάβλατος, ἀμετάβολος
Philol. fr. 21: 70f.
ἀμήτωρ
Philol. fr. 20: 67f., 75.
ἀμιγής 355, 359.

ἄμορφον 265, 274, 383.
ἀμυδρόν
χαλεπὸν κ. ἀ. εἶδος: 187.
ἀνισότης 275f.
ἀνυπόθετον 185, 187, 216.
ἄνω
Philol. fr. 17: 63f.
ἀόριστος
– δυάς: 264-274.
τὸ – ν, τὰ – α: 264, 383.
ἀπάθεια 407.
ἀπαθής 359, 363 n. 3, 403, 408, 410.
ἄπειρα
Philol. fr. 1: 31f.
– fr. 2: 32ff.
– fr. 6: 37ff.
– fr. 11.10: 44.
concl.: 75.
ἄπειρον
in Pl.: 190, 261, 264-277, 378-395.
theory of a double –: 388-395.
in Plotinus: 411ff.
See also: indefinite and ὕλη.
ἀπόρρητα, τὰ –, 58.
ἀργός
– βασιλεύς: 360.
ἀρετή
δημοτικὴ κ. πολιτική: 13;
in the *Protr.*: 319.
in the *EN.*: 338.
ἀριθμός
Philol. fr. 4: 35f.
– fr. 5: 36f.
– fr. 11: 44-54.
Aristox.: 87.

INDEX OF GREEK WORDS

Sextus Emp.: 282f.
ἄριστον
τὸ – ἐν τῇ φύσει πάσῃ: 336.
ἁρμόζων
Philol. fr. 10.8: 44, 49f.
ἁρμονία 30
Philol. fr. 6: 37, 39f.
– fr. 10: 42f.
– fr. 11.16: 52ff.
ἄρρητος 363, 366.
ἄρτιον
Philol. fr. 5: 36.
ἀρτιοπέριττον 36f.
ἀρχά. (ἀρχή)
Philol. fr. 3: 35; fr. 8: 42.
ἀρχαί, Philol. fr. 6: 37ff.; fr.13: 56f.
ἀρχὰ κ. ἀγεμών, Philol. fr. 11: 44.
– τᾶς κινήσιος, Philol. fr. 21: 69f.
– αἱ πάντων: 269; cf. 272, 273.
– ἡ τῶν ὄντων: 282.
– γραμμῆς: 284.
– αἱ: 333ff.
two kinds of – αἱ: 339f.
– in Albinus: 363f.
in Plotinus: see First principle and monism.
ἀρχέτυπος
τὸ – ν εἶδος: 361 n. 2.
ἄστατον 159, 265, 274, 383.
ἀσύμβλητος 246.
ἀσώματον 390 n. 1, 410.
ἀταραξία (ataraxia) 427.
ἄτομοι γραμμαί 284f.
αὐτὰ ἕκαστα 188f., 318.
αὐτὰ τὰ πρῶτα: 320.
αὐτὰ τὰ ἀκριβῆ: 320.
αὐτόζῳον (αὐτὸ τὸ ζῷον) 181; cf. 193f., 200, 208, 277-281.
αὐτοτελής 363 n. 7.
ἀφασία (aphasia) 427.
ἀχλύς 323.

Βασιλεύς
– ἀργός: 360.
βίος
the three βίοι: 7f.;
– θεωρητικός: 311, 318.

βουλεύσασθαι 407.

Γενατόν, τὸ –,
Philol. fr. 21.16: 71ff.
γεωμετρία, γεωμετρική (ἱστορία) 86, 87.
γιγνόμενα
τὰ – opposed to ὄντα: 178f., 188ff.
τὸ – ον: 378.
γιγνωσκόμενα, τὰ,
Philol. fr. 4: 35.
γνώμων
κατὰ – ονος φύσιν, Philol. fr. 10: 44, 49f.
γνῶσις
θεία κ. ἀνθρωπίνη, Philol. fr. 6: 37ff., 50ff. (fr. 11).
γνωσούμενον, τὸ –,
Philol. fr. 3: 35.

Δαιμόνια κ. θεῖα πράγματα
Philol. fr. 11.12: 50ff.
δέ
archaic usage of –: 31, 74.
δεκάς
Philol. fr. 11: 44ff.
δεύτερος θεός 358.
δεχόμενον
τὸ –: 379.
See also χώρα.
δημιουργός
Philol. fr. 21.22: 73.
term used in *Rep*. X: 235f.
in Numenius: 360; in the Hermetics: 362.
See also Demiurge.
διάνοια
Philol. fr. 16: 60ff.
in Plato: 202.
διαστατόν
τὸ πάντῃ –: 370.
δίεσις
Philol. fr. 6: 40.
δι' ὀξειᾶν
Philol. fr. 6: 40.
δι' οὗ 372f.
διπλόον
Philol. fr. 6: 40.
δόξα 189.

INDEX OF GREEK WORDS

δυάς
  Philol. fr. 20: 67f.
  – ἀόριστος: 269; 282f., 384.
δύναμις
  ἐν τᾷ δεκάδι, Philol. fr. 11: 44ff.
  – εἰς (Hermetica): 361; (Plotinus) 408.
  – ἄπειρος: 390 n. 1, 410f., 412.
  – τῶν πάντων: 405 n. 7.

Ἑβδομάδες,
  π. – ων: 63, 67 (De hebdomadibus).
εἶδος 125, 272, 283.
  the soul – τι: 314.
  361 n. 2, 363 n. 3, 373 n. 1, 401.
εἴδωλον 411.
εἰκών 189f., 206, 238f.; 359 n. 2, n. 7; 401, 404 n. 5, 422.
εἰκὼς λόγος 381.
εἰλικρινής 359 n. 7.
ἔλλειψις
  ὑπεροχὴ καὶ –: 159, 384.
ἕν, τὸ –,
  Philol. fr. 7: 40ff. cf. fr. 8: 42.
  Cf. 55, 101.
  Ar. on Pl.: 272, 273f., 279ff.;
  in Sextus Emp.: 282.
  in the Parm.: 370ff., 392.
  – / πλῆθος: 388.
  See also One and ἀγαθόν.
ἐναντία
  – ων συναρμογή – Philol. fr. 10: 42f.
  πρὸς –: 383.
ἐνδέχεται
  Philol. fr. 6: 37f., 50ff. (fr. 11).
ἐνέργεια 402, 406.
ἔννοιαι
  κοιναί: 376.
ἐν ᾧ
  τὸ –: 379.
ἕνωσις
  πολυμιγέων ἕ.: 30, 42f., 74.
ἐξερρύη 405.
ἐξ οὗ 373 n. 1.
ἐόντα, τὰ –,
  Philol. fr. 2: 32ff.
  – fr. 6: 37ff.
ἐπέκεινα

  – τῆς οὐσίας: 186, 216, 380.
ἐπιστήμη 183, 332.
ἐπίτριτον
  Philol. fr. 6: 40.
ἐπόγδοον
  Philol. fr. 6: 40.
ἐποπτικός
  – ν μέρος τῆς φιλ.: 314ff.
ἐράσμιον 403.
ἔργα
  Philol. fr. 2: 35.
  τὰ – τῶ ἀριθμῶ, fr. 11: 44, 50ff.
  ἔργον, man's particular –: 319, 338.
ἑστία
  Philol. fr. 7: 40ff., 74, 75.
ἑστώ
  Philol. fr. 6: 37ff.
ἕτερον 187, 261f., 275f., 389.
  πρὸς – α: 383.
ἑτερότης 275f., 390, 399.
εὐδαιμονία 319; cf. 428f. (eudaemonia).
εὐθυμία 10.

Ζῷον
  λογικόν, Philol. fr. 13: 56f.
  the cosmos as a ζ.: 70f., 408.
  ὅλον τὸ ζ.: 164f.
  παντελὲς ζ.: 176ff., 198ff., 368ff.
  αὐτὸ τὸ ζ., see αὐτόζῳον.
  – α ἄλογα: 362.
  – ἀίδιον: 369 n. 1.

Ἡμιόλιον
  Philol. fr. 6: 40.
ἡρμοσμένον
  τὸ –: 265f., 383.

Θεάματα
  τὰ ἐκεῖ –: 308-314.
θεῖον 203f., 211, 212, 217, 350.
  θ. θεωρίαι: 216 n. 3.
  τὸ –: 404.
Θεολογούμενα ἀριθμητικῆς 64ff.
θεός 350, 358f., 363 n. 3, 404.
  δεύτερος –: 358; τρίτος –: 360;
  πρῶτος –: 358 n. 1, 363 n. 7.
  See also God(s).
θεωρήματα 88, 89.

447

INDEX OF GREEK WORDS

θεωρία 216 n. 3, 409.
  See also contemplation/and contemplative life.
θιγεῖν 314ff.

'Ιδέα 125.
  – τοῦ ἀγαθοῦ: 184ff.
  in Albinus: 363 n. 4.
ἴσον
  τὸ –: 265f., 268, 383.
  ἰσότης: 269.
ἰσότης
  γεωμετρική: 84.
  –/ἀνισότης: 269.
ἰσοταγῆ
  Philol. fr. 6: 37ff.

Καθαρός 355, 359 n. 7.
κάθαρσις
  by math. studies: 82ff.
καθ' αὐτά
  τὰ –: 264, 383.
καθόλου
  τὰ –: 332.
κάτω
  Philol. fr. 17: 63f.
κινέον, τὸ –,
  Philol. fr. 21.10: 71ff.
  πρῶτον κινοῦν – see πρῶτον.
  κινοῦν οὐ κινούμενον: 339.
κοιναὶ ἔννοιαι 376.
κοινὰ τὰ τῶν φίλων 102, 145 n. 1.
κοινωνία 84.
κοσμηθῆναι
  Philol. fr. 6: 37ff.
κοσμιότης 84.
κόσκινος
  Philol. fr. 14: 59f.
κόσμος
  Philol. fr. 1: 31f.
  – fr. 6: 37ff.
  – fr. 17: 63f.
  – fr. 21: 68-73.
  κ. and τάξις: 84.
  – νοητός: 359, 390, 401, 404, 412.
  – αἰσθητός: 359.
  – ἀπεριόριστος: 361.
  one great living being: 408.

See also ζῷον.
κτῆσις - χρῆσις 320 n. 4.

Λογισμός 407.
λογισμῷ τινι νόθῳ 187, 263.
λόγος
  ἱερὸς –:
  Philol. fr. 19: 64ff., 74.
  ὁ θεοῦ λ.: 358f.; cf. 373 n. 4.
  – αὐτὸς καθ' ἑαυτόν: 359 n. 7.
  εἰκὼς –: 381.
  κατὰ – ν: 408.
λόγοι
  Philol. fr. 16: 60ff., 75.

Μᾶλλον καὶ ἧττον 159f., 264-277, 378.
μανὸν κ. πυκνόν 273f.
μέγα καὶ μικρόν 264ff.
  See also: great-and-small and: indefinite.
μεγαλόψυχος 17.
μεικτὸν γένος 378f., 382.
μεσίτης 358.
μέσον, τὸ –,
  Philol. fr. 17: 63f.
μέσση
  Philol. fr. 6: 40.
μεταβλατικὰ φύσις
  Philol. fr. 21.18: 73.
μεταληπτικόν 260, 264.
μεταξύ 177, 179.
  See also intermediates.
μετεμψύχωσις 317.
μέτριον
  τὸ –: 379.
μέτρον 363 n. 4.
μὴ ὄν 261ff., 275ff., 389, 410, 413, 422.
  See also ἕτερον.
  Cf. οὐκ ὄν.
μίμημα 239, 320.
μονάς
  Philol. fr. 8: 42.
  ἡ πρώτη – (in Sextus Emp.): 269, 282f.
  See also monade (monad).
μουσικά, ἃ –,
  Philol. fr. 11.15: 50f.

448

INDEX OF GREEK WORDS

Νεάτα (νήτη)
Philol. fr. 6: 40.
νείατος
— ἄλλων: 185, 230.
νόημα 363 n. 3.
νόησις 314, 363 n. 4.
νοητόν
τὸ ν., τὰ ν. ά: 183 ff., 194-209, 379 ff., 404.
ν. ά —/αἰσθητά: 191.
— ὁς τόπος: 216.
τὰ ν. ἀ κ. τὰ θεῖα: 310 f., 323.
πρῶτον —: 363.
νόμῳ
—/ φύσει, Philol. fr. 9: 42.
νοῦς
see intelligence.
ν. : τὰ νοητά: 183, 194-209, 401 f.
in *Protrept.* 10c: 224 n. 1.
in *Metaph.* Θ 10 en *An.po.* II 19: 314 ff.
— is a man's "self": 319.
in Anaxagoras: 355;
in Plutarch: 360;
in Valentinus: 361;
— the Hermetica: 361 f.;
— Albinus: 363 ff.
— always in a soul? 369 f.
— is αἴτιον: 378 f.
— = τὰ ὄντα: 401 f.; τὰ πάντα: 402, 405.
a great God: 403.
always active: 409.

Ὀλκάς 30, 54 ff., 74.
ὁμοῖος
Philol. fr. 6: 37 ff.
ὁμοίωσις θεῷ 220.
ὁμόφυλος
Philol. fr. 6: 37 ff.
ὄν
ὄντως — ("la vraie Réalité"): 156 ff., 215 ff.
τὸ παντελῶς —: 160, 176 ff., 194-209, 369, 380 f.
ὄντως - τα = αὐτὰ ἕκαστα: 188 f.
μὴ ὄν: see μὴ —.
τὰ ὄντα divided into three parts:

264 ff., 268 ff.
οὐκ ὄν: see οὐκ —.
νοῦς = τὰ - τα: 401.
the — of Parm.: 413.
See also Being.
ὁρατόν
opposed to νοητόν: 185.
ὄργανον 373 n. 4.
Also τὸ ὀργανικόν: 373 n. 1.
οὗ ἕνεκα 335 ff.
οὐκ ὄν 265, 383, 389, 422.
οὐσία
τῷ ἀριθμῷ, Philol. fr. 11: 44-54, 74.
ἐπέκεινα τῆς — s: 186 f., 216.
ἡ ὄντως —: 195.
— ι πρῶται κ. δεύτεραι: 333 f.
the — ι are πρῶτα: 338, 340 f., 346 f., 350.
the idea is —: 363 n. 4.
a real being: 412.
ὕλη an — (Stoa): 415.
οὐσιότης 393.
ὄχημα 55 f.

Πάθη
Philol. fr. 16: 60 ff.
παιδεία 86, 88 ff.
πανδεχές 379.
παντελὲς ζῷον see ζῷον.
παντελῶς ὄν see ὄν.
παράδειγμα 238, 363 n. 4, 373.
παρθένος
Philol. fr. 20: 67 f., 75.
πάσχον
τὸ —: 415.
πατήρ
κ. δημιουργός: 73.
See also Father.
περαίνοντα
Philol. fr. 1: 31 f.
— fr. 2: 32 ff.
— fr. 6: 37 ff.
— fr. 11.11: 44.
Concl.: 75.
περαιοῦται
Philol. fr. 21: 70 f.
πέρας - ἄπειρον 81, 99, 101, 190, 261, 264-274; 378 ff.

449

τὸ π. identified with ἀγαθόν and
ἕν: 281-285.
περίλαμψις 405.
περισσόν
  Philol. fr. 5: 36.
ποιοῦν
  τὸ –: 373 n. 1, 415.
πολλά
  τῶν – ὧν ἕνωσις, Philol. fr. 10: 42f.
  See also many.
πολυκοιρανίη
  οὐκ ἀγαθόν –: 342.
πολυμιγέων ἕνωσις
  see ἕνωσις.
ποσόν
  τὸ –: 378, 392.
πρᾶτον, τὸ –, (πρῶτον)
  Philol. fr. 7: 40ff., 63f., 74.
προαίρεσις 408.
προλήψεις 376.
προσθῆκαι 403.
πρὸς ὅ 373.
πρός τι
  τὰ –: 268, 383.
πρῶτα,
  αὐτὰ τὰ –: 320ff.
  τα – κ. αἴτια: 332ff., 336.
  νοῦς = τὰ –: 402.
πρῶτον κινοῦν 329, 336, 338, 342ff.
πρῶτος θεός 358; cf. 360 (first God) ff.
πυκνότης
  καὶ μανότης: 273.

Σημεῖον 284.
σκιά 359 n. 3.
σκότος 393, 412f. (darkness).
σοφία
  – σαφεία: 310, 323.
  in *Met.* A 1: 331ff., 346ff.
στιγμή 284.
συλλαβά
  Philol. fr. 6: 40.
συμπάθεια 407.
συμφρόνησις
  δίχα φρονεόντων σ.: 30, 42f.
συναμφότερον, τὸ –, 165f.
συναρμογή
  Philol. fr. 10: 42.

[σύνευνος]
  Philol. fr. 20a: 77 (épouse)
συστοιχία 37, 53, 75, 391f., 413.
σφαῖρα
  Philol. fr. 7: 40ff.; cf. fr. 17-19:
  63f., 74.
  – fr. 12: 54ff.
σφαῖρος 56.
σχίζων
  τοὺς λόγους τ. πραγμάτων, Philol.
  fr. 11.10: 44, 49f.
σῶμα
  πέμπτον σ.: 30, 54ff., 74.
  πέντε – τα ;, Philol. fr. 12: 54ff.
  σ. σῆμα: 57ff.
σωματῶν
  Philol. fr. 11.9: 44, 49f., 74.

Τάξις 84.
ταὐτόν 275f.
ταυτότης 187.
τέλειος 363 n. 7.
τέλος 335ff., 339, 340, 373 n. 1.
τερετίσματα 328.
τέχνη
  and ἐπιστήμη: 332.
τιμωρία 58f.
τόλμα 399.
τόπος 260.
  νοητὸς –: 216.
τρίτα
  Philol. fr. 6: 40.
τρίτον γένος
  in the *Tim.*: 379, 389.
τρίτος θεός 360.

Ὕβρις 399.
υἱὸς θεοῦ 359.
ὕλη 264, 272, 373 n. 1, 401.
  – νοητή and αἰσθητή: 389ff.; cf.
  395, 411ff.
  the – a μὴ ὄν: 392, 410f., 414.
  the origin of – explained in Iambl.
  De myst.: 393.
  – in the Stoa: 415.
  See also: material principle, matter
  and: indefinite.
ὑλότης 393.

INDEX OF GREEK WORDS

ὑπάτα
   Philol. fr. 6: 40.
ὑπερερρύη 405.
ὑπεροχή (and ἔλλειψις) 159, 268 ff., 272 ff., 384.
ὑπόθεσις, ὑποθέσεις 185; cf. 284 (hypothesis) f.
ὑποκείμενον 412.
   See also ὕλη.
ὑφ' ὅ 373 n. 1.

Φανότατον
   τοῦ ὄντος τὸ φ.: 185 ff., 230.
φιλία 84, 355.
φιλόσοφος, φιλοσοφία 3-24.
   Cic., *Tusc.* V 3, 8-9: 7 f.;
   Christian use of the term: 19-22.
   first use: 81 f.
   in Plato: 214 f.
φιλοσώματος 214.
φιλότιμος 214.
φιλοχρήματος 214.
φρόνησις 202, 213, 214, 318 ff., 369.
φρόνιμος 319.

φρουρά 57 ff.
φύσις
   Philol. fr. 1: 31 f.
   – fr. 6: 37 ff.
   φύσει, Philol. fr. 9: 42.
   ἁ φ. ἁ τῶ ἀριθμῶ, Philol. fr. 11: 44-49, 52 ff.
   ἡ – τέλος κ. οὗ ἕνεκα: 336 n. 4.
   κατὰ – ν ζῆν: 337.
   creative activity of –: 409.
φῶς 393.
   See also Light.

Χώρα 260 ff., 379.

Ψεῦδος
   Philol. fr. 11.16-20: 52 ff.
   in Plotinus: 411.
ψυχή
   Περὶ – s of Philol.: 68 ff.
   in Plato: 202 ff.
   See also soul.
Ὡρισμένον
   τὰ – α: 264, 383.

LIBRARY OF DAVIDSON COLLEGE

Books on regular loan may be checked out for **two weeks**. Books must be presented at the Circulation Desk in order to be renewed.

A fine is charged after date due.

Special books are subject to special regulations at the discretion of the library staff.